Stuart Macintyre's history of the Communist Party of Australia

The first volume in Stuart Macintyre's history of the Communist Party of Australia is *The Reds: The Communist Party of Australia from origins to illegality*. It covers the period 1920 to 1939. *The Party: The Communist Party of Australia from heyday to reckoning* is the second volume, covering 1940 to 1970.

The Reds was the winner of the *The Age* Non-Fiction Book of the Year Award 1998, and shortlisted for Best Australian History Book in the NSW Premier's History Awards 1998.

Praise for *The Reds*

'This fascinating remembrance of the first two decades of the Communist Party of Australia [is] both erudite [and] infused with moral vision. A combination of courage, impeccable judgement and assiduous research.'
Ross Fitzgerald, *Australian Book Review*

'This is a masterful book.'
Tom Sheridan, *Academy of Social Sciences Newsletter*

'Takes the history of the CPA to an entirely new plane.'
Kerry Taylor, *Labour History*

'There is no doubt that Stuart Macintyre's *The Reds* will be the definitive work on Australian communism up until the early 1940s.'
Robert Mackie, *Journal of Australian Studies*

THE PARTY

The Communist Party of Australia from heyday to reckoning

STUART MACINTYRE

ALLEN&UNWIN
SYDNEY • MELBOURNE • AUCKLAND • LONDON

First published in 2022

Allen & Unwin
83 Alexander Street
Crows Nest NSW 2065
Australia
Phone: (61 2) 8425 0100
Email: info@allenandunwin.com
Web: www.allenandunwin.com

NATIONAL LIBRARY OF AUSTRALIA

A catalogue record for this book is available from the National Library of Australia

ISBN 978 1 76087 518 3

Internal design by Julian Mole, Post Pre-press Group
Set in 11/15.5 pt Bembo by Post Pre-press Group, Australia
Printed and bound in Malaysia for Imago Group

10 9 8 7 6 5 4 3 2 1

FSC www.fsc.org MIX Paper from responsible sources FSC® C005748

The paper in this book is FSC® certified. FSC® promotes environmentally responsible, socially beneficial and economically viable management of the world's forests.

Contents

Abbreviations

AASW Australian Association of Scientific Workers
ABC Australian Broadcasting Commission
ACCL Australian Council for Civil Liberties
ACP Australian Communist Party
ACT Australian Capital Territory
ACTU Australian Council of Trade Unions
ADB Australian Dictionary of Biography
AEU Amalgamated Engineering Union
AGPS Australian Government Publishing Service
AIF Australian Imperial Force
ALP Australian Labor Party
AMIEU Australasian Meat Industry Employees' Union
ANU The Australian National University
ARU Australian Railways Union
ASIO Australian Security and Intelligence Organisation
ASSLH Australian Society for the Study of Labour History
ATMOEA Australian Tramway and Motor Omnibus Employees' Association
AWU Australian Workers' Union
BHP Broken Hill Proprietary Company Limited
BLF Builders Labourers Federation
BWIU Building Workers' Industrial Union
CIA Central Intelligence Agency (US)
CIB Commonwealth Investigation Branch
CIS Commonwealth Investigation Service
Cominform Communist Information Bureau
Comintern Communist International

CPA Communist Party of Australia
CPA (M-L) Communist Party of Australia (Marxist-Leninist)
CPC Communist Party of China
CPGB Communist Party of Great Britain
CPSU Communist Party of the Soviet Union
CPUSA Communist Party of the United States of America
CRTS Commonwealth Reconstruction Training Scheme
CSIR Council for Scientific and Industrial Research
CSIRO Commonwealth Scientific and Industrial Research Organisation
CUP Cambridge University Press
DP displaced person
ECCI Executive Committee of the Communist International
EYL Eureka Youth League
FBI Federal Bureau of Investigation (US)
FEDFA Federated Engine Drivers' and Firemen's Association
FIA Federated Ironworkers' Association
GPU State Political Directorate of the Soviet Union
GRU Soviet Military Intelligence Organisation
ISGS Intelligence Section, General Staff
IUS International Union of Students
KC King's Counsel
KGB Committee for State Security (USSR)
MCG Melbourne Cricket Ground
MGB Ministry of State Security (USSR), later KGB
MHR Member of the House of Representatives
MS motor ship
MUP Melbourne University Press
NAA National Archives of Australia
NATO North Atlantic Treaty Organization
NBAC Noel Butlin Archives Centre, Australian National University
NKGB People's Commissariat for State Security (USSR)
NKVD People's Commissariat for Internal Affairs (USSR)
NLA National Library of Australia
NSW New South Wales

NUAUS National Union of Australian University Students
OUP Oxford University Press
PCF Parti Communiste Français
PCI Partito Comunista Italiano
PKI Partai Komunis Indonesia
QC Queen's Counsel
RAAF Royal Australian Air Force
RSL Returned Sailors', Soldiers' and Airmen's Imperial League of Australia
SLNSW State Library of New South Wales
SLP State Labor Party of New South Wales
SMWIU Sheet Metal Working Industrial Union of Australia
SUP Sydney University Press
THC Victorian Trades Hall Council
UCL University College London
UNESCO United Nations Educational, Scientific and Cultural Organization
UNSWP University of New South Wales Press
UQP University of Queensland Press
USSR Union of Soviet Socialist Republics
UWA University of Western Australia
UWAP University of Western Australia Press (later Publishing)
VE Victory in Europe (8 May 1945)
WEA Workers' Educational Association
WEB Women's Employment Board
WFTU World Federation of Trade Unions
WWF Waterside Workers' Federation

Preface

This book follows an earlier one, *The Reds*, which covered the first two decades of the Communist Party of Australia from its foundation in 1920 up to the Second World War. *The Reds* appeared in 1998, so I cannot be accused of rushing the sequel. One reason for the delay was beyond my control: in the following year I took on an administrative post at my university, which drew me into a number of related activities. Unable to give the second volume of communist history the sustained attention it required, I turned to other, more manageable, research projects. The last and most substantial of these, a study of Australia in war and reconstruction during the 1940s, took me back to the point at which *The Reds* ended with a greater appreciation of that momentous decade in which communism exerted its greatest influence in this country.

I cut my teeth as a historian with two books on the British left, *A Proletarian Science* and *Little Moscows*. My first substantial exercise in writing Australian communist history came at the end of the 1970s, when I returned to Australia and embarked on a biography of Paddy Troy, a legendary figure in the port city of Fremantle. I drew heavily on oral history to supplement union records, which then could be read in the union office with members only too happy to answer my questions, and other primary sources. Members of the Troy family and a number of Western Australian informants—some identified below—gave me insight into the lived experience of communism 70 and 80 years ago.

I began work on a national history after historian Andrew Wells asked me to join him in an expression of interest to the trustees of the Communist Party in writing its history. We obtained a grant from the Australian Research Council, which enabled us to employ Beverley Symons as our research assistant. As well as compiling a comprehensive bibliography, Beverley collected, organised and indexed a very large body of primary sources on which I have continued to draw. *The Reds* lists a large number of informants, archivists, librarians and scholars who assisted me as I wrote that volume. Invidious though it is to single out one from so many, I was particularly indebted to the late Bob Gollan for his encouragement, support and close reading of drafts.

It is not possible to simply resume a history of communism after an interval of twenty years. I put it aside just a few years after the fall of the Berlin Wall and the hoisting of the Russian tricolour over the Kremlin in place of the flag bearing the hammer and sickle. Apart from five countries that are grotesque parodies of the cause they continue to profess, communism is now a distant memory. Back then I was in touch with many who had lived through the events with which this volume is concerned; very few now remain. *The Reds* showed the growth over two decades of a tiny political venture into a party of modest proportions. *The Party* covers three decades during which this party grew rapidly in size and influence, entered into an extensive range of activities, had a much greater presence in national affairs and incurred much greater hostility. In writing this phase of its history I have necessarily used a smaller scale. And in relating its subsequent decline, I have wrestled with the paradox that as the Communist Party of Australia shed some of its least attractive qualities, its fortunes dwindled.

Most of those who shared their recollections for *The Reds* also spoke about the years that followed. More recently, others whose involvement began after 1940 have provided testimony. But from the time I joined the Communist Party in 1971 as a young historian, my interest in the past overlapped with friendships and acquaintanceships to the point that I have difficulty compiling a full list of those who helped me. Marking the deceased with a ★ (they would not appreciate the conventional +) and apologising to those overlooked, I thank Annette Aarons★, Brian Aarons, Eric Aarons★, Laurie Aarons★, Mark Aarons, Hugh Anderson★, Zelda D'Aprano★, Pauline and Bruce Armstrong★, Les Barnes★, Jean Blackburn★, Audrey and Jack Blake★, Bob Boughton, Joe★ and Hazel Butorac, Eileen Chapman, Lloyd Churchward★, Mick Counihan, Pat and Noel Counihan★, Ruth Crow★, Ann Curthoys,

Barbara Curthoys★, Dave Davies, Lloyd Davies★, Geoff Davis, Miriam Dixson★, Gwyn and Hume Dow★, Lloyd Edmunds★, Geoff Evans, Judy Ferguson, Eric Fry★, Rivo Gandini★, Ralph Gibson★, Bill Gollan★, Bob Gollan★, Daphne Gollan★, Norma Grieve★, Gerry Harant, Evelyn Healy★, Pat Healy, June Hearn, Tom Hills★, Jack Hutson★, Amirah Inglis★, Audrey Johnson★, Monty Johnstone, Bill Latter★, Margaret Lindley, Jack Lindsay★, Penny Lockwood, Les Louis, Wendy Lowenstein★, John McKenzie★, David McKnight, Max Marginson★, Jack Mundey★, Nita and Stephen Murray-Smith★, Ken Norling, Max Ogden, John O'Leary★, Penny Pollitt, Barbara Purse, Ted Roach★, Mavis and Alec Robertson★, Betty Searle★, George Seelaf★, Dawn and John Sendy★, Nonie and Geoff Sharp★, Carmel Shute, Bernard Smith★, Jim Staples★, Joyce Stevens★, Carl Stubbings, Bernie Taft★, Mark Taft, Lal Troy★, Pat Troy, Ann Turner and Edgar Waters★, Ian Turner★, Bob Walshe★, Judah Waten★, Ted Zeffert★ and Sandra Goldbloom Zurbo.

As with *The Reds*, I benefited from having much rare or restricted material to hand in my study. Copies of documents assembled by Beverley Symons sit on the shelves alongside large collections of pamphlets given by Miriam Dixson and Gwyn and Hume Dow. Nicholas Brown, Rowan Cahill, Craig Campbell, Penny Pollitt and Andrew Reeves lent or gave further material for this volume, while Phillip Deery and Michael Lazarus made long runs of the *Communist Review* available.

As the result of the COVID-19 lockdown and my own treatment for cancer, I lost access to the principal repositories during the final year of research and writing. I am indebted to Brendan Somes of the State Library of New South Wales and Luke Whitington of the Search Foundation for making digital copies of documents in the national records of the Communist Party; to Katie Wood and Sophie Garrett for doing the same with the Victorian records of the Communist Party and papers of Bernie Taft in the University of Melbourne Archives; to Nicholas Brown, Emily Gallagher and Graeme Powell for locating and copying material in the manuscript collections of the National Library of Australia and Noel Butlin Archives Centre at the Australian National University; and to Ashley Sutherland of the University of Melbourne Library for arranging a long-term loan of its holding of the Melbourne *Guardian*. My debt to

Emily Gallagher increased as she took on much of the pictorial research at short notice. Elizabeth Weiss was as supportive at Allen & Unwin as her predecessor John Iremonger was in publishing *The Reds*, and I greatly appreciated the skills of Samantha Kent and Nicole Young.

I have been assisted by information and advice from a large number of friends, colleagues and correspondents. These include Hugh Anderson, John Arnold, Peter Beilharz, James Bennett, Jude Bloomfield, Bill Bunbury, Pamela Burton, Craig Campbell, David Carter, Lynn Dalgarno, Phillip Deery, Alex Ettling, Ross Fitzgerald, Sheila Fitzpatrick, Charlie Fox, Barry Jones, Ben Kiernan, Julie Kimber, Andrew Lemon, Peter Love, Martie Lowenstein, Janet McCalman, Iain McIntyre, Mark McKenna, David McKnight, the late John McLaren, Laurence Maher, Greg Mallory, Ken Mansell, Philip Mendes, Julian Meyrick, Stephen Moline, Kevin Morgan, Mary Mortimer, Doug Munro, Martin Munz, John Myrtle, Greg Pemberton, Angela O'Brien, Bobbie Oliver, Carolyn Rasmussen, Andrew Reeves, Jan Richardson, Anne Richter, Lyndall Ryan, Tom Sheridan, Carmel Shute, Paul Strangio, Carl Stubbings, Lesley Synge, Peter Thompson, Gary Werskey and Sally Young.

Brian Aarons, Phillip Deery, Stephen Moline, Andrew Reeves, Sean Scalmer, Mark Taft and James Walter read all or part of the manuscript and made valuable suggestions. It is fitting that Brian Aarons and Mark Taft should have done so, since from the time I began work on the party's history I had long conversations with Brian's father Laurie and uncle Eric, as well as Mark's father Bernie. While taking a keen interest in *The Reds*, they were even more interested in how I would deal with the events that followed—as they came together to play a decisive role in the party's fortunes, only to fall out over intractable disagreements. That the three of them allowed me to form my own judgements on these events was not the least of their services.

Introduction

Communism was a political movement like no other, unique in its scope and in the commitment it demanded, utterly different from conventional parties. When the Communist Party of Australia (CPA) began in 1920 as a small and distant section of the newly formed Communist International, it was required to adopt a revolutionary program and repudiate any suggestion that workers could be emancipated by piecemeal reform. Still in its strident infancy, this tiny party was castigated in 1922 for isolating itself from a local labour movement wedded to reformism. At the end of the decade the CPA was ordered to end all collaboration with these reformists and embark on unremitting revolutionary agitation. In 1935 it had once more to redirect its efforts, this time in pursuit of a broad alliance against the threat of fascism and war.[1]

Each reversal of direction came with a fresh appraisal of the changing fortunes in the class struggle. Here communists drew on Marx's understanding of capitalism as an oppressive system based on the exploitation of labour. The single-minded pursuit of profit was invading every corner of life, turning everything into a commodity, while the unprecedented productive powers that capitalism released were punctuated by crises of mounting severity. Since capitalism knew no territorial limits, the class struggle spread from the industrial heartlands to encompass every part of the world. As early as 1848, Marx and Engels traced the consequences in their *Communist Manifesto*, which concluded with the rallying cry: 'Workers of the world, unite!'

A half-century later, Lenin added the further stipulation of a dedicated revolutionary party to channel the discontent of workers into effective action. At his insistence, every kind of opposition to capitalism had to be brought under the control of this vanguard party, as he described it, which in turn must exercise absolute authority over its members' activities. Lenin's Russian followers operated initially as a faction of that country's socialist party, styling themselves the Bolsheviks (or members of the majority). After seizing power in 1917 they adopted the title of the Communist Party. This was a party of a new kind, and one that was imitated all round the world. It attracted adherents who gave no quarter in their revolutionary fervour and withstood hardship, victimisation and repression. Their Australian opponents, who denounced them as fanatics, wreckers and traitors, used various terms of opprobrium: they were the Reds, the Commos or simply the Comms. The members themselves had no doubt as to their allegiance: they belonged to 'the Party'.

The Communist International (or Comintern), established after the Russian Revolution, embraced every national party in a single, unified whole. Delegates who attended its world congresses adopted resolutions that an executive committee and secretariat drawn from the constituent parties administered—Lance Sharkey, president of the CPA, was a member of the executive committee from 1935, and other Australians worked in the secretariat alongside comrades from many countries. But the congresses were held in Moscow, the capital of the Union of Soviet Socialist Republics (USSR), where the executive committee met and the secretariat worked. This was a matter of practical necessity since no other country would allow such a hostile presence. The Soviet Union stood alone until the Second World War as the only land under communist rule.

Lenin, its founder, was the creator of twentieth-century communism and instigator of the Communist International. He codified Marxism into a science that disclosed the laws of social change, allowing communists to predict and hence control the course of history. He invested the party with an infallible authority and bequeathed the terminology and symbols—vanguard and rank-and-file, hammer and sickle—adopted by comrades in other lands. The Russian Revolution was at once the inspiration for communists everywhere, a universal model applied to their own country's circumstances, and a form of political activity grafted onto its history and traditions. The implications of this dual legacy form one theme of the history of Australian communism.

At least initially, adherents did not feel any conflict of loyalties. The unshakeable unity of all proletarians was a central tenet of communism, so the Australian party supported the struggles of workers and victims of imperialism everywhere. In upholding the achievements of the Soviet Union and dedicating themselves to defend it against any threat, they did not see themselves as serving the interests of another country, for the socialist sixth of the world was the homeland of all communists.[2] But its rule by a single party degenerated after Lenin's death into rule by a single person, and Stalin's dictatorship of the Soviet Union carried over to the Communist International. The Terror he unleashed on his compatriots also swallowed up the foreigners who worked for the International in Moscow, as one national group after another disappeared from the Hotel Lux on Gorky Street, where Jack and Audrey Blake were living in 1937 as Australian representatives.[3] Under Stalin, the Communist International became an appendage of Soviet foreign policy, completely subordinated to its interests.

So it was that Australian communists were informed in late August 1939 that the Soviet Union had signed a treaty with Nazi Germany. Ostensibly, this Non-Aggression Pact was an agreement that neither country would wage war on the other, nor give any assistance to its enemies. In itself, this was an astonishing reversal of the campaign for collective security against fascist aggression to which all communists had directed their efforts since Hitler came to power in Germany. Stalin justified it by claiming to have outwitted Britain and France, with which the USSR had been negotiating an agreement to guarantee Poland's security from German demands. He accused the two Western powers of procrastinating to encourage Hitler to unleash his armies through Poland onto Russian soil. He failed to disclose the secret protocol to the pact that divided the lands separating Germany and the Soviet Union between the two signatories, so that Germany's march into western Poland at the beginning of September was followed within a fortnight by Soviet occupation of the eastern half.

Though taken by surprise, the Australian party readily embraced the feeble rationalisation of the Non-Aggression Pact. Within a week, however, Germany's invasion of Poland forced it to abandon the pretence that Stalin had secured peace in Europe, and the subsequent declaration of hostilities against Germany by Britain and France discredited his specious allegation they were conspiring to allow Hitler free rein. Soon Australian communists were told to drop their support for Polish independence and stop championing Australia's participation in the war against the Nazi aggressor. The conflict must no longer be treated as defending democracy against fascism, they were told; rather, it was an 'unjust, reactionary, imperialist war' that must be rejected by communists everywhere.[4]

The CPA again complied. As instructed, it also made public acknowledgement that it had erred in its initial appraisal of the war because of what it described lamely as an 'over-simplified, anti-fascist' stance. In a characteristically brazen statement, the party president Lance Sharkey dismissed any suggestion that Australian communists were betraying the defence of democracy on the grounds that 'the role of democracy changes with the march of events' and 'what is revolutionary today can be reactionary tomorrow'. The party would accordingly raise its theoretical level to ensure members understood democracy more 'dialectically'.[5]

The pact with Hitler, betrayal of Poland and precipitate abandonment of any reference to the threat of fascism were too much for some comrades, who shed their membership. Others freely admitted bewilderment, but Australia remained free of the divisions that occurred within the Communist Party of Great Britain and Parti Communiste Français at this time.[6] From its Bolshevisation at the beginning of the 1930s until the early 1960s, the CPA was notable for unquestioning adherence to a monolithic communist orthodoxy—though the subsequent break from conformity would take it further into heterodoxy than other communist parties. The reasons for its prolonged compliance, as well as the subsequent independence, make up a further theme of this history.

When Bulgarian exile Georgi Dimitrov, who became head of the Communist International after defying a Nazi show trial in 1933, asked Stalin how he should frame its statement on the outbreak of war, he was told that there was nothing to choose between the two sides. 'We have no objection to their having a good fight,' Stalin told him, and they should be encouraged to do so in the expectation that 'the position of the richest capitalist countries (especially England) were shattered'. That calculation did not find its way into Dimitrov's declaration, which was published by the Australian party at the end of 1939, but the actions of the Soviet Union were sufficient to arouse increasing hostility.[7]

Especially after the USSR invaded neighbouring Finland at the end of November 1939, the CPA encountered violent opposition. Street meetings were broken up, property destroyed, speakers assaulted. Jean Devanny, an accomplished platform performer who took pride in her ability to deal with an abusive audience, admitted to fearing for her safety. She welcomed the dismemberment of Poland, writing to her friend Miles Franklin that 'ever since the Red Army marched into White Russia and the Ukraine, a little engine seems to be pulsating in my breast, an engine of pulsating joy'. In a subsequent letter to Katharine Susannah Prichard, another communist writer of equal fidelity to the cause, she dismissed press reports of unruly affrays at the party's pitch in the Sydney Domain. 'My spirits are sky high', she wrote, even though her memoirs attest to the opposite.[8]

Communists were used to threats and abuse, indeed they wore them as badges of honour that testified to their prosecution of the class war. Those active in the Depression had experienced treatment at least as rough as they encountered at this time, for there was limited popular enthusiasm for Australia's involvement in the opening phase of the Second World War, when the lack of military action on the Western front gave rise to the description 'Phoney War'. That inaction ended in May 1940 as German forces swept through the Low Countries and pushed deep into France, forcing it to capitulate by the end of June. In the same month the Soviet Union annexed the Baltic States. With Britain and its Dominions now fighting alone and Italy joining Germany to launch its own offensive in the Mediterranean, the government led by Robert Menzies stepped up Australia's military effort. The Communist Party's continued anti-war activity brought a ban on its newspapers in May and declaration of illegality on 15 June, accompanied by raids on communist premises and followed by prosecution of members for a range of offences under the National Security Act.

The conditions of illegality were not rigorous. Members continued their agitation through a range of other organisations, and a number even stood for parliament in the federal election of September 1940. *Tribune*, the national newspaper, reappeared in a reduced format within two months, and other underground presses produced a range of further publications that were more outspoken since they no longer underwent wartime censorship, and probably aroused greater interest because of their clandestine nature. More than one security officer thought the Communist Party was assisted, rather than hampered, by its illegal status. Membership had fallen from 4421 in mid-1939 to 3569 at year's end, but held up in the first year of illegality. By early 1941 there were 4000 or more—the circumstances of the time prevented a precise count.[9]

The CPA continued to condemn Australia's participation in this 'capitalist conflict', though the military defeats that precipitated its illegality also brought an adjustment of policy. Stalin, who had expected a long war of attrition, was shaken by Germany's speedy conquest of Western Europe since it freed Hitler to turn to the East. While not abandoning condemnation of the belligerents, the Communist International now called for the replacement of their rulers by 'people's governments' that would work for peace—or, if necessary, wage a people's war against any threat of invasion.

Stalin had ample warning of Hitler's intention to launch an invasion, and not just from British intelligence sent to him by Winston Churchill, for Soviet agents in Berlin and Tokyo confirmed the Nazi preparations.[10] Still hoping to conciliate Germany, he insisted that Britain was again trying to 'switch the war' against the Soviet homeland, a claim the Australian party reiterated throughout the first half of 1941. On 22 June, the very day that Hitler ordered 150 army divisions to begin Operation Barbarossa, Nazi Germany's codename for the invasion of Russia, *Tribune* derided any suggestion the Soviet Union would be attacked as 'wishful thinking'.[11]

'Without any warning', the CPA's national secretary, J.B. Miles, wrote on the following day, Hitler had 'launched the Nazi hordes against the peaceful Soviet socialist people', and he called on all workers to rally to its defence. Three weeks later, Lance Sharkey emerged from hiding to give a press conference in which he stated: 'We will support every effort to defeat Fascism and Hitlerite Germany.' Asked if his pledge of complete assistance to the efforts of the Allies meant a change of communist policy, he replied, 'We have always opposed Fascism.'[12]

Such barefaced denial of a previous position was the stock-in-trade of Australian communism. Refusal to admit any error, this one affirmed so recently, only drew attention to its expediency. Given the transformative effects of the Soviet Union's entry into the war at a time when the outcome hung in the balance, few dwelt at this time on the CPA's earlier anti-war stance; it was later, when the wartime unity ended, that its record of following the dictates of a capricious parent body was held up to hostile scrutiny. Even so, the series of abrupt changes of policy made at this time had a cumulative effect. They taxed the loyalty of members, who were expected not just to fall into line but to uphold the new line without any public acknowledgement the previous one was mistaken. Obedience required pliancy, and too many calls on pliancy resulted in cynicism. A further theme of this history is the debilitating effect of this habit of denial.

★

The entry of the Soviet Union into the war brought enormous relief to Australian communists. A short time after it was reported, two young members attended a symphony concert in Sydney where the orchestra began with the customary 'God Save the King' before the conductor swept it unexpectedly into 'The Internationale'. For those used to hearing that fugitive anthem reproduced in scratchy recordings or sung in meagre choruses in half-empty halls, the effect of hearing it filling a concert theatre was electrifying. 'From 22 June,' one of them recalled, 'we were on the side of the (red) angels, and yet we were on the side of the rest of Australia. Without sacrificing our ideals, we belonged.'[13]

There was an immediate growth of membership that accelerated throughout 1942: 3000 were recruited between June 1941 and May 1942, 9000 more by the end of the year.[14] Branches sprang up in most suburbs and regional towns, many with their own bookshop, office and meeting rooms. Newspaper circulation increased proportionately, and you could listen to a communist radio program on a daily basis. This enlarged party championed the war effort: communist-led unions spear-headed the drive for increased production and many leading members went into the armed services.

There was also an immediate public response to Australia's new ally. A large crowd gathered at the Sydney Domain on the Sunday following the German invasion—police said 11,000, the organisers claimed 40,000—to hail the Soviet Union's entry into the war. Four days later, 4000 citizens packed the Sydney Town Hall to affirm their support, with another 1500 listening outside to a broadcast of proceedings. The lord mayor presided as Ernest Burgmann, the Anglican bishop of Goulburn, declared 'we are here tonight to pledge our solidarity with the great Russian people in their struggle first for existence and then for freedom to develop their great work'. Even before Sharkey appeared to pledge support for the Allied war effort, this Christian socialist was calling for communists to forgive the capitalists and capitalists the communists.[15]

In the following month the redoubtable Jessie Street drew on her extensive range of contacts in the Sydney establishment to form a Russian Medical Aid Committee. It had the chancellor of the city's university as president, with the governor's wife, the Anglican archbishop of Sydney and the state premier among the patrons. Street paid the rent for the organisation's city office.[16] John Curtin, a few days into office as prime minister, sent a message of support for its first major appeal, a 'button day', later in the year. Volunteers sold the buttons, depicting Soviet leaders, on streets and in workplaces at prices ranging from sixpence to a pound (Marshal Timoshenko was particularly popular), with hammer-and-sickle earrings also on offer. A procession then marched from the city to a fete at Kings Cross, led by returned soldiers carrying portraits of King George VI, Churchill (deprived of the trademark cigar) and Stalin (who kept his pipe). There were mounted Cossacks in national dress, along with contingents of the Free French, Poles, Greeks and participants from other German-occupied countries, all bearing their national flags. Banks helped collect donations, bookmakers from Tattersall's Club conducted raffles, and bands from the Eastern Command and the city fire brigade entertained the crowd.[17]

After the outbreak of the Pacific War in December 1941 made it difficult to obtain medical supplies, the committee concentrated on sending sheepskins to help those fighting on the Eastern Front survive the northern winter—and subsequently amended its title to the Russian Medical Aid and Comforts Committee. With assistance from a host of voluntary organisations and free rail transport to city warehouses, the sheepskins were purchased, tanned and dispatched by ship, half a million of them by war's end, along with ambulances and other items.

Among the fundraising efforts for the Medical Aid and Comforts fund was a 'Racing for Russia' meeting organised by the Newcastle Jockey Club in August 1942 with the support of the Trades Hall Council. The program had six events, including the Stalin Flying Welter, the Timoshenko Three-Year-Old Novice and the Molotov Improvers' Handicap. It raised £2000 and also stimulated a well-to-do country trainer to register a promising colt as Russia. Ridden by David 'Darby' Munro, Russia ran away with the 1946 Melbourne Cup.[18]

Ostensibly, the Medical Aid and Comforts Committee was non-political, although the communist journalist Rupert Lockwood served as its publicity agent and another party member, Doris Beeby, became principal organiser. A separate Aid Russia Committee was therefore launched at the Sydney Town Hall on 30 August 1941 at a Congress for Friendship and Aid to the Soviet Union. After Canon Arthur Garnsey, head of Sydney University's Anglican college St Paul's, opened proceedings with a prayer, churchmen, parliamentarians, academics, writers and feminists, including Jessie Street, were among the speakers who endorsed a resolution urging complete cooperation with the Soviet ally. The highlight of the congress was a presentation to the Sydney City Council of a Soviet flag, carried down the body of the hall by six returned soldiers as the 2400 delegates stood to sing the Internationale.[19]

Soviet flags flew from all public buildings for the anniversary of the Russian Revolution on 7 November 1941, when the Australian Broadcasting Commission (ABC) arranged a special program of talks, music and drama.[20] The next rally, in February 1942, this time organised jointly by the Aid Russia and Medical Aid committees, bore the title Congress for National Unity for an Allied Victory. The list of office-holders of the Aid Russia Committee had grown to include the secretaries of the NSW Rugby League and Soccer associations, and among the speakers were two members of the federal Cabinet, business leaders, the state president of the Returned Sailors', Soldiers' and Airmen's Imperial League of Australia (RSL), the headmaster of Sydney Grammar and an assembly of consuls. The congress opened to the strains of 'Advance Australia Fair' as a guard of honour marched up the hall with massed flags, the Australian and Soviet ones flanked by the Union Jack, Stars and Stripes and those of the other Allied nations. The second day began with Canon Garnsey conducting a ceremony at the Cenotaph for the fallen of the Red Army and the Australian Imperial Force (AIF).[21]

Similar organisations in other states raised funds for the Soviet Union and marked its national days. An event in Melbourne to celebrate the anniversary of the Russian Revolution in 1943 was also billed as a rally to promote the latest Australian war loan. Brass and pipe bands led marchers, banners and floats through the city to the West Melbourne stadium, where the stage was bedecked with heroic depictions of Allied leaders, a capacity crowd of 12,000 participants all rising to sing the Internationale. General Blamey, the Australian commander-in-chief, sent a message to the organisers hailing 'the courage and unforgettable spirit of the Russian people', and the head of the Soviet legation was welcomed to the podium by the Labor politician Bill Slater, who had recently returned from representing Australia in the USSR.[22]

In the same year the Australia–Soviet Friendship League of Victoria set about creating a rest and recreation centre for members of the armed forces that would foster closer relations between the two countries. The organising committee assembled an impressive list of patrons and paid £16,300 for a bluestone warehouse in Flinders Lane. A public appeal to convert and fit it out was launched at the Town Hall in 1944, and the lord mayor opened Australia–Soviet House later that year, when the guests of honour included the Anglican archbishop of Melbourne and Sir John Latham, chief justice of the High Court.

The renovated building had a bookshop at the entrance with Australian and Soviet flags in the window, and there was a small kiosk alongside. Behind them were rest rooms and a large dining room that served cheap meals to servicemen and women. A hall on the first floor was used for dances, lectures, concerts and film screenings. Reading rooms, an art gallery and a library stocked with Russian educational and cultural material occupied the top floor. Apart from the voluntary labour that went into Australia-Soviet House, a sum of £22,000 was raised to create and staff this 'monument to our victorious fighting alliance with the Soviet peoples'.[23]

How deep ran the support for the Soviet Union? For some Australians it was a matter of self-interest, a calculated judgement that my enemy's enemy is my friend. This was the position of Winston Churchill, whose wife Clementine headed the British Aid to Russia Fund. It is noticeable also that these friends used the designation Russia in preference to the more politically laden Soviet Union. Stalin himself invoked past patriotic struggles against foreign invaders to rally his compatriots, and as the war proceeded he replaced the Internationale with a new state anthem, 'Be Glorious, Our Free Motherland'—the Second World War is still known in Russia as the Great Patriotic War.

The epic battles that accompanied the siege of Leningrad, the defence of Moscow and the destruction of a whole German Army at Stalingrad undoubtedly compelled admiration, as did the extraordinary sacrifices endured by the civilian population. In one of his exhortations to greater effort, John Curtin called on Australians to emulate the defence of Leningrad, where 'the people still stand fighting because of the reborn patriotism which has marked Russian history ever since the Bolshevik Revolution'. Communists who had long extolled the Soviet unity of purpose now found themselves in unfamiliar company. In marking the 25th anniversary of the Russian Revolution at the end of 1942, the *Sydney Morning Herald* attributed the country's survival to the 'constructive strength of the Stalinist regime'.[24]

The party continued to grow. By the end of 1944 it had 22,052 members, and the classes held to induct the flow of recruits into an understanding of communist theory and practice had become a major undertaking. Earlier in that year the party paid £30,000 for a substantial commercial building at the upper end of George Street in Sydney, which 'shock brigades' of members transformed into the national headquarters.

There was a basement for storage, a large bookshop and a cafeteria on the ground floor, then lecture halls, meeting rooms, various specialist departments, and offices for the principal functionaries, with editorial facilities for the newspapers and periodicals on the fifth floor. Seeing Marx House for the first time when posted to a Royal Australian Air Force (RAAF) training course in Ultimo, an interstate member wrote to a comrade that he was 'stunned by its greatness'.[25]

Several hundred 'cadres' gathered there every Saturday afternoon to hear reports and discuss plans. Some were full-time party organisers; an increasing number were union officials as communists won posts in many of the largest and most powerful trade unions. *Tribune* appeared twice a week from early 1945 and there were plans to make it a daily. It was here also that an exhibition was opened in August to mark the 25th anniversary of the Australian Communist Party. Paintings, murals, convict leg-irons, a musket from the Eureka stockade, an edition of the handwritten newspaper published at William Lane's 'New Australia' socialist colony in Paraguay and the rotary press built to produce the illegal *Tribune* between 1940 and 1942 were among the exhibits that traced 'The Story of Australian Labor History' from colonial settlement to 'the further unfolding of the story' in a commitment to achieve 'real post-war security—for jobs, homes, health, more rapid expansion of education, culture, recreational facilities—in short . . . what kind of Australia we should live in'.[26]

★

On the morning of 8 July 1949, less than five years after this national headquarters opened, an officer of the Commonwealth Security Service entered it with a warrant issued under the Crimes Act. Assisted by customs officials and members of the police force, the Commonwealth Investigation Service searched the building and carried off all its contents. The action was conducted in conjunction with emergency legislation that froze union funds in order to end a strike of the communist-led Miners' Federation that was crippling industry and denying both heat and light to households in the depths of winter. Already under financial stress, the Communist Party sold Marx House in September. Australia–Soviet House in Melbourne lasted little longer. Beset by dwindling membership and mounting debts, the party sold the building at the end of the year.[27]

Efforts to promote friendship with the Soviet Union now fell on stony ground. In 1948 the Sydney City Council denied the use of its town hall to the Australian–Russian Society, and the prohibition was subsequently applied to a reception for the Reverend Hewlett Johnson, the celebrated 'Red Dean' of Canterbury, when he visited Australia for a peace conference. An alderman explained that such functions were sponsored by 'misguided people and could serve no useful purpose'.[28] The Melbourne City Council applied the same ban in 1949 to a booking by the Australia–Soviet House organisers: the council clerk explained that the town hall was not to be let to the Communist Party or any of its auxiliaries.[29]

Later in the same year a Victorian royal commission was told that those who had assisted in the establishment of Australia–Soviet House were 'dupes of the Communist Party'. The secretary of the organisation produced a list of the patrons associated with the 1944 appeal for funds and the first name he read out from the witness box was that of the royal commissioner. 'I am not going to sit here and listen to such innuendoes,' Sir Charles Lowe interrupted, even though the inquiry was occasioned by the allegations and innuendoes of a former communist who was paid a large sum to publish them in the Murdoch press. 'I lent my name as a patron,' Sir Charles explained, 'because I was told that Australia–Soviet House was a club to which Soviet and allied soldiers could resort' and 'any suggestion I have ever had sympathy with communist aspirations is entirely devoid of foundation'.[30]

Good will towards the Soviet Union turned rapidly into mistrust and hostility at the end of the Second World War as Stalin imposed communist rule in Eastern Europe. Churchill's address in March 1946 at a college graduation ceremony in Fulton, Missouri, is widely regarded as heralding the advent of the Cold War. 'From Stettin in the Baltic to Trieste in the Adriatic,' he declared, 'an iron curtain has descended across the continent.' Less often quoted is his warning that 'in a great number of countries, far from the Russian frontier and throughout the world, Communist fifth columns are established and work in complete unity and absolute obedience to the directions they receive from the Communist centre'.[31]

The Chifley government initially resisted the confrontational foreign policies of the United States and Britain, though Australia's strategic dependence on the Western alliance forced accommodation by the end of the decade. At home a change of mood was evident from the end of the war and not just within civic bodies that expelled communists and proscribed any association with activities deemed sympathetic to the USSR. A concerted campaign to drive communists out of the trade unions coincided with a wave of strikes that began in the second half of 1945 and culminated with that of the coalminers in 1949.

As communist support for the Labor government turned to overt hostility, the Australian Labor Party (ALP) enforced strict rules of loyalty on its members. Jessie Street was one of the victims. She had contested the federal seat of Wentworth as an ALP candidate and in 1943 came close to defeating the sitting member for this conservative electorate in Sydney's eastern suburbs. Her chances of success in the new and adjoining electorate of Phillip were good, but in 1948 the ALP made its endorsement conditional on her resigning from the Australian-Russian Society. Street refused to do so, stood as an independent in 1949 and attracted barely a tenth of the votes of the successful Labor candidate.[32]

By then the Commonwealth had passed legislation prohibiting any interference with defence projects and, in response to evidence of Soviet espionage in Australia, created a new security agency to hunt out fifth columnists. At the time of the miners' strike, the party's leader, Lance Sharkey, was in gaol. Asked by a reporter to explain how the Communist Party would respond to a war involving the USSR, he had replied that 'If Soviet forces, in pursuit of aggressors, entered Australia, Australian workers would welcome them.' Sharkey was charged with sedition, convicted and sentenced to three years in prison.

★

Communism's abrupt changes of fortune in the 1940s had a lasting effect. The party weathered the initial adversity with a grim determination. Then, after the transformation of the war into a concerted effort to destroy fascism, communists around the world enjoyed unprecedented legitimacy. In occupied countries they led resistance movements.

In Australia their strong presence in unions covering industries vital to the war effort brought them into the counsel of the prime minister. His government regularly consulted communist union leaders and appointed them to commissions that controlled crucial sectors of the workforce; they in turn accepted wage controls, condemned recourse to strike action and threw their weight behind the government on measures such as conscription that divided the labour movement.

The growth of the Communist Party after 1941 also broadened its composition. Ever since the unions had created the Labor Party to improve the lot of workers, it had been dominated by male wage-earners. There was little place in this milieu for women or middle-class progressives. Both were drawn into the country's war effort, but the tertiary-educated professionals who contributed their expertise to vital tasks of planning, coordination and administration were still looked upon with suspicion—hence Ben Chifley's observation that there were 'enough bloody B.A.s' working for the government—while the influx of women into war industries was seen as a temporary expedient.[33]

By contrast, the Communist Party embraced each of these two increasingly important constituencies. When male cadres enrolled for military service, female ones took on organisational tasks. Communist unions were the most responsive to the needs and concerns of women in the paid workforce. Scientists, doctors, architects and other professionals were drawn into party committees that planned the new post-war order, while journalists, writers and artists contributed to an upsurge of cultural activity. More than any other political movement, the party linked the transformative effects of a people's war to winning a people's peace.[34]

Some of these expectations were realised in Australia's program of post-war reconstruction, though the onset of the Cold War reduced the opportunity for communists to participate. And the decision in 1945 to prosecute an industrial offensive put the party on a collision course with the government. The previous insistence of communists on wage restraint and avoidance of stoppages had strained the patience of union members, so they relished the chance to improve their pay and conditions. In a series of disputes initiated in the abattoirs, the metal industries and the rail and maritime transport sectors in 1946, 1947 and 1948, communists used their influence to bring about general stoppages and in most cases secured their demands. But the cost of such repeated disruption was heavy, eroding public sympathy and taxing the loyalty of the working-class families that went without pay for lengthy periods. Laurie Aarons, who later led the party but was then a young organiser in Newcastle, has recalled how this wave of militancy and the increasingly intransigent language that accompanied it prevented the leadership from understanding the consequences: 'all the time our political support was eroding and we didn't know it'.[35]

The coal strike of 1949, the last and most costly of these industrial confrontations, put an end to that ignorance. It also confirmed a narrowing of communist activity. The non-industrial forms of involvement continued but were more difficult to sustain in the face of Cold War hostility, while the fight in the unions absorbed a growing proportion of the party's energies. Moreover, the effort to maintain its industrial base returned the Australian Communist Party to the conundrum with which it had wrestled from the beginning. Trade unions, according to communist doctrine, existed to improve the wages and working conditions of workers under the illusion that capitalism could satisfy their needs. The task of communists was to raise this 'trade union consciousness' to a fuller, political understanding, and strikes were the principal means of winning union members to the revolutionary cause. From this perspective, an unsuccessful strike was as efficacious as a successful one.[36]

For those communists who held union posts, however, defeat had serious consequences—both for their members and for their own standing. The party had always directed industrial activity so that a senior organiser met regularly with communist union leaders to determine strategy, but these leaders had to reconcile the party's expectations with the circumstances of their industry and the willingness of their members. We shall see how communists who rose to national leadership of powerful unions became less amenable to direction.

The failure of the 1949 coal strike figures as a watershed in communist memoirs that appeared many years later, when the cause to which their authors dedicated their lives was passing out of existence. 'It is only four years since the war has ended,' one wrote of this ruinous defeat, 'but it might have been a century ago. The interlude of hope has passed.'[37] The cultural historian of Australian communism David Carter has observed that such testimonies are not concerned with self-justification; their purpose is to tell a now obscure history that otherwise will not get told, one of ordinary men and women caught up in a great historical movement and living, for a time, 'on the side of history'.[38]

The story they relate begins with the Depression of the 1930s, which ruptured the established order and initiated a political awakening. The abject surrender to fascism of so many countries advanced the cause as proof of the death of the old order and confirmation that the Soviet Union was the sole bulwark against barbarism. This narrative faltered with the Nazi–Soviet Non-Aggression Pact, but without breaking the conviction of imminent revolution. 'War-time brings difficulties and dangers,' a leading Australian communist wrote in a Christmas message to his mother at the end of 1939. 'But the whole pace of history is hurrying up, the new order is coming rapidly near, and we can afford to face what lies between.'[39]

The conviction strengthened after 1941, when the tension between support for the Soviet Union and democracy, the party and patriotism, was seemingly resolved. With the war now a people's war for a new social order, communists believed that they were indeed working with history and about to realise their historical mission. But at some point after the war the correlation between history and communism began to come unstuck. For some, the break occurred with the coal strike, for others it was Khrushchev's revelations in 1956 of Stalin's crimes or the later schism between Soviet and Chinese communists. These narratives are thus personal stories of a journey from innocence to experience that culminates in a decision to choose 'the broad left' over the narrow left. As Carter observes, no one wrote Stalinist memoirs.[40]

As the communist project was uncoupled from history, it became common to distinguish two kinds of communists—those forged in the Depression and those who joined during the Second World War. The art historian Bernard Smith, for example, states in his biography of the artist Noel Counihan, whose lifelong party membership began in 1931, that he had seen 'a much uglier side of capitalism' and was thus prepared to accept the party's discipline. Smith, on the other hand, did not join until 1939 and found the 'petty intolerances' more irksome. Both visited Eastern Europe after the war, and Counihan admired the new people's democracies whereas Smith discovered a police state and gave up his party card soon afterwards.[41] The rigours of the Depression certainly instilled an unyielding form of commitment; almost all the Australian leaders in the 1940s were products of this era, and they remained in charge into the 1960s.

In this typology the war communists are young men and women with broader intellectual horizons seeking an outlet for their progressive sympathies. Patricia Thompson provides an instructive example. Educated at Sydney Girls High, she travelled as a young woman to London in 1936, where she worked for the Left Book Club, and married John Thompson, an Arts graduate from Melbourne pursuing a literary career in England. They returned in 1939 to Perth, where John worked for the ABC and Pat became active in the Workers' Art Guild. She wanted to join the Communist Party but Katharine Susannah Prichard warned her 'not here and not yet', so her enlistment did not occur until the Soviet Union entered the war. By her own admission, it owed little to communist ideology (she had read neither Marx nor Lenin), and John later described Marxism as 'perhaps the last Christian heresy'. Rather, she explained, Australia did not offer the 'many shades of grey between the black and white of political extremes' that were available in England, and the CPA seemed the only organisation that grasped the full implications of the war against fascism. Though Pat was sometimes described as 'an intellectual bourgeois ratbag', she threw herself into party work and edited its Western Australian newspaper, the *Workers' Star*.[42]

Patricia Thompson also observed that most middle-class recruits did not stay on after the war. Her break came when John was transferred to Melbourne in 1945 and the party secretary there directed her to work as a country organiser. New to Victoria and with young children, she thought the proposition ludicrous and left. Membership statistics indicate that at least 20,000 men and women joined the Communist Party between 1941 and 1945, and also disclose that there was already a higher turnover than during the 1930s. More left and fewer joined with the onset of the Cold War, but precisely how many came and went remains a matter of conjecture. It has been suggested that at least 100,000 Australians passed through the ranks over the life of the Communist Party.[43]

The dramatic changes in the Communist Party's standing during the 1940s caused the greatest exodus, and some who departed were permanently embittered. Hence the philosopher John Passmore was grateful that he escaped the fate of contemporaries at the University of Sydney who, as ardent communists, adopted a 'vituperative style' of thought and expression, which they carried over into a subsequent career of anti-communist polemics. 'There are many anti-communists I mistrust,' he wrote, 'as much as I mistrust communists and for much the same reasons.'[44] But such apostates were atypical. John Thompson was a generous, self-effacing man who for some years gave lunchtime lectures on music at Australia–Soviet House. Later he combined foreign assignments for the ABC with documentaries that recalled the warm-hearted impulses of those who set about creating a new social order from the misery of the Depression and wartime sacrifice. He and Pat became community activists who defended the environmental and social amenity of inner-Sydney Paddington from the depredations of developers. The various causes taken up by ex-communists form an integral part of communist history.

Other war communists were cut from a different cloth. Here we find recruits who stayed the course and kept their convictions intact. Hal Alexander, an electrician who worked mostly in heavy industry, began his 50-year party membership as a teenager in 1941 and during the 1950s was a party organiser in what was called the 'red belt' of Sydney—the railway workshops, power stations, factories, breweries, foundries, brickyards and oil refineries that stretched from Redfern and Newtown down to Mascot and Botany. Why did he and other wage-earners in the red belt throw in their lot with the Communist Party? 'Because it gave us a rationale for the madness that was. Because it changed us from headbutting incompetents to some kind of thinking strategists. Because it gave us self-esteem. Because it educated us in the knowledge that WE were better than them.'[45] This dimension of communism as a transformative life experience that endowed adherents with knowledge, confidence and an unshakeable conviction is an essential component of its history.

★

Such a dimension is seldom captured in Australian studies of the subject. When research into the Communist Party of Australia began in the 1950s, it concentrated on policy, strategy and tactics. As with the studies of Soviet communism undertaken at this time, there was an emphasis on the hierarchical structure of the party and a corresponding concentration on the inner workings of its leadership. Such Kremlinology was employed to take the measure of an organisation that had an appreciable effect on Australian politics in the post-war period. Two political scientists went further. John Playford's 1962 doctoral thesis was a historical study of changes in communist policy. Alastair Davidson traced the tension between communist doctrine and local circumstances in a history published in 1969.[46]

As the party's influence declined, that way of writing about its predicament gave way to closer attention to what communists had done. Labour historians were first to investigate their work in industry, and subsequently there were studies of other areas of activity—among women and national minorities, in support of Aboriginal activism and against colonialism, as community activists and in local government, through the New Theatre and the Realist Writers, within university and artistic circles, the Eureka Youth League, the peace movement, campaigns for conservation and the environment, and many other endeavours.

The passing of the Cold War also made it possible to consider anti-communism as a subject with its own history. My earlier account of the first two decades of Australian communism paid limited attention to this aspect because it was derivative and peripheral to the party's fortunes. It was the Second World War that transformed the Soviet Union into a plausible threat to world security, just as it solidified the strength and ambition of the United States. The military and ideological rivalry of these two superpowers dominated world politics, and the Cold War infected Australian public life with a virulence from which few forms of radical belief or association were immune.

The Labor Party set up a dedicated organisation to drive communists out of the labour movement, and the failure to do so allowed its opponents to kick the communist can. Robert Menzies made a ban on the Communist Party a centrepiece of Coalition policy when he won office in 1949, and again to consolidate his control of parliament in the double-dissolution election of 1951. The setback later in the year when the referendum to allow this measure was rejected might even have worked to his advantage, since it allowed the Coalition to reap the electoral dividends of continued red-baiting. The schism in the ALP that followed in 1955 created a breakaway party whose raison d'être was the elimination of communism.

Cold War anti-communism went far beyond electoral politics. It reached into intellectual and cultural life and was projected onto many anxieties of the post-war era. Big business invested heavily in initiatives that promoted free enterprise as a bulwark against the threat to freedom. Eastern European émigrés kept the international dimension before the Australian public. Above all, there was the crusade of the Catholic Church against a doctrine of godless materialism. A lay organisation, Catholic Action had been formed before the war to advocate the church's social doctrine, but as the war ended the Australian bishops lent their authority to a new and far more combative Catholic Social Studies Movement. Sworn to secrecy, the members of this movement had their own full-time organisers and newspapers, a zeal that matched that of the communists, and a much larger base of support. The progeny of this arm of the church militant—including Tony Abbott, Gerard Henderson and Greg Sheridan—remain active in public life to the present day.[47]

Finally, from the 1990s there has been a plethora of publications on communist espionage. The upsurge of interest on this aspect might seem paradoxical since the appearance of these publications coincided with the disappearance of communism in Europe and the abandonment of any revolutionary intent among communist states elsewhere. It was in fact the end of the Cold War that opened the archives—albeit selectively—and allowed the conspiratorial heritage to be examined. In particular, the release by the United States' National Security Agency of decrypted messages sent from Australia to Moscow during the 1940s revealed that a senior Australian communist, Wally Clayton, had assembled a network of party members to gather classified information, which he then passed on to the Soviet legation in Canberra.[48]

The limitations of this source will be considered in later chapters. A more damaging shortcoming is the unfamiliarity with the host organisation of the intelligence experts who have used it. Taking the Communist Party of Australia's structure and rules at face value, they have portrayed it as an organisation intrinsically inclined to such activity. Identifying Wally Clayton as the master spy, they overestimate his standing in the CPA. He was put in charge of its arrangements for wartime illegality, but these proved much less effective than he claimed, while his lack of tradecraft greatly concerned those directing the espionage operations to which he volunteered his services. It is likely that some CPA leaders knew what Clayton was doing, but others didn't and the membership at large had no idea.

The very fact that in 1949 Clayton was once more put in charge of making arrangements for the party to operate should it again be declared illegal suggests a lack of awareness of the full import of his espionage, for it is a basic principle of underground activity that those who direct it should attract no suspicion. Still, it suited Clayton to go into hiding and, apart from briefly reappearing to deny all to a royal commission on espionage, he remained underground until 1957. By then his isolation and secrecy were so deeply ingrained that he was incapable of understanding how he had mired the Communist Party in a morass of suspicion. It was only when Laurie Aarons persuaded him to break his silence a few years before he died in 1997 that Clayton came to realise what he had done. In anguish, he told Aarons: 'I think I've done a lot of damage to the party.'[49]

That the Communist Party of Australia was doomed to decline from its wartime high point was not apparent to those who persisted. They went on the offensive willingly at the end of the war, undeterred by the mounting cost. Having experienced earlier vagaries of fortune, they ignored the setbacks and drew inspiration from victories won in other countries. Shaken by the purges and show trials in the new communist regimes as well as the mounting evidence of Stalin's tyranny, they suppressed their doubts and closed ranks. Each crisis in international communism—Khrushchev's secret speech in 1956, the Sino-Soviet split of the early 1960s, the crushing of the Prague Spring in 1968—brought hopes of renewal. There were still causes to fight, still the fading hope that history might once again go their way.

Communism charged the lives of its adherents with significance. It was a way of thinking and acting that claimed jurisdiction over every dimension of activity. If the party made inordinate demands on members' time and energy, they were proud of the sacrifices they made—the jobs lost to victimisation, the career opportunities passed up, the leisure and comforts set aside. The party also provided the training, confidence and staying power that made them such dedicated political activists. Towards the end of his life, the Marxist historian Raphael Samuel evoked these qualities of his fellow communists during the 1940s as 'the lost world of British communism', a world that defined and sustained them. 'To be a communist,' he explained, 'was to have a complete social identity, one which transcended the limits of class, gender and nationality.'[50]

To understand Australian communism it is also necessary to imagine a lost world of political engagement. Communists were not alone in their conviction that a new order would follow the Second World War, for it was manifest there could be no going back to the old order of economic mismanagement and neglect of social welfare. Despite fundamental differences over how these maladies were to be eradicated, all political parties proposed a new and better future. These parties, moreover, allowed for a level of popular participation that is unimaginable today—indeed, they depended on it. There was no public funding of elections, no electoral allowance for members of parliament, no support staff, not even an office in which to work. The secretaries of both the ALP Federal Executive and the Australian Council of Trade Unions still worked on an unpaid, part-time basis. Public opinion polls were in their infancy, the techniques of media management rudimentary. Election campaigns were conducted face to face in public meetings and assemblies. If communists went further with their open-air oratory, rallies and demonstrations, they were practising a form of participatory politics with which Australians were familiar.

★

In my earlier study of the Communist Party from its foundation in 1920 to illegality in 1940, I wrestled with the volume of the evidence.

It is even greater for the years covered here. Communists produced an extraordinary body of books and journals, newspapers and pamphlets; they used posters, cartoons, radio and cinema, organised rallies, marches and demonstrations, and fostered culture and enlightenment through theatre, art, literature and music. There are hundreds of boxes of national records, as many again of state ones, large personal and union collections, thousands of files in government archives. It would take many months to listen to all the recorded interviews. The search term 'communist' produces more than a million articles in the digitised newspapers available through the National Library's online aggregation, Trove, and the books, journal articles, research theses and other studies of particular aspects of communism are hardly less daunting. I have cited only some of these secondary sources, just as I have drawn on only a fraction of the primary ones. Even the full bibliography accompanying this volume and available online at the SEARCH Foundation is incomplete. While further research would no doubt yield additional discoveries, for the most part it would merely provide further instances of the party life described here.

As with *The Reds*, I set out with the intention that *The Party* would go the full distance and finish along with the CPA itself in 1991. It soon became apparent that this was impossible if I was to provide an adequate treatment of the decades in which communism was most active and influential. Accordingly, the first half of the book deals with the party during its heyday in the 1940s in six chapters that follow a chronological sequence but overlap in order to draw out patterns of initiative and response.

Three chapters then explore how it withstood adversity in the first half of the 1950s. Although the party learned from its misfortunes, there was a failure to resolve the disjunction between its espousal of revolution and the decidedly non-revolutionary activities that gave it a place in Australian politics and society.

The last two chapters deal with the consequences of that failure. Caught between members who urged the need for radical change and others clinging to outworn dogmas, it suffered a wave of resignations in the late 1950s and two schisms in the 1960s. Some might feel that in concentrating on this turmoil, I have skimped treatment of campaigns and activities, and it is true that the book allocates most space to those aspects in the earlier period when the party flourished. My primary purpose, however, has been not to attempt a comprehensive account but to explain the breakdown of older certainties. A brief epilogue sketches the new directions taken after 1970.

The book ends at the point when I joined the CPA. I had many conversations with party veterans in the years that followed, and indeed with ex-party ones. In the acknowledgements I identify some who shared their memories with me, though the list is far from exhaustive. If only I had known what questions I should have asked! Stephen Murray-Smith made me the fall guy for a memoir he wrote in 1983, recalling how I told him 'in kindly but academic tones' early in our friendship that he had talked and written of his becoming a communist but had not 'accounted for it'. 'What does the dear man want,' Stephen continued, 'a list of books I read? My views on the labour theory of value?' I probably was interested in some reflection on his understanding of communist doctrine, but it was only as I conducted research for this book that I came to realise how much more he had to tell.[51]

And the same holds for so many others. With rare exceptions, they were not withholding information. Rather, as their communist hopes became uncoupled from history—to use David Carter's metaphor—so their memories settled into a form that made sense of that outcome and left little room for other, more discordant aspects of their lived experience. They remembered their involvement in the light of communism's failure, passing over the flux of events when it seemed history might still go their way. So Stephen recalled taking leave from the director of the press agency in Prague for which he worked until 1951, who reportedly said, 'I wonder if I should have had him arrested after all', yet passed over a pamphlet he wrote the following year dismissing all criticism of the Eastern bloc.[52] It was only as I conducted research to write this book that I became aware of such inconsistencies—and by then it was too late.

Some further explanation of the book's coverage is needed. It concentrates on the two south-east states of New South Wales and Victoria, which were the most populous, the most industrialised and shared a rivalry that extended to their versions of communism. This orientation is partly a matter of practical necessity to keep the book to a manageable length. Queensland twice sought to impose a more militant policy than the Sydney-based leaders wanted, first in the late 1920s and then the late 1940s, but for reasons that need to be investigated it fell away more rapidly from the 1950s. The other states are also neglected. Western Australia, then still heavily reliant on gold and farm exports, suffered from isolation. The party had a lively presence in the 1940s and sent many able comrades east, but also served as a whipping boy for its alleged backwardness. Communism in South Australia was marked by that state's distinct liberal tradition, later by a marked dogmatism. Tasmania, cut off from the mainland, had few party members, as did the Northern Territory. All invite closer attention than they are given here.

My earlier history, *The Reds*, ended with a chapter on the opening years of the Second World War and the Communist Party's illegality. It provided a perspective from which to appraise the growth of a tiny and beleaguered circle of dissidents into a substantial movement that built a union presence after the Depression and cultivated a popular front to combat the threat of fascism and war. This history opens by going over the same ground with a different perspective. The party's opposition to the 'imperialist' war lasted from late 1939 to mid-1941, and its illegality was not lifted until the end of 1942. The underground activity, however, effectively ended more than a year earlier, when the entry of the Soviet Union into the war transformed the party's fortunes. This was a period of rapid change, strain and uncertainty, some aspects still shrouded in obscurity. It also had lasting consequences for much of what followed, and is therefore where this history begins.

1

Illegality, 1940–41

In the 1920s communism was a beleaguered movement on the fringes of Australian politics. It grew during the 1930s and by the end of the decade communists had won leadership of a number of trade unions: first the coalminers, then the ironworkers, waterside workers and seamen. State branches of the powerful Australian Railways Union, and smaller unions covering the metal trades, transport, construction, the meat industry, clerks and even teachers, all had communist officials. *Tribune*, the party's national paper, appeared twice a week in Sydney, and there were weekly papers in three states.

The Communist Party maintained a number of auxiliary or 'fraternal' organisations. Some were based on a particular category, such as women and youth, and some pursued causes, such as the Friends of the Soviet Union, the League Against Imperialism and the Movement Against War and Fascism, which in 1938 was turned into the League for Peace and Democracy. These were known as 'fronts', since they had prestigious office-holders who were not communists while party members served as their organisers. By 1939 there were additional auxiliaries serving further purposes, such as the Workers' Art Club, the New Theatre and the Left Book Club. Communists also played the leading role in them, but because they attracted a larger following, and perhaps also because cultural and intellectual activity was less amenable to direction, they were more loosely supervised.

The constitution of the Communist Party of Australia (CPA) adopted by the Twelfth Congress at the end of 1938 declared it to be a 'working class political party carrying forward today the best traditions of Australian democracy'. Rule 6 explained that the CPA's practices were based on the Leninist principle of democratic centralism, according to which all members were bound to accept the will of the majority, and the decisions of 'higher bodies' were 'absolutely binding on lower bodies'.[1] This was a form of democracy quite different from Australian tradition, which accepted the right to disagree. Once the Communist Party made a decision, it had to be embraced by all members. Any lingering reservation, any failure to implement it unquestioningly, was a breach of discipline.

Every higher body was elected from below, but from a list of candidates it nominated. A national congress met every three years after all levels of the party discussed draft resolutions circulated from above. The congress elected a central committee (which had more than 30 members in 1938) that met quarterly. It in turn elected a central executive, which had eight members and met every few weeks, while a secretariat of just three—the party secretary (J.B. Miles), president (Lance Sharkey) and assistant secretary (Richard Dixon)—completed the chain of command. The central committee had a number of specialist departments responsible for different aspects of its work: a political, an industrial and an agrarian department, with others that dealt with finance, organisation, agitation and propaganda, and a control commission that oversaw discipline and security.

The same structure was replicated at the state level. Each state held an annual conference that elected a state committee, executive and secretariat to supervise the work of the same specialist departments. Larger states were divided into districts with a similar arrangement of functions. Finally, there were the local branches, perhaps 500 of them in 1939. These were of two kinds, one based on the workplace and the other on the locality, though there were also some special branches for ethnic groups (such as the Italian members) or professions (such as teachers and journalists). The task of the branches was to carry out the work of the party: take up its campaigns, organise public meetings, assign duties to members, recruit and train new members, sell the press, collect funds and conduct the social and cultural activities that sustained party life.

This was an elaborate structure for an organisation of 4000 members, and one that demanded an extraordinarily high level of activity. It was made possible by full-time party workers who were described as 'functionaries' or 'cadres', a term that carried military connotations of core staff training a larger force for the class war. Most members of the central committee worked on this basis, as did those on the state executives and the leading members of district committees. A record of payments made by the Victorian executive at the end of 1939, when there were fewer than 1000 members, listed 24 functionaries in receipt of 'sustenance payments', as they were known—and with good reason, since the amounts were barely sufficient to sustain them with food and lodging. Jack Blake, the Victorian secretary, was paid £2 10s weekly and most others just £1 10s, when the basic wage was a little over £4.[2] Unsurprisingly, the majority were young, since the financial strain on those with family responsibilities was particularly severe.

All communists were expected to make sacrifices, for they lived in a hostile environment that exposed them to vilification and victimisation. The party supported them with rituals and practices that guided their personal, educational, cultural and even moral development. Intermarriage created family networks that gave comfort and support. Partly because of the sacrifices cadres made and partly because they were the confidants and aides of an austere and demanding leadership, they carried an unusual authority. Their dedication to the party's fortunes was both a strength and weakness. With well over 100 full-time functionaries, the CPA could staff the specialist departments, supervise the work of branches and maintain a much higher level of activity than the national membership of 4000 would suggest. Living and working within a tightly enclosed circle of fellow communists, finding purpose and fulfilment in meeting the party's demands, these cadres were conditioned to withstand adversity. Yet precisely because they worked within the structured lines of the organisation, they were susceptible to a dogmatism and rigidity that cut them off from the outside world. That nearly all of them were men also reinforced the masculine character of the organisation.[3]

This model of the professional revolutionary had its origins in Lenin's argument that workers would not become conscious they belonged to a class at war with the established order spontaneously, and that a vanguard party of dedicated revolutionaries was needed to educate them in the realities of capitalism and direct their efforts to overthrow it. In this model, first expounded in his tract *What Is to Be Done?* (1902) as the basis of the Bolshevik faction of Russian socialists, Lenin made the party the guiding intelligence of the working class.

'We communists are people of a special mould. We are made of special stuff,' Stalin proclaimed in a speech to mark the death of Lenin in 1924.[4] The Australian communist was a special kind of worker who shared the injuries of their class but rose above them. The spontaneity that they tried to correct went beyond what Lenin called trade unionism and reformism to more primitive forms of rebellion. In Australian parlance this was the larrikin who asserted his defiance in drinking, gambling and fighting, scorned all authority and regarded any form of learning as a poor substitute for native cunning. Larrikinism flourished in the working-class communities in which communism had its base, and was a constant challenge to the patient, purposeful, disciplined effort the party demanded.

Yet members were by no means immune to its effects. Many came to the party from such a background and did not throw off the rebellious impulse; some, indeed, cultivated a larrikin style of activism. A good example is Stan Moran, probably the most celebrated orator at the Sydney Domain, who combined two years of training at the Lenin School in the Soviet Union and work as treasurer of the Sydney branch of the Waterside Workers' Federation (WWF) with a calculated irreverence. It was Moran who dubbed Robert Menzies 'Pig Iron Bob' for prosecuting the waterside workers who refused to load a ship for Japan in 1938. In similar vein he stood for federal parliament in 1946 with posters declaring 'Stan Moran Exposes the Cigarette Paper Shortage'.[5]

The party placed inordinate stress on educating members in the theory and practice of communism, the doctrines that gave them an objective knowledge of the world and the methods whereby they put that knowledge into effect. Meetings of the central committee customarily began with a lengthy survey of international, national and local developments in order to explain the correct strategy to guide members in their tasks, and the same practice was imitated at the branch level. Buttressed with various pronouncements of Marx, Engels, Lenin and Stalin, these reports were described as going 'three times round the world and twice up George Street'. The effect, as Eric Aarons, the son and grandson of communists, put it, 'was to make it seem as though the whole of world history had been moving inexorably towards this particular point and these particular tasks'. This was a discourse of the initiated that then had to be translated into the language of the working class. The danger was that those who directed the party's work engaged with workers—the 'proletariat' in communist terminology, the 'toilers' in communist rhetoric—as a class in need of direction rather than as members of an organic community of which the communist was part.[6]

That was not possible for the communists who worked as trade union officials. They won their posts by persuading workmates they could improve pay and conditions as the union movement recovered from the setbacks suffered during the Depression. They retained them by providing effective leadership. The present state of industrial relations, with such diminished and marginalised trade unions, makes it difficult to appreciate their significance 80 years ago, when they represented a substantial majority of the workforce. Every trade and industry had its own union, and in many workplaces a union ticket was compulsory. Unionists carried bitter memories of how employers crushed the Waterside Workers' Federation in a protracted strike and locked out the miners on the country's principal coalfield for more than a year. As unemployment rose to more than 20 per cent in 1931, all wages were cut, and by 1933 union membership had fallen by a fifth.[7]

Communist activists typically experienced long spells of unemployment before they found work in basic industries where labour was expendable: denied job security, these manual workers were at the mercy of management, so a first step was to rebuild collective strength. That made it possible to bargain more effectively and win improvements during the slow recovery from the Depression. Communists initiated such action through planned campaigns and prepared their resolutions in conclaves known as 'fractions' for adoption at mass meetings, but no union had more than a small minority of party members. Their influence always relied on the support of other militants and the preparedness of the membership at large to follow their lead.

The rise of communists to industrial leadership during the 1930s thus required attentiveness to their base of support. They also had to devise strategies for conducting offensives within the confines of an arbitration system that replaced direct bargaining with enforceable industrial awards. Communists were adamant that arbitration shackled the working class. They appealed to militant traditions using the argument that any improvement would only be won by industrial action, but in practice they took their claims for better wages and conditions to the Arbitration Court for it to make them legally binding. While prepared to back those claims with industrial disruption, they were loath to lose the court's registration of their union since that would end the union's right to cover the occupation. Then there was the additional object of drawing union members into political campaigns, such as the ban on shipments of scrap iron to Japan that the WWF imposed in 1938. This again required a prescient calculation of the members' willingness to use the strike weapon for non-industrial purposes. All this is to say that the Australian communists set themselves to work within the existing trade union structure rather than attempting to form their own unions along communist lines.[8]

The party's industrial strength lay in unions covering the working-class communities that formed around the ports, railways, coalfields and centres of heavy industry. The officials who rose to prominence in the 1930s were products of these occupational communities and immersed in their distinctive traditions of solidarity. Bill Orr and Charlie Nelson, respectively secretary and president of the Miners' Federation, had worked underground in Scotland before emigrating to cut coal at the Lithgow State Mine. Idris Williams, the principal communist in the mining town of Wonthaggi, was steeped in the lodge culture of the South Wales Miners' Federation. These men understood the devolved structure of the union and were able to mobilise its highly localised pits for concerted campaigns. Ernie Thornton, a broad-chested Yorkshireman, pursued a more aggressive strategy in expanding the Federated Ironworkers' Association (FIA), which covered the less skilled grades in the steelworks and foundries.

Tom Wright, another Scot, was a shrewder, less self-aggrandising leader of the smaller Sheet Metal Working Industrial Union. Eliot V. Elliott of the Seamen's Union (his baptismal name was Emmanuel and his friends called him Vic) was a New Zealand seafarer who came to national office from the Brisbane branch. With a tongue like a razor and a carefully groomed appearance that some likened to Trotsky, he established a firm discipline over a notoriously unruly workforce. Combining a keen appreciation of the forces at work in his industry with a burning socialist conviction, he was a skilful negotiator. The most impressive was Jim Healy, who had worked as a wharf labourer in North Queensland after migrating from the United Kingdom and was elected general secretary of the WWF in 1937. A large, companionable man of deliberation, insight and integrity, he won the respect of all who dealt with him. Wharfies venerated 'Big Jim'.[9]

These communists worked methodically to strengthen their unions. In contrast to the smaller craft unions, whose secretaries operated out of rooms in the Trades Hall, they had their own premises and full-time organisers to service the membership. They recruited research officers to help prepare campaigns, and journalists to produce union journals of superior quality—so that more communists found full-time industrial posts. They were the pacesetters in the revival of the union movement, and wielded significant influence in peak bodies such as the NSW Labor Council, Victorian Trades Hall Council and Queensland Trades and Labor Council. And since their unions were affiliated with the Labor Party, they influenced it too—albeit indirectly, because communists were barred from participating in the ALP.

The Labor Party's prohibition of communists extended to members of front organisations such as the Movement Against War and Fascism, and presented a barrier to the CPA's efforts from 1935 to build a united front. In an effort to overcome it, the party encouraged some members to withhold their communist identity and work within the ALP. The number of such undeclared communists is not known, but there was a substantial body in New South Wales, where the ALP had split into two rival parties, one following the domineering Premier Jack Lang, who brought down the Scullin Labor government in 1931, and the other made up of his opponents. Communists played a significant part in this anti-Lang campaign, which finally achieved success in 1939, and thus gained leading positions in that state's branch of the Labor Party.[10] One of them was Lloyd Ross, who worked in adult education before he was elected secretary of the NSW branch of the Australian Railways Union in 1935. He proved as active and effective as his openly communist comrades and, like them, was a member of the central committee.[11]

Lloyd Ross was probably the country's first union secretary to hold a university degree (as did his brother Edgar, who worked for the Miners' Federation). Indeed, he had postgraduate experience in England and was awarded a doctorate for his research on Australian labour history. Ross was also an oddity in the insistently proletarian Communist Party. Despite the privileged family origins of Marx and Lenin, the CPA's leaders emphasised their humble origins and proclaimed the historic mission of a working class that held firm in combat with capitalism, unlike the vacillating middle class.

After 1935, when the party reached out to progressive members of the middle class, it attracted an increasing number of university-educated men and women—teachers, lawyers, doctors and scientists—as well as journalists, writers and creative artists. While these recruits put their expertise at the service of the party, they were expected to perform the full range of duties of any branch member. By doing so they proved their commitment and entered into a close association with working-class comrades. Yet their education exposed them to other influences, just as their professional lives involved them in systems of knowledge and value that required independent judgement. Some subordinated such ways of thinking to party discipline and remained lifelong members. Others reached a point at which their own interpretation of contentious issues could no longer be reconciled with the party's demands. The leadership kept a close eye on its middle-class members.

Similar reservations applied to those who took on full-time party work. Lloyd Ross's undergraduate contemporary Ralph Gibson, the son and brother of professors of philosophy at the University of Melbourne, who served as state secretary in Victoria and editor of the *Guardian*, was widely admired for his selfless dedication to the cause. Even so, Gibson's precise manner and distinctive diction—his r's were easily confused with w's—betrayed his origins as a bourgeois intellectual whose role was to justify and propagate communist policy rather than to determine it.[12] Fred Paterson, a former Rhodes scholar, barrister and the only communist candidate ever elected to parliament, incurred frequent criticism from the dour national secretary, J.B. Miles.[13] Bill Wood, another Rhodes scholar whose father had been professor of history at the University of Sydney, worked for a pittance as a party journalist and publicist without ever being admitted to the inner circle.[14]

The Communist Party was formed in Sydney, the leadership was based there and the NSW section of the party was always the largest. With some 1850 members in 1939, the NSW section was held up as a model for others to follow. Victoria was often criticised for failure to do so, despite the organisers sent down to bring it into line, until Jack Blake was installed in 1934. Blake, a Lithgow miner who had trained at the Lenin School in the USSR, was a tall, austere and formidable dialectician. Under his leadership a weekly newspaper became a biweekly, union activity increased and membership grew to nearly 1000, only to fall back during his absence as CPA representative in Moscow to 860 by the end of the decade. Victoria lacked the heavy industrial strongholds of New South Wales, though the party had a greater presence in Melbourne's more socially engaged intellectual and cultural life—an aspect the Sydney leaders thought symptomatic of its laxity.

The Queensland branch of the CPA grew rapidly to more than 1200 members by 1939. Queensland was a Labor state, dominated by the powerful and vehemently anti-communist Australian Workers' Union, and party members worked with other militants to challenge its repressive stranglehold. They achieved greatest success in the north, among the miners, canecutters, mill-hands, shearers and meatworkers, as well as those who worked on the railways and ports. Much employment in North Queensland was seasonal, and it fostered a distinctively confrontational style of activism. Jack Henry, who led a major strike in the sugar industry, came down to Brisbane as state secretary in 1937, followed by the young men he installed as organisers: Doug Olive, Albert Robinson, Jim Slater, Les Sullivan and Claude Jones from Toowoomba. 'We were larrikins,' Jones declared, 'bush larrikins with a militant don't give a bugger attitude.' If Victoria was insufficiently proletarian, the Sydney leaders chided Queensland for a tendency to anarchism.[15]

Progress elsewhere was slow. There were no more than 40 members in Tasmania, fewer still in the Northern Territory and a fledgling branch in the ACT. South Australia languished until an organiser was sent from Melbourne, and had just 105 members in 1939. Western Australia made the greatest headway, building membership to 350 and the weekly circulation of the *Workers' Star* to 2000. There, as in Queensland, the party offered an alternative to a conservative state branch of the Labor Party that was accustomed to office. Furthermore, the ALP officials coordinated the unions—there was no separate trades and labour council in the west—so that communists provided the lead for industrial activism. As in the east, the party was also attracting university students and young professionals through cultural activity and promotion of international causes.

The CPA enjoyed particular success with its campaign against fascist militarism. As Germany, Italy and Japan committed repeated acts of aggression during the 1930s, the Lyons government remained resolute in appeasement while the Labor Party was hopelessly divided on foreign policy. Communists stood out in warning of the danger to world peace and the need to confront the belligerents—for the war that most concerned the Movement Against War and Fascism was an assault on the Soviet Union. Initially, the Communist International saw fascism as an instrument of the ruling class, a sign that capitalism was nearing collapse and dispensing with the cloak of democracy, just as social democrats were being forced to come out openly as collaborators or 'social fascists'. Then, after the Nazis destroyed the Kommunistische Partei Deutschlands, came recognition that fascism was something more: it was 'the open, terroristic dictatorship of the most reactionary, most chauvinist and most imperialistic elements of finance capital'.[16]

The Comintern now called for a united front of all workers and all countries to rally to the defence of democracy—as in the international campaign to defend the Spanish republic from an attempted military coup in 1936. With Hitler and Mussolini providing munitions, soldiers and air support to the insurgents, and the Western democracies maintaining a policy of non-intervention, the republican forces were ground into submission over more than two years of fighting marked by civilian atrocities. The Spanish Civil War pricked the conscience of a new generation chafing against the repressive insularity of public life in Australia.

The Soviet Union called on the European democracies to resist fascist aggression wherever it occurred, and ultimately sought a military pact with Britain and France to protect Poland from German invasion. At least it did so until suddenly the two sworn enemies, the USSR and Germany, announced on 24 August 1939 that they had settled their differences.

★

The sudden reversal of communist policy shook many Australian communists. 'I was stunned' by the Nazi–Soviet pact, recalled Bernie Taft, a young refugee from Germany who would rise to become national secretary. 'I was shocked,' testified Laurie Aarons, who preceded Taft in the same office. He said so at the time to a senior party member and 'a real nasty argument' ensued, Aarons unable to see how such an accommodation could be reconciled with Lenin's rejection of all military agreements, his antagonist insisting that the actions of the Soviet Union were not to be questioned. There was no suggestion Laurie Aarons would refuse to follow the Comintern instructions. Nor did the public hostility directed at party members for doing so deter him. 'Especially when you're young,' he explained, 'you don't mind so much being in a minority; in a way you feel it's good.'[17]

The party threw itself into a campaign to justify the new Soviet policy and oppose Australia's participation in the war, which began a fortnight later. Hundreds of meetings were organised in September, hundreds more in the following months. By November the CPA had distributed 295,000 copies of the pamphlet *War, What for?* and 700,000 copies of other publications denouncing the imperialist conflict.[18] For a movement that believed in the inexorable force of history and insisted that objective conditions determined the level of class consciousness, communism attached remarkable importance to the written and spoken word. The party's newspapers and a continual flow of pamphlets, leaflets, handbills and stencilled local bulletins combined persuasion and denunciation, justification of current policy and exhortation to greater effort. The same charged language was employed in hall meetings and on street corners.

Since many venues were denied to communists opposing the war, the street meeting became all the more important. Speakers would set up a stand with a portable loudspeaker in an inner city suburb on Friday evening when the streets were busy with shoppers, and attract an audience by dint of their oratory. Larger open-air meetings were conducted on Sunday afternoons in places set aside for that purpose—the Domains of Sydney and Brisbane, the Yarra Bank across from the business district of Melbourne, the Perth Esplanade and the Botanic Gardens in Adelaide. Here they competed with a range of other speakers—rationalists and evangelical Christians, anti-communists and Trotskyists—so the party assigned its most accomplished performers to the task.

Until the closing months of 1939 the communist campaign went largely without incident. Australia had entered the war reluctantly, hostilities lapsing after the dismemberment of Poland, and the prime minister himself declared that the country should maintain 'business as usual'.[19] That interlude ended when the Soviet Union demanded territorial concessions from Finland and then, in late November, launched an invasion of its northern neighbour. As France and Britain contemplated intervening in support of Finland, sentiment against the Soviet Union increased. 'Tear down that flag, you rats,' an interjector shouted at communists in the Sydney Domain on the Sunday following the Soviet offensive. A fortnight later, six members of the AIF carrying the Union Jack marched on the party's stand, followed by some 500 men and women of like mind. Thereafter the Sydney Domain became a weekly battleground, communists defending their platform and giving the clenched-fist salute, their opponents drowning out the speakers with patriotic and popular songs ('God Save Our King', 'Rule Britannia', 'Roll Out the Barrel', 'South of the Border'), pelting them with overripe tomatoes and, on more than one occasion, seizing and burning the communist flag.[20]

It was the same in Melbourne. 'What about Finland?' hecklers shouted, and soon there were running battles along the Yarra Bank, with at least one combatant ending up in the river. Street meetings became increasingly hazardous, the police commonly refusing to provide protection from assault and instead charging the victims with obstruction. Restrictions were imposed on open-air assemblies in Brisbane and Adelaide; the communist rooms in Wollongong were ransacked, and there were full-scale assaults on the party headquarters in Sydney and Melbourne.[21] The number of public meetings fell away, from 299 nationally in November to 196 in December, only 42 of them outside New South Wales and Victoria.[22]

The invasion of Finland was too much for James Rawling, national organiser of the League for Peace and Democracy. In mid-December party leaders discovered an article he had written for the league's journal criticising the Soviet action, summarily expelled him and pulped all 6000 copies of *World Peace*. Rawling had discussed his concerns with Guido Baracchi and Betty Roland, the former a foundation member and former editor of the *Communist Review*, the latter a playwright for the New Theatre. They too were excommunicated with bell, book and candle, the central committee's condemnation of their 'anti-Party, anti-Soviet agitation' and 'political and moral cowardice' followed by similar denunciation from district committees and local branches.[23] The party explained that all three were bourgeois intellectuals 'of the type that has frequently deserted the revolutionary movement in times of stress'. Sharkey compared the faint-hearted left intelligentsia with the steadfast resolution of proletarian members: 'Not a single leading or important functionary of working-class origins has deserted the party.'[24]

He spoke too soon. Bob McWilliams, the secretary of the Sydney district committee, stopped appearing at public meetings shortly after the war began. *Tribune* explained he was being treated in hospital, and he resumed speaking duties in the New Year, only to drop out altogether when the pressure mounted in May 1940. Ernie Knight, the chairman of the NSW state committee, was also reported in November 1939 to be 'under strict instructions from his medical adviser' to relinquish duties. He returned to work at the end of January but lasted only until April. Both men were expelled for 'desertion of post'. Three other members of the central committee would suffer a similar fate.[25]

The CPA kept up as much of its other activity as it could through auxiliaries. On the outbreak of war, the New Theatre in Sydney was staging a revival of *Till the Day I Die*, US playwright Clifford Odets' powerful drama of German communists risking all to withstand the Nazi terror; it was replaced by an anti-war play as a 'counter-blast to jingo propaganda'.[26] With both the Friends of the Soviet Union and the League for Peace and Democracy struggling to make headway, a No Conscription League was created in early 1940. As with the denial of venues to communists, most radio stations no longer allowed them to buy broadcasting slots; in any case, scripts had to be submitted to the censor in advance of any talk going to air. There was a row in February 1940 when Richard Dixon, the party's assistant secretary, was allowed to appear on an ABC discussion program a week after Rawling used it to recount his expulsion. The compere, Hermann Black of the University of Sydney, gave Dixon ample opportunity to justify the actions of the Soviet Union and insist the CPA determined its own policy with no instructions from Moscow. 'In the first couple of days,' Dixon conceded, 'some of our members, taken by surprise, were a little hesitant', but it soon became apparent that Britain and France wanted war while Germany and the USSR sought peace.[27]

In March 1940 three members of the NSW branch of the ALP prepared a resolution for its annual Easter conference that denounced the war as an imperialist conflict 'pursued in the interests of big finance and monopolists', and warned against any effort 'to change the direction' of the war 'by an aggressive act against any other country with which we are not at war, including the Soviet Union'. The authors of this resolution were all members of the ALP state executive and one of them, Jack Hughes, was also president of the powerful NSW Labor Council. On the eve of the conference, the state parliamentary leader, William McKell, called him to a private meeting to go over a list of communists he had obtained and ensure none was re-elected to the executive. Hughes expected his own name to be on the list. It wasn't, nor was that of Lloyd Ross, even though he was challenged as an undercover communist while moving the 'Hands Off Russia' resolution. The conference adopted it by 195 to 88 votes.[28]

With a federal election imminent, this declaration created uproar. John Curtin, the national leader of the Labor Party, demanded it be expunged from the record; the Federal Executive subsequently dissolved the state executive and appointed a new one. The Easter resolution also allowed the discredited former state leader, Jack Lang, to revive his fortunes by forming an ALP (Non-Communist). The architects of the 'Hands Off Russia' resolution carried on regardless as the 'Australian Labor Party, State of New South Wales'—sometimes known as the State Labor Party (SLP) and sometimes as the Hughes–Evans Party after Jack Hughes, its driving force, and Wally Evans, its secretary. The SLP began with the backing of left-wing unions, active branches and a pungent weekly paper, *Progress*, but failed dismally in federal and state elections and dwindled until it merged with the Communist Party in 1944. This was a clear case of communists overplaying their hand. Having won their long-held objective of achieving influence in the Labor Party through dual membership, they threw it away in a quixotic display of Soviet apologetics.

That left trade unions as the principal outlet for communist agitation. In September 1939 the NSW Labor Council declared its opposition to the war measures of the Menzies government. Communist delegates, who formulated the declaration, contributed characteristically defiant statements: 'I have never apologised for the Soviet Union,' said Tom Wright, 'because there is no need to do so.' The Labor Council also adopted a 'Hands Off Russia' resolution in March 1940 and a similar declaration was only narrowly rejected at the congress of the Australian Council of Trade Unions (ACTU) in the following month.[29] The union movement at large was critical of participation in a distant war under an unsympathetic prime minister. The appeals for labour discipline were overshadowed by his ill-considered call at the outbreak of the war for business as usual, which for unions meant pursuing industrial claims. An unemployment rate of 10 per cent made it difficult for all but the strongest unions to do so immediately, but others would follow as the rapid build-up of war industries improved their bargaining position. Just 456,000 working days were lost in strikes in 1939 but 1,716,000 in 1940.[30]

All but 121,000 of the days lost in 1940 were in the coal industry, which at this time was the only source of gas and electricity. But the miners' strike that began in March 1940 was not political in nature, despite a forged letter that purported to show the communist union secretary instructing the comrades to keep it going until every industry was tied up as a means of 'sabotaging the Menzies Government's war schemes'.[31] It was rather a resumption of an earlier strike in 1938 that had secured a 40-hour week, resumed because the mine owners continued to resist applying the award to surface workers. This 'second-round' campaign lasted 67 days and, after the government threatened to send in volunteer labour, was settled in consultation with the ACTU on terms that provided for adjudication of the miners' claims.[32]

The other major dispute arose from the shortage of coal. BHP had mechanised operations in its vast Newcastle steelworks during the 1930s to reduce labour costs, and even though it was increasing production in 1940 to fulfil war orders, the company took advantage of the mining dispute to undertake further improvements. In laying off workers, the management used a list of suspected communists provided by the Commonwealth security service—the strike at Newcastle was to defend them. BHP had always resisted union coverage, but Ernie Thornton's reorganisation of the Newcastle office of the FIA at this time brought a major recruitment drive that enabled the union to establish a strong presence in the steelworks. Although the FIA was unable to secure reinstatement of the victimised workers, the continued expansion of war production set the stage for its campaign to improve wages and conditions.[33]

Contrary to conservative myth, very few days were lost in the maritime industry during the period communists opposed the Second World War: 18,000 days in 1939 (or about one day for every member of the workforce), and 7000 in both 1940 and 1941. Nevertheless, a stoppage in April 1940 by a gang of waterside workers in the port of Sydney brought accusations of sabotaging the war effort. The wharfies were loading flour on a merchant vessel to supply an AIF division dispatched to the Middle East. Bagged flour was both heavy and dusty, and the men wanted a quarter-hour 'smoko' break during each shift, as they were entitled to when loading wheat. Since their claim had been before the Arbitration Court for twelve months, those working this vessel took the break and in response to fines they walked off the job. The shipowners blamed the Communist Party, the government threatened to invoke the Transport Workers Act (which would allow it to remove the men from the industry) and Jim Healy played a straight bat, denying the dispute was political in nature. He prevailed. Work resumed after five days of indignation, the workers still taking their smoko and the Arbitration Court formalising it shortly after.[34]

But since the Communist Party was calling for action to stop the war, this sequence of events—the miners' strike followed by the 'Hands Off Russia' resolution and then further industrial action—seemed to establish a clear pattern of disruption. It coincided, furthermore, with the collapse of the Western Front. Germany invaded Norway and Denmark in April 1940, advanced into Belgium and the Netherlands in May, and forced evacuation of the British force by the end of the month. Paris fell on 14 June. With Britain now fighting for survival, communist opposition to the war became a threat to national security.

*

A number of security agencies were keeping watch on the Communist Party. First in the field was the Investigation Branch of the Commonwealth Attorney-General's Department (CIB), which inquired into breaches of federal law and enforced controls over immigration, aliens and the issue of passports; a section of the CIB dealt with espionage and subversion. The army, navy and air force all had intelligence sections to assist their operations, and all three interpreted intelligence to include counterintelligence on domestic threats to national security. The army's Military Intelligence assumed additional responsibility for censorship of communications at the commencement of the war, though civilian staff of the Ministry of Information conducted the press and radio censorship. Special branches of the state police forces paid close attention to communist activity, and the one in New South Wales worked with the army in a Military Police Intelligence Section.

While sharing security responsibilities, these organisations resisted attempts to coordinate their efforts. The CIB, with only 39 staff at the outbreak of war, held the largest collection of files and clung to its exclusive relationship with the British Security Service, MI5. It also had a number of informants (known as 'agents') inside the Communist Party, though they were the confidants of particular field officers, who refused to share access to them or even divulge their identities. The practice of paying agents according to the significance of the information they provided encouraged exaggeration. In early 1940, Agent W provided the CIB's Sydney office with a list of 47 communists that included four clergymen as well as Brian Penton, the editor of the *Daily Telegraph*; Cyril Pearl, the editor of the *Sunday Telegraph*; Sydney Deamer, who edited the ABC's weekly magazine; Brian Fitzpatrick, the notoriously independent secretary of the Australian Council for Civil Liberties; and John Kerr, the future governor-general. When Harold Jones, the director of the CIB, expressed concern about the 'scanty evidence of communist leanings' contained in its files on these men, he was assured that Agent W was reliable.[35]

Police in the special branches had greater familiarity with the party, since they attended its public meetings and took down the speeches, but most of these officers were also familiar to communists, so that the police too relied on infiltrating members of the force into the party, with mixed success. Rupert Lockwood has recalled how the two leading members of the Victorian special branch, who would sit in a Melbourne restaurant to eavesdrop on the conversations of communists, were welcomed with a song to the tune of 'The Red Flag':

> Oh Sergeant Birch, Oh Constable Gooden,
> We all know your heads are wooden.[36]

Military Intelligence decided soon after the war began that the CPA was sending members into the armed services to stir up trouble and urged stronger action. If the government was not prepared to ban the party outright, it wanted raids to seize all incriminating evidence and launch prosecutions.[37] Contrary to popular legend, Menzies did not favour such draconian action. Initially he resisted Cabinet members arguing for a crackdown and instructed the security agencies to confer and recommend more appropriate measures. The defence force representatives who pressed their concerns at this conference in January 1940 found little support. W.J. MacKay, the commissioner of the NSW police, said there was nothing to justify repression and added that from his extensive experience 'the best advertisement for the C.P. was to take notice of them'. Most of the other commissioners agreed and the CIB warned against giving communists the status of martyrs. The conference resolved it was 'not desirable at present' to declare the CPA illegal but that censorship should be tightened and action taken against members who transgressed National Security Regulations.[38]

The miners' strike and the deterioration of the Western Front brought additional pressure, but it was probably the need to reconstruct his ministry after losing a by-election that forced Menzies' hand.[39] In March 1940 he re-established a coalition with the vociferously anti-communist Country Party, and in the following month the government introduced new national security regulations that required communist newspapers to submit all copy to censorship before publication: they were forbidden to write on the war, recruit or train, to make any reference to the Soviet Union or report any industrial dispute—even the Sermon on the Mount was blue-pencilled. In May there was a total ban on nine newspapers, and on 5 June the Cabinet approved further regulations to proscribe the Communist Party. These regulations allowed the government to declare any organisation deemed 'prejudicial to the defence of the Commonwealth or the efficient conduct of the war' unlawful and prohibit its activities.[40]

The new regulations were to be gazetted as soon as the government was ready to conduct a nationwide raid on communist premises and the homes of members, for it did not want to give advance warning of its intentions. But the Communist Party anticipated illegality. In March 1940 it issued instructions on how members were to work under such circumstances, and it was tipped off in late May when a proofreader in the Canberra printing office, which was preparing to publish the regulations, rang Lance Sharkey with full details of their wording.[41]

The raids began across the country on the evening of Saturday 15 June, when the special issue of the *Commonwealth Gazette* appeared. The scale of the exercise required the CIB and Military Intelligence to call on hundreds of police officers in addition to those of the special branches. In Sydney, Commissioner MacKay addressed more than 200 uniformed and plainclothes policemen before they set out in pairs to enter over 100 offices, bookshops and homes, and there were similar raids in Newcastle, Wollongong and other regional centres. In Melbourne over 100 detectives, using 40 cars, left from the Russell Street police headquarters on a similar search of city buildings and suburban residences. A larger number went into action in Brisbane from Roma Street, more than 50 houses were raided in Toowoomba, and as many more in Cairns and Rockhampton.[42]

The purpose of the raids was to find evidence of unlawful activity, so the police seized all records and publications that seemed to fit the bill. Truckloads of material were removed from the party's national and state headquarters, as was the equipment in its printeries. The police conducting house searches took away whatever seemed incriminating, so that all communist publications were seized (though some members would claim they persuaded officers that Stalin's *History of the Communist Party of the Soviet Union*, which used the abbreviation CPSU on its cover, was no more than a history of the Commonwealth Public Service Union). Any Russian literature was likely to go, as were the writings of other foreign authors. Hundreds of play scripts were carried from the New Theatre, even the works of Shakespeare. Some constables simply swept up all books with red covers, which included publications of the Left Book Club and commentaries on current affairs in the distinctive red livery of Penguin Specials. Afterwards, party members traded stories of how Shelley's *Poetical Works* were mistaken for political works, while *Engels on Dialectics* was passed off as a dietary manual and his *Origin of the Family* as a guide to family planning.[43]

Most made light of their experience. Some members would claim they felt slighted to have been overlooked, while Jean Devanny rebuked the two policemen who raided her room in Cairns, telling them 'you ought to be going after crims' and warning 'I've got a little black book of names for after the revolution'.[44] Others were clearly shaken to have police ransack their homes in the small hours of Sunday morning. The library had pride of place in the communist home as what Raphael

Samuel has called 'a kind of secular shrine'. Even if it were just a single bookcase, the collection of Marxist texts, political pamphlets, communist periodicals and progressive literature bore testimony to the knowledge and understanding that defined a communist. With no indication that possession of incriminating items would not result in arrest, some had already burned or buried valued possessions. John Oldham, an architect, was returning by ship from work on the Australian pavilion at the New York Trade Fair when he learned the party had become illegal; he threw overboard the portfolio of artwork he had produced over the previous decade.[45]

The books, pamphlets and periodicals seized on 15 June failed to provide any information about communist doctrine and policy that was not freely available. Some publications were returned to their owners, some were sold by auction, and subsequent police raids took away many of the same books—a distraction of effort the CIB condemned as 'ludicrous'. It had hoped to obtain documentary evidence of communist subversion along with organisational records and membership lists, and thought these slipped through the net because of a 'lack of effective co-operation' from the state police forces. A better explanation was that the police were brought in too late and told too little. For its part, Military Intelligence complained it was denied sufficient notice of the government's plans and that the CIB's direction of the raids 'left the Military and Police in a most invidious position'.[46]

Communist leaders, on the other hand, congratulated themselves on their vigilance. Wally Clayton, whom they put in charge of preparations for illegality in 1939, took credit for arrangements that became more effective every time he boasted of them. He claimed to have gone into smoke before the axe fell. In fact he was found on the evening of 15 June hiding in the backyard dunny of the house of a party member in Petersham, in Sydney, with the very communist literature he had ordered members to hide. 'The police found little, but they found more than they should have,' the party acknowledged, 'because some members failed to carry out repeated advice to keep home and person free from documents.'[47] It was the advance warning that allowed the party to remove records from its principal offices, and the laxity of the raids that left other material in members' homes undisturbed. Possibly inadvertently, the head of the CIB in Queensland tipped off Ted Bacon, a member of the state committee, but he failed to clear the shelves in the flat he shared with his mother at New Farm. The caretaker told the coppers who arrived early Sunday morning that Ted was away surfing and his mother at Mass, then replaced the communist literature with pulp fiction. Similarly, when the police escorted Bacon on the following Monday to the tax office where he worked, the senior tax assessor turned them out. Eva Goldner, a Jewish refugee who would marry Ted in 1944 and had recently arrived from working for the communist underground in Vienna, regarded the CPA's illegality as a 'complete joke'.[48]

By European standards it was undoubtedly light. The new set of National Security Regulations dealing with Subversive Associations gazetted in June 1940 made it an offence to collect funds, organise meetings, or publish or broadcast on behalf of the Communist Party. Some twenty prosecutions were brought under these regulations, but they did not cover activity that was not conducted in the party's name. About as many more prosecutions used Regulation 42 of the general regulations issued at the start of the war, which prohibited attempts to influence public opinion against the defence effort, and another score arose from Regulation 17A, which was added to the general regulations in May 1940 as part of the ban on the communist press and made it an offence to print, publish or even possess any newspaper that did not include the names of the printer and publisher. Altogether, around 70 Australians ran afoul of these security regulations, including two Trotskyists, three pacifists and four supporters of enemy powers.[49]

Why so few? The National Security Regulations provided for a summary trial, with a maximum penalty of six months' imprisonment or a fine of £100, but any prosecution had to be authorised by the attorney-general, and the senior officers of his department who had drafted the regulations were extremely cautious in interpreting them. Harry Whitlam, the Crown Solicitor (and father of Gough), held it was not enough to provide evidence of criticising the government or denouncing conscription, since these were legitimate subjects of public debate, and he drew a distinction between 'invective' against the war and 'advocacy' of opposition to it. A summary trial had the advantage that it was conducted by a magistrate, it being thought juries were less likely to convict, but not all magistrates upheld the charges. Both the police and Military Intelligence chafed at these restrictions, as they did when censors insisted that industrial and political criticism was not necessarily subversive.[50]

There was also awareness of the potential for public sympathy with victims. In an early illustration, Phyllis Johnson, the national women's organiser, was prosecuted under General Regulation 42 for a speech at a no-conscription street meeting at Chatswood a week after the CPA was declared illegal. When she was arrested, the police found two anti-war pamphlets down the front of her dress, so she was also charged with a breach of Regulation 17A. Johnson was convicted of both offences and fined £30 for each. An appeal to the Quarter Sessions dismissed the charge of possessing illegal literature on the grounds that she had been handed the pamphlets and did not know their contents, and her fine for a speech prejudicial to the war effort (the police had tendered a transcript) was reduced. But she refused to enter into a recognisance of £50 to comply with all National Security Regulations for the duration of war and undertook a sentence of hard labour for two months in Long Bay Gaol.[51]

Johnson's case attracted growing controversy. Leading party members spoke on her behalf at the Sydney Domain. Women supporters rallied at the appeal court but were prevented from attending by plainclothes police, who occupied all the public seating. Johnson was unwell when she went into Long Bay, and a medical examination found tumours in her ovaries, yet the prison doctor advised they were not an immediate threat, so she was placed on light duties. News of her condition fanned calls for release. 'You talk as though Mrs Johnson had been imprisoned by the order of the Gestapo of Germany or the Gay Payoo [GPU] of the Soviet,' Billy Hughes, the unyielding attorney-general, told the secretary of the NSW Labor Council. When Johnson completed her sentence, the Women's No Conscription League presented her with a gold brooch as a martyr to the cause.[52]

Most of the subsequent prosecutions in New South Wales arose from attempts to stop the distribution of literature. The head of the CIB in that state engaged a group of officers to work with the special branch of the police and patrol the streets by night. They picked up a number of distributors and prosecuted around a dozen, but the location of the principal press remained a closely guarded secret.[53] The most serious case involved Max Thomas and Horrie Ratliff, the secretary and treasurer of the St George district of the CPA. Both went underground on 15 June and set up operations in a secluded house on the banks of the Georges River, where a police raid in November found them in possession of a typewriter, stencils and a duplicating machine. They were charged and convicted under Regulations 17A and 42, and each was given six months' hard labour. While they were serving their sentences, Military Intelligence decided that further punishment would have a 'salutary effect' on the party's illegal activity. On its advice, the Minister for Defence ordered their internment.[54]

The arrest of the two men indicated the failure of the party's own security arrangements. Ratliff, affectionately described by Thomas as 'a real bloody larrikin', had previously busked with his bugle around the pubs in the area, and there was always a danger that someone would recognise him on his sorties to the local railway station. Moreover, the party decided the isolated refuge was an ideal venue for a meeting of leading members—an elementary mistake, since several were under observation—and shortly after it occurred a rowboat was spotted lingering on this stretch of the river.[55]

The response to the internment testified to the party's determination to withstand repression. Both men were picked up six weeks after release from prison in May 1941 and taken to the Holsworthy military camp. No one was allowed to visit until party member and journalist Edgar Ross went to explain the need for them to publicise their mistreatment by embarking on a hunger strike. They did so and continued to refuse the tempting meals put before them when taken to hospital a fortnight later—both men had to be wheeled on trolleys before the tribunal that rejected their appeal. By then Germany had invaded the Soviet Union and the two internees offered an undertaking that they would not disrupt the war effort. On instructions from the Labor Council, they also terminated their hunger strike, but still the government refused to relent,

Menzies insisting their detention was not a punishment but a protective action. Ratliff and Thomas were released as soon as Labor took office in October of the same year.[56]

A rare instance of prosecution under one of the Subversive Associations regulations that prohibited meetings from advocating unlawful doctrines arose in New South Wales when six communists, including Harry Gould of the central committee and several union officials, were found in the Bondi School of Arts. Gould, who was conducting a training class, claimed they were meeting as members of a tennis club—to which the policeman leading the raid was said to have replied, 'Balls!' Two who had communist literature in their homes were charged under General Regulation 17A, the others placed on a bond for contravening Regulation 8 of the Subversive Associations regulations. Gould refused to enter into the bond and served 40 days.[57]

There were fewer prosecutions in all but one of the other states. Several Queenslanders were convicted for possession of illegal literature, but the principal case there was the prosecution of Fred Paterson for statements he made at a meeting of the Townsville City Council in May 1941. In response to a motion farewelling citizens leaving for service in the AIF, Paterson was reported to have said that the war was being waged by 'kings of finance and industry' to determine 'which millionaires and exploiters will dominate the world'. Charged with endeavouring to influence the other aldermen in a manner prejudicial to the efficient prosecution of the war under Regulation 42, he proposed to subpoena the prime minister. Paterson had stood for the state parliament as an 'Independent Socialist' two months earlier and narrowly failed to win the seat of Bowen, so Inspector Wake of the CIB warned that 'every effort should be made' to prevent him from using the trial as a 'propaganda exercise' and several of the charges were withdrawn. The case, which was heard after the Soviet Union entered the war, resulted in a fine along with a bond to comply with National Security Regulations. Paterson was happy to provide an assurance he would support an Allied victory, and members of the public donated money to pay the fine.[58]

Victoria was more tranquil. Several party members were convicted of distributing communist literature, but others found in possession of illegal publications escaped prosecution. In one such instance, a raid on a boarding house in Hawthorn found a copy of the *Guardian*, but Whitlam advised against pursuing a breach of the Subversive Associations regulations on the grounds that it would be difficult to prove the paper contained doctrines advocated by the CPA. A more controversial case concerned Frank Deakin, president of the Geelong branch of the Amalgamated Engineering Union, who had chaired election meetings for the Labor parliamentarian John Dedman. Communist books and two copies of the *Guardian* were found when Deakin's home was raided in November 1940. Whitlam advised there was little likelihood of sustaining an infringement of Regulation 42 since mere possession (Deakin claimed the newspaper had simply appeared in his letterbox) did not show he was attempting to influence public opinion against the war, though prosecution might have been brought for a breach of a Subversive Associations regulation. The attorney-general declined to proceed.[59]

The principal case in South Australia came early, with prosecution of two men who spoke at a meeting of the League Against Conscription at the Prospect Town Hall on 26 June 1940. Both were found guilty and fined for having tried to influence the public in a manner prejudicial to the efficient prosecution of the war in contravention of Regulation 42. One, Francis Rowan, a member of the Rationalist Society, won an appeal against his conviction, though it was eventually upheld by the High Court. The other, Tom Garland, communist secretary of the Gasworkers' Union, was defiant, complaining that the government had recently 'stolen' a collection of books 'that cost me quids to get together', and comparing his long opposition to fascism with the record of the 'fifth-columnist' prime minister.[60] In Tasmania, the state secretary of the CPA was charged with vagrancy after asking repeatedly for the return of possessions seized on 15 June and in later raids. The magistrate dismissed the case.[61] These prosecutions were clearly aimed at leading party members, and little effort was made beyond them.

Western Australia presents a striking contrast. Repression there began several weeks before 15 June with five convictions for possession of illegal literature. More arrests followed in Perth, spreading over the following year to regional towns and the goldfields. By my count there were

23 prosecutions in the west, ten of them using the Subversive Associations regulations and all successful. Only three escaped a prison term, whereas most convicted in other states got off with a fine or a bond.[62]

Some of the sentences were extraordinarily harsh. The five men found guilty in early June of possessing or distributing communist publications served months of hard labour in Fremantle prison, which consisted of carrying lumps of limestone from one pile to another and back again. A hitchhiker who told his driver that 'a man was a fool to go away and fight for this country' was given three months in an exceptional instance of prosecution relying on the testimony of an informer. Frank Owen, a returned soldier from the Great War, and his wife Dorothy were found guilty of distributing communist literature after they lent two books to a tradesman visiting their house in Geraldton. They were not party members, the communist newspapers found in their possession had been published before the ban and the books were freely available in public libraries, but both served six months. Dorothy Owen, who was clasping her infant in the courthouse, broke down as the sentence was delivered.[63]

Western Australia, with a population of just 470,000 spread over a third of the continent, felt its wartime isolation. The police commissioner had disagreed with his eastern states counterparts at the security conference in January 1940 by urging drastic action: he said his special branch had a list of 'Communists and Russian agents' who should be interned immediately with no provision for appeal. The head of that branch was Detective Sergeant Ron Richards, an English immigrant of saturnine appearance and knowing manner; he was also a drinking companion of the CPA state secretary, Bill Mountjoy.[64]

The police obtained both a membership register and list of subscribers to the *Workers' Star* from the party's Perth office on 15 June, and Richards extracted additional information from an early victim. More than one defendant alleged that members of the special branch planted copies of the *Star* in the course of subsequent raids. 'I hope you have nothing in your pockets that can be planted on me,' Bill Mountjoy's brother Don told the officer who knocked on his door, and John Oldham requested that the same man turn out his pockets before entering.[65] Richards also recruited an agent of notorious unreliability to infiltrate the party. The same man later acted as agent provocateur to incriminate the members of Western Australia's Australia First movement in a fantastic plot to murder both communists and Richards himself.[66]

Richards' greatest triumph was to track down an experienced party organiser sent from Sydney to replace the loose-lipped state secretary. Jack Simpson, using the name Maurie Flynn, moved his accommodation frequently but was apprehended in a city hotel room with literature and a large sum of party dues in his possession, convicted under Subversive Associations Regulation 7A and given six months. The Military Intelligence section of Western Command wanted to intern him and place restriction orders on a number of local communists, but by then the Soviet Union was an ally and the request was denied.[67]

★

Military Intelligence suffered similar rebuffs elsewhere. Dr Ian MacDonald was both the director of the Northern Territory Medical Service and a captain in the Medical Corps attached to the army base in Darwin. After arriving from Melbourne in late 1939, he and his wife built up the local branch of the CPA. The army acknowledged MacDonald was 'a man of the highest character and an idealist' but thought that made him all the more dangerous and sought termination of his appointment. The solicitor-general advised there was no evidence that MacDonald was endangering the security of the Commonwealth. A further attempt to obtain an order under the National Security Regulations to remove him from the Territory was made in January 1941, but this required the Minister for the Army to secure Cabinet approval, and it judged further evidence was needed. Finally, in March, the Minister for Social Services transferred him back to Melbourne.[68]

The Australian government went further than the United Kingdom in curtailing communist opposition to the war: although the *Daily Worker* was banned there, the party itself remained a lawful organisation. Other Dominions went further still. The raids began earlier in New Zealand and took in a larger proportion of a much smaller party. The ban on the Communist Party of Canada was accompanied by internment of many leading members.[69] Political circumstances here inhibited such a drastic course of action. If Robert Menzies' reconstruction of his ministry in early 1940 allowed the Country Party to argue for a crackdown, he still hoped to draw the ALP into a national government, and Labor was mindful of the way similar measures had been used against it in the last war. Moreover, the CPA had a strong presence in unions vital to the war effort; any move on their leaders would have set back efforts to secure the cooperation of the ACTU.

These unionists were therefore immune from the raids that accompanied the declaration of the CPA as a subversive association in June 1940, and there was no attempt to apply its provisions to them. On the contrary, most prosecutions were directed at relatively unimportant party members on the initiative of state police. We have seen how the Attorney-General's Department took a narrow reading of the National Security Regulations in approving these prosecutions, as it did in dealing with other police action. The solicitor-general insisted, for example, that the printing machinery used by the CPA in Queensland could not be seized since it was owned by a separate company, and repeatedly ordered police to return to their owners any books that were not subversive.[70]

Although Military Intelligence complained of the lost opportunity to round up more communists, the CIB accepted the restrictions set by the Attorney-General's Department in which it was located—its rivalry with other security agencies contributed to Australia's light regimen of illegality. Nor is any groundswell of public opinion apparent in favour of complete suppression of all communist activity, for there was still a conspicuous absence of national resolve at this stage of the war. Accordingly, the government seems to have felt it sufficient to give communists a salutary reminder of the limits of its tolerance. But if that was the intention, the Communist Party did not heed the warning. The effect of making the party unlawful was to drive it underground and harden its resolve.

2

Underground, 1940–42

'The general view seemed to be that nothing in the party's lawful life became it like the leaving of it.' Written in 1956 at the height of the Cold War, this is an unlikely observation from Brian Fitzpatrick, who as secretary of the Australian Council for Civil Liberties fought the suppression of the Communist Party in 1940—and did so with even greater urgency a decade later. Looking back on the period of wartime illegality, he claimed the National Security Regulations occasioned 'dislike, resentment and scorn' among non-communists who had experience of them: the 'wide swathe of book-readers incensed by ill-directed police raids on their private libraries' and the 'young persons who on weekend leave interrupted the tedium of life in the armed forces by distributing, under cover of the black-out, the illegal *Tribunes* and *Guardians* and *Stars*'. At the time, however, his council was kept busy publicising the misuse of these regulations and providing legal assistance to their victims.[1] He wrote afterwards that 'every foolish act of restriction, detention or prosecution' attracted fresh sympathy to the banned Communist Party, which maintained its organisation and activities 'despite, but also because' of the ban. Back then he regarded it as a grave threat to democratic freedom.[2]

The party's own evaluation of its experience of illegality underwent a similar transformation. It worked at the time under constant fear of prosecution, exposed members to significant risk, hectored them to be more vigilant and expected them to remain defiant. When a Western Australian member was convicted in June 1940, comrades at the back of the courtroom stood to give the communist salute—there was much less of such bravado over the following twelve months.[3] Looking back, members made light of their tribulations. The stories they told were of a trial that only steeled their determination and of a stand vindicated by the party's disciplined unity in support of the anti-fascist war after June 1941.

Not all subscribed to such rosy nostalgia. Ted Hill, an intensely suspicious disciplinarian who was in charge of underground arrangements in Victoria, argued later that the methods adopted in the period of illegality sowed the seeds of the CPA's capitulation to revisionism—the pejorative term for any deviation from communist orthodoxy. Unable to work openly, it relied unduly on propaganda at the expense of mass agitation, and the fact that communists were still able to work in trade unions exacerbated a 'one-sided emphasis' on industrial activity.[4] But Hill flourished under these restrictions. The exigencies of illegality, the clandestine nature of the party's work and the heightened vigilance against infiltrators gave full rein to his talent for conspiracy.

The CPA's conspiratorial work did not begin with wartime illegality. It was part of the Leninist inheritance, having begun as a necessary condition of political activity under the Tsarist regime and then become a defining characteristic of a vanguard revolutionary party. David McKnight has argued that this conspiratorial thread runs through the history of the Communist International and it was certainly there in the original conditions for membership: communist parties could place no trust in 'bourgeois legality' and 'must everywhere build up a parallel illegal organisation' that would assist the party to fulfil its revolutionary duty at the decisive moment.[5] The Australian party had practised covert activity in the 1930s. It made frequent use of pseudonyms, dissembled in its use of fronts and withheld disclosure of the identity of members so that they could infiltrate the Labor Party. But the resort to underground activity in 1940 went much further. It involved the whole of the party in techniques of deception.

The secretariat issued instructions in March 1940 on how to work underground. Members were to clean up all traces of their communist activity, destroy notebooks, remove all lists of contacts and go through their pockets to ensure that nothing was overlooked. If any information had to be recorded, it should be written on the smallest piece of paper and a fire kept burning until it was discarded. Outside the home, they were to 'get into the habit of talking in a low voice', not wear distinctive clothing and give no sign of recognition when they met other comrades. If arrested, they should say nothing and remember they would be under observation when released from custody.[6] Some branches practised using false names. When Daphne Gollan was asked what pseudonym she would use, she proposed Cleopatra Sweatfigure. 'That's enough, comrade,' said a member of the central committee, 'we are not joking.'[7]

Further precautions were added following the proscription of the party. If arrested or questioned, members should now say that since the CPA was illegal their membership had automatically ceased. They should keep away from party rooms and hold meetings in safe places: the homes of people not suspected of communist association, hotel bars and lounges where every entrance could be watched, or open spaces where any approach could be observed. All messages would be delivered by word of mouth, and members were not to discuss party matters with their families, for that bred 'carelessness and chattering'. They should avoid using terms that might betray their political identity such as 'trade union bureaucrat', 'leftist', 'agitprop' and—apparently an incriminating phrase—'democratic rights'.[8]

At the same time the party had to demonstrate it was still operating. Branches must produce and distribute leaflets, and send copies to the prime minister and premier, the police commissioner and head of the Commonwealth Investigation Branch (CIB) as a show of defiance. Stickers and posters were to be fixed to telegraph poles, footpaths chalked and walls painted—especially those outside police stations. Party 'fraternals' (fronts) should be used, work in the unions stepped up 'as the government will hesitate at putting too great a ban on them', and every opportunity taken to get publications about the war into the armed forces. In short, the party was to respond to illegality by 'resuming in full swing its former programme'.[9]

It was expected that the government's next move after the raids of 15 June would be the arrest of party leaders. They were removed immediately to safe places, Miles and Sharkey initially to the Blue Mountains, Richard Dixon to Victoria, Jack Henry to North Queensland, Ralph Gibson to Brisbane, and Jack Blake to the outskirts of Melbourne. Preparations had been made well in advance, so that Gibson stayed the night with a friend and was then driven to Albury, where another party member took him on to Culcairn; he then boarded a train to Junee and went on by rail through Sydney to a disused garage behind a house on the Brisbane River. The arrangements were sometimes over-elaborate. Dorothy Gibson was to join Ralph later in the year, when he was sharing a house in Toowong, to which a party member would direct her when she reached Brisbane; but the contact was away and Dorothy wandered the city with suitcase in hand until by chance her husband appeared on a street corner. On this occasion Ralph relaxed the rule of giving no sign of recognition, unlike an earlier encounter when he was in Cairns and spotted by Roy Dalgarno, an artist who had joined the party in Melbourne. Roy approached him to say hello but was met by an angry stare before Ralph turned away and hurried on.[10]

Some adopted disguises. Miles grew a moustache, the well-groomed Blake was covered with whiskers and Henry simply became dishevelled. The leaders of the youth organisation in Victoria resorted to school uniforms, the diminutive Audrey Blake wearing a tunic and school hat, her colleague Harry Stein a Scotch College cap.[11] Much communication was by courier, and messages to the central committee went to the Commercial Hotel at the Circular Quay end of George Street, where Len Donald, a reliable organiser, worked behind the bar, while Ted Hill used his legal chambers in Melbourne to receive and pass on instructions. It soon turned out that there was no danger of arrest. Sharkey and Gibson both came out of hiding in September 1940 to conduct their campaigns in the federal election, and others joined them in subsequent public appearances. But since party meetings remained illegal, the leaders went back into smoke after such events. By now they were residing in the homes of metropolitan sympathisers, which made it possible to organise secret meetings of the central committee, though less often and with reduced numbers. There was no attempt to convene a full meeting of the central committee with all its interstate members (known as a plenum). Holding state conferences, let alone the national congress due in the first half of 1941, was out of the question.[12]

In preparation for illegality, the party had set up secret printeries with stockpiles of paper, type and ink. Initially they used flat-bed platen presses, which were cumbersome, slow and noisy. But among the party members Clayton recruited to work underground was a young man with a technical bent, John O'Reilly, who in the 1930s had helped his father produce suburban newspapers. He thought he could build a better machine and was taken to a workshop where he designed and constructed a rotary press that was faster, quieter and much easier to transport. O'Reilly then built an improved version, and another that was taken down to Melbourne. When the party celebrated its 25th anniversary with an exhibition at the Sydney Town Hall in 1945, one of his presses was on show and used to run off souvenirs of the occasion. Another is now part of the collection of the Powerhouse Museum.[13]

The first illegal *Tribune* appeared on 29 July 1940, a meagre affair of a single sheet handset in a rudimentary font and folded to make four small pages. It remained in this format until well into 1941, but gradually increased in size, coverage and regularity. The party's theoretical monthly, the *Communist Review*, resumed publication in January 1941, and three policy statements by Miles and Sharkey, writing as Mason & McShane, were produced.[14] One of these gave the Communist Party as the publisher, whereas *Tribune* was variously ascribed to T. Tucker of Gundagai and T. Grace of Cato Street; the *Communist Review* purported to be a publication of John Fairfax of the *Sydney Morning Herald*. Newspapers were distributed in pubs and worksites with the instruction to 'pass it on'. As the hunt for the source intensified, distributors were enjoined to ensure every recipient was reliable. Other copies were pushed under doors or rolled tight with a string and thrown over fences. Fred Paterson advised Queensland members to read all banned publications at the front gate and keep them in the letterbox: 'Anybody can drop anything in your letterbox'.[15]

In Victoria the party bought several flat-bed presses in the early months of 1940. The largest of them, used to produce the illegal *Guardian*, was installed in the Kew house of a party member who worked as a printer for the *Argus*. He directed operations in a chamber constructed under the veranda that was lined with insulation to reduce the noise. His wife, the artist and historian Marguerite Mahood, regretted only that their comrades did not understand why the couple dropped out of open activity. The Brunswick organiser, Les Barnes, also had printing skills and set up other presses, though the carrier used to transport one of them told friends that Les was going back into the trade and the special branch was soon on his trail. The party instructed him to grow a moustache, but he thought it made him look like Hitler, so carried on clean-shaven and on 'tiptoe'.[16]

Queensland had the most exotic printery, a cave now known as the Communist Cave overlooking Thunderbolt Creek in the rugged ranges north-west of Townsville. A donkey carried in the press that was used to produce the *Spark* (in place of the *North Queensland Guardian*), and it took members two hours on horseback to reach it, though most spent longer backtracking to avoid detection. There were other printeries on the outskirts of Brisbane, including one on a poultry farm that was visited by police—Ted Bacon, who was responsible for them, decided there was greater safety in the anonymity of the city than in the country, where newcomers aroused curiosity.[17] Western Australia took longer to recover from the police onslaught: a cyclostyled version of the *Workers' Star* reappeared in October 1940 with a print run of just 300 copies.[18]

Underground work tested nerves, some enjoying the intrigue and others finding it oppressive. The historian Russel Ward and his wife Margaret, who were recruited at this time through activity in the New Theatre, had to meet a party member at the GPO in Martin Place to receive careful instructions on how to find their way to the local branch. He refused to be intimidated by surveillance; she was less comfortable and eventually suffered a nervous breakdown. Betty Searle and two other members were sheltering a visiting Adelaide member, Joan Finger, in their Cremorne flat in 1941 when two policemen appeared at the back door. They locked their guest in a wardrobe before discovering the visit was to inform Joan of lost property. She immediately contacted Len Donald and was whisked away to a safer refuge.[19]

Public activity was unavoidably risky. Those who ventured out at night with a bucket of paint or paste were advised to take an additional member to act as cockatoo, but you could never know when a police patrol might appear. Some members of the force turned a blind eye. The sergeant in charge at Toowoomba bought the party's illegal newspaper. Jim Cairns' unpalatable duties as member of the special squad in Melbourne helped set him on a life on the left. Alf Hughes, a detective sergeant of the NSW police, was a special case since he was involved with the CPA before joining Military Intelligence in June 1940, from where he was able to provide Wally Clayton with advance warning of hostile operations.[20]

Much ingenuity was exercised in the organisation of party meetings. The central committee met late at night or in the small hours of the morning, sometimes in safe houses and sometimes in remote shacks or tents, changing the venue after each meeting. The Victorian state committee adopted similar methods, on one occasion meeting in a rowboat in Port Phillip Bay with rods in hand. Members of the Queensland state committee planned their work in the compartment of a railway carriage of a suburban train making the morning trip to the city.[21] Party branches disguised meetings as card games or picnics in the park, with bottles of beer for authenticity. With the restrictions on public meetings, there was an emphasis on intra-party activity. Dixon and Blake conducted three one-week schools, each involving a dozen members who were put up in the cottage of Ralph Gibson's mother in the Dandenong Ranges. Sharkey came up from Sydney for a similar gathering of 30 Queenslanders at a seaside resort.[22]

A great deal of this clandestine activity was known to the security agencies. Even though the central committee used post office boxes for interstate mail, much of its correspondence was intercepted and copied. Despite the party's instructions, members did share confidences, allowing informants to report on underground activity. The party in turn knew that the security agencies were planting agents in its ranks. As best it could, it sought to reduce the risk by restricting participation in decision-making. Hence, when the Western Australian state committee told Sydney in 1941 of its inability to identify an informant, it was instructed to hold its state conference at a place and date kept confidential, to elect a new state committee of no more than seven members and not to announce the results. The danger was that preoccupation with security would paralyse the party. Hence the political committee advised the Western Australians that 'Whether you like it or not, you have to work on the assumption that even at a conference there is a pimp.'[23]

★

To circumvent restrictions, the party conducted much of its public campaigning through auxiliaries. The Friends of the Soviet Union, for example, remained a legal organisation and was used for organising 'cottage lectures' (meetings at a member's house to which sympathisers were invited), as was the Left Book Club. The No-Conscription Committee was formed in February 1940 and launched at the Sydney Town Hall in April with a Southern Cross draped on the platform bearing the Eureka oath: 'We swear by the Southern Cross to stand truly by each other, and fight to defend our rights and liberties.'[24] It too escaped the prohibition of subversive organisations and was able to hold public meetings. A Budget Protest Committee followed at the end of the year, to campaign against the government's proposal to finance additional war expenditure through increased income tax on lower-income-earners and higher duties on items such as beer and tobacco.

The use of fronts did not overcome the threat of prosecution. Phyllis Johnson was arrested when speaking at a street meeting of the No-Conscription Committee because her words were judged to influence public opinion against the efficient prosecution of the war. The party had to draw a fine line between using auxiliaries 'for spreading propaganda of a legal character to the masses' and ensuring that they were not linked too closely to its illegal work. On the one hand it called for greater use of opportunities for public agitation, on the other it warned against the involvement of known party activists: 'our line should be alertness, initiative, persistence, relentless attack, gain, retreat, attack'.[25]

That did not save the Australian Youth Council, an umbrella organisation through which the communist youth organisation worked with a broad range of similar bodies, including the Student Christian Movement. The council was added to the list of subversive organisations in August 1940, though oddly the CPA's own League of Young Democrats was allowed to continue until February 1941. The banning of the Youth Council was precipitated by its sponsorship of an Australian Youth Parliament, which was to meet in Canberra and discuss an anti-war resolution, but Audrey Blake spoke with impunity three weeks later at a meeting of the Youth Parliament in Melbourne on civil liberties.[26]

The State Labor Party (SLP) also retained its legality and provided a platform for communists in New South Wales. Initially it lacked a newspaper, but in November 1940 was able to acquire *Progress*, the makeshift publication of a moribund unemployed organisation that came with a permit (for the government had imposed a licence system on newsprint as a wartime measure). Bill Wood, the editor, drew on a talented group of writers to transform *Progress* into a lively tabloid weekly with a circulation that reached 20,000.[27] Contributors included Rupert Lockwood, who had been a feature writer in the 1930s for Keith Murdoch's Melbourne *Herald* before travelling overseas, and John Fisher, son of a former Labor prime minister, who followed the same path, including a stint in Moscow. Both were recently arrived in Sydney, new to the Communist Party and hence able to work more plausibly through the SLP—Lockwood and Fisher, as well as Wood, represented it in the 1940 federal election.[28]

Not one of the SLP candidates was successful in this or the 1941 state election, and as its membership fell away few regarded it as more than a communist front. The security services watched it closely, including tapping the phone in a back room of the Sydney Trades Hall that served as *Progress*'s editorial office. Bill Wood had managed to obtain the number of Military Intelligence and in idle moments would ring and inquire of the man who answered: 'Hello, Major, how's it going?' Invariably ordered to hang up immediately, Wood came to realise that until he did so the line was not available for Military Intelligence to eavesdrop. With the censor also taking a keen interest in the paper, the party's lawyer Jack Sweeney was kept busy.[29]

The decision of the SLP to contest the federal election confirmed the breach with the Labor Party. It was also the parting of the ways for Lloyd Ross, who had moved the original 'Hands Off Russia' resolution but now wished to withdraw it and return to the ALP. Lloyd had been close to his brother Edgar, the dour editor of the Miners' Federation's paper

Common Cause, and the two men played tennis regularly with Lockwood and Sweeney at Lloyd Ross's home in Hunters Hill. Now he was yet another 'middle-class intellectual' who had gone over to 'the camp of the class-collaborators'.[30]

The party's attitude to the Labor Party at this time was ambivalent, but then so too was Labor's attitude to the war. With great difficulty, John Curtin had persuaded the ALP Federal Conference to support Australia's participation, but there were members of the parliamentary caucus who remained hostile. They opposed the government's war measures, including its budget proposals, and the Communist Party called on Curtin to do the same even as it denounced him as a 'lackey of capitalism'. In one of their pseudonymous pamphlets produced at this time, *What Is This Labor Party*, Miles and Sharkey exhumed Lenin's 1913 article characterising the ALP as a 'liberal-bourgeois party' representing the interests of Australian capital.[31] Yet the central committee vehemently repudiated a leaflet distributed in Curtin's seat of Fremantle during the September 1940 election calling on workers to 'Throw Curtin Out', for the party's policy was to put Labor into office as a first step towards a people's government. This was a departure from the Comintern line, which insisted that all such collaborators must be exposed as traitors to the working class.[32]

The same condemnation was applied to Curtin's caucus critics, who wanted him to challenge Menzies for office after the election left the ALP just short of a majority. Bert Evatt, the most outspoken, was described as a 'liberal flunkey to the Australian warmongers'. Even Edgar Ross conceded that a cartoon in *Progress* showing Judas and Pierre Laval, the Vichyist collaborator, with the caption 'Move over mates, here comes Jack Curtin' was unnecessarily sectarian. Jessie Street remonstrated with Bill Wood about the savagery of these attacks and was assured that *Progress* bore the ALP leader no ill will: 'If I may paraphrase Brutus on Caesar: As Curtin loved Labor we weep for him; as he was fortunate, we rejoice at it; as he was valiant, we honour him, but as he betrayed the case of Labor we must (politically) slay him.'[33]

These polemics mattered less in New South Wales, where the party had sacrificed its presence within the ALP, than in other states where it continued to cultivate influence. Twelve local branches of the Labor Party in Victoria were identified as having a significant communist membership (three had adopted 'Hands Off Russia' resolutions) and the state executive reconstituted several of them. It also required all delegates to the state conference to declare they were not members of the Communist Party or attached to any of its auxiliaries. Every one of the communists who participated in the Easter conference in Sydney had signed a similar declaration. Ted Laurie was a dual member in Melbourne when the party ordered him to give the same assurance in 1941. He did so, though the lie continued to trouble him.[34] There is little evidence that other communists felt the same compunction.

The fallout was probably greatest in Western Australia, where an unlikely conjunction of events threw communist infiltration into the spotlight. A by-election in the federal seat of Swan resulting from the death of the Country Party incumbent shortly after the 1940 election opened the possibility that Labor might gain an additional seat and deadlock the House of Representatives. Jim Dinan, the ALP candidate, was an ex-farmer who had performed well two months earlier in this sprawling electorate, which ran from Midland-Guildford into the wheat belt, but Dinan had come under suspicion from the state executive for communist sympathies. As Curtin made no effort to assist Dinan's candidature, Evatt travelled west to do so and complained at the lack of support from local officials. Following his narrow defeat in the December by-election, Dinan alleged the ALP had sabotaged the campaign because of his criticism of its 'sell-out' in not opposing the federal budget. And following his expulsion in January, he called a meeting of supporters to form a Western Australian branch of the Budget Protest Committee.[35]

The state executive of the ALP saw this as an attempt to create an offshoot of the 'Hughes–Evans' State Labor Party, and there were grounds for that view. The secretary of the Budget Protest Committee, June Carder, came to Western Australia in September 1940 after working for the Federated Ironworkers' Association (FIA). Jack Simpson, who later came from Sydney as party organiser, was found with budget-protest material when arrested—and he was working with Dinan, who used the party name of 'Norman'. John Oldham, who also returned from Sydney at this time, played a leading role in the protest campaign. And a joint statement from Jack Hughes and Wally Evans following Dinan's expulsion likened his stand to their own.[36]

There was an important difference, however, between the SLP's origins as the NSW branch of the Labor Party and a committee of dissidents within the Western Australian one. Their support petered out when the state executive of the ALP expelled the ringleaders, and Dinan embarked on a tour of the eastern states organised by the party.[37] The irony is that the Labor candidate who won Swan in the following 1943 election was Don Mountjoy, brother of the former state secretary of the CPA and himself a secret member.

★

'We made strikes our business,' Ernie Thornton boasted of this passage in his union's history.[38] The CPA's opposition to the war included disruption of war industries, but Thornton greatly exaggerated his influence. Industrial conflict dropped sharply with the settlement of the mining dispute in May 1940, not because communists fell quiet but because the gravity of the fall of France put a dampener on their efforts. There were more disputes in the later months of the year and more still during 1941, notwithstanding the party's support for the war following the German invasion of the USSR.

The disputes that did occur at this time were principally in industries with a strong communist presence, but they were not conducted as protests against the government's policies, as was the case with the waterside workers' refusal to load iron for export to Japan in 1938. Rather, they arose from changes in the workplace as part of a drive for increased production, coupled with the unwillingness of the government to relax wage controls and the refusal of employers to make concessions. Fifty hands at a brass shop in the Melbourne suburb of Maidstone stopped work in July 1940 in protest against a speed-up, and 300 builders of defence facilities in nearby Deer Park and Maribyrnong did the same in November until they obtained improved overtime rates. More than 2000 employees of the Lithgow munition works downed tools for six days in the same month after one of them was victimised, as did nearly 1500 at the Port Kembla steelworks for a fortnight in a dispute over classifications, and 600 women who had been introduced to the shipyards of Cockatoo Island and Mort's Dock but wanted better pay. An overtime claim closed the Mt Isa lead, zinc and copper mine for six weeks, and there was a seventeen-day stoppage at the BHP steelworks in February 1941.[39]

The coalminers in the southern district of New South Wales were out for eight days over a new award in October 1940, and disputes continued to arise sporadically at particular collieries, but otherwise the coalfields remained conspicuously quiet. The party suffered a setback in September 1940 when Bill Orr, the Miners' Federation secretary, resigned. He had been on leave for stress earlier in the year but now told the press he had opposed the 'second round' stoppage that began during his absence. When elected in 1933, Bill Orr was the CPA's first national leader of a major union, though his involvement in party work had declined and his resignation followed its decision not to renominate him for the union post. To make matters worse, the party's candidate lost the ballot to replace Orr.[40]

A similar problem arose in April 1941 when the Miners' Federation president, Charles Nelson, joined with the president of the NSW northern district in a public undertaking of uninterrupted production for the war effort. Nelson, who defied the instruction of the federation's national council to retract his statement, was subsequently found to have accepted a government payment of £300 to help pacify the coalfields.[41] This was a distasteful conclusion to a long career of service to the union, though Nelson too had been drifting out of the party and drinking heavily. Although the party's candidate won the ballot for the presidency, its influence in the federation was shaken.

The CPA's industrial propaganda was directed at profiteering, the cost of living, wage controls and the erosion of working conditions. Members were instructed to avoid any suggestion that these grievances could be used to hinder the war effort. All talk of the 'imperialist war' was to be confined to the party's illegal work, and public statements of trade union leaders had to be 'carefully considered' to determine the degree to which they linked industrial demands to an anti-war message. Even so, the policy of fomenting strikes was straining relations with union activists who had previously supported the party's lead. Lloyd Ross and his supporters won a fierce battle for control of the NSW branch of the Australian Railways Union, and there were setbacks in other union elections. Jack Hughes lost the presidency of the NSW Labor Council in February 1941 to the anti-communist secretary of the bootmakers' union, James Maloney.[42]

*

From late 1939, when the CPA fell into line with the Communist International's instructions, it gave up any acknowledgement of Nazi Germany's aggressive intent. Abandoning the earlier call to defend democracy against the fascist powers, the party insisted there was nothing to choose between the combatants. All of them were engaged in an imperialist war of conquest and plunder fought in the interests of monopoly capital. All were equally culpable of inciting bellicose hatred, repressing dissent and placing the burden of sacrifice on workers.

Until the middle of 1940, the party called for an end to Australia's participation and warned especially against any Allied attack on the Soviet Union. Then, after Germany's rapid conquest of Western Europe alarmed Stalin, communist policy took a new turn. Fascism was once more identified as the enemy of democracy, and not just within the countries where it had originated: the Allies were accused of adopting similarly dictatorial methods to serve their equally reactionary purposes. At the same time the CPA now accepted that Australia was under threat and supported defence measures, except that these required a 'people's defence of Australia against both foreign and native fascism'. All troops must be brought back home, the people armed, Menzies driven from office, democratic liberties restored and workers put in charge of industry. The party accordingly called for Labor to take office as a first step towards establishing a 'People's Government' representing 'toilers, small farmers, soldiers and middle-class democrats', and campaigned 'to force Curtin to take a stand on behalf of the workers'. After he persisted with his 'spine-lessness', the task was to expose 'the Labor servants of imperialism' and 'drive the traitors out of the Labor movement'.[43]

Thus from mid-1940, the party's denunciation of the imperialist war was accompanied by a politically expedient program of national defence. Much propaganda was directed at the failure of the Menzies government to safeguard the country, its 'bungling incompetence and betrayal of national security', the subservience to Britain in dispatching the AIF to the Mediterranean theatre and especially the ill-fated expedition to Greece in April 1940. Criticism of domestic precautions concentrated on the inadequacy of air-raid shelters.[44] And while Australian communists still refused to take sides in an imperialist conflict, they placed increasing emphasis on Menzies' record of appeasement and their own opposition to the fascist regimes. There were reminders of how communists had fought to save the Spanish Republic and placed an embargo on the export of war materials to Japan. The continued appeasement of Japan attracted particular criticism as the CPA warned of *The Coming War in the Pacific*.[45]

All this is to say that the party put the best possible face on the Comintern's instructions to maintain opposition to the war. Hitler's conquest of Western Europe, followed by his pact with Italy and Japan in September 1940 and then the German thrust into the Balkans, sent shockwaves through the Kremlin. Hoping still to avert an attack on the Soviet Union, Stalin resisted an open breach with Hitler. If the call for a 'people's defence' provided communist parties in those countries that had not fallen to the Axis powers with some relief from the accusation they were oblivious of the danger of invasion, then the argument that 'only a People's Government and a free people, ruthlessly crushing the enemy at home, can defend the nation' was an ominous indication of the grim fantasy that overcame the CPA's underground leadership.[46]

From places of hiding, the national leaders chided comrades who undertook the party's illegal activity without adequate concealment. Various examples of 'gross carelessness or thoughtlessness' were castigated in a November 1940 directive. In one case a member had been out with a car pasting up posters when apprehended and party literature had been found in his car. 'Some casualties are to be expected,' the central executive stated, but this was 'criminal stupidity'. In March 1941 the executive warned that the northern spring was likely to bring an escalation of the war and a new drive against communists. 'There must at once be a tightening up of the struggle against provocation, a check and improvement in all areas of precaution', it advised, and all legally issued material had to be 'careful and subtle'. At the same time, mass work had to be increased and a survey made 'to ensure that each member with any degree of freedom of movement is active'.[47]

The security services noticed no decline in activity. Military Intelligence in particular judged 'it was far more difficult to deal with the Communists' after they were forced underground. The periodic discoveries of illegal presses and prosecutions for breach of security regulations seemed to have no deterrent effect, and most of those who were convicted resumed agitation as soon as they had served their sentences.[48]

The circumstances made it impossible to keep accurate membership records, even if the party secretariat had been inclined to do so. Some members certainly dropped out following the declaration of illegality, and a recruitment drive was launched at the end of 1940. Revealingly, it took the form of a competition in which branches were awarded three points for every new member in a war industry, two for recruits in other industries and just one for housewives and others not in the workforce—the results were not reported. Sharkey's report to the next CPA congress acknowledged there was 'a noticeable fluctuation' at this time and attributed a 'drift out of the Party' to the difficulty of maintaining organisational contact with smaller branches.[49]

The principal problem of illegality, according to Sharkey, was a weakening of democratic centralism. Because the central committee met less frequently and without its interstate members, state committees had greater latitude to find their own way. With the central committee largely confined to discussion of general policy and its leading members struggling to supervise the work of the specialist departments, collective decision-making declined. And with those leading members all underground and reliant on the information provided to them, they became 'divorced from the practical direction of the work of the party'. As soon as circumstances allowed, he abolished the NSW committee so that the central committee could supervise work in that state.[50]

There is some suggestion that Sharkey fell out with the trade union leaders in Sydney who were able to work freely. A CIB agent with connections to the upper echelons there reported in July 1941 that Tom Wright, Ernie Thornton, and Ted Roach and Stan Moran of the Waterside Workers' Federation, had taken over responsibility for the party's industrial work and that Sharkey, who disagreed with them, was sidelined. This is implausible. It is true that the party annulled the assurance he gave in his press interview following the German invasion of the Soviet Union that communists were 'opposed to frivolous and unnecessary strikes'. It is also likely that the unionists were responsible for the corrective statement that the party would not surrender the right to strike—for no union leader could forgo the right to withhold labour.[51]

Sharkey might well have employed greater licence than other comrades wanted at this juncture, but there is nothing to suggest that his place as party president was challenged during the period of illegality—on the contrary, he seems to have gained authority at the expense of the CPA's general secretary, J.B. Miles, to whom he was nominally subordinate. John Bramwell Miles, known as JBM or more informally as the 'Old Man', was a Scots immigrant, slight in stature, hard of hearing and deliberate of speech, deeply read in Marxism–Leninism but in failing health. Lance Sharkey, on the other hand, was a rough-hewn orator of Irish Catholic descent, red-haired and built like a footballer. If there was dissatisfaction with Sharkey's 'dictatorial attitude', as the CIB agent suggested, it derived from the fact that at this time he had to issue instructions rather than administer them. His report to the following congress made it clear that party discipline would not be relaxed.

Underground activity, then, weakened the party's hierarchical structure. With messages relayed by word of mouth on a personal basis by comrades known to each other, it was inevitable that members exercised greater personal initiative. The circumstances of illegality, the prohibitions enforced so inconsistently, only added to the uncertainty. Audrey Blake provides a telling example. She recalls being summoned in early June 1940 to the office of Roland Browne, the head of the CIB in Victoria, who began by asking after her husband Jack. He had gone into hiding and Browne wanted Audrey to get a message to him that he had to stop producing the illegal party newspaper or he would be spending the war in gaol. Sitting behind a desk laden with security files, Browne went further, intimating that Audrey's youth organisation, the League of Young Democrats, would soon be declared illegal, along with the party itself, but asking her to keep this information to herself. Knowing that preparations had been made for underground activity, she said nothing. Nor did she report the conversation to the party. Sixty years later she could still recall the look in Browne's eyes.[52]

3

The Leading War Party, 1942–45

News of Germany's invasion of the Soviet Union, which reached Australia on 23 June 1941, confounded the Communist Party. Only the previous day *Tribune* had derided the suggestion that Hitler would turn east as 'wishful thinking'. Bruce Miller, then an undergraduate at the University of Sydney and later a distinguished political scientist, recalled attending a lecture given at that time by the young historian Bob Gollan that demonstrated conclusively that all talk of war between Germany and the USSR was a capitalist plot—and the next day reading that it had begun. Richard Dixon, who was in South Australia for a meeting of the state committee, is said to have dismissed the initial reports as rubbish.[1]

There was never any doubt the CPA would rally to the defence of the Soviet Union. A meeting was hastily convened at the Sydney Trades Hall, the crowd spilling into the street and those inside singing the Internationale before communist union delegates moved and the NSW Labor Council unanimously adopted a resolution to give every possible assistance to the socialist homeland. The mass meetings at the Domain and Sydney Town Hall in the following days, described in the Introduction, did the same.[2]

It took longer for Australian communists to grasp the implications of Hitler's fateful decision to launch Operation Barbarossa. Notwithstanding Churchill's immediate pledge of support, the party leaders still suspected that 'Anglo-American imperialists' were responsible for 'switching the war' and would leave the USSR to fight alone. J.B. Miles rejected any suggestion of 'swinging in behind the imperialist enemies of Germany as some naïve people, wishful thinkers, hope, imagine and suggest we will'. 'We would not help, we would harm the Soviet Union and socialism,' the central executive maintained, 'by ceasing to fight the class enemy in Australia.' 'Defend the Soviet Union! Down with the Nazi gangsters! Down with all Imperialists!' were the slogans that accompanied Miles's instruction that 'the main blow' of communists must still be struck at the imperialists in their own country.[3]

Two interstate members of the executive, Jack Blake (the Victorian leader) and Dixon (still based in Melbourne), could see that this position, supporting the war effort of the USSR while opposing that of Australia, was impossible. Blake claimed that they prevailed at a subsequent meeting of the inner circle, and there is supporting evidence. On 5 July the central committee issued a circular acknowledging that the 'just and progressive war' being waged by the Soviet Union 'intermingles' with the imperialist war. Four days later it changed the party's slogans to 'Victory for Soviet Russia, Defeat the Nazi Armies', and withdrew a call for the return of Australian troops from North Africa.[4]

The initial confusion was indicative of the CPA's organisational difficulties. There was also uncertainty about the progress of Operation Barbarossa—if the German and Russian communiqués were to be believed, both sides were winning easily. Accustomed to claims that Stalin had used the past two years to build an impregnable line of defence, Australian communists placed their faith in the Soviet reports. As one put it, they thought the Red Army was so strong it would go through the Wehrmacht 'like a pack of salts through a sick shearer'. Indeed, *Tribune* insisted that 'wise, farseeing Stalin' had always known of Hitler's intentions and been ready to resist aggression at any time. It soon became apparent that this confidence was misplaced. In the first month of the German offensive, armoured columns punched through the defences, inflicting three-quarters of a million casualties and penetrating hundreds of kilometres into Soviet territory.[5]

By then an Anglo-Soviet Agreement had been concluded and Sharkey had come out of hiding to pledge CPA support for the Allies to defeat Hitler. In September he went further, burying all reference to an imperialist war. With the 'aggression of the Nazi beasts against the Soviet

Union', he explained, the nature and course of the war had changed to a people's war for the defeat of fascism.[6] Yet this new enthusiasm for the Australian contribution still remained equivocal, as the party found it necessary to correct 'distortions' in press reports of Sharkey's July press interview. He was quoted as pledging 'full aid for the war effort', but the statement of clarification derided those 'softheads' who thought the party would 'swing in behind Churchill and Menzies'. The Australian prime minister was still serving the interests of monopoly capitalism, still oppressing workers and suppressing democratic rights: 'Menzies fears a Hitler victory but he also fears a Soviet victory.'[7]

The CPA called for Menzies to be driven from office and replaced by a Labor government, but did not expect that to bring about the changes needed unless the new administration was held to account. To this end it arranged in September 1941 for fourteen trade union officials to propose an agreement to John Curtin. They would use their influence to eliminate strikes if he undertook to impose control of monopolies, replace the businessmen in charge of munitions production with union representatives, restrict profits, open diplomatic relations with the Soviet Union and remove the ban on the Communist Party. This was a hopelessly misjudged ambit claim. Curtin, still leader of the opposition until two independent members made him prime minister shortly afterwards, could only reject it as blackmail and was then roundly abused as a capitalist lackey.[8]

Behind the scenes, however, the party's union leaders entered into discussions with Labor ministers as soon as Curtin took office, and gave an assurance of full support for the new government's plans to mobilise all available resources. In October the central executive instructed state and district leaders they must intervene when strikes were threatened to ensure uninterrupted production. The party welcomed Curtin's call for an 'all-in effort', and told members that 'support for the Allied cause must be absolute, there can be no conditions or reservations'. Care should be also taken in propaganda to go beyond 'the great struggle of the Red Army' and recognise 'the grim courageous struggle of our Australian forces at Tobruk', for this was a war 'to preserve the independence of Australia, Britain and other Dominions' as well as 'the social system in the Soviet Union'.[9]

In communist terminology, the policy had changed from a united front from below (aiming to win workers to the revolutionary cause by exposing the duplicity of their reformist leaders) to a more expedient united front from above, through alliance with the Labor Party. Indeed, the policy went further in calling for a popular front of all progressive and patriotic forces against the fascist enemy, such as had been pursued between 1935 and 1939.[10] The change required communists to temper their zeal. Hence the central executive advised against pursuing nationalisation of industry on the grounds that any such campaign would alarm capitalists and weaken national unity. Even so, the party condemned the appointment of Essington Lewis, the managing director of BHP, who was already in charge of munitions, to direct aircraft production, and flatly rejected any idea of an all-party national government—in striking contrast to the Communist Party of Great Britain (CPGB), which with the Comintern's approval supported the one led by Churchill. It saw the need to support Curtin against critics in the ALP but reserved its own right to criticise him. With Japan's entry into the war in December 1941, it accepted that the Pacific was Australia's sector of the 'anti-Axis front', but was already arguing the need to ease the pressure on the Soviet Union by opening a second European front.[11]

These reservations fell away during 1942, though for reasons that will be explained the Labor government did not restore full legality to the CPA until the end of that year. By then the Communist Party had declared itself to be 'the leading and most active war party'; indeed, it had thrown its weight behind Curtin on conscription and other emergency measures that some sections of the labour movement resisted. The united front policy would hold to the end of the war, but was never free of tension: even at the height of the Japanese advance, the leadership acknowledged 'a noticeable lack of enthusiasm for it throughout the Party'.[12] The rapid growth of membership, activity and influence made adherence to the united front all the more demanding, for it required setting aside much of what distinguished revolutionaries from reformists. But in doing so, communists found a place in national affairs they had never before occupied.

★

The party began to grow as soon as the Soviet Union entered the war. 'The situation was never more favourable for a mass recruiting drive,' the central committee announced in July 1941, and more than 1000 new members were enrolled over the following three months. The advent of the Labor government in October removed most of the obstacles to recruitment, and membership increased to 6850 in May 1942. At that time the central committee opened a campaign to build the party to 15,000 by the end of the year.[13]

This Build the Party campaign was supervised by Len Donald, an experienced member of the central committee, and conducted as an interstate competition. A quota was set for each state: New South Wales was to win 3600 new members, Victoria 1600, Queensland 1150, Western Australia 250, South Australia 220, Tasmania 40. There were sub-quotas for industrial workers, women, farmers and youth, though the aim was for two-thirds of the new branches to be in factories and just a third local branches. Monthly tallies were reported in a new organisational bulletin, the *Party Builder*. Queensland won the competition by reaching its quota in October, and by December the national membership approached 16,000.[14]

With the influx of recruits came the problem of keeping them. Donald drew attention at the outset of the party-building campaign to the high turnover: 3000 new members were won in New South Wales between June 1941 and May 1942 but 1000 had been lost. Every branch was therefore to appoint a membership director who would induct new members, arrange their enrolment in a study class and 'weave a comradely atmosphere around them'. They should immediately be given an active role and any absence from a branch meeting must be followed up. Meetings were to keep routine business to a minimum, encourage full participation and finish punctually at 10 p.m. To deal with the proliferation of branches—1214 of them by December 1942—they were grouped in zones, the zone committee reporting to the district committee and it in turn to the state committee.[15]

Reviewing the party-building campaign in early 1943, Richard Dixon observed that many new members lacked knowledge of communist theory and organisation. Joining was only the first step in a further membership drive conducted during the second half of 1943; it was called 'Strengthen the Party' and 'the task was to make real communists' of recruits through rigorous training. But the goal of 6000 new members was not achieved: just 3500 joined between July and December 1943. Hence the third recruitment effort in the second half of 1944, the Victory Campaign, returned to the methods of the first. Quotas were set for all states, 'recruiting shock brigades' appointed in all districts, and Red Star certificates awarded for zones and branches that did best. There was a greater emphasis on welcoming newcomers through 'cottage lectures' in members' homes and open meetings where those interested could sample party life. But again the goal of 6000 new members was not achieved; just 2751 were enrolled by late 1944, when the Victory Campaign was extended for a further six months. Momentum was slowing, and the 22,052 members at the beginning of 1945 probably represented the high point.[16]

The growth was remarkable, nevertheless. In under four years the CPA increased more than fivefold to approach the size of the two major political parties. Both the Labor and the Liberal Party had around 60,000 members in 1945, though the latter was still new and would expand rapidly to more than 100,000 members by 1947.[17] But the Communist Party had a much higher rate of attendance at branch meetings, which occurred more often (every fortnight) and its members were far more active—in auxiliaries, campaigns and rallies, in their workplaces and unions, and in community and civic organisations. It had far more organisers, its publications outsold those of the Labor Party, its training was of a different order of magnitude.

Until 1943 the national newspaper, *Tribune*, remained an undersized affair. In that year the party was granted licences to publish newspapers in Sydney, Melbourne, Brisbane and Perth, and with the licences came an allocation of paper from the country's newsprint pool. Simultaneously, the State Labor Party (SLP) paid £25,000 for a Sydney trotting weekly along with its substantial printing works in Forest Lodge, which was used to produce *Progress*, *Tribune* and a number of other party and union publications as well as the profitable betting guide. *Tribune* expanded its staff and coverage, added graphics, cartoons, greater foreign coverage, a literary page and sporting column. It claimed a circulation of 50,000 when it went biweekly in 1945 and arranged for distribution through newsagents with the intention of becoming a daily. The circulation of the Melbourne *Guardian* grew to 18,000 in 1945 and the Brisbane *Guardian* sold 10,000.[18]

Current Book Distributors, the party's publishing arm, produced between twenty and 30 books and pamphlets annually, and claimed sales approaching three million by 1945. An abridged local edition of *The Socialist Sixth of the World* (1939) by Hewlett Johnson, the 'Red Dean' of Canterbury, was the bestseller with 210,000 copies; and Len Fox's *Australia's Guilty Men* (1943), an Australian adaptation of an English exposé of ruling-class appeasement, sold more than 50,000.[19] The separate publishing arms of the state committees were also active, Victoria's especially. Its reminder of the long history of fascist aggression, *You Remember?* (1942), was a montage of images and text, using colour backgrounds overprinted with a variety of fonts in a strikingly modern design.

The same professionalism was apparent in the party's leaflets, posters and use of radio and cinema. Until legality was restored, weekly radio programs were conducted in Sydney by the SLP, the Aid Russia Committee and the Legal Rights Committee, along with a five-minute news commentary delivered each weekday morning and evening by Syd Jordan, a party member employed by the station 2KY owned by the NSW Labor Council. Such programs expanded from 1943 with Rupert Lockwood, Bill Wood and Edgar Ross among the commentators, a regular New Theatre program, Phyllis Johnson's weekly *Women for Freedom*, and *Voice of the People* presented by the party organiser Adam Ogston—there was even a Sunday-night *Soviet Quiz*. In Sydney the party bought time on the Macquarie network stations 2GB and 2UE as well as local stations in Newcastle, Wollongong and country districts (*Voice of the Countryside* was widely broadcast), while other states produced their own programs.[20] There was increasing use of journalists (scores of party members worked for metropolitan dailies), dramatists (from the New Theatre) and announcers (the Actors' and Announcers' Association was a communist union). *Australia Marches On*, the party's flagship program from 1945, employed leading writers and actors for a fully scripted half-hour presentation.[21]

The cost of such publicity was substantial, and the party outlaid further sums as it expanded. The purchase of the Newsletter printery in 1943 was financed by a payment of £12,000 and two promissory notes of £6500. Two businessmen associated with the party arranged the acquisition of Marx House in George Street for £30,000 in 1944, and donations helped raise the £22,000 needed to buy and fit out Australia–Soviet House in Melbourne in the same year. The sums involved were unprecedented. As the central executive discussed the financial details for buying the printery, Sharkey recalled how 'we had to battle to get a threepenny tram fare'. 'Yes,' Len Donald replied, 'and I can remember the time when the party bought you a push-bike to get around on.'[22]

We do not know the full magnitude of communist income and expenditure. A financial statement for 1942 shows income of £20,465 made up principally of £4791 in dues (which were sixpence a week, threepence for non-wage-earners), £2398 in donations and £5830 in literature sales; publishing costs were £5041 and £4962 went on wages.[23] A subsequent statement was published in 1945 for the 30 months following restoration of legality in December 1942. It gives an income of £56,361, made up principally of £20,100 in dues and £14,000 in quotas (additional dues levied for specific campaigns and projects). Expenditure included £9300 on radio and publicity, £8900 on wages and £4300 on travelling expenses. But this second statement is for the central committee only. It does not include accounts for the party press, Current Book Distributors, or state operations. Dues by this time would have yielded more than £20,000 a year, and most of this sum supported the work of state committees and local branches. There is no entry for donations, and we know that well-to-do members made substantial contributions. At a conservative estimate, the CPA's annual turnover was at least £50,000 by 1945, approaching $4 million in current values.[24]

The second financial statement showed expenditure of £4490 on the Marx School. This was established in Sydney early in 1943 to cope with the influx of new members by training a cadre of members who would conduct elementary courses in communism at the branch and district level. A *Handbook for Tutors* covered the elementary course, which was a catechism in communist terminology ('What is a class?' 'What is the state?' 'What is a revolution?' 'What is the Communist Party?') taught in conjunction with a *Glossary of Marxist Terms*. Then followed a more advanced course covering the party, trade unions, political economy and the state, and after that an exegesis of works by Lenin and Stalin.[25] The *Handbook* was adapted from a British equivalent and the *Glossary* was the work of Harry Gould, a widely read member of the central committee. Born in Dublin, he had spent time in the United States and was memorable for an accent in which 'overlays of broad Australian and Brooklynese rasped against the Irish bass tones'. His wife Diana, on the other hand, was an elocutionist of English origins and an equestrian. As a women's organiser, she was known to participate in rallies on a chestnut mare and in full riding kit.[26]

A Marx School opened in Melbourne shortly after the Sydney one, though the other states still ran their educational classes in party offices. In return for an annual subscription, the two schools offered additional courses that ranged from practical training in the duties of a branch president, secretary and treasurer to educational classes in history, literature, art, musical appreciation and even Russian language, and there were also guest lectures and concerts. For the most part the classes ran in the evenings and on weekends, with special training of organisers and union officials conducted intensively over a week or a fortnight.

A paradox of the Marx School was the limited attention it paid to Marx. Some of his shorter statements were covered, including *The Communist Manifesto*, but not the major theoretical works; Eric Aarons, who took up work at Sydney's Marx School in 1945, was most unusual in tackling the three volumes of *Capital*. Harry Gould's *Glossary of Marxist Terms* is more accurately described as a primer in Marxism–Leninism. The party leaders, who paid close attention to training and regularly reviewed the curriculum, had no interest in Marxism as an intellectual method, and communists made a very limited contribution to intellectual life in Australia. If the party training imparted a set of fixed truths, the larger educational effort probably yielded a greater reward as members acquired a capacity and confidence that assisted them in a wide range of activities.[27]

★

One of these was military service. Earlier, when the party opposed the war, it sent members into the armed forces to foment discord. Most were quickly identified and discharged. In a similar vein, some communists became air raid wardens, the better to criticise the inadequacy of arrangements to protect the civilian population. At a rally to recruit more wardens in Martin Place at the end of 1940, with the governor of New South Wales among the spectators, a group of communist women unfurled banners inscribed 'Give Us More Bomb-Proof Shelters'. Police quickly confiscated the banners.[28]

Such agitation fell away after Hitler attacked the Soviet Union, but it was not easy to reverse the past eighteen months of virulent opposition to the imperialist war. One reason for the party's equivocations in the months that followed its change of policy was an ingrained resistance to militarism. It was all very well for the leaders to proclaim the need to fight fascism, another for members to overcome their bitter memories of the last war and repugnance for the military ethos. Jack Hughes recalled the response of one old comrade at the Sydney Domain to his announcement of the new line: 'Jack, I never thought you'd rat. Become a bloody war-monger, an imperialist, another Billy Hughes!'[29]

Some thought that a people's war needed a people's army, and the emergency that followed Japan's entry into the war in December 1941 encouraged such thinking. With the air force, navy and all but one division of the AIF deployed far from home while the enemy advanced rapidly towards Australia, there were grave doubts about the capacity to resist invasion. From January 1942 the CPA began calling for a 'people's defence' of Australia by training and arming 'the masses'.[30] It was not alone. A number of daily newspapers promoted the formation of a voluntary civilian force that would 'dispense with uniforms, salutes and the exasperating parade ground detail' in favour of improvised weapons and guerrilla tactics to fight the enemy in the bush and, if need be, street by street in the cities. These enthusiasts took their lead from Tom Wintringham, who had commanded the British Battalion of the International Brigade in the Spanish Civil War and was calling for similar measures of home defence in Britain.[31] The popular writer Ion Idriess adapted them to Australian conditions in a series of manuals (*Shoot to Kill*,

Sniping, *Guerrilla Tactics*, *Trapping the Jap*, etc.), as did Rupert Lockwood in *Guerrilla Paths to Freedom*.[32]

Idriess, Lockwood, Bill Wood and Jessie Street were among the office-holders of the Australian People's Defence Auxiliary, formed in February 1942 and sponsored by the SLP, but with initial support from ex-army officers and local government representatives. A number of groups had already begun training, but the government was opposed from the outset. As communist participants appreciated and the resistance movements in Europe and Asia would demonstrate, guerrilla warfare was an extreme case of von Clausewitz's dictum that war is the continuation of politics by other means; besides, as Lockwood would put it, 'guerrilla armies after victory are terribly difficult to disband'.[33] But in the face of the Curtin government's refusal to entertain any unofficial force, little was be gained by persisting. To do so, Richard Dixon judged, would jeopardise unity. Accordingly, he instructed members to transfer into the official Volunteer Defence Corps and build up activity in the armed forces.[34]

There was little need to direct members to join the armed forces. Some were called up for compulsory home service in the Militia at this time, others were anxious to enlist for overseas action in the AIF or RAAF. Max Thomas, only recently released from internment in the Holsworthy military camp, was one who signed up. The central executive placed no restrictions except on leading cadres, instructing some to join the AIF and forbidding others from doing so. One in the first category, George Gowland, was a member of the central committee. Despite the party publicising his enlistment in a pamphlet, *I Have Joined the AIF*, he went AWOL while in training camp and was expelled. A number in the second category who enlisted regardless were left in no doubt of the party's displeasure but escaped sanction.[35]

Communists who went into uniform were expected to keep up their party work. Though constrained by the forces' prohibition on political activity, they busied themselves with the concerns of the lower ranks, took up grievances, promoted discussion of war aims and post-war aspirations, sold literature and recruited new members. A series of publications as well as newspapers such as *Citizen Soldier* set out the improvements that were needed: adequate leave, better medical attention, improved catering, elimination of profiteering from canteens, provision for recreation, equal pay for servicewomen and a 'battle bonus' for those in action. With these went calls for democratisation of the military through removal of 'Blimps', 'brass hats' and 'fascist-minded martinets', promotion based on ability, and representative committees to resolve grievances—but always with the proviso that such measures would improve morale and efficiency 'without in any way interfering with discipline'.[36]

The scale of these endeavours varied. Some isolated members relied on intermittent contact with those back home and exercised caution in seeking out other comrades: one used to whistle the Internationale while strolling around the training camp. The party set up service welfare committees that kept track of members in uniform, and the three women who ran the Brisbane one had around 1200 men on their cards. These committees also provided comforts, arranged billets and hospitality for men on leave (hence Melbourne's Australia–Soviet House), sent literature and received dues. Communists serving abroad established further connections. Those in the AIF 9th Division linked up with British and local party members in Palestine, and a strong branch on Morotai Island made contact with Indonesian independence fighters later in the war. The large numbers in Papua New Guinea led to the creation of a district committee and kindled a critical awareness of the colonial regime.[37]

Communists were particularly active in the Army Education Service, established in 1941 to sustain morale. Apart from providing books, films and course materials for instructors to use in weekly educational sessions, it published a *Current Affairs Bulletin* and a popular magazine, *Salt*, which grew to a peak circulation of 180,000. At least 40 university-educated communists worked as unit instructors, and a majority of the journalists, writers and artists who produced *Salt* were party members. The Melbourne communist Helen Palmer held a senior post in the educational arm of the RAAF.

The party made much of its military contribution, publishing regular news of comrades in action and parading an honour guard of uniformed members at the national congresses of 1943 and 1945. Towards the end of the war, the central committee sought to compile a complete record of all who had served and asked veterans to send full details to Marx House. Not all did so, but the party settled on a figure of 4000 enlistments and installed an honour board in Marx House recording as many as it could. It also paid considerable attention to the problems of repatriating and rehabilitating members of the armed services, conscious of how the grievances of ex-servicemen had been directed against the left after the previous war.[38]

Communists cultivated an alternative account of military service in which the citizen soldier exemplified the best democratic instincts of the Australian people. They praised a unity of purpose, love of freedom and contempt for sham and hypocrisy, which were often likened to the qualities that fortified the Red Army. While both were fighting a 'democratic people's war', it was acknowledged that the Australian military was not yet a people's army. For one thing, it lacked political commissars to make sure that all soldiers knew what they were fighting for—though Bill Wood pointed out that Oliver Cromwell's New Army was the first to employ them in a British tradition that Australia might well follow. Here party members had to lead by example as they instilled a fuller appreciation of what was at stake.[39]

This figure of the communist soldier as the wise outsider was most fully developed in the war novels of Eric Lambert, who fought with the 9th Division in the Middle East and New Guinea, rising to the rank of sergeant. Lambert was an active supporter of the party, though he did not join until 1947, and *The Twenty Thousand Thieves* (1951) was his first and most successful work, with sales of more than half a million. It tells of a battalion recruited from resentful victims of the Depression. Their commander, Colonel Ormond Fitzroy, is a reactionary pastoralist and most of his officers are sadistic cowards, but the rebellious spirit of the hard-bitten diggers is vindicated by their heroism in the siege of Tobruk and battle of Alamein—and their grievances are resolved as a new private shows them how to stand up for their rights. This is Slim Sullivan, a communist steeled by his experience as an unemployed organiser who is able to make sense of the war: 'We're fighting to preserve what little democracy we've got from fascism.'[40] Slim Sullivan was based on Les Sullivan, a party organiser in Queensland who volunteered for the AIF in

1939 and was secretary of the party's branch in the 9th Division during the North African campaign.

★

Communists working in industry far outnumbered the 4000 members in military service. Among them were coalminers, metalworkers, munitions hands, waterside workers and seamen, occupations crucial to the war effort and thus restricted from enlistment. The principal unions covering these occupations were all led by communists and, with the party's support for the war, it is hardly surprising that the national officers were appointed to authorities the government created to iron out any grievances. Eliot Elliott represented the Seamen's Union on the Maritime Industry Commission established in January 1942 to regulate that industry, and Jim Healy represented the Waterside Workers' Federation (WWF) on the Stevedoring Industry Commission. Harold Wells was a member of the Central Reference Board, which performed a similar function in the coal industry.

Other communists made additional contributions to the war effort. Norm Jeffery, the central committee member who had organised the No Conscription League, now headed the industrial panel of the NSW war loans committee, so that J.B. Miles appeared alongside Labor ministers at war rallies in Sydney. Phyllis Johnson, who had served time for promoting the no-conscription campaign, worked with Jeffery as women's organiser for the panel. But it was the CPA's strength in the vital war industries—far greater than that of the communist parties of other Allied countries—that gave it an unprecedented influence.

The party's assistance in ensuring maximum production was acknowledged in other ways. Its union officials were exempt from the call-up, and so too were those party organisers it made representations to keep. They were able to travel interstate at a time when rail journeys were tightly controlled, and 50 delegates were issued with permits to attend the 1943 national congress. Newspaper proprietors complained of favoured treatment when the party received a generous newsprint allocation in the same year to re-establish its newspapers.[41]

How communists gained such favours remains unclear. Even after Curtin restored the CPA to legality at the end of 1942, he kept its leaders at arm's length. That did not hold for the union officials who participated in his meetings with the ACTU—and sprang to his defence when other unionists complained of the government's draconian measures. We also know that he talked with these communist union leaders when their paths crossed, and that they had regular dealings with particular members of his Cabinet. Bert Evatt and John Dedman, Minister for War Organisation of Industry, were often helpful. So was Eddie Ward, the Minister for Labour, especially after he appointed Jock Garden as his union liaison officer, for this fixer was a former secretary of both the NSW Labor Council and the CPA. Ernie Thornton could open many doors, given his Federated Ironworkers' Association (FIA) covered the great bulk of munitions workers, but the most important negotiations were conducted by Jim Healy, who held the respect of both Curtin and Ben Chifley, his treasurer and closest confidant.[42]

The privileged access to the government of these leading unionists upset the hierarchical order of democratic centralism. The secretary, president and other members of the central executive—all of them full-time party workers apart from Thornton—were meant to formulate policy for adoption by the central committee and then implementation by the party's departments. Its industrial department oversaw the campaigns of communist unions, watched over the performance of officials and intervened when necessary to straighten the line. But now these party leaders relied on the union officials to advance its claims as the leading war party and conduct negotiations with government leaders. The united front was made possible by their ability to keep the wheels of industry turning.

Initially, there was no disagreement over industrial policy. The central executive gave full support to the government's production drive, accepted the need for longer work hours and condemned stoppages. 'We must have discipline,' it insisted after a number of workers refused to forgo the usual Christmas break at the end of 1941. Union leaders took the same stand. 'It is necessary to tighten up union discipline on absenteeism,' Thornton warned in mid-1942, and his union fined members for unauthorised stoppages. Both also recognised the impracticality of ignoring legitimate grievances. It was impossible to 'simply brush aside' management provocation, Richard Dixon explained, for 'otherwise we will become completely isolated from the workers'. The communist policy was therefore to confine industrial disputes to brief, union-controlled stoppages designed to solve the problem by securing government intervention. The number of days lost in industrial disputes fell from 984,000 in 1941 to just 378,000 in 1942.[43]

This agreement on industrial policy began to fray in 1943. By then the war was clearly turning in favour of the Allies and the willingness of wage-earners to accept long working hours, let alone the privations imposed by wage controls and rationing, was falling away. The days lost in disputes jumped to 990,000 in that year, and the union leaders were becoming resentful of the party's criticism of their failure to maintain discipline. The party leaders attributed the disruption to the usual suspects—'Langites' (supporters of Jack Lang, who was hostile to the Labor government as well as the CPA), 'Trotskyites' and 'anarchists'.

The union leaders often used the same scapegoats, but they appreciated that the unrest was more widespread. 'Sometimes we have to adjust our stand to keep with the workers,' Thornton said. He gave vent to his frustration when reporting on union work to the party congress in March 1943. Deploring the 'tendency to adopt an anti-trade union official attitude', he warned that he and his fellow unionists 'are just not going to take too much of this sort of thing . . . we know how to look after ourselves, and give a warning to Party members generally'. Ernie Thornton was habitually outspoken but he was supported in the ensuing discussion by Tom Wright, the quietly effective secretary of the Sheet Metal Workers: he too was 'not going to put up with contemptuous attitudes to trade union officials'. Their criticism was clearly aimed at the censorious main report to the congress given by Lance Sharkey, whose knowledge of union work was restricted to a brief period in the Miscellaneous Workers' Union during the 1920s (he relied on the expertise of Thornton and Wright for his recent tract *The Trade Unions*). J.B. Miles did his best to smooth over this unusual display of animosity.[44]

There was a further reason for the union officials' resentment. While doing their best to avoid disputes, they continued to press their members' interests. The circumstances of the war—the employment regulations that removed employers' power of dismissal, the influx of new workers, and the need to sustain morale and secure cooperation—made it possible to win significant improvements. This was particularly the case in industries where communist unions were able to work through the new bodies that controlled wartime industrial relations.

Jim Healy of the Waterside Workers was determined to abolish the notorious 'bull system' in this casual occupation, whereby the stevedoring companies engaged the most compliant workers at the expense of the others. His goal was a system of regular workgroups (or 'gangs') that would be allocated work in rotation, thus depriving the company foremen of the ability to pick and choose. The chaotic condition of the ports at the onset of the Pacific War, when a shortage of labour allowed men of dubious repute to evade the military call-up by enrolling as wharf labourers and working irregularly, enabled Healy to persuade Curtin to establish the Stevedoring Industry Commission and introduce the rotary system. He and the other communist officials of the WWF had to overcome opposition from employers and many of their own members. The Melbourne branch of the Federation voted approval by a narrow majority; the Sydney branch refused and there was a sixteen-day stoppage in April 1943 that ended only when Curtin threatened to withdraw the rebels' exemption from military service. The communists were defeated in the following branch election, though Healy easily withstood a challenge as general secretary and the party regained control of the Sydney branch in 1944. With the rotary system came more regular employment, greater job control and a number of improvements to working conditions.[45]

Healy had the Stevedoring Industry Commission in the palm of his hand, but Eliot Elliott walked out of the Maritime Industry Commission in June 1943 because of the 'anti-working class attitude' of its chair, and continued to boycott it for ten months. His style was always more confrontational—indeed he had physically ejected the previous secretary of the Seamen's Union from his office after winning the ballot for the position. In particular, Elliott resisted the creation of a labour pool along the lines of the waterside workers' roster on the grounds that it would weaken union control of the selection of crews. Yet his aggression won gains, including a 44-hour week and a bonus for war risk (more than 600 seamen died as the result of enemy action). For the most part he and the equally belligerent state secretaries confined disputes to grievances on particular vessels in order to keep the mercantile marine moving.[46]

The FIA pursued a similar war policy. It too preferred to bargain with employers and keep members working, calling strikes as a last resort after negotiations failed or when it judged an organised stoppage might forestall a lengthy dispute. But the rapid expansion of the metals and munitions industries presented this union with problems that did not arise in the smaller maritime ones. It grew from 23,000 members in 1940 to 63,000 in 1944, a third of whom were women. To overcome the entrenched prejudice against these women working in men's occupations, the FIA supported the Labor government's creation of a special tribunal, the Women's Employment Board (WEB), and accepted its determination that they should be paid 90 per cent of male rates. Many employers refused to do so, and their employees were not always prepared to wait for the union to bring them to account.[47]

Hence the women at a foundry in Marrickville, where the manager was contesting the WEB determination, walked out in protest in May 1943 against the refusal of ten workers (all but one of them women) to join the union. 'I think I am overpaid as it is,' said Gwen Cassidy, a society matron whose husband was a wealthy barrister. The FIA was unable to prevent this dispute, which continued for ten weeks and was settled only when Thornton persuaded the prime minister to threaten the company with loss of government contracts unless it sacked the non-unionists. It was the same at the BHP steelworks in Newcastle, where members of several unions took unofficial action against the company's refusal to pay penalty rates for time worked during the Christmas of 1942 until the FIA ordered its members to lift their overtime bans. A year later the company flouted National Security Regulations (on legal advice from Robert Menzies) to retrench 1700 ironworkers when a few assigned to a furnace refused to work with a staff member. This time Curtin ordered the company to resume operations and the union recovered £15,000 in back pay.[48]

The FIA entered the war with an incomplete coverage of a poorly paid workforce. Its rapid expansion was accompanied by a strengthening of the union through streamlined administration, centralisation of finance and many more paid officials. In 1945 the union moved into its own building, a former department store in George Street, which boasted a research bureau, publishing department, bookshop, gymnasium, child-care centre, snack bar and a licensed club for members of this and other unions.[49] Thornton delegated much of the work in industrial tribunals to Jack McPhillips, the overbearing assistant secretary, and used communist branch secretaries, Charles McCaffrey in Newcastle, Pat McHenry in Wollongong and Bert Flanagan in Victoria, to ginger up other branches. He achieved growth through amalgamation with the Munition Workers' Union, despite legal challenges, and sought further membership by claiming coverage of other workers—an irate official of the Transport Workers' Union alleged the FIA wanted to enrol 'even the parson who married their members'. Thornton faced growing opposition from anti-communists in the Balmain branch, allegations he was diverting union funds to the Communist Party (he sued Jack Lang for libel in 1945) and the party's censure for his defiance of policy. But his vaulting ambition made him the country's most powerful union leader by 1945.[50]

That could not be said of Harold (Bob) Wells, the hapless president of the Miners' Federation. He was at a disadvantage since his experience was as a pit-top carpenter—union leaders traditionally came from the coalface—and the general secretary who succeeded Bill Orr was an easygoing Labor man. On the coalfields, moreover, the party's pledge of increased output ran up against primitive working conditions and a legacy of bitterness and mistrust. Wells gave full support to the agreement formulated by the prime minister in mid-1942 for all disputes to be settled by conciliation. He harangued, cajoled and threatened his members, but absenteeism and localised, unofficial stoppages continued to plague the industry, as did the owners' refusal to conciliate. The problem was largely confined to New South Wales, since communist officials had greater success in Queensland and Victoria, whereas they faced growing opposition in the Hunter Valley and Illawarra. After Henry Scanlon, another communist, lost the presidency of the northern district at the end of 1943, Wells's authority was in tatters. His subsequent novel,

The Earth Cries Out, speaks eloquently of the difficulties the leading war party encountered in this run-down and recalcitrant industry.[51]

The no-strike policy caused particular difficulties in Sydney's southern 'Red Belt', where women working in the knitting and spinning mills lost patience with the delays of the Arbitration Court in settling their claim for better wages. A walkout began at the beginning of February 1943 in two factories producing military uniforms, and spread quickly as the women took their message to adjoining ones. The strikers voted down the recommendation of the male officials of the Textile Workers' Union that they return, and the stoppage grew to 9000 workers across the state by the end of the month. There were prosecutions and fines for absenteeism until Eddie Ward secured a return in early March by expediting the wage claim.[52]

The party opposed this strike from the outset, and Sharkey publicly condemned it on the very eve of the Thirteenth Congress in a statement that can only have exacerbated the ire of Thornton and Wright. To make matters worse, eighteen months earlier party activists had managed to obtain a foothold in this notoriously exploited industry and led a similar general stoppage to obtain a war loading; now these same activists were on the other side. Six years later, when Dorothy Hewett was put into the Alexandria Spinning Mills to establish a party presence, she found 'the Communist Party was a dirty word'.[53]

Communists made rapid gains in other industries. Tom Wright was already the national president of the Sheet Metal Working Industrial Union as well as NSW secretary, and by 1945 the party had strengthened its position in the Amalgamated Engineering Union. Jack Hughes led the Clerks' Union in New South Wales, and communists won control of its Victorian branch in 1943, giving the party a majority on the federal council. The pattern here was extension to smaller unions in industries where there was already a strong communist presence, so that the Ship Painters' and Dockers' Union swung left with the assistance of the Waterside Workers and Seamen. Similarly, the communist faction in the Clerks' Union was assisted by support from the waterfront tally clerks. Amalgamation of previously separate unions sometimes served the same purpose: in 1942 communists brought the bricklayers and carpenters together in a Building Workers' Industrial Union. And sometimes the assistance crossed industries, as in the office space the FIA made available to Topsy Small and Flo Russell as they built up the NSW branch of the Hotel and Restaurant Employees' Union.[54]

Some effort was made also to strengthen alliances of unions. Hence the Metal Trades Federation allowed the Engineers, Sheet Metal Workers, Boilermakers, Engineers and smaller unions to coordinate their campaigns, as a similar Building Trades Federation brought together the Carpenters, Bricklayers and Builders Labourers. Workshop committees served the same function in large factories and the party also encouraged the formation of production committees to reduce inefficiency and mismanagement. Workshop committees were made up of shop stewards drawn from all the unions with a presence in the factory. Elected directly from the shopfloor, they allowed greater initiative at the local level, though for that reason many union officials discouraged them. By turning them into production committees the party blunted that opposition.[55]

The Northern Australian Workers' Union provides a striking example of missionary activity. It had nominal coverage of almost the whole of the Northern Territory workforce, but languished with a membership of no more than 1000 until Jack McPhillips arrived as secretary in 1940 along with Gordon (Bugs) Burgoyne, a communist dismissed from the *West Australian* who took charge of the union's newspaper. McPhillips and his successor Mick Ryan established a stronger presence in the pastoral industry (including, for the first time, Aboriginal stockmen) and the port of Darwin, and began to organise the large camps of labourers working on defence projects. That proved hazardous. The army, which took control of the Territory following the bombing of Japan, expelled Ryan (after a tug of war with Labor ministers that provides further evidence of their appreciation of communist support), but by then there were local organisers able to sustain the union's work.[56]

The party also established a presence in a number of professional associations. Sam Lewis claimed there were 500 communist members when his NSW Teachers' Federation affiliated with the Labor Council at the end of 1942 (though he did not declare his own membership). This gravel-voiced primary teacher became president in 1945, and Bill

Gollan, a high-school principal, held the presidency of the federation's Secondary Teachers' Association. The NSW branch of the Australian Journalists' Association underwent a similar radicalisation, with A.E. Crouch winning presidency of the Sydney district in 1944. In that year the party's printery was used to produce a daily paper for the journalists and members of the Printing Industries Employees' Union during a dispute with Sydney's press proprietors, and Gavin Souter, the historian of the *Sydney Morning Herald*, judged the union paper to be better produced and distributed than the composite effort of the employers. Actors' Equity also took a leftward turn under the leadership of Hal Alexander, a colourful former professional dancer (whom security often confused with the party organiser of the same name). Gladys Moncrieff was among the performers who capitulated to Alexander's insistence on a union ticket.[57]

The industrial advance remained uneven. There was no union in which the party controlled all the state branches. It was strong, for example, in the Queensland and Victorian branches of the Meat Industry Employees' Union, weak in New South Wales and South Australia. The Victorian branch of the Builders Labourers Federation was communist, the New South Wales one anti-communist. Despite a concerted effort to recapture the NSW branch of the Australian Railways Union, it remained in the hands of Lloyd Ross's supporters, whereas J.J. (Jack) Brown won the secretary's position in Victoria in 1942.[58] Nor was there any union in which communists held all the leading positions. The support of other militants remained essential, and even where the party might have put up a complete slate, the united front required it to include others.

The same held for peak bodies. Mick Healy was elected secretary of the Brisbane Trades and Labor Council in 1943, and Tom Garland became president of the South Australian one, in both cases with support from non-communist delegates. Smaller craft unions preserved non-communist control of the NSW Labor Council and Melbourne's Trade Hall Council, but the party's strength was evident at the biennial congress of the Australian Council of Trade Unions in June 1943, which adopted a resolution in favour of the united front. Communists also secured a vote to move the organisation to Sydney, change the composition of the executive so that it was no longer controlled by the state councils, and make congress resolutions binding rather than subject to ratification by the councils.[59]

★

A party meeting would open ritually with reports on the present state of the class struggle and the tactics required to advance the communist cause. A report on the international situation came first, then the national and local position, and finally attention turned to women, youth and culture. This account follows that sequence.

The movement of women into war industries brought party women into a more active union role. Della Xenodohos, from a Greek communist family, became an organiser (later assistant secretary) of the Clerks' Union. Doris Beeby, the daughter of an Arbitration Court judge, who worked as his associate for over a decade, undertook the same organisational tasks for the Sheet Metal Working Industrial Union, and Linda Chapple, daughter of the federal secretary of the Australian Railways Union, became women's organiser of the Victorian branch—indeed, she married Jack Brown, its secretary, in 1946. The FIA, with the largest female membership, was less responsive. 'Organisation of women is one of our biggest problems,' Thornton told the union's general council in June 1942, because of 'the backwardness of women and the hostility of a large section of them to trade unionism.'[60]

Such attitudes were deeply ingrained in the party's ranks. Joyce Deans, a young communist assigned to work in the textile industry, found employment in the Alexandria Spinning Mills and played the leading role in organising the 1941 strike. 'As a young militant,' she recalled, 'I never intended to get married,' but through her work in the industry she met and married Bob Batterham and in the course of the strike she became pregnant. When she told the organiser Len Donald, he was furious. 'It's taken us all these years to get any organisation in textiles and now you're going to have a baby! You and Bob, you both ought to be expelled!'[61]

Equal pay was party policy, but it readily accepted the determination of the WEB that gave most women in war industries 90 per cent of the male rate. That brought it into conflict with the Council of Action for Equal Pay, which had been formed in 1937 at a union conference convened by Jack Hughes' Clerks' Union and was demanding 100 per cent. Emphasising the overriding need to support the war effort, communists argued that 90 per cent was as far as the government would go and that the WEB had to be defended against employers' challenges to its rulings. Hence communist union officials—the women as well as the men—condemned Muriel Heagney, secretary of the Council of Action for Equal Pay, for her criticism of the WEB and turned instead to a Council for Women in War Work formed at the end of 1942 by Jessie Street's United Associations of Women.[62]

Communists were strongly represented at the national conference convened by Street in November 1943, the Women's Conference for Victory in War and Victory in Peace, which adopted a comprehensive Women's Charter. Noting that many proposals in the charter were to be found in the party's own program, a communist women's organiser reiterated the dictum of J.B. Miles that 'only the abolition of exploitation of man by man will make it possible for women to be economically, socially and politically the equal of man'. Nevertheless, she claimed, 'the Women's Charter reflects the growing association of middle-class women's organisations with the real leadership of the people—the working class'.[63]

The party conducted its membership drive in 1942 with the goal of increasing the proportion of women to a quarter. There were 980 of them at that time and they made up 14 per cent of all members. A central women's committee embarked on a substantial round of activity, including a national conference in 1943 that attracted more than 200 delegates, but the outcome fell short—1900 women were recruited in the three rounds of the party-building campaign, bringing the proportion up to just 18 per cent.[64] The reasons for this shortfall are not difficult to identify. Len Donald, the director of the membership campaign, still thought of women following men, with his advice that members should reach out to 'every wife, mother, sister, daughter or sweetheart'. Katharine Susannah Prichard, a special guest at the national conference, hardly assisted with her advice that 'party women must study' if they were to acquire the theoretical knowledge and organisational experience required to take their place alongside men in positions of responsibility.[65]

Party women already filled such positions, if only because so many male cadres enlisted that females replaced them. Leah Healy became state secretary in Western Australia in 1942, Joan Finger a year later in South Australia. Twenty of the 28 district organisers in Melbourne were women by 1944, ten of the twelve in Western Australia. Some had to be talked into accepting such responsibilities; most quickly gained confidence as they undertook them. Gloria Garton, organiser of the East Sydney district, gave a particularly revealing account of her experience. Educated at a business college, she had worked for an insurance company before recruitment in 1941, when she took on clerical duties with the Australian–Soviet Friendship League until Norm Jeffery appointed her an organiser. Her memory was that she was always busy, always out doing something somewhere, too busy to question the sexism she encountered. She knew that feminism was a 'bourgeois concept' and yet was 'pissed off' when Jeffery recruited a bevy of young, personable women to persuade men in the factories to buy war bonds. 'I guess I was a bit full of myself and my own importance,' she later reflected, but she was soon put back in her place—when the war ended and the men returned, Garton went from organising to typing for the blokes in Marx House.[66]

There were some awful attitudes to women, Dorothy Hewett recalled, and she encountered them when she joined the party in Perth in 1941, but still felt it attracted women who were 'strong, passionate and revolutionary'. Those who challenged its authority, as she did, were dealt with harshly, yet at this time of such high expectations its discipline held. For all the authoritarianism, Hewett thought 'it was possible within the party for women to act with more force than in any other political area'.[67]

Women had principal responsibility for the party's youth work. Following her time in Moscow, where she was Australian representative in the Young Communist International, Audrey Blake broadened the youth movement by forming a League of Young Democrats. Previously, a Young Communist League had catered to the children of party members. Now, using a range of cultural, recreational, sporting and social activities, the league reached out more widely and cultivated an anti-fascist united front with other Victorian youth organisations. That came to an end with the onset of the imperialist war, and the league was banned in early 1941, though it continued to operate through offshoots such as the Workers' Sports Federation and youth committees in factories. Then, in June, the imperialist war became the anti-fascist war, and the party's youth movement swung over to full support.[68]

To circumvent the ban, a new organisation was created in Victoria at the end of 1941, the Eureka Youth League (EYL). From the beginning it emphasised support for the war, with classes in first aid, working bees to dig trenches, collection of scrap metal, promotion of war loans and recruitment of city youth to help bring in the harvest. A shock brigade movement within the EYL aimed to eliminate absenteeism and increase production in the war industries; another section, the Friends of the Services, sent letters and parcels to those serving. A party man, Malcolm Goode AIF, was the initial president, and others such as Harry Stein and Ken Miller contributed their organisational skills, but Audrey Blake had a genius for this activity. Within a year the EYL acquired headquarters in North Melbourne for concerts, dances and socials, and soon it was building Camp Eureka on a large block of land near Warburton. By 1945 it even had a ski club.[69]

Such was the success of the EYL that it was taken up nationally. Audrey Blake and Rivkah Brilliant, who joined the party through the Labour Club at the University of Melbourne, went up to Sydney at the beginning of 1943 to assist the establishment of the league in New South Wales, and other states followed. Blake was the national secretary, and the state secretaries of Queensland (Connie Healy and Kath Olive), South Australia (Hazel Stoyle) and Western Australia (Julie Marks) testified to women's leadership.[70]

Audrey Blake's guiding principles, taken from a passage by Lenin, were the organisational independence of the youth movement and its socialist character—as she put it, 'our League aims to draw into its ranks the clearest-thinking youth of our generation'. This was not an easy combination. Kath Olive thought that one of the greatest pieces of miscasting the party every perpetrated was to give J.B. Miles responsibility for overseeing the party's youth work, for Miles was 'never young', and in her dealings with him he was an irascible, elderly gentleman who terrified young people. He did respect the EYL's organisational independence, but Blake and other officers were repeatedly chastised by party leaders for the irregularity of the league's activities and the lax supervision of its camps. Still, with some 5000 members by 1945, the party's youth arm was strong.[71]

The same was true of cultural activity. Workers' theatre, art and literature had begun in Australia as a stridently oppositional form of agitprop before turning in the later 1930s to the cultivation of national traditions that served the party's united front against war and fascism. Although the underground party had little opportunity to engage in such work—a publication prepared by the Fellowship of Australia Writers condemning the suppression of the CPA was itself suppressed—the leading war party made it a priority. Noting the influx of 'the intellectuals and the artists' into the party at the Thirteenth Congress in March 1943, J.B. Miles called for 'a raising of the cultural level of communists'. He had no doubt that the executive committee could give a lead in the interpretation of literature, though he was less confident about music (indeed, he confessed that he was unable to sing the Internationale), art, theatre and film. It was the task of the party's practitioners to lift the appreciation of culture as a progressive force.[72]

That was already happening. An Artists' Unity Congress in late 1941 was followed by major exhibitions of anti-fascist art. The New Theatre flourished, despite a shortage of male actors, with satirical reviews and full-length Australian plays. Partly in response to the intense interest of American servicemen in Australiana, Oriel Gray dramatised the life of *Lawson* in 1943—'how they took to Henry Lawson!' In the same year the party published the first collection of *Australian New Writing*, linking the people's war to the new order that would follow: 'A war effort in this struggle does not mean only the production and use of guns [and] Austerity campaigns. It means a new approach to life.'[73]

In these and other activities the party drew on the release of energy that came with national mobilisation and a new awareness of how Australia was connected to momentous world events. At this stage there was no attempt to lay down a party line on art, except that it must draw its strength from the people and guard against 'anything that is stiff, effete and formulistic', as Harry Gould put it in preparation for a People's Conference on Culture in the War and the Peace following the Thirteenth Congress.[74] There was already bitter infighting in the Contemporary Art Society between the communist exponents of social realism and their opponents' experimental modernism, and similar arguments would spread into other cultural forms. But with the assistance of bodies such as the Army Education Service, the impulse for a fuller and more democratic culture flourished. As the war grew to become a global conflict that demanded the country's complete commitment and called on its full creative capacity, communism attracted cultural practitioners, intellectuals and scientists as never before.

*

Although the party had to wait until the end of 1942 to be restored to legality, it suffered few restrictions after Labor came to government in October 1941. There were no further prosecutions and no attempt to close down the illegal presses, so that communist newspapers circulated freely and remained free of censorship, an anomaly one state censor thought was 'simply bringing the law into contempt'. The celebrations organised in Sydney for May Day in 1942 were larger than ever before. The principal disability was that this party could not operate publicly as a communist party. Hence Jack Blake was able to call himself a communist when he stood in a parliamentary by-election for the Victorian electorate of Port Melbourne in April 1942, but he was unable to issue election material on behalf of the party or summon a communist meeting. Of necessity, the party conducted much of its public activity during 1942 as the Political Rights Committee.[75]

This was clearly an impediment to the aim of forging an identity as the leading war party, and there were repeated efforts to persuade the government to lift the ban. Curtin was reluctant to do so, principally because of the political consequences. Opposition members repeatedly denounced the favours given communist union officials. 'If I had my way,' one said, 'I would put them up against a wall and shoot them.' Even though the ACTU called for the party to be legalised, public opinion polls indicated that a minority of voters (though a narrow majority of Labor voters) favoured this step, and opinion ran strongly against it in marginal electorates.[76]

Accordingly, the government indicated that the lifting of the ban would have to wait upon the establishment of diplomatic relations with the USSR. Australia had suggested an exchange of representatives at the beginning of 1942, and in May Bert Evatt pursued it in his capacity as Minister for External Affairs at a meeting with his Soviet counterpart, Vyacheslav Molotov, while in London. But Stalin was in no hurry, and it was not until October that the Soviets nominated a head of their legation. Meanwhile, the ban on the *Daily Worker* had been lifted in Britain, Canada had released its internees, and an avalanche of petitions and letters to the prime minister accompanied the Australian party's renewed campaign for legality.[77]

The catalyst was a federal conference of the ALP in November 1942 at which Curtin announced his intention to remove the restriction preventing members of the Militia from serving outside Australian territories. This decision, which broke with Labor's longstanding opposition to conscription for overseas service, encountered strong resistance, and the necessary change to the party platform had to be accepted by a majority of the state branches. Communists did all in their power to back conscription in the heated deliberations that ensued; their influence in left unions affiliated to the ALP might well have tipped the balance in New South Wales and South Australia, which both endorsed the change and allowed Curtin to prevail when the ALP conference reconvened in January 1943.[78]

At the same November conference, South Australian delegates proposed the ban on the CPA be lifted, and a suitably worded resolution was carried by twenty votes to fourteen. With communists supporting him so strongly, Curtin was ready to accede. He had Evatt as attorney-general draw up an appropriately worded undertaking—in consideration of the order of unlawful association being set aside, the CPA was to pledge that until the end of the war it would observe the requirements of other National Security Regulations, do all in its power to assist in the prosecution of the war, and use its best endeavours to minimise absenteeism, work stoppages, strikes or other hold-ups in industry. Miles, Sharkey and eleven other members of the central committee were happy to attach their signatures. From 18 December 1942 the party was once more a lawful organisation.[79]

This allowed the long-delayed congress to meet in March 1943. It was designed to promote the united front, so that most sessions were open to the public, as were the preceding state conferences. The one in South Australia had commenced in the Adelaide Town Hall to the strains of 'Advance Australia Fair'; a cynical reporter acknowledged 'the charm of Comrade Joan [Finger]'s smile' as she gave the opening address, but added that the conference closed with clenched fists and the Internationale. The national congress went much further, spending nearly £1000 on advertising hoardings, posters, newspaper advertisements, a promotional 'talkie' featuring J.B. Miles shown in 30 cinemas and a national broadcast of his opening address in the Sydney Town Hall on the Friday evening of 19 March. Every metropolitan district was required to provide contingents of factory workers, soldiers, women and youth to fill out the audience. Sixty-five 'girls' were drafted, in black skirt, white blouse and red sash, to act as ushers.[80]

The central executive determined the congress slogans: 'Everything for the Victory of Democracy' and 'Return a Stronger Labor Government'. The principal resolution depicted a world divided into two camps: the 'freedom loving nations' and the 'fascist hordes'. The overriding need was for a 'maximum war effort'—that formulation was preferred to the earlier 'total war effort' because of the unfortunate associations of total with totalitarianism, a term originally coined by fascists but already being applied by others to the Soviet Union. The Curtin government was best placed to lead such an effort, and it was hastening Australia's progress towards 'a united independent, capitalist nation', thereby laying the foundations for a transition to socialism, though to raise that prospect now would imperil national unity. In the course of discussion of this resolution on 'A United Working Class and a National Front For Victory', Ernie Thornton revealed that Bert Evatt had rung him on the conference eve to say, 'I hope your fellows at the Congress on the weekend will behave themselves.' He need not have worried. Discipline was the catchcry. Even as Jim Healy acknowledged the unrest in essential industries, he admonished wavering party members. Ninety-nine per cent support of the war effort was not enough; it had to be 100 per cent.[81]

The restraint extended to elections. The party planned to run sixteen candidates in the federal election later in the year, but its overriding objective was to ensure the return of the Curtin government with a strong majority. To this end it would direct its preferences to Labor and support ALP candidates in all other electorates; Phyllis Johnson withdrew from contesting Wentworth to give Jessie Street a clear run. Miles quashed a suggestion there should be more party candidates. What communist imagined there could ever be 'a communist government in a bourgeois parliament?' he asked. 'If such a situation should be approaching, I am not going to worry about parliament, I am going to worry about the proletarian dictatorship.'[82]

Even so, there were hopes that communists might be sent to Canberra. Fred Paterson had fallen narrowly short of winning the Queensland seat of Bowen in the state election during the period of illegality, while Jack Blake won 40 per cent of the vote in a by-election for the state seat of Port Melbourne in April 1942, and 39 per cent in the Victorian election of June 1943 when other communist candidates in Carlton, Clifton Hill, Collingwood and Footscray all attracted a fifth of the poll. Jim Coull, the secretary of the Liquor Trades Union, was not yet a party member but spoke regularly for it every Friday night at Red Square, his pitch on the corner of Bridport and Montague Streets, Albert Park. He won 43 per cent of the vote in that suburb.[83]

Although the party ran an intensive federal campaign, the results of the poll on 21 August 1943 were disappointing. Seventeen communist candidates attracted 82,000 votes and six SLP contenders in New South Wales another 30,000. Paterson gained 34.2 per cent of the vote in the North Queensland seat of Herbert, but Stan Deacon's 11.4 per cent in Newcastle was the next best effort, and Sharkey and Miles received only 6.9 and 4.2 for the Sydney seats they contested.[84] The political committee (as the recent congress had renamed the central executive) found various reasons for this 'relatively poor' performance. The party was thought to have 'submerged' its own identity to Labor, which won a record majority, and Miles warned of the need to 'guard against the masses getting a "great man" theory over Curtin'. Sharkey argued it was time to adopt a more critical attitude to Labor 'in a constructive way'.[85]

The election campaign had not so much submerged the party's identity as presented it in the most reassuring terms. Hence communists were not opposed to religion, nor to private property; they were loyal to Australia and had no intention of imposing socialism by force. Above all, they backed Curtin's national leadership and argued he would be 'strengthened by the inclusion of tried and tested anti-fascist champions of the people'.[86] Curtin studiously avoided any acknowledgement of these unwelcome endorsements, however, and while both the NSW Labor Council and the ACTU carried resolutions in 1943 calling for the establishment of a united front, neither he nor the Federal Executive of the Labor Party would entertain any alliance.[87]

During this impasse the Australian party learned that the Communist International was to be dissolved. A resolution of its executive committee, published in *Pravda* on 22 May 1943, announced that members were to be released from their obligations to the statutes that bound them as 'a single world Communist Party' and become wholly independent national parties. These parties, the resolution explained, had attained the maturity to chart their own course without further guidance from a 'directing centre'. Furthermore, it had become apparent that there were 'deep differences of the historic paths' of the member countries, differences in their economic and social development, the problems they faced and the political consciousness of their workers, which made central direction a fetter on their further progress. In particular, the war against fascism had created a 'deep dividing line' between the resistance activities of communists in occupied territories and the parties that were able to work freely in countries fighting alongside the Soviet Union. The latter, in effect, were to emulate its patriotism and reinvent themselves as champions of national unity rather than proletarian internationalism. To this end, abolition of the International would give the lie to 'screams' about Soviet interference in the affairs of other countries.[88]

Stalin had been contemplating dissolving the Communist International for some time. Now, as he prepared for his first meeting with Roosevelt and Churchill at the end of 1943, he had pressing reasons to do so. At this meeting in Tehran he hoped to obtain their definite commitment to launching a second front against Germany, and he wanted their agreement on post-war arrangements. By dispelling the spectre of world revolution he could profess his support for the 'patriots of all countries' and proclaim the unity of 'all freedom-loving people' in a common cause.[89]

The Comintern's lengthy suicide note was notable for its silences. It made no reference to Stalin's intention of allocating the spoils of victory among the great powers. It said nothing of the 'freedom-loving peoples' of China or the subjects of the British, French and Dutch empires and their interest in national liberation. It passed over the previous twenty years of Russia applying a revolutionary model derived from its circumstances to other countries, and made no mention of the disastrous consequences. As Fernando Claudin has argued, the belated acknowledgement of different historical paths to socialism was an admission of the bankruptcy of a monolithic communist model. And removing the fig leaf provided by the Communist International only revealed more starkly that the directing centre was in fact the Politburo of the Communist Party of the Soviet Union.[90]

In keeping with the ostensibly independent status of the Communist International, all sections were requested to ratify its self-destruction. Since there was no time to reconvene the recent congress, the Australian secretariat asked all state and district committees to circulate the Moscow statement and indicate their endorsement within three weeks. Most met the deadline, but by then the undertakers had appended the CPA's acceptance to that of 30 of the 66 member parties (apart from China, all the Asian ones were overlooked). In public statements Sharkey was at pains to refute press speculation that the demise of the Comintern signalled a retreat. Miles emphasised the responsibility it placed on the Australian party 'to study, really study' the *Pravda* statement and 'the whole history of the Third International', though there was little evidence of it doing that. Dixon was most forthcoming. When interviewed for the *Daily Telegraph* by Bert Birtles, a writer who had witnessed the rise of fascism in Europe, he was asked if the party felt 'deserted by the Russians and left out in the cold'. On the contrary, Dixon answered, 'we think this move will be an advantage to us' in establishing a stronger united front with the Labor Party.[91]

Following the federal election, the party embarked on a new path to unity. It had already arranged a united front with the State Labor Party—though since communists controlled that party, the common platform announced with such fanfare in April 1943 was little more than a gesture. Reduced to just a few thousand members, the SLP was in any case a declining force that no longer presented a challenge to the NSW branch of the ALP; indeed, its very existence was a reminder of the schism communists had provoked at the 1940 Easter Conference and thus an impediment to rapprochement. The party now decided on an amalgamation of the two organisations to build momentum for a more ambitious overture.

The leaders of the CPA and SLP hammered out arrangements at meetings in October 1943: the two parties would amalgamate as the NSW branch of the Communist Party, their local branches would be merged, five members of the SLP executive (Jack Hughes, Bert Chandler, Edgar Ross, Bill Gollan and Alan Wilson) would join the central committee, and Hughes would also become a member of the political committee.[92] An SLP conference agreed unanimously to these arrangements on 27 November; 200 delegates of the NSW branch of the Communist Party did the same on 15 January 1944, and on the following day they joined with 100 SLP delegates to complete the formalities.

The purpose from the outset was to renew an approach to the Labor Party, though the prospects were not auspicious. Bill McKell, the Labor premier of New South Wales, derided the amalgamation as simply indicating the Communist Party was 'going to make an honest woman out of the wench'. Miles, who attended the SLP's November conference, hardly helped with his boast that the unity of these two 'genuinely socialist parties' would allow them to draw the mass of the workers 'away from the capitalist agents inside the Labor Party'.[93]

But a fortnight later, Stalin, Roosevelt and Churchill concluded their meeting in Tehran with a grandiloquent declaration that their 'nations shall work together in the war and in the peace that will follow', confident their concord 'in spirit and in purpose' would bring a lasting peace in which 'all people of the world' could live 'free lives untouched by tyranny'.[94] Stalin attached enormous importance to the agreement struck at Tehran, and communists around the world hailed its communiqué as confirmation that history was moving rapidly in their favour. 'Teheran' (as the name of the city was spelt at the time) quickly became a shorthand term for both international and domestic unity to secure a lasting and democratic peace.[95]

For Earl Browder, the head of the Communist Party of the United States of America (CPUSA), the Tehran meeting was 'the greatest, the most important turning point in all history'. Gaoled for a passport offence in 1941 and released by Roosevelt in the following year when he pledged full support for the war effort, Browder interpreted the enduring peace proclaimed at Tehran as holding out the prospect of a new post-war order of cooperation, prosperity and progress. It had particular significance in the United States, he said, because it was there that capitalism was strongest and Roosevelt's program of domestic reforms and liberal internationalism was already under assault. The greatest point of danger would come when the war ended, and for that reason Browder announced that the Communist Party would not raise the divisive question of socialism in the foreseeable future. Nor would it continue as a separate political party: it needed to change its name and activity so that it could operate alongside other progressive forces through the American two-party system. Browder proclaimed these changes in January 1944 and developed them in a book published in April, *Teheran: Our Path in War and Peace*, a month before the CPUSA turned itself into a Communist Political Educational Association.[96]

Browder had tested his proposals with Dimitrov and received tacit approval, since the Soviet Union still hoped for favourable relations with the United States. Their appearance attracted international attention, especially the abandonment of socialism, and the Australian party sought immediately to play down Browder's statements. Contrary to the 'hysterical reporting' in the capitalist press, it claimed, he had not repudiated socialism but merely said he would not raise it in the immediate post-war period. In any case, American communists faced tasks different from those in Australia and Britain. Their labour movement was weaker, their party proportionately smaller (80,000 in a population of 140 million, compared to the CPA's 20,000 in a country with barely 7 million). Teheran certainly raised the possibility of a peaceful coexistence that allowed for a gradual transition to socialism, but Australia would undertake that in its own way.[97]

Here, it might seem, the CPUSA was exercising the independence of all national communist parties, granted so recently, to determine their own policy. But Browder's understanding of Teheran was not restricted to his own country. He persuaded a number of South American communist parties to follow his course, and pressed it on the British and Australian ones. Some Australian communists wanted to do so, especially after the party here publicised his principal statements.[98] The extent of Browder's influence is disputed, especially since his denunciation the following year brought a discreet silence among those who had flirted with the heresy of 'Browderism'. We shall see that one notable enthusiast created particular difficulty for the Australian party.[99]

Browder's startling proposals certainly left their mark on the Unity Conference of SLP and CPA delegates. Even though this was strictly a state conference, it was attended by leading communists from the other states and adopted a new national program and a new name—the Australian Communist Party (ACP). The program, *For Victory, Peace and Security*, hailed the decisions taken at Tehran for peace and cooperation as influencing the course of history 'for generations to come'. It also warned that ruling-class interests were working to undermine international and national unity. 'If the great people's war against fascism has demonstrated anything, it is the identity of interests between the working class, the farmers and the town middle classes and their joint responsibility to combat and defeat reaction.' The Communist Party was a working-class party and it stood for socialism, but in the immediate future it proposed only the nationalisation of the banks and big monopolies in a form of common ownership that 'fully accords with the history and traditions of the people'. The communist program also held out the possibility of a peaceful transition to socialism: it would not be imposed on the country but 'come into being only when a majority of people want it'.[100]

The change of name, similarly, indicated that it was an *Australian* Communist Party and had the further advantage of euphony with the Australian Labor Party. Following the conference, Miles lodged a request for the ACP's affiliation to the ALP. It proposed the party would abide by Labor's constitution and rules while maintaining its own organisation and activity. Communists claimed such an arrangement would be similar to that of unions affiliated to the ALP, but a better analogy would be the earlier affiliation of the Victorian Socialist Party to the Labor Party as a ginger group providing it with greater vigour and purpose. Somewhat imprudently, Sharkey told the conference that 'affiliation would be a safeguard against another Labor betrayal, such as in 1916 and 1931'. Affiliation, then, was a strategy quite different from the course pursued by Browder: not the abandonment of a separate party but its relocation into a larger one in order to exert greater influence upon it.[101]

Sharkey again invoked Browder in a radio broadcast to launch the party's campaign for affiliation. The American had formulated principles that were generally applicable, especially that the Teheran agreement allowed 'each people to decide their own form of government and social order for themselves without outside interference'. In Australia the Labor and Communist parties had 'long since stood shoulder to shoulder for the defeat of fascism'. They were as one in support of post-war plans for social improvement, and they both had socialism as their long-term objective. Now that the 'great people's war has purchased in blood and tears the possibility of a peaceful social development throughout the world', the question of whether capitalism would give way to socialism or have to be overthrown was no longer a stumbling block. 'Affiliation would make the labor movement an invincible force.'[102] This statement, made at the high point of the party's fortunes, was not so much deception as self-deception.

4

Headwinds, 1943–45

The war raised the Soviet Union from pariah status in the West to the standing of a great power and indispensable ally. It also brought a rapid growth in communist parties around the world. Those that resisted enemy occupation benefited most. The French party had 270,000 members at the outbreak of war and a fraction of that number when the country surrendered, but more than 900,000 following liberation; the Italian party shot up to approach two million; there were 40,000 in the Chinese party when it began fighting Japanese invasion in 1937 and 1,200,000 in 1945. These were the three largest parties, but the Australian one matched those of India, Latin America and most Western European countries on a population basis, and its fivefold increase surpassed that of the other Anglophone countries. None of these approached its industrial strength.[1]

The CPA prospered as never before. Yet even as it flourished its credentials as the leading war party, the leaders saw worrying signs. Stalin, it is said, was once asked what was the most dangerous tendency, 'right-wing opportunism' or 'left-wing adventurism', and replied 'whichever we are not keeping our eye on at the moment'. His Australian followers kept an eye on both. The problem arose from the constraints that support for the war imposed, especially curtailment of industrial militancy. 'In varying degrees in the ranks of our Party', the resolution proclaiming 'A United Working Class and a National Front for Victory' adopted at the 1943 congress warned, 'there has been capitulation to harmful "Left" moods' that resulted in strikes, stoppages and absenteeism. Members had to distinguish between 'listening to the masses' and following them.[2]

The need for communists to suspend the class war at the point of production, to suppress combative instincts that were deeply ingrained and oppose workplace disputes they had always encouraged meant that this left deviation remained a constant threat. The right deviation, on the other hand, arose episodically as some members sought to go further in support of the war. There was an early instance at the beginning of 1942, when a group of Victorians wanted the CPA to propose an all-party national government such as that led by Churchill in the United Kingdom. Ted Laurie raised this possibility with Lance Sharkey on a visit to Sydney and was told that unlike Winston Churchill, Robert Menzies remained an incorrigible reactionary.[3]

Yet Ted and his wife Bonnie continued to discuss the need for greater national unity with friends, who included his brother Bob, a journalist; Dave Aronson, another party lawyer; the artist Noel Counihan and his wife Pat; the writer Judah Waten and teacher Hyrell Ross, his future wife; and Ian Milner, a lecturer in politics at the University of Melbourne, along with his wife Margot, who was also a schoolteacher. This was more a social circle of young, middle-class communists than a dissident faction, and they were not so much contesting the party's policy as sharing their frustrations with the turgid qualifications that accompanied its initial statements of support for the war. Even that was too much for the state committee, which in April 1942 denounced their 'persistent right opportunism and underhand anti-party activity'. Judah Waten had form—suspended in 1930 for bohemianism, expelled in 1935 for 'petty-bourgeois irresponsibilities'—and was expelled once more, along with Hyrell Ross and the Counihans, though Pat was readmitted on appeal six months later and Noel allowed back in 1943. Ted Laurie was too valuable to lose, so he and the others escaped with a reprimand.[4]

Greater latitude was afforded those members in South Australia who in early 1943 helped establish a movement to combat 'the apathy, selfishness and mistrust' that was impeding the war effort. It began when Tom Garland, the communist secretary of the Gasworkers' Union, who had been convicted in 1940 for opposing the war, came together with the Reverend Guy Pentreath, headmaster of that bastion of the Adelaide establishment St Peter's College, the one a diminutive Glaswegian firebrand and the other a high-minded English cleric. They formed a coalition of academics, ministers of religion, members of the professions, progressive businessmen and trade unionists, and named it Common Cause—the cause being to 'forge from all our disunited wills a single sword for victory and a new world of free and happy peoples'.[5]

Neither Garland nor the other communist participants consulted the party on this initiative, and while the leaders of the CPA in South Australia extended a public 'hand of friendship' to Common Cause as an expression of the 'heightened social consciousness of the middle class', they made clear that its stance of political neutrality differed from the unified endeavour they sought, one led by the working class. As the state secretary explained at the Thirteenth Congress, the 'platitudes about the new post-war world' that Common Cause promoted were likely to cause confusion, but 'we cannot stand aloof from this organisation, nor can we attack it', so the comrades within it would have to provide stronger direction. Garland, who was president of the Trades and Labor Council from 1944, was not prepared to do so and left the party in 1945.[6]

'Submergence' was a common failure in the communist pursuit of a united front. As we have seen, it was first detected during the 1943 federal election, when the party called for the return of the Curtin government with a strong majority, strengthened further by the election of communists. Since the CPA put up seventeen of its own candidates for the House of Representatives (which then had just 75 members), it could hardly be accused of passing under the radar. Even so, the central committee detected a failure to bring out the communist position: 'We are fighting to return Labor to office, but mustn't for one moment forget our own independent role and organisation.' Similar criticisms were made of recruits who were drawn to the party as a force for progress but reluctant to declare their allegiance. It was one thing to safeguard members in positions that made them vulnerable to victimisation, another to hold back from publicising the party. Such backsliding was usually found in hostile environments: 'submergence has been a deep-rooted disease in the Western Australian section of our Party', J.B. Miles told the state conference there in 1944. A similar weakness was also detected in New Theatre productions and other forms of cultural work that failed to 'show the face of the party'.[7]

The most serious instance of right deviation arose during 1944 at the highest level of the party. Midway through that year Ernie Thornton set off across the Pacific as one of two ACTU delegates for a world conference of trade unions in London. On reaching Los Angeles he learned the conference was postponed because of travel difficulties created by the D-Day landings in Normandy, and decided to stay on in the United States and familiarise himself with the labour movement there. He soon met Earl Browder, fell under his spell and immersed himself in the work of the Communist Political Educational Association. Even before Thornton returned to Australia, the *Sunday Telegraph* was predicting he would press for similar changes to be made here, and he did so in September in a lengthy submission to the political committee.[8]

It began with the new possibilities for peace and prosperity opened by the Teheran agreement. The overriding task was to preserve national unity and guard against threats that would plunge the country back to the pre-war evils. Any dispute, Thornton said, would 'tear holes' in national unity and the party had too often supported them—he cited the ban imposed by Actors' Equity on non-union productions, the recent strike of Sydney journalists, and his own boasting of the £15,000 in back pay secured for his members from BHP. More than this, Thornton argued that the Communist Party's continued existence was an obstacle to the unity the labour movement needed to lead Australia through the difficult post-war years. Its application for affiliation to the ALP had stalled, and its standing of parliamentary candidates put it in opposition to Labor. It should therefore 'abandon the field as a political party' to work through large, consolidated branches with a principally educational role. Similarly, industrial members should work directly within their unions and give up the factory branches and divisive union fractions.[9]

Thornton's proposals came as no surprise, since his union colleague Jack McPhillips, to whom he wrote from America, had reported his heretical views to the party secretariat. It sought to persuade him of his errors at a meeting of the political committee on 8 October, but he remained adamant and supplemented his submission on the following day with a long account of his American discoveries, extolling the wisdom of the communists there who had opened his eyes to the real significance of Teheran. In their company, he declared, 'I felt like an apprentice in the presence of first-class tradesmen.' So the secretariat summoned the two interstate members of the political committee, Jack Henry and Jack Blake, to drive home the lesson. Thornton remained unrepentant: 'there are a million miles between us', he said, though he did not intend to pursue the fruitless argument. And despite an assurance that he would refrain from criticising party policy during a national speaking tour later in the year, he used it to urge greater cooperation between unions and employers.[10]

Miles and Sharkey were caught in a quandary. They had reproached Thornton in the most scathing terms for his 'inability to see where he was going politically', and secured an undertaking he would not persist. To go further and 'force the matter into the open' was likely to lose the party's best-known union leader, who, moreover, was due to attend the delayed world conference of trade unions in London the following year. They could not foresee that Thornton would embarrass them further by urging Browder's course of action on the leaders of the CPGB.[11]

A persistent feature of Thornton's argument was the growing disunity as the end of the war approached and capital and labour prepared to resume combat. His misgivings began before the trip to the United States—he warned the Thirteenth Congress of a 'war weariness' and cynicism among workers and that they would reap the benefits of their forbearance—but gained force after his conversion to Browderism. 'People are losing confidence,' he asserted, and the 'standard of morale' was 'lower than it has ever been in any other period of Australia's history'.

He was not alone in this concern. The party's press warned against the black markets, gambling dens and sly-grog outlets that were crippling the war effort. Its policy statements were poised between welcoming the unprecedented opportunities opened by the defeat of fascism and sombre warnings of the forces of reaction that threatened to thwart them. 'The enemy is busy,' Miles warned the Thirteenth Congress, and would be defeated only by 'unity of will, discipline and vigilance'.

He worried that a large majority of party members had no experience of adversity, and had not learned to detect and struggle against provocation. 'Even experienced comrades become less vigilant in the liberal, democratic conditions of today. It will be a dangerous thing, indeed, if this is not corrected.'[12]

The enemy came in many forms. There were the monopoly capitalists seeking to restore their control of the economy, and the politicians and press proprietors who served them. There were military officers who sought to direct the resentment of returned soldiers against those who had not served. And there were reactionary elements within the labour movement itself: the corrupt Australian Workers' Union, the Langites who sabotaged the Curtin government, the right-wing Laborites who obstructed unity, and 'the Trotskyite fifth column with its pseudo-revolutionary phrases . . . All their roads lead to Fascism.'[13]

★

The enormous prestige of the Soviet Union put anti-communists at a disadvantage. In epic battles fought on a scale that dwarfed other theatres of the war, the Red Army held and then turned the German advance. These victories seemed to vindicate both its economic system and form of government. Alarming reports of Stalin's Great Terror in the 1930s were set aside, as were more recent memories of his complicity with Hitler. One reason for Stalin's anxiety as he prepared for the Tehran conference was that the corpses of thousands of Polish officers and officials executed following the Soviet invasion of that country had recently been unearthed in the Katyn Forest. There was no mention of this grim discovery at the summit. On the contrary, the formal proceedings were suspended so that Churchill could present Stalin with a gift from King George VI, a ceremonial sword of the finest steel, its handgrip bound in gold, the scabbard encrusted with jewels, as a 'token of homage of the British people'. Stalin took the Sword of Stalingrad, kissed the scabbard and passed the gift to Marshal Voroshilov, who dropped it.[14]

The willingness to overlook the crimes that Stalin inflicted on his people is difficult for a later generation to comprehend. Despite a stream of publications paying homage in the most extravagant terms to his success in building socialism, there was unmistakable evidence of a brutal dictatorship. The French author André Gide went to the Soviet Union as a warm admirer and discovered a climate of fear that he described in his book *Retour de l'URSS* (1936). The comprehensive report on the Moscow trials, Stalin's 1930s show trials of leading communists, issued in September 1937 by a commission of inquiry chaired by the American philosopher John Dewey, made clear that the confessions extracted from Stalin's rivals lacked any credibility. Novels by two former communists, Victor Serge's *Midnight in the Century* (1939) and Arthur Koestler's *Darkness at Noon* (1940), made the same point more graphically. Australian communists were not unaware of these revelations. The artist Roy Dalgarno lent his copy of Gide's book in English translation, *Back from the USSR*, to the Queensland leader Jack Henry, and sometime later asked for it back so he could pass it on to another member. 'Oh you can't lend that book out', he was told, it was 'a rotten liberal approach' and Henry had destroyed it.[15]

The executions and extrajudicial killings were conducted by the People's Commissariat for Internal Affairs, or NKVD. In August 1940, a Spanish communist working for the NKVD gained entry to the Mexican home of Stalin's chief rival, Leon Trotsky, and drove an ice pick into his skull. The Australian party explained that Trotsky's death was the result of a quarrel among his circle of 'bandits, murders and spies' over the 'blood money' they received from the capitalist class to destroy the USSR. The Moscow trials had cast Trotsky as a fascist agent plotting against the Bolsheviks. Posthumously he was accused of planning to assassinate the Soviet leadership, sabotage its war industries and disrupt its defences so that he could be installed as Hitler's *gauleiter* for Russia.[16]

The virulence of the language used against Trotsky is shocking. 'To turn from the heroic deeds of Moscow and Stalingrad' to Trotsky's 'fifth column', Harry Gould and Bill Wood wrote in 1943, 'is like putting aside Homer's *Iliad* to study the details of a rat-hunt'. He was 'human refuse' that had to be eliminated. More alarmingly, since the caricatures that appeared in the party press emphasised his Jewish appearance: 'Judas had first to be a disciple before he could earn his thirty pieces.'[17] The mendacity of the allegations is brazen. Although Trotsky had described the Soviet Union in *The Revolution Betrayed* (1937) as a degenerated workers' state disfigured by Bonapartism, brutality and a deadening bureaucracy, he insisted it had to be defended unconditionally against its enemies—and accordingly justified the invasion of Poland and Finland.[18]

Vilification of Trotsky served several purposes. First, it protected the party's monopoly on Marxism: 'Of all the contemptible, treasonous fascist fifth columns, the Trotskyites are the most despicable because they parade themselves as "socialists".' Second, it demonstrated the need for the most severe measures. Gould and Wood claimed that Australia was spared invasion only because Stalin had destroyed this gang of 'atrocious criminals'. Above all, it established Stalin as a wise leader and teacher, modest and austere, vigilant and implacable in eliminating the enemies of the people.[19]

A Stalin cult arose in the 1930s in hagiographies that placed him at the right hand of Lenin, with codification of his writings, constant citation of his canonical pronouncements, and regular rituals of veneration.[20] This laudatory ode by a leading Australian communist appeared several months before the war:

> They fear him, the silent one, the unscrupulous one,
> For he is no scribbler, no vain talker, no senseless screecher,
> He is more powerful than they,
> He the big-hearted one, the invincible will of the Party.[21]

The wider public interest created when the USSR entered the war brought more popular accounts of Stalin. Bill Smith, who had left the party after leading the Friends of the Soviet Union, thought the cult of 'Stalin-worship' did a grave injustice to a great man but did not disguise his ruthlessness: 'Stalin dealt with enemies and waverers in a characteristic manner: by the firing squad.' That trait was absent from the subsequent popularisation of an avuncular 'Uncle Joe', Generalissimo of the Red Army and world statesman, as in the portrait that appeared on the cover of *Australian Women's Weekly* in 1945, where he was painted in a plain military jacket, pipe in mouth, gazing resolutely into the future.[22]

John Curtin acknowledged the Soviet ally in speeches and ceremonies. The opposition was less enthusiastic but generally resigned to the Grand Alliance. When Robert Menzies moved a motion of censure against the government's 'encouragement of communist activities in Australia', he regretted the growing number of 'warm-hearted, but rather soft-headed people who are easily led to call themselves communists by sentimental appeals to the valour and heroism of Russia in this war'.[23] They differed, he said, from the 'highly intelligent, utterly unscrupulous revolutionary whose real ambition is to have blood in the streets', but even these fanatics were portrayed as a disease within the Australian labour movement, a cancer invading a receptive host. Similar accusations were made by established conservative organisations such as the Sane Democracy League and new ones such as the Institute of Public Affairs, formed by leading businessmen in late 1942 to combat the rising tide of socialism. It was not until 1945 that a right-wing organisation dedicated to the exposure of communism was created, the Political Research Society, with Jack Cassidy KC as its chairman and W.C. Wentworth as the research officer.[24]

Long before then an assault came from a different quarter. A lengthy pamphlet, *Red Glows the Dawn*, appeared at the end of 1942 with an urgent warning of the communist threat. Although the CPA had failed in earlier attempts to capture the labour movement, it said, the danger arose from the cloak of respectability it had acquired now that the Soviet Union was an ally. Hundreds of thousands of Australians had been lured into admiration of the Soviet regime through the fundraising efforts of the Medical Aid and Comforts Committee and the propaganda of the Australia–Soviet Friendship League. Radical bishops, barristers, medical and military men, and 'that mysterious section of the community known as the "intelligentsia"', had shifted the propagation of communism from the Domain and the Yarra Bank to Potts Point and Toorak, drawing in fellow travellers heedless of the materialist philosophy of these 'totalitarian monsters' and their bloody record of tyranny. Communism would tear down freedom and democracy in this land 'unless you and I and those who hold our beliefs are prepared to gird on our armour and enter the conflict' before 'the day glows red over the hill-tops'.[25]

Although the author used a pseudonym, Michael Lamb, he was soon identified as Herbert Michael Cremean, the deputy leader of the parliamentary Labor Party in Victoria. Along with the longstanding anti-communist Arthur Calwell, the legendary numbers man Pat Kennelly and Dinny Lovegrove, whose antipathy went back to his expulsion from the party in 1933, Bert Cremean led a faction that held tight control of the ALP in that state. Faced by a rebellion at the 1940 conference, they closed down a number of local branches. In 1941 they proscribed the Australia–Soviet Friendship League for exploiting 'the magnificent effort of the Russian people' and expelled the federal parliamentarian Maurice Blackburn for his continued association with its activities. In 1942 they took a strong stand against Curtin's call for conscription. In 1943 they decreed that any union with an official who campaigned against a Labor candidate would forfeit its affiliation to the Labor Party—a tactic that enabled them to turn away conference delegates who might have challenged their control.[26]

This inward-looking, intensely suspicious junta treated John Curtin with a thinly veiled hostility and made John Cain's life as parliamentary leader in Victoria a torment. It overreached itself in November 1943, when on the eve of celebrations of 'Russia's National Day'—a grand ceremony described in the Introduction—Lovegrove informed the Labor participants, in his capacity as state president, that they were not to attend. The prime minister had arranged for a Cabinet member, Don Cameron, to represent the Commonwealth, while Bill Slater, who had recently returned from heading the Australian legation, was to introduce his Soviet counterpart, Andrei Vlasov. Cameron submitted to the Victorian executive's ban, Slater ignored it with impunity. Shaken by criticism of this public affront to an ally, Lovegrove called on Vlasov and then issued a misleading report of their conversation to the press that the Russian promptly corrected. As a political commentator described this debacle, 'with elephantine finesse, the executive tried to slap the ASFL in the eye with one hand and to pat the Soviet minister on the back with the other'.[27] The next annual conference replaced Lovegrove as president and, in a sign of tensions within the inner circle, the state secretary Pat Kennelly mislaid Bert Cremean's nomination for re-election as vice-president. The same conference condemned the Communist Party's affiliation campaign and expelled a further batch of rebels.[28]

Cremean, a former mayor of Richmond, was well practised in the black arts of branch stacking that were a way of life in Labor's inner-suburban strongholds. He was also a devout Catholic and a member of Catholic Action, the lay organisation established in 1937 to promote Catholic social values. In that same year, Cremean attended the stormy meeting at the University of Melbourne where B.A. (Bob) Santamaria, who was about to become assistant secretary of Catholic Action, debated the Spanish Civil War with communists. Impressed by the young man's fervour, Cremean introduced Santamaria to other members of his ALP inner circle who explained that a similar battle was occurring in the labour movement. Santamaria said later that they asked him to help defend their shrinking industrial base—though this and other parts of his account are disputed.[29]

In any event, the two men obtained approval from Archbishop Mannix early in 1942 to conduct operations. They were also given £3000 to assist their efforts, and *Red Glows the Dawn* was one of the first publications. Soon there would be a weekly newspaper, *Freedom* (its licence obtained by Calwell), and a growing network of anti-communist cells. At this stage those in the know referred to their organisation as 'the Show'; by 1945, when it was formally constituted as the Catholic Social Studies Movement, it was dubbed 'the Movement'.[30]

The Labor right in Victoria used other ploys in its anti-communist crusade. There was a Workers' Rights Association that commenced a radio campaign against left-wing unions in 1943, and there was Loyd Ring Coleman, head of the Australian branch of the American advertising agency J. Walter Thompson, whose attacks on international communism appeared under a pseudonym in the Victorian ALP's newspaper *Labor Call*, as did the criticisms of Soviet policy in Eastern Europe contributed by a recently arrived refugee, Richard Krygier, on behalf of the Polish government in exile.[31] But the Movement was a venture of a new kind, attaching the authority of the Catholic Church to a lay organisation that intervened directly in the affairs of the labour movement. It was modelled, moreover, on the very organisation it sought to destroy—highly select, centrally directed and even more secretive: as Santamaria put it, pitting 'cadre against cadre, cell against cell, fraction against fraction'.[32]

Catholic hostility intensified as the party's membership and influence grew. Of particular concern were the public support for the Soviet Union and its popularisation in works such as Hewlett Johnson's *Socialist Sixth of the World* as an exemplar to all people of good will. First published in 1939, this bestseller extolled the building of a wholly new economic and social order that had replaced scarcity with abundance, selfishness with service, the chaos of competition with cooperation, and stunted lives with the fullest development of human potential. Perhaps the most credulous of such panegyrics, the book's authority was enhanced by its author's standing as the Dean of Canterbury, the archdiocese of the primate of the Church of England, and his conviction that God's work was being done in Russia.[33]

Australian clergymen who appeared at war rallies proclaimed a similar redemptive message, and Stalin's relaxation of restrictions on religion during the 'patriotic war' encouraged dialogue with Australian communists. 'Communism had wrought the most amazing achievements in social regeneration the world had ever seen,' said the Dean of St Paul's Cathedral in Melbourne. 'If God looked down this year on Melbourne and Moscow,' asked the Brotherhood of St Laurence's Frank Coaldrake, 'which in His judgement would be considered closer to the right?'[34]

Catholic publicists were scornful of such apologetics. Cremean observed in *Red Glows the Dawn* that the prayer Canon Garnsey offered in opening the Congress for Friendship and Aid to the Soviet Union in Sydney on 30 August 1941 was composed by 'Bishop Burgmann, the Australian equivalent of the Red Dean of Canterbury'. Father Paddy Ryan, director of the Lay Apostolate in the Catholic archdiocese of Sydney, wrote a widely read condemnation of Hewlett Johnson: 'his Christianity is not the Christianity of Christ. It is a diminished, truncated and hopelessly muddled thing.' This drew a response from Lance Sharkey, who insisted that communism enshrined a higher morality. But Ryan was adamant: communism was materialistic, atheistic and incompatible with Christianity, so no Catholic who joined the Communist Party could remain a member of the church. As for those brethren who sought to justify communism, Judases were to be found in every age, and whether their price was 30 pieces of silver or 'the myth of a Soviet Paradise', the betrayal was the same. Bill Wood subsequently chipped in as a deacon of the Congregational Church with a plea for toleration and a prediction that God's division of the sheep from the goats would be on lines different from those Father Ryan drew.[35]

The most prominent clerical sympathisers were Anglicans. A few ministers of the Nonconformist denominations, which allowed greater freedom of conscience, even joined the party. The Catholic hierarchy remained utterly antagonistic, and its mobilisation of the laity presented a serious threat. 'Religious strife must be kept out of the Labor movement', Sharkey warned; 'it splits the workers and is therefore a boss's weapon'. The party's response was to try to separate Catholic workers from their bishops. Thus the Thirteenth Congress condemned the 'reactionary, pro-Fascist, Roman Catholic leaders who must be distinguished from the people of the Catholic faith who work for victory', and there were regular reports in *Tribune* of recruits who continued to attend church. 'This is a lie, a deliberate lie', a pastoral letter read in every NSW church on Sunday 23 May 1943 warned: 'no Communist may receive the Sacraments or expect a Christian burial'.[36]

The sponsors of the Movement were themselves economical with the truth. When asked in 1944 about his connection with its newspaper, Archbishop Mannix said that 'Personally, I do not know of any connection between *Freedom* and the Catholic Church.' It purported to be published by a group of laymen 'independent of all church bodies', yet Santamaria was working under the umbrella of Catholic Action and reporting directly to the archbishop.[37]

By this time he had organised cells of anti-communists in a number of Victorian unions, and similar ones were formed in Sydney, Newcastle, Adelaide and North Queensland. They achieved some success, but depended on the endorsement of like-minded bishops and parish priests. Santamaria's goal was 'a disciplined national organisation' backed by the full authority of the church.[38] Mannix advised him that the support of

Sydney's Archbishop Gilroy, who held that such activity needed clerical direction, was essential, but with Paddy Ryan's assistance he was able to put his proposals to a meeting of the Australian bishops in September 1945. He wanted them to establish the Movement as an arm of Catholic Action. They decided it should be a separate Catholic Social Studies Movement under the supervision of its own episcopal committee and with Santamaria as liaison officer—though he also became director of Catholic Action at the end of the year. The bishops provided £10,000 for the first year of operations.[39]

Secrecy was essential if the Movement was not to arouse sectarian hostility, and Santamaria produced just 30 copies of a report on his progress in the fight against communism, one for each bishop, in preparation for their September meeting. Three months later the Communist Party reproduced most of it as a pamphlet, *Catholic Action at Work*. In his autobiography Santamaria attributed the lapse in security to a bishop who left a copy under the pillow of his sleeping compartment on the rail journey to Sydney, and suggested that a cleaner must have taken it to Marx House. More plausibly, the document was given to Jack Blake in Melbourne by a Catholic who disagreed with the bishops' endorsement of this clandestine organisation, and Blake had Ted Hill check the authenticity of the report's detailed account of Movement work in scores of unions before sending it to Sydney.[40]

The publication of *Catholic Action at Work* disclosed the sums of money the church had provided to initiate the Movement, the tactics it had used and the future plans. With a membership of 3000, Santamaria claimed the Movement had been able to overturn communists in a number of union ballots, though he conceded there were instances when opponents raised a 'sectarian cry' to rebuff its efforts. It had the advantage in Victoria, he acknowledged, of operating with the support of the Labor Party. That was not the case in New South Wales, though he welcomed a recent decision that would allow the Movement to join up with other anti-communists there and give it the benefit of working under 'the cover of the Labor Party'.[41]

★

Santamaria's claims were greatly exaggerated. It suited some trade union officials to enlist assistance in repelling a communist challenge to their positions. Vic Stout, secretary of the Melbourne Trades Hall Council, met the Movement's union coordinator regularly from 1942, to advise of impending elections where additional numbers were needed to rustle up an anti-communist majority. The support was welcome, but few of the beneficiaries shared the religious fervour that accompanied it. Other union leaders, who felt secure from challenge, resisted any interference in their affairs. The claim that the Movement rescued the country's unions from an imminent communist takeover, sedulously promoted by Santamaria and his admirers, is difficult to sustain. It came late to a struggle between left and right that was already under way, and with many points in between.

Growing industrial unrest in the final years of the war exacerbated the contest. The number of working days lost in disputes rose to 1,112,000 in 1944 and 2,120,000 in 1945.[42] Most occurred in industries with a strong communist presence, though that does not mean communists directed them. Many arose as the result of union members' impatience with wage controls at a time of full employment; some, indeed, were initiated as an act of rebellion against communist leadership of the union. But the party's policy of industrial cooperation was coming under strain: if only to hold its union following, it needed to give a lead. We see this in the coalmining industry, where communist union officials had particular difficulty in preventing stoppages. It was the prosecution of recalcitrant miners, as the government lost patience with the constant hold-ups in production, that brought a change, since communist officials felt compelled to defend their members, if only to repair their own standing. Unrest in the metal industries contributed to a growth of communist influence in the Amalgamated Engineering Union. Ted Rowe, who came from the Ballarat railway workshops, emerged as the leading militant in this traditionally exclusive craft union.[43]

Communists made advances in some unions at this time and suffered reverses in others. The contest between left and right was growing, though the adversaries still based their arguments on industrial issues and within the conventions of a union movement that guarded its autonomy jealously. There was a reaction against outside interference in the Clerks' Union when Jack Hughes obtained a letter circulated by the Movement in New South Wales that invited 'advanced members only' to a meeting to promote an Association of Non-Communist Clerical Workers at which Father Ryan would speak. Communists also kept control of the Victorian branch of the Clerks in 1945 after a protracted dispute with Movement supporters there.[44]

Control had many meanings. The confidential Movement report the party obtained in 1945 distinguished unions under communist control from those with 'moderate control' and 'genuine control', by which it meant its own. The party also spoke of controlling unions, though we have seen that there were very few in which communists held all the positions on a state executive, let alone every state branch. Control also carried undesirable implications of directing a union regardless of the wishes of its members, for both communists and their opponents claimed to respect industrial democracy. Where communists held office, they promoted workplace involvement, encouraged participation in a wider range of activities, issued regular reports, took modest salaries and held themselves accountable through regular elections (it was not uncommon in more conservative unions for secretaries to hold office for life).[45] They also pursued amalgamations, streamlined administration, strengthened central decision-making and discouraged dissent.

J.B. Miles warned at the Thirteenth Congress against the temptation to run 'a full party ticket for all the official positions of a union'. Even where this was possible, he said, it was better to include non-communists.[46] His warning might well have been meant for Ernie Thornton, who undoubtedly sought complete control of the Federated Ironworkers' Association (FIA). Thornton used the national executive's powers to intervene in any branch that resisted its authority and install new branch secretaries to ensure compliance. Opposition to the amalgamation with the Munition Workers' Union was crushed, the dissident communist organiser of the South Australian branch cast aside in 1944 and driven out of the party.[47]

There were already doubts about the union's conduct of the ballots used to elect officials. Kate Challis, a member of the Kings Cross branch of the party, resigned when she was expected to help fill in a batch of

FIA ballot papers. Bernard Smith, her husband, took the matter to Miles, who replied 'to the effect that he knew that kind of thing happened'. Those who engaged in ballot rigging described the practice as 'adjustment'. The union-appointed returning officer, who was responsible for both issuing ballot papers and counting them, would hold a number of additional ones in reserve to make up any deficit and secure the desired result. We do not know how widely such chicanery occurred or how many communists were involved. That Kate Challis, a recent recruit and a high-minded teacher, was called on suggests it was widespread in the FIA and that she was not alone in her abhorrence.[48]

Crooked ballots were a way of life in the labour movement, as was stacking meetings at which members voted by show of hand. Tipped off by Vic Stout, the Movement sent a large contingent of ring-ins to a meeting of the Shop Assistants' Union in Melbourne early in 1945; the meeting usually attracted no more than 30 members, so the 164 it provided seemed more than enough, but 'the Opposition, working on the sectarian cry', had mustered 187. Ballots were usually confined to election of office-holders on the grounds that they took too long for industrial matters requiring speedy decision. Besides, Thornton remarked, 'There's one great disadvantage about a secret ballot. You can't ask a question.'[49]

Many questions were asked of 'the Czar of the Ironworkers', who attracted greater opprobrium than any other communist union leader. Attacks came from Labor as well as non-Labor politicians in both federal and state parliaments (a deputation of Victorian Labor parliamentarians asked the non-Labor premier to conduct an inquiry into the FIA), from anti-Labor publications such as *The Bulletin* and anti-communist ones such as Jack Lang's *Century*. There were persistent claims that Thornton diverted union funds to the Communist Party and refused to publish a balance sheet, despite his belated production of audited accounts. Lang went furthest, with allegations that Thornton had not been a bona fide worker when he joined the FIA, that he used it for his own nefarious purposes, and even that he conspired with the manpower authorities to control membership of the workforce.[50]

'Don't tangle with me,' Thornton warned the leader of another union pleading against absorption of his members into the FIA, 'the Ironworkers are well known for knocking over people who oppose them.'[51] He withstood formidable opponents, only to be brought undone by a handful of Trotskyists working in the shipyards scattered round the Balmain peninsula in Sydney. The FIA had its origins in this close-knit community, and the Balmain branch had always guarded its independence. The small organisation of Australian Trotskyists, which never exceeded 100 members, had recently split over tactics, and those in the Balmain branch of the union adopted a policy of working within the Labor Party.[52] Their insistence that the working class should refuse to make sacrifices for the imperialist war struck a chord with the substantial number of unionists in Balmain who shared Jack Lang's hostility to Labor's war measures. Nick Origlass, the pugnacious leader of the Trotskyists, was elected shop delegate at Mort's Dock; Laurie Short, more diminutive but no less combative, won the same post at Cockatoo Island.[53]

The national executive acted with characteristic high-handedness, suspending the Balmain branch executive in August 1943 to install its own officials. The effect was to inflame the rebellion. The next monthly meeting of the branch shouted Thornton down, and soon there was a war of legal proceedings, battles over occupancy of the union premises, fist fights, blatant manipulation of meeting procedure and rigged ballots, all publicised by Thornton's critics. The party condemned 'the alliance of Langites, Trotskyites and other unprincipled factionalists who undermine the organisation and authority of the trade unions'. It overplayed its hand in early 1945 when, in Thornton's absence at the trade union conference in London, Jack McPhillips removed Origlass from his position as Mort's Dock delegate for encouraging a stoppage. This resulted in a six-week strike that ended in the election of a new branch executive with Origlass as assistant secretary, which obtained legal recognition from the Arbitration Court. By this time the Movement was involved, providing money to support the strikers. More ominous was the studied silence of the Labor government as a union led by one of its chief industrial supporters struggled unavailingly to quell a strike.[54]

There was also restlessness in the ACTU. In June 1944, when it met with members of the federal Cabinet for one of their periodic discussions, both Eliot Elliott and Jim Healy complained about the government's lack of attention to their members' concerns. But this complaint was by no means confined to the left. Throughout the war, the Curtin government had excluded the unions from any involvement in the determination of policy, and it was Albert Monk, the ACTU secretary and a pronounced moderate, who scolded ministers at this meeting for disregarding the viewpoint of the industrial movement. Despite their grievances, the leading communists continued to urge cooperation in the war effort.[55]

A similar spirit was apparent at the 1945 congress of the ACTU, which called for an immediate wage increase, a 40-hour week and a remodelling of the arbitration system. The strong contingent of communist and other militants were in agreement with the other delegates on these demands. The left succeeded in securing two rule changes, one to the composition of the executive (allowing direct election of five of its ten members instead of them all being chosen by the trades and labour councils) and the other making congress decisions binding rather than subject to ratification by the councils. Furthermore, the left won all five of these executive positions, with Jim Healy, Bob Wells and Tom Wright among them. But communists withdrew a challenge to the president, Percy Clarey, and had one of its successful candidates for the executive stand down to make a place for Charlie Crofts, yet another of the old guard. Though the congress met in Sydney, Monk and Clarey had simply ignored the 1943 decision to move the ACTU's secretariat there. And although they were unable to prevent congress from voting for a partly elected executive, they prevailed when the trades and labour councils of New South Wales, Victoria and Tasmania rejected the necessary alteration of the ACTU's constitution.[56]

The left was disadvantaged in these state councils, partly because they included right-wing unions such as the Australian Workers' Union that were not affiliated with the ACTU, and partly because a sliding scale of representation put a cap on the number of delegates from large unions in which the left was strongest. Communists had a majority following in the Brisbane Trades and Labor Council and could sometimes carry motions in Adelaide, but were consistently outvoted in Melbourne and losing ground in Sydney. Bob King, the secretary of the NSW Labor

Council, was moving to the right, along with previously sympathetic delegates alarmed by the party's growth and estranged by Thornton's aggrandisement. Communists no longer bothered to contest the presidency after 1944.[57]

The leaders of the Labor Party in New South Wales shared this concern—indeed, most members of the ALP state executive came from the Labor Council. A motion at the 1944 Labor Conference that the Communist Party be allowed to affiliate was ruled out of order, the challenge to the president's ruling defeated by 271 votes to 77. In the immediate aftermath of the 1945 ACTU Congress, the state conference went further and decided to establish Industrial Groups in trade unions to promote the policies and principles of the ALP. Earlier in the year the premier had opened a Henry Lawson Labor College and bookshop in competition with the Marx School, and initially the Industrial Groups conducted propaganda to shore up unions against communist influence. But very quickly they went further by running their own candidates in union elections. The Victorian and South Australian branches of the ALP created Industrial Groups in the following year, Queensland in 1948.[58]

To take such a step, at odds with deep-seated traditions of union independence and solidarity, was a measure of the polarisation of the labour movement. Jack Ferguson, secretary of the NSW branch of the Australian Railways who left the Communist Party along with Lloyd Ross in 1940, insisted as late as 1945 that 'communism as a political belief possesses much that is acceptable' and that communists were among the 'builders' of his union. A year later he was decrying 'the communist saboteurs' for their 'diabolical attempt to wreck the union'.[59]

The intention in forming Industrial Groups was to safeguard Labor's industrial base, for affiliated unions made up the majority of conference delegates. And since there was no way of preventing unions with communist leaders sending delegates of like mind, the groups were not open to all ALP members. This restriction did not apply to those who belonged to the Catholic Social Studies Movement, which had cells in most of the Industrial Groups and was thereby able to work in unions with the authorisation of the Labor Party. The two organisations were often conflated, the term Grouper used to describe members of the Movement, but there was an important difference. The groups were loosely coordinated by an ALP official, the Movement directed by a man claiming the authority of the Catholic Church who had no standing in the ALP. The effect was to create a faction to combat the left within which another, secret one flourished. Devised to protect the ALP, the Industrial Groups became a means of capturing it.

*

The mines and foundries, factories and wharves where large teams of workers sold their labour were always the principal site of the class struggle. Other kinds of activity, in the community and at the ballot box, through national and international campaigns, by means of the party press and engagement in a wide range of social and cultural pursuits, were of undoubted importance in sustaining communism as an all-encompassing form of political engagement. These too prospered in the middle years of the war, then became more embattled as victory drew in sight.

In its cultural activity, the party promoted work that was popular and progressive, gave expression to the people's experience and aspirations, and above all served the war against fascism. By pressing culture into this purpose, however, it created a division between its own writers and artists and those who rejected politicisation of their creativity. Paradoxically, at the very time communists celebrated the way that the people's war produced a new unity in common endeavour, they uncovered fresh enemies of the people—those intellectuals who cultivated an obscurantist, undemocratic and ultimately fascist depiction of life. This hostility was encouraged by the call at the Thirteenth Congress in 1943 to raise the cultural level of the party, after which Harry Gould produced a ponderous formulation of art as an expression of social conditions and a weapon in the class war. Such pronouncements from on high, replete with references to Marx and Lenin, were not new. It was only as the party demanded complete support for the war effort that the artistic freedom demanded by the avant-garde became synonymous with reaction.[60]

The tension between the realist style favoured by communist artists and those who turned to expressionism, surrealism and primitivism can be traced back before the war, though initially they worked together in the Contemporary Art Society's challenge to the conservative art establishment. Charles Merewether, who in 1984 curated the most comprehensive exhibition of the work produced in this period, demonstrated that leading communists had themselves drawn on the more experimental genres to depict the human predicament of the outcast in the modern city.[61] It was their enlistment in the war against fascism that created an open breach with a group of young Melbourne artists, Sidney Nolan, Albert Tucker, Arthur Boyd and John Perceval, whose experience of army life strengthened a hostility to regimentation and a conviction that the true artist must stand outside society in order to capture its pathology. Tucker, who read most widely in the literature of alienation, was the most articulate in rejecting communism as but another form of mental slavery, and Noel Counihan, the most theoretically adept of the communist artists, quickly denounced this 'metaphysical claptrap'.[62]

Counihan had begun an association with Bernard Smith, who had joined the teachers' branch of the party in Sydney, where the first NSW exhibition of the Contemporary Art Society was held in the Teachers' Federation's city building during 1940. At the suggestion of Sam Lewis, Smith extended his lectures on art to encompass Australian painting; these would lead to *Place, Taste and Tradition* (1945), the first serious history of Australian art and one that gave lavish praise to the social realists—though the book's publisher refused to include Smith's chapter on 'the fascist mentality in Australian art'.[63] Writing under the pseudonym 'Courbet' (for he was now working for the NSW Art Gallery), Smith condemned 'the chamber of synthetic horrors' painted by the modernists. Counihan posed the choice starkly in the *Communist Review*. Art could progress with 'a sensitive, uncompromising realism' or 'decay, sterile and impotent, in the ivory tower of formalism'. Artists could inspire 'a sincere love for our country, our people and our own traditions' or encourage 'demoralisation, pacifism and defeatism'.[64]

These polemics spilled over into the field of literature after John and Sunday Reed, who supported Tucker, Nolan and other artists at Heide, their home on the outer fringes of Melbourne, threw their weight behind an experimental magazine, *Angry Penguins*. Max Harris launched this publication in 1940 as an undergraduate at Adelaide University while he was a communist (and thrown into the River Torrens by loyalist students), though he moved on quickly in his career as an enfant terrible and formed a partnership with the Reeds to produce *Angry Penguins*. It was one of a number of such periodicals to spring up during the war, and by far the most iconoclastic, but became the victim of a celebrated literary hoax in late 1943, when two poets passed off a parody of its portentous modernism as the work of Ern Malley, a young man who supposedly had recently died in obscurity.

John Reed was at this time close to the party in Victoria and hoped it would get behind *Angry Penguins*, but any possibility of cooperation disappeared after *Angry Penguins* devoted a special issue to Malley's poems. Here was confirmation of the Heide coterie's 'blind obedience to an art ideology that exalts obscurantism and fantasy above meaning and profundity', an illustration of their descent into 'anti-Marxist, anti-communist and anti-Soviet propaganda'. It should be noted that it was the party's artists who issued this ukase. Jack Blake, the Victorian secretary, was more conciliatory.[65]

'We believe it is high time Australian writers faced up to the present day,' proclaimed Bernard Smith, Katharine Susannah Prichard and George Farwell in launching the first issue of *Australian New Writing* in 1943, for 'art is a means of coming to grips with reality, of understanding the processes of society and the human heart and mind.'[66] Practitioners called this social realism, a category that Smith would later distinguish from socialist realism. He saw the one as concerned with telling the truth as seen and experienced, the other serving the political project of winning and maintaining power. Socialist realism would be laid down after the war as the duty of party artists, but the term was not yet in common use. Noel Counihan was one who invoked it at this time, though his canvases had little to do with the socialist realism of the Soviet Union and its heroic depiction of the new socialist performing monumental tasks with unflagging ardour; his was an art of sympathy and compassion for those wronged by capitalism.[67] It was not to all party members' tastes. The 1944 exhibition of the Contemporary Art Society had an 'appallingly depressing effect' on Bernice Morris, a young Melbourne recruit. She found Arthur Boyd's paintings 'hideous beyond description', and even though she understood what those of Counihan and Vic O'Connor were trying to convey, 'felt the message could have been said just as well if the pictures had been a little less ugly and grotesque'.[68]

There was keen argument in other cultural fields. What kind of music should communists encourage, Nadine Dalgarno, Roy's wife, asked. She advocated 'a music arising from the people' that included Aboriginal chants as well as ballads of bushrangers and goldminers. The party conducted a weekly radio program in Melbourne, 'Stories in Song', that ranged across Eureka ballads, 'Negro spirituals' and recordings of Fats Waller (claimed as a member of the CPUSA). Jazz was popular in the Eureka Youth League but the classical repertoire was also promoted, especially Shostakovich. The highlight of a concert that Nadine Dalgarno organised at Marx House in early 1945 was a reading by Peter Finch of Mayakovsky's epic poem 'Lenin' accompanied by orchestral music.[69] John Oldham and his wife Ray made the case for modern dance as 'a weapon in the people's struggle for freedom' against other communists who defended the favoured Soviet form, ballet.[70]

It was common to disparage popular entertainment as 'bourgeois escapism', but an article by a young British historian, Eric Hobsbawm, appeared in *Tribune* in 1944 making the case for taking commercial cinema seriously. The most successful Australian film of 1945 was *The Overlanders*, an Ealing studio production based on Dora Birtles' novel of a cattle drive to safety across northern Australia from the Japanese advance, which involved a number of New Theatre actors. There was also experimental local cinematography. Ken Coldicutt had toured Australia with a 16-millimetre projector in the late 1930s to screen documentaries on the Spanish Civil War, and he used his severance pay from the RAAF in 1945 to establish a Realist Film Unit that applied the techniques of Sergei Eisenstein to social life in Melbourne.[71]

The party sought a broad alliance in its cultural work. A People's Conference on Australian Culture, held in Sydney in mid-1944, drew in leading musicians, writers, architects and scientists. It gave way to the Council for the Encouragement of Music and the Arts, founded by the visionary Dorothy Helmrich upon her return from Britain, 'to bring art, in all its forms, to the people'.[72]

But vigilance towards real and imagined opponents continued. In 1944 Jack Blake commenced legal proceedings against the writer Kylie Tennant and Angus & Robertson, the publisher of her novel *Ride on Stranger*, which gave a hostile portrayal of a domineering communist organiser.[73] The publisher settled out of court and withdrew the book. This was of a piece with the legal challenge in the same year to the award of the Archibald prize to William Dobell for a portrait that was hardly realist but was defended nevertheless by party artists, and the conviction of Max Harris for publishing an 'indecent' work. Communists were frequent litigants at this time, with Jack Brown, Claude Jones, Ted Laurie and Ernie Thornton all bringing actions for defamation, all unsuccessfully.[74]

The most striking instance of the party's intolerance was its campaign against the Workers' Educational Association (WEA). Late in 1942, members working in a railway workshop in Sydney appear to have drawn the leadership's attention to a course offered there by Percy Partridge on 'Political Theories and Movements of Today'. Partridge was then a lecturer in philosophy at the University of Sydney, and his WEA course, known as B40, cast doubt on the proposition that the Soviet Union was a socialist state in which workers enjoyed economic equality or exercised political control. The party demanded the course be withdrawn. Rebuffed, it mobilised delegates at a meeting of the NSW Labor Council in April 1943 to carry a resolution, moved by the FIA, which withdrew the unions' affiliation to the WEA. This was accompanied by far-fetched accusations of Trotskyist 'anti-Soviet lies' designed to discredit the Soviet Union and sabotage the war effort. Partridge's offence consisted partly of his inclusion of Trotsky's *The Revolution Betrayed* as reading for the course, and partly his association with John Anderson, a professor of philosophy who had turned briefly to Trotskyism in the 1930s after leaving the party. 'One cannot reason with these human jackals,' Sharkey proclaimed, 'they can only be dealt with by being punished and suppressed.'[75]

Given that the ban on the CPA had only recently been lifted, its refusal to allow any criticism of the USSR—more precisely, any discussion of the nature of the Soviet regime—was startling. Speaking at the Labor Council as a delegate of the Teachers' Federation, Bill Gollan said the issue was not one of free speech but whether middle-class professors should use the cloak of the WEA to disseminate their anti-Soviet hatred. Bill Wood, who also taught for the WEA, said there was no question of preventing fair criticism, only preventing the propagation of lies. A decision by the Teachers' Federation to endorse the disaffiliation on the grounds that the WEA was aiding the enemy only reinforced the impression of heresy hunting. The federation backed down in the face of public condemnation, but Sharkey persisted in what he called 'the essential defence of democracy against its enemies and the people against their foes'. As Partridge observed, 'our local communists' were given to 'hurling the word "Fascism" at anyone—even members of the working-class movement—who ventures to disagree with them'.[76]

★

The establishment of diplomatic relations with the Soviet Union brought further complications. Evatt, as Minister for External Affairs, chose Bill Slater (the speaker of the Victorian Legislative Assembly) to head the Australian mission, and Slater recruited Max Crawford, professor of history at the University of Melbourne, to accompany him as first secretary. Slater was on the left of the Labor Party and Ted Hill was only one of several communists working in his legal firm, Slater and Gordon, while Crawford was prominent in the Australian Council for Civil Liberties. Offsetting them were two impeccably conservative career diplomats, Keith Officer as counsellor and Peter Heydon as second secretary, but two additional appointments were highly unusual. John Fisher, the press attaché, had been *Tribune*'s correspondent in Canberra until 1939 and was already working as a freelance reporter in Moscow. Irene Saxby, the archivist, had taught English in Moscow for most of the previous decade and was also close to the party. The Australian legation (it was not yet an embassy) began at the end of 1942 in Kuibyshev, the wartime seat of government on the River Volga. The trying conditions soon broke both the health and the resolve of Slater and Crawford. For reasons that remain unclear, Evatt chose James Maloney, from the right of the Labor Party in New South Wales, to replace Slater. Maloney's lack of diplomacy was soon painfully obvious.[77]

The Russians arrived in early 1943 and established their residency in Canberra. They diverged from the other diplomatic missions by locating it in Kingston, rather than on Mugga Way, and bringing their own domestic staff. The few members of the legation who had proficiency in English were unaccustomed to the local version and puzzled by the informality of the locals. Apart from Andrei Vlasov, the head of the legation, they seldom ventured beyond Canberra, in contrast to the representatives of TASS, the official Soviet news agency, the first of whom had arrived in Sydney six months earlier and mixed more freely as an accredited war correspondent. As was customary, the diplomatic staff included officers of two intelligence agencies, the NKVD (known from 1943 as the NKGB) and Military Intelligence, the GRU. The NKGB resident was Semyen Makarov and he relied on a new TASS representative, Fedor Nosov, for contacts. Working in Sydney and frequenting the Journalists' Club in Phillip Street, Nosov was familiar with communist and other sympathetic journalists. Since the Australian government was seeking closer relations with the Soviet Union, Nosov was also welcome at Evatt's office in Martin Place.

Australian intelligence officers followed these developments closely. Conscious of the need for increased vigilance in the war against Japan but mistrustful of both the calibre and political sympathies of existing agencies, the Labor government had given responsibility for domestic security in 1942 to a new Commonwealth Security Service. Led initially by Commissioner MacKay of the NSW Police Force and later by William Simpson, a legal colleague of Evatt, it was soon at loggerheads with the intelligence sections of the three armed services, which continued to conduct their own domestic operations—there were indeed cases of agencies spying on each other and even burgling their rivals' safes. Military Intelligence still intercepted mail; tapped telephones, including those of government ministers; and monitored the cable traffic between the Soviet legation and Moscow.

By 1944 it reached the conclusion that the legation was sending information on Allied military operations in the Pacific that found its way to the Soviet legation in northern China and thence to the Japanese. Neither the source of this information nor the means whereby it passed to Japan was ever established. The Chinese military attaché in Australia was suspected of obtaining some of it, and some came from reports issued by the Australian Department of Information, but none of the enciphered cable traffic from Canberra to Moscow that Military Intelligence collected and was subsequently deciphered by the US Army Security Agency confirms the claim that the legation sent it. Suspicion fell on the USSR because it was not fighting Japan, and one reason for Australia establishing diplomatic relations was to encourage it to do so. While Stalin argued that the demands of his western front made it too risky to open an eastern one, critics alleged he meant to prolong the Pacific War so that he could make greater gains in Europe. Handicapped by the need to protect the secret that the United States was reading Japanese signals, the Australian Army could not persuade the Cabinet or the Security Service that Soviet diplomats were to blame.[78]

Our knowledge of Soviet espionage in Australia at this time relies on a small number of messages to and from the legation that were deciphered after the war. In communicating with Moscow, Soviet diplomatic missions used a one-time cipher code that was almost impossible to penetrate, but some code-pads had been duplicated in the turmoil created by the German invasion, and these enabled US analysts to break the code in 1946 and read a substantial body of the Australian material collected since 1943. Most of it was routine stuff concerning diplomacy and trade, but some 400 of the messages passed between the NKGB resident in Australia and Moscow Centre. Of these, some were copies of British material and some were merely administrative. That left a little over 100 that contained intelligence material, and they were released after the Cold War ended to document America's success in what it called the Venona program. Australian security was at first denied access to these messages. It spent much time afterwards trying to identify those referred to in the messages by their operational names. EFIM was Semyen Makarov and TEKHNIK was Fedor Nosov, but who were KLOD, BEN, SESTRA, TOURIST, PODRUGA, ACADEMICIAN and BUR?[79]

The picture of communist espionage these messages provide is fragmentary. More details were assembled later through interrogation of those involved, but much of their testimony was given under duress and is exculpatory in nature. Here I use some of these retrospective accounts to take the measure of a subject that is still open to dispute. There is no doubt that Wally Clayton recruited informants to collect intelligence for the NKGB. Clayton (KLOD) first appeared in March 1945 when Makarov had Nosov ask him if the NKGB could use Alf Hughes (BEN), his informant in the Security Service, to obtain a better picture of its operations. Clayton had evidently been assisting Soviet espionage for some time as a 'talent spotter', but we do not know when he began to do so or whether he had the blessing of the party. He was a secretive man, marked by his years in the underground. There is no mention of him ever invoking the authority of the CPA's leaders, but since his recruits were minor figures and he was a member of the central control commission there was little need for him to do so.[80]

In April 1945, Clayton informed Nosov that he had placed Frances Bernie (SESTRA) in Evatt's ministerial office in Sydney. Bernie, then 22, was a former member of the Eureka Youth League who worked from November 1944 as a stenographer-typist under the supervision of Evatt's private secretary, Allan Dalziel. It was her habit to make an additional copy of any document she thought might interest Clayton and take it to him at his office in Marx House—though she claimed not to have realised he might pass it on to the Soviet legation. She recalled Clayton as a hard taskmaster, often dismissive of the material she showed him, cold and evasive; 'he wouldn't look at me when I was reporting to him'.[81]

A fortnight later, Makarov informed Moscow that he had given Clayton £15 on the 'plausible pretext' of compensating him for expenditure incurred in performing assignments, that Clayton was taken aback as he considered it his duty to assist the Soviet Union, but cheered up when assured that his efforts were appreciated. In July Moscow had Makarov ask Clayton to provide the names of party members who might be enlisted in gathering information. He agreed to do so—though we do not have this document—but Moscow remained concerned with the Australian's lack of training in 'operational work' and the danger that he would attract attention by indiscriminate recruitment of informants. Precautions were tightened in July 1945 after the defection of a Soviet cipher clerk in Ottawa brought a Canadian spy ring to international attention: Moscow Centre ordered that Nosov cut down meetings with Clayton to one a month and that he was not to take any documents from Clayton to Canberra until further notice. Makarov himself was coming under criticism for his laxity.[82]

By this time Clayton had made contact with several officers of the Department of External Affairs in Canberra. One was Jim Hill (TOURIST), a younger brother of Ted Hill who was working in the Post-Hostilities Division and provided copies of a British report on south-east Europe. Another was probably Dorothy Jordan (PODRUGA), who worked in the department's archives. Her husband, Ric Throssell, was also working in the Post-Hostilities Division but about to be posted to a mission in Europe. There is no evidence of any contact between Clayton and Throssell; rather, Clayton worked on Throssell's mother, Katharine Susannah Prichard (ACADEMICIAN), who was then living in Sydney, urging her to persuade him to seek a European appointment. Prichard, however, insisted it must be the Soviet homeland she so greatly admired. The third contact was Ian Milner (BUR), acting at this time as head of the Post-Hostilities Division, and he provided copies of two British reports on post-war defence arrangements in the Mediterranean, Atlantic and Indian oceans. The transmission of these lengthy and closely guarded documents elevated the security risk, and Clayton was put on ice soon afterwards.[83]

There were other informants who came to light in the Venona documents, and there was a good deal of inconsequential information. For example, the legation passed on the comments of John Crawford (a senior public servant who would rise to eminence after the war) on Ben Chifley when he succeeded Curtin as prime minister in 1945, which Clayton had overheard in the bar of a hotel in Canberra. There is no doubt that Clayton created a network of sources, but the diagram given in the principal book on the subject fails to distinguish what it calls his 'willing agents of the Soviet Union' from the '"in-the-dark" or unwitting informants'.[84] It shows Ric Throssell, who was not an informant, and his mother, who was but hardly a compliant one since she defied Clayton over the posting of her son. Prichard and other friends of the Soviet Union often gathered socially, and Nosov was in their company more often than Clayton. Similarly, Nosov was a friend of Dalziel, and Evatt encouraged him to drop in at Martin Place (where he met Bernie), but so did other foreign nationals. Evatt was notoriously careless with documents. His style was open diplomacy and the cultivation of good will.

⋆

There was another source that Makarov wanted to tap, a textile merchant in Sydney named Mark Younger who had migrated from Poland in 1926 and was active in a local Committee of Polish Democrats. Since Younger was an habitué of the Russian Social Club in George Street and ran a press agency on behalf of the provisional government the Soviet Union intended to install in Warsaw, he was a person of interest to security and Moscow ordered he not be used.[85] The Committee of Polish Democrats was only one of a number of national associations supporting the war against fascism and the liberation of their countries. Italia Libera, the Greek Democritus League, the Yugoslav Immigrants Association, the Free Albania Association, Free Austria League and other similar organisations participated in war rallies and marched in national dress on May Day. Some were also at loggerheads with the consuls representing governments in exile that did not share their politics, and the contest for legitimacy increased as the struggle for control of their homelands intensified. The party supported its European counterparts in that struggle and encouraged the efforts of their supporters in Australia.

The largest group of immigrant communists were Jewish. They also had a disproportionate presence in the international communist movement, though their contribution to the Australian party has been understated. Bill Rubinstein, the author of the most substantial history of Jews in Australia, contends that the diasporic community here lacked the engagement shown elsewhere and that Australia's Jewish left was always weak. But the community was closely engaged in left-wing politics in the 1940s. Philip Mendes, who has written most extensively on the politics of Australian Jewry, suggests there were never more than a few hundred Jews in the CPA. That is a pronounced underestimate of their numbers.[86]

There were Jewish communists from the outset, including the Aarons family, though Laurie and Eric Aarons, like their father Sam, did not maintain Jewish practices or consider themselves Jewish. That was not the case with those who arrived in Australia as refugees between the wars, for whom the Holocaust would make their Jewishness paramount. Some of the Yiddish-speaking newcomers from Eastern Europe were attracted to the Gezerd, an organisation that supported the creation of Jewish homelands, and the Gezerd in Melbourne had a cultural centre, the Kadimah, in which communists were active. They supported Jewish homelands, including one proposed for the Kimberley region of Western Australia, but were less enthusiastic about a Jewish state in Palestine unless the national rights of Arabs were recognised.[87]

Jewish support for the party increased after the Soviet Union entered the war. Communists had always stressed the link between fascism and anti-Semitism, and now they continually publicised the Nazi regime's murderous hatred of Jews. In 1942 the CPA initiated a Jewish Council to Combat Fascism and Anti-Semitism (based on the one that Stalin expediently created in the USSR after the German invasion), which attracted substantial support: it was recognised as the public relations arm of the Jewish Board of Deputies in Victoria, and the NSW board sponsored the republication of Len Fox's 1939 work *Australia and the Jews*.[88] At this stage communists sought the broadest possible alliance to assist refugees, combat anti-Semitism and mobilise support for the war—with considerable success, so that Jewish donors contributed most of the funds to establish Australia–Soviet House in Melbourne. Yet there were already strains. In 1942 Stalin executed two leaders of the Bund, the Jewish socialist party in Poland, and the Australian party dutifully published a justification of 'why the Soviet Union shot these two traitors'.[89] The Zionist wing of Australia's Jewish community became increasingly concerned with communist influence. Bundists were vehemently opposed to Zionism, but after 1945 the two would make common cause against the council.

The war also brought foreign nationals to Australia as temporary residents. Seamen working on Chinese ships stranded here by the Pacific War formed a Chinese Seamen's Union in 1942, and with the help of the Australian union gained four-fifths of the Australian wage. Their leaders linked up with members of the local Chinese community, and party branches were formed in Melbourne and Sydney.[90] When the Dutch were driven out of the Netherlands East Indies by Japan, they brought several thousand Indonesian officials, public servants and seamen, a number of whom were imprisoned for striking against inferior wages and working conditions. The Seamen's Union helped secure their release and assisted the formation of an Indonesian Seamen's Union. Five hundred political prisoners interned in Dutch New Guinea came later. They were held as prisoners of war in Cowra and included members of the Partai Komunis Indonesia (PKI), who soon established contact with Australian communists. The party was already calling for an end to colonial rule in the region, including Papua New Guinea.[91]

With support for national liberation went unrelenting hostility to all forms of racial prejudice. In early 1942 a jumpy government sought to strengthen resolve through a publicity campaign inciting hatred of Japan; the material portrayed the enemy as 'loathsome creeping creatures' of a 'bespectacled, ape-like race'. The party deplored such chauvinism. Just as it condemned disparaging references to the Germans and Italians, it rejected all talk of the 'Yellow Peril': 'we do not fight the Japanese because their skins are yellow' but because of their fascist aggression. 'The Japanese is not by nature a bully, a cheat or a sadist, any more than the German is; both have been warped by their rulers.' Similarly, it objected to the prejudice against African-Americans serving in the US Army and the segregation measures that kept them from mixing freely with Australians.[92]

The party had a strong record of opposition to racism, even if some of its anti-Japanese material lapsed into indiscriminate hostility—notably Rupert Lockwood's pamphlet *Japan's Heart of Wood*, which endorsed the incendiary bombing of Japanese cities.[93] As the government began planning its post-war immigration program, communists called for abandonment of the White Australia policy. The labour movement had traditionally resisted mass migration as a device for driving down wages, and for that reason the party wanted entry numbers regulated to ensure full employment. But it rejected selection on the basis of race. White Australia was criticised as a policy based on racial, not economic, considerations, and 'an outrageous insult' to the people of China, India and Indonesia whose friendship Australia needed. Accordingly, communists called for a program of immigration with quotas specifying the number to be taken from each country on a non-discriminatory basis.[94]

As was often the case, Thornton's advocacy generated the greatest controversy. There was an outcry from anti-communists in the Labor Party after he gave a forthright address to the annual conference of the FIA in June 1945, arguing that the White Australia policy isolated Australia from the countries of the region. Jack Beasley, a senior federal minister, led the denunciation with his claim that communists planned to break down living standards and destroy 'the Australian way of life' by introducing 'cells of non-Australians'. That Thornton represented Australian unions at the world conference in London only added to the indignation of the leaders of the Australian Workers' Union, Jack Lang and Movement publicists. The threat of an alien influx became one more argument for driving communists out of the labour movement.[95]

These and other controversies testify to a growing resistance to communism in Australia in the closing years of the war. It was brought about partly because of the party's success: as its influence increased, so too did the temptation to overreach. It was not so much communist policy that stimulated the antagonism, for the newly renamed ACP presented itself as distinctly unrevolutionary in its commitment to the war against fascism, its call for national unity in the tasks of post-war reconstruction and its eagerness to affiliate with the Labor Party. It was more the way it pursued these objectives by vilifying its opponents and repeatedly seeking to impose control over the organisations in which it worked.

There was also a growing suspicion of Soviet intentions. Stalin's abandonment of the Comintern and the Tehran conference at the end of 1943 affirmed amity between the great powers. Subsequent international conferences at Bretton Woods and Dumbarton Oaks in the United States created a framework for post-war cooperation, but the mood had changed when the Big Three next met, at Yalta in February 1945. Recognising the strong position of the Red Army, Churchill and an ailing Roosevelt made territorial concessions to the Soviet Union and agreed to its hegemony in Eastern Europe. But the British had already intervened to put down communists in Greece, and by the time the three leaders next met, at Potsdam in July 1945 with Truman in place of Roosevelt, any good will had vanished.

Jim Maloney, the second head of the Australian legation in the Soviet Union, took up the post at the end of 1943 proclaiming his 'friendly feelings' for Australia's ally. He returned briefly in July 1945, and Evatt had to deny reports of diplomatic disharmony. Among the material that Makarov obtained from Clayton and sent to Moscow by diplomatic bag in the following month was a photographic copy of Maloney's scathing report on conditions in the Soviet Union. At least publicly, Maloney would neither confirm nor deny rumours of his criticism until he completed his tour of duty at the beginning of 1946. He broke his silence at a function of the Empire Parliamentary Association to welcome him home. There was no democracy in Russia, he said; it was a dictatorship even more severe than had existed in Hitler's Germany.[96]

5

The Offensive, 1945–49

Expectations were high as the Australian Communist Party opened its Fourteenth Congress on the evening of 9 August 1945. The May Day celebrations earlier that year coincided with the German surrender, and John Curtin had issued a message from his sickbed in the Canberra Lodge praising the international labour movement for 'leading the masses towards emancipation'. Roosevelt, the American president, did not live long enough to witness the final victory in Europe and the party mourned him as 'a noble friend'. Curtin in turn was praised on his death in July as the country's greatest prime minister, a man of humble origins who had 'sacrificed his life in the stress and strain of leading his people to victory over fascism'.[1]

The party combined the congress with commemoration of its 25th anniversary. John Oldham created an exhibition of Australian labour history to mark the occasion, drawing on skills he acquired in designing the Australian pavilion at the New York Trade Fair of 1939. A large team of writers, graphic designers, carpenters and technicians installed the display in Marx House, where it was opened by the president of the NSW Labor Council, then taken to South Melbourne Town Hall and afterwards to other cities. Records, artefacts and memorabilia from Sydney's Mitchell Library, government departments and union collections were on display. Party artists provided paintings and (on the urging of Bernard Smith) the party purchased six of them that traced a sequence of landmarks in Australia's radical tradition: Ray Wenban's *The Tolpuddle Martyrs*, Herb McClintock's *The Oath at Eureka*, James Cant's *The Bread*

Line, Rod Shaw's *Unemployed Shack*, Harry Macdonald's *King's Cross Riot* and finally Noel Counihan's *Head of a Liberal*.[2]

The party had come into being in October 1920 when 26 men and women gathered in a shabby building in nearby Liverpool Street. This congress filled Sydney's Town Hall and, by what J.B. Miles called a 'joyful and important accident', it spanned the very last days of the War in the Pacific. Two days before the congress began, a nuclear bomb was detonated over the city of Hiroshima, and news that the Soviet Union had declared war on Japan reached Australia shortly before the delegates assembled.

Japan surrendered two days after the congress concluded and, as on VE Day, revellers gathered that evening on George Street in front of Marx House. Leading members celebrated with a supply of pure alcohol brought by some young scientists from the University of Sydney and mixed with lemon squash—Laurie Aarons recalled that one of them was so elated he began to eat his glass beaker. Tea was the beverage of delegates during the congress, but such was the euphoria that similar acts of bravado punctuated the proceedings.[3]

Like the Thirteenth Congress of 1943, this one put the party on display. There were just 92 delegates, but 3000 members and friends joined them at the Town Hall for the public sessions. As was customary, the congress elected honorary members to a presiding committee whose portraits looked down on proceedings: Stalin, Molotov and Dimitrov, the new heroes Mao Tse-Tung[4] and Marshal Tito, along with a brace of leaders of other communist parties. Miles, Sharkey and Dixon spoke first, at considerable length, followed by other delegates who were allocated time commensurate with their importance; all were spruced up for the occasion, the men in lounge suits, the women in skirts and jackets. Miles introduced the only resolution—'Jobs, Freedom, Progress'—while other members of the political committee presented reports on different aspects of the party's work.

The starting point was that the defeat of fascism opened the prospect of a lasting peace. The Soviet Union had emerged triumphant, new democracies were installed in Eastern Europe, movements of national liberation were on the march in Asia, and communist parties were growing all round the world. The opportunity thus arose for the working class to consolidate its advance and for the party to unite the people in securing 'a strong, democratic and independent Australia'. This involved 'the provision of jobs, the raising of living standards, rehabilitation of servicemen and women, better education, and a fair deal for farmers, professional workers, small businessmen and others' along the lines laid down in the Labor government's plans for post-war reconstruction.[5]

The chief threat arose, as always, from the capitalists. Big business in Australia, as in Britain and the United States, had been compelled to play its part in the war against fascism, but with the coming of victory it was once more revealing its reactionary character—hence the formation of a new and revitalised political arm, the Liberal Party. In opposing Chifley's program of post-war reconstruction, it constantly raised the 'red bogey' with the aim of dividing the labour movement and winning over large sections of the farmers and middle class. Assisted by anti-communist elements in the labour movement itself, it was producing what Miles called 'weaknesses in Labor's policy' that included a 'tendency to capitulate to the pressure of reaction instead of vigorously combatting it'. The Communist Party must therefore redouble its efforts for affiliation with the Labor Party in order to shore up the united front.[6]

It was common for speakers who followed a party leader to begin by expressing full agreement with his masterly analysis and then proceed to agree in their own way. Hence Jack Blake's speech made clear that he rejected the federal government's White Paper on Full Employment, a keystone of its economic policy, since it propagated the illusion that capitalism could eliminate crises and depressions, and he took this as indicative of the 'class collaborationist views of the Labor Party leadership'. The struggle for working-class unity, Blake asserted, required constant exposure of such errors, along with a unity in action 'led and conducted in such a way that the inevitable conclusion . . . will be that socialism is the only final solution'.[7] Similarly, Richard Dixon argued that 'its very nature as a bourgeois Labor Party' made the ALP 'incapable of meeting and solving the problems of peace in a progressive and democratic way', and he too anticipated the onset of intense class struggle.[8]

Blake's criticism of the white paper signalled differences with the Sydney leadership that would become more pronounced, but it would be going too far to suggest that there was serious disagreement within the political committee. It was wrestling with the problem of adjusting the party's policy towards the ALP to the new circumstances, for if the Labor Party had resisted a united front for the war effort, it was hardly likely to entertain any closer relationship now that emergency had passed. Even so, the Chifley ministry had an unprecedented opportunity to implement measures that would advance the interests of wage-earners. Accordingly, the party threw its weight behind the post-war reconstruction program (full employment, social welfare, public housing, a national system of health care, rural rehabilitation) and urged the federal government to go further with its banking controls and limited plans for nationalisation of industry. To this end, the draft resolution for the congress stipulated that 'production had to be maintained, strikes avoided and disruption of national unity opposed'.[9]

So too Miles was at pains in his opening speech to play down any call for socialism. Such was the enthusiasm at this, the peak of the party's membership and influence, that delegates talked freely of its imminent achievement. When Bernie Taft, who was attending his first congress, demurred from another functionary's prediction of a socialist Australia within five years, he was derided as a terrible pessimist. 'We are not putting forward Socialism as an immediate slogan,' Miles insisted, for to do so would be 'to get ahead of the masses'. Not one delegate uttered the word revolution.[10]

But if this was reformism, it was reformism without illusions. Earlier that year, in welcoming the government's plans to nationalise the air transport industry, Lance Sharkey and Ernie Campbell felt compelled to point out that nationalisation differed from socialisation: the one was a form of state capitalism, the other an entirely different system based on use rather than profit. As Blake put it at the congress, the years following the war held out no 'idyllic prospect' such as Labor promoted 'of workers, farmers, middle class people and capitalism sharing the benefits of a planned and regulated capitalist economy'. On the contrary, the party predicted sharper class conflict here and elsewhere. It was in this connection that

Miles acknowledged the Australian party's good fortune to have avoided entanglement in Earl Browder's repudiation of the class struggle.[11]

That was a close-run thing, with Browder pressing his position on the Australian party as late as March 1945 and Thornton having recently canvassed it in London. The Australians would have heaved a sigh of relief at the end of May when they received a copy of the statement that cast Browder into the wilderness. Written by the leading French communist Jacques Duclos and published in that party's *Cahiers du communisme* in April 1945, its use of documents that were unavailable in France made clear it originated in Moscow.[12] The article branded Browder as a revisionist who had changed the Teheran agreement from a diplomatic document into a political program, and liquidated the workers' party in order to appease monopoly capitalists. His American comrades duly condemned Browder and re-established their party. Happily, Duclos praised the ACP for rejecting Browder's errors, and the political committee instructed all members to root out any lingering traces of his pernicious influence. Congress delegates greeted the inclusion on their presiding committee of Browder's successor, William Z. Foster, with particular enthusiasm.[13]

The spectre of Browderism nevertheless hung over the proceedings. The party was committed to securing the re-election of the Labor government, and it had determined to refrain from advancing immediate demands for socialism. For that very reason the leaders found it necessary to criticise sections of the party for revisionist tendencies: the Marx School was neglecting Marxist–Leninist theory; the Eureka Youth League was downplaying socialism for sport, recreation and entertainment; and some members wanted to drop articles expounding policy from the party's papers and confine them to 'tabloid news reporting'.[14]

In the light of the news from America, the political committee itself drew back from organisational changes prepared for the congress. It had intended to transfer members from industrial branches to locality-based ones in which they could be drawn into greater political activity, but that bore an unfortunate resemblance to Browder's abolition of factory cells. Miles now withdrew the proposal. The party would retain its two basic organisations, factory and local. The factory branches were to be confined to large workplaces, the local branches were to be consolidated (they should have at least 50 members and their own meeting place), and they must engage in mass work and 'not be mere clubs and educational centres'.[15]

The emphasis on the locality was indicative of the number of communists recruited during the war from outside the working class. Some of the biggest and most active branches, such as Camberwell in Melbourne, Mosman on the lower north shore of Sydney and Claremont-Nedlands in Perth, had substantial numbers of salaried and professional men and women. Moreover, the party hoped to go beyond industrial campaigns. Many of the breakthroughs made during the war came from taking up community concerns, and the provision of housing, services, health care and family welfare took priority in post-war reconstruction. In 1944 all local branches were instructed to prepare a comprehensive plan for improving their locality—and most did so, drawing on the reports and proposals of the Department of Post-War Reconstruction to create detailed blueprints for a revitalised neighbourhood. These plans, moreover, were to assist the campaign for a united front. Since the Labor Party blocked all formal overtures, unity was now to be pursued by going directly to the people. Miles explained at the congress that local branches would 'take up the problems of the people, develop unity in mass work for local demands'. Here was a new strategy for a united front from below.[16]

★

The scope of such community initiatives can be seen in three particular localities. The first is the resort town of Katoomba in the Blue Mountains, where branches of the Labor and Communist parties cooperated during the war in schemes of civic improvement. A children's library was established in 1942, followed by a day nursery and play centre, free milk for the local school and from 1945 an Oslo lunch canteen. Eric Dark, the local doctor, was involved, along with several teachers at the school, the pharmacist, an accountant and some retailers, but the driving force was Bruce Milliss, an astute businessman who had a large mercer's shop in Katoomba and also ran a guesthouse.

Milliss convened a committee to deal with the influx of evacuees from Sydney in 1942 (and turned his guesthouse over to them); he organised the air-raid shelters, conducted the War Loans appeals, and recruited volunteers to assist the depleted agricultural workforce. His wife Edith headed the mothers' club of the infant school, he the parents and citizens association of the primary school. An inveterate organiser, he held office in the state council of parents and citizens, and led the formation of a NSW association to combat tuberculosis.[17]

Milliss was a leading member of the ALP in Katoomba, and as vice-president of the federal electoral assembly he ran election campaigns in the Blue Mountains for the local member, Ben Chifley. From 1937 he was also a communist, entrusted with a large sum of money when the CPA was declared illegal in 1940, and one of the purchasers of its Newsletter Printery in 1943. Though undeclared, his party membership was hardly a secret following the 1943 federal election, when he turned the shop that had been used as campaign headquarters into a bookshop and lending library that distributed *Tribune* and other communist publications. This local united front came to grief at the end of 1944 after a dissident Labor councillor accused the team of ACP and ALP candidates contesting the municipal elections of 'white-anting' Katoomba. All five 'Progressives' were defeated, albeit by narrow margins, and soon the state executive of the ALP required Milliss to answer allegations he was a communist.[18]

While steadfastly denying belonging to the Communist Party, Milliss championed the united front at state ALP conferences and spoke out against Father Paddy Ryan, who came up to Katoomba early in 1946 to denounce 'the treacherous anti-Christian, anti-democratic, anti-British, anti-Australian, foreign-controlled conspiracy that threatens to destroy our country'. Milliss repeatedly criticised the Labor government's failures at meetings of the Macquarie ALP district assembly, but went too far at the end of the year when he accused the prime minister of acting as 'an apologist for the capitalist system'. Although there is no indication that Chifley took umbrage, the ALP expelled Milliss for his 'personal and repeated attacks', and in the following year he announced he was joining the Communist Party. But he was a diminished figure in Katoomba, pushed out of a number of the civic organisations he had established, his business ostracised, the family vilified. They sold up and left in 1951.[19]

The Darks suffered a similar fate. Eric, a socialist doctor, and Eleanor, a well-known writer, were among Katoomba's most celebrated residents. Early in 1946, Bert Evatt nominated Eric Dark to replace James Maloney as Australia's minister to the Soviet Union—after first canvassing his name with Ernie Thornton, according to information Wally Clayton passed to the Soviet legation. It was hardly surprising that the Cabinet overruled Evatt, since Dark was already in trouble with the ALP for his outspoken criticism of the government's failings. He was not a member of the Communist Party, he declared, but had known many communists and they were among the finest people he knew, morally or spiritually, a theme he developed in a book later that year, *Who Are the Reds*. As for the Labor right, 'compared with them Judas was a gentlemen'.[20]

Dark was called before the NSW Labor executive to explain that slur but escaped expulsion. Instead, the executive revoked the charter of its Katoomba branch in March 1947, allowing the Movement to capture the positions of president and secretary in a reconstituted branch.[21] This came after Joe Abbott, a grazier and noted red-baiter, used parliamentary privilege (and, in all likelihood, a dossier provided to him, since his own electorate was in distant New England) to name the Darks, the Millisses and seventeen other residents of Katoomba as dangerous communists. He likened Dr Dark, who headed his list, to Dr Alan Nunn May, the British physicist recently convicted of espionage. By this time Dark was receiving threatening letters, his medical practice melting away, and in 1948 he and Eleanor closed up their house to embark on an extended holiday—it is now a writers' centre. The dwindling number of declared communists in Katoomba persisted. As one put it, they were hardened to withstand such attacks; it was well-meaning activists such as the Darks, who believed in justice, honesty and fairness, who were most vulnerable.[22]

Communists worked in the Blue Mountains with men and women of good will in practical schemes of civic progress. In tropical Queensland they fought for the necessities of everyday life. It was there, in the far north, that the Australians and Americans concentrated their forces for the Pacific War in numbers that caused acute shortages of accommodation, food, fuel, transport and other basic requirements of civilian life. Fred Paterson won election to the Townsville city council in 1939 on the basis of an extensive legal practice, and led it in developing a range of municipal services during the war: an ice works (the armed forces exhausted available supplies), a firewood depot, a fruit and vegetable market, a ladies' restroom with a free 'baby-stroller' service for mothers shopping in the city, and a legal aid department. The party benefited from the neglect of North Queensland by an indolent Labor Party that dominated state politics, brooked no dissent and expelled the ALP branch in Townsville's working-class suburb of Hermit Park for refusing to sever links with the Russian Medical Aid and Comforts Committee. The 'Hermit Park ALP' ran a joint ticket with communists in the 1943 municipal elections and consolidated its majority.[23]

Paterson first contested the state seat of Bowen in 1935 and built his support to 47 per cent of voters by 1941. Bowen took in only a small part of Townsville, and Doug Olive had contested its principal electorate of Mundingburra in 1941, but the party stood aside in 1944 to allow Tom Aikens, leader of the Hermit Park ALP, a clear run (as Queensland used a first-past-the-post voting system at this time). Bowen, on the other hand, was a sprawling electorate that extended down the coast from Tully to Bowen, and inland to Charters Towers and Collinsville. There were militant branches of the Australian Railways Union and Waterside Workers' Federation in the port towns that, together with the region's meatworks, sawmills, sugar mills and coalmines, supported a large number of party branches. Paterson won a three-cornered contest with 44.4 per cent of the vote.[24]

The new member of the Queensland parliament was farewelled at a widely attended concert in Townsville, and a public appeal raised funds to build a Paterson playground and library in his honour. He enjoyed substantial personal popularity as a former Rhodes scholar and champion of the underprivileged, though support for the party was not restricted to Bowen: the AIF veteran Les Sullivan attracted 43 per cent of the vote in nearby Herbert in the same 1944 election, and two other communist candidates, in Kennedy and Tablelands, won 26 and 23 per cent. Such was 'the dissatisfaction with the dictatorial Australian Labor Party' in North

Queensland at this time, a local newspaper remarked, that it seemed to be taking the place of the 'Tory party', leaving communists to represent 'the genuine toiler'. But their support fell away sharply in the 1947 election, whereas Paterson retained his seat.[25]

The party made much of its first member of parliament, who spoke at the opening session of the Fourteenth Congress and whose parliamentary speeches were publicised nationally. He proved a remarkably diligent local member, returning regularly from Brisbane to tour the electorate and report on his work. Yet he found great difficulty in catching the speaker's eye, and the Labor government punished the voters of Bowen with a conspicuous lack of response to his representation of their needs.[26] In his absence, furthermore, the progressive local government alliance withered. Although the Hermit Park ALP retained control of the Townsville City Council in 1946, both communist councillors lost their positions. The party blamed local organisers for relying on the prestige of its union officers and municipal representatives and failing to bring forward 'the face of the party'.[27]

By 1949 the ALP had won back Townsville and other North Queensland towns. Meanwhile the Industrial Groups made gains in the trades and labour councils of Townsville and Bowen after Paddy Ryan came up from Sydney to warn of the Red Menace. Leaving nothing to chance, the government broke up the electorate of Bowen, so that Paterson had to contest the new and less favourable one of Whitsunday in 1950. It was won by the Country Party, with Paterson attracting just 12.7 per cent of the poll.[28]

The high tide of communist success in local government came in 1944. Many branches had prepared their plans for civic improvement, and the party issued a manual on how to conduct a municipal campaign. It ran 70 candidates in the NSW municipal and shire elections in that year, with sixteen successful. The highlight was the shire of Kearsley on the northern coalfield, where communists won five of the eight positions. Kearsley, which took in Abermain, Branxton, Kurri Kurri, Rothbury and Weston (but not Cessnock, which had its own municipal council), thus became the country's first communist-led local government authority. Its 'New Deal' called for extensive renovation of the severely deprived mining townships and envisaged tree-lined streets, parks and playgrounds, and new housing equipped with electric stoves and washing machines.[29]

Local government in Australia was constrained in both its powers and revenue. The Kearsley Council was determined to go further, to provide 'leadership of the people's needs' and speak on their behalf on all manner of progressive causes—at its first meeting the new council issued a declaration condemning British intervention in liberated Greece. Yet despite repeated efforts to link up with other councils and constant appeals for funds from the state and federal government, Kearsley struggled to realise its program. The council planted trees, created parks and play centres, improved the garbage collection and purchased a bulldozer to regrade the unsealed roads, but failed to renegotiate the bus service with the private operator or to municipalise the electricity supply. It took until 1947 for the first baby health centre and swimming pool to be completed. As in Queensland, the communists encountered growing hostility from the ALP and were disadvantaged by the introduction of compulsory voting for the 1947 local government elections. Labor regained control of Kearsley and all five communist candidates were defeated.[30]

At the end of the war the party looked to activity of this kind as the 'spearhead' of its advance, and convened regular conferences on local government. While early results were encouraging, it soon became apparent they could not be sustained. An alternative was to form citizens' committees to agitate on grievances such as the shortage of housing, evasion of price controls, black marketeering and beer rackets. These committees were constructed as united fronts, wherever possible including the local branches of the ALP and ex-service organisations, but usually succumbed to allegations of communist control.[31]

Again at a local level, communists also encouraged squatting in empty houses. A notable example was the occupation in early 1946 of the twenty-room Maramanah mansion in Kings Cross, which the city council had bought and planned to demolish. This squat was organised communally, the inhabitants contributing a weekly 'rent' to meet expenses and sharing in the household tasks. It lasted some years, whereas others were short-lived.[32] The shortage of housing was a burning issue after the war as ex-servicemen were reunited with their wives and children, and the party encouraged them to help themselves to residences in empty military buildings and munitions factories. In instances where the government itself established such accommodation, such as Camp Pell in Melbourne's Royal Park—there were 40,000 on the Victorian Housing Commission's waiting list—communists agitated for improvement of the squalid living conditions and established a medical service. Direct action of this kind was accompanied by public protest, such as the group of activists led by Laurie Aarons, who interrupted proceedings of the South Australian parliament in 1946 and threw leaflets publicising the housing shortage from the gallery.[33]

A pamphlet produced in Victoria contrasted the inner suburb of Richmond, where 'the factories seem to be crushing out the little homes' left in disrepair by absentee landlords, with the mansions of Toorak (illustrated by a photo of Keith Murdoch's residence). This was 'the story of how Richmond has built Toorak and how Toorak has robbed and ruined Richmond', the 'fat dividends' earned from noxious industries enriching their owners on the other side of the Yarra. In similar vein, Ralph Gibson described the transformation of Richmond in a future Socialist Melbourne, the derelict terraces replaced by a modern housing estate, the noisome abattoirs closed down and a community centre with library, theatre, meeting hall and swimming pool occupying the site of the Pelaco shirt factory. Toorak's mansions had been turned into rest homes and municipal government was thrown open to representatives of the people.[34]

Gibson's pamphlet, first published in 1937, was community planning on a grand scale and utopian register. By the time a revised and enlarged edition appeared in 1951, communists had been driven out of local government and many councils would no longer allow them to use the town hall for their meetings. They had lost their positions in various civic bodies, some of which went further and refused membership to communists. With the very legality of the Australian Communist Party again under threat, any prospect that it could mobilise communities had passed. The party's principal site of activity, the organisations in which it was able to exercise effective leadership, had shrunk back to its industrial base.

★

There was no intention at the end of the war of launching an industrial offensive. On the contrary, delegates were warned at the Fourteenth Congress of the need for caution. As Edgar Ross of the Miners' Federation put it, the party's avoidance of strikes during the war had resulted in a widespread feeling among workers that it had been 'sitting on them'; they were now 'raring to go', and the danger was that they would do so in a 'disruptive and premature manner'. At the same time, the end of hostilities brought a modification of party policy, from 'production for victory' to 'production for improved living standards'. On the motion of communist delegates, the 1945 ACTU Congress resolved to seek an immediate wage increase and reduction of working hours.[35]

The labour movement at large was convinced these claims were fully justified. During the war, workers had put up with wage controls, long shifts, tax increases, rationing of food and clothing, and the unavailability of many consumer goods. Memories of the Depression strengthened their determination to finally hold employers to account for past injustices, and full employment gave them the opportunity to do so. Higher wages and a 40-hour week were to be a down payment on their entitlement.

This was precisely what Ben Chifley, the new prime minister, was determined to prevent. His government was wrestling with the tasks of demobilisation, retraining and re-establishment, converting war industries to civil production, restoring run-down plant and equipment, and making good the acute shortage of housing. At its height the war had absorbed two-fifths of the country's output, and the changes needed to redirect this enormous military effort back into civil production were daunting. Everything was in short supply—labour, materials, power, equipment, imported goods and foreign exchange—and with the winding back of wartime controls the government exercised through its defence power, the danger of inflation was acute. Hence Chifley, who remained treasurer after he succeeded Curtin as prime minister, would countenance no wage breakout, and employed all of his authority, charm and guile to resist the unions' claims.[36]

He managed to do so for several years, though at considerable cost. The second half of the 1940s was marked by industrial turmoil. In lost working days the strikes that occurred between 1945 and 1950 were matched only by those conducted between 1917 and 1920 and then at the onset of the Depression—this was in fact the last episode of such sustained militancy in the country's history. Lost production is more difficult to measure, but output of energy and basic materials fell sharply from their peak war levels. The principal disputes lasted for months and involved the mining, gas, electrical and transport workforces, disrupting other industries and affecting large numbers of consumers and commuters. Communist union leaders were prominent throughout, and it suited the other parties—employers, industrial tribunals and hostile unionists—to accuse them of plunging the country into chaos. The party in turn was happy to claim the credit, even for strikes it did not initiate, as proof of its influence. The role of a vanguard party, after all, is to lead rather than follow.

The historian Tom Sheridan has challenged the view, widely held then and since, that communists caused the conflict. In a detailed examination of industrial relations in the Chifley years, he draws attention to the legitimate grievances of the workforce, the determination of employers to take back control as restrictions on their employment practices ended, the cumbrous conservatism of the arbitration tribunals, and the spoiling operations of the ACTU and state labour councils. Above all, he relates Chifley's masterful manipulation of the system of industrial relations to keep the unions waiting until finally, in 1949, he resorted to draconian powers to crush the striking coalminers and punish the communist leaders of unions that supported them. Sheridan acknowledges the delusions of grandeur that overcame the Australian Communist Party in its industrial campaigns, the limits of its ability to control left-wing unions and the miscalculations that brought it to the ruinous miners' strike. Of necessity, he concentrates on the party's involvement in the major disputes; the emphasis here is on evaluating their effect on its fortunes.[37]

Communists did not instigate the rash of disputes that broke out at the end of the war. At least initially, they opposed a crippling strike in September 1945 at Sydney's Bunnerong Power Station, initiated by the shop stewards, and a prominent Victorian union leader travelled to Adelaide in November to persuade its tram workers to return after they had struck in defiance of their moderate officials. The point at issue here was the Commonwealth wage-pegging regulations that prevented industrial tribunals from granting better pay or shorter hours, and Chifley averted the paralysing consequences of these two stoppages by allowing them to be treated as special cases.[38]

That was not the case with a dispute that began in the steel industry in September 1945 after BHP dismissed a job delegate of the Federated Ironworkers' Association (FIA) from its Port Kembla plant and spread to its Newcastle operations in October with the retrenchment of union activists there. By November, 13,000 workers were idle and the decision of the Miners' Federation and the Seamen's Union to support them placed another 500,000 jobs at risk. The enlargement of the strike, together with the extension of the strikers' demands to include a 40-hour week and wage increases, brought allegations that communists were waging industrial war on the nation, as did the striking unions' rejection of efforts by the NSW Labor Council and ACTU to arrange a settlement. But BHP had brought on the strike by victimising unionists, and the stumbling block to any settlement was its refusal to negotiate with the FIA, which had been deregistered by the NSW Industrial Commission over a separate demarcation dispute. It took all of Chifley's finesse to secure reinstatement of the unionists and re-registration of the union, so that operations could resume at BHP in the new year.[39]

At least publicly, the party put a brave face on the outcome of the steel strike. It claimed that in the face of provocation by the country's largest and most powerful company, and despite the strikebreaking efforts of the Labor right, the workers held fast and returned 'in an organised and disciplined fashion with their morale improved'. At a meeting of the central committee, however, Sharkey acknowledged mistakes. The steelworkers had been drawn into a costly stoppage lasting three months. They were unable to win the 40-hour week or wage increases. With Christmas approaching, the miners showed signs of wavering and the hardship that resulted from the lack of coal was straining public support. And despite the party's intention that the steelworkers return together with the miners and seamen, the FIA remained out until mid-January, with Jack McPhillips (the acting national secretary in the absence of Thornton) 'inclined to be a bit left'. It was evident that the party needed to build greater support for its program of jobs, homes and improved living standards before pressing industrial demands through mass strikes. There should be no strikes whatsoever for the next 'six to twelve months'.[40]

Just three months later communists were embroiled in a similar fight against victimisation that resulted in an even longer stoppage. The Queensland branch of the Australasian Meat Industry Employees' Union (AMIEU) had served a log of claims on the meat companies, including a 40-hour week and improved wages; the employers refused to discuss it and instead sought to restore the power to hire and fire they had lost during wartime labour controls. A walkout from a bacon factory in Brisbane in early March 1946 following the dismissal of four union members became a statewide strike by the end of the month as other companies cancelled their union agreements. With many meat-works obtaining alternative labour, the AMIEU was forced to drop its log of claims, though that did not save it from deregistration by the State Industrial Commission for refusing to return to work without the reinstatement of pre-strike conditions. In desperation, the meatworkers called on other militant unions for support, including the coalminers, whose refusal to produce coal crippled local industry. After the premier declared a state of emergency and a stormy mass meeting of the meat-workers, the strike ended in July.[41]

The party had a strong presence in the AMIEU, as well as the Queensland Trades and Labor Council, whose disputes committee coordinated support for the strikers, and it was widely condemned for inflicting hardship on the community. In fact, the communist leadership was highly critical of the union for embarking on such an ill-considered and poorly prepared strike across the entire industry on an issue of the employers' choice.[42] Once the meatworkers were out on a limb, however, it felt compelled to call on other communist-led unions to support them—though the reluctance of some to do so was telling. Of particular concern was the mass meeting at the Brisbane stadium on 10 July, where two AMIEU organisers accused the disputes committee of seeking to establish a communist dictatorship. Bob Wells, the national president of the Miners' Federation, who had come up to lend support, was counted out. The party lost ground in the AMIEU and other unions as a result of the strike. A further consequence was the decision of the state executive of the Labor Party to form Industrial Groups in Queensland.[43]

The party drew several lessons from the steel and meat strikes. It needed to avoid defensive battles provoked by employers and concentrate on winning improvements. There were dangers in lengthy, general strikes that alienated farmers (such as Queensland livestock producers) and the urban middle class (deprived of essential services). A further concern was that public exasperation with the constant disruption might damage the prospects of the federal Labor government, which faced an imminent election. Communist union officials were chastised for their ill-directed militancy and instructed to consult more closely with the party's state and central committees.[44]

Attention then turned to Victoria, where transport and metalworkers took up the campaign on hours and pay. Early in 1946, Chifley had diverted the ACTU's demand for a wage increase and a 40-hour week to determination by the Arbitration Court. Since any review of the basic wage was likely to take into account the cost of reducing the length of the working week, the ACTU chose to begin with the 40-hours case, which commenced in April 1946 in the expectation of a decision within six to eight weeks. The hearings dragged out for eighteen months and held up any consideration of the basic wage.

The Victorian branches of the Australian Railways Union (ARU) and Australian Tramway and Motor Omnibus Employees' Association (ATMOEA), both resentful of long hours and unsatisfactory overtime rates, had meanwhile commenced an industrial campaign. Repeatedly rebuffed, they came together in October 1946 to hold Melbourne's first combined tram and rail stoppage. Although this occurred after the federal election returned Chifley to office, it threatened John Cain, the Labor premier, so Chifley came down to Melbourne to offer a concession. If the ACTU agreed to a simultaneous hearing of wages and hours, the Arbitration Court would declare acceptance in principle of a 40-hour week, then conduct a speedy hearing of an interim wage increase before resuming the hours case to determine when the shorter working week would begin.[45]

The party leaders saw the transport strike as a vindication of their instruction to concentrate on winning improvements. Chifley's intervention followed negotiations between John Cain and leading communists that were conducted discreetly (the premier in one suburb, the communists in another, with Ted Hill relaying messages between them); and even though the prime minister rejected allegations of instructing the Arbitration Court on hours and wages, he rang Hill to confirm he was doing so. The Melbourne press portrayed J.J. Brown, the forthright secretary of the ARU (and a fitness fanatic who set world skipping records in the gymnasium of the Victorian Railways Institute), as a villain second only to Ernie Thornton, but Brown increased his majority in the following union election. Another communist, Clarrie O'Shea, defeated a right-wing candidate in the subsequent ballot for secretary of the Tramways Union.[46]

This apparent victory proved nugatory, however, since the court offered just a tiny wage increase, continued to hold up the 40-hour week and refused to ratify the concessions won by the transport workers. Hence a new wave of overtime bans and stoppages broke out across the country, among which a lengthy strike in the Victorian metal trades proved decisive.[47] It strictly began as a lockout in November 1946, when a number of employers dismissed members of the Amalgamated Engineering Union (AEU) who had imposed overtime bans as part of a campaign for higher pay. The engineers stayed out after the employers reopened the gates in January 1947, and stepped up their campaign for improved margins in April by halting public transport and cutting supplies of gas and electricity. Cain, close to despair, again secured Chifley's intervention, so that the metalworkers obtained a substantial increase of their margins. Subsequently the federal government also had to yield on the 40-hour week, its hand forced by the Labor governments of New South Wales and Queensland, which introduced it for workers on state awards by legislation, and the threat of the ACTU Congress to implement it unilaterally for workers on federal awards.[48]

The skilled tradesmen of the AEU traditionally held aloof from campaigning with other unions, relying on their considerable bargaining power to maintain higher rates of pay. This time they cooperated with the

Sheet Metal Workers, the FIA and other unions through a Metal Trades Federation, and made common cause in their campaign with the ARU and Federated Engine Drivers' and Firemen's Association (FEDFA). The militancy was commonly attributed to the influence of Ted Rowe, who in 1943 became the first communist to hold national office in the AEU. But 'Red Ted' worked closely with the head of the union, Joe Cranwell, who was steeped in the Engineers' traditions and a widely respected vice-president of the ACTU.

The allegation that communists directed the metal strike cannot be sustained, yet that was precisely how the party's leaders interpreted it. At a meeting of the central committee in May 1947, Sharkey discerned a mounting discontent with Chifley's wage pegging, the fetters imposed by arbitration, and the treacherous role played by the junta that dominated Trades Hall Council and the Victorian ALP executive. The party's aim was to unmask and overcome these forces of resistance, though at this point it was not prepared to abandon the united front. As Sharkey put it, they needed to be 'very, very careful', for the campaign had to be conducted in such a way that did not endanger the federal or state Labor governments. Since the metal strike was paralysing the city of Melbourne and the public mood was volatile, he judged that the unions had to settle for the increased margins and not pursue their full claim for a £1 increase in the weekly wage. Besides, the court was about to deregister the AEU and the ACTU was threatening to disaffiliate it.[49]

This post-mortem, delivered a fortnight after the unions returned to work, gave no indication of how party leaders deliberating in Sydney had determined the decisions of the Victorian unionists. Also missing was any recognition of the cost to the unions of a stoppage that lasted five months. The FIA had exhausted its capacity to support members with strike pay and Ernie Thornton was urging a return to work. The AEU persisted, drawing on all of its substantial reserves, sustained by the leadership of Cranwell and fortified by the determination of members of all political hues to see it out. The fact that a large proportion of them found other jobs probably saved the union from insolvency. This was a novel feature of the post-war strikes because of the acute shortage of labour, and placed pressure on employers if they were not to lose their skilled hands, but it also thinned the picket lines. As Jack Blake pointed out, 'it does become a little trying after a while to conduct a strike without strikers'.[50]

Another strike tested this adage, that of the Aboriginal pastoral workers in the Pilbara region of north-west Australia. It began on May Day 1946 with demands for better pay, housing and food as well as the right to organise. The workers had begun to do that four years earlier at a meeting to which they invited a sympathetic white contractor, Don McLeod, who was radicalised by the unyielding obstruction he encountered in his subsequent campaign. On joining the party in 1944, McLeod made contact in Perth with Katharine Susannah Prichard, who put him in touch with the editor of the *Workers' Star*, Graham Alcorn. Small and wiry, with blazing blue eyes, a black beard and wild hair, McLeod made a striking appearance at a party school in 1945 and was manifestly no conventional recruit. The party expected him to build a branch, whereas he regarded work on behalf of the Aboriginal people as his mission—and to do that he needed the party's assistance.[51]

In 1945 his two principal collaborators began spreading word of the planned strike. Dooley Bin Bin, a Nyamil man from the Western Desert, covered the more remote pastoral stations on a bicycle; Clancy McKenna, his kinsman and a contractor, dealt with the 'settled areas'. Some pastoralists agreed to pay the higher rates but most refused, and on 1 May 1946 workers from about twenty stations stopped work. Within a week, McKenna and Dooley Bin Bin were gaoled for 'enticing Aborigines from service'. McLeod was convicted of the same offence in June and, with the secretary of the Committee for Defence of Native Rights who came up from Perth, found guilty in August of entering a native reserve without permission. By then the strikers had walked off the stations to establish two camps, one near Port Hedland and the other close to Marble Bar—the weekly train service between them took eight hours. With the state administrators backing the pastoralists and the maritime unions refusing to ship their wool, this long industrial campaign was inconclusive. As a consequence, the inhabitants turned to mining and other cooperative enterprises to support themselves. Their strike became a venture in autonomy.[52]

The party had been agitating on behalf of Aboriginal people since the late 1920s. Tom Wright of the Sheet Metal Working Industrial Union took the keenest interest and, as a member of the central committee, he formulated communist policy. This distinguished between those he called 'full-bloods' or 'natives', who were living in remote areas, and others suffering discrimination in places of European settlement, whom he called 'half-castes'. As historian Tim Rowse has explained, the terms were not used with pejorative intent but to distinguish levels of social organisation and political capacity. Those Aboriginal people living on their tribal lands were seen, in communist jargon, as a national minority whose future lay in maintaining their way of life with complete control of their territories and resources. Those who had lost that connection to land, on the other hand, were seen as an oppressed section of the working class who must have full citizenship rights.[53]

Communists frequently drew attention to the prejudice and discrimination that such 'detribalised' Aboriginal people suffered. In Western Australia, for example, they took up the cause of those who camped on the outskirts of Perth in unsanitary conditions, harassed by the police and denied access to education and health care.[54] The events in the Pilbara, however, seemed to involve self-organising tribes. That is how Tom Wright understood them when Don McLeod enlisted his support and confirmed, in answer to his question, that the pastoral workers were predominantly full-blood Aborigines. On the other hand, the fact that they were demanding better wages seemed to upset his typology. This point had been made two years earlier by another party member, Alec Jolly, who was one of several communist doctors to graduate from the University of Melbourne in the 1930s and worked during the war as medical officer in Broome. Jolly rejected the hard-and-fast distinction between 'tribalised' and 'detribalised' Aboriginal people, arguing that all of them were affected by European colonisation. Even in the Western Desert, he pointed out, they used metal spearheads and tobacco, and suffered from tuberculosis and venereal disease.

The war had drawn many Indigenous people in northern Australia into new forms of employment, their experience of better wages and greater freedom spurring demands for improvement when they returned to the pastoral industry.[55] 'We can no more revive their culture,' Jolly argued, 'than we can revive feudalism.' He developed this argument in partnership with Fred Rose, a Cambridge-educated anthropologist who also worked in Broome during the war for the Bureau of Meteorology. Wright restated his position in a new edition of *A New Deal for Aborigines* in 1944, and remained adamant that the struggle of 'Aborigines' was completely different from that of 'mixed-bloods'.[56] This remained party policy, though it is doubtful if most members bothered with the distinction. They supported the aspirations of remote Aboriginal and Torres Strait Islanders with the same feeling of solidarity that marked their relations with Aboriginal workmates.[57]

*

A similar commitment to fight exploitation and oppression wherever it occurred was apparent in the party's campaign for Indonesian independence. As the European powers returned to their Southeast Asian territories at the end of the war, they faced the daunting challenge of rebuilding colonial administrations, reviving shattered economies and above all restoring control over their subjects. The military disasters they suffered in 1941 and 1942 had dispelled the aura of Western supremacy, just as the Japanese occupation fractured the collaborative networks that sustained colonial rule. Britain was able to reimpose rule of Malaya, but not Burma.[58] France prevailed in Vietnam by armed force—for the time being. The Netherlands, which had been laid bare by German occupation and was suffering a domestic famine by 1945, encountered the greatest difficulty in the chain of islands that made up the Dutch East Indies.

Two days after the Japanese surrender, nationalists in Java declared an independent Republic of Indonesia. They did so in the vacuum of power created by Japan's sudden surrender, for it took six weeks before British forces of the South East Asia Command were able to land in the capital of Batavia with the intention of restoring order pending the Dutch return. Part of that return involved administrators, officials, armed forces and merchants stationed in Australia, along with the transfer of political prisoners back to internment in Dutch New Guinea, but the majority of Indonesian nationals had no intention of participating in restoration of the colonial regime. Acting in concert with communist union leaders, Indonesian seamen walked off merchant vessels and the Australian waterside workers refused to load them. Some got away and an attempt was made to man others with Indian crews, but they too came ashore. By the end of September 1945, dozens of Dutch vessels were tied up in the ports of Brisbane, Sydney and Melbourne.[59]

The party was at the forefront of this boycott. In Queensland, where the central committee of the Indonesian Independence Committee was based, Mick Healy, the secretary of the Brisbane Trades and Labor Council, and his wife Connie had taken language lessons from a former political prisoner and arranged for the striking seamen to bunk down on the dance floor of the Trades Hall. Similar accommodation was provided in the ARU's Unity Hall in Melbourne for seamen there. In Sydney the secretary of the Indonesian Seamen's Union worked closely with Eliot Elliot and Jim Healy, while C.H. Campbell (known variously as Clarrie and Steve), a businessman with Indian interests and party connections, assisted the seamen from that country. But most of the Indonesians were not communists and their cause had wide public support, not least because of the high-handed actions of Dutch military police stationed in Australia. Fifteen unions backed the boycott, as did the NSW Labor Council and the ACTU.[60]

The Australian government was reluctant to intervene. Although Chifley did not yet support Indonesian independence and in any case was bound by formal obligations to a war ally, he made clear his opposition to restoration of the old order. Hence he scuttled a Dutch plan to train troops here for operations in the East Indies, just as he refused demands from The Hague that the Indonesians in Australia be returned to ports under Dutch control. Instead he arranged passage to ports of their choice and withstood British pressure to offload those the Dutch wanted to reimprison in New Guinea; a handful did end up there but with safeguards. Similarly, while insisting that the union boycott should not apply to ships carrying medical and other essential supplies, Chifley drew attention to the consignments of weapons and other military equipment that wharfies discovered in the holds of such 'mercy ships'.[61]

The first contingent of Indonesians departed on the troopship *Esperance Bay* on Saturday 13 October 1945 after a farewell dance on the previous evening. Eliot Elliott told a large assembly on the Pyrmont wharf that 'We—Indonesians, British, French, Americans and Russians—fought this war for freedom', led three cheers for the Indonesian Republic and handed over a republican flag for presentation to President Sukarno, while those on board sang their new national anthem.[62] Recording this triumphant occasion was Joris Ivens, a Dutch film director who had been recruited to make a documentary on the restoration of colonial rule but instead threw in his lot with the nationalists. Using a borrowed camera and working with his American partner and Catherine Duncan, a New Theatre playwright, Ivens shot further incidents and re-enacted others to produce a short but dramatic documentary, *Indonesia Calling*.[63]

Those subsequent incidents included a mutiny by Indian seamen as their ship passed out through the Sydney Heads and then returned, followed by a march on the Dutch shipping office to demand their back pay; violent demonstrations when a British vessel, the *Stirling Castle*, brought Dutch troops to Sydney; and the desertion of ten British seamen from the *Moreton Bay*, which was to take them on to Java. The most serious confrontation was on a Woolloomooloo wharf in early November, when Dutch soldiers on board the *Stirling Castle* hurled bottles, tins and other missiles onto the crowd below. An appeal to the soldiers in their own language from a small launch by Jack Zwolsman, a veteran communist who had migrated from the Netherlands as a boy, only inflamed his compatriots, who turned the ship's fire hoses on the demonstrators.[64]

Disturbed by the party's widening of the campaign for Indonesian independence, the NSW Labor Council relaxed the ban on Dutch shipping and the ACTU lifted it when talks between Republican and Dutch leaders began in February 1946. Chifley still hoped for a negotiated settlement and, while fulfilling Australia's treaty responsibilities to transfer naval vessels and release military equipment, was determined that Australia not be used as a platform for the Dutch to crush the Republic. 'The old order in Indonesia,' he stated, 'will not go on.' In regular contact with Jim Healy, he arranged for the maritime unions to handle medicine, food and clothing while conniving in their refusal to load the military equipment. The prime minister's sympathies were made clear when the Commonwealth film censor banned the export of the film *Indonesia Calling*. After arranging for the Cabinet to see it, he overruled the censor.[65]

Australia welcomed the agreement between the two sides in November 1946 whereby the Dutch recognised the Republic's control of Java and Sumatra. Their termination of that agreement by a 'police action' in July 1947 that deployed more than 100,000 troops exhausted Chifley's patience, and Australia referred the conflict to the Security Council of the United Nations. It ordered negotiations, with each side to choose a representative on the committee that supervised them. The Dutch chose Belgium, the Indonesians chose Australia.

In response to the 'police action', the Australian unions also reimposed their ban on Dutch shipping and, as part of the protest campaign, students from the University of Sydney marched down Broadway and George Street on 25 July 1947 for a demonstration at Wynyard Park in front of the Dutch consul's office. The assembly was addressed by members of the Labour Club, and by Hal Alexander as an organiser of the Eureka Youth League, and Ted Roach, the assistant secretary of the Waterside Workers' Federation, who had returned from a union congress in Indonesia. But as a delegation approached the consulate, a squad of plainclothes police fell on the demonstrators. Even the *Sydney Morning Herald* expressed criticism of the police brutality. Fourteen students were arrested, two charged with assault and the others with offensive behaviour. The magistrate acquitted the first two defendants and, although finding the others guilty, recorded no conviction.[66]

★

The Sydney Labour Club and its counterparts in the country's five other universities provided fertile ground for the united front. As societies recognised by the university, they had access to the facilities that supported student activity, and since most universities insisted that such societies had to be autonomous, it was not possible for the Labor Party to exclude communists. All were affiliated to an Australian Student Labor Federation, set up in late 1940 on the urging of Margaret Paul, the wife of a lecturer in philosophy (and sister of a future archbishop of Canterbury), who had been active in a similar British body before the war.[67]

Melbourne's Labour Club, the oldest and largest, was a source of party recruits from its formation in the 1920s. Sydney's came later, in 1939, and then only because communist students formed it. It limped on through the early years of the war, whereas the one in Melbourne remained strong: there were seven or eight communists at Sydney, whereas the party branch at Melbourne had 40 in a club of more than 100 that was always more inclusive.[68] Alan Barcan, the assiduous historian of the Sydney club, has drawn attention to a striking difference between the two student bodies: the University of Sydney, with a much larger number of bursaries, scholarships and free places, was more socially inclusive than Melbourne, where private schools had a stranglehold on access to higher education—yet some of the most ardent communists came from the most prestigious private schools.

This difference narrowed during the war as the Commonwealth government introduced financial support for undergraduates in courses regarded as vital to the war effort, and all Australian universities were transformed from 1945 by an influx of ex-servicemen and women studying free of charge and with a living allowance under the Commonwealth Reconstruction Training Scheme (CRTS). Enrolments doubled, from 15,000 in 1945 to 30,000 two years later.[69] More mature than the school-leavers and often radicalised by their 'gap years' in uniform, these CRTS students provided the leadership and much of the membership of the Labour clubs—half of the Wynyard Park defendants wore their ex-service badge to court.

Nevertheless, the differences between communist activity in the two largest universities (they had two-thirds of all Australian enrolments at this time) persisted. The Melbourne club grew rapidly from 1945 with members drawn from the full spectrum of the left. Until the end of the decade it held leadership of the students' representative council and provided editors of the student newspaper and magazine. It organised lunchtime meetings for outside speakers in the university's largest lecture theatre, produced a regular newsletter, ran conferences in vacations, turned out for city demonstrations and marched in academic dress on

May Day. It also participated in the city's cultural and intellectual life, taking up the radical nationalist tradition as part of the aspiration for a new, socialist Australia.

There were faculty committees and study groups, including tutorials in university subjects, for Melbourne communists took their studies seriously. 'The first task of any Labour Club,' Ian Turner, AIF veteran, student activist and later historian, declared, 'should be to ensure that not only good doctors, engineers and architects, but also good socialists, go out from the University to the community.' Above all, there were parties, dances, concerts, revues and a camaraderie that transcended political loyalties: as Turner, Melbourne's most charismatic figure, put it: 'we worked and struggled together, certainly—but we also talked and studied and ate and drank and slept together'. When members turned out at Station Pier on Port Phillip Bay in 1947 to see off the historian Geoff Serle, just one of the club's Rhodes scholars, the harbourmaster had to order them to take down its Red Banner on the grounds that incoming ships might mistake it for a danger signal.[70]

Communists worked within the Melbourne Labour Club in the party's usual fashion, caucusing off-campus to determine their strategy and tactics. Turner recalled that the branch 'heavies' were Ken Gott, a commerce student rejected for military service, and Rex Mortimer, who commenced a law degree in 1943, along with three ex-service comrades who resumed studies in 1945: Noel Ebbels, Turner himself and his close friend Stephen Murray-Smith, an ebullient ex-commando.[71] He acknowledges legitimate complaints from female comrades about their lesser status, for women provided the leadership during the war, but those active after it included Miriam Brilliant, Miriam Dixson and, for a time, Helen Gintz (later Helen Hughes), none of them inclined to deference. Nor were Amirah Gust (who married Turner), Nita Bluthal (who married Murray-Smith) or Beth Noye (who married Gott). At its height, the branch had well over 100 members. A number of communists also secured teaching posts in this period: Dan Taylor in philosophy, Ian Milner and Lloyd Churchward in politics, Alan McBriar in history, and Fred Emery and Geoff Sharp in the psychology department. The branch also sought permission in 1946 to enrol Jim Cairns, then a senior tutor in economic history. The state executive quashed that proposal: an ex-copper was unacceptable.[72]

Murray-Smith's loft down a lane off Grattan Street served as a base of operations for recruiting and inducting recruits; according to an intelligence agent who infiltrated the branch, it had a large map of Moscow on the wall. But communists did not conceal their loyalty; on the contrary, they argued openly for their policies and made a conscious effort to reach agreement with the several hundred other members of the Labour Club as well as the large branch of the Student Christian Movement. It was this capacity to build consensus that Bob Gollan, a founder of Sydney's Labour Club, thought distinguished the Melbourne one. A leading member of the Melbourne branch described its approach in a 1947 report to the party's national youth committee. 'Largely because of the class composition of the university,' he explained, students would not accept direct party leadership, so it was necessary to work through the Labour Club. In doing so, however, there was no 'attempt to dominate the Club, or run it as a party show. It must make its own decisions.' Sharing office in the students' representative council with other Labour Club members, communists concentrated on issues that directly affected students such as improved facilities, accommodation and allowances, as well as the defence of academic freedom. By winning the confidence of the student body through such campaigns, they gained greater acceptance for their political initiatives.[73]

The communists at the University of Sydney pursued their own united front but found it harder to achieve. The Labour Club there was in constant dispute with followers of John Anderson, the ex-communist professor of philosophy who propagated a radical scepticism towards all creeds and institutions. Members of the Freethought Society competed with the Labour Club in student politics, and while they lost ground after the war, free thinking exercised a pervasive influence. Hence Sydney's Labour Club did not follow Melbourne in campaigning for greater government support for universities, but resisted such intrusion as a threat to academic freedom—with the conspicuous exception of Bob Walshe, a CRTS student who transferred from the Sydney Technical College at the end of 1946 and led the campaign for improved allowances. As president of the NSW Council of Reconstruction Trainees, Walshe regarded the Labour Club as 'an effete grouping of leftish dilettantes, useful only for staging the occasional talk'. That was a harsh judgement, for we have seen that members did more than talk at Wynyard Square. Even so, the Sydney club was more fractious, its communists more doctrinaire.[74]

The clubs at the other universities were smaller, and Bob Walshe's 1947 manual of student politics gives a good picture of how communists worked within them.[75] Their significance lay in the federal structure of the National Union of Australian University Students (NUAUS). Labour Club members were prominent at its annual conferences, filled most of the executive positions after 1945, and in turn promoted Australia's participation in the International Union of Students (IUS). This was established in the Czech capital of Prague in 1946 after an initial conference in London that Alan McBriar attended, but was beset from the outset by disagreement between Western European representatives who wanted it to be a service organisation, and those from Eastern Europe who wanted it to play a political role. A critical report on the founding conference from the accredited Australian delegate brought a narrow vote by NUAUS against membership, but Jack Redrup of the Sydney Labour Club went to the 1947 one. Noel Ebbels, Ken Gott and Stephen and Nita Murray-Smith all took up work in Prague.[76]

★

At some point during 1945 the Australian Communist Party began to shrink. The last Victory recruiting campaign took the membership to 22,052 at the end of 1944 but only 16,280 cards were issued twelve months later and there was a further decline to 13,450 at the end of 1946. While some members were lost in the transfer from the armed services to local branches, the great majority resigned or simply dropped out as the demands of adversity increased. There were also more departures than the membership tallies suggest, for the party continued to attract a substantial number of recruits: 2030 in 1946 and 1850 in 1947, so the loss in those two years amounted to more than 8000 members.[77] The turnover seems to have been greatest among the wartime recruits, the smaller states and outlying districts, leaving a core of more experienced and determined comrades in the major centres. Membership stabilised at 12,108 in 1947.[78]

The party continued to plan for growth. In early 1945 the Queensland state committee launched an appeal for £15,000 to expand the weekly *Guardian*, so that it was able to buy a three-storey building in Adelaide Street with a press in the basement. Ted Bacon, the editor, went down to Sydney to learn layout and other skills from *Tribune*'s chief of staff. The party was confident the improved *Guardian* would achieve a circulation of 15,000, but it managed only 10,000, and a further press appeal was needed by the end of 1946 to stabilise the paper's finances.[79] In Victoria the party opened an appeal for £10,000 at the end of 1945 'to lay the foundations for a daily *Guardian*' and bought a printing works in Corrs Lane, off Little Bourke Street. As with Sydney's Newsletter Printery, the Federal Press in Melbourne obtained additional revenue by producing a trotting guide and printing union papers, but was unable to lift *Guardian* sales beyond 18,000 and lost money by publishing it twice a week.[80] Western Australia had its own printery for the *Workers' Star*, as did South Australia for the edition of the Sydney *Tribune* it supplemented with local reports.

Sydney trams at the end of the war carried an advertisement for the communist press, 'If it's in Tribune, it's True', a claim that a university member suggested should have read 'If it's in Tribune, it's Correct'. That stipulation applied to every party publication, so that editors often took copy over to the leaders' offices to make sure it was on the line. *Tribune* was under direct invigilation from Ernie Campbell, who replaced Harry Gould as editor in 1945. Its principal journalists, Rupert Lockwood, Len Fox, George Farwell and Bill Wood, wanted it to be a more popular paper of the left than the propaganda tool their 'political commissar' demanded. Close oversight prevented the party from lifting the circulation of its newspapers beyond four or five times the number of members.[81]

Tribune also suffered a setback when the party arranged for its sale by newsagents in 1945, since many branches reduced the bulk orders that members sold in their workplaces, at street pitches and through door-to-door canvassing. With falling sales, the paper was incurring a loss of £1100 a month by early 1946. The party nevertheless pressed ahead with plans for a daily by forming a People's Printing and Publishing Company with a capital of 50,000 £1 shares, of which 20,000 were offered as a first issue. It took six months to sell 16,500 of them in small lots to many hundreds of party members (and the security service found the list of subscribers it obtained in 1949 from Marx House very useful), but the company's application for an increased paper ration was rejected. For the time being, the plan for a daily paper had to be postponed.[82]

Richard Dixon, who as assistant national secretary kept the party's books, was first to sound the alarm. 'The recruiting figures over the last few months,' he told the central committee in May 1946, 'are amongst the lowest for years ... The finances of the Party are in a most unsatisfactory condition, the sales of our pamphlets have declined seriously, and even the press was declining until the recent sales drives.' J.B. Miles, no less parsimonious, stressed the need to plan, budget, record and account for all expenditure. Spending on radio and publicity was cut, the number of cadres reduced and drastic economies foreshadowed if the slide was not arrested.[83]

The electoral performance was also disappointing. After the ALP rejected the proposal for an exchange of preferences in the federal election of September 1946, the party proceeded to stand sixteen candidates for the House of Representatives. As in 1943, a substantial effort went into the campaign: a month out from the election, it had 100 members working for each candidate and aimed for 200.[84] Only two of them, Jack Henry in the North Queensland seat of Herbert and Alan Finger in the South Australian seat of Hindmarsh, won more than 10 per cent of the vote, and there was a marked decline from support in the 1943 poll for all but two of the candidates. Sharkey acknowledged that 'the Party vote was most unsatisfactory', and 'it is no use our baulking [at] the fact'.[85]

The same was true of the five state elections that communists contested in the following year. Alan Finger attracted 17.4 per cent of the vote for Port Adelaide in the South Australian election of March 1947 and Alec Jolly (the two had studied medicine together at the University of Melbourne) 18.9 per cent for Midland-Guildford in the Western Australian election on the same day, but except in Fred Paterson's seat of Bowen there were substantial falls in the Queensland election held in May: Les Sullivan's vote in Herbert dropped from 43 to 21.6 per cent. The most encouraging results in the concurrent NSW election were in the mining districts (20.1 per cent in Bulli, 15.3 per cent in Hartley, 15 per cent in Cessnock and 14.1 per cent in Kurri Kurri), but Sydney saw steep falls (Stan Moran's vote in Balmain dropped from 28.2 per cent in 1944 to 8.9 per cent). The party stood just one candidate in the Victorian election of November 1947, Port Melbourne, where Ralph Gibson had obtained 23.6 per cent two years earlier but managed just 6.2 per cent this time.[86]

Throughout its immediate post-war offensive the party remained committed to a united front. The aim was to win over the workers through unity in action by fighting for improved wages and conditions, and to secure closer relations with the Labor Party by exposing the treachery of its right-wing leaders. But this strategy of building a united front from above and below became increasingly tenuous. While the major strikes of 1946 and 1947 had substantial union support, they caused disunity with the ACTU. Moreover, they brought the party up against the prime minister's determination to prevent a wage breakout. When Chifley canvassed the party's views on assuming the Labor leadership after the death of Curtin, the two communists sent to meet him urged him to do so because in their judgement 'he was the best man for the job'.[87] There is no indication of any change of mind. On the contrary, communist union leaders continued to appeal for his intervention when strike action went awry. The growing criticism of his government's failures went far beyond the avowed purpose of discrediting the Labor right; it called into question the character of the ALP as a reformist party propping up the capitalist system. Yet still the Communist Party persisted with the united front.

It did so in conformity with international communist policy. As we shall see, the Soviet Union was at this time instructing Western communist parties to curb any revolutionary impulses and work wherever possible in partnership with reformists. Stalin still hoped to avoid confrontation while consolidating the 'people's democracies' of Eastern Europe and rebuilding the war-torn Soviet Union. His principal concern was the mounting hostility of the United States, whose global power revived communist denunciation of a monopoly imperialism that threatened the independence of lesser nations and the livelihood of their small producers. The expectation at the ACP's Fourteenth Congress of 'Jobs, Freedom, Progress' soon gave way to warnings of an imminent capitalist crisis that would destroy Australian living standards.[88] Where did that leave a united front meant to bring gains to workers as they advanced on the path to socialism?

The first to pose the question was Jack Blake in a resolution issued by the Victorian executive ahead of its state conference in early 1946. As was expected, a draft of the resolution was sent to the political committee in Sydney, which objected to a passage that stated workers would gain from Labor governments only what they fought for. Disregarding the political committee, the Victorians circulated their resolution to the conference unchanged. Blake argued at a subsequent meeting of the political committee that the imminent economic crisis was turning the party's policy of 'constructive criticism' and conditional support of Labor into an obstacle to the leftward movement of the workers. He found no support and Dixon went down to Melbourne to correct the Victorians' leftist sectarianism.[89]

The political committee was already hardening its own attitude to the Labor Party. 'It is necessary for us in every way to sharpen our criticism of the Government and rally the working class to bring about a change of their policy,' Dixon stated in June 1946. But that was precisely what communists had been doing in their industrial and other campaigns, with a conspicuous lack of success. While the 'masses' were deemed to be 'moving to the left', the failure of the party to recruit them, win their votes or mobilise their dissatisfaction with the Labor Party brought no reconsideration of strategy other than instructions to broaden and deepen the united front—and always with the injunction to avoid sectarianism.

The united front from above fared no better. 'We have proceeded per medium of threats and ultimatums and what not,' said Sharkey in February 1947, without shifting the Chifley government from its course of action. He added that 'of course we can undoubtedly bring down the

Chifley Government'; the more difficult task was to apply pressure on it through a combination of strikes and negotiation in a way that avoided the danger of a Menzies government. In a rare show of humility he confessed: 'I have no plan to say how this is going to be done.'[90]

6

The Chill, 1947–49

The fortunes of the Australian Communist Party were bound up after 1945 with the onset of the Cold War. George Orwell coined the term at the end of Second World War when he predicted that the terrible nuclear weapon used to terminate hostilities would freeze the post-war order in a state of constant tension. The United States and the Soviet Union had emerged from that war as the two dominant powers, each proclaiming the universal validity of its economic system, form of government, social structure, values and way of life, and they embarked almost immediately on a struggle for control of places each considered vital to its interests: Germany, the Middle East, and soon Northeast and Southeast Asia. While the danger of an unrestricted 'hot war' was never absent, an additional novelty of this cold one was that it was conducted through client states on which the adversaries in turn sought to impose their competing ideologies.

Long before the Soviet Union collapsed in 1991, it became apparent that the Cold War was not the all-encompassing, bipolar contest its adversaries imagined. Apart from differences within the Western alliance and even among the Soviet Union's European satellites, the newly independent countries of Asia and Africa had their own aspirations, and the People's Republic of China was charting a divergent course that would eventually make it a third superpower. Even so, the effects of the Cold War were felt all round the world during the post-war decades in an arms race that threatened nuclear annihilation, a preoccupation with domestic as well as external security, an increased surveillance of people's lives, and a battle of ideas that imposed new tests of loyalty.[1]

Even today there is no agreement how this Cold War began or who was responsible for it taking hold. Its origins lay in mutual misunderstanding of the agreements reached by the Allied leaders at the Tehran conference of December 1943 and a subsequent meeting at Yalta in February 1945. Roosevelt and Churchill accepted the westward expansion of the Soviet Union back to Russia's pre-revolutionary borders as well as its dominance of neighbouring European countries, which in any case the Red Army already occupied. Stalin, in return, agreed that these countries would enjoy freely elected, representative governments. He regarded this undertaking as no more than a diplomatic fig leaf, for in his view the war to eliminate the threat of fascism had established a new principle of international relations: 'whoever occupies a territory also imposes on it his own social system'.[2] But the Soviet dictator greatly underestimated his Allies' determination to hold him to his word, so that the next summit at Potsdam in July 1945 was far less cordial. He was further discomfited by changes of leadership in the United States and United Kingdom following the death of Roosevelt and the electoral defeat of Churchill. President Truman, inexperienced and insecure, talked tough, while the taciturn Clement Attlee and his belligerent foreign minister, Ernest Bevin, revived a long history of hostility between British Labour and Soviet Bolshevism. Subsequent conferences were confined to foreign ministers and marked by mounting acrimony.[3]

Roosevelt, a committed internationalist, had been confident he could manage the Grand Alliance. His country, after all, held a preponderance of power. Its factories produced half the world's manufactures at the end of the war and it held almost all the financial reserves. The US Navy and Air Force were larger by far than those of any other country, and it alone possessed the nuclear bomb. Moreover, it had devised new international institutions, including the United Nations and the International Monetary Fund, as a rules-based system for safeguarding peace and promoting trade. The United States had no intention of remaining in Europe; its goal was to ensure a lasting settlement in the war-torn continent so it could extricate itself.

Stalin's immediate objectives were more limited. He aimed to repair the devastation left by the war and consolidate control of his buffer zone of Eastern European countries, most of which had no desire for that to happen. The USSR had suffered too much to risk a further war; it needed a breathing space during which there should be no confrontation. Hence he instructed Western European communist parties to participate in governments of national unity, as they did in Italy and France, discouraged the Chinese party from taking power, and proclaimed a broad alliance of progressive forces along the lines that the Australian party attempted to implement. At this time Stalin was actively rethinking the universal validity of the Russian model of a revolutionary seizure of power, which had been imposed so unsuccessfully on other communist parties following the First World War. His strategy in Eastern Europe was to establish a transitional order, using rural and industrial reform to displace the old elites while the communist parties won popular acceptance by working through national fronts with social democrats and peasants' parties. These regimes were designated initially as 'new democracies', since only Czechoslovakia had any real experience of that form of government, and later as 'people's democracies'. In practice they were marked from the beginning by the removal of 'enemies of the people' along with censorship, intimidation and ballot rigging.[4]

This rough wooing created alarm in the West—hence Churchill's warning in March 1946 that an Iron Curtain had descended across Europe, and the 'long telegram' that George Kennan, the American chargé d'affaires in Moscow, sent the Secretary of State a month earlier urging vigorous containment of further Soviet expansion. Stalin did have designs in Iran and Turkey but not in Greece, where it was the Yugoslav leader, Josip Broz Tito, who encouraged the local communists to renew their civil war against the authoritarian regime Churchill had installed. Since Britain was militarily overstretched and financially crippled, it fell to the United States to prop up the Greek dictatorship in a commitment that President Truman announced to the congress in March 1947: to 'help free peoples to maintain their free institutions and their national integrity' against the threat of 'totalitarian regimes'. The language of the Cold War had taken hold.[5]

Three months later came the Economic Recovery Program, more commonly known as the Marshall Plan after the Secretary of State who announced it, which provided the huge sum of $12 billion to assist European reconstruction. In contrast to the Soviet Union, which had stripped its occupied territories of plant and machinery, this was an act of extraordinary generosity, though not without ulterior motives. The benefaction was in credits to buy American goods that would otherwise remain unsold. It was designed to deal with the severe hardship in Western Europe that threatened political stability—the governments of both Italy and France had recently ejected their communist ministers. And by offering assistance to any country willing to open its markets, it tempted the people's democracies—Poland, Czechoslovakia, Hungary and other members of the Soviet bloc had to be ordered to desist. Finally, the Marshall Plan exacerbated the dispute over Germany. Stalin, who was determined that this country must never again be able to threaten Russia, accepted its division into zones, but was angered in 1946 when first the United States and then the United Kingdom ended the payment of Soviet reparations from their zones. Now the Marshall Plan would integrate the larger part of Germany into the Western European economy.[6]

In response, Stalin convened a meeting of communist parties in Poland in September 1947 to consider 'the tasks of democratic organisations against attempts by American imperialism to enslave economically the countries of Europe'. The meeting established a Communist Information Bureau (Cominform). Unlike the earlier Comintern, the Cominform was not a fully international organisation—China was not admitted to membership when communists took power there in 1949—but rather a limited European one. Only two Western parties were invited, those of France and Italy, so that they could be castigated for following the parliamentary course of action that Stalin had imposed on them. They complied by embarking on mass strikes and violent confrontations. The Eastern European communists, in turn, were given the green light to eliminate their remaining opponents, so there was a brutal coup in Czechoslovakia in February 1948, and soon Stalin turned on the only country where communists had made their own revolution. Yugoslavia was expelled from the Cominform in 1948.[7]

In a report to the founding conference of the Cominform, Andrei Zhdanov, Stalin's assistant secretary of the CPSU and leading ideologist, announced that the world had split into two irreconcilable camps, the one an 'imperialist and anti-democratic camp' led by the United States, and the other the 'anti-imperialist and democratic camp' led by the Soviet Union. He gave no explanation why the Grand Alliance in which Stalin had invested such effort had ended, other than to claim that the capitalist powers took fright at the rapid progress of communism. The United States certainly gave considerable assistance to anti-communist politicians, trade unionists, newspapers and cultural organisations in countries such as Italy where communism had a mass following, but that hardly accounts for the disarray into which Western communist parties were thrown as a result of the 'two camps' theory. From the Grand Alliance had come a division of the world into spheres of influence. When this gave way to the unremitting hostility of the Cold War, it consigned the communist parties in the Western camp to what historian Tony Judt called 'a secondary, spoiler role'.[8]

Their continued operation was indicative of a further asymmetry in the Cold War. The communist regimes allowed no opposition, but freedom of association and expression was a precondition of liberal democracy, so Western communists were able to meet, organise and campaign against the policies of their governments. They did so, however, under increasing duress, as their support for the Soviet Union marked them out as threats to national security.

The subordination of Western communist parties to the Soviet camp was emphasised by the journal issued by the Cominform, a body in which they had no voice, which appeared in fourteen languages and was distributed in some 60 countries. Its cumbrous title, *For a Lasting Peace, for a People's Democracy!*, was taken from Zhdanov's two-camps statement. Party members commonly abbreviated the name to *Forfor*, but could do nothing about the contents. Eric Hobsbawm has remarked on the 'sensationally unreadable reports' issued by the international communist movement, which was 'almost viscerally anti-rhetorical' in its turgid and jargon-ridden statements. He considered *Forfor* the 'all-time champion of unreadability'.[9]

★

Criticism of the Russians began immediately the war ended, with press reports of atrocities committed by the Red Army in occupied Germany. The transformation in reportage from gallant ally to brutal conqueror was sudden and relentless. Australian newspapers relied on British press agencies for their coverage of the stormy meetings between foreign ministers in which Vyacheslav Molotov, the unyielding Soviet representative—his adopted surname meant hammer-man—personified their narrative of a humourless and unbending adversary bent on world domination. (Such was his habitual nay-saying at these meetings that my wife's parents dubbed their adamant little girl 'Mrs Molotov'.)

Condemnations of the Soviet regime also reappeared, though these relied on familiar descriptions of an oppressive police state since Western journalists were barred from entry soon after the war and so missed important developments such as the renewed persecution of national minorities.[10] For that reason, the picture of life 'Inside Russia Today' given by J.J. Maloney, the recently returned head of the Australian legation, attracted wide attention—including in Moscow, which denounced his slanders. Maloney wrote six lengthy articles under this rubric that were published in 1946 simultaneously by the *Sydney Morning Herald* and the metropolitan dailies published by Keith Murdoch's newspaper chain: the Adelaide *Advertiser*, Brisbane *Courier-Mail*, Melbourne *Herald* and *West Australian*. Maloney's account traversed the repression, the backwardness of agriculture and industry, the low wages, high prices and deplorable housing, and the privileges enjoyed by the *nomenklatura*, drawing on official statistics and personal testimony to buttress the author's authority.[11]

There were immediate rejoinders from Ernie Thornton and Jessie Street (both of whom had returned from recent visits to the Soviet Union) and two former members of the Australian legation, Irene Saxby and Max Crawford.[12] Crawford, who had resumed the chair of history at the University of Melbourne and intended to write a book on Russia, was president of Australia–Soviet House. His was the most substantial response, though the *Sydney Morning Herald* cut it back to just 700 words, and the full version appeared as part of Australia–Soviet House's reply to Maloney entitled *The Real Facts About Russia*. Those real facts consisted of brief extracts from wartime admirers such as Joseph Davies and Averell

Harriman, along with credulous pre-war visitors such as Hewlett Johnson and Sidney and Beatrice Webb.

Crawford took a different tack. It was not so much that Maloney misstated the facts, though some were untrue, as the way he used them selectively to present a distorted picture 'out of relation with history', for 'no country can ever build except on its own past'. Crawford conceded there had been 'bad mistakes' and 'bad deeds' but argued the task of building a modern industrialised nation from the ruins of two world wars entailed severe hardship and 'a discipline that in the ordinary way we would prefer to dispense with'. Such justification of Soviet communism by reference to its unique difficulties was not uncommon; Crawford added (in truth, greatly exaggerated) his ability 'to speak to the Russian people in their own language' to illustrate 'the tremendous vitality and good humour of that overstrained and tired, but delightfully individualistic people'.[13]

He had another brush with Maloney later in the year when a function at Australia–Soviet House to commemorate the Russian Revolution, at which the Soviet ambassador was to be the guest of honour, clashed with an address on the same evening in the Melbourne Town Hall by Maloney on 'The Soviet Myth Exploded'. Crawford drafted a letter of protest to the lord mayor against the diplomatic discourtesy, which four other Melbourne professors signed along with Bishop Burgmann, Dean Langley and Canon Maynard. This brought allegations Crawford was misusing his academic post to disseminate 'mischievous propaganda'—and the prominence of Labour Club members among the history students who came to their professor's defence only added fuel to the fire. Justice Lowe, who was unhappy about Australia–Soviet House's publication of *The Real Facts About Russia*, took the opportunity to resign as a patron; Crawford confided that he too regretted its composition and intended to give up the presidency. He also abandoned his planned study of the interplay of freedom and necessity in modern Russia.[14]

The onset of the Cold War revived allegations that the Australian Communist Party was a seditious organisation serving the USSR's plans for world conquest. Organisations such as the Sane Democracy League, the Institute of Public Affairs, the Graziers' Association and soon the

League of Rights produced a rash of publications to publicise the danger within: *Communism, Australia's Fifth Column*; *Betrayal: Being a Short History of Australia's Fifth Column*; and *The War Has Ceased but Australia Still Has a Fifth Column.*[15]

A new generation of anti-communists built their political careers by banging the communist drum and denouncing anyone suspected of serving the enemy's purpose. Hence Frederick Edmunds, a schoolteacher elected to the Victorian Legislative Assembly in 1945, broadened his attack on Max Crawford to other 'pink professors and puce pedagogues', and Douglas Evelyn Darby, another teacher, who entered the NSW Assembly in 1945, railed against communist subversion.[16] The blue blood William Charles Wentworth entered federal parliament in 1949 as a red-baiter whom even Robert Menzies thought excessive. Miles Franklin bailed Wentworth up at a family wedding in 1947, saying 'a member of *my Gestapo* told me that *your Ogpu* takes the form of a blacklist and that my name is on it'. (The emphasis is Franklin's.) Wentworth replied that she was 'a stooge for communists' and then harangued her throughout the reception. In relating the incident to a friend, she commented: 'I think he's cracked.'[17]

There was an upsurge of attacks on communist premises. A brick was thrown through the window of the party's Paddington office in December 1945, and a glazier was needed twice in the same month to replace the windows of the bookshop on the ground floor of Marx House. A shop in the Melbourne suburb of Prahran suffered the same treatment in 1946, and on the second occasion lit cigarettes were dropped through the opening. Subsequently it was plastered with stickers: 'Send All Commos Back to Russia', together with a somewhat confusing additional exhortation to 'Kill All Commos' and 'Strangle All Commo Women'. Repeated attacks on the party bookshop in Geelong under cover of darkness culminated in a break-in and destruction of much of the stock.[18]

There were numerous cases of harassment and assault. Two young men on a suburban Sydney train spotted a teenage girl wearing a hammer and sickle on her lapel. 'Look what we've got here, a—Communist,' they exclaimed, seizing her party badge and threatening to push her from the carriage. An ex-serviceman landed punches on a party member at a wedding reception who gave himself away by refusing to stand for the singing of 'God Save the King'. Such incidents were deemed newsworthy because of their unusual circumstances as ordinary cases of abuse and intimidation became commonplace.[19]

An index of the increasing hostility was expulsion of communists from ex-service organisations. The party had worked hard during the war to build support among the armed services with an eye to its aftermath, and with good reason, since the principal ex-service body, the RSL, had a record of unremitting hostility to the left and was already at loggerheads with the Labor government over the question of preference in employment for its members. Laurie Aarons was put in charge of the party's work among former members of the armed forces and wrote its guide to demobilisation. *Civvy Street* gave a comprehensive explanation of the range of benefits to which veterans were entitled, confident that 'they will come back into the economic, social and political life of the community with the full force of the real Digger spirit of democracy and solidarity'. Far from the party fearing their return, *Civvy Street* claimed these ex-servicemen would be 'a vitalising force in national life' and 'strengthen those who work and struggle for progress'.[20]

Aarons had not served overseas and was therefore ineligible for membership of the RSL, so he joined the Australian Legion of Ex-Servicemen and Women, a new organisation for those in the domestic forces. Indeed, he played a leading role in its creation and was a member of the state council. But he overplayed his hand in 1945 by distributing a ticket for the annual election of officers, which brought to light a faction that met in Marx House. A general meeting of the state branch resolved to bar communists and Aarons was expelled. The legion's federal conference banned communists from holding office in the following year and in 1947 it excluded them from membership. Some state branches did not enforce this rule; the left-wing Queensland branch openly defied it and was expelled from the legion in 1949. By then suspects were required to make a sworn declaration denying any communist association, with the threat of prosecution for any false statement.[21]

The party fared no better in the RSL. While it had some initial success at the local level, communists were unable to shift the league's antagonism to the labour movement. Arthur Bergeest, president of the

Paddington–Woollahra sub-branch, proposed cooperation with trade unions at the NSW congress at the end of 1944; but since he was president of the Painters' Union and well known for producing the party's banners, this was taken as evidence of communist 'white-anting'.[22] The RSL's Victorian branch was first to announce a ban on communists, in 1946, and more than 80 members were expelled. Not all were communists: two young economists who had served in the RAAF wrote in protest to the state president, reminding him that 'Liberals, Labourites, Socialists and Communists fought together as comrades for freedom to express their thoughts and ideas' and abhorring the 'fascist attitudes' that were 'slowly seeping into this country'. Their membership was terminated and their letter forwarded to the security service. Many more went quietly, fearing the stigma that followed press reports of expulsion.[23]

Other states followed Victoria's course, though New South Wales resisted and instead expelled the right-wing publicist Frank Browne for throwing a red flag on the official table at the 1946 RSL congress. The tide turned as the Cold War intensified. A resolution adopted at the 1948 national congress urged the government to ban the Communist Party, remove all communists from the public service, prevent them from holding union office and deport all foreign-born members. The NSW executive introduced a ban on communists in the same year and expelled Arthur Bergeest, who by this time was a member of the state council. Although he obtained an injunction from the Supreme Court, the full court upheld the state branch's right to expel any member for communist activities or sympathies.[24] The drive to do so was opposed by Bill Yeo, a Gallipoli veteran elected state president in 1949 who believed the league should serve as a welfare organisation without divisive tests of political allegiance. His stand brought an accusation from a Returned Servicemen's Anti-Communist Vigilance Corps that he was part of a group of communists seeking election to the state council. After further legal manoeuvres, the council expelled another dozen members. Some were communists, including Jack Zwolsman and Charles Davidson, a life member from Katoomba. Others, such as Eric Dark, were not.[25]

The strongest protest came from Arthur Gietzelt, who worked in his father's industrial products business and was the elder brother of the Miscellaneous Workers' Union activist Ray Gietzelt. Arthur lived in Caringbah, where he became active in local government, helped Gough Whitlam win the federal seat of Werriwa in 1952, and in the fullness of time represented the ALP in the Senate from 1971 to 1989. Throughout his parliamentary career, Arthur Gietzelt denied allegations of a communist past (and obtained substantial damages from the ABC after a *Four Corners* program accused him of working with the Communist Party in a preselection contest). In fact, he directed the party's ex-service work for a number of years following Laurie Aarons' expulsion from the Legion of Ex-Servicemen and Women, and used the cover name Arthur James in party circles as he made his way in the ALP.[26]

★

The Chifley government was a conspicuous absentee from the early Cold War. It rebuffed Britain's statements on the communist threat at meetings of the Commonwealth prime ministers in London and criticised the United States as well as the Soviet Union for not using the United Nations to resolve their disputes. Evatt, as foreign minister, was an internationalist who championed the rights of smaller nations; Chifley, who acted in his stead during the minister's long absences abroad, refrained from commentary on Soviet actions. When pressed on the subject in parliament, he expressed regret at the 'flood of communism' sweeping Europe, but insisted it arose in both old and new democracies as a result of poverty and misery that went back hundreds of years, just as it flourished in Asia because of colonial oppression. The only remedy was to improve the conditions of the people. Hence Chifley rejected British and American support of the 'repressive and reactionary' Greek government, just as he dismissed the 'sheer utter hypocrisy' of abstract appeals to freedom that became a hallmark of anti-communist rhetoric, for he had witnessed the 'freedom to starve' during the Depression when thousands of workers lined up outside a factory in his electorate to secure the only job on offer. When asked in 1947 if Australia would follow the United States and subject public employees to a loyalty test, he said little was to be gained by 'setting up the equivalent of a gestapo'.[27]

There were limits to the prime minister's forbearance. His government responded firmly in 1947 to the threat of industrial action against a rocket range it was building in South Australia. The facility was to test British guided missiles as part of a defence agreement between the two countries that included the development of atomic weapons and would allow Australian scientists to work in the Harwell nuclear research facility in Oxfordshire. Chifley embraced this arrangement because, apart from strengthening Australia's military capacity, it provided an opportunity to acquire advanced technology and share in its industrial benefits.[28]

The problem was that the long flight path needed to test missiles would pass over the Presbyterian mission established at Ernabella in 1937 to provide education and medical services to the Anangu people in the north-west of the state. Dr Charles Duguid, the mission's founder, protested that the range's observation posts and service roads would intrude on the lands reserved for Aboriginal people and disrupt their traditional way of life. After religious and humanitarian bodies took up Duguid's crusade and Doris Blackburn, who succeeded her husband Maurice as an 'Independent Labor' member of the House of Representatives, raised the concerns there, the government appointed a committee to recommend safeguards. It did so, but failed to anticipate the greater danger—nine nuclear devices were exploded on Aboriginal homelands in South Australia between 1953 and 1957, with scant regard for those living there and lasting effects from nuclear contamination.[29]

The Communist Party supported Duguid's campaign, initially on the same basis as it championed protection of the traditional way of life of all living on country. The playwright of *Rocket Range*, staged by the New Theatre at this time, spelt out its message in *Tribune*: 'The central core of tribal unity, tribal culture and the tribal will to live is based on the rocks, lagoons and sacred places of the tribal domain.'[30] Communists went further, however, in condemning the guided missiles project as a threat to peace, and in March 1947 they secured a resolution by the South Australian Trades and Labor Council proposing an ACTU ban on the principal facility 450 kilometres north of Adelaide that was to be known as Woomera (after the Aboriginal device to extend the distance a spear can be thrown). This threat embarrassed the government, which was already under notice from both Britain and the United States for its lax security. Alarm increased in May when the communist secretary of the Building Trades Federation announced that building unions would be asked to support a complete ban on construction.[31]

This was a step too far and quickly disowned by party leaders. The comrade concerned had apparently been warned not to act precipitately, and especially not to link any union action to a claim that Australia was to serve as a base for future wars. Such was the adverse reaction to his doing so that the political committee felt compelled 'to make it clear that we are not out to sabotage the defence of Australia'. Its attempts to provide such reassurance were nullified, however, by an earlier pamphlet written by the party's South Australian secretary. Miles and Sharkey claimed in a press statement that communists were motivated solely by the welfare of Aboriginal people, and the Communist Party had no desire 'to deny Britain and Australia legitimate equipment for defence purposes'. The South Australian publication *Rocket Range Threatens Australia* declared that the project was to be opposed, along with the 'whole armaments program and every aspect of the foreign policy of which the rocket range is a part'.[32]

The government moved quickly to limit the political damage by making it an offence to obstruct or advocate obstruction of any approved defence project. Evatt, who oversaw the Approved Defence Projects Protection Act, explained that the Communist Party's threat of a boycott required this safeguard but that the government had no intention of going further. Chifley continued to distinguish between communism as a creed and a political movement that had a legitimate presence in Australia, however repugnant he found it, and acts of subversion. Nothing was to be served, he said, by driving communism underground. Communists should be free to proclaim their beliefs and pursue their cause, subject only to prohibition of illegal conduct.[33]

The controversy over the rocket range drew attention to the country's security arrangements. As part of a more general pruning of the public service at the end of the war, a review found no reason for the Commonwealth Security Service to continue, since the greater part of its responsibilities, such as internment and surveillance of aliens, were no longer needed. It recommended that the sections concerned with counterespionage and subversive organisations be transferred to the attorney-general's Commonwealth Investigation Branch (CIB). This did not satisfy the Joint Intelligence Committee of the armed services, which pressed for a separate defence security organisation, but Evatt was adamant that any monitoring of Australian civilians must be undertaken by a civil agency under his control. The rocket range controversy brought replacement of the CIB by a dedicated Commonwealth Investigation Service (CIS), but that made little difference. With no money to mount operations or attract capable officers, the CIS was held in low regard; its director-general, Eric Longfield-Lloyd, a softly spoken and self-effacing man, was known as 'Linger Longer Lloyd'.[34]

For all that, the Communist Party was under surveillance. The CIS obtained advice on its nefarious activities from ALP contacts and exchanged unreliable information with the Movement. It intercepted letters and telephone calls, despite a lack of authorisation, and planted agents, including in Marx House—though Evatt's repugnance for such illicit methods meant that little of this intelligence found its way to the government, which continued to insist all was well. That became more difficult as members of the federal opposition kept up a barrage of accusations.

Chifley's hand was forced by new evidence of communist espionage. During 1947 the US Army Security Agency deciphered a number of the messages sent from the Soviet Embassy in Canberra two years earlier that revealed the leakage of British post-war planning documents from the Department of External Affairs. This information was passed on to the British security agency, MI5, and its head arrived in Australia in early 1948 to urge action. The prime minister was sceptical until Attlee obtained permission from the United States to tell him (and very few others) how it had been obtained. The United States went further in June and suspended the flow of virtually all classified information to Australia, an embargo that placed the rocket range in jeopardy. Even then, the government baulked at the measures its allies demanded.[35]

American diplomats, already censorious of Labor's foreign policy, were convinced that communist penetration extended to the highest levels of the government. Like their Soviet counterparts, security officers in the US Embassy gathered information from local sources—which in their case included opposition politicians, leading businessmen, Military Intelligence officers and the aggrieved Dutch consul. In turn the American operatives leaked intelligence to well-placed Australians, including Keith Murdoch. It was no secret that Sir Frederick Shedden, the head of the Department of Defence, was at loggerheads with Evatt's departmental secretary, John Burton, and that he thought the country's security arrangements were seriously inadequate. We do not know who gave Artie Fadden, the leader of the Country Party, copies of two classified documents that revealed the United States and United Kingdom had stopped sharing information with Australia, but he used them in a parliamentary debate on 30 September 1948 to discredit the government's denial of an embargo. That two officers of the CIS who sought to interview Fadden in his parliamentary office beat a retreat when journalists were summoned only compounded impressions of its ineptitude.[36]

★

Fadden used parliamentary privilege to breach security during the House of Representatives' consideration of the budgetary appropriation for the Council for Scientific and Industrial Research (CSIR), more specifically a sum to support its research on nuclear fission. Established in 1926 to undertake work in agricultural science, the CSIR had grown during the war to a staff of more than 2000 covering a broad spectrum of biological and physical science, and it was also Australia's principal source of defence science. Accusations the council was a security risk were fanned by a university address its chair, Sir David Rivett, delivered in March 1947, decrying the pall of secrecy that prevented the free exchange of scientific research and impeded the advancement of knowledge. That Rivett was a distinguished chemist who had led the CSIR from its establishment only magnified his offence: 'in a period almost of war', Fadden's colleague Joe Abbott charged, 'he preached wickedly and wrongly the most dangerous doctrine to our young scientists'.[37]

A bull of a man with a matching bellow, Abbott repeatedly gored the CSIR. A red rag was the appointment to its governing body of an ALP parliamentarian, Don Mountjoy, following his loss of the seat of Swan in the 1946 election. Mountjoy's brother Bill was a former state secretary of the Communist Party in Western Australia who now worked in Canberra for *Tribune*; another brother, Henry, was active in the party and Don himself was an outspoken left-winger. Along with other members of the opposition, Abbott linked allegations of Don Mountjoy's disloyalty to a Soviet spy ring in Canada that obtained nuclear secrets from scientists working there. 'I can swear categorically that Mr Mountjoy has no connection whatsoever with the Communist Party,' the minister in charge of the CSIR replied. That was a rash claim, for in all likelihood Mountjoy was an undercover member.[38]

A further provocation was the participation of CSIR scientists in an international body that promoted science as a force for social progress. Beginning in Britain as a trade union at the end of the First World War, the Association of Scientific Workers developed into a much broader movement of scientists wanting to put their expertise at the service of humanity. The Australian Association of Scientific Workers (AASW) flourished during the war, and Rivett was just one of the dignitaries who participated in its 1944 conference on post-war planning. The onset of the Cold War turned this commitment to international cooperation and unfettered inquiry into an object of suspicion, especially as the president of the Canadian Association of Scientific Workers was among those arrested there in early 1946 for passing his research on explosives to the Soviets.[39] The Australian one protested against such infringement of scientific freedom, as well as the conviction of the British physicist Allan Nunn May for espionage, at its conference on 'Atomic Power and the International Co-operation of Scientists' held shortly afterwards; and Joe Abbott cited the Canadian spy scandal when he named five communist members of the AASW and called for the CSIR to be safeguarded from a similar betrayal of secret information.[40]

The government resisted any such interference until the clamour that resulted from the US embargo on sharing classified information with Australia forced its hand. As a first step it transferred the scientists working on defence projects to a separate organisation. The CSIR itself was then reconstituted as the Commonwealth Scientific and Industrial Research

Organisation (CSIRO) to give the minister greater powers, with conditions of employment determined by the Public Service Board. Scientists would be subject to the same security screening as other public servants and required to take an oath of allegiance.[41]

David Rivett resigned upon the passage of the legislation that made these changes in April 1949, and the AASW wound up its affairs shortly afterwards. Membership had fallen away as the Cold War took hold, leaving a rump of scientists whose refusal to bow to the new circumstances was taken as evidence they were security risks. The CIS opened a file on communist activity in the CSIR following the US embargo, linking its inquiries to extensive personal files it had compiled on those who worked for it. They included Shirley Andrews, who was employed as an information officer; John Pomeroy, a photographer in the plant industry division; and Arthur Rudkin, a chemist working on forest products. All were known communists (Rudkin, a former editor of the *Workers' Star*, had been gaoled in 1940 for a breach of National Security Regulations), though none handled sensitive information. Suspicion also fell on others who were not party members, such as the administrator Frank Nicholls and the dietician Margaret McArthur, later a distinguished anthropologist, because of their association with communists.[42]

The scientists who worked in the radiophysics laboratory in Sydney were of particular concern, since it had been established to conduct wartime research on radar. Eric Burhop was seconded to the laboratory from the Department of Physics at the University of Melbourne, but left in 1944 to work at the University of California, Berkeley on the Manhattan project to build the atomic bomb. Others to come under suspicion were William Berry-Smith, Ron Bracewell, Joan Freeman, Len Hibbard, Tom Kaiser, Bernard Mills, Ruby Payne-Scott, Wilbur Christiansen and Kathleen Makinson—though Military Intelligence prevented the CSIR from recruiting her husband Richard, a lecturer in physics at the University of Sydney.[43]

Dick Makinson was the first university-based communist to suffer from an adverse security assessment, rejected for the University of Sydney chair of physics in 1946 after he declared his party membership at a meeting of the AASW.[44] Eric Burhop, who came to the notice of Military

Intelligence in 1941 because of a lecture he delivered for the Army Education Service judged too sympathetic to the Soviet Union, was deemed unsuitable for the physics chair at the University of Adelaide in 1948. Ruby Payne-Scott, a pioneer in radiophysics and radio astronomy, was subsequently driven out of the CSIRO, and others were denied advancement until they forsook their AASW past. Dave Morris, an army scientist, was recalled from experimental work on long-range weapons in England because of his party membership and rendered unemployable by the constant intervention of security services. Harry Medlin, a University of Adelaide graduate sent to work on the same project in 1949 while concurrently pursuing doctoral research in nuclear physics at Cambridge, was also recalled because his earlier activity in the Adelaide University Socialist Club made it impossible to provide a security clearance, but since he was not a communist, this was written off as a youthful indiscretion and he was able to resume his academic career in Australia.[45]

Many scientists were drawn to communism in the 1930s and 1940s as a doctrine proclaiming an objective knowledge of the laws of natural as well as human history. The Soviet Union deployed science on a massive scale as part of its central planning, and admirers saw this state patronage as demonstrating its potential to liberate humanity; indeed, they claimed that the quest for knowledge free of vested interests was an essentially socialist enterprise. Australian communists frequently cited the most forceful exposition of this argument, *The Social Function of Science* by J.D. Bernal, a leading British scientist known as 'The Sage' for his erudition and acuity; and *Tribune* and the *Communist Review* regularly reprinted the popular articles on 'Science for the People' that J.B.S. Haldane, an equally renowned polymath, wrote for the *Daily Worker*.[46]

A difficulty was that communist scientists here lacked the eminence of their foreign counterparts. Party members such as the physicists Dick Makinson of Sydney and Syd Williams of the University of Western Australia, or the biochemists Jack Legge at Melbourne and John Callaghan in Queensland, were still establishing their careers. If the AASW attracted some influential senior figures, the statements issued by the party's own Arts and Sciences Committee were confined to practical matters such as housing and soil erosion. The medical doctors were more active, making submissions to public inquiries on population and social welfare, and offering advice on diet, milk pasteurisation, industrial health, free medicine, immunisation, dental care and a range of other public health concerns. It did not help that the party officials who supervised the Arts and Sciences Committee were so ill equipped for the task—the scientists felt compelled in 1946 to correct the mistakes and misunderstandings of an organiser's attempt to explain nuclear physics.[47]

More embarrassing still was the Lysenko controversy. Trofim Lysenko was a Soviet agronomist who claimed that plants could acquire and pass on characteristics in response to their environment. On the basis of bogus experiments showing spectacular increases in grain production, he was appointed director of the Institute of Genetics of the Russian Academy of Sciences, from where he condemned the bourgeois science of genetics and victimised those researchers who refused to renounce it. More than any other blow to the reputation of Soviet science, this imposition of a patently false dogma estranged scientists in the West, and Stalin's decision in 1948 to put Lysenko in charge of Soviet biology proved too much for many communist ones.

While the Australian party hailed Lysenko for showing 'how environment kayoes heredity', the party scientists expressed grave misgivings. They urged Harry Gould, the member of the political committee responsible for Arts and Sciences, not to publish a *Pravda* article condemning 'bourgeois geneticists' until they could discuss the subject with party leaders. Gould appealed to John Callaghan as secretary of the science committee to take a stand against the 'capitulationist' attitude of his comrades. Admitting he had no knowledge of biology, Gould insisted that 'we are not dealing with a scientific discussion of genetics' but the slanders of ideological apologists for imperialism.[48]

A lack of scientific training did not deter Jack Blake, who embarked on an intensive study of the Russian material along with some works on genetics in order to settle the doubts of scientists in Victoria. Addressing a large meeting of them in March 1949, he hailed the victory of 'Academician Lysenko' over the Soviet biologists who had attempted to sabotage his leadership with a sterile adherence to bourgeois science. Their concentration on chromosomes as 'dominating the heredity of an organism' was likened to the inability of the ruling class to recognise the possibility of revolutionary change. So just as Comrade Stalin had demonstrated how to change 'the political contours of the world', so Lysenko now pointed the way to the task of remaking nature. Blake enjoyed respect for his dedication and intelligence (Ian and Amirah Turner gave him a copy of the *Proceedings of the Soviet Academy of Biological Science* as a birthday present) but was clearly out of his depth. Max Marginson, a young tutor in biochemistry, could still recall 30 years later the shock and dismay of Melbourne's scientific comrades regarding the party leader's dogmatism.[49]

★

The denunciation of bourgeois science followed a similar crackdown on writers and artists. In 1946 Andrei Zhdanov unleashed a tirade against two Leningrad literary journals that had adopted 'a tone of servility and cringing before philistine foreign literature'. As with Lysenko's assault on his reactionary scientific opponents, Stalin personally supervised this statement and it was followed by similar attacks on theatre, film, art, music and opera.[50] Zhdanov was put in charge of the propaganda and agitation department of the CPSU to direct the campaign, for he had helped formulate the doctrine of socialist realism proclaimed at the first Congress of Soviet Writers in 1934 that called on them to be 'engineers of human souls'.[51] His new duties signalled Stalin's decision to restore the barriers to dangerous foreign ideas that had been relaxed during the wartime Grand Alliance.

The intense ideological crusade within the Soviet Union during the second half of the 1940s was known as the *Zhdanovshchina* (though its namesake died in 1948). It punished writers, dramatists, artists and composers who betrayed their patriotic obligations by succumbing to the decadent modernism of the West, and it exalted national traditions with a patriotic fervour that rejected all vestiges of cosmopolitanism—a term that acquired increasingly anti-Semitic undertones. It also drew on the formulation of a world divided into two hostile camps that Zhdanov laid down at the founding conference of the Cominform in 1947. Just as the Soviet Union had saved European high culture from Hitler's onslaught, it was now defending it from the meretricious popular culture propagated by American imperialism.[52]

Australian communists caught up in the discussion of cultural policy at this time have observed that 'Zhdanov's brutal and vulgar criticism' had limited influence here.[53] The party did publish several of his decrees, though at noticeable intervals after they were issued, and while those who wrote on the subject in the *Communist Review* made the obligatory gestures, the editor allowed considerable latitude to contributors who were clearly uncomfortable with the crudity of Zhdanov's attacks.[54] Hence John Oldham defended Pablo Picasso from Soviet condemnation of his 'morbid, revolting pictures'; Len Fox and Paul Mortier preferred the less reprehensible charge of 'obscurity'; and Rod Shaw, a leading member of the Studio of Realist Art, deplored the inference that all forms other than realism were to be torn down and reviled.[55]

J.B. Miles concluded this discussion with a restatement of the party's line that art was a weapon in the class war and had to be judged by its standpoint: 'progressive or reactionary, for my class or against my class, for the people or for the imperialists'. But Miles was no Zhdanov. When Joan Williams, a young party member in Perth, criticised the first volume of Katharine Susannah Prichard's goldfields trilogy, *The Roaring Nineties*, for its failure to go beyond social to socialist realism and show 'the new and the good growing out of the old', Miles travelled west to rap the zealot over the knuckles. It is also noticeable that both the critics and defenders of Picasso appealed to a dictum of Harry Gould, who was much more comfortable handling the arts side of his responsibilities than science: 'Comrade artists, what we ask of you is to be communists.' Even Jack Blake, that stern guardian of the party line, counselled cultural practitioners in Victoria that 'it is essential to avoid any narrow, doctrinaire approach'.[56]

The principal publicists of Zhdanovism in Australia were not communists but their opponents. 'No longer may poets praise the unideological beauties of nature and the loveliness of unideological women', ran a press commentary on the initial rebuke of the Leningrad writers; 'they must get back to their true ideological business of verses in praise of greater tractor production'. Lloyd Ross was an early combatant on the

Cold War's cultural front. Writing in the *Sydney Morning Herald* in 1946, he linked the Soviet denial of artistic and intellectual freedom to the treatment of ex-communists such as Arthur Koestler, John Dos Passos, James T. Farrell, John Strachey, Ignazio Silone, Stephen Spender and Victor Gollancz—'they chose freedom and were called reactionary'. The Australian journalist and war correspondent Godfrey Blunden, who had reported from Moscow, now related the fall from grace of Prokofiev, Shostakovich and Khachaturian after Stalin stormed out of the premiere of an insufficiently lyrical opera portraying his partnership with Lenin.[57]

The party's two most successful initiatives, the Studio of Realist Art in Sydney and the Realist Writers' Group in Melbourne, felt no need to specify what kind of realism they practised. The Studio, which began in the basement of an old potato store in Sussex Street in early 1945 and later moved to more spacious premises in George Street, was open to all who strove to capture 'some aspect of reality and to face the problems set by life'. James Cant, Dora Chapman, Roy and Nadine Dalgarno, Russell Drysdale, Herb McClintock, Hal Missingham, John Oldham, Bernard Smith and Rod Shaw were among the participants who gave lectures and conducted classes; William Dobell, Margaret Preston and Jeffrey Smart contributed to its exhibitions.[58]

The Melbourne Realist Writers' Group began about the same time and with a similar emphasis on collective development of form and content, the members submitting their writing for workshop discussion of its strengths and weaknesses. It too was open to non-communists and included critics as well as practitioners. Jack Coffey, a reporter on the *Sporting Globe*, was secretary, and Les Barnes, a party organiser with an interest in history, Deirdre Moore, an Arts graduate down from Sydney, and Frank Hardy, fresh from the Army Education Service, were founding members. Max Brown, Eric Lambert and Bill Wannan joined after demobilisation, as did Judah Waten and John Morrison, a former wharfie and jobbing gardener who won the Fellowship of Australian Writers' short story competition in 1943. They wrote from personal experience, telling stories of everyday life and consciously building on the radical nationalist tradition, though the realist writers included two Jewish refugees—David Martin, who had fought in the Spanish Civil War, and

Walter Kaufmann, who came to Australia on the *Dunera*—along with the Trinidadian Ralph de Boissière.[59]

Running alongside the Realist Writers' Group was the Dolphin Press, a venture of Judah Waten and the Melbourne artist and lawyer Vic O'Connor. It published two collections. *Southern Stories* included pieces that Waten translated from Yiddish and an essay in which he set out the tasks of a new realism 'rousing the people of all freedom-loving nations', while *Twenty Great Australian Stories* traced the radical nationalist canon from Marcus Clarke, Joseph Furphy and Henry Lawson to the present. The Dolphin Press also aimed to produce cheap but well-designed editions of Australian works (as in its publication of Raffaello Carboni's *The Eureka Stockade*) but had to be wound up in 1947 for lack of capital and effective distribution arrangements.[60]

The party was tightening up on cultural work by the end of the decade. The Studio of Realist Art came under fire for bohemian laxity. After Miriam Hampson, a sister of Sam Aarons and aunt of Laurie and Eric, replaced Vic Arnold on the management committee of Sydney's New Theatre in 1948, a number of 'arty hangers on' were shown the door. The Arts and Science Committee condemned its 1949 revue for an allusion 'in very bad taste' to Stalin: 'art must truthfully reflect life'. Melbourne New Theatre deemed Oriel Gray's 1950 drama *Had We But World Enough*, exploring racism in a country town, to reveal a 'Tolstoyan individualism' and a failure to show how unity of the Aboriginals, white workers and small farmers would bring 'a positive solution'. Ken Coldicutt and his colleagues in the Realist Film Unit were expected to screen films imported by the Soviet Legation that were laden with clichés of Stalinist heroism.[61]

This move towards a more stringent form of socialist realism contributed to growing hostility to communist practitioners. In 1948 the *Sydney Morning Herald* stopped reviewing New Theatre productions or accepting its advertisements. In the same year a Coalition government in Victoria introduced legislation that restricted the screening of films to licensed theatres and cinemas. The Commonwealth Literary Fund, the principal source of financial support for writers, came under fire for awarding fellowships to left-wing authors—not just Jean Devanny and Katharine Susannah

Prichard but other members of the Fellowship of Australia Writers, such as Frank Dalby Davison and Marjorie Barnard, even James Rawling, who had been expelled from the party at the beginning of the war. At least Chifley kept his head: in response to opposition allegations that the Commonwealth was sponsoring communist propaganda, he declared the government would impose no political test on recipients of its support.[62]

But the party did. The Eureka Youth League (EYL) took up jazz in the post-war years, holding Saturday night concerts and record sessions in a number of suburban venues. The most successful was the EYL's Victorian headquarters in North Melbourne, where the country's first jazz convention was held in 1946. On Saturday nights Eureka Hall became the Uptown Club, where Graeme Bell's Dixieland jazz band attracted large numbers. Harry Stein, an EYL organiser who sometimes filled in as drummer, persuaded the band to perform at the inaugural World Festival of Youth and Students in Prague in 1947, a trip made possible by donations from the communist movement. The Bell Band proved enormously successful with numbers such as 'Walking Wenceslas Square', so it toured Europe for several months before returning to Australia and accepting a regular engagement with the ABC. A condition of the contract was that the members sever their links to the EYL. 'We gladly accept their resignations,' Audrey Blake declared. 'People with such a lack of principle have no place in our ranks.'[63]

Excessive demands cost the EYL another prominent member. Shirley Strickland, a Perth schoolteacher, was selected to represent Australia in hurdle and sprint events at the London Olympics of 1948. The party immediately claimed Strickland as one of its own, quoting her statement that 'The League has helped me very considerably to understand what is going on in the world.' When her success in winning three medals drew attention to this connection, she found it necessary to explain she was not a communist, even though she had 'definite socialist leanings'. At that time she said she would resume offering physical instruction to league members, but upon her return told reporters she would give the matter further thought and by 1949 she felt compelled to state that she had not been involved in the organisation since 1945.[64]

★

Among the victims of the *Zhdanovshchina* was Jenö Varga, Stalin's economic adviser who accompanied him to the Potsdam conference in 1945. Varga's mistake was to acknowledge the improved fortunes of the advanced capitalist economies after their governments learned under pressure of war how to manage their economies. In his book *The Economic Transformation of Capitalism at the End of the Second World War*, Varga predicted that the United States would enjoy several years more of increased prosperity.[65]

It was in this spirit that the Australian party welcomed the Labor government's 1945 White Paper on Full Employment setting out the measures it would use to maintain full employment and raise living standards.[66] There remained the caveat that the respite could only be temporary, since profits came at the expense of wages so that a crisis of overproduction was bound to recur. Australian communists embraced Varga's analysis as they embarked on their campaign for an immediate wage increase. His claim that the capitalist state had altered its relationship to the economy also served the political strategy they adopted at the Fourteenth Congress. Whereas monopoly capital had dominated the United States and United Kingdom between the wars, Varga argued, the Democratic administration in the US along with British Labour government—and, by implication, the one in Australia—had a broader, more popular base.

This suited the ACP's call for a progressive alliance of workers, farmers and the middle class to contest the dictates of big business. 'Twenty men who can meet in a secret room and dominate the whole population of Australia' were the subject of Len Fox's 1946 pamphlet *Wealthy Men*, which described the network of companies controlled by Australia's richest families. Such exposures of the concentration of wealth commonly drew on share registers and company reports, as Brian Fitzpatrick had in his recent exposure of how *The Rich Get Richer*. Taken up at the onset of the Cold War, the party's campaign had a more pointed message—to advance the interests of the people against an oppressive oligarchy.[67]

Fox's wealthy men owned newspapers and radio stations. They were the instigators of the Institute of Public Affairs and the paymasters of the

Liberal Party. Their business empires, run from Sydney and Melbourne, dominated the other states. Here Fox distinguished the 'Sugar Daddies' of Sydney, where the Colonial Sugar Refining Company was based, from the 'Steel Kings' of Melbourne, the home of BHP.[68] Later elaborations described a 'southern bloc', which had installed Liberal governments in South Australia, Victoria and Western Australia, and a northern 'bloc' that was unable to shift Labor from office in New South Wales and Queensland, so that the southerners were now setting their sights on Canberra.[69]

Their dominance was also given a more precise identity. They were the men who shared offices in a building on Collins Street in the financial quarter of Melbourne, 'the biggest and most ruthless group of monopolist parasites now preying on the people'. Beginning with the mining and smelting of non-ferrous metals, the Collins House companies had expanded in the first half of the twentieth century into a number of other industries, though communists greatly exaggerated the cohesion and reach of the Collins House group when they listed its range of interests: iron and steel, coal and shipping (here they confused it with BHP), gas, glass, chemicals, brewing, banks and newspapers. Lance Sharkey took up the denunciation of Collins House at the Fifteenth Congress, likening it to 'the 400 families' that French communists had made a 'great bogey' during the Popular Front of the later 1930s; scarcely an issue of *Tribune* thereafter failed to remind readers of Collins House's perfidy.[70]

The party continued to publish Varga right up to his fall from grace in 1947, when Soviet authorities accused him of 'subservience to bourgeois science' and closed his research institute. By then, however, the ACP was using his more recent writings to warn of an imminent depression.[71] Varga's forecast was in fact directed at the overheated US economy, which did suffer a short recession in 1949, but there was no sign of that in Australia. Rather, the ACP had fallen back into the habit of pinning its fortunes to a breakdown of capitalism that was always about to occur but somehow never did. In the course of its industrial offensive, the endorsement of Labor's reconstruction program gave way to an insistence that the government's tight controls of wages and prices could not stave off a crisis and served only to obstruct a working-class advance. Much was made of Ben Chifley's prediction during the 1946 election that Australia would enter a 'golden age' of prosperity so long as discipline was maintained. Although committed to his re-election, the party insisted the golden age was an illusion and continued to deride the prime minister's pipe dream at every opportunity.[72]

Criticism of the government mounted as the Cold War took hold. Just as it was blamed for betraying the workers in every industrial dispute, so the party drew attention to any sign that Labor was falling in behind the imperialist powers in its foreign policy. As the reprimands became more censorious, however, they only emphasised the contradictions in the communist position. It proposed a united front with a party that by its very nature served the interests of capital. Despite repeated rebuffs, moreover, it directed its electoral efforts towards keeping that party in office. Both in its public statements and private deliberations, the Australia Communist Party was unable to resolve these contradictions.

Until the end of 1947, all Western communist parties were enjoined to work in concert with labour and socialist parties. Ostensibly, the aim was to strengthen progressive forces in the period of reconstruction. Hence Lance Sharkey declared in July 1946 that the party was 'the enemy of that which is rotten in the ALP'—the Industrial Groups and 'right-wing stooges'—and that communists would strive to 'keep the ALP strong and progressive, and moving towards the acceptance of socialist principles'. Within the political committee he acknowledged that 'the Government is going more and more to the right'.[73] Dixon confirmed this assessment, noting how the party's relations with Labor's leaders had deteriorated. Although Evatt and some other ministers still gave communist union leaders confidential assurances of their good intentions, Chifley had brought right-wing members of the Cabinet to his most recent meeting with these unionists. It was necessary to sharpen attacks on the government.[74]

A further expectation was that Labor's pusillanimity would draw workers over to the Communist Party. This was always an aspect of the united front but not at first canvassed openly, and for that reason the political bureau quashed Jack Blake's 1946 call to build the united front from below. The early results were not encouraging. Despite growing disillusionment with the ALP, Dixon reported, there was no evidence of a swing to the party. On the contrary, membership, recruiting and press sales were falling. More worrying still was the growing electoral support for the Liberal Party—and, it would seem, an increasing restlessness among members. The central committee felt it necessary to warn against a tendency to say that Chifley was no better than Menzies.[75]

Then came the meeting in Poland that established the Cominform, proclaimed the division of the world into two hostile camps and instructed Western communist parties to expose all reformist illusions. The Australian one responded immediately by repudiating any suggestion of a peaceful transition to socialism, condemning the Chifley government as 'in the camp of the most reactionary section of the bourgeoisie', and calling for a popular front that would unite all those who were 'flocking away in disgust at the Labor Government'.[76] The political committee anticipated an intense period of struggle and discussed the need to prepare once more for illegality. Here, it would seem, was a final break with the strategy that had prevailed from the early 1940s—yet the party persisted with its call for a united front and continued to argue that Labor must be kept in office. As Blake acknowledged, it was an 'extremely complicated situation'.[77]

To see the Australian party as simply falling into line with the Cominform's declaration of two camps in yet another instance of dutiful compliance is to overlook clear signs of its impatience. This was expressed obliquely through condemnation of the CPGB. Tension between the two parties went back to the inter-war period, when the Communist International used the CPGB to supervise the CPA; more recently, Ernie Thornton had embarrassed the Australians by pressing Earl Browder's views on his trips to London in 1945. Neither party was free of sympathy for Browder's claim that the Teheran agreement opened up new possibilities for a lasting peace and peaceful transition to socialism, though both declined to follow his course of dissolving their own party.

Harry Pollitt, the general secretary of the CPGB, went furthest in his declaration that all countries could now find their way to socialism. A party leader more authentic and compelling than Miles or Sharkey, Pollitt believed the war had changed everything and even called for a continuation of Churchill's national coalition in the hope that the spirit of Dunkirk and D-Day would carry over into post-war recovery to speed the socialist advance. Just as his party took a stronger line than the Australian one against strikes in the later years of the war, so it went much further in avoiding them after the war, calling instead for a maximum work effort. Pollitt's emphasis on national unity did not go uncontested. There was open criticism during the lead-up to the CPGB's congress in November 1945, where a tenth of the delegates withheld support for the policy. That some complained of the 'top-down' nature of decision-making was a measure of the difference between the two parties—such dissent was unthinkable in Australia. And while the CPGB became increasingly critical of the Labour government's foreign and domestic policies, even in 1947 Pollitt continued to assert that 'the essence of the period we were now in is that of a transition stage towards socialism'.[78]

Sharkey first voiced his misgivings at the beginning of 1946. The British party lacked 'sufficient punch', he told the central committee, adding that 'after our little experience with Browderism it is better to say what one thinks rather than keep on thinking'. The political committee went further later in the year by setting out its concerns in a letter that Jack Henry took to an Empire Communist Conference in February 1947. The very fact that the CPGB summoned such a meeting, attended by delegates from eleven countries in various parts of the British Empire and observers from another fifteen, seems to have provoked the CPA, which felt it had outgrown such tutelage. Henry was constrained in his criticism during the conference since it was open to the public, but spoke more candidly at a meeting with the British leaders and found Pollitt's response platitudinous and patronising.[79]

Sharkey opened hostilities in October 1947 with a scathing review of Pollitt's recent policy statement, *Looking Ahead*. By this time Pollitt was openly critical of the Attlee government but he still talked of forcing it to follow a 'real socialist policy' in a constructive drive to solve the country's economic problems. His timing was unfortunate. A month later the Cominform put paid to any collaboration with the imperialist camp, so that Sharkey was able to accuse Pollitt of failing to understand the true nature of social democracy. Pollitt eventually fell into line with the two-camps position, though with a conspicuous lack of self-criticism (he'd had his fill of that after being forced to apologise for opposing the Nazi–Soviet pact in 1939). The most he would concede was that 'we were late in appreciating the full drift to the right of the Labour Government'.[80]

It was this failure that encouraged the Australians to go further. Some dissidents in the British party had already made contact with the ACP, and Sharkey was dismissive of Pollitt's attempt to justify his errors with 'effusions' that only created 'fresh illusions'. He saw no hope for the British party but 'to get rid of Pollitt' and rebuffed an invitation to attend the British party's congress in February 1948. Instead the ACP dispatched a long letter accusing the CPGB of 'reinforcing social democratic illusions among the masses'. This time the Australians were caught out by an unexpected development. In condemning the British party for seeking to push the Labour government to left, they invoked Marshall Tito's strategy of building a popular movement from below, but a month later Stalin condemned Tito for pursuing a nationalist road that downplayed the leading role of the revolutionary party.[81]

It was hardly surprising that in their reply to the Australian political committee the British central committee observed 'no doubt in view of the events in Yugoslavia you will be reviewing your opinions', and added it was a 'little ironical' to be accused of Browderism since Comrade Thornton had urged that error on them. Beyond these ripostes, the British rejoinder denied the sins of which it was accused. Indignant at these 'evasions and distortions', the Australians restated all the charges (the role of social democracy, the illusion of a peaceful transition to socialism, the reactionary nature of the production drive, the failure to support the anti-imperial struggle) and sent copies of the full correspondence to the Cominform and all communist parties.[82]

One of the objections Pollitt raised to the Australian party's polemics was its encouragement of factionalism.[83] The secretariat in Sydney was in touch with sympathetic members of the CPGB (including Edward Upward, whose novel *The Rotten Elements* relates the consequences), and although Sharkey warned Australians living in Britain against becoming involved, they kept him informed of the feeling there. So too did a well-placed party official (most probably William Rust, the hard-line editor of the *Daily Worker*), who said he could not become involved in the dispute but kept Sharkey abreast of the attitudes of leading comrades.[84] There is no indication that the Cominform sanctioned, let alone initiated, the Australian campaign, and there was not even a remote possibility Pollitt would lose his post. It makes more sense to see the ACP treating the CPGB as a scapegoat for errors it had shared, and perhaps also asserting a more prominent place in the communist firmament. Richard Dixon raised the errors of the CPGB with leading communists in Italy and France in 1949. They let him down gently, saying they shared the Australian party's concerns but were unable to intervene since the British party was not a member of the Cominform.[85]

The Australian ambitions were evident in its relations with Asian parties. In February 1948 Sharkey attended the congress of the Communist Party of India, which replaced its general secretary, Puran Chand Joshi, and embarked on revolutionary struggle. The ACP welcomed this turn to the left and published a statement by the new leadership that attributed Joshi's 'right opportunism' in pursuing a popular front with the Congress Party to the revisionist influence of the CPGB—in particular, Rajani Palme Dutt, its theoretician, who was usually a stern guardian of orthodoxy but at this time was lagging behind the Cominform on the colonial question.[86]

Then, following the congress, Sharkey travelled to Singapore and met leaders of the Communist Party of Malaya. It too had pursued a popular front with nationalist parties until mid-1948, when it turned to a campaign of insurgency against the British administration. It is doubtful that Sharkey determined this change, which occurred in other Asian countries following Zhdanov's declaration of the two camps, but he certainly encouraged it. The Communist Party of Malaya published two articles Sharkey wrote during his March visit, which stressed the need to mobilise against the 'Anglo-American bloc' and criticised the CPGB for failing to give a lead. Pollitt protested to Sharkey against 'the uncomradely and un-Communist action' of failing to consult his party. Sharkey, addressing Pollitt with the distinctly uncomradely title of

'Secretary', replied that the Cominform had not consulted Tito over its condemnation of his un-communist errors.[87]

Sharkey's role became a matter of public controversy when the British declared a state of emergency in Malaya in June to put down the uprising. Accusations in the Australian parliament that he had instructed the party there to embark on armed struggle were followed by British reports to the same effect and then claims by some captured Malayan communists that he had chided them for their caution. Sharkey insisted that he had done no more than meet them and encourage their struggle for independence, leaving the question of armed insurrection up to them. Compounding the accusation that the Australian party president had abetted the Soviet Union in fomenting revolution in a British territory was the threat by the Seamen's Union to prevent any Australian assistance to the British forces.[88] Chifley had no intention of being drawn into the conflict. He saw the unrest in Malaya as part of 'a great upsurge of nationalism' and an economic rebellion against exploitation, and while acknowledging that communists were exacerbating the discontent, saw no purpose in pursuing the matter further. The pressure to do more was mounting.[89]

Coming hard on the heels of this controversy was another concerning a proposed air service to Southeast Asia. Asian Airlines Ltd was registered as a company in January 1948 with Clarrie Campbell as its managing director. Campbell had helped arrange the purchase of Marx House and then played a prominent part in the boycott of Dutch shipping, while Fred Wong of the Chinese Seamen's Union was one of several Chinese shareholders. They proposed to operate a freight service from Australia to nationalist-controlled regions of Indonesia with Catalina flying-boats purchased from the Commonwealth Disposals Commission, and by June the plan included flights to Malaya. The British administration refused landing rights there after the CIS divulged the scheme to opposition politicians, and the sale of nine Catalinas did not proceed. But Asian Airlines became further evidence of the sinister intrigues of Australian communists.[90]

*

'Today capitalism is in crisis, fighting its doom, its foundations shattered. There is no other way out for toiling humanity than Communism, there is no leadership capable of leading nations to liberation other than Communist Parties.' With these closing words at the Fifteenth Congress in May 1948 Sharkey completed the ACP's adoption of the intransigent position laid down by the Cominform. In keeping with the growing hostility it faced, there was no attempt to make this congress a public occasion of the kind held just three years earlier and there were no press reports of the proceedings. One hundred and fourteen delegates assembled, and their average age had increased to nearly 40. That just seventeen were women was waved aside with the explanation that the end of the war reduced the need for them to serve in leading positions. A new recruitment drive had failed to arrest the decline of membership, finances were still shrinking, press and pamphlet sales were 'shocking'.[91]

The principal resolution noted the division of the world into two camps: 'the peace-loving, truly democratic socialist forces' and the 'reactionary camp of the American imperialists', which included 'the British, French and Dutch imperialist slave-drivers' and the 'surviving remnants of fascism everywhere'. The United States was undermining Australia's independence 'and threatening to drag us into a new war', yet Labor was 'capitulating before the reactionary offensive'. It had to be kept in office, for 'a victory of reaction would unleash an offensive of monopoly capital against the living standards and democratic liberties of the Australian masses', but the party would not restrict its efforts to that end in the federal election due next year. Rather, it would create a 'People's Front' to secure a 'People's Democracy'.[92]

The nature of this people's front remained unclear. It would involve an alliance between workers, farmers and the middle class around immediate demands taken up by local committees, though the prospects of spreading these across the country were remote. But the people's front would not come at the expense of pursuing a united front, against which the door was bolted and barred. 'We cannot separate the two', Dixon insisted, since 'people's unity would strengthen the united front just as working-class unity would strengthen the people's front'. The problem with united fronts was that they relied on partnership with other parties that, as recent events in both Western and Eastern Europe showed, consistently betrayed the people. The great advantage of the people's front was that it arose from the struggles of the mass of the people, as demonstrated in the liberation of Yugoslavia. There were many references to this model. 'Our understanding of the People's Front has been clarified a great deal', Jack Henry explained, by the 'excellent report of Marshall Tito' to the Cominform.[93]

Consternation followed a few weeks later when the ACP learned that Marshall Tito was an ungrateful anti-Soviet revisionist. This was 'one of the worst developments since Trotsky', Sharkey told the political committee, and 'the results could be disastrous'. Allowing that Tito had been 'high in our estimation', Dixon insisted that all members of the central committee had to share responsibility for any mistake, and issued a denunciation of the errors that resulted from Tito's denial of the leading role of the party. Did this mean the Australian party had made a mistake in embracing the people's front? He did not think so, and the political committee resolved to proceed with it—or at least with its preparation, as it was clear much preparation was needed.[94]

There was a notable absentee from the 1948 congress. Fred Paterson was still convalescing from injuries he suffered at a protest march in Brisbane two months earlier. The protest arose from a strike of rail workers in early February 1948 to secure a flow-on of the increased margins in the metals trade granted by the Commonwealth Arbitration Court, which quickly escalated. The Queensland Labor government declared a state of emergency at the end of the month, followed by an Industrial Law Amendment Act in March that authorised severe penalties for all activity that prolonged the stoppage. Charges were laid against six communist picketers, including the barrister Max Julius. All participated in the protest march on the morning of 17 March, with Julius and Paterson standing on a footpath as observers, when it was attacked by a large contingent of baton-wielding police. A policeman struck Paterson from behind as he went to the assistance of a wounded demonstrator, and he was taken to hospital with severe lacerations to his scalp, brain damage and a suspected fractured skull. Max Julius's brother Solomon stitched his head at the Brisbane General Hospital, but it was several months before Paterson was able to resume parliamentary duties.[95]

Although the government settled the dispute by granting the increased margins and subsequently repealed the Industrial Law Amendment Act, it refused to withdraw the prosecutions. Ted Rowe, who had gone to Queensland on behalf of the federal council of the Amalgamated Engineering Union, defied a summons for interfering with a government-conducted ballot and went into hiding before being smuggled across the border. 'Some of these police could not trace an elephant in the snow even if it wore gumboots,' Stan Moran boasted, but Rowe gave himself up after returning to Brisbane and speaking at Trades Hall, and discharged his offence with an apology within five days of imprisonment. Mick Healy, the secretary of the Trades Hall Council, Ted Englart, secretary of the Brisbane branch of the Waterside Workers' Federation, and Max Julius held firm. They were gaoled in August for refusing to pay their fines, which came to more than £650; the threat of a renewed industrial campaign was averted by anonymous payment of the outstanding amount.[96]

The party hailed the Queensland railway strike as a victory over repressive anti-strike legislation that revealed the true nature of a Labor government, though the party neither initiated the dispute nor anticipated the consequences. Sharkey had to explain to congress delegates that Ted Rowe was instructed not to apologise to the court, but was placed under great pressure by Joe Cranwell and other Amalgamated Engineering Union leaders to do so. Jim Healy revealed that the prime minister had dissociated himself from the sanctions imposed by the Queensland government. More particularly, Healy warned of a feeling among many workers that 'our Party is a severe one', and made impossible demands. He was signalling the difficulty the new line created for union members. They were to step up their campaign against the reformists, and Ernie Thornton announced to the congress that his union would no longer pay its full political levy to the ALP; instead members could choose to direct it to the ACP. But communist officials dominated the Federated Ironworkers' Association, whereas in other unions they relied on allies whose support would be strained to breaking point by such a step.[97]

Thornton himself bridled at the persistent censure of the party's trade unionists for 'economism', by which was meant their pursuit of industrial demands in ways that encouraged the illusion capitalism could meet their needs. This was a charge levelled at some of the most highly respected leaders, including Tom Wright, who was told that as his leadership of the Sheet Metal Workers was secure he should devote his efforts to political campaigns. The party's expectations were myopic. Union officials were ordered to 'develop activity of a broad political character, not confining themselves only to activity on behalf of their own members'—in fact, they were encountering increasing difficulty in persuading their members to take industrial action. Public sympathy was waning, and the fact that strikes had to be fought out to the bitter end imposed a growing burden on workers' families. It was also evident that solidarity strikes were more difficult to conduct than those arising from workplace grievances. Thornton appealed at the congress for 'a bit of balance in this matter'. There were some union officials 'who are being economist' and some with 'illusions about their scintillating personality', but blanket condemnation was unhelpful. You might as well condemn all party officials, because there are 'some real weaknesses' in their ranks. Six months later he was again rebuked for complaining that party functionaries were dictating to trade union officials.[98]

The Fifteenth Congress also brought Sharkey's replacement of J.B. Miles as general secretary. In a brief statement on the final day, Miles explained that he had turned 60, suffered from poor hearing and had decided the post required greater energy and mental vigour than he was able to provide. There was no conflict or power struggle, he added; rather, he had discussed his intention to resign with the other members of the secretariat—Sharkey, Dixon and Jack Henry—who agreed. Sharkey followed with a brief acknowledgement of the leadership Miles had provided, and delegates accorded him a standing ovation.

It was a sudden end to two decades of unchallenged authority, though signs of Miles's decline had been evident since the war, when Sharkey became the party's public spokesman. Neither he nor Dixon wanted to suggest it was time for the 'Old Man' to go, so Henry was brought down from Queensland in 1947 to do so. The decision was taken at a meeting of the political committee on the eve of the congress, with a marked lack of regret—it was Ted Rowe who insisted on a statement of appreciation. Afterwards, Sharkey in his cups became sentimental about 'poor old J.B.'. 'Oh Lance, don't give me the shits,' replied Henry, 'you know bloody well that he's been making messes.'[99]

Henry came to Sydney as organising secretary with the clear purpose of invigorating the cumbrous national apparatus. He told his Queensland intimates that he was going to 'clean out the whole nest of bludgers' working at Marx House, and a number were soon shown the door. The district structure was overhauled so that their full-time organisers were given wider responsibilities, and Claude Jones was brought down from Brisbane to direct their work, with Doug Olive coming later to supervise the industrial committee. Two veterans, Norm Jeffery and Ted Docker, were dropped from the central committee. Younger organisers were installed further afield: Laurie Aarons took charge of South Australia and then the Hunter Valley, his brother Eric went to the South Coast. Moving cadres about was intended to shake up settled ways and strengthen national oversight.[100]

Henry's criticism did not stop there. He was privately censorious of Sharkey and ridiculed Dixon among his close associates as 'just a pedantic school master who knew nothing about the working class'. But Dixon had assumed the presidency vacated by Sharkey, and these two men continued to issue the party's public statements. It suited them to have Henry effect some of the organisational changes they thought necessary, and also to have him close at hand rather than sniping from Brisbane, but they had no intention of surrendering control. For the same reason, Jack Blake was added to the secretariat at the end of 1948 and expected to come up from Melbourne as soon as possible. To prepare the party for the tasks ahead, an extended national school was conducted following the congress at which leading members spent three months discussing how the obstacle of social democracy would be cleared from the path to a people's democracy.[101]

7

Showdown, 1949–50

The circumstances in which the party set about building a people's front for a people's democracy could hardly have been less favourable. Any authenticity the people's democracies of Eastern Europe had as newly liberated countries finding their own way to socialism was lost as their communist rulers snuffed out all opposition. A show trial early in 1949 of Cardinal Mindszenty, the Catholic primate of Hungary, was followed later in the year by the confession of Laszlo Rajk, the communist minister of the interior, that he too was an agent of Western imperialism. Similar proscriptions and purges were conducted in the other people's republics, invariably justified by the Australian party. From mid-1948 the USSR blocked the West's road and rail access to its sector of Berlin, an exercise in futility since it could not prevent a round-the-clock airlift that kept the city supplied. By the time the blockade was abandoned a year later, Germany was divided into two rival states.

Stalin's brutal imposition of communist rule in Eastern Europe and clumsy attempt to force the West into an amenable settlement in Germany had brought about the very outcome he feared, the consolidation of the 'imperialist camp' in a military alliance that ensured American forces remained in Western Europe. The North Atlantic Treaty Organization (NATO) did not dispel fears the Red Army might still overwhelm these defences, but even after the Soviet Union successfully tested its own nuclear bomb in 1949, Stalin had no intention of risking another war. His calculations were based on the strategic interests of his own country rather than communism as a world movement, so that he actively discouraged the Chinese party from taking power until the US-backed regime of Chiang Kai-shek was on its last legs.

The belligerent statements issued by the Cominform made no mention of any strategy for winning power in capitalist countries—the task of their communist parties was simply to prevent further consolidation of the anti-Soviet alliance by championing peace and national independence. They complied with strikes, demonstrations and provocations that were accompanied by vehement denunciation of American imperialism and vitriolic attacks on the social-democrat lackeys who served its interests—but as the Spanish communist Fernando Claudin later observed, the violence of the language could not conceal the absence of any consideration of how these communist parties were to revive their flagging fortunes.[1]

The Australian party readily took up vilification of its own social democrats. 'We are not fooling around with milk and water sentimental reformists', Sharkey told the central committee in February 1949, 'but people who today are the definite allies of warmongers and imperial aggressors', rank opportunists who 'would betray their own grandmothers if it helped to ingratiate themselves with the capitalist class'. 'In all the history of the past,' Jack Henry added later in the year, 'there are no greater scoundrels anywhere in the world, whose hands are redder with the blood of the working class, than the reformists.'[2]

Despite such bombast, the party realised it would not be easy to uproot a reformism that was so deeply embedded in the country's system of politics and industrial relations. The venture into community activism had stalled. The work among farmers yielded a meagre harvest. A campaign against the rising cost of living (the Chifley government was finally dismantling price controls) was launched at the end of 1948 through the New Housewives' Association, but it was tiny and needed unionists to fill out the first and last mass protest in Martin Place. And how could a party that slavishly supported every twist and turn of Soviet policy claim to be defending Australia's independence? Dixon told the central committee in February 1949 that much preparatory work was needed before the peace movement could be launched, especially to persuade the 'masses' that the Soviet Union was genuine in its desire for peace.[3]

★

'You put that film on and you'll be looking for trouble.' The manager of Hoyts cinema company claimed to have received this anonymous phone call on the day he arranged a private screening of *The Iron Curtain* for parliamentarians and representatives of the Victoria police, the defence forces and the RSL. Produced by Darryl Zanuck for Twentieth Century-Fox, the feature film was based on a book by Igor Gouzenko, the cipher clerk who had defected from the Soviet Embassy in Ottawa, and dramatised his choice of freedom. It also showed how well-meaning Canadians were lured through organisations such as the Association for Scientific Workers and the Friends of the Soviet Union into betraying their country.[4] After protests against the screening of *The Iron Curtain* in North America and Europe, it opened at the Capitol Theatre in Melbourne in September 1948, with a substantial number of communists in the audience hissing, booing and laughing derisively. As fights broke out, a large detachment of police bundled the protesters into vans and took them away.[5] A closer watch was kept on the patrons of the Plaza Theatre in Sydney, where two men were arrested, and the Regent Theatre in Brisbane, where the Trades and Labor Council had imposed a boycott and a girl wearing bright purple slacks and a yellow jumper sold copies of the *Guardian* to patrons who queued for the first public showing there.[6]

By this time municipal bans on communist use of town halls were spreading to other organisations promoting friendship with the Soviet Union. In June 1948 the Sydney City Council rejected a request from the Australia–Russia Society for a town hall meeting that was to be addressed by its president, the Reverend E.J. Davidson, and Bert Evatt's brother Clive, who was a minister in the NSW government.[7] Six months later the town clerk of the Melbourne City Council cancelled a booking for Canon Maynard to chair a report by John Rodgers, the organiser of Australia–Soviet House, on his recent tour of Eastern Europe and the USSR. After unsuccessfully contesting the cancellation of the booking in the Supreme Court, the organisers proceeded to hold their meeting outside the town hall, with amplifiers broadcasting a short address by Rodgers to a large crowd before the meeting adjourned to the Unitarian Church in East Melbourne.[8]

Rodgers was able to speak at the Moonee Ponds, St Kilda and Camberwell town halls but a growing number of municipalities denied their facilities to communists in any guise. With this came tighter restrictions on street meetings. From late 1948, police in every state were enforcing council by-laws against speaking at suburban shopping centres, selling newspapers, distributing pamphlets or painting slogans on footpaths. The sale of literature was also prevented at public spaces traditionally used for open-air meetings on Sundays. The Perth City Council went further in September 1949 with a ban on the use of amplifiers at the Esplanade, which the party circumvented by addressing the crowd from a small boat on the shore of the Swan Estuary.[9]

Taken together, the restrictions on gatherings hampered the party's ability to promote the people's front. The party made a determined effort to overturn Melbourne City Council's refusal of the town hall to Australia–Soviet House. Several left-wing unions applied in March 1949 to use the main auditorium for a meeting on 'Trade Unions and Peace', and threatened to impose their own boycott if this request or another by Australia–Soviet House was denied. Rebuffed, the Building Workers' Industrial Union stopped construction of the council's new electricity substations, and Jim Coull's Liquor Trades Union withdrew services from council functions. As a further reprisal, signs were painted on the streets outside the homes of the councillors who had voted in favour of the ban. 'Disney the Warmonger Lives Here', read the message outside the lord mayor's house.[10]

The resort to such clandestine abuse was a sign of the increasing hostility the party encountered. Speakers at the Yarra Bank once more faced large numbers of hecklers, including men in uniform, and John Arrowsmith, the Victorian organiser, hardly served the cause of peace when he told a group of naval ratings, 'You will need your full rum issue to stand up to the Russian Navy.' He needed a police escort to reach his car. A fortnight later, provosts had to hold back servicemen from storming the Australian Railways Union's Unity House following another confrontation on the Yarra Bank.[11] It was more difficult still to obtain a hearing outside Melbourne. Two members were run out of Leongatha when they organised a public meeting in late 1948 and a planned tour of Gippsland had to be cancelled. Disruptors prevented John Rodgers from speaking at meetings in Shepparton and Wonthaggi in March 1949.

By this time the trouble had spread to other states. Hedley McMeekin, a Broken Hill doctor (yet another of the communists from the University of Melbourne medical school), was campaigning in a state by-election for the seat of Cobar when he appeared at Bourke on the evening of 9 March. Opponents stormed his platform, beat up local supporters and laid siege to the police station where he and Norm Jeffery took shelter. A similar affray occurred at Rockhampton later in March, when vigilantes assaulted the speakers and then invaded the party office to wreak destruction.[12] Ralph Gibson ran the gauntlet in his tour of Western Australia in April, with violent affrays at Boulder, Fremantle and Midland Junction before he was arrested for addressing a meeting at the railway workshops.[13] In the same month Richard Dixon wrote as ACP president to the federal government to complain about incitements to violence, citing the particular example of a suburban Sydney newspaper that stated 'we know a lot of citizens who would slit every communist's throat on sight'. Senator Nick McKenna, acting attorney-general while Evatt was overseas, replied that the statement did not incite the commission of an offence.[14]

A common thread ran through these refusals to allow communists a hearing—the RSL. It was present in strength at Leongatha, Shepparton, Wonthaggi, Bourke, Boulder and Fremantle, having adopted a policy that communists should be refused use of any town or shire hall. Where the local council permitted such meetings, the RSL reserved the right to disrupt them by bringing in members from further afield—while attributing outbreaks of violence to the spontaneous feeling of residents. The league went further later in the year, when its national president declared the days from 4 August to 3 September (the dates on which Australia entered the two world wars) to be 'anti-communist month' with the object of 'driving communists out of public life'.[15] Another ex-service body remained in the shadows. This was the 'Association', a paramilitary organisation led by Thomas Blamey and directed by officers who had served on his staff during the Second World War. Some local units of the

Association took part in the RSL's shows of strength, though its avowed purpose was to stand ready to put down a communist uprising.[16]

★

The Association regarded the Chifley government as wilfully blind to the communist threat. For its part, the government knew from Commonwealth Intelligence Service (CIS) reports of the Association's antagonism to the labour movement and disregard for democracy and the rule of law. It had no intention of bowing to the clamour to suppress the Communist Party as the opposition demanded, but several states were entertaining that step. The Victorian government established a royal commission into the Communist Party following revelations from a leading member about its nefarious activities.

Cecil Sharpley was a communist organiser, until recently a member of the state executive and in charge of the party's industrial work in Victoria. The introspective son of an Anglican clergyman, he came to Australia after losing his faith, joined the party in 1935 and claimed to have wrestled with his conscience before abandoning it at the end of 1948. His former comrades said he was drinking heavily and sponging on party members after abandoning his wife, but these and other allegations were made after he defected. Fearing retribution, he went fruit picking in Shepparton under an assumed name and entered into negotiations with Keith Murdoch to tell his story. He claimed he was offered £10 an article but in fact was paid much more and provided with a senior journalist and a bodyguard while he prepared them, with other reporters checking their accuracy and a lawyer vetting them for libel. The articles, which appeared in the Melbourne *Herald* (and were syndicated nationally) over seven days from 16 April 1949, caused a sensation. Tipped off in advance, the Victorian government announced immediately there would be a royal commission. Legislation was enacted in May to authorise a Supreme Court judge to conduct an inquiry into the origins, aims, objects and funds of the Communist Party in Victoria, and determine whether it engaged in subversive activities.[17]

Even though Sharpley had gone missing more than three months before his accusations appeared, they took the party by surprise. It responded with writs for libel against the *Herald* and Sharpley, and soon arranged an application for maintenance of the wife he had deserted, but was fighting another charge even before the royal commission began sitting. On 7 May Ken Miller, the editor of the *Guardian*, was charged in the city court with carnal knowledge of an eight-year-old girl. The police alleged she had gone with her brother to the flat in Richmond that Miller occupied with his wife Pat adjoining another in which Amirah and Ian Turner lived (Amirah's father, Itzhak Gust, owned the block of flats), and that Ken had sent her younger brother away and then committed the offence. The case collapsed when the girl changed her testimony repeatedly in court before admitting 'a lady' had told her to tell the story to the police. Having featured Miller's arrest on its front page, the *Herald* gave a perfunctory report of his acquittal. It had also provided readers with the Millers' address, so his wife Pat had to be shifted to safer accommodation while Ken was on remand pending the trial. Amirah and Ian moved into the Millers' flat to prevent anything being taken or planted. It was not an easy time to be a communist.[18]

The royal commission opened on 20 June in Melbourne's largest courtroom, the gallery packed with members of the public. Counsel assisting the commission called 80 witnesses. First was Malcolm Ellis, an anti-communist publicist who appeared at the invitation of the premier. He furnished a selection of documents that demonstrated the Communist Party's subservience to the Communist International, but that had been dissolved in 1943. James Rawling subsequently tendered a vast mass of material in pedantic detail, but his membership had ended in 1939. Other ex-communists made a poor impression, including 'Mrs X', who had been a branch secretary until leaving the party in 1939 and spent nine days recounting her subsequent persecution along with accusations against a number of alleged communists. She had previously been accused of perjury.

The appearance of Sharpley brought a storm of abuse from the public gallery—'You dirty rat', 'Scum', 'Renegade'—so the commissioner ordered it be cleared. Over the following 28 days the star witness presented a detailed account of the operation of the party and front organisations, its subservience to Moscow, use of violence and intimidation, and widespread rigging of union ballots. Many witnesses were called to corroborate his claims, some suggested by him and others by B.A. Santamaria, who advised one of the counsel assisting which members of his Industrial Groups would best bear out the allegations of corruption in union elections.[19] Little of this information was new and there was no expectation the royal commission would result in legal proceedings against the party or its members—indeed, the terms of reference made no provision for any recommendations. Tom Hollway, the Liberal premier, had recently broken with his Country Party coalition partner over its demands for more drastic measures, and he continued to resist calls to proscribe the party. But precisely because of accusations that the premier was soft on communism, it suited him to turn Sharpley's allegations over to a public inquiry.[20]

At first the party leadership made light of the turncoat. 'They have Sharpley, we have Shanghai,' Sharkey boasted in April, but privately he was highly critical of the Victorian executive's failure to anticipate the danger that this wavering functionary might defect. With a recent Gallup poll indicating that 70 per cent of voters believed the Communist Party should be banned, the prospect of a detailed exposure of its operations lasting right up to the federal election at the end of the year threatened to do substantial damage.[21] The secretariat dispatched funds to Melbourne to help answer the charges, which allowed extra editions of the *Guardian* to be produced along with leaflets and pamphlets. There were attempts to discredit Sharpley, not just through his wife's testimony of abuse in the maintenance case but with a statement from Ted Hill that he had been expelled for 'theft, lying, drunkenness and gross immorality'—by which was meant a conviction in 1947 for urinating in the doorway of a building in North Melbourne. There was also an ill-judged attempt to discredit the royal commissioner, Sir Charles Lowe, on the grounds that he had shares in Collins House companies, and even talk the party would boycott the hearings.[22]

This truculence changed as it became apparent that Lowe was far from convinced of Sharpley's reliability. Sharpley faltered under relentless cross-examination from Ted Hill, which caught him out on many points of detail. Hill's cold implacability unnerved Sharpley, who had recruited his tormenter and taken umbrage as the younger man overtook him in the party hierarchy. But Hill himself had a torrid time in the witness box when counsel assisting alleged that he had acted improperly when defending a union against a ballot-rigging charge. And because Hill appeared as a witness, it was Ted Laurie who led the examination of the communist witnesses. All were carefully coached to present the party in the most favourable terms: it was an organisation that sought to emancipate the workers, grounded in Marxist theory but rooted in Australian traditions, prepared to work by all available means but peaceful, democratic and as open as circumstances would permit. Ralph Gibson, who stuck to this script over seven days, impressed Lowe; some leading members departed from it under cross-examination; all were economical with the truth.[23]

The hearings dragged on for nine months, so that Lowe's report did not appear until April 1950. In dispassionate terms it laid out the origins, aims and objects of the Communist Party, found no evidence it was controlled from abroad, cited instances of violence, intimidation and defamation (the *Guardian* had to apologise for its attacks on Sharpley and the royal commission), but was not satisfied the numerous allegations of ballot rigging were established beyond doubt, except in one case. Lowe judged Sharpley an unreliable witness on many points, his credibility impaired by the 'munificent' reward he received for acting as an informer.[24] Both the *Herald* and the *Guardian* greeted Lowe's findings in the report as a vindication of their claims, but the public had lost interest and the report was overtaken by events: it appeared the day after Menzies brought down federal legislation to outlaw the Communist Party.

By then the damage was done. Even before the royal commission sat, Sharpley's seven original articles for the *Herald* were given wider circulation in a booklet entitled *I Was a Communist Leader*. He was interviewed on its national radio network, then in a special production of 'Movietone News' screened in all cinemas, and began a string of public appearances at the Pleasant Sunday Afternoon conducted by the unctuous Irving Benson at Melbourne's Central Methodist Mission, which was also broadcast to an Australia-wide audience. Throughout the hearings, the *Herald* unfailingly reported the allegations made by Sharpley and other witnesses against hundreds of men and women, wherever possible with photos to identify them, while passing over evidence to the contrary. The victims included Molly Inge, a party donor, who had the windows of her house smashed; Itzhak Gust, who lost his contract as a supplier of slippers to Coles; Brian Fitzpatrick, who lost a newspaper column; Clem Christesen, who was told by his printer that his literary magazine *Meanjin* would be boycotted; five journalists working for the *Herald*, whom Murdoch summarily dismissed; and Ted Laurie himself, who found briefs hard to come by for years afterwards. He also learned things about the party that deeply dismayed him. Although the party was pleased with Lowe's report, it suffered serious damage.

Among those named by Sharpley was a group of communist teachers. There was indeed a communist fraction in the Victorian Teachers' Union, though its leaders had been driven from office in 1948 following a concerted campaign against them. As the Cold War took hold, the threat of communists subverting the loyalty of impressionable young minds aroused particular anxiety, so there was a furore when Sam Lewis, the union's federal president, attended a 1947 UNESCO conference on education in Mexico as an official Australian delegate. His NSW Teachers' Federation was able to withstand the efforts of a Teachers' Anti-Communist League, whereas the Victorian Teachers' Union succumbed. The principal victim was Doris McRae, headmistress of Flemington Girls School and president of the high school section of the union. She was accused, under parliamentary privilege, of using a social studies course to disseminate communist propaganda, and then subjected to a campaign led by a local Catholic priest to remove her from the school, culminating in allegations that she had preached communism at a school assembly. The royal commission found no evidence that McRae or the other communist teachers had in any way used their positions to serve the party, but by then both her health and spirit were broken and she resigned from the Education Department in June 1950.[25]

Ben Chifley described the Victorian royal commission at the outset as 'completely futile', and continued to resist calls to outlaw the Communist Party. 'We shall not begin to chase shadows,' he insisted in response to the Liberal parliamentarians' decision in March 1948 to make this part of their party platform, for there was nothing to be gained by driving communists underground. Moreover, his government would never support any policy that deprived minorities of the right of expression 'unless—I qualify that statement—those expressions are subversive, seditious or in some way detrimental to the safety of the country'.[26]

Five months later the government prosecuted a communist for making a seditious utterance. Gil Burns, a member of the Queensland state executive, had taken part in a debate on the proposition 'That communism was not compatible with personal liberty' on the evening of 15 September 1948. The event was organised by the Queensland People's Party (shortly to become the Queensland division of the Liberal Party), in conjunction with the RSL and the League of Rights (a new organisation that saw communism as part of a Jewish conspiracy), with the intention of incriminating Burns, and to this end stationed a shorthand writer in the hall. During the question period at the end of the debate, a leading member of the RSL asked what the Australian Communist Party would do if war broke out between Russia and the West. Burns replied that such a war would be fought by the imperialist powers, but his questioner demanded a direct answer. 'All right,' Burns added, 'we would oppose that war. We would fight on the side of the Soviet Union. That's a direct answer.' A delighted Jim Killen, Burns' adversary in the debate and future Minister for Defence, said that 'if we had a Federal Government worthy of the name', Burns would be treated as a traitor.[27]

There were two officers of the CIS in the audience as well as two members of the special branch of the police force, and the Queensland director of the CIS sent their reports to the director-general, Commander Longfield Lloyd. Under fire for failing to curb communist activity, Lloyd urged that Burns be prosecuted. The difficulty, as the solicitor-general and other legal officers saw it, was that an answer to a hypothetical question seemed to fall outside Section 24D of the Crimes Act, which made it an offence to write, print or utter words with a seditious intent. They so advised the acting attorney-general (Evatt was presiding over the General Assembly of the United Nations), only to be instructed they were to launch a prosecution immediately. Burns was tried in the court of petty sessions on 11 October, found guilty of uttering seditious words and sentenced to six months' imprisonment.[28]

This was not the first time communists had made such statements. Earlier in the year, for example, Freda Brown said that the Communist Party would support Russia in a war against America.[29] The difference was the heightened risk of hostilities following the Soviet imposition of the Berlin blockade at the end of June 1948 and the increased pressure on the government to respond firmly to any threat to national defence. Senator Nick McKenna, the acting attorney-general, had strong anti-communist convictions, but he was close to Chifley and consulted him on the decision to prosecute. The crackdown clearly took the party by surprise. Richard Dixon, as party president, issued a statement that Burns' views were not those of the Australian Communist Party, which were to defend national independence against any aggressor, and Burns followed instructions to say at the trial that he was in error. The party secretariat notified all state committees he had muddled the party's line, which was that the Australian people would not go to war with the Soviet Union, and warned them to avoid any 'nonsense about the Party fighting for the Soviet Union'.[30]

Lance Sharkey came a cropper when he endeavoured to draw this distinction. He too was a victim of entrapment when rung at his home on the evening of Friday 4 March 1949 by a reporter for the *Daily Telegraph* seeking comment on recent statements by communist leaders in Western countries that were preparing to sign the North Atlantic Treaty. Did Sharkey agree with French communist leader Maurice Thorez's claim that if the Red Army entered France in pursuit of an aggressor, the workers would side with it? Sharkey felt compelled to meet the challenge and said that in the unlikely event of Soviet forces entering this country for the same purpose, Australian workers would welcome them. He insisted several times that the reporter ring him back to verify his statement, corrected several passages to indicate that the goal of communists was to prevent war and to emphasise the 'very remote and hypothetical' nature of war reaching Australia. He made further qualifications to a reporter from the *Sydney Morning Herald* who rang him in the early hours of the morning, and two from the *Daily Mirror* who visited him later in the day—though what good he thought would come of speaking off the cuff to these newshounds remains a mystery.[31]

The CIS immediately contacted the management of the three newspapers, obtained the reporters' notes of their conversations with Sharkey and collated the various passages. Within a fortnight McKenna decided to prosecute. Apart from an important difference between the statements of Burns ('fight') and Sharkey ('welcome'), Fred Paterson argued at the trial in June that Sharkey could not be found to have uttered his statement since he merely spoke on the telephone and had not used all the words that appeared in the composite statement given in the indictment. But a jury found him guilty and, after the High Court dismissed an appeal, he was sentenced in October to the maximum penalty: three years' gaol.[32]

A third prosecution for the same offence was brought against Kevin Healy, the chairman of the Western Australian state committee, who issued a statement on 7 March 1949 in support of Sharkey. His trial was delayed until the High Court considered the appeals of Sharkey and Burns, and the chief justice of the Supreme Court allowed him considerable latitude to argue that the prosecution was political in nature. The jury acquitted Healy, though the special branch of the Western Australia police raided the party's office and members' homes on 1 May seeking evidence of seditious activity.[33]

Commentators then and since have made similar criticisms. Perce Partridge, by this time professor of government at the University of Sydney, said the law of sedition was arbitrary, since a large number of statements, both for and against communism, were 'calculated to promote ill-will and hostility between different classes of His Majesty's subjects' (defined as sedition in Section 24A of the Crimes Act), adding that Sharkey had been singled out because he was general secretary of the Communist Party 'and the present administration dare not ignore the present outcry' for its suppression. There is evidence to support this claim: from March 1949 the Liberal Party was running press advertisements proclaiming 'Chifley is afraid to smash Communism'. The legal scholar Laurence Maher has observed that the press was replete at the time with statements (such as the one Richard Dixon drew to the attention of McKenna) that clearly fell within the provisions of the Act and yet were not prosecuted; indeed, McKenna was advised not to reply to Dixon, since communists would take advantage of any explanation he gave for the discrepancy.[34]

By 1949 the government was feeling the pressure of the United States and United Kingdom to get tough with the Communist Party. When Sir Frederick Shedden, the head of the Department of Defence, was sent to Washington to reassure the Americans about new security measures, he made much of the prosecutions of Burns, Sharkey and Healy.[35] But the principal reason for the crackdown was not to placate the leading Western powers, nor to reassure electors that the government would not tolerate sedition. It was an outcome of an escalating conflict between the Labor and Communist parties that culminated in their showdown over industrial relations.

★

In the immediate post-war years the federal government relied on its wage-pegging regulations (soon to expire) and the unwieldy system of industrial arbitration to hold down wages, intervening only when major disputes forced its hand. The states strengthened their own industrial powers in the course of this union offensive. Queensland made a secret ballot to strike compulsory at the end of 1946 and passed draconian legislation to deal with the 1948 rail strike, though this was subsequently repealed.

Like Queensland, Victoria enacted its own emergency legislation in the course of a tram strike there in early 1948. The Essential Services Act outlawed strikes unless a secret ballot was conducted by the chief electoral officer, and introduced harsh fines for both union officials and members who embarked on illegal strikes. Communists were not alone in opposing the measure, and Hollway reached a compromise with the leaders of the Trades Hall Council: he would not withdraw the legislation but neither would he proclaim it. In Hollway's absence overseas at the end of the year, however, the acting premier responded to a brief stoppage of gasworkers by proclaiming the Act and then commenced proceedings against the leaders of a number of other unions that stopped work in protest. Once more the Trades Hall Council negotiated a settlement: the prosecutions were dropped, the unions returned to work and it was agreed that any future industrial claim likely to cause serious disruption should be submitted to the council.[36]

This settlement precipitated a schism within the Victorian union movement. Eight left-wing unions—the Railways, Tramways, Seamen, Ship Painters and Dockers, Building Workers, Builders Labourers, Ironworkers and Meatworkers—accused the council's leaders of selling out the campaign to defeat the Essential Services Act. After stormy meetings at the Trades Hall in December 1948, with police in attendance, all were suspended from membership. They remained suspended until the end of 1951, allowing the council to accept the affiliation of two anti-communist alternatives (the Carpenters and Joiners and a breakaway from the Clerks). A further consequence was that the militants had no voice in the council during the industrial showdown of 1949.[37]

Meanwhile the Commonwealth had overhauled the federal arbitration system. The principal innovation, a large panel of lay commissioners each responsible for a particular industry, was seen as reducing the legal formality of the Arbitration Court, though the court retained control of the basic wage, minimum rates for women, standard hours and annual leave. In closing off appeal to the High Court, furthermore, the legislation made the Arbitration Court a superior court with the power to punish contempt. The ACTU executive was by no means happy with the new arrangement, but it did respond to the prime minister's call for a new spirit of cooperation in industry. At a conference he convened with employers, ACTU representatives accepted the need for increased production, expressed disapproval of unauthorised strikes, and were even prepared to consider dropping their opposition to incentive payments. As communists stepped up their militancy, the ACTU leadership was drawing closer to the Labor government.[38]

One remaining point of contention was the unions' application for an increase in the basic wage. In 1948, when the court finally granted the 40-hour week, the ACTU was at last able to proceed with its case for improved wages. It suffered an immediate setback in February 1949, when the Arbitration Court heard applications from the Commonwealth and employers for representation by legal counsel; their involvement threatened to drag out the hearings in the same way as the 40-hour case—and after the court acceded to the request, it took another eighteen months to reach a decision on the basic wage. The early sign of delay drew criticism from Jack McPhillips, assistant secretary of the Federated Ironworkers' Association (FIA), and one of three unionists representing the ACTU in the basic wage case. Speaking at a meeting in Melbourne's Unity Hall in early March as part of the communist campaign on prices and wages, he said the wage claim would be settled 'outside the Arbitration Court', since 'we do not trust the people in charge of the Court to play the game'.[39]

The first of these statements was consistent with what communists had always said about arbitration: that it gave nothing the workers did not win for themselves. The second also had a long lineage, going back to the Wobbly (i.e. union) song 'Bump Me into Parliament', which singled out H.B. Higgins, president of the Arbitration Court from 1907 to 1921, as a capitalist lackey. Nevertheless, McPhillips was charged with contempt and brought before the court. He denied saying he did not trust the judges to play the game, pointing out that the audience would have laughed at him if used such a phrase 'associated with the old school tie', but the Crown solicitor had obtained sworn statements from three journalists and he was found guilty. One of the judges would have imposed a fine (as the court had when an employers' organisation accused it of partisanship in the 40-hour case); the other two were adamant that such a grave contempt had to be punished by a gaol term of a month.[40]

The severity of the penalty shocked the union movement. The ACTU executive sought without success to have McPhillips released, though its subsequent removal of him from its panel of advocates in the wage case created further difficulties since a number of left-wing unions withdrew their authorisation for the ACTU to act on their behalf. The party also initiated a number of stoppages in protest at the gaoling, and there was talk that these too should be prosecuted. The CIS gathered affidavits from journalists against Tom Wright of the Sheet Metal Workers for describing the conciliation commissioners as 'dilutee judges whose main activity appears to be strikebreaking', though the president of the court ruled that the commissioners were not protected from criticism.[41]

The Waterside Workers' Federation (WWF) was the next to feel the government's resolve. Jim Healy had enjoyed good relations with Richard Kirby, a judge of the Arbitration Court who also headed the Stevedoring Industry Commission. Although Kirby turned a blind eye to the union's protest stoppage on 28 March 1949 over the prosecution of Sharkey, he took strong exception to another on 11 April in support of McPhillips and, after failing to receive an undertaking the union would refrain from such action, recommended that Healy and Ted Roach, the assistant secretary, be removed from the commission. Not at all sure the government would agree, Kirby was surprised that the Minister for Shipping (the prime minister was overseas) told him 'Healy has to go'. Indeed, the government went further, abolishing the Stevedoring Commission and thereby abandoning any provision for consulting the union.[42]

Then came the showdown with the miners. They had been seeking better wages and conditions since the war in what remained a troubled and fractious industry, but could not have chosen a less propitious time than April 1949 to serve a log of claims that included a wage increase, a 35-hour week and three weeks of annual leave. The government, which had spent large sums on improving amenities without any lift in production, regarded this as a direct communist challenge. It did not have to look far for confirmation of that assessment: Edgar Ross, who edited the Miners' Federation's newspaper *Common Cause*, had boasted at the party congress in May 1948 that that miners could play a decisive role in the coming crisis.[43]

Yet the party remained censorious of the chronic lack of discipline among miners, which Bob Wells had been powerless to control. He abandoned the presidency of the federation in 1947 without consulting the party, and although communists secured the election of Wonthaggi's Idris Williams as his replacement, they had since lost several other positions and held only the narrowest of majorities on the central council. Not that the party had to persuade the miners to demand action on their log of claims. On the contrary, the other members of the federation's central council (and the Coal Mining Unions' Council, which embraced the craft unions) did so with enthusiasm. After subsequent negotiations with the employers proved fruitless, aggregate meetings voted overwhelmingly to commence a general strike on 27 June 1949.[44]

The government responded immediately by freezing the federation's funds. The National Emergency (Coal Strike) Act, introduced on 29 June and completed on the same day, prohibited the use of its funds or those of any union to support the strikers and it was backdated to the announcement of the strike on 16 June. A week later the secretary of the western district of the federation was sentenced to a month's imprisonment for refusing to answer questions about money drawn from its account. Then thirteen officials of three unions, the Miners' Federation, the FIA and the WWF, were brought before the court and found guilty of contempt for refusing to reveal the location of large sums they had withdrawn. Five miners' leaders (two of them members of the ALP), along with Jim Healy and Ted Roach, were given twelve months, and McPhillips of the FIA began a new term of six months. This was a dramatic escalation of the dispute, since the union movement had always upheld the right to strike and the president of the ACTU, who was endeavouring to persuade the miners to resume negotiations, warned that the gaolings would make his task far more difficult.[45]

Although the judge who sentenced them claimed to be simply upholding the law, he went much further in his condemnation of the defendants: 'you have imposed upon the community intolerable hardships', 'you have caused the economy to suffer very great loss', 'you have prejudiced and attacked two Labour governments'. Both the Commonwealth and NSW governments made similar claims. In full-page advertisements that appeared in more than 80 newspapers over the course of the strike, the prime minister presented it as a communist-inspired attempt to 'smash the arbitration system', 'sabotage Australian industry' and 'destroy the democratic way of life'.[46]

On 8 July federal and NSW police raided Marx House and took away a truckload of material. The ostensible purpose was to find evidence that the party had used funds to support the strike, though since it was not an incorporated organisation the subsequent proceedings were taken against members of the central committee, including McPhillips and Healy, who were brought into court from Long Bay Gaol handcuffed together. Ordered to pay the missing money to the Industrial Registrar, the party was in a cleft stick: if it refused to do so, the allegation the strike was a communist plot would gain credibility; if it complied, the leaders could be accused of deserting the miners they had duped at the first sign of personal danger. It chose the latter option, claiming the wrathful howls of its enemies were a vindication of its dexterity.[47]

The miners' leaders had seriously misjudged the prime minister's determination to break the strike. Even though he warned them in early July it would be 'boots and all' if they continued to wage their 'callous war on the community', they thought the crippling effects of the lack of coal for industry, transport and households, families reduced to just a few hours of power a day for cooking and heating in the depths of winter, would force his hand. Chifley remained adamant he would not negotiate, and few members of the government challenged the severity of his measures: the prevention of any support for mining families, and the use of the navy to unload a ship carrying coal from India and then the army to operate open-cut mines. A threat to give the Australian Workers' Union coverage of these mines broke resistance. After aggregate meetings voted overwhelmingly against the central council's recommendation to persist with their demands, the miners returned to work on 15 August.[48]

The magnitude of the defeat is difficult to exaggerate. It exposed the party to new levels of execration. Communists who attempted to rally support outside the mining districts ran a gauntlet of abuse that shook even the most resolute. As secretary in Newcastle, Laurie Aarons arranged public meetings on three consecutive Sundays during the strike that attracted thousands of workers. The only trouble, he observed, 'was that nine hundred out of every one thousand wanted to stamp us into the ground'.[49] The defeat set back the party in the Miners' Federation and other unions, increased their isolation within the ACTU, exacerbated the antagonism of the ALP and strengthened the influence of the Industrial Groups.

Even while the miners were on strike, the government gave the Arbitration Court increased powers to regulate unions. Legislation enacted in July 1949 allowed any member of a registered union to seek rectification of any irregularity in the conduct of its affairs. The court could, for example, order reinstatement of an expelled member, and it could direct a flawed election of officers to be held again under the supervision of the Industrial Registrar. An ALP industrial committee on which Groupers were well represented suggested these changes, which were directed at unions with communist leaders. Some of these communists had used charges such as disruptive conduct or bringing the union into disrepute to suspend or expel their opponents, and Sharpley's allegations of ballot rigging were fresh in the public mind. That the ACTU supported the legislation was indicative of the new mood, for it had always resisted outside interference in union affairs. Responsibility for the new jurisdiction was given to a new member of the court, Edward Dunphy. Recently, as the president of Western Australia's Arbitration Court, he had ruled that communists were not 'fit and proper persons to hold executive office in a union' and refused to allow any who did to participate in basic wage hearings. His appointment to the federal tribunal made it clear the gloves were off.[50]

As it happened, the only union in which Royal Commissioner Lowe was satisfied there had been ballot rigging in Victoria, the Building Workers' Industrial Union, had been deregistered in 1948, so the court could not investigate it. It did, however, take up complaints from members of the Industrial Group in the Victorian branch of the Clerks' Union. They had been seeking to win back control ever since communists evicted them in 1945 from the union office in Elizabeth Street, and Ted Peters, the group's leader and a member of the state executive of the ALP, was censured by the union executive in 1948 for criticising the conduct of a recent postal ballot. During the ballot at the end of 1949, the Groupers foreshadowed an application to the Arbitration Court over alleged irregularities but were forestalled when Fred Farrall, the returning officer, cancelled the election. Farrall claimed to have done so after discovering some forged votes in favour of left candidates that he thought would be used to frame the union executive and, on the advice of Ted Hill, took the ballot box to the backyard of his cottage in South Yarra, doused it with petrol and burnt the contents.[51]

Unsurprisingly, Dunphy declared the election void and ordered a new one under the supervision of the Industrial Registrar. It turned out, however, that the court did not have the power to replace the returning officer, so he and the registrar had to jointly issue the new ballot papers.

Farrall once more proved an unhelpful returning officer, claiming that illness prevented him from authorising more than 200 of the 6000 ballot papers in any day, and then resigning before the result was declared so that the process would have to begin again. He was delaying the inevitable. A team of Groupers won the election by more than two to one, and followed precedent by forcing their way into the union premises. For good measure they expelled several communists. The union would remain in their hands for the next 40 years of increasingly autocratic leadership, which ended only when a young Lindsay Tanner restored democratic control.[52]

Farrall was procrastinating with an eye to the federal conference of the Clerks' Union set for late March 1950, at which numbers were tight. Western Australia, Queensland and the separate taxation branch were anti-communist, while New South Wales, South Australia and Victoria supported the communist federal secretary, Harry Thorne. He and Jack Hughes, the NSW secretary, managed to have delegates from the old Victorian executive admitted to the conference. The new Victorian officers appealed to the Arbitration Court, which eventually found in their favour but not until the end of 1951.[53]

Hughes' hand was strengthened by an ill-judged venture of the Group in the NSW branch of the Clerks' Union. In early 1949 it engaged a new organiser, Bill Dobson, to gather evidence of ballot rigging. He quickly came to grief when he was discovered trying to plant a radio transmitter in a meeting of the union executive. Undeterred, Dobson attracted sensational press coverage when he was found on the evening of 6 August on the shore of Rose Bay, semi-conscious, blue with cold and mumbling about three communists on a Manly ferry who had bashed him, stolen his briefcase and thrown him over the rails. The police were sceptical, especially when the CIS advised them of his record. Dobson was a fantasist who had posed as an RAAF veteran and war correspondent, a petty criminal with convictions for burglary, fraud and possession of an unlicensed firearm, and a confidence man who had fooled many who should have known better—including Arthur Calwell, who arranged for him to be given telephone facilities for his work of national importance. As Dobson's story fell apart, the Group leaders repudiated 'Diver'

Dobson, who headed for the bush. From there he rang Laurie Aarons in Newcastle, who brought him to Jack Hughes in Sydney, where for a sum he disclosed the plot to discredit the party.[54]

That was a rare win in a year of reverses. The party was losing ground in the FIA, partly because the union was contracting as munitions work ended, partly because veteran iron workers and munition hands who had fought for improvements were leaving the industry, and partly because of growing resistance to protest action—the great majority of branches refused to stop work when Jack McPhillips was gaoled. Ernie Thornton's frequent absences abroad did not help. Laurie Short of Balmain challenged Thornton in the election for federal secretary and attracted widespread publicity in August 1949 when he was bashed at the entrance of the union headquarters. The national officers foolishly tried to discredit him, alleging that, like the claims of 'Diver Dobson' several days later, it was all a publicity stunt.

Thornton secured a narrow victory over Short in the election of late 1949, though he was clearly worried that the ballot would not withstand scrutiny as he undertook to hold an inquiry if Short suspended an appeal to the Arbitration Court. This offer, which Short rejected, widened the rift between Thornton and McPhillips, who continued to crack the whip while the federal secretary strutted the stage at meetings of the World Federation of Trade Unions (WFTU). Following a decision by Dunphy in June 1950 to hear the appeal against the disputed union election, Thornton resigned from his union to work for the WFTU. Although McPhillips defeated Short in the ballot for the vacancy, the union was embroiled in an almost continuous series of legal challenges that culminated in a decision by Dunphy in November 1951 that the disputed election was rendered invalid by 'forgery, fraud and irregularity on a grand scale' and a declaration that Short was the national secretary. Short dismissed the office staff and evicted a number of tenants from the FIA's headquarters in George Street (including the Hotel, Club and Restaurant Employees' Union, the Association of Scientific Workers, the Australian Union of Women and the trade union club that since 1945 had served as a meeting place for the left). This communist bastion had fallen.[55]

The biennial congress of the ACTU in September 1949 confirmed the party's weakened industrial influence. The union leaders gaoled for contempt during the miners' strike were there, released following the return to work, and communists made up perhaps a third of the delegates. In contrast to the previous congresses of 1945 and 1947, however, they attracted almost no support from other delegates. Hence congress endorsed the actions of the executive in the miners' strike and, for good measure, resolved that any similar dispute must be referred to the ACTU. It rejected a campaign of action for an increased basic wage, and endorsed the removal of McPhillips from its panel of advocates. A measure of the officers' confidence was their invitation to the US Embassy's labour attaché, who sat alongside them on the platform; a motion to remove him was defeated by 209 votes to 148. Also present was the young Donald Horne, a sardonic feature writer for the *Daily Telegraph*. He described the studied cheerfulness of leading communists as one vote after another went against them, the twinkle in the eyes of Jack Hughes, the geniality of Jim Healy and the fixed grin of Tom Wright. Only the 'scowls and dark mutterings' of Ernie Thornton gave the game away. This congress marked the complete defeat of the party's hopes of winning leadership of the union movement.[56]

It also revealed the delusions that overcame the party as it stepped up its industrial campaign. Through their zeal and dedication, communists had achieved considerable success in the drive for better wages, hours and conditions following the war. The effect was to reinforce a belief that they were not simply leading workers impatient to share in the benefits of economic growth after years of wage-pegging and consumer rationing, but directing and controlling them. As labour historian Tom Sheridan has argued, these illusions were encouraged by the rising tide of anti-communism that blamed the communists for every dispute.

In 1948, when the party embarked on an all-out attempt to expose reformism, it was further misled by the conviction that Australia was about to experience a serious economic crisis—an illusion encouraged by Soviet denunciation of the Marshall Plan, which was applied here without any consideration of local circumstances. With this miscalculation went an insistence that the party's leading trade unionists must combat all forms of economism. This too was a gross overestimation of their influence. They held office because they were able to secure economic gains for their members, and it was in doing so that they found common cause with other militants. A direct assault on the ACTU could only isolate them.[57]

*

The left suffered one other rebuff at the 1949 congress that no doubt exacerbated Thornton's scowls, a decision to withdraw from the World Federation of Trade Unions. He had represented the ACTU at the founding conferences of this body in London and Paris during 1945, defended it from British and American criticism, regularly attended meetings and was vice-president of the metalworkers' section. The WFTU's decision to oppose the Marshall Plan caused a split that culminated in the formation of an alternative body, the International Confederation of Free Trade Unions, in 1949. The ACTU declined to send delegates to the WFTU's Milan congress in June of that year, at which Thornton was elected to the executive committee, and voted to withdraw in September by 231 votes to 134, leaving only the FIA, the Miners, Seamen, Waterside Workers and Building Workers as affiliates of its industrial sections. In 1950 Thornton took up a post at the WFTU's Asian Bureau in Beijing.[58]

Similar arguments engulfed other international bodies founded at the end of the war in the spirit of optimism engendered by the Grand Alliance. They also rapidly succumbed to the divisive effects of the Cold War. In 1946 the National Union of Australian University of Students applied for membership of the International Union of Students (IUS). Based in Prague, its initial membership included a number of Western student organisations, though most dropped out following the Czech coup in early 1948. The Labour clubs were able to delay Australia's withdrawal until 1949, by which time a number of communists had worked for it there. Ken Tolhurst and his wife Moira did so until the end of 1949, when a growing apprehension of the purges led him to 'extricate' himself.[59] The Tolhursts were followed to Prague by Noel Ebbels, Ken Gott and Stephen and Nita Murray-Smith, who gave no indication of any reservations before they left in 1951—though we saw in the Introduction that Stephen later claimed to have had misgivings. By this time the Labour clubs had lost any influence in Australian universities and these ardent Melbournians no longer represented anything more than the party.[60]

The same applied to a parallel organisation, the World Federation of Democratic Youth, which held a founding conference in London in 1945 before establishing its secretariat in Paris and then Budapest. An Australian, Bert Williams, was one of the organising secretaries and in 1947 the Eureka Youth League (EYL) raised a delegation of 23 Australians to attend the first of its biennial World Youth Festivals in Prague and to participate in a 'Shock Brigade' to assist in the reconstruction of a Yugoslav rail line. Most were party members, though not all, as the subsequent parting of ways with Graeme Bell's jazz band demonstrated. A larger contingent of 40 went to the 1949 festival in Budapest, mostly from trade unions but including Nita Murray-Smith's brother John Bluthal, together with Bernard Rechter and Miriam Rechter (later Dixson) from the Melbourne Labour Club and Frank Hardy.[61]

Each national delegation was expected to provide a display of its own democratic culture, and the Australians decided to sing 'Waltzing Matilda'—the only trouble was that none of them knew all the words. They were not alone in their predicament: the best the British could offer at Prague was 'D'Ye Ken John Peel?', and their contribution to a work brigade concert was 'My Old Man Said Follow the Van'.[62] The Australians also took reels of *The Overlanders* and *Indonesia Calling*, recalling the glory days before the Cold War took hold. And although Audrey Blake persuaded some members of other youth organisations to make the journey, by this time those organisations had terminated any association with the EYL. The opening ceremony in Budapest, in which 1000 white doves were released while the 10,000 delegates cheered Stalin as 'The Guardian of World Peace', showed the clear alignment of the World Federation of Democratic Youth with the Soviet camp. So did the closing ceremony, when thousands of delegates leaped to their feet chanting 'Stalin! Stalin! Stalin!' as his portrait appeared on a screen. The playwright Mona Brand looked on this novel spectacle with 'something like horror'.[63]

Such ostentatious homage came at the expense of credibility. The federation claimed to represent the common interests of the freedom-loving people in all countries, but invariably supported the Soviet interpretation of world events. It professed to be democratic, but the resolutions adopted at its festivals were prepared in advance and discussion was tightly confined. The internationalism it espoused was that of the two camps, one peaceful and progressive, the other bellicose and reactionary, with no middle ground.

This meant that Yugoslavia was excluded from any involvement after its expulsion from the Cominform in 1948. Tito's original offence was subordinating the leading role of the party to a people's front of workers and peasants, but his continued defiance brought rapid escalation of the charges. He and his comrades were a 'gang of imperialist spies and murderers' conspiring with the West to sabotage neighbouring people's democracies. The Australian party fell into line with these preposterous claims, and members of the EYL who had worked there in 1947 on the railway construction project handed back the badges awarded to them. The vilification caused particular difficulties for Yugoslavs living in Australia. While a significant number who had taken refuge between the wars returned to their homeland following its liberation, the party retained a following here. Dissidents, including sympathetic Australians, now had to form their own Society for Cultural Relations with Yugoslavia.[64]

After Yugoslavia was made a pariah for rejecting Soviet tutelage, the other Eastern European regimes took care to distance themselves from earlier claims that they too were following their own paths to socialism. Paradoxically, Yugoslavia was a federation whereas the other people's democracies (except for Czechoslovakia) were dominated by a single nationality, and became more nationalist as they expelled ethnic minorities after the war. Stalin himself had promoted Russian patriotism during the war, and Zhdanov's ideological crusade against errant artists, scientists and intellectuals had a strong xenophobic component. Russia's Jewish community was singled out for its rootless cosmopolitanism. Yiddish culture was suppressed, the Jewish Anti-Fascist Committee dissolved and its leader murdered. Romania, Hungary and other people's democracies followed suit, purging their communist parties of Jewish members and uncovering Zionist plots in a wave of anti-Semitism that culminated

Max Thomas and Horrie Ratliff were arrested in November 1940 for breach of wartime security regulations. They served six-month gaol terms and were later interned at Holsworthy military camp, where they embarked on a hunger strike. This demonstration in Sydney was part of a nationwide campaign for their release. SLSNW

After Germany invaded the USSR in June 1941, the outcome of the war was determined on the Eastern Front. Despite frequent assurances from the other Allies that they would relieve pressure on the Soviet Union by opening a second, western, front, Churchill and Roosevelt delayed doing so. This procession along the Yarra in 1942 linked the demand for a second front with an increased Australian war effort. Note the respectability of the participants. AWM

The artist Albert Tucker, briefly a party member, took this shot of Victorian Secretary Jack Blake addressing an evening meeting on the Yarra Bank in 1942. Behind Blake stands Ralph Gibson, the state president. The police helmets draw attention to the restrictions on communist activity. NLA

Albert Tucker also took this shot of a march of the Australia–Soviet Friendship Society along Queen Street, Melbourne, in 1943. Banners of Lenin and Stalin pass by Queen Victoria Market. SLVIC

Audrey Blake, chief organiser of the Eureka Youth League, launched the New Deal for Youth campaign in 1945. The principal demands were for better wages and conditions, raising the school leaving wage, improved vocational training, the franchise for all citizens aged 18 and equal rights for men and women. The use of national dress reflects the call for wartime unity. SLSNW

Marx Schools were established in the closing years of the war to meet the needs of the influx of new members. In addition to short courses on communist doctrine and practice, they offered advanced courses on Marxism–Leninism as well as classes in history, literature, music, art and foreign languages. This photo shows a class immersed in their studies. NAA

The party's candidates for the New South Wales parliamentary elections in May 1944 appear here with Fred Paterson (who had been elected to the Queensland legislature earlier that month). From left they are Jack Martin, Harold Wells, Paterson, Adam Ogston, Stan Coulton and Stan Moran. NAA

May Day march in Melbourne, late 1940s, with female members of the Eureka Youth League heading from Trades Hall through the city to Yarra Bank. Olga Silver, later a stalwart at the party's International Bookshop, comes before the man carrying the Eureka Flag. But who was responsible for the women's dress? UMA

A demonstration in support of the Red Army in its defence of Stalingrad, the city that ensured Soviet access to the Caucasus oilfields. German and other Axis forces besieged Stalingrad from August 1942 until February 1943, when they were themselves cut off and forced to surrender. With two million casualties, this was a turning point in the war. SLNSW

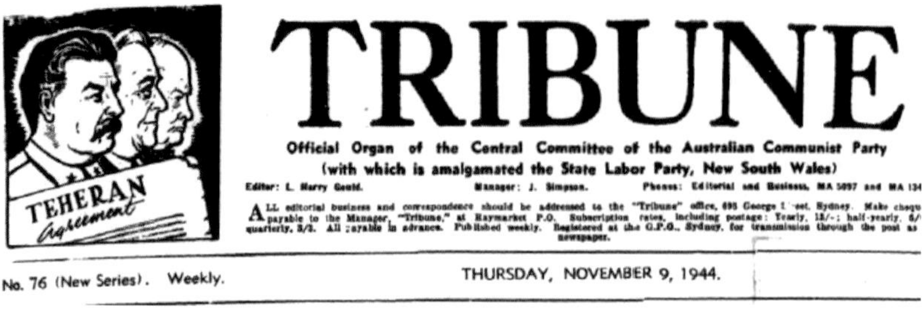

TRIBUNE

Official Organ of the Central Committee of the Australian Communist Party
(with which is amalgamated the State Labor Party, New South Wales)

Editor: L. Harry Gould. Manager: J. Simpson. Phones: Editorial and Business, MA 5097 and MA 134

ALL editorial business and correspondence should be addressed to the "Tribune" office, 695 George Street, Sydney. Make cheques payable to the Manager, "Tribune," at Haymarket P.O. Subscription rates, including postage: Yearly, 13/-; half-yearly, 6/-; quarterly, 3/3. All payable in advance. Published weekly. Registered at the G.P.O., Sydney, for transmission through the post as a newspaper.

No. 76 (New Series). Weekly. THURSDAY, NOVEMBER 9, 1944.

This triptych of Stalin, Roosevelt and Churchill appeared on the masthead of *Tribune* on 9 November 1944, recalling their summit meeting in Tehran at the end of the previous year. It marks the high point of optimism within the party for a peaceful post-war order. NLA

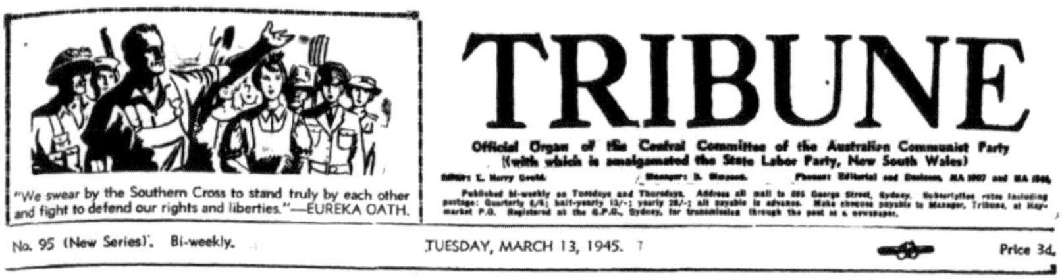

"We swear by the Southern Cross to stand truly by each other and fight to defend our rights and liberties."—EUREKA OATH.

TRIBUNE

Official Organ of the Central Committee of the Australian Communist Party
(with which is amalgamated the State Labor Party, New South Wales)

No. 95 (New Series). Bi-weekly. TUESDAY, MARCH 13, 1945. Price 3d.

The *Tribune* masthead of 13 March 1945 invoking the oath taken by the Eureka rebels to affirm the alliance of servicemen, servicewomen, workers and farmers. NLA

The Thirteenth National Congress in Sydney Town Hall, March 1943. Richard Dixon as assistant secretary presents Western Australian delegates with the cup for winning the recruitment competition. Note the delegates in service uniform and women wearing blouse and sash. SLNSW

The New Theatre movement originated in Britain and the United States during the 1930s, and branches of the New Theatre League were formed in Sydney, Melbourne, Brisbane, Perth, Adelaide, Newcastle and Lithgow. This 1945 photo shows the dressing room at the Castlereagh Street (Sydney) theatre when the company was performing the play *All Change Here* by the British communist (and future Labour peer) Ted Willis. SLNSW

Ernie Thornton, the national secretary of the Federated Ironworkers' Association, resigned in 1950 to work in Beijing for the World Federation of Trade Unions. With his union covering the munitions industry, he was a dominant and domineering leader during the war, repeatedly at odds with party policy. SLNSW

Marx House was established in 1944 after the party acquired a building at the southern end of George Street, Sydney. Members converted it into the headquarters of the central committee and its specialist departments, with a bookshop, meeting rooms, and editorial facilities for *Tribune*. NAA

Shortly after the miners' strike began on 27 June 1949, the federal parliament passed legislation that made it illegal to give financial assistance to miners and their families. Executing a warrant issued under the Crimes Act, members of the Commonwealth Security Service, customs officials and NSW police raided Marx House and took away records and publications. Marx House was sold shortly afterwards. SLNSW

In 1948 the Labor government of Queensland passed legislation to prohibit support for striking railway workers. Fred Paterson, acting as legal observer of a protest march on the morning of St Patrick's Day, appears here taking notes. The policeman with baton poised is about to strike him from behind. SLQLD

Miners playing cards at the poppet head of the State Mine at Wonthaggi, Victoria, during the strike of 1949. UMA

The impassioned speaker, the hammer, sickle and star, and the vigilant policeman in the background suggest this outdoor meeting was held during the party's opposition to the Second World War. However, the advertisement for the Eureka Youth League meeting with Joyce Barnes (Joyce Stevens) places it at the beginning of 1950, in the aftermath of the miners' strike. UMA

John Bramwell Miles (left) was general secretary of the party from 1931 to 1948, when he was replaced by Lance Sharkey (right), previously the national president. Neither studio portrait is dated, but Miles shows the signs of ageing that contributed to his resignation. SLNSW/NAA

Jim Healy was the general secretary of the Waterside Workers' Federation from 1937 until his death in 1961. Widely admired for winning improvements in wages, conditions and job security, Healy was the party's outstanding trade unionist of that era. PAT HEALY

Lance Sharkey, general secretary, was prosecuted for a seditious utterance after he said the Australian people would welcome the Red Army to Australia in pursuit of an aggressor. Following conviction and appeal, he was brought handcuffed from Long Bay gaol in February 1950 for final sentencing. Supporters expecting a rousing address did not reckon on the absence of his false teeth. Phyllis Johnson, who had served a gaol term herself in 1940, is to Sharkey's right.

Faith Bandler on board MV *Australia* on the voyage to the third World Youth Festival in East Berlin, 1951. Her father had been blackbirded from Vanuatu. After working during the war in the Australian Women's Land Army, Bandler was recruited to Margaret Walker's dance group to perform in East Berlin. NLA

The Graeme Bell band on a semitrailer float leading the Eureka Youth League contingent in the 1947 May Day march in Melbourne, before it appeared at the World Youth Festival in Prague. Graeme Bell appears on the far right with Harry Stein second from right. Roger Bell, lower centre, is on cornet, and Ade Monsbourgh, on trumpet, is to his right. UMA

Helen Palmer in her uniform as a WAAAF education officer during the war. She became the most influential dissident as a result of Nikita Khrushchev's secret speech in 1956 and established the journal of the 'first' New Left, *Outlook*.

Marj Nunan lived with her parents in Brunswick from the 1930s and was secretary of the local party branch. Suffering from Ehlers-Danlos syndrome, a painful condition that affects connective tissue, she was an invalid pensioner. In 1954 she formed the Combined Pensioners' Association to campaign for better support of pensioners and was foundation treasurer of the Commonwealth Pensioners' Federation. UMA

Top left: Ted Hill, Victorian state secretary, kept up a practice at the bar, often briefed by Cedric Ralph, who followed him into the Communist Party of Australia (Marxist–Leninist). Hill leads Ralph in this 1954 ASIO shot taken at the Royal Commission on Espionage. NAA

Top right: Fred Paterson represented Dave Morris before the Royal Commission on Espionage. Again, Paterson leads. NAA

Eliot Elliott, the federal secretary of the Seamen's Union, at the Royal Commission on Espionage in 1954 with Bill Bird, the defiant Victorian secretary. NAA

A conference of the Melbourne University Labour Club at the seaside resort of Point Lonsdale in 1952. Miriam Rechter (later Miriam Dixson) is on the right, with her husband Bernard Rechter behind her. ASP

Knowledge is power. This float promoting the Marx School uses a Carlton and United Breweries lorry for a May Day procession in Melbourne. The disparity in ages of the instructor and the student is marked. UMA

A large group of wharfies in 1960 at the compound where they were picked up for work. The space was being used for a stop-work meeting, which has voted to refuse to work a vessel. Facing the camera at bottom right is Dave Rubin, who had fled Nazi Germany and at this time was a union organiser. UMA

Ralph Gibson speaking in Melbourne in the early 1960s with John Arrowsmith behind him. Gibson, who became a communist in the depths of the Depression, spent more than 40 years as a full-time organiser. Notorious for his self-abnegation, he served at various times as Victorian secretary, president and editor of the *Guardian*. UMA

Paul Robeson, African–American football player, actor and opera singer, was to attend a peace congress in Australia in 1950 until the US government confiscated his passport. After its restoration, he made several concert tours, including to Australia in 1960. The Building Workers' Industrial Union invited him to sing to workers on the Sydney Opera House site on 9 November 1960—famously the first performance there. SLNSW

The party's organisation for children, the Junior Eureka League, consisted largely of the children of members. These children are shown riding in the tray of a Holden utility through the streets of Melbourne for a May Day procession in the early 1960s. UMA

Mourners of the death of Jim Healy process through the city of Sydney in 1961. SLNSW

Roger Wilson, then Victorian assistant state secretary of the Seamen's Union, sells the *Guardian* in the retail centre of Melbourne. UMA

In 1966, some 200 stockmen, domestic workers and their families went on strike over wages and other injustices, walked off the Wave Hill pastoral station and moved to traditional lands at Wattie Creek/Daguragu, claiming their land back. The writer Frank Hardy, who promoted their claims and helped raise support, is shown here in conversation with the Gurindji leader Vincent Lingiari. NAA

Claude Jones (at the podium) and Ted Bacon (at the table), leading members of the party in Queensland, shown here at a state conference in the early 1960s. UQ

ASIO's surveillance section picked up these leading members meeting in Sydney in 1965. From left, Jim Moss of South Australia, Bernie Taft of Victoria, Sam Aarons of Western Australia and Bill Brown of New South Wales. NAA

Another surveillance photo, showing Judah Waten (right) in conversation with Rex Mortimer at a cultural conference in Melbourne. They are an unusual pair: Mortimer a full-time organiser and reformer; Waten an unyielding supporter of the Soviet line. NAA

ASIO photograph of Eddie Koiki Mabo, a Torres Strait Islander, at the 1965 North Queensland district conference. Trained in the Meriam customs of his home island, Mabo moved to Townsville in 1959 and pursued land rights for his people, vindicated in the landmark High Court decision of June 1992. NAA

Pallbearers at the funeral of Lance Sharkey, Sydney, May 1967. On the right-hand side, from front, Laurie Aarons, national secretary of the CPA; Bill Parkinson, president of the Miners' Federation; and Alec Robertson, editor of *Tribune*. SLNSW

The meeting of the national executive on 21 August 1968 that discussed and condemned the invasion of Czechoslovakia earlier that day. Left to right: Claude Jones, Jim Moss, John Sendy, Laurie Aarons, Richard Dixon, Eric Aarons, Ted Bacon, Bernie Taft and Alec Robertson. SLNSW

Richard Dixon and Bernie Taft meet Alexander Dubček in Prague in March 1969, seven months after the Soviet invasion and just one month before he was forced to resign as first secretary of the Czechoslovak communist party. Dixon, who followed Lance Sharkey as president, was more influential than his quiet, self-effacing manner suggested. SLNSW

Rex Mortimer (left), a long-serving cadre, and Rupert Lockwood, the most accomplished communist journalist, at a party function in the early 1960s. Both dropped out of the party at the end of the decade. SLNSW

In June 1969 Laurie Aarons and Bernie Taft attended the last world meeting of communist parties in Moscow and defied CPSU attempts to prevent discussion of the invasion of Czechoslovakia. Beforehand they spoke with Yugoslav president Josip Broz Tito, shown here at left with Aarons. SLNSW

Audrey Blake speaking from the floor at the Left Action Conference in April 1969 as the party explored common ground with the New Left. SLNSW

in the 1952 trial of the Czech general secretary, Rudolf Slánský, and discovery of an alleged plot among Jewish doctors to assassinate the Soviet leadership.[65]

The growing evidence of this venomous anti-Semitism would cause increasing difficulty for Jewish communists in Australia. During the war they had championed the Soviet Union as the saviour of European Jewry from extermination at the hands of the Nazis. Afterwards, they dismissed reports of persecution as the fabrication of Zionists. In doing so they employed a circular argument: none of the charges brought against the victims of these purges referred to their Jewishness, for race had no place in the communist lexicon, and any form of anti-Semitism was incompatible with Marxism–Leninism. 'Trying to prove that the Soviet Union practices anti-Semitism,' Judah Waten would claim, 'is as impossible task as proving that the world is flat.'[66]

The Australian party consistently championed the creation of the Jewish state of Israel. Here, indeed, it was in advance of Soviet foreign policy, which did so in 1947 in order to undermine British imperialism in the Middle East. Working through the local Jewish Council to Combat Fascism and Anti-Semitism, Australian communists continued to reject Zionism as a form of reactionary nationalism and argue that the emancipation of both Jews and Arabs from British rule was a step towards the creation of a single, free and independent Palestine.[67] This policy came under fire from Australian Zionists and more conservative members of the Executive Council of Australian Jewry, who were disturbed by the criticism of Britain, but it had considerable support within the Jewish community. That was also true, at least initially, of the campaign the council launched in 1949 against the entry of German nationals to Australia. The ensuing controversy would isolate the council from the Executive Council of Australian Jewry.[68]

Denunciation of German migration followed the campaign the party was already conducting against the entry of refugees from Eastern Europe. They came in large numbers from the end of 1947 under an agreement between Australia and the International Refugee Organization, which allowed the government to choose from residents housed in refugee camps in Germany and Austria and direct them to work here for two years in basic industries unable to attract sufficient local labour. To allay domestic concerns, the government selected those least likely to inflame prejudice against aliens, and therefore favoured refugees displaced from Estonia, Latvia and Lithuania, who were suitably fair-haired, faired-skinned and blue-eyed, along with Poles, Hungarians and Ukrainians. For the same reason, very few Jews were selected. Political screening was perfunctory, and a number of Nazi collaborators were accepted. In any case, the great majority of those seeking resettlement had fled before the advancing Red Army and were understandably hostile to the Soviet Union.[69]

The party condemned the introduction of these displaced persons (DPs) from the outset. At first it argued they would displace Australian workers and be used to erode wages and conditions—and, at least initially, the government tried to meet these concerns, so that Arthur Calwell gave Ernie Thornton an undertaking that any introduced to BHP's steelworks in Newcastle and Port Kembla would join the FIA and be assigned the least desirable jobs. Similar complaints were raised against 'luxury hostels' built to house the newcomers at the expense of working-class Australian families still waiting for homes.[70]

Along with such arguments about favoured treatment, there was constant criticism of the refugees' political views. The very fact that they had supposedly deserted their socialist homelands was taken as evidence of fascist sympathies. Many of these 'Balts' (the derogatory term was used indiscriminately) were said to be former quislings and concentration camp guards, some to have tattoos that identified them as members of the SS. Soon there were reports of them proclaiming their Nazi loyalty and intimidating those who objected. From time to time the party distinguished between 'good Balts' and 'bad Balts', and applauded those who objected to their inferior working conditions, but the blanket condemnation of DPs persisted. When the question was raised at the central committee, Sharkey insisted the party should 'treat them all as bloody one'. Communists, who had long proclaimed their internationalism, succumbed to a national prejudice that only reinforced a reputation for intolerance.[71]

★

The severity of government sanctions imposed during 1949 caught the party by surprise. Having embarked on a course of uncompromising defiance, it incurred a flurry of blows—the Crimes Act prosecutions, the Victorian royal commission, the gaoling of McPhillips and then other union leaders, freezing of funds, raids and the introduction of court-controlled union ballots—for which it was unprepared. Above all, it failed to appreciate Chifley's determination to break the miners' strike.

The party's capacity to mount such a challenge to the Labor government was weakening. Membership had continued to fall—it no long reported precise numbers but there would have been no more than 11,000 by the beginning of 1949. Finances were strained, so that a National Fighting Fund had to be launched in February to sustain operations. The major industrial campaigns of 1948 had failed to achieve significant gains. Indeed, the mining strike might be seen as a final attempt to wrest back the initiative with an all-out offensive that left nothing in reserve and no room to retreat. Failure to anticipate the consequences betrayed the *folie de grandeur* to which the party had succumbed, for a nationwide stoppage of coal production was bound to bring severe sanctions. Even at the aggregate meetings in June 1949, when the miners voted to embark on an indefinite strike, some communist organisers on the coalfields detected a lack of enthusiasm, but since Marx House did not want to hear of such defeatism these organisers withheld their misgivings.[72]

The decision to persist as the strike dragged on into a fifth and sixth week with no sign of a settlement was even more foolhardy. With the government starving the miners of financial support, sending in the army and threatening to replace them with members of another union, the willingness to continue was clearly faltering. Some leading communists apparently attempted to negotiate a backdoor settlement: Edgar Ross claimed later that he met an official of the Coal Board and Ernie Thornton was said to have talked to Evatt. It has also been suggested that Idris Williams and Lance Sharkey both wanted to call it off, but Williams was behind bars with the other leaders of the Miners' Federation and unable to communicate his view, while the implication that Sharkey was overruled strains credulity.[73] There are no transcripts of the central or political committees to shed light on the deliberations; this source dries up in 1949, probably because it was judged imprudent to keep such records after the July raid on Marx House. We have only the retrospective claims of some of those involved, each of whom blamed others for the disastrous miscalculation.

Throughout the strike there was not the slightest outward sign of any second thoughts. On the contrary, the party urged the miners to stand firm, insisting right up to the end that they would prevail. It maintained the same bravado when they voted to return to work, asserting that 'far from being a defeat, it is a great working-class victory'. Jack Blake enlarged on this claim shortly afterwards in an appraisal of *The Great Coal Strike of 1949* that praised 'the skill and boldness of the Communist leaders' for ensuring the miners resumed work with their ranks 'more solid than ever' after a 'magnificent seven weeks struggle' that had exposed the 'treachery of the right-wing Labor leaders'.[74]

At this point a divergence of views does become apparent. In an article published concurrently with Blake's pamphlet, Lance Sharkey disputed the proposition that the right wing of the ALP was discredited. That would only come, he stated, as the party won the majority of the working class over to a united front from below, and in the meantime it must not allow 'the slightest tinge of sectarianism' to poison relations with the supporters of the Labor Party. Allowing that comrades were 'burning with righteous anger' at Labor's betrayal of the miners, Sharkey warned that 'merely bawling out that reformists are traitors' would be a serious blunder. This interpretation was taken further at a plenum in October 1949, where Richard Dixon condemned those who thought it sufficient to 'tip the can' on Labor strikebreakers. He introduced two new criticisms of the party's conduct of the strike: it had failed to mobilise the miners at the outset, and it should have called for a termination in the last week of the struggle so that it could have directed the resumption. There was no suggestion at this plenum that Blake was responsible for the second of these mistakes.[75]

Jack Blake's extravagant justification of the sacrifices made by the miners has been interpreted as evidence that he and Jack Henry gained control of the party in the course of the strike. Both had joined the secretariat after conducting major industrial campaigns in their respective states, and we have seen that Henry made no secret of his intention to shake up the national leadership. But Henry played little part in the miners' strike, while Blake remained in Melbourne until the last fortnight; he wrote *The Great Coal Strike of 1949* in consultation with other members of the secretariat, and the political committee endorsed it.[76]

In their recollections of the confusion that followed the strike, some participants emphasise a leadership vacuum.[77] Dixon had left the country in May to attend the national congress of the Czech party and visit other peoples' democracies; his absence until the strike ended was costly. But Sharkey remained at large until mid-October, when he was taken to Long Bay Gaol to begin his sentence of three years. Despite this clear indication he was free to participate throughout the strike, he plays no part in the account that several leading members of the central committee gave many years later.

They tell of a breakdown in the party's decision-making. Henry had gone into hiding to prepare an underground apparatus in the conviction the party would soon be declared illegal, and was communicating with others only through a messenger. As part of these preparations he was liquidating the party's assets, so that Marx House and the various printing works were put up for sale over the head of the political and central committees. In desperation, they say, some leading members called on Blake to come up to Sydney and take charge. Jack Hughes, who went down to Melbourne on their behalf, recalled that Blake was cynical about this belated appeal for his assistance, though one reason for his reluctance was that Audrey would not return from the Budapest Youth Festival until early the next year, leaving him as sole carer for their teenage daughter. Even so, he answered the call and began to restore a semblance of order at the party headquarters.[78]

Apart from failing to account for Sharkey's activities during and after the coal strike, the tellers of this story of a leadership vacuum used Jack Henry as a convenient scapegoat. They told it in interviews with Laurie Aarons 25 years after Henry passed from the scene, and were understandably anxious to absolve themselves from responsibility for a disastrous miscalculation from which the party never fully recovered. An alternative explanation was given even later by someone who had no involvement in the fateful decision to fight the miners' strike to the bitter end, even if he had his own axe to grind. This was Cedric Ralph, a communist solicitor practising in Melbourne who would leave the party with his friend Ted Hill. He told in his memoirs of going up to Sydney in July 1949 to prepare the defence case for the members of the central committee charged with illegal withdrawal of funds. In doing so he quickly formed the impression that these party leaders had failed to anticipate the consequences of their actions—'and then, having done that, panicked'. He was particularly startled by conversations with Lance Sharkey whom he thought 'naïve in the extreme'. Panic and naïvete, in Ralph's opinion, made a disastrous combination, and he 'never really recovered full confidence in the central committee'.[79]

Blake's arrival did not stop the sale of Marx House along with other properties. These included the various printing works, though the new owners of the ones in Sydney, Melbourne and Brisbane were associated with the party—the intention here was to protect the press from any confiscation of communist assets. Marx House, on the other hand, was sold in September 1949 for £50,000 to the Coal Board, a trophy of its victory over the miners. So late in October, two lorries took the equipment and records left over from the raid to a smaller building in Market Street where the Eureka Youth League was housed, which now became the new national headquarters. Another lorry took unwanted material to Malabar, where a fire burned on a sand dune throughout the night to destroy it. The creation of Marx House in 1944 had signalled the public presence of an ascendant party. Its disappearance five years later indicated the rapid decline in its fortunes.[80]

'It is difficult for those who did not experience Party work in 1949 and the following years to appreciate the extent and fury of the attacks,' John Sendy wrote later, 'the constant barrage in the daily papers and in parliament, the violence at Party public meetings.'[81] He was a young organiser in South Australia at the time, running the gauntlet there. The federal election at the end of 1949 was a particular ordeal. The party planned to run no fewer than 76 candidates, for its intention was to present an alternative to the Labor Party, which the director of the communist campaign dismissed as offering no more than a 'Tweedledee' variant of the Liberal

Party's 'Tweedledum' policy.[82] By the time nominations closed, the number had shrunk to 56 and a decision was taken to allocate preferences to Labor.

There were limited funds to support the campaign, and a change to the broadcasting regulations deprived the party of radio time. It relied on open-air meetings to drum up support, and these met an unprecedented level of opposition. It was as if the setbacks suffered during the year culminated in an unprecedented fury. Election meetings in the cities were difficult, those in country towns well nigh impossible. A mob pushed Bill Gollan, candidate for the Riverina electorate of Farrer, from the tray of a truck on which he was speaking in Ganmain and then pursued his car to the nearby town of Coolamon, where he was pelted with missiles. The Senate team in Queensland had several narrow escapes from ambushes as they travelled along the north coast. Eight communist bodyguards fought to protect the platform from a hostile crowd of several thousand in Rockhampton armed with stink bombs, firecrackers and stones; the police confiscated an air rifle.[83]

The election, on 10 December, confirmed the fall in communist support. Its 35 lower house candidates received 62,000 votes, whereas 14 candidates had won 65,000 votes in 1946. The best results were in two NSW mining seats, where Evan Phillips (a Miners' Federation official) won 9.5 per cent of the poll in Hunter and Eric Aarons (the South Coast organiser) 7.6 per cent in Cunningham. The 21 Senate candidates attracted 88,000 votes from the 4,700,000 Australians who cast a vote, though nearly half of these were gained in Victoria, where the party drew first place on the ballot paper. None of the communists saved their deposit. Where their preferences were distributed they flowed strongly to Labor candidates, but the ALP's primary vote dropped to 46 per cent and it was decisively defeated.[84]

Fighting Menzies' accusation that it was riddled with communism, the Labor Party spurned any assistance from that quarter and directed its own preferences to Liberal ahead of Communist candidates. The party's election program, 'For Peace, Democracy and Higher Living Standards', proclaimed that communists stood alone in defending Australia's freedom and independence from subservience to Western imperialism. The principal difference between the two major parties was that the Liberals openly supported the Collins House capitalists in their collaboration with Wall Street counterparts, whereas Labor cloaked its defence of these interests. There was a further difference. Chifley and Evatt had used the Arbitration Court and the Crimes Act to discipline workers and attack the Communist Party, while the 'Menzies-Fadden clique' intended to launch an offensive against unions and ban the Communist Party. As in 1940, the party took the threat to its legal existence as a vindication of its stand and undertook that members would 'learn to trade blow for blow and to give two or three blows for every one we receive'. But the threat it now faced was far greater, its ability to trade blows much diminished. The party was on the ropes.[85]

8

Survival, 1950–55

'For some years now,' Robert Menzies explained to the House of Representatives on 27 April 1950, 'I and other persons resisted the idea of a Communist ban on the grounds that, in time of peace, doubts ought to be resolved in favour of free speech.' But, he continued, 'we are not at peace today except in a technical sense'. The Soviet Union was waging a Cold War on all Western democracies and local communists were assisting its designs. Hence the need for the legislation he was now introducing, the Communist Party Dissolution Bill.[1]

Menzies' biographers have traced how he came to the conclusion that the Australian Communist Party should be suppressed. He had not been comfortable with the prohibition on its activities in 1940 and rejected the Country Party's call for a ban during the 1943 and 1946 elections. He began to argue that communism could no longer be tolerated from early 1948, after the parliamentary party made such a ban Liberal policy, but it was not until he made a lengthy visit to the United Kingdom and witnessed the Berlin blockade that he threw off all reservations. 'I have come back from abroad with no doubts whatever on this subject,' he told a rally in the Melbourne Town Hall in January 1949. There must be no more temporising, no more talk of communism as a legitimate political philosophy. 'The fact is that it is not a philosophy. It is a form of high treason.'[2]

However reluctant he and some other Liberals might have been to take such a drastic step, by this time they were convinced of its necessity. The Czech coup and the Queensland transport strike were uppermost in the minds of parliamentarians who voted for the ban in March 1948, and subsequent events magnified their alarm: the crushing of democracy in Eastern Europe, the Berlin blockade, the acquisition by the USSR of its own atomic bomb, the fall of China, uprisings in Indochina, Burma, the Philippines, Malaya and Indonesia, and at home the continued disruption of essential industries. Partly because of their distaste for the measures that were proposed, partly because the Coalition played up the Red threat long after the Australian Communist Party ceased to be a credible source of danger, historians on the left have dismissed Menzies' claim that he was a reluctant convert to suppression. They recall his earlier record of appeasing fascist dictators and penalising their Australian opponents, as well as his lasting sympathy for authoritarian regimes. But they also overlook the distinctive nature of Menzies' anti-communism and the particular shape this doctrine took in Australia.

Judith Brett, a close student of Menzies' political rhetoric, has suggested that he regarded communism as an alien intrusion into a harmonious and homogeneous society, a foreign virus that threatened its political and racial integrity. Ours was a more parochial anti-communism than that of the United States, she argues, lacking the same religious intensity and more inclined to characterise communists as foreign than as evil. She points also to the theme of duplicity in Menzies' second-reading speech on the Communist Party Dissolution Bill: communists disguised their destructive purpose behind a façade of progressive causes in order to draw innocent dupes into their designs. This distinction between the true communist and the gullible trade union member or woolly-minded peace activist ran through Menzies' anti-communist measures. It allowed him to claim that there was no danger of punishing the innocent since the real communist stood out unmistakably from the naïve fellow traveller.[3]

To these attributes I would add another: a profound ignorance of socialist history, theory and practice. Like the communists themselves, Menzies did not see that you could be a socialist and not a communist, a Marxist but not a Leninist. In warning in his second-reading speech that communism threatened Australia with a violent revolution that would impose a dictatorship of the proletariat, he explained that 'the word "proletariat" is one of those dreadful words that Communists have forced on to the world'. It was in fact the ancient Roman term for a propertyless citizen, revived in the early nineteenth century to describe a new kind of worker created by the industrial revolution who was completely dependent on the sale of labour; the political economist Sismondi, among others, popularised this usage decades before Marx adopted it. Similarly, Menzies treated the word 'bourgeoisie' as no more than a barbarous neologism for the middle class, unaware that here again Marx was adapting an established term to denote the class that had come to own the means of production.[4]

The prime minister also ignored deep differences within the international labour movement. Albeit with an eye to discrediting the Labor Party, he contended there was no difference between the 'ultimate objective of the Communist Party and the ultimate objective of the Socialist Party'—they differed only over the method of achieving it. It is doubtful if he ever read any of the principal works of Marx and Engels, or for that matter Lenin. In preparing the Communist Party Dissolution Bill the government relied on a lengthy compilation of excerpts from a miscellany of sources—Lenin, Stalin, Litvinov, Molotov and other members of Stalin's inner circle past and present. Soviet statutes and Comintern theses were filled out with passages from Sharkey and ACP training manuals—all of them evidence of an unchanging and universal doctrine.[5]

Other leading anti-communists in the Coalition ranks employed even more unreliable sources. As president of the Liberal Party, Richard Casey commissioned Father Paddy Ryan to compile the booklet *Facts About Communism* and sent 500 copies to General Blamey, head of the paramilitary 'Association'. Casey knew less about communism than Menzies; as his biographer put it, insofar as he had a picture of them, communists seemed to be 'seedy, violent and alienated people'. Like Menzies, he swung over from distaste to vehement antagonism as the Cold War took hold, and seemed unaware of the impropriety of his use of ministerial office to request information from the security service so that he could denounce disloyalty. He found McCarthyism vulgar and hysterical, oblivious to the similarity of his own denunciation of 'a nest of traitors' in the public service to the wild accusations of Senator McCarthy.[6]

It was one thing to agree on the need to ban the Communist Party, another to work out how to do it. A committee of the Parliamentary Liberal Party considered ways and means in 1948, fruitlessly, and a new committee headed by Menzies laboured without success right up to the 1949 election. It was safer for him to simply declare in his policy speech that 'Communism is an alien and destructive pest' and that 'if elected we shall outlaw it'. The Communist Party would be declared illegal; its assets would be confiscated and the same action would be taken against any other organisation deemed to serve the party's purposes. Members would be ineligible for employment by the Commonwealth or for union office.[7]

The new government had little difficulty in drafting a statute containing these provisions. It took longer to determine the basis on which the Commonwealth could impose them. The method chosen was to set out in the preamble of the legislation the grounds on which parliament held the banning of the party to be necessary. There were four such recitals, as they were technically known: that the Australian Communist Party engaged in actions to bring about a revolutionary seizure of power and a dictatorship of the proletariat; that it pursued its objectives by force, violence, intimidation and fraudulent practices; that it engaged in espionage and sabotage; and lastly that it used strikes and stoppages to disrupt vital industries.[8]

The bill that Menzies tabled on 27 April also contained a number of disturbing features. First, the government would be able to declare any organisation illegal on the basis of evidence that remained confidential. The organisation could appeal to the courts that it was not in fact affiliated to the Communist Party, but in a striking departure from a fundamental principle of justice, the presumption of innocence, it would carry the burden of proof. Second, the government could declare individuals whom it deemed to have been members of such organisations since 10 May 1948 (the last day of the most recent party congress) and judged to be engaged or 'likely to engage' in subversive activities. Again they could appeal against the declaration but needed to prove it was false. Those who persisted would be subject to five years' imprisonment.[9]

As Menzies anticipated, the legislation divided the Labor Party. Its federal conference had declared as recently as 1948 that Labor was opposed to banning political parties, and the broad scope of the bill was especially repugnant to Chifley. As he declared at the outset of the debate on the second reading, 'it opens the door for the liar, the perjurer and the pimp to make charges and damn men's reputations, and to do so in secret without having either to substantiate or prove any charge they might make'. But Chifley no longer commanded the loyalty he had enjoyed as prime minister. The 1949 election had brought a new crop of parliamentarians from Victoria, some replacing sitting members as a result of the Movement stacking local branches, all strongly anti-communist. Several openly declared their support for the ban. Rather than oppose the legislation outright, therefore, the Labor caucus decided to press for amendments in the knowledge that it still held a majority in the Senate.[10]

There was a feeling that Menzies might have overreached. In introducing the bill he read to the House a list of 53 communist union officials, and within days had to admit he was wrong about five of them—if the government could be in error about such well-known figures, how could it be trusted with the power to declare lesser-known ones? To make matters worse, the *Sydney Morning Herald* published photographs of some of the more prominent, and had to apologise for substituting a portrait of J.W.R. Hughes, the deputy tax commissioner, for Jack Hughes, the secretary of the Clerks' Union.[11]

Equally damaging was an exchange provoked by the Labor firebrand Eddie Ward during an evening sitting of parliament in May. As Menzies discussed the problem of securing a Senate majority, Ward suggested he could simply declare a couple of Labor senators. Menzies replied that he could think of at least one whom it would be easy to declare and then added he could also think of a member of the House—he meant Ward—who might escape only by the skin of his teeth. It has been suggested the prime minister had dined a little too well, and he later passed off his indiscretion as jocular banter. Chifley, who was appalled by the members on the ministerial benches baying in delighted approval of their leader's loose talk, took the incident as betraying the government's willingness to use its draconian new powers against political opponents.[12]

Labor therefore persisted in the Senate with its amendments, notably restoration of the onus of proof, and would have been encouraged by an opinion poll showing that while an overwhelming majority of Australians thought communism should be banned, 56 per cent believed the government needed to justify allegations against individuals.[13] Undeterred, Menzies laid the bill aside in early June with the intention of reintroducing it in the next session, when a failure by the Senate to pass it would serve as a trigger for a double dissolution and—he had good reason to believe—give him control of both houses.

The government's stocks were boosted at the end of the month when the Korean War broke out. This regional conflict drew both China and Western countries (including Australia) into fierce fighting that took the world closer to an all-out war than ever before. By strengthening Menzies' claims of an imminent threat to Australian security it also fanned Labor's fears of a double dissolution and, in a backdown that dismayed Chifley, the ALP Federal Executive instructed federal parliamentarians to allow the bill to pass through the Senate. It became law on 20 October but was immediately challenged in the High Court by the Communist Party and a number of communist-led unions, and was found unconstitutional in March of the following year. Menzies persisted and fought a double-dissolution election (triggered by Labor refusing to accept his changes to the central banking system) on the question. Having won control of the Senate, he proceeded to a referendum that would authorise his Dissolution Act. This time Labor opposed the measure, which against expectations was narrowly defeated on 22 September 1951.[14]

Chifley was not able to enjoy this final vindication of his stand, as he died of heart failure in June 1951 after overtaxing his health in the double-dissolution election held two months earlier. Evatt, his successor, incurred criticism for representing left-wing unions in the High Court case, but fought the referendum with courage and tenacity. He had the backing by this time of moderates such as Jack Ferguson of New South Wales, the federal president of the Labor Party, along with Pat Kennelly, the Victorian federal secretary, who together secured a resolution of the Federal Executive instructing the parliamentary party to oppose the referendum. Some anti-communists defied the instruction and there was talk afterwards of retribution against the Victorian branch of the ALP, where the Movement was most powerful, for sabotaging the referendum campaign. That did not happen, but the Federal Executive declared the Movement's paper *News Weekly* to be an enemy of the Labor Party akin to the Communist Party's *Tribune* and Jack Lang's *Century*.[15]

The long and tortuous argument within the labour movement over the Dissolution Bill thus checked the influence of the Groups, just as the Australian Communist Party manifestly owed its continuing legality to the persistence of Chifley and Evatt. But that brought no softening of Labor's hostility. On the contrary, when Jim Healy sought out Chifley in May 1950 to discuss the legislation, the Labor leader made clear that he blamed the waterside workers along with the miners for his loss of office. Each time Labor declared its opposition to banning any political party as a violation of democratic principles, it also made clear that the policies and activities of the Communist Party were repugnant. And as fast as the party created new bodies to circumvent Labor's prohibition on its members cooperating with communists, Labor declared them to be subsidiary organisations and warned that participation in their activities was incompatible with membership of the ALP. This applied from May 1950 to the Australian Peace Council and from September even to the Democratic Rights Council, whose declared objective was to defend freedom of association.[16]

The party responded to the Dissolution Bill with a range of initiatives. A group of churchmen had established a Democratic Rights Council in Melbourne after the Melbourne City Council cancelled their booking of the town hall in 1949. With the encouragement of the party, they organised a conference in May 1950 that adopted a Charter of Freedom. Offshoots of the Democratic Rights Council were then formed in other states. It held rallies, produced literature and organised delegations to lobby federal parliamentarians, including a convoy to Canberra on the day Menzies introduced the Communist Party Dissolution Bill, though police prevented all but a handful of representatives from entering Parliament House to meet the few Labor members prepared to speak to them. Restrictions on public venues hampered attempts to publicise the charter, and an ambitious Australian People's Assembly for Human Rights in Melbourne's

Exhibition Building, timed to coincide with the reintroduction of the bill in September and to which international speakers including scientist J.D. Bernal and actor Paul Robeson were invited, had to make do with a much smaller venue and disappointing attendance.[17]

The Democratic Rights Council relied for its credibility on public figures who had no formal connection to the Communist Party, such as Doris Blackburn, Maurice's widow and successor in the federal parliament until 1949; Brian Fitzpatrick, the secretary of the Australian Council for Civil Liberties; and the 'peace parsons', of whom more later. But it failed to attract a broad membership and fell into inactivity after the passage of the Dissolution Act. 'No' committees, formed to fight the referendum, suffered similar difficulty in attracting support. Although the party set a fundraising target of £50,000 for its own referendum campaign and produced a huge volume of posters and leaflets, it was largely excluded from the national debate.[18]

Attempts to organise direct action against the Dissolution Bill were also unsuccessful. Stop-work meetings in June 1950 of the Building Workers, Engineers, and Ship Painters and Dockers rejected calls from their communist officials for rolling stoppages. Most lodges of the Miners' Federation and a number of branches of the Waterside Workers' Federation voted against a proposal to shut down the economy, if necessary, to defeat the 'fascist legislation'. The Seamen's Union, the third member of this 'triple alliance', had to back off after its persistence brought a serious challenge to the communist leadership.[19] The party took some time to come to terms with the extent of its isolation.

★

Although the government failed in its attempt to outlaw the Communist Party, confiscate its assets and remove its supporters from positions of importance, it had other weapons. The Crimes Act was used to prosecute both political and industrial offences, changes to the Arbitration Act provided new sanctions against strikes, and plans were made for even more drastic measures in the event of war.

During the second half of 1950, the prime minister moved rapidly to put the country on a war footing. His discussions in Washington after the outbreak of fighting in Korea in June of that year convinced him of the need to rebuild the armed forces, stockpile strategic resources and make ready for war. China's entry into the Korean War later in the year gave greater urgency to these preparations, and Menzies warned upon his return to Australia of the danger of a third world war. Unlike the Minister for External Affairs, Percy Spender, he did not think the principal threat to Australia came from Asia, for he shared the US assessment that China was incapable of attempting a seaborne invasion. In his view Korea was a preliminary test of strength and resolve pending a full-scale Soviet assault. He allowed three years at most for the West to be ready for the global conflict that would ensue.

Menzies gave this warning in a series of national broadcasts in September 1950 that were entitled 'Defence Call to the Nation'. As part of the defence preparations, Edmund Herring, the chief justice of Victoria, took leave from his duties to serve as director-general of recruiting. A little over a year later, on Remembrance Day 1951, Herring launched a more comprehensive 'Call to the People of Australia' that was endorsed by four other chief justices and the country's religious leaders. 'Australia is in danger,' it began, 'we are in danger from abroad. We are in danger from moral and intellectual apathy, from the mortal enemies of mankind which sap the will and darken the understanding and breed evil dissension.' Coming less than two months after the defeat of the referendum, this call disavowed any partisan intent. But its author was an adviser to Menzies, who put him in touch with Herring and arranged for the support of business leaders at a preparatory meeting in Melbourne's Windsor Hotel. The well-funded campaign that followed used a mixture of modern communication techniques and old-fashioned moral uplift, with meagre results. A crusade with the rallying cry 'Fear God, Honor the King' was unlikely to fire anti-communist fervour.[20]

As part of its defence preparations the government devised a scheme, codenamed Operation Alien, to safeguard essential supplies and services from domestic disruption. Under this scheme members of the army were trained to perform wharf labour, and naval ratings used in 1951 to break union bans on ships carrying troops and supplies to Korea. As late as 1953, troops were sent to the Queensland port of Bowen to replace members of the Waterside Workers' Federation delaying the loading of sugar.[21]

A further war precaution was to be internment of communists and their supporters. Enemy aliens with adverse security records would be rounded up and placed in detention camps on the commencement of hostilities, as in the two earlier world wars, but this time Australian citizens would also be interned. These included members of national, state and district committees of the Communist Party, union officials, leaders of auxiliaries and others in 'key' public service and scientific positions. Since internment would rely on regulations made under the National Security Act, it was necessary to collect evidence that would satisfy a court in the event of an appeal, and this task fell to the new security agency the Labor government had established in 1949 to meet British and American concerns.

More particularly, it fell to Colonel Charles Spry, whom Menzies appointed director-general of the Australian Security and Intelligence Organisation (ASIO) in July 1950. Spry quickly realised that the files he inherited from his predecessor were 'utterly inadequate' and struggled to advise the army, which would be responsible for running the internment camps, of the numbers involved. Around 1000 Australian citizens was the usual estimate, though it remained unclear whether provision needed to be made for dependants. ASIO continued to compile lists of alien and domestic subversives, along with briefs to justify their internment, into the 1970s.[22]

The Menzies government also launched a series of raids on communist premises and residences, which continued at a brisk rate for several years. Most sought evidence to support Crimes Act prosecutions, though some were fishing expeditions and at least one was part of a frame-up. And in contrast to the previous period of illegality, trade unions were no longer immune. Industrial provisions of the Crimes Act were proclaimed in March 1950 against members of the Waterside Workers' Federation in Brisbane for conducting rolling stoppages, and a year later there were raids on the Melbourne and Sydney offices of the Seamen and Waterside Workers, along with the communist printery in Melbourne, for banning New Zealand shipping in support of their counterparts there. Jim Healy was convicted under the Crimes Act and gaoled for six weeks, a sentence reduced on appeal to a fine. Raids were also conducted on party offices in all state capitals following the passage of the Communist Party Dissolution Act, though the legal challenge to the legislation stopped further action.[23]

The Menzies' government's first prosecution for sedition was brought in July 1950 against William Fardon Burns, the publisher of *Tribune*, after it ran articles calling for opposition to Australia's participation in the Korean War. It was a moot point whether the party's slogan 'Not a man, not a ship, not a plane, not a gun for the oppressive imperialist war' constituted incitement threatening the peace, order or good government of the Commonwealth, as section 24(a)1 of the Crimes Act stipulated, and Burns was in any case a purely nominal publisher who worked on the Sydney waterfront. Even so, he was found guilty and sentenced to nine months, reduced to six after a long and acrimonious series of appeals. Eliot Elliott and Bill Bird, secretary of the Seamen's Union of Australia and its Victorian branch, were to be prosecuted for their campaign against the Korean War, but a lack of corroborative evidence caused the cases to be dropped.[24]

There was a raid in August 1952 on the party's Sydney headquarters and the home of Rex Chiplin, a *Tribune* journalist, in response to an article he published nine months earlier on negotiations for an economic treaty with the United States. ASIO had long suspected Chiplin was receiving secret information from inside the government, and his account of the treaty bore the hallmarks of a report prepared by the Department of National Development. More than this, ASIO had recruited a *Daily Telegraph* journalist, Mercia Masson, to cultivate Chiplin and it now arranged for her to be placed in that department and offer him further information. This attempt at entrapment foundered because Masson developed divided loyalties, and would have rested there had not William Wentworth raised the breach of security in parliament in May 1952, prompting Richard Casey's allegation as Minister for External Affairs that there was a 'nest of traitors' in the public service. The raid that followed shed no light on the identity of any of them.[25]

There was a sequel in 1953 when Colonel Spry ordered an investigation of an article in the *Communist Review*, thought to be by Chiplin, that disparaged the monarchy. A subsequent raid on party premises, Chiplin's office and the homes of two leading communists found no evidence of his authorship, and a magistrate dismissed the charge of sedition against the publisher and printer of the *Review*. But this raid was far from fruitless. ASIO's search of the home of H.B. Chandler, the party's business manager, found central committee records, financial accounts and—most damningly—typed extracts from the confidential diary of Casey.[26]

As these episodes revealed, ASIO did much more under its new director-general than collect intelligence on threats to security. Charles Spry, a career soldier, had no doubt that the Communist Party posed the greatest threat, and in his earlier capacity as director of military intelligence had called for a secret service that would undertake clandestine operations against it. Since ASIO was established by prime ministerial decree rather than legislation, it operated without any semblance of public accountability, and Spry made the most of his direct access to the prime minister. He built up staff numbers, brought the heads of the various branches of the organisation together in its new Melbourne headquarters and strengthened operational practices. The persistence of military habits, such as subordinates addressing senior officers as Sir, would have surprised ASIO's British counterpart MI5, though Spry also recruited a number of university graduates.[27]

We will examine more closely some of the methods ASIO used to combat communist activity: the vetting of recruits to the public service and universities, restrictions on overseas travel, the placing of agents within the party and its auxiliaries, the leakage of information to opponents. Surveillance of communists extended to intercepting telephone calls and illegal entry to party offices to install bugs and photograph documents. ASIO quickly acquired a level of knowledge of communist operations that compounded the party's fears of repression.[28]

In 1949, when Jack Henry disappeared from view, Wally Clayton once more built an illegal apparatus. This involved the establishment of secret printeries and workshops to service them, safe houses and hidden meeting places, along with drop-offs and cut-outs to avoid detection. Clayton was responsible for the national apparatus, leaving state and district committees to make their own arrangements. So it was that Laurie Aarons had a duplicator and other gear smuggled out of the party's Newcastle office and into hiding. As district organiser, he was to make his way with appropriate precautions to a safe house when the party was proscribed. On the day the High Court was to hand down its decision on the Dissolution Act he therefore caught a train to Tamworth and then the evening express to Sydney with the intention of doubling back to Newcastle and entering a secure hiding place. But Aarons arrived in Sydney to read newspaper placards announcing the High Court had thrown out the Red Bill, so instead spent the day at the Rosehill races before rejoining his family.[29]

Six months later, on the eve of the referendum, Aarons made the same journey, again to discover it was unnecessary. Many other cadres had similar experiences. Eric Aarons, the South Coast organiser, went into hiding in October 1950 when the Dissolution Bill was enacted, and waited several days for the High Court to issue an injunction against its enforcement before he reappeared. John Sendy, who was responsible for security in South Australia, travelled by car and train to Sydney at the same time to liaise with Jack Henry. Ted Bacon, in charge of the party's work in Sydney, told four organisers to go into hiding on the eve of the referendum and they chose to do so in a cave overlooking the Cowan River in Ku-ring-gai Chase National Park, taking a frying pan and store of tinned food. Cooking over an open fire filled the cave with fumes (as one observed, they had certainly gone into smoke), the nights were bitterly cold and one of the men's snoring kept the others awake. They gave it away after five or six days.[30]

The party had expected that on coming to office Menzies would use the Crimes Act to arrest leading members, and did not anticipate the lengthy hiatus over the legality of the Dissolution Act. It turned out that the elaborate underground arrangements were superfluous. Just four clandestine numbers of the *Communist Review* were produced between December 1950 and March 1951, declaring the Henry Lawson Press of Eurunderee as their publisher. Apart from seeking to locate Wally Clayton, who by this time had been identified as the head of the espionage network, ASIO made little attempt to track down others.

Keith Wilson, an organiser who spent three years underground, thought the hospitality that so many comrades willingly and unquestioningly provided vindicated the party's stand. He also acknowledged the strain that resulted from avoiding any contact with family and friends.[31]

The isolation was particularly severe on John O'Reilly, the builder of printing presses, who once more accompanied Clayton into hiding and remained there for most of the 1950s. Such was O'Reilly's ingrained reticence and inability to share his life that his marriage foundered and he was estranged from his parents. He did not know the real name of his closest underground friend and thus lost contact with him afterwards. Even when he moved to Melbourne under an assumed name, correspondence with friends in Sydney went by courier. And although I visited him at his home in the southern suburbs of Melbourne during 2006 by prior arrangement and in the company of a former member of the central committee, he still felt it necessary to ring Sydney and check it was appropriate for him to talk.[32]

Going underground nurtured political delusions. Jack Henry envisaged a period of illegality lasting several years from which the party would emerge to establish a people's democracy, as it had in Eastern Europe. A group of communists went for extended training in China in June 1951 on the understanding that should the leadership be eliminated, they would form the nucleus of a 'leadership in exile'. Some other functionaries were scornful of such fantasies. Jack Beasley told the four men who returned from the cave in Ku-ring-gai Chase National Park that it was 'a bloody lot of rot people disappearing and going off the face of the earth—how can you lead a bloody struggle like that?'[33]

Carrying on the struggle with the threat of illegality hanging over the party imposed its own strain. Many members were shaken by the outcome of the miners' strike and the animosity it created, even among previously sympathetic workmates. Many felt it necessary to destroy incriminating records and hide their collections of books and pamphlets. Police action against the usual forms of public activity—open-air addresses, sale of literature, marches, banners, even the heckling of government speakers—made it hard for communists to contest allegations of subversion. They were reduced to acts of defiance that did little to reassure the public of their legitimacy. Hence the 85,000 spectators who queued outside the Melbourne Cricket Ground for the 1950 Grand Final found slogans denouncing the prime minister's dictatorial conduct painted on the fences and gates surrounding the stadium. As the referendum approached, a rash of such messages appeared on buildings, bridges, hoardings and any other suitably conspicuous landmark.[34]

The infiltration of security agents into the party and its associated organisations was particularly disconcerting. The Commonwealth Investigation Branch and special branches of state police had used informers to gather intelligence ever since the 1920s, but most were readily detected. ASIO worked far more systematically to create a large network of agents. They had first to join the party, though some quickly made their way into advantageous positions. Anne Neill, a kindly widow in her fifties, entered through the peace movement in 1950 and two years later was able to provide a first-hand account of the World Peace Congress in Moscow. As typist for the South Australian state secretary, Elliott Johnston, she also obtained a mass of reports and documents. Much of the information that officers compiled, especially when they relied on informants, was unreliable, some little more than gossip, but ASIO built up a substantial body of information, including copies of state and district documents.[35]

Attempts to recruit disaffected communists holding more senior positions were less fruitful. The unlikely modus operandi was to offer such potential sources a few pounds a week to provide information, and there is little evidence that such approaches were successful.[36] Even so, by August 1951 ASIO was able to compile the names and descriptions of every delegate to the party's Sixteenth Congress. This congress, on the eve of the referendum, was held under the tightest security, so that delegates did not even learn the venue until they arrived in Sydney. ASIO was nevertheless able to track the interstate delegates from Mascot airport to their billets, along with the registration numbers and owners of the cars used to take them there, and to produce a lengthy summary of the proceedings. Towards the end of the congress, in a move calculated to increase delegates' unease, officers let them know they were under surveillance. Spry went further, suggesting to Menzies that he make reference to the penetration of the congress in opening his referendum campaign in the expectation it would 'cause an intensification of their current verification purge, and leave us less of these people to watch'. The prime minster obliged, except that he attributed a statement made at the preceding NSW state conference to what he described as the party's '13th annual congress'.[37]

The verification campaign opened in April 1951, ostensibly to reclaim those who were faltering in their commitment. As part of a 'thorough political ideological examination' of the work of every branch and every member, some who failed to measure up would have to be removed from their posts, but there should be no 'wholesale expulsions' or any 'heartless treatment'. Even so, the fear of penetration was palpable, discussed at length during the Sixteenth Congress and accompanied by a revision of the party's constitution to tighten disciplinary provisions. As Spry anticipated, the heightened vigilance did little for morale. Members became more preoccupied with guarding their secrets, more isolated and suspicious. Fighting and winning the referendum provided some relief from this despondency without solving the problem of restoring the party's fortunes.[38]

★

As the new government embarked on its campaign to expunge communism from Australia, the priority was survival. Partly because Jack Henry placed such emphasis on the underground apparatus, normal routines were curtailed, including recruitment. In 1951 Colonel Spry advised Menzies that membership had dropped to 7000 and there was a corresponding decline in financial resources. It was not until 1952, when membership had fallen further to 6120, that the party was in a position to mount a 'Build the Party' campaign. The decline was apparent in every state, though New South Wales had held up best with 2954 members, followed by Victoria (1463), Queensland (1032), Western Australia (320), South Australia (279) and Tasmania (72). This and subsequent campaigns employed the methods that had brought such success a decade earlier. Quotas for recruitment, press sales and fundraising were set for each state, which in turn set quotas for districts, sections and branches.[39]

The results were persistently disappointing. The first campaign, from July to September 1952, fell well short of the goals, so that a second one ran from February to May 1953. That took membership to 6842 in mid-July, with New South Wales (3282) and Victoria (1850) showing the best outcomes, but subsequent efforts yielded meagre results and Laurie Aarons told the Seventeenth Congress in 1955 of 'a small but disturbing decline in Party membership' that had persisted since 1952 as the number of recruits failed to compensate for the departures.[40]

Keeping up sales of the party press required constant attention. The Western Australian *Workers' Star* ceased publication at the end of 1950, leaving that state, South Australia and Tasmania reliant on editions of *Tribune* with a page of local items. *Tribune* became a weekly in the same year and needed constant sales drives to sustain an eight-page edition. It was losing £150 on every issue in 1950 and initiated an appeal for donations that fell well short of this amount. But a newspaper was one of the few outlets open to communists at this time, and a special effort was made to publish a twelve-page edition in the lead-up to the referendum.[41]

The first 'Build the Party' campaign set a target of an increase of 7000 in *Tribune* sales. Its circulation at that time was 19,774, of which 11,069 were sold directly in New South Wales, 3865 through newsagents and subscriptions, several thousand in South and Western Australia, and a smaller number in Queensland and Victoria. These states continued to produce their own newspapers with greater local coverage and a full page of readers' correspondence, the Victorian *Guardian* with a circulation of around 8000 and the Queensland one a little under that. The first campaign brought the circulation of *Tribune* up to 24,344, though it fell back to 23,315 by early 1953. The second campaign was less successful and sales slumped further in 1954. All three of the papers required the party to make good persistent losses, around £100 for every edition of *Tribune* and £50 for each of the *Guardian*.[42]

This in turn exacerbated a shortage of funds. Marx House and the Newsletter Printery were sold in late 1949 and the proceeds were split into bundles of banknotes and salted away for safekeeping. In early 1950 Claude Jones confessed that he was unable to repay money owed to creditors; he had taken charge of the party's new headquarters in Market

Street but all he could find was debts. In July a campaign was launched to raise £35,000 for the campaign against the Dissolution Act, then £40,000 in April 1951 to fight the double-dissolution election and subsequent referendum—the sum was raised with great difficulty.[43]

In 1952, after dues were raised (to 1/1 a month for those earning less than £5 per week, 4/4 a month for others) finances stabilised, except that the state committees ran up large debts by failing to remit the portion of dues that was payable to the central committee and pay for their purchases on credit from the Central Book Depot. A debt of £15,000 was gradually brought under control and substantial economies made in expenditure. The party could no longer count on support from as many communist-led unions as before, and would appear to have drawn on assistance in cash and kind from the Soviet Union. Though it would dispute the claim of Vladimir Petrov after he defected from the Soviet Embassy that US$25,000 was handed over to Lance Sharkey in 1952 (Petrov said the money was in $25 notes, a denomination the United States never used), it seems clear that the party asked for substantially more and did receive other payments.[44]

A feature of the balance sheets presented to state conferences was the importance of donations. In the financial year 1952–53, for example, the Sydney District Committee raised £4000 in dues and recorded £24,378 in donations. The Victorians recorded around £300 per month in dues during 1952, while donations were often over £2000. It is possible that overseas payments might have been fed into the party's accounts in this way, but most of the donations came from local members. Itzhak Gust was by no means the wealthiest Melbourne communist, but he provided £500 annually and other Jewish families gave more. The largest single item of expenditure was salaries of officials and cadres, £1800 a month in New South Wales, about half that in Victoria and as much again for the national secretariat. Financial exigency forced rationalisation in 1953, principally by making cadres responsible for particular districts and sections in addition to their specialist roles. The other states had fewer full-time officials, four or five in South and Western Australia, more in Queensland.[45]

While the threat of illegality preoccupied the party until the end of 1951, it brought no agreement on how to proceed. On the one hand the central committee appealed to the Federal Executive of the Labor Party for a united front to defeat the Coalition government's war plans and attacks on the labour movement. On the other it warned against the illusion that the Labor parliamentarians would take a stand on the Dissolution Bill: their subsequent backdown on the amendments to the legislation was further evidence they were ardent defenders of capitalism.[46] The party's appeal for cooperation during the 1951 federal election was again spurned, though the political committee regretted that its approach to Labor was 'sometimes narrow and sectarian'. The groundwork for the 'reactionary, anti-democratic policy of the Menzies-Fadden government' had been laid by the right-wing leadership of the Labor Party, 'in particular by the Chifley Labor Government', yet Chifley was praised on his death as an honest reformist who had fought the right wing on the issues that mattered most.[47] There was little rhyme and less reason in this sophistry other than to ensure that, in pursuing a united front, communists did not in any way encourage reformist illusions.

By the time of its Sixteenth Congress in August 1951, the ACP had adopted a new program that, if it stopped short of acknowledging the ruinous consequences of the showdown with the Labor government, set out a less confrontational approach. The failure of the Chifley government to build a new social order after the war was deemed unsurprising since 'the so-called "democratic socialism"' of its leaders was 'only a camouflage for their real defence of capitalist exploitation'. It was therefore futile to expect that any future Labor government would defend Australian independence from US imperialism, protect living standards or resist the drive for war. That would come only when the Australian people won political power and began an advance to socialism through a 'People's Government'.[48] Such a government would be established by a people's movement of workers and farmers, along with 'professional and clerical workers, technicians and teachers, small shopkeepers and business people', all of whom were threatened by monopoly capitalism. As had the people's democracies of Eastern Europe, it would use existing political institutions, suitably democratised. Above all, 'Australia also will find her own path to Peoples' Democracy and Socialism in accord with her own historical conditions, her own level of economic, political and cultural development and political institutions and organisation.'[49]

Australia was not alone in proclaiming a form of socialism attuned to national conditions. A very similar program, *The British Road to Socialism*, had appeared almost a year earlier and assumed talismanic significance in later debates there over revisionism with its claim that peaceful existence between the two rival camps made it possible for all countries to find their own way forward without a revolutionary seizure of power. There was little new about such a perspective. It marked a partial return to the confident expectations of the immediate post-war period, except that the call for a people's democracy now conjured up images of show trials and secret police. Furthermore, the initiative for the program came from Stalin, who pressed Harry Pollitt on the need to rebuild the CPGB's credibility when the British leader visited Moscow in 1950.[50]

Australia's Path to Socialism largely bypassed the question of the Labor Party, except to note that the working class had 'the glorious mission' of leading the people's movement and that this required a united front of the Communist Party and the ALP. Sharkey suggested how in a pamphlet on *The Labor Party Crisis* that appeared following the referendum. He was confident the mounting unpopularity of Menzies would soon bring a new Labor government, and that its inability to restore prosperity would lay bare the bankruptcy of reformism and thus open the prospect of a people's government. The Communist Party should therefore seek the widest possible measure of agreement with ALP members; while continuing to expose the treacherous role of the right wing, it must 'avoid sectarian, negative attitudes like poison'.[51]

In the lead-up to the Sixteenth Congress, the Australian party engaged in an intense discussion of the mistakes that had led to its difficulties. It began with an article by Jack Blake in the *Communist Review* in April 1951 condemning the lingering sectarianism that cut the party off from other workers. Such sectarianism took the form of doctrinaire statements and leftist declarations that passed over the heads of their intended audience. At the same time he warned of a second deviation, economism, a deep-seated malady 'which penetrates every pore of the labour movement and colours much of the work of the party'. Economism took the form of confining the party's work to industrial campaigns and encouraging the illusion that capitalism could be tamed. As Blake acknowledged, this was an unusual combination, since sectarianism was usually understood as a form of left adventurism, economism as a hallmark of right-wing opportunism. Although the two errors were commonly regarded as occupying opposite poles, he argued that at this juncture they were linked and later cited no less an authority than Stalin for his claim that sectarianism and opportunism were in fact twins.[52]

Blake's argument dominated the next meeting of the party plenum. It found support from Jack Henry and qualified support from the other two members of the secretariat, Lance Sharkey and Richard Dixon. They and other party leaders laid emphasis on the danger of sectarianism, though Dixon allowed that economism was also a danger. This understanding found its way into the resolution on *Australia's Path to Socialism* that was adopted by the Sixteenth Congress. Communists were to avoid a frontal assault on the Labor Party, relying instead on its inability to resolve the contradictions of capitalism to bring workers over to the program of the 'People's Government'.[53]

Nevertheless, Blake's stress on the danger of economism undercut the party's rejection of sectarianism. There was little likelihood the latter error would recur: after communists had estranged so many supporters and sympathisers, they would never again embark on such a disastrously ill-judged confrontation with the rest of the labour movement. In any case, they were incapable of mounting any serious challenge to the Menzies government. To do so they would have needed to embark on a new industrial offensive, and there was no chance of that; the most they could manage was localised, rolling stoppages in a very restricted range of industries.

Why, then, did Blake emphasise the danger of economism? The short answer is that he thought the peace campaign must have priority. Until world peace was secured, the Cold War would continue to set West against East, the Menzies government would maintain its war preparations and repression, Labor's right-wing leaders would persist with their anti-communism, and a broad coalition of workers, farmers, professionals and small business proprietors would not be possible. The struggle for peace was therefore 'not just another campaign, it is part of the very essence of all activity of the Communist Party and it will be so until complete victory over imperialism is won'.[54]

As he put it later, the atmosphere of the party in 1950 was that of a besieged fortress, so that the campaign for peace was also meant 'to turn the vision of party members outwards' towards the broadest possible movement that would provide the best conditions to defeat Menzies. This had particular significance for the party's work in trade unions. It was not unusual for communists to include peace as an agenda item in union meetings, and as often as not a resolution would be carried to support it—but at that point the meeting would return to the real business, the industrial concerns that exercised the workers. These unionists did not understand that without peace Australia would remain in thrall to Wall Street and monopoly capitalism, rendering their campaigns for better wages and conditions futile.[55]

His warning of sectarianism had a similar purpose. Cynics might have suspected he was covering himself against allegations that this was but another instance of his leftism, but Blake was incapable of such guile. Rather, he worried that some communists regarded the peace movement as no more than a party front that needed to be inculcated with communist doctrine. This would negate the broad composition that Blake thought essential if it was to embrace all elements of the people's movement. Drawing on an address given by the Italian party leader Palmiro Togliatti, he argued that for peace to be a mass movement it must avoid all indoctrination, manipulation and numbers games. There was no need to instruct the Christians and pacifist participants on the realities of imperialism; they should be allowed to find their own way to that realisation.[56]

The strictures against economism were aimed particularly at the party's union leaders. Unions, after all, were the natural habitat of this illusion, and neither Blake nor his colleague Jack Henry had backgrounds in industry—Blake had been a party official ever since returning from the Lenin School in Moscow in 1933, while those close to Henry, who had led an unofficial strike in the sugar industry in 1934, regarded his impatience with unions as verging on syndicalism—a form of industrial militancy that dispensed with formal structures. Since both men were new to Sydney, they had limited familiarity with the mettlesome comrades there who occupied the federal offices of the principal left-wing unions.

The dual responsibility of these union officials, to the party and to their members, had long been a source of tension. That tension was acute in the early 1950s for, unlike the period of illegality a decade earlier, union leaders were no longer immune from sanction. On the contrary, they were expected to spearhead resistance to Menzies' measures and thus took the brunt of the government's repressive measures. Ted Roach, the assistant general secretary of the Waterside Workers' Federation, had particular reason to feel aggrieved. He was one of the unionists who went to gaol in 1949 for refusing to hand over funds withdrawn to assist the miners, whereas the party's leaders purged their contempt to avoid similar treatment. In January 1951 he was charged with contempt by the Arbitration Court for failing to get waterside workers in Mackay to resume loading sugar, found guilty, sentenced to twelve months in Long Bay prison and held in isolation for all but a few hours of the day. A group of wharfies carried Roach shoulder-high to a stop-work meeting at Sydney's Trades Hall on his release in December, but he was extremely disappointed by the failure to mount a stronger campaign for early release and complained that the party had let him down.[57]

We see an early indication of the strain the union leaders were under when the political committee reprimanded Roach, Jim Healy, Jack McPhillips and Idris Williams for excessive drinking in a hotel near the Waterside Workers' Sydney headquarters in the first days of 1950. These men were formidable drinkers. Itzhak Gust was shocked by their intemperance when he hosted them while they were in Melbourne for the 1947 ACTU Congress in Melbourne, though he conceded their local counterparts were just as thirsty. But in 1950 they drank for relief rather than conviviality.[58]

No allowances were made for those who fell short. In August 1950 the South Australian state secretary announced the expulsion of Andrew Newell. He had come to Adelaide from Sydney four years earlier to take up the post of state secretary of the Gas Employees' Union and in March 1950 was elected federal president of the union. The party's statement, circulated within the union movement, explained that Newell was guilty of excessive drinking, gambling and 'gross neglect of his political and industrial responsibilities'.[59] He was followed in April 1951 by Charlie Morgan, who, after losing his post as secretary of the Newcastle branch of the Ironworkers, was refused re-employment in the industry and in desperation became industrial officer for a local firm against the instructions of the party. Laurie Aarons, the district secretary, noted that Morgan had also failed to give sufficient help with the party's peace campaign.[60]

Don Thomson, the federal secretary of the Painters and Decorators and Victorian secretary of the Building Trades Federation, fell victim in 1952. A major figure in Melbourne's post-war industrial disputes, he gave up leadership of the Building Trades Federation because of constant interference from party officials. Thomson was not alone in this resistance. Joe Chandler, the state secretary of the Building Workers' Industrial Union, retired after resisting party instructions and bridling at allegations he was guilty of economism. Bert Flanagan and Pat Malone of the Builders Labourers Federation, even Clarrie O'Shea of the Tramways, were under fire for failing to follow instructions. Citing nervous strain, Thomson said he was prepared to carry on providing he was relieved of so many other calls on his time. The party was reluctant to incur the publicity his resignation would attract, but refused his application for leave and expelled him when he applied with his wife for a hotel licence.[61]

These unionists were self-made and CPA-made men with little formal education. Their horizons were by no means narrow, such as George Seelaf of the AMIEU, and some had a marked interest in cultural pursuits, but few were attuned to the arcane jargon of communist theory. Take Bill Parkinson, the president of the southern district of the Miners' Federation, who succeeded Idris Williams as national president in 1954. Parkinson was a rough-hewn Geordie and steeped in the traditions of the industry. He was also a natural orator capable of inspiring an audience, though he could get his members to think strategically. He joined the party in 1943 after reading Johnson's *The Socialist Sixth of the World*, hardly a reliable guide to Marxism–Leninism. Eric Aarons, who was the party's organiser in Wollongong during the late 1940s, recalls taxing Parkinson with an indifference to theory and describing him as an empiricist. 'What did you say I was?' Parkinson demanded. Swallowing hard, Eric said he had called him an empiricist. 'That's all right,' Parkinson assured him, 'I thought you had called me an imperialist.'[62]

The demands on these men were relentless. In addition to their union duties they were expected to support the party and its auxiliaries, appear on the public platform in support of worthy causes, and use their influence to resolve all manner of difficulties. It is hardly surprising that they found difficulty in discharging the additional duties of an ordinary branch member, and there were complaints at this time of absence from classes at Marx House; one, indeed, was said to have offered his volumes of Lenin's *Collected Works* for sale. The admiration union leaders won for their achievements turned the heads of some. Tom Brislan, who had worked as an organiser for the Ironworkers, blamed the 'terrible examples of sectarianism and conceited and arrogant methods of work' for the loss of that union to Laurie Short. Nancy Wills, a party member who moved to Sydney with her mariner husband after the war, worked in the union office for Eliot Elliott. She found he had a very arrogant attitude to women: 'I can see him now with that half smile, half curled lip saying with his cultivated stammer that women were at their best in a horizontal position.'[63]

The party made an effort to keep the unionists onside by including them in its decision-making bodies. There were ten of them among the 40 members of the central committee in 1950, and three on the twelve-man political committee (Jack Hughes, Ted Rowe and Tom Wright). With rare exceptions such as Wright's contribution to the party's Aboriginal policy, they were seldom involved in discussions outside their own area of expertise, industry, but they were capable of putting their foot down. In 1952 Jim Healy asked Richard Dixon to release a journalist from *Tribune* so that he could help Rupert Lockwood produce the weekly *Maritime Worker*. When Dixon said he would need to discuss this with *Tribune*'s editor Alf Watt, Healy told him: 'They have got Chiplin, Brown, Watt, Joyce Metcalfe, Barbara, Bill Wood, enough to eat it, and yet Lockwood gets our paper out on a weekly basis.' He obtained the additional assistance. Healy would also exert increasing influence in discussions of policy.[64]

★

Until 1954 the debate that followed the Sixteenth Congress failed to resolve the contradictions inherent in Blake's coupling of sectarianism and economism. Sometimes, as the party pursued a united front with Labor, sectarianism was the main danger. At other times it was necessary to guard against economism and expose the illusion that Labor could be won for the people's program. In 1951 Ted Rowe had warned of what he called the party's 'kiss-kick philosophy' in building the united front: 'you either kick their heads off or embrace them'.[65]

Insofar as a more constructive policy began to emerge, it was principally due to Richard Dixon. He had long exercised a moderating influence, and at a plenum in mid-1952 he emphasised the need to correct 'sectarian mistakes'. Members should not regard those workers who opposed communism as enemies of the working class, for the great majority—even those who belonged to Industrial Groups—were honest in their opposition and it was possible to work with them. Yet Dixon never repudiated the view that the purpose of the united front was to 'wrest the masses of the working class from the grip of the treacherous Labor Party leaders' and that 'the Labor and Liberal parties merely compete with each other to decide which of them will manage the State and run it in the interests of the monopolists'. It followed that the approach to the rank-and-file Labor member had to be completely different from the approach to the 'top leaders': endless patience was needed to build relations with the former, 'whereas in the case of the right-wing leaders our aim is to undermine them'.[66]

One reason for the equivocation was that there seemed every chance Labor would regain office. Menzies' loss of the 1951 referendum dented his popularity, and the government suffered from its mishandling of the economy as the soaring demand for wool following the outbreak of the Korean War brought rampant inflation. To make matters worse, the treasurer did not bring down a contractionary 'horror budget' until some months after the federal election of 1951, when the export boom had collapsed. The party's expectation of an imminent economic crisis seemed far from implausible at this time. With Labor well ahead in the polls, Menzies delayed the election due in 1954 for as long as possible—and then rescued his fortunes with the defection of the Petrovs, discussed in the next chapter.[67]

The extended debate over how the party should proceed was complicated by leadership tensions. They are not easy to follow because there are very limited records of the party's upper-level deliberations after 1950. Before then a full stenographic record was kept of the proceedings of the central and political committees, and we know that practice continued. But none of these lengthy documents, which recorded verbatim the contribution of every participant, are lodged in the party's archives—until 1966, when more systematic record keeping resumed. We do not know what happened to the 1951–65 ones. Some have suggested that the seizure of such highly sensitive documents in security raids during 1949 and the years immediately afterwards made it too risky to keep them in the national office, but that was no longer the case by the end of the 1950s. The most likely explanation is that the transcripts were held in safekeeping and knowledge of who had them was lost.

Some of the arguments advanced at these meetings found their way into the *Communist Review* after they had been cleaned up and differences of opinion eliminated, but the unavailability of what was actually said makes it difficult to follow the patterns of decision-making. We do not even know who was responsible for the party reverting to its original name, the Communist Party of Australia, or why the one used since 1943, the Australian Communist Party, was jettisoned. The change was made at the Sixteenth Congress with no prior notice and no explanation. Sharkey seems to have initiated dropping the descriptor Australian Communist Party because it was a nationalist formulation.[68]

The leadership tensions went back to the arrival in Sydney in 1947 of Jack Henry as national organising secretary. We have seen that he was brought down to do what the Sydney leaders could not do, tap J.B. Miles on the shoulder, and was critical of what he saw as the top-heavy and bureaucratic set-up at Marx House. He made no secret of his contempt for Sharkey falling into the trap that journalists laid in 1949, and told Ted Bacon, one of the Queenslanders he brought down to Sydney, that 'the doddery old bastard' deserved to go to gaol; moreover, he should be installed in a safe house upon release because he had been in the hands of the authorities and 'no matter how good a man is, you can never be sure of him after that'.[69]

Jack Blake was linked with Henry after he took up duties in the secretariat in the second half of 1949, though differences between them were already apparent. When Audrey joined Jack in early 1950, she saw immediately that Henry and his fellow Queenslanders were moving against the NSW leaders. She was not particularly interested in this contest, though the Sydney old guard 'really did give me the shits because they were so terribly inefficient and very poor organisers'.[70]

With remission for good behaviour, Sharkey was released from Long Bay penitentiary at six in the morning of 27 November 1950. He was met by a small group, including his wife, Richard Dixon and Claude Jones, and welcomed by a large crowd at the Domain on the following Sunday. Though clearly affected by imprisonment, which left him with high blood pressure, he immediately began sounding out members of the political committee.[71]

Over the following months he would re-establish his supremacy; indeed, it was at this time that the party adopted the overseas practice of greeting his public appearances with chants of 'Shar-key' punctuated by rhythmical handclapping in the manner since popularised here by soccer followers. Sharkey prepared the way at a plenum in April 1951 when he said such displays were not personal but rather allowed members to express confidence in their leaders. Similarly, in closing the Sixteenth Congress, Sharkey told delegates that Comrade Stalin interpreted the homage paid him not as servility but as an expression of communists' pride in their party. Afterwards, members spoke of their distaste for the practice: 'you felt bloody embarrassed while you were doing it', Claude Jones said, 'you wanted to crawl away'. At the time a claque of sycophants led the chanting. There was consternation when the result of the election to the new central committee was announced and it turned out that Blake had attracted one vote more than Sharkey; much effort was made to discover which of the 95 delegates had failed to support the general secretary.[72]

This was a volatile situation ripe for exploitation by Ted Hill, who succeeded Blake as Victorian state secretary in 1949. Blake supported his appointment, though with reservations, for he thought Hill exercised an unhealthy influence over the state committee and needed stronger restraint than his acolyte Frank Johnson could provide as state president.

Hill polarised opinion like no other communist. A stocky, myopic man with a round, boyish face, he would look deep into your eyes with a cold, penetrating stare that unnerved those who incurred his displeasure. A cold fish with no small talk, he was capable of acts of generosity in his capacity as a barrister (he had a large industrial practice) and inspired admiration from cadres whose careers he nurtured for selfless commitment to the cause. Even his critics allowed Hill could be a skilful tactician, though they also recalled his cutting remarks to those who disagreed with him. Nancy Wills, one who did, was told 'Comrade, I'm here to do the thinking' and relieved her of her responsibilities.[73]

During 1950 Blake criticised Hill and Henry, who was quick to cultivate the new state secretary, for taking too narrow a view of the peace movement, and towards the end of the year went down to Melbourne to participate in a discussion of the state committee on the make-up of the Australian delegation to the Berlin Youth Festival. Hill invited him to dine beforehand at his home in Flemington and, while driving into the city for the meeting, stopped the car and said that Sharkey had discussed with him how Blake could be 'politically destroyed'. So long as Blake did not intervene in the state committee's discussion, they could remain friends. But Blake did intervene. This led to a savage attack by Jack Henry at a meeting of the political committee in February 1951 on Audrey Blake, who was organising the Berlin delegation and responsible for the party's youth work. Blake again intervened, calling it a disgraceful report and referring the matter to the central control commission. It made no adverse finding apart from 'that Audrey Blake was inclined to be impetuous'. Blake later claimed that Henry realised Hill had taken him for a ride. He was wrong.[74]

Hill had already initiated another thrust. Citing evidence of a leak from the trade union committee headed by Richard Dixon, he told Blake that Dixon was an ASIO informer. Why the attack on Dixon? Principally because this able administrator was an obstacle to Hill's ambitions. The information put Blake in a quandary. He was not close to Dixon, even though the two had both joined the party as young men in Lithgow and then trained in the Lenin School. Back in 1946, when Blake had come under fire for his leftist statement at the Fourteenth

Congress, he compiled a document showing Dixon was under the influence of Browderism—and naïvely gave it to Sharkey, who held on to it to keep Dixon in line. On the other hand, Blake could not credit the proposition that Dixon was a traitor and took no action other than to give Dixon the letter in which Hill set out his allegations. But Hill had also told Henry of Dixon's perfidy, and Henry told Claude Jones, who in turn told others.[75]

Sharkey outmanoeuvred Blake and Henry after the Sixteenth Congress. He had the knack of listening to other party officials rather than instructing them. He had a high regard for Ted Hill and was also close to Bert Chandler, the party's business manager who ran the printery at Forest Lodge. Jack Hughes, who had been put in charge of the central control commission in 1949, was concerned about Chandler's business dealings—especially trade with China, for which he raised funds from party sympathisers—and wanted to audit the printery, but Sharkey would not allow him to do so. One of Chandler's other ventures was betting large amounts of money on horse races, and among the members of the central committee in his syndicate was the general secretary.[76]

Sharkey was ready to bring the leadership struggle to a head by 1952, but waited until he returned from treatment in the Soviet Union for hypertension at the end of the year. At a meeting of the plenum that December, Blake had to apologise for the 'narrow state parochial outlook' he and Henry had brought to their national duties, which led to mistakes endangering the unity of the party, and expressed gratitude to Sharkey and Dixon for correcting his errors.[77] But he fell into dispute with Hill once more over the peace campaign, and when he criticised Hill at a meeting of the central committee, the Victorian demanded an investigation. The secretariat sent Dixon down to investigate. Although Blake was allowed to accompany him, Hill had lined up the state committee to support his version of events.[78]

Dixon's report occasioned a special meeting of the political committee in December 1953 that lasted six days. It produced a comprehensive statement, 'For Party Consolidation', which rehearsed the sectarian errors of Blake in discouraging trade union members from pursuing economic demands and the 'anarcho-syndicalist mistakes' of Henry, who overestimated the militancy of workers, along with the rumours and slanders against Sharkey and Dixon that left 'a heritage of bitterness and mistrust'. Dixon called for censure of the two men, Hill demanded their expulsion and Sharkey favoured demotion, so they were both removed from the secretariat. Blake issued an anguished and abject self-criticism, Henry a perfunctory one. The Queenslander returned to his home state, accompanied by several of his followers. Blake remained in Sydney as a member of the central committee, but with greatly reduced responsibilities.[79]

Hill was rewarded by appointment to the secretariat vacancy along with Laurie Aarons, who replaced Henry. It was a rapid rise for Aarons, who had served previously in Adelaide and Newcastle and was put in charge of New South Wales only in 1952. He gathered much of the oral history on which we now rely to follow the convoluted story of Consolidation, sympathetic to Blake while conscious that he was a beneficiary of the outcome. Blake himself was aware that he was ill suited to such a ruthless leadership contest. 'I have never been able to dissemble . . . or intrigue in any way,' he told Aarons. Hill was 'cleverer in these things' while 'old Shark' was a past master.[80]

9

Revival? 1950–56

Following their downfall, Blake and Henry were blamed for the misfortunes the party had suffered from the late 1940s by cutting itself off from the rest of the labour movement. As members sought to repair the damage, they were warned repeatedly of the perils of sectarianism. Laurie Aarons, who conducted a question and answer column in *Tribune* at this time, explained that the everyday meaning of sectarianism was bigoted attachment to a religious sect and that communists had borrowed the term to describe 'a condition of the isolation of the Communists from the masses' that unfortunately had yet to be eliminated.[1]

He was putting the best possible construction on a tendency to dogmatic intolerance that was widespread within the CPA, perhaps inherent in Lenin's model of a vanguard revolutionary party. Keith Wilson, an organiser with the Seamen's Union, would recall trying to arrange a unity ticket in 1953 for elections to the Newcastle Trades Hall Council that foundered because an ALP member of the Waterside Workers' Federation declined to participate. On his way home with Len Donald that night, Wilson saw the miscreant's car at the side of the road and another party member trying to help start it. 'Leave him there, don't help the scabby bastard,' Wilson told his comrade, and Jim Healy had to come up from Sydney to smooth the row that resulted.[2]

A contributor to *Tribune* conducted a 'critical quiz' on sectarianism that captured its characteristic traits. When your workmates are discussing an important question, do you come in to set them right or listen? When one talks about conditions on the job, do you keep saying 'Yes, I know' or reply 'That's interesting, tell me more'? When they turn to pastimes, do you talk politics? Do you use jargon or the language of the people? Do you attempt to give a Marxist explanation for every subject under the sun?[3] So entrenched were these habits that anyone who has ever been a branch member will readily recall instances of such pig-headed rectitude. The phrase 'politically correct' originated within the American left to satirise those who made a fetish of their ideological zeal. Here in Australia they were mocked as 'ideologically sound'.[4]

Another party member cited the Chinese communist Liu Shaoqi's aphorism that 'the masses make their own history' to argue that 'no-one who really loves the people can be sectarian'.[5] Jim Healy was a prominent exponent of this proposition. His Waterside Workers' Federation (WWF) was made up of many branches that differed widely in their politics, and since each one elected delegates to the federation's central council, Healy could not ignore their concerns if he was to maintain the union's cohesion. In 1949 there were ten communists on the federal council and eleven Groupers who showed open resistance to the WWF's support for the miners' strike. The rolling stoppages in protest against Menzies' Dissolution Bill further strained relations between the communists and their opponents, but Healy had general support for the union's black ban on New Zealand shipping in 1951 and won a vote to continue it at a mass meeting in Melbourne, even though Groupers controlled the branch executive.[6]

In this instance union solidarity outweighed internal differences. Healy used his considerable personal following to cultivate it and restrain party members who put it at risk. He was not always successful: communists were voted out of their positions in the Brisbane branch as a result of what he called their 'sectarianism, individualism and general leftism'. But he outmanoeuvred an attempt by the government and employers in 1954 to break the union by removing its control of entry to the industry, and in the same year the Groupers lost control of the Melbourne branch after it was discovered that the secretary was embezzling funds. By then an alliance with ALP supporters had been formalised by agreeing on a slate of candidates for office in the annual elections. Such 'unity tickets' were issued in Sydney in the name of the United Trade Union, in

Melbourne by the United Federation, and other branches had their own names for the arrangement. The right did not even bother to contest Healy's re-election in 1955.[7]

The left's control of the union remained contentious, however. Groupers raided the branch offices in Melbourne and Sydney as their fortunes faded, and fist fights were still used to settle differences or intimidate opponents. But wharfies cultivated their traditions of solidarity. After extensive renovations to their head office in Sussex Street in 1952, which included a canteen, art studio (where Rod Shaw and other realist artists encouraged members to develop their talent), film studio (for the union's film unit), library and reading room, volunteers began painting an elaborate mural depicting passages in the union's long history of militancy.[8]

Above all, Healy insisted that communists had to reach out to all their workmates. Despite success in the 1952 union elections, he told a plenum of the central committee, an investigation of the eight party branches that covered the Sydney waterfront revealed gossipers who were forever criticising the failures of leadership, the arrogant who said it was no good talking to the backward workers, and the exclusives who saw no need to do so. A member from Port Kembla commented that 'the trouble with our fellows is they do not love the workers . . . they do not understand the workers, they do not want to understand'. Hence it was common for party members to drink in one bar, other unionists in another.[9]

Healy reiterated at the Seventeenth Congress in 1955 that too many communists formed coteries who talked in language other workers did not understand or didn't like. 'They sit with themselves instead of getting out and talking to others.' They also needed to attend to their personal appearance and set a good example of working-class dignity. Building unity required conviction, confidence ('How often do you see or hear members of our party saying that their workers are hopeless?'), flexibility and patience.[10] In his address to the same congress, Ernie Thornton took full responsibility for the loss of the Federated Ironworkers' Association to the Groupers. He spoke of talking down to the union members and treating anyone who criticised his leadership as an enemy.

At the other end of the spectrum was the Seamen's Union, where Eliot Elliott practised a quite different style of leadership. Short, aggressive and histrionic (he had been active in the New Theatre), Elliott worked in conjunction with a team of state secretaries and vigilance officers, most of them communists, who attended to the grievances of the seafarers. Though the regular stop-work meetings could be lively, most officials and Elliott himself were returned unopposed in the annual elections. This general secretary polarised opinion. Some thought him unnecessarily abrasive, and he would prove increasingly defiant of party discipline. Others admired his energy, intelligence and internationalism: even though the Seamen's Union was forced to abandon affiliation to the World Federation of Trade Unions, Elliott remained very active in its maritime transport sector. Bill Bird, the Victorian secretary, matched his belligerence. Although the state executive of the party regarded Bird as a loose cannon, it turned to him and his seamen more than once to prevent their opponents breaking up meetings.[11]

Elliott's partner softened his asperity. Kondelia (Della) Xenodohos (her Greek father changed the family name to Nicholas) joined the party in the early 1930s and was married for a few years to Laurie Aarons. A trained stenographer-typist, she worked as Jim Healy's secretary and during the war became assistant secretary of the NSW branch of the Clerks' Union. She liaised with Elliott after resuming at the WWF head office, when the two smuggled union donations to support the New Zealand watersiders during their lockout, and moved to the Seamen's Union in 1955 to help produce its journal and organise the federal office.[12]

The excesses of the later 1940s took a heavy toll on the party's industrial influence. Changes made by the Menzies government to Commonwealth laws governing trade unions compounded the problem. Legislation passed in 1951 simplified the imposition of fines for breach of awards and strengthened provisions for court-controlled ballots: a relatively small proportion of aggrieved unionists could now take their complaints to the Arbitration Court and obtain a new election under its control. The ACTU, which was not consulted, opposed these changes as an attack on union autonomy, and the party kept up a chorus of allegations of malpractice in court-controlled ballots. Anti-communists, especially Groupers, made use of them, and even the threat to do so served as a constraint on unions that conducted their own elections.[13]

It was possible for left-wing unions to escape these provisions since they applied only to federally registered bodies. Hence they did not govern the Building Workers' Industrial Union, which was deregistered in 1948 for persistent defiance of court orders. This mattered less in the NSW branch, where the union kept its state registration, than in Victoria, where it allowed an alternative union to be formed and recognised: the Amalgamated Society of Carpenters and Joiners, formed originally in Tasmania with the assistance of Groupers, and a thorn in the side of the Victorian branch throughout the decade. The Building Workers' 1952 application for federal re-registration foundered because it refused to give an undertaking to bring all disputes to arbitration, as well as the Arbitration Court's adoption of the rule Judge Dunphy brought from Western Australia that a union represented by communist officials could have no standing. Even the NSW branch, where Pat Clancy, the state secretary, had strong support, was constrained in its industrial campaigns by the threat that the Master Builders' Association would persuade the state tribunal to cancel its registration. The building workers did not win back federal recognition until 1963.[14]

Historian John Playford suggested in his pioneering study of the CPA in this period that it met the threat to its industrial influence with defences he likened to a fortress protected by an inner and an outer defensive ring. The 'fortress' unions were the Waterside Workers' Federation, Seamen's Union, Miners' Federation, Ship Painters and Dockers, Ironworkers, Boilermakers and Sheet Metal Workers. His inner ring consisted of state branches of powerful unions such as the Australian Railways Union and the Amalgamated Engineers. Finally, the outer ring consisted of some smaller craft and white-collar unions such as the Clerks and NSW Teachers' Federation. In the years from 1950 to 1952, he argued, Groupers were able to sweep through the outer defences, capture leading positions in the inner ring and even penetrate the fortress unions. Thereafter, he argues, the communists fought back with a new appreciation of the importance of unity.[15]

Some qualifications of Playford's generalisations can be briefly noted. Of the unions making up the outer ring, the Teachers' Federation did come under assault from a large Industrial Group, which used a court-controlled ballot to unseat Sam Lewis from the presidency in 1952. But Actors' Equity remained under communist control in New South Wales, and although a court-controlled ballot, along with a concerted campaign in Keith Murdoch's newspaper chain (which included the *Listener In*), brought down Dick Diamond's leadership of the Victorian branch, Vic Arnold of the New Theatre succeeded him.[16]

Until finally succumbing to Laurie Short's well-funded challenge in 1952, the Federated Ironworkers' Association was perhaps the most powerful fortress union. Efforts to win back some of its branches were unavailing in the face of a new national leadership that was as ruthless as Ernie Thornton had been. Short refused to allow the former general secretary to be employed in the industry after he returned to Australia in 1954 from his work for the World Federation of Trade Unions, and thus disqualified him from standing for union office.[17]

Of the state branches making up the inner ring, the Groupers used court-controlled ballots to win effective control of the Victorian branch of the Australian Railways Union, with J.J. Brown losing his post as secretary in 1953. The Railway Commissioners bolted the door by refusing him employment, but Brown established his right to stand for office and won the assistant secretary's position in an election in 1955 that returned a majority of unity candidates to the state executive. He regained the secretaryship in the following year. Lloyd Ross resumed the secretary's position in the NSW branch in 1951, threw in his lot with the Industrial Groups, and saw off all challenges from a left-wing rank-and-file movement. But there was little change in other states: hence Queensland and Tasmania remained militant, Western Australia conservative.

Variations on this pattern can be found in the Meatworkers', the Builders Labourers, and the Tram and Bus unions, where the left lost some state branches in the early 1950s but held others. The North Australian Workers' Union fell to the Groupers in 1951. 'Red Ted' Rowe lost his position on the Commonwealth Council of the Amalgamated Engineering Union in 1952, but the Groupers overplayed their hand by petitioning for a court-controlled ballot out of fear he would win the vacancy Joe Cranwell's retirement created in 1953. Although he didn't, the court's intervention caused great resentment in this traditionally independent union. While communists remained strong in the NSW branch and their opponents in other states, the engineers continued to resist outside interference.[18]

Playford's implication that the fortress unions had formerly been under communist control is also misleading. We have seen that the Waterside Workers' Federation was always marked by a diversity of political views, and it was communist excess that allowed Groupers to win elections for the Brisbane and Adelaide branches at this time. Similar challenges occurred in all the fortress unions except the Sheet Metal Workers, where the support for Tom Wright's leadership made him almost impregnable. The Seamen's Union was probably the only communist-led union that could get away with refusing to share positions with non-communists.

The use of unity tickets to regain ground was at first hampered by ALP rules that forbade any association with communists. This prohibition would not be eased until the Groupers broke with the Labor Party in 1955, and until then the party's recovery was limited. It remained at loggerheads with all the state peak bodies except the Queensland Trades and Labor Council, and continued to accuse the ACTU of betraying the labour movement until the end of 1951, when the need for greater unity was acknowledged. Communist delegates exercised conspicuous restraint at the ACTU Congress in that year. Lloyd Ross, admittedly no neutral observer, wrote of how Tom Wright 'cooed his views on international trade union unity' and Jim Healy was so benign and reassuring that a new delegate asked, 'Is this the face that stopped a thousand ships?' The only exception was Eliot Elliott, who 'tried hard not to be Elliott but the real man would persist in coming out, arrogant and authoritarian, as contemptuous of his comrades as of his foes'.[19]

The communists were unsuccessful in their principal proposals, though they attracted considerable support for a call for an immediate boycott of the new secret ballot provisions and an amendment that called for greater cooperation between the International Confederation of Free Trade Unions, to which the ACTU had switched its allegiance, and the World Federation of Trade Unions. In the immediate aftermath of the congress, however, the executive ruled that all affiliated unions must sever links with the World Federation. The Seamen's Union was last to come into line, defiant until its affiliation to the ACTU was suspended in 1953.[20]

Laurie Aarons gave the CPA's Seventeenth Congress a rare glimpse into the occupational composition of the membership in New South Wales. Fifty-five per cent were industrial workers, 17 per cent housewives and 14 per cent professionals. Of the industrial workers fully 79 per cent worked in the mining, metal, transport and building industries, indicating a much smaller presence in the light manufacturing, processing and service sectors. This was a narrower base than in the party's halcyon days, and one that did not help it respond to the changing composition of the workforce.[21]

★

We come now to the other ways the party sought to break out of isolation and rebuild influence. These relied heavily on auxiliaries and fronts, some of which were directly under the party's control and others nominally independent. Those in the second category did best, but even so struggled in the face of government measures and the prohibitions imposed by the ALP. Insofar as these activities were able to develop their own momentum, party officials were likely to intervene. It was in this period, for example, that communist cultural activity was most vigorous, influential, contested and so closely subjected to party invigilation. Finally, all such non-industrial activity required support that the party's diminished membership and finances made difficult to sustain.

By far the most ambitious was the peace movement. There had been earlier attempts to promote peace, but this one had its origins in a 1948 Congress of Intellectuals in Wrocław, Poland, that led in April 1949 to a World Congress of Partisans for Peace in Paris at which the Nobel prize–winning chemist Frédéric Joliot-Curie chaired the executive and Louis Aragon, Heinrich Mann, Henri Matisse, François Lafitte, W.E.B. Du Bois, Paul Robeson and Charlie Chaplin were among the 2000 delegates. Picasso contributed a drawing of a white dove on a soft blue background that became the movement's symbol. A second World Congress in Warsaw in 1950 formally established the World Peace Council. The emphasis from the outset was on the non-partisan support needed to prevent the Cold War becoming open preparation for war: thus the importance attached to the dazzling array of scientists, artists, intellectuals and men and women of conscience.[22]

Preparations for an Australian Peace Council began immediately after Paris. Following meetings of party intellectuals and ministers of religion in Melbourne, the council was constituted on 1 July 1950 at the home of the Reverend Vic James of the Unitarian Church and launched at a rally in the Town Hall in September. Jim Cairns, then a young lecturer in economic history, was in the chair. Melbourne founders assisted the formation of branches of the council in other states later in the year. Clergymen held the principal offices, while communists served as the full-time organisers.[23]

Even before the World Peace Council made an effort to involve the churches, clergymen provided the public face of the Australian peace movement. The most prominent were Melbourne's three 'peace parsons', the Methodist Frank Hartley, the Presbyterian Alf Dickie and the Unitarian Vic James. While James came from Wales with established anti-war views, the other two had trained in the theological seminaries attached to the University of Melbourne's Methodist and Presbyterian colleges, which taught a liberal theology with emphasis on the social gospel. Both came from working-class backgrounds, with personal experience of the effects of the Depression and a hostility to war that was strengthened by service as chaplains in the Second World War.[24] They had counterparts in other states, though none with the same prominence. Anglican clergymen were also active. The only Catholic to become involved seems to have been Vernon Rice, a Melbourne philosopher who was to attend a peace conference in China but could not obtain a travel permit ('No Rice for China', declared the *Catholic Worker*).[25]

The peace parsons were prepared to accommodate the party's heavy calls on their services. Refusing the Manichean logic of the Cold War, they attended meetings on both sides of the Iron Curtain, formed friendships with churchmen of different allegiances, and gave credulous accounts of what they found in the Soviet Union and Eastern Europe. As they declared at the inaugural Australian Peace Congress in April 1950, socialism's 'youthful vigour and ideals' offered more opportunity for the practice of Christianity than monopoly capitalism. The Reverend George Van Eerde, the leading NSW churchman, said that the thought had occurred 'time after time' during a trip to China in 1952 that 'maybe this is how the Kingdom of God will come on earth'. Alf Dickie stated on returning from a trip to the 1951 celebrations of the Russian Revolution that 'the people of the Soviet Union love Stalin so deeply that no power on earth can separate them'.[26]

The Australian Peace Council quickly established a pattern of national congresses. The first was held in Melbourne and opened at the Exhibition Building in Carlton on Sunday 16 April 1950 with more than 600 delegates and an overflow crowd of 10,000. There were three international dignitaries: the Red Dean, Hewlett Johnson, making his first visit to Australia; Joseph Fletcher, the head of the Episcopal Theological College in Cambridge, Massachusetts; and Fred Stover of Henry Wallace's National Progressive Party. The congress then broke into commissions representing trade unions, ministers of religion and laity, youth, women, scientists and writers before adopting an Australian Peace Manifesto that condemned the arms race, called for the abolition of nuclear weapons and emphasised the need for self-determination in Asia.[27]

This pledge was put to the test with the outbreak of war in Korea three months later. The Peace Council was opposed to the use of force to settle disputes and in favour of using the United Nations to resolve them peacefully. Since the United States, and eventually twenty other countries including Australia, fought in Korea under the auspices of the United Nations, the decision to accuse the Allies of aggression and omit any criticism of communist belligerence was manifestly specious. The decision was in fact taken by the party and implemented unhappily by Ian Turner, the council's organiser, at a stormy meeting in the Melbourne Town Hall a few days after North Korean forces swept into South Korea. Hartley, Dickie and James were most unhappy with this flouting of the council executive's decision to take a neutral position but accepted it. Other ministers did not and resigned, as did Jim Cairns and some lay sponsors.[28]

Partly because of such damaging instances of communist direction, a group of Protestant clergymen decided in late 1950 to establish their own

Peace Quest Forum with the object of promoting open discussion among 'all men and women of goodwill'. They put a full-page notice in the *Age* in March 1951 and commenced a series of Friday lunchtime meetings at a city venue. These led to a Citizens' Conference on Peace and Disarmament in Melbourne during 1952 and a National Convention on Peace and War in Sydney the following year. While both had communist involvement and were accused of being under communist control, this arrangement allowed the ministers to determine the basis of their peace activism.[29]

The Peace Council relied on local groups to publicise the cause. Their staple activity was peace petitions. The first of these, calling for the abolition of nuclear weapons, was launched at Stockholm in April 1950 and gathered 500 million signatures (a fifth of the world population) by the end of the year. Most were obtained in communist countries—100 million in the Soviet Union, 200 million in China—though Italy produced 17 million, France 15 million and the United Kingdom 1.5 million. Judged by these lofty standards, Australia struggled to reach its goal of 200,000 signatories. The second petition, launched in February 1951 and expressing support for a peace pact between the five principal powers, relied even more heavily on communist countries to reach 600 million signatories, since it lacked the emotional simplicity of doing away with the most terrible of all weapons. Besides, the peace pact was proposed by the Soviet Union and three of the powers, the United States, United Kingdom and France, had already rejected it. This time the Australian goal was 250,000 signatures and it took a year to obtain 125,000. A third petition, an Appeal Against Preparations for Atomic War, did better in 1955, with more than 300,000 signatures, but overuse was robbing the device of import.[30]

Australians were also regular participants in the congresses and assemblies of the World Peace Council. Since there was no time to send a delegation to the first congress in Paris, Rupert Lockwood (then working in London as *Tribune*'s foreign correspondent) rounded up a group of expatriates who included Noel Counihan (studying art), Daphne Gollan (accompanying Bob during his doctoral studies at London University) and Stephen and Nita Murray-Smith (back briefly from Prague). Credentials were hastily arranged from left-wing unions and cultural organisations so they could be among the 1700 delegates from 72 countries, and Counihan was elected to the praesidium. There was an unexpected sequel. Noel wrote regularly back to Pat Counihan, who had yet to join him in England, and she left the handbag in which she kept a recent letter (complaining of Stephen Murray-Smith's pompous manner) at a tram stop, so that it was handed in to the local police station and forwarded to security. Henceforth his letters were intercepted before delivery and copies placed on file.[31]

The second world congress was planned for the English city of Sheffield at the end of 1950, but had to be moved to Warsaw as the British government refused entry to many of the delegates. Jack Hughes led a group of more than 30 Australians who included Jim Healy, Elliott Johnston and other leading communists, as well as Jessie Street, who became a member of the council's executive. There was an Asia-Pacific Peace Conference in Beijing that a number of Australians planned to attend in 1952, but only eleven managed to overcome travel restrictions. A larger delegation went to the third congress in 1953, which was notable for a broadening of the participants and the greater emphasis it placed on peaceful coexistence.[32]

By this time, however, the peace movement had passed its peak. It encountered government hostility from the outset, with restrictions imposed on passports issued to peace activists wishing to travel to communist countries during the Korean War and again during the 1954–55 Royal Commission on Espionage. A number of overseas activists invited to conferences here were denied entry.[33] While Menzies disparaged the Protestant clergymen as naïve dupes, their involvement caused particular concern, and a spoiling operation was mounted against their 1953 National Convention on Peace and War. Menzies had Spry brief the Reverend Eric Owen, moderator of the Presbyterian Church in Victoria and principal supporter of the Sydney organisers, with a dossier of information obtained in raids on communist premises—except that it referred to a different gathering the party had abandoned to give the ministers a clear space.[34]

Both the NSW and Victorian ALP state executives placed a ban on their members participating in the Peace Council, followed by the

Federal Executive. Among those punished for defying the ban was Bill Morrow, the Tasmanian secretary of the Australian Railways Union who had won election to the Senate in 1946. He was the senator whom Menzies said it would be easy to declare a communist during the debate on the Communist Party Dissolution Bill and he became a leading figure in the Australian peace movement. Morrow was lucky to keep his seat in 1951 when the ALP executive in Tasmania decided to draw names from a hat to determine each candidate's place on the ballot paper: the penny dropped when Morrow's name was not called for a winnable position and he grabbed the hat to find the paper with his name was stuck inside the band. Morrow lost his endorsement in 1953.[35]

The involvement of ministers of religion and people of good will was meant to reduce the isolation of the party at the height of the Cold War. But after both major parties dismissed the Peace Council it was itself marginalised, too beholden to the patronage of the CPA and too supportive of Soviet foreign policy to break out of its own isolation. This was compounded by the absence of press reportage of its activities and the denial of public venues. The council was hampered further by a shortage of money. All organisers were expected to raise the cost of its operations, including their own salaries, and the third issue of its journal, *Peace News*, was held up because there was no money to pay the printer.[36]

The problems of the peace movement shed further light on the stance taken by Jack Blake in the early 1950s. Since he was the member of the central committee responsible for peace work, Amirah Inglis sought him out to urge that the Peace Council should call for an end to the fighting in Korea, not argue who was to blame. He and Audrey were adamant that condemnation of the United States was necessary. After Ian Turner returned from the Warsaw congress in the following year, he was dismissed as Victorian organiser of the Peace Council and sent to work as a railway cleaner. The idea was that after being satisfactorily proletarianised, he would help J.J. Brown ward off the Groupers in the Australian Railways Union, but when he stood for office in 1954 the Railway Commissioners sacked him.[37] There were other cases of such movement into industry. Dave Bearlin, who joined the party while a student at the University of Melbourne, worked as a teacher for just a year before becoming a waterside worker and by 1955 was assistant secretary of the Melbourne branch of the WWF. Vic Williams also taught before becoming a member of the Fremantle branch, and the anthropologist Fred Rose had a year on the wharves in 1955–56. Jim Mitchell, a journalist, became vice-president of the Port Adelaide branch.

Turner's replacement as national peace organiser was Alec Robertson, then working for the *Argus*, who in turn was succeeded by Stephen Murray-Smith. There was a marked difference between the peace movement in New South Wales and Victoria. Its backbone in New South Wales was the unions, whereas in Melbourne the leaders were unmistakably middle class and, according to one participant, 'looked with some disdain at the rough and ready Sydney methods'. Since the NSW movement obtained most signatures on peace petitions at worksites, it regularly surpassed the more community-oriented approach in Victoria.[38]

Blake was not alone in calling for communists to remove barriers to the broadest possible participation in the peace movement, though he found it difficult to persuade the other party leaders of its priority. His own position was that peace was the overriding consideration, since peaceful competition between capitalism and socialism would demonstrate the superiority of the socialist system; indeed, he flirted with the idea that local committees of the Peace Council could serve as embryonic soviets during the transition to socialism. It followed that 'any attempt to "impose" Communist policy would be counterproductive' and the party 'must never arbitrarily "use" broad non-Party people at any level'. These views were expressed in 1953 and increased his vulnerability to censure in the party's consolidation statement in the following year.[39]

★

The people reached through communist cultural activity exceeded those who put their name to a peace petition. Four hundred and fifty thousand Australians paid to see a performance of the musical *Reedy River* after it was first produced in 1953, and hundreds of thousands read Frank Hardy's 1950 novel *Power Without Glory*, which also appeared in various foreign-language editions.[40]

The cultural front took in a variety of activities that by their nature were difficult to control. Even so, attempts to popularise a progressive and inclusive artistic practice repeatedly ran up against the party's expectations. We saw in Chapter 6 the crackdown in the Soviet Union at the end of the war against all bourgeois culture, and how the Australian party acknowledged the *Zhdanovshchina* but with a conspicuous lack of enthusiasm for heresy hunting. This changed at the end of the 1940s, especially when Jack Blake arrived in Sydney and assumed responsibility for directing the party's cultural work, as he laid down a far more rigorous version of socialist realism.

Of all leading Victorian communists Blake had the least involvement in *Power Without Glory*. A request in late 1945 to Frank Hardy to write this book has been attributed to both Ralph Gibson and Ted Hill; in both versions of the book's genesis, its purpose was to expose the Movement and discredit the newly formed Industrial Groups. A number of fellow members undertook research for Hardy, and the novel that resulted used thinly disguised pseudonyms for the principal figures, though he conceded that 60 per cent of *Power Without Glory* was fiction. One of the many critics who have debated the book's merits has suggested that, rather than follow the established literary form of the historical novel, it can be seen as a long and complicated version of a form of narrative in which Hardy excelled: the yarn.[41]

Power Without Glory follows the rise to power of real-life businessman John Wren (John West in the novel), a working-class resident of Collingwood (Carringbush) who opens an illegal betting shop at the opening of the twentieth century and builds a business empire by practising corruption on a grand scale, especially corruption of the labour movement, where he colludes with Archbishop Mannix (Malone) and eventually B.A. Santamaria. Leaving aside the embellishment of Wren's influence within the ALP, a fundamental problem is that the Movement was itself highly critical of his involvement.

Much of the book's impact derived from the author's self-promotion. He spent four years gathering material and wrestling it into shape, using pseudonyms of his own while pursuing inquiries, then acquired a press to produce the first edition of 5000 copies, with a variety of printers and volunteer binders producing a larger second edition. A gratuitous episode relating an adulterous affair of Wren's wife (Nellie West) brought prosecution for criminal libel. Against the background of the threat to the party's existence (Hardy was arrested five days after passage of the Communist Party Dissolution Act and acquitted less than three months before the referendum), his case was emblematic of the threat to artistic freedom, and a broad-based Hardy Defence Committee headed by Clem Christesen of *Meanjin* magazine and including Walter Murdoch, Vance Palmer, Kylie Tennant and Manning Clark raised funds to pay for his legal expenses.[42]

The trial launched Hardy as a larger-than-life character whose career spanned four decades of writing, popular entertainment, trouble-making and erratic politics. His subsequent account of his tribulations, *The Hard Way*, conveys his energy and ambition, but gives no hint of the controversy that invariably followed him. Hardy was a gambler, heavy drinker and womaniser who borrowed money from other party members as freely as he appropriated their research. 'For years,' a member of the control commission committee recalled, 'we sat in more or less permanent session hearing complaints against Hardy.' He undoubtedly had a talent for yarn-spinning—some thought 'bull-shit artist' a better description—while wanting literary recognition and claiming to be an authority on socialist realism. His redeeming features were encouragement of younger writers and a willingness to use his celebrity to promote the party's cultural activity.[43]

Hardy was a founding member of Melbourne's Realist Writers' Group, which began at the end of the war. Although similar groups emerged afterwards in other cities, he regarded this one as distinctive in the breadth of its membership and the practical assistance it offered participants. Unlikely though it might seem, Judah Waten facilitated links to other writers who were not interested in socialist realism, such as Leonard Mann, Frank Dalby Davison and Alan Marshall. Jack Coffey, the secretary, acted as a conduit between the participants and the state executive, but had no literary talent of his own and is remembered chiefly for circulating a denunciation of the shortcomings of György Lukács, a leading Marxist theorist and literary critic, by József Révai, his jealous former pupil and Hungarian Minister for Culture. Moreover, a number of the realist writers themselves baulked at socialist realism. John Morrison allowed that knowledge of dialectics and a working-class outlook might make a good writer better but alone would not make a good writer. David Martin came to the conclusion that it violated a fundamental law of fiction, that characters must not be invented to dramatise heroic revolutionary qualities: 'real heroes are constantly at war with their unheroic elements'.[44]

It was Hardy who suggested the formation of a book club to promote the work of the realist writers, characteristically leaving others to make it happen. The Australasian Book Society was incorporated as a limited liability company in March 1952, with Bill Wannan working as secretary from a room in Collins House and the publishing operations conducted in New Theatre's Flinders Street building. Members paid 50 shillings a year for six books and were offered a discount on other left-wing publications. Undercapitalisation exacerbated a persistent problem of unpaid subscriptions, but the society built a membership of several thousand.[45]

Although the party did not initiate the society, all its directors were communists and the state executive intervened on several occasions to determine what was produced. Its insistence that the society publish *Journey into the Future*, Hardy's tediously eulogistic account of his visit to the Soviet Union following acquittal on the charge of criminal libel (some suggested he made the trip because of threats to his personal safety in Australia), was a costly flop. It also brought the resignation of the society's selection committee (A.A. Phillips, Leonard Mann and Alan Marshall), who were not consulted.[46] The subsequent condemnation by *Tribune* of a fictional trilogy deemed insufficiently militant provoked its author to ask whether Sydney had a monopoly on political acumen. Jack Blake closed that discussion with a statement that the society was moving in the wrong direction.[47]

Such pointed criticism brought the resignation of Bill Wannan, who was replaced in 1954 by Ian Turner. He hustled the books in factories and workshops, on building jobs and the waterfront, with a NSW functionary keeping watch over the precarious finances. Turner and Stephen

Murray-Smith were also members of the Realist Writers' Group, and Murray-Smith edited its journal, a makeshift duplicated publication until 1954, when Judah Waten obtained a modest amount of money to turn it into a printed quarterly, *Overland*. Murray-Smith set out to attract a popular audience for *Overland* and quickly built a circulation of several thousand.[48]

Painting, so acrimonious a topic of debate in the 1940s, was less troubled by arguments over matters of style, more concerned with discussion of the role and purpose of the communist artist. Art was a weapon, Blake insisted, that awakened and intensified the consciousness of the people, but Marxism had also made a science of aesthetics.[49] Its principles were equally applicable to popular artistic initiatives, such as the Studio of Realist Art (and later the art classes that Rod Shaw conducted among the Sydney waterside workers) and to the work of professional artists.

That left unresolved the question of how worker practitioners were to acquire the necessary technical skills, and how full-time artists were to fulfil their communist obligations. As Frank Hardy demonstrated, it was possible for an untutored neophyte to become a successful novelist, a transition made possible in his case by the support of trade unionists such as George Seelaf of the Meatworkers as well as more formally educated members of the Realist Writers' Group. As Hardy came to regard himself as an authority on cultural policy, he treated his own experience as generally applicable. Budding writers should begin with short sketches for factory bulletins, and then compose reports and stories for the party press. Those aiming further should join a Realist Writers' Group and work on their grammar, sentence structure, punctuation and literary technique—on condition that they not succumb to bourgeois notions of merit. Communists pursuing artistic careers had to remain 'organically connected' to the party lest they hanker for the plaudits of the critics and drift away. Yet they also needed the understanding of branch members of the time their craft demanded and recognition that it was contributing to the party's political work just as much as other branch duties. Here Hardy contrasted the deep and growing interest of workers in literature and other cultural forms with the disdain that many communists displayed for 'culture vultures'.[50]

The musical *Reedy River* served the impulse for a popular, participatory culture as well as providing a riposte to the lavish American musicals that flourished here in the 1950s. It drew on three kinds of such cultural activity: the well-established New Theatre, the more recently formed Unity Dance Group and a burgeoning interest in folk culture. Loosely supervised by the party, the New Theatre's repertoire included musical revues. The Unity Dance Group performed at factories, street parades and all manner of party events. Some of those who started it came from a ballet background, but they soon developed a strong interest in reviving traditional forms of the Australian bush dance, and shared this interest with collectors and performers of the Australian version of the folk song, the bush ballad. The Great Patriotic War had seen the cultivation of this musical genre in Russia, and it was taken up by communists in a number of Western countries, notably the United States, where Pete Seeger formed his first group soon after joining the party in 1941. The most active Australian was John Meredith, who collected ballads on journeys through the bush and formed the Bushwhackers' band (with two aitches) to promote them.[51]

Meredith and other communists were not the first to collect such material: Andrew Barton ('Banjo') Paterson's *Old Bush Songs* (1905) was a basic resource. Nor were they alone in the field, though neither Percy Jones, the musician who also collected traditional bush songs at this time, nor Douglas Stewart and Nancy Keesing's collection of *Australian Bush Ballads* (1955) made any claims as to their political significance. It was the left that worked the ballad into an authentic expression of the Australian egalitarian ethos. Edgar Waters, then working in the State Library of New South Wales, began field recordings with the encouragement of Meredith and established the Folklore Society in that state. Ian Turner, Wendy Lowenstein (an activist in the New Theatre and Eureka Youth League) and Hugh Anderson (a collaborator of Meredith's) initiated the Victorian one, and the poet John Manifold played a similar role in Queensland.

Waters would continue to make field recordings for the rest of his life, but he also completed a doctoral thesis at the Australian National University (ANU) on 'the popular arts' in Australia in the late nineteenth and early twentieth centuries. Russel Ward undertook his thesis at the same university on the ethos of the pastoral worker, which he extended into a seminal book on *The Australian Legend*. It traced a tradition of protest and solidarity from the convicts and bushrangers to the diggers of the goldfields, the itinerant workers of the pastoral industry and ultimately to the people at large. One of the attractions of local folklore was to rebut Cold War allegations that the left was in thrall to a foreign ideology.[52]

John Gray of the New Theatre asked Dick Diamond, the former secretary of Actors' Equity who had previously written agitprop pieces, to provide a script for the musical. He set it in 1891, after the epochal strike of the Queensland shearers had been crushed. One of the shearers, Joe Collins, returns to the settlement of Reedy River after release from prison and incurs the censure of his workmates and sweetheart by working with non-union labour—until the whole shed goes on strike for union conditions. In constructing this plot Diamond drew on advice from Turner, Ward, Meredith and Waters, just as he used a mixture of bush ballads, the verse of Henry Lawson and Paterson and new songs such as 'The Ballad of 1891', written by Helen Palmer and set to music by Doreen Bridges. A feature of the production was the interaction between actors and the audience, and the live performance of the music with instruments such as the lagerphone, mouth organ, concertina and upright piano. A notable absence was any acknowledgement of the original owners of the Queensland pastoral country who had been dispossessed only a few decades earlier. Joe's conflict with his sweetheart Mary and subsequent reconciliation remain subordinate to masculine solidarity.[53]

In striking contrast to the promotion of a popular culture uncontaminated by professionalism was the communist interest in sport. This received greater coverage in the Melbourne *Guardian* than the Sydney *Tribune*, with particular interest in athletics in the lead-up to the Melbourne Olympics of 1956. If Australia was to do well, it must provide better coaching and training facilities, and support to enable athletes to gain international experience. The opportunities provided by sports carnivals organised behind the Iron Curtain by the World Youth

Festival were held up as of particular value, and much was made of the training advice provided to Dave Stephens, the 'flying milko', by the Czech long-distance record-holder Emil Zátopek. Percy Cerutty, not a party member but active in the peace movement, took a similar approach in his athletics coaching, as did Freddy Lester, a German refugee who later established the annual 10,000 metres championship named after Zátopek.[54]

A persistent theme of communist cultural activity in the 1950s was the need to defend Australia from the pernicious effects of American imperialism. 'Australian people today are being subjected to a vicious and unprecedented flood of foreign decadence,' Stephen Murray-Smith warned in 1953. It consisted of comics, movies, jukebox music and syndicated journalism, all 'preaching pornography, sadism, sex, violence, hatred between nations'.[55]

Similarly, progressive writers (the term used to describe those who favoured a literature of social engagement but baulked at socialist realism) had to be defended from discrimination. Communists believed, with good reason, that ASIO vetted all applicants for assistance from the Commonwealth Literary Fund, which was then the only source of public support. The prime minister defended Vance Palmer, who chaired its advisory committee, against an attack in parliament during 1952 by two cold warriors, Stan Keon of the Labor right and William Wentworth, but in private expressed grave misgivings over the award of a fellowship to Judah Waten and instructed ASIO to investigate all future applicants. For more than a decade it did so and drew the most tenuous connections: Thea Astley had nominated a referee who had contributed a tribute to *Overland* on Dame Mary Gilmore's ninetieth birthday; Eric Lowe nominated Colin Roderick, who was patron of an organisation affiliated to the Union of Australian Women.[56]

Keon, Wentworth and, for good measure, Laurie Short were original members of the Australian Committee for Cultural Freedom, formed in 1952 by Richard Krygier, who by this time had a book-importing business in Sydney. His object was to gain recognition and support from the Congress for Cultural Freedom, a Paris-based organisation (generously, though covertly, funded by the CIA) designed to counter the influence of left-wing intellectuals. To this end he recruited Sir John Latham, who had recently retired from the High Court, as president to help him assemble a prestigious executive. Latham was disconcerted by Krygier's plan to have ASIO run security checks on prospective members, even though he himself had Spry reassure him of Krygier's credentials. Similarly, the congress secretariat advised Krygier to tone down his aggressively anti-communist polemics and reminded him that the organisation was meant to promote cultural freedom. Yet when the congress provided additional funding so the Australian association (as it had become) could produce a quarterly magazine, *Quadrant*, Krygier was guided by B.A. Santamaria in choosing as editor the poet, Catholic convert and deeply conservative James McAuley.[57]

Although the party condemned the Congress for Cultural Freedom as yet another example of American interference in Australian cultural life, it was left to Clem Christesen, the editor of *Meanjin*, to grasp the significance of its Australian arm. His literary quarterly, committed to liberal humanism and high culture, exercised precisely the fellow-travelling pernicious influence on intellectuals that Krygier was determined to combat. Krygier encouraged Wentworth to seek security information on Christesen and was delighted to find ASIO documents identifying communists and fellow travellers pushed under his door.[58]

⋆

Other auxiliaries enjoyed far less success. The Eureka Youth League had just a few hundred members scattered in 50 branches when Audrey Blake took charge as national secretary in Sydney at the beginning of 1950. She sought to popularise the youth movement and make it less self-enclosed, but was hamstrung by an unresolved contradiction in the league's structure and purpose. According to the constitution it was an independent youth organisation, and Blake emphasised the need to recognise 'the non-party character of the EYL' and maintain its organisational independence. But the same constitution declared it to be a Marxist youth organisation that based itself on the principles of scientific socialism; all the officers were communists and Blake herself worked under the direction of a member of the secretariat, Jack Henry.

She wanted to expand the membership by offering social, cultural and sporting activities ('socialism through socials', as a later league organiser put it) and broaden its work through mass campaigns. The Sydney leadership expected it to draw ideological guidance from the party, operate as a 'revolutionary socialist youth organisation' and win young workers to the united front under its leadership.[59]

There was a special effort to attract non-party members to the biennial Festival of Youth and Students for Peace. Drawn from the Labour clubs, the Student Christian Movement and other organisations, they made up a substantial minority of the 135 Australians who attended the Berlin festival in 1951. The main contingent made its way to Italy on the Lloyd Triestino shipping line's MS *Australia* and then broke into smaller groups to evade restrictions on treks that took them through Switzerland and Austria, and eventually to the Soviet zone of Berlin. While the delegates (who included a large number of union representatives) raised support from sponsors and the party spent a considerable amount, some made considerable sacrifices to attend. Thus Shirley Andrews of the Unity Dance Group had to resign her position with the CSIRO and had great difficulty in finding employment upon her return. There was an Indigenous delegate, Ray Peckham, and Faith Bandler, a Pacific Islander. Rivkah Brilliant was there, along with her husband Bob Matthews and John Walker of the Realist Film Group (his wife Margaret led the Unity Dance Group) to make a photographic record, which was supplemented by another Victorian, Joyce Evans.[60]

The expectation was that the excitement and spectacle of an assembly of 26,000 delegates from 104 countries would draw those with no connection to the party into its ambit, and to this end delegates visited communist countries when the festival ended. The expectation backfired when the chair of the Australian delegation and another influential delegate refused to follow the official itinerary in the Soviet Union and made open criticism of conditions there upon their return in 1952. Even the festival opening ceremony was too much for Joyce Evans, who recoiled in dismay from the mass hysteria and abandoned plans to join the party.[61]

The Berlin festival was the inspiration for a Youth Carnival for Peace and Friendship in Sydney in March 1952, the first of its kind held outside the communist bloc. Audrey Blake conceived it on a grand scale, with a packed program of sport, song, dance, art and literary competitions, a film festival and much else. It foundered when the government denied passports to delegates from communist countries and local government authorities withdrew the use of their facilities. There were 2300 registered delegates and a total attendance of 25,000 over the week's events, a meagre return on an outlay of more than £16,000 that increased criticism of Blake's leadership. She and Harry Stein were replaced as national officers of the Eureka Youth League immediately after the festival, though this brought no improvement in its fortunes.[62]

The women's auxiliaries fared no better. The first of them, the New Housewives' Association, began in 1947 after the failure of attempts to overturn conservative control of the established Housewives' Association, which took a strong anti-communist stand after the Second World War. The new one campaigned on a range of issues, including prices and living standards, peace, women's rights and child welfare, and threw its weight behind the miners during the 1949 strike.[63] Partly to repair the damage created by vitriolic denunciation of the Labor government and partly to serve the party's call for a people's movement, the party abandoned the New Housewives' Association in early 1950 in favour of a Union of Australian Women. The decision to do so, taken on high without consulting the women, removed leaders such as Mary Wright, who had served the party for as long as her husband Tom; as she put it, 'we weren't young enough'. It also offended younger women such as Jean Blackburn, the president of the New Housewives in South Australia, who was told there was no place for her in the new organisation as the party did not want any more 'bourgeois leadership'.[64]

No longer tailoring its program to housewives, the Union of Australian Women took up an extensive range of causes. Apart from the peace campaign, these included prices and wages, equal pay, child care and kindergartens, housing, health care, education and support for Indigenous Australians and movements of national independence, all tailored down to a suburban ordinariness that found expression in columns such as 'Over a Cuppa' and 'Down Any Street' that appeared in its journal *Our Women*. Kath Williams was the principal advocate of equal pay, and helped to keep that cause alive within the ACTU.[65] But she was an official of the Liquor and Allied Trades Union, whereas most of the Union of Australian Women's members were not in the paid workforce and many of the meetings were held during the working day. Like the Eureka Youth League, it sent delegates to meetings of a world body, the Women's International League for Peace and Freedom, and took the lead in Australian celebration of International Women's Day on 8 March. While there are no precise figures, the membership never exceeded a few thousand.[66]

The 1950s also brought increased questioning of gender roles. It had been common enough for party members, male and female, to deprecate the attitude of male superiority among many communists. Miles, Sharkey, Dixon and other leaders were married men whose partners were conspicuous by their absence from party life; indeed, it was not unusual for wives of activists to resent the constant demands that robbed them of their husbands' companionship. (Conversely, Jessie Street, Australia's most famous fellow traveller, spent most of the 1950s overseas to avoid embarrassing her husband, Sir Kenneth Street, the chief justice of the NSW Supreme Court.) Such division of labour was by no means always the case, as the partnership of Audrey and Jack Blake demonstrates, and in-marriage created extensive kinship groups in which the women were as involved as the men.

By this time women were beginning to challenge the party's patriarchal practices. As secretary of the party's disciplinary body, the central control commission, Wally Clayton had been notorious for interfering in members' marital arrangements. That ceased to be the case after he went underground in 1949 and Jess Grant became a member of the commission. She decided that watching over 'who slept with whom' was not part of its responsibility.[67] In a further reform, the commission adopted a less menacing name: it became the central disputes committee.

Jean Blackburn's experience was indicative of the changes at work. She joined the party while studying economics at the University of Melbourne and subsequently worked for the Department of War Organisation of Industry. Marriage to Gerard (Dick) Blackburn, the son of Maurice and Doris, led to resignation from the public service ahead of the birth of their first child—part of a broader movement of women back into the home in the aftermath of the war. But when Dick Blackburn, an agricultural scientist, accepted a research post in South Australia with the CSIRO in 1946 without consulting her, she found herself marooned in two rooms in Adelaide while he was away on long periods of field-work. Impoverished, isolated and subject to depression, she returned to the paid workforce as a teacher—just as other women of her generation did during the 1950s—and began a remarkable career as an educational reformer. Her earlier spell as president of the New Housewives in South Australia can be seen as an indication of this desire to go further, just as two leading organisers of the Union of Australian Women had their own aspirations: Ailsa O'Connor in Victoria as an artist, Dorothy Hewett in Sydney as a writer.[68]

Zelda D'Aprano, an embattled party member in Melbourne, might well have had such educated, enterprising female comrades in mind when she railed against the middle-class 'elite' in the party that kept those such as herself on the outer. D'Aprano's parents were Jewish refugees from Poland living in a run-down area of Carlton; she left school early to work and married an Italian communist. At considerable physical and emotional cost, she contested the Groupers' control of her union but could not bring herself to speak up at party meetings, conscious of her lack of education and poor elocution. Initially D'Aprano did not question the men in positions of authority but directed her ire at their partners, who seemed to relish the limelight. In time she would sheet the blame home to the men, especially those who held union office.[69]

There was limited success too in the party's work among national minorities. It drew back from hostility to displaced persons in 1951 with an enhanced awareness of the need to break down its isolation from these newcomers. And although communists called for a pause in the immigration program when the government's deflationary budget in the same year brought a recession, they recognised that unemployment was hitting the migrant workers more harshly than the local ones. As part of this reorientation, the party took up the grievances of assisted migrants arriving from Britain and living in migrant hostels, as well as Italian and other nationals housed in former displaced persons camps such as

Bonegilla in Victoria. This in turn brought reconsideration of the policy of closing the party's 'foreign branches' and transferring the 'foreign-born comrades' into ordinary branches, where some complained of a less than warm welcome.[70]

The Jewish Council to Combat Fascism and Anti-Semitism lost ground as a result of its opposition in the early 1950s to a migration agreement with West Germany. The council was no means alone in its repugnance for these German settlers, but came up against Israel's desire for closer relations with West Germany and mounting evidence of the anti-Semitism practised by communist regimes. Maurice Ashkanasy, a prominent Melbourne barrister, denounced the council's failure to acknowledge, let alone condemn, this crude xenophobia, and secured its expulsion from the Jewish Board of Deputies in 1952. Meanwhile, the Bundists won control of the Victorian council's meeting place, the Kadimah, and evicted it. A similar split occurred in Sydney, where the Jewish Council fell out with Bundists and established their own Peretz Centre in 1953.[71]

The party gave limited attention to the council's activities, which were determined in Victoria by an alliance of communists such as Judah Waten, Saul Factor and Itzhak Gust and non-communists such as Norman Rothfield and Sam Cohen. A belated attempt to use the execution of Julius and Ethel Rosenberg, arrested by the FBI for spying in 1950 and finally electrocuted in 1953, as an antidote to the damaging effects of Soviet anti-Semitism on the Jewish community came too late.[72] By then the misgivings of Jewish communists were so apparent that a meeting was organised in Sydney for Jack Blake to admonish them, warn that any traitor in the party's ranks who raised the problem of Soviet anti-Semitism would be sought out and destroyed, and order a renewed campaign against Zionism. Blake was conscious he was misleading members. Much as he came to regret laying down the line on the Lysenko controversy, he was far more ashamed of justifying the victimisation of Stalin's Jewish doctors.[73]

The CPA continued to promote international solidarity with national independence movements, especially in Asia. This was particularly controversial while the Korean War was being fought, and the actions of Wilfred

Burchett, who reported on that war and also interrogated captured Allied soldiers to buttress his claims of atrocities, brought allegations of treason that would dog him for the rest of his life. Following the Korean armistice, the anti-imperial movement revived as the French were driven from Indochina in 1954 and as the Indonesian party grew rapidly. When Laurie Aarons represented the Australian party at the Eighth Congress of the Partai Komunis Indonesia in that year, he was struck both by the size of the meetings he addressed (many of more than 100,000) and open threats to kill its leaders.[74] Burchett arranged for Len Fox to work in Hanoi assisting the Vietnamese news agency with English translations, while Mona Brand and Dick Diamond did the same for the radio station known as The Voice of Vietnam.[75] They were followed by Malcolm and Lorraine Salmon: she had worked as a broadcaster in Melbourne for fifteen years and he served as *Tribune*'s Vietnamese correspondent.[76] But solidarity movements with these peoples' democracies attracted no more than an earnest minority.

The most successful solidarity movement was the one pressing for protection and emancipation of Indigenous Australians, which found expression in campaigns against the Woomera rocket range, support for the Pilbara pastoral workers' walk-off and demands for improvement of conditions of those living on the fringes of white Australia. Nominally, the party remained committed to the distinction laid down in Tom Wright's *New Deal for the Aborigines* (1939) between 'full-bloods' in remote areas, who had to be protected in their traditional way of life, and 'half-castes' who should enjoy the same conditions and rights as other Australian workers; but this distinction made little sense of a case that arose in Darwin in 1950, when residents of the Berrimah Reserve struck for better pay. As part of the administration's crackdown, one of them, Fred Nadpur (better known as Fred Waters), was convicted and transported to Haasts Bluff, 2000 kilometres away.[77]

Waters was in touch with members of the North Australian Workers' Union and other Darwin communists who had Melbourne connections. They took the lead in arranging for protest meetings in the southern city, which led almost immediately to the formation of a Council for Aboriginal Rights. It began, like so many communist auxiliaries, with churchmen, humanitarians and Aboriginal activists prominent among the office-holders, and the biochemist Shirley Andrews was principal organiser. She had no prior involvement in Indigenous affairs, and took on this responsibility only because the party had assigned her to proselytise among the scientists, an uncongenial task for this woman who guarded her dignity. The Council for Aboriginal Rights had been allocated to John Walker, an architect and husband of her friend Margaret, the founder of the Unity Dance Group, so the two simply swapped responsibilities.[78]

Andrews proved a remarkably effective organiser. Having suffered discrimination because of her sex, she had a deep-seated hatred of injustice, while her scientific training made her scornful of racism. Though uncomfortable with mass agitation, she excelled in establishing a network of informants and advisers that spanned political differences. Such was her dedication that she welcomed Don McLeod as a houseguest on his visits to Melbourne, even though he kept talking at the breakfast table long after she was due at work.[79]

It was noted in Chapter 5 that Fred Rose, the Cambridge-trained anthropologist, and Alec Jolly, a doctor who worked in Broome during the war, had challenged Tom Wright's distinction between tribalised and detribalised Indigenous Australians. Rose continued to advance his views after the war and he also assisted the fieldwork of Peter Worsley, a young British anthropologist who reached similar conclusions as a research student at the ANU in 1954. Worsley was invited to address the central committee on the subject and published his argument that even remote Aboriginal people were by now 'proletarians, not nomads' in the *Communist Review*. Ted Bacon, at this time secretary of the Queensland state committee, took up Worsley's argument in a paper he had Richard Dixon submit to the political committee, and waited patiently outside the room as it met to hear the outcome. 'Total political and ideological rejection,' Dixon informed him.[80]

Shirley Andrews showed little interest in such doctrinal disputes. Her object was to document, publicise and lobby for the recognition of Aboriginal rights whenever and wherever they were denied. Nor did she seek to build the council into a large front organisation under the party's control. If she brought any distinctively communist approach to its work, it was the importance of organisation. The council was successful precisely because it was an outward-looking body of shared goals.[81]

★

By 1954, then, the party had stabilised its industrial fortunes and pursued a range of initiatives designed to rebuild communist influence. If these taxed its declining capacity, the party seemed to have weathered the storm—at least until early April, when Vladimir Petrov, an intelligence officer working as third secretary in the Soviet Embassy, defected with claims that implicated the Communist Party of Australia in an extensive spy ring. A fortnight later his wife Evdokia was taken from the custody of two burly Soviet couriers at the Darwin aerodrome to join him in political asylum. Menzies established a royal commission to investigate his claims, which sat from 19 May 1954 until 31 March 1955. The inquiry damaged the reputation of many of the 119 witnesses it examined and inflicted major political damage on the Labor Party, which seemed to have had a good chance of winning the federal election due in 1954 and held on 29 May. Just a few days of preliminary hearings before the poll raised sufficient doubt about entrusting Labor with national security to keep the Coalition in office.

The subject of keen controversy then and since, the Royal Commission on Espionage has generated a large literature. Investigative journalists have argued it was a conspiracy against the left, part of a pattern that went back to the conscription split in the First World War whereby a contrived crisis cheated the labour movement of its rightful due. The Petrov affair had a resonance as powerful to the generation who lived through it as that of the Dismissal of the Whitlam government. Academics working on the security state have followed the journalists' lead. Their principal criticisms are the timing of the defection to suit the government's election prospects, the draconian conduct of the commission and the fact that no prosecutions followed—this spy hunt caught no spies.[82]

Several of those involved in the Petrov case (including Michael Thwaites, ASIO's then director of counterintelligence) have contested these allegations, and in 1987 the political scientist Robert Manne used recently released security records and extensive conversations with Charles Spry to publish a forensic examination of the whole episode.[83] He was successful in rebutting some of the wilder accusations, though questions remain about when Menzies learned of a likely defection and the way the commissioners used their extraordinary powers.[84] The Communist Party has a secondary role in this controversy, which is concerned with the clash between Menzies and Evatt, the Labor Party and those seeking to discredit it.

For communists, on the other hand, the terms of the commission were a direct threat. It was to inquire into the information provided by Vladimir Petrov, and to determine whether agents of the USSR were conducting espionage in Australia and if any Australian 'persons or organisations' were involved in such espionage.[85] The party leaders knew that Petrov, who was in charge of the KGB's operations, was drinking heavily and behaving erratically. They also knew he was a singularly inept spymaster who relied on local assistance to obtain even the most basic information Moscow requested. Finally, they knew from a bungled interrogation of External Affairs officer Jim Hill conducted by British security in 1950 that Australian intelligence had the names of a number of party members who had provided official secrets for Wally Clayton to pass on to Moscow. Particularly embarrassing was the realisation that the undercover ASIO agent who cultivated Petrov and persuaded him to defect had stood high in the party's regard: this was the mysterious refugee Dr Michael Bialoguski, aptly codenamed Diablo, who served for a period as treasurer of the NSW Peace Council.[86]

The party's immediate response was therefore to discredit the Petrovs and the inquiry. Hence Richard Dixon called the defection a provocative stunt designed to smear communists with lies and forged documents. Soon it was linking Vladimir Petrov to the discredited head of Soviet intelligence, Lavrenty Beria. The subsequent revelation that the Petrovs were paid £5000 to defect, information that Menzies instructed the commission to withhold during the preliminary hearing before the election, encouraged such allegations.[87]

A determined effort was made to discredit the documents that Vladimir Petrov brought with him from the Soviet Embassy. Some of these, labelled Exhibits A to F in the royal commission, were instructions sent by Moscow Centre after he arrived in Australia in early 1952. Exhibit G consisted of documents that Petrov's predecessor Ivan Pakhomov bequeathed, though they were mostly created by Pakhomov's predecessor Valentino Sadovnikov and Petrov had no involvement in the intelligence-gathering they described. Exhibit H was an appraisal of Australian journalists written by Fergan O'Sullivan in 1951 when he was a member of the Canberra press gallery; its sensitivity increased when O'Sullivan became press secretary to the leader of the opposition in 1953.[88]

Of greatest sensitivity was Exhibit J, composed and typed by Rupert Lockwood at the request of a TASS journalist in 1953. Described by counsel assisting the commission as 'a farrago of fact, falsity and filth', it was a 20,000-word compilation of information and scuttlebutt on Japanese cultivation of prominent Australians and American espionage in Australia, with notes on other subjects, including Evatt, and it identified some of Lockwood's informants. Aware of the hostile interpretation likely to be put on this document, Lockwood produced a bowdlerised version of *What Is in Document 'J'* in June 1954 and, when that was suppressed, a second version purporting to be a publication of the Freedom Press of Everglades, Canberra. These were meant to show that the one submitted to the commission was a forgery.[89]

When summoned before the commission, Lockwood prevaricated, dissembled and lied about his authorship, for he realised that by naming his informants, who included three members of Evatt's staff, he had placed them at risk. Worse, he persuaded Evatt himself that Exhibit J was a forgery, setting the Labor leader on a collision course with the commissioners that culminated in them withdrawing his leave to appear. As they examined a number of Clayton's informants in the remainder of 1954, their powers to subpoena witnesses and compel them to answer questions had been strengthened, and a new provision made it a criminal offence to bring the commission into disrepute.

Even so, most witnesses followed a strategy similar to that of Lockwood. Richard Dixon, on behalf of the party, insisted it would have nothing to do with espionage, that he had not seen Clayton for years and that the party kept no records—not even a wage book for income tax purposes. When pressed, witnesses refused to name associates and in many cases claimed not to remember activities that ASIO had documented. This applied even to witnesses who cooperated with ASIO in earlier interrogations. Hence June Barnett, who left the party on joining the Department of External Affairs in 1948, spoke frankly of how she was invited to the home of a party member in Canberra in 1950 so that Clayton could visit and ask her to assist him by gathering information—except that she could not confirm it was Clayton, not even when shown photos of him. Similarly, Frances Bernie was keen to tell her story of taking Clayton documents from Evatt's office but passed over other dealings.[90]

The most truculent witnesses were likely to come undone, though the commissioners were happy to see the back of Bill Bird. He appeared at a Sydney sitting of the commission at the end of 1954 to reject the allegation he had told Jack Skolnik, a businessman who assisted Clayton financially, that the authorities would never find him since he had been taken by sea to New Zealand. Bird came to Sydney, moreover, with members of his Melbourne branch of the Seamen's Union and made his attitude clear from the beginning. Did he know Clayton? Not if he fell over him. Was he a member of the Communist Party? 'I am, and proud of it.' As the seamen applauded, the exasperated chairman cleared the public gallery to allow counsel assisting to proceed. He wanted to know if Bird met Clayton when the two men lived in Melbourne in 1935. 'Why don't you get your facts right before you ask questions?' demanded Bird, who had not taken up duties there until 1941, and then 'Just a minute: I'm not finished,' which prompted the chairman to hope the Crown Law authorities were keeping a record of his contempt. 'It doesn't worry me,' Bird replied and then told the commissioners how he had berated Skolnik for his mistake. They released him after just 30 minutes.[91]

By this time it was apparent the commission would make no reference to the Venona information. Charles Spry was briefed on it in 1950 and Ron Richards, whom he recruited from the Western Australian police, used several months in London during 1952 to study the files. To avoid tipping off Soviet intelligence that the West could read its communications, however, the case against the Australians had to stand up independently, so Richards spent much of 1953 assembling it. The irony was that the MGB (as the NKGB then was) had already learned of Venona through two sources, one an agent in the US Army Security Service and the other a celebrated mole in Britain's MI6, Kim Philby.

Klod, or Claude or simply K, had been identified as Clayton, but Wally Clayton went underground in 1949 and slipped further from view in the following year after learning of the interrogation of Jim Hill. The party leaders maintained contact. Laurie Aarons took over this responsibility in 1954; he wanted to bring Clayton out of hiding, particularly after the government launched a manhunt in the national media, but did not prevail until March 1955. Clayton then walked over the hills behind Milton on the NSW south coast to a rendezvous with a party member who took him to the solicitor Cedric Ralph in Melbourne, who in turn took him by car to the commission hearing in Sydney.[92]

Represented by Ted Hill, Clayton explained that he had come forward to clear his name, refused to say where he had been, denied suggestions he had ever sought government secrets from Bernie, Barnett or George Legge of the Department of External Affairs, and mixed platitude ('I am of old English stock. My ancestors are Kentish peasants') with conceit ('I am a worker. Our battle is hard'). Warned by the chairman not to shout, he insisted 'I am calm—calm!' Spry wanted to know if Clayton could be prosecuted for refusing to answer the commission's questions but the Attorney-General's Department thought not.[93]

As the commission dragged on with little sign that any prosecution would follow, the party stepped up its attack. A Christmas social at the end of 1954 where the Petrovs, the counsel assisting the commission and ASIO officers mingled over drinks provided inspiration for a demonstration by wharfies when the commission resumed in the new year. Dressed up in character, Menzies identifiable by his glass of brandy, they sang and danced their contempt on the lawn outside the courthouse. Similarly, much was made of Petrov's statement that he arranged for Lance Sharkey to receive US$25,000 in $25 notes, not a denomination of that currency. Reports of such incidents were nearly always accompanied by calls for the commission to be terminated, for the press coverage of its proceedings was inflicting considerable damage on the party's reputation.[94]

The consequences for some forced to appear before it were devastating. Hardened party leaders such as Audrey Blake, who was said to have provided Moscow with information on Eureka Youth League members, were less likely to lose sleep over a subpoena than communists with careers at stake. Bruce Milliss's trading enterprises, for example, were damaged by the commission placing his earlier activities in Katoomba in the most sinister light. Dave Morris, an engineer, appeared in the G series of documents that Petrov handed over to Ron Richards because (unknown to him) he had been deemed a security risk while conducting military research in Britain in 1946. After his appearance before the commission in 1954, ASIO ensured Morris was unable to find employment and he moved with his family to China in 1959. Ric Throssell was sidelined in the Department of External Affairs after his ordeal in the witness box. Then there were victims of guilt by association, including Clem and Nina Christesen.[95]

Dorothy Hewett provides the most atmospheric account of the commission. She was summoned to appear as an organiser of the Union of Australian Women, until it was decided that her heavily pregnant condition might win sympathy. But appear she did after a drunken legal officer informed her the night before the hearing she was not wanted. Entering the courtroom, she saw 'little fat Petrov' sweating profusely, Evdokia, an attractive blonde woman in an ill-fitting Soviet costume, and the dark-jowled and heavy-shouldered Ron Richards, familiar to her from her days in Western Australia. The mood reminded her of *Alice in Wonderland*, and at any moment she expected the Red Queen to scream 'Off with their heads'. Instead 'the three old, desiccated men nodding away on the bench carried out their appointed tasks like senile marionettes, conferring and muttering to each other in a travesty of justice'.[96]

It was harder to sustain that bravado after the adrenalin wore off and you were back at home, still under surveillance, your phone tapped, ostracised by neighbours and subjected to anonymous abuse, threats and broken windows, the children bullied at school. Such notoriety strained marriages. The allegations against the party nagged away at even the most resolute comrades.

★

Evatt's decision to defend members of his staff and portray the royal commission as a conspiracy against the labour movement attracted mounting criticism within the Labor Party. Hitherto he had cultivated the Movement to shore up his leadership; now it condemned him. Meanwhile, B.A. Santamaria gave a speech to the Movement's annual convention in which he suggested it could increase its control of the ALP by discrediting 'the Chifley legend' propagated by those who resisted the Cold War, and cultivating the 'Curtin legend' of looking to America. A prominent opponent of the Movement drew this address, all the more provocative since Santamaria was not even a member of the Labor Party, to Evatt's attention.[97]

Mindful of the problems that Christian Democrats caused for Italian and other European communist parties, Sharkey and Dixon did not want Labor's division pressed to breaking point. Santamaria had already told Archbishop Mannix that the Movement was in a position 'to implement a Christian social programme in both the State and Federal spheres' and within five or six years could 'completely transform the leadership of the Labour Movement'. This was the first time, he boasted, that such work had become possible in Australia and, as far as he could see, 'in the Anglo-Saxon world since the advent of Protestantism'. The danger, as the party saw it, was that if the leading Groupers were to defect, they would take a substantial number of their fellow Catholics with them.[98]

Evatt would not be deterred. In early October he released a statement that condemned the disloyalty of a small minority of members, who he said were located particularly in Victoria and directed from outside the labour movement. A war of words erupted in which the name of Santamaria became familiar and many Catholics discovered the existence of his clandestine organisation. Evatt won the support of a number of unions, including the Australian Workers' Union, and officers of the Victorian Trades Hall Council and NSW Labor Council who had been happy to call on Groupers to defeat communists in union elections but now saw them as threatening their own positions.

He thus secured a decision by the ALP Federal Executive to hold a special conference of the Victorian branch and elect a new executive to participate in a special meeting of the federal conference in Hobart in March 1955. The old Victorian executive rashly decided to boycott the federal conference, which in turn voted narrowly to withdraw all support from the Industrial Groups. The Movement fought this out to the bitter end in Victoria, so that seven members of the House of Representatives broke away, along with a group of state parliamentarians who brought down the government headed by John Cain. In New South Wales, where the church was increasingly critical of Santamaria's lack of accountability, the Movement's leaders decided to continue the fight from within the Labor Party. There were no Groups in Western Australia, the Labor firebrand Clyde Cameron had long since brought those in South Australia to heel, and the battle in Queensland had still to be resolved. Accordingly, the Victorians were alone in forming a new party, the Australian Labor Party (Anti-Communist), and it took several years for a national Democratic Labor Party to emerge.[99]

The Communist Party remained an onlooker during the Labor split. Although Dixon's concern was borne out when a significant proportion of Victorian voters followed the breakaways, the party was a beneficiary. The Hobart conference dropped a number of anti-communist shibboleths (it called for a ban on atomic weapons, an end to Australian military involvement in Asia and recognition of the People's Republic of China) and softened the ALP's prohibition on unity tickets in union elections.

At its Seventeenth Congress, the party therefore welcomed the growing signs of unity. That congress had been planned for September 1954—the draft resolutions had been circulated and discussed; the delegates had been chosen; and Sharkey had issued the report on the work of the central committee over the past four years—and then was suddenly postponed. No explanation was given; the delayed congress assembled in Sydney in May 1955 as if that had always been the intention. The most likely reason for the delay was that the commission was pursuing cases of espionage that went back to the Venona period, and the party was still unsure whether it would use the incriminating transcripts.

The reports and policies taken to the CPA's delayed congress differed little from those prepared almost a year earlier. The central policy document, *Australia's Path to Socialism*, was in any case a revised version of that adopted by the Sixteenth Congress four years earlier. It repeated the argument that the Labor Party would not embrace socialism, which would come only from a people's movement led by the organised working class. It again claimed that Australia would find its own way to a people's government aided by the peaceful coexistence of East and West that the peace movement would secure, and now cited the Bandung Conference held the month before in Indonesia as evidence that a non-aligned movement of Afro-Asian countries would further dissipate Cold War tensions.[100]

There was frank admission of the setbacks suffered over the past few years and the need to restore membership, press and finances. An underlying problem nevertheless remained unexamined. The socialist program advanced for a people's government proposed to nationalise the big monopolies, re-equip basic industries and 'secure an unparalleled growth of the productive forces, free from the crises inseparable from [a] capitalist economy' that would allow better pay, improved social welfare, modern housing and higher living standards. At the same time the party remained committed to the view that Australia faced an imminent economic crisis: after being propped up by the post-war economic boom, it was now 'tottering on the brink of the abyss'.[101]

The party's proposals for a people's government fell well short of a fully socialist program. They were more in the nature of a mixed economy such as social-democratic governments created after the war, one that took control of the 'commanding heights' of the economy (a phrase Lenin coined to justify his turn to a market-oriented policy in 1921). The people's democracies of Eastern Europe had mixed economies until Stalin ordered them to follow the Soviet model, but there was no suggestion of that happening in Australia. Although the CPA was nominally a revolutionary party committed to the abolition of capitalism, in practice it advanced a clearly reformist program. Claiming to pursue a course of action in keeping with national traditions, it nevertheless continued to uphold a dictatorship of the proletariat. Here and throughout the communist world, the events of 1956 brought these contradictions into the open.

10

A House Divided, 1956–60

The Twentieth Congress of the CPSU in February 1956, the first since the death of Stalin, occupied ten days. Nikita Khrushchev, the party's first secretary, set the tone when he proclaimed in an opening speech of more than six hours that the communist countries were prospering as never before. After years of resisting Western confrontation and containment they now governed a third of the world. In contrast to the capitalist powers whose colonial empires were being swept away, they enjoyed high rates of economic growth and rising living standards. There was still much to be done, the first secretary warned, to step up the battle against moribund ideas, shake up decayed practices, and restore life and vitality to inner-party democracy. Yet even if the official description of the delegates' response to the first secretary's speech ('Stormy, prolonged applause and cheers. All rise') stretched credulity, the note of optimism was clear.[1]

As the congress wound up on the evening of Friday 24 February 1956, however, delegates learned that a further session would be held at midnight from which foreign delegates and journalists were excluded. Apart from the absence of portraits of Stalin in the congress hall, the presence of around 100 of his victims who had been recently released from imprisonment signalled the dramatic revelations that followed. Khrushchev had referred in his earlier report to a 'cult of the individual' that was inimical to Marxism and belittled the role of the party. He now explained how Stalin used this cult to justify gross abuses of power. The first secretary had also talked of the need to strengthen socialist legality, but only now revealed how torture had been used to obtain false confessions from victims of the Great Terror. Though Khrushchev did not say so, Stalin had consolidated his rise to supremacy at the end of the 1920s not simply by taming the party but annihilating it, hence the show trials that discredited the Old Bolsheviks and their removal from history in the textbook he had produced.[2] The first secretary did point out that a majority of delegates to the Seventeenth Congress in 1934 and two-thirds of those who served on the central committee were subsequently arrested as counter-revolutionaries.[3]

Khrushchev has been described as 'the last true believer in the ideals of Communism': he genuinely believed his country could defeat its foes with superior ideology, organisation and economic performance. It was on this basis that he pursued détente with the West and urged a peaceful coexistence in which the superiority of the socialist bloc would become evident. His colleagues were not so confident. As survivors of Stalin's malignant tyranny, they shared a desire to put the bloodletting behind them—the execution in 1953 of Lavrenty Beria, who oversaw state security, was the last time a loser in Kremlin power struggles paid with his life. They differed, however, in their preparedness to break with Stalin's legacy. Besides, they were all complicit in his crimes and understandably reluctant to have them aired in such chilling detail. That the boorish, uncultured Khrushchev prevailed over more cautious veterans such as Molotov and Malenkov surprised many, who underestimated his energy and earthy authenticity.[4]

There had been earlier signs of Khrushchev's new course. In 1955 he visited Belgrade to repair relations with Yugoslavia and began releasing prisoners from the Gulag. He would press on with agricultural reform, rebalance the economy in response to consumer demand, invest heavily in housing, education and social services, and repudiate Zhdanov's doctrine of socialist realism. In foreign as well as domestic policy he lived dangerously, narrowly surviving a challenge from the old guard in 1957.

His 'secret speech' to the Twentieth Congress placed both Eastern and Western communist parties in a quandary. If the formation of the Cominform at the end of 1947 put paid to the brief experiment with multi-party people's democracies, those who now ruled Eastern Europe lacked the legitimacy—and in most cases the willingness—to undertake the changes needed when the Cominform was abolished in 1956. An exception was Poland, where the general secretary of the communist Workers' Party responded to mass protests against economic hardship by admitting the party's failure of the working class. The rehabilitation of Władysław Gomułka, a survivor of the purges in 1948, and the reforms that followed his restoration to the leadership, brought the USSR to the brink of intervention, but Khrushchev was assuaged by Gomułka's reassurance of loyalty to Moscow. Hungary initially followed a similar course as another rehabilitated communist, Imre Nagy, announced sweeping reform and restoration of a multi-party people's front. But Nagy lacked Gomułka's political skills and was unable to prevent a popular uprising in October 1956 that toppled the eight-metre statue of Stalin in Budapest's central square. The Red Army put down the uprising at the cost of 2000 lives.[5]

The leaders of Western communist parties faced a similar dilemma, too complicit in the past to accept the implications of the secret speech, unable to deal with its consequences. Harry Pollitt resigned the leadership of the CPGB in May 1956, ostensibly on grounds of ill health but in reality because he was not prepared to join in the condemnation of Stalin. The CPUSA was alone in publishing Khrushchev's revelations in its daily paper, though the old guard prevailed there too.

Palmiro Togliatti, the Italian party leader, studiously ignored the secret speech until the text appeared in June 1956, when he responded with a characteristically bold sally. No longer turning a blind eye to Stalin's crimes, Togliatti argued they could not be explained simply by a personality cult. A deeper and longer perspective was needed that reached into how Stalin had won power (off limits in Khrushchev's account because it raised Trotsky's allegations of a revolution betrayed) and why he faced so little opposition. Finally, Togliatti extended Khrushchev's argument that every party had to find its own path to socialism into the assertion that each country had to forge its own form of socialism. Beyond national parties and national paths, he introduced the concept of a polycentric communist movement. Togliatti's response, made without consulting the party's leadership, reduced the fallout in the Partito Comunista Italiano (PCI), whereas the British party lost a quarter of its membership in 1956 and the American party half.[6]

That year presented the communist movement with its most serious crisis. For decades every communist party had followed policies laid down by the Soviet Union and dismissed all allegations of dictatorship, purges and terror as capitalist propaganda. As the lamentations that followed the death of Stalin in 1953 attested, he was the wise, all-seeing guide, the implacable foe of any deviation from orthodoxy, the great and beloved leader of communists everywhere.[7] Now, according to Khrushchev, he was a bloody monster who had made grievous mistakes, including leaving the Soviet Union unprepared for German invasion. Yet if the secret speech caused shock and consternation, it also brought relief to some communists that they would no longer have to deny or excuse atrocities that disfigured their cause, and even kindled hopes of renewal. The brutal repression in Hungary crushed any such hope. Every single Western communist party, including the PCI, upheld the Soviet action, and it occasioned a greater exodus: 2000 members left the CPGB following the Twentieth Congress, 5000 after the invasion of Hungary.[8]

We have no official membership figures for Australia but it is generally thought to have suffered a similar loss. Alastair Davidson wrote in his short history of the CPA of a 'revolt of the intellectuals' that reduced the membership by a quarter.[9] This claim has been challenged on two grounds: first, that many who left would not have identified themselves as intellectuals (the term was used to discredit them); and second, that there was no revolt—instead, the party members who rejected the CPA's response to the secret speech and the invasion of Hungary one by one resigned, were expelled or simply dropped out.[10]

While the first argument is undoubtedly correct, the second is seriously misleading. A significant number of dissidents did not turn their backs on the party. On the contrary, they set out to change it from within and persisted long past 1956. They did so, moreover, by sharing their objections, canvassing aims and tactics, in a conscious challenge to the party's rules. Although this activity alarmed the leaders, they were by no means agreed on how to deal with it. There were relatively few expulsions. Many dissidents declined requests to recant or resign. The fallout from 1956 revealed a remarkable impairment of the discipline that had been a hallmark of communism—back in the 1930s and for much of the 1940s, resignation was not an option, expulsion the only way out. Democratic centralism was already breaking down, but 1956 brought the unrest into the open and ended decisively the CPA's claim to monolithic unity.

★

The secret speech was hardly secret. How could it be when the text was read to a million members of the CPSU and copies given to a number of other communist parties? Many of the foreign delegates to the congress were already aware that the ground was shifting and soon learned what Khrushchev had said. Australian communists were slower to pick up the significance of the changes made following Stalin's death (though a few, such as Lloyd Churchward, who was a scholar of the Soviet Union and subscribed to *Pravda*, were aware of them). The first response of the party here was therefore to warn members not to trust the reports of Khrushchev's speech appearing in the capitalist press. Ted Hill, who represented the CPA at the congress, is said to have told Dixon and Sharkey that the reports were almost entirely accurate but that little need be done since Molotov and Malenkov were likely to overthrow the upstart revisionist. It is impossible to verify this claim but since Hill remained in the Soviet Union for medical treatment until well after the middle of the year, he would surely have let other members of the secretariat know the contents of the secret speech. It has also been suggested that the delegate of the New Zealand party briefed the Australians as he returned via Sydney.[11]

The CPA acknowledged it for the first time in late March, when *Tribune* reproduced an account by Sam Russell, the Moscow correspondent of the CPGB's *Daily Worker*—one that its editor toned down but nevertheless conceded the 'many serious mistakes and injustices' that accompanied Stalin's cult of the individual. The Australian party adopted an even more cosmetic response, allowing that Stalin had made 'mistakes' while calling for them to be treated 'in a balanced way'. Sharkey advised a large meeting of cadres in Melbourne on 26 March that 'we all make mistakes' and that the lies being printed in the capitalist press must be vigorously denied. Moreover, the 'line which some party members in Australia were thinking along', namely 'what were other party leaders doing to allow this cult of the individual to flourish', had to be 'stamped out ruthlessly'.[12]

Probably in April, the party obtained a copy of the secret speech. According to Jack Blake, it was made available only to members of the political committee, who had to read it at the national headquarters in Sydney before handing it back. The implications of the document were judged too damaging to share beyond this inner circle, and the leaders continued to play down its contents: hence Sharkey declared in May that although Stalin had committed 'grievous mistakes' he remained an 'outstanding leader'. It was possible to go a little further behind closed doors. Eric Aarons told an audience of Sydney communists in a lecture on the Twentieth Congress how Stalin had become so puffed up in self-importance as a result of fawning praise that the 'whims and desires of one man' replaced the application of Marxist theory, while his treatment of opponents took a 'monstrous form'. Even so, a group of Jewish members pointed out there had still been no acknowledgement of the wave of Soviet anti-Semitism in Stalin's last years.[13]

With the appearance of the text of Khrushchev's secret speech in early June in the international edition of the *New York Times*, it was no longer possible to keep members in the dark. Even though the leaders rejected it as the work of the US State Department (as indeed it was), they were soon confronted with Togliatti's acceptance of its authenticity. The CPA therefore took comfort in a recent statement by the central committee of the CPSU, which by this time had forced Khrushchev to tone down his attack on Stalin's legacy, and declared the efforts made to eradicate the cult of the individual had already yielded positive results. The political committee of the CPA went further, expressing relief that there had been no violation of the principles of collective decision-making here: congresses had been held regularly and decisions reached on the basis of free and frank discussion.[14] They passed over the fact that there had been no such free and frank discussion of the secret speech—not even acknowledgement of calls for it to occur, as had already appeared in other Western communist parties.

A number of Australian communists obtained a copy of the *New York Times* with the supplement giving the text of the secret speech, though at first they read it surreptitiously. Stephen Murray-Smith brandished a copy at a meeting of members in Melbourne, said he believed the report was authentic and requested that Ralph Gibson (who chaired the meeting in the absence of Ted Hill) explain it. Studiously blank-faced, Gibson refused to respond. There, for the moment, the challenge rested.[15]

★

From August, Bill Brown, editor of *Tribune*, published a series of articles in the *Communist Review* critical of the party's handling of the cult of the individual. Just as past 'adulation' of Miles and Sharkey had inhibited disagreement with the leadership, he wrote, so the failure to provide access to the secret speech betrayed a lack of faith in the rank and file. The party could only benefit from freer discussion. Other leading cadres such as Paul Mortier joined in these criticisms, which were kept within bounds (and thus expressly rejected factionalism); it is difficult to imagine that they appeared without permission from on high.[16]

Some Sydney members were already preparing to go further. As soon as he obtained a copy of the *New York Times*, Jim Staples took it to the home of Bob Walshe. Staples was a young lawyer, Walshe a teacher and friend from their days in the University of Sydney branch in the 1940s. Both were convinced the report was genuine, and Walshe raised it in his local branch. Staples, who according to Walshe 'had a shorter fuse than me', took a more direct approach: he wrote a letter to *Tribune* that accused the central committee of deliberately withholding its prior knowledge of the secret speech and taking an 'unprincipled, dishonest and un-Marxist' position on the cult of the individual. When publication of this letter was rejected, he enlarged on his charges with a 6000-word 'Statement on the Attitude of the Central Committee, Communist Party of Australia, on the Stalin Issue', submitted to the secretariat on 2 July 1956 with a request that it be published in either *Tribune* or the *Communist Review*.[17]

The statement alleged the secretariat had decided soon after Khrushchev delivered his secret speech to prevent discussion of it. Indeed, he said, the leadership refused even to acknowledge the speech until Togliatti's interview forced its hand. Even then, there was no recognition that in their veneration of Stalin the leaders of all communist parties had 'blood on their hands'. Nothing was to be gained, Staples argued, by refusing publication of all the documents and allowing a 'complete, detailed, honest and painstaking description' of the source of these crimes—'how else do we ensure that our revolution will be a democratic one?' Finally, Staples contended that the prohibition of discussion violated rule 4(a) of the party's constitution ('It is the right of a Party member to participate in full and free discussion at Party meetings or in Party publications on questions of Party policy').

Staples distributed more than 50 copies of this statement to comrades in Sydney. Since it was not authorised by the party, he was in violation of rule 9 on democratic centralism. Accordingly, he accepted an offer from the secretariat that it would permit discussion of the secret speech providing he hand over all his material. This undertaking was barely observed. The pages of *Tribune* and the *Guardian* were opened in the first two weeks of October to a handful of letters critical of the CPA's handling of the secret speech before the discussion was declared closed. Staples now called for a special national congress to consider his charges against the secretariat and threatened once more to circulate them.[18]

The secretariat referred his 'serious anti-working class and anti-Party activities' to the principal disciplinary body, the central disputes committee, and he was expelled at the end of the year after refusing to appear before it. That did not put an end to his agitation, however, and in February 1957 he notified the secretariat of his intention to appeal. The disputes committee noted that Staples was spreading dissent among a number of party members and had recently produced 500 copies of the secret speech in an edition produced by the publishing company of another dissident, Rod Shaw, who also designed the cover. Among those seen distributing the publication was Helen Palmer.[19]

Palmer, following the path taken by her sister Aileen, joined the party in the 1930s as an undergraduate at the University of Melbourne. Following war service as an educational officer in the Women's Auxiliary Australian Air Service, she taught in Victorian schools and then transferred in 1952 to Sydney. A historian and occasional poet (her 'Ballad of 1891' was a highlight of the musical *Reedy River*), she was active in the Teachers' Federation and the peace movement. A greater contrast with the headstrong and abrasive Jim Staples could scarcely be imagined. Palmer, a sturdy woman of medium height and acute intelligence, was modest, tolerant and had a seemingly endless reserve of patience. David Martin recalled her smiling like a Cheshire cat as Staples leaned across at one of the meetings of dissidents she held in her Kirribilli flat to nibble her ear.[20]

She submitted a letter to Bill Brown as editor of *Tribune* in July 1956, well before the perfunctory discussion of the secret speech was permitted, asking him to publish her request that it be allowed. Brown replied that the party had no authorised version of the speech on which to base such a discussion. She repeated her request in September, just a week before the pages of *Tribune* were briefly opened, again without success. Meanwhile, she appealed to Ted Rowe, a sympathetic member of the political committee, arguing that the Twentieth Congress gave the CPA 'tremendous opportunities' to persuade Australians it could enlarge, rather than fetter, their freedom providing it went beyond the confines of the cult of the individual and undertook 'a fuller, really Marxist analysis of what happened'.[21]

Although Palmer made her request in a personal capacity and without any reference to fellow dissidents, it clearly transgressed the narrow limits the party set when it permitted a handful of letters to appear at the beginning of October. Even before Soviet troops invaded Hungary, this fortnight of licence ended with the return in early October of Ted Hill from China, where he had attended the Eighth Congress of the Chinese Communist Party following medical treatment in a Soviet sanatorium.[22] Hill set out his rejection of any latitude in a blistering attack on Bill Brown's articles in the *Communist Review*: by pitting the leadership against the rank and file they denied the organic unity of the party, so that the freedom they sought was 'freedom from the Party to attack the Party'. Besides, the mistakes made in the Soviet Union were 'mere incidents in the great progress of Communism' and Stalin's errors were far outweighed by his achievements. It was appropriate that the Australian party should acknowledge the 'problems' caused by the cult of the individual, but that had been done and no useful purpose was served by further discussion.[23]

In the absence of Sharkey (attributed to illness), Hill represented the secretariat at the party's state conference in New South Wales at this time, quelling the unrest that marked the preceding district conferences and demoting a number of senior cadres who had failed to enforce discipline. Even though Bill Brown retracted his errors, he was relieved of his *Tribune* duties; Harry Hatfield, secretary of the Sydney district committee, was returned to industry; and Adam Ogston was stripped of all other responsibilities to work as sales organiser for *Tribune*.[24]

That the door had closed on any questioning of either the secret speech or the Soviet Union's suppression of the 'counter-revolution' in Hungary was made clear in a report Sharkey presented to the central committee at the end of 1956. He insisted the party had always guarded its unity and would continue to do so against those 'few individuals' who had 'lost their balance'. The party's refusal to take Khrushchev's secret speech seriously and its uncritical support of the Soviet invasion would not change. Its ability to deal with the misguided individuals, on the other hand, would be tested to the limit.[25]

★

Some members left the party as an immediate response to the secret speech. These included Jean Blackburn in Adelaide, who was already fed up with the constant grind of bringing up children while performing political duties in the absence of her husband Dick on agricultural fieldwork. She had no one with whom to discuss her conviction that the press reports of the secret speech were accurate, though she had harboured doubts about Stalin ever since friends at the University of Melbourne drew her attention to the published transcripts of the show trials of the late 1930s. Furthermore, she made up her mind while Dick was working in Borneo for three months, much to his chagrin, and had to suffer being cold-shouldered by many former comrades who expressed sympathy to him for being married to a 'renegade'. There is no evidence Blackburn sought to persuade others to follow her, though she later linked up with Helen Palmer, a friend from their days in the Melbourne University Labour Club.[26]

Others were determined to kick up a fuss. Hence Bob Walshe mobilised a number of members of his Como branch as well as the communist fraction of the Teachers' Federation. He won election as a delegate to the Sydney district conference and from there to the state conference, where he was allotted five minutes to raise his concerns while Ted Hill was given as long as he wanted to deliver a crushing rebuke. Sometime afterwards, in late 1956 or early 1957, Alf Watt, a Sydney organiser, knocked on Walshe's door with the news he had been expelled. By his own account, he had been determined not to leave quietly, but felt 'relieved' and 'unburdened' to be out of it.[27]

Walshe was not alone in uncertainty about the timing and circumstances of his departure. Most historians, relying on the recollection of dissidents, have Staples' publication of the secret speech appearing in 1956, before his condemnation of the party's handling of it. In the absence of reports in the party press or proper records of the central committee, we are heavily reliant on such testimony and information obtained by ASIO. There are inconsistencies in both sources. A circular from the NSW state executive in mid-1958 listed fourteen expulsions, including Jim Staples, Rod Shaw, Bob Walshe and several others in his Como branch, along with Helen Palmer and others of her circle. An additional eighteen were reported to have 'lapsed', including Ken Buckley of the University of Sydney and Edgar Waters, who was then working in the State Library (though his wife Ann was expelled).[28] With the passage of time it is hardly surprising that these two forms of departure were often confused or that a protracted process was compressed into a much shorter period of time.

It is also clear that some in the party hierarchy were reluctant to see wholesale expulsions. Alf Watt asked Laurie Aarons in early 1957 how he should proceed with two dissidents (one of them, a 'joker' making statements on behalf of the party, might well have been Walshe). Laurie advised Watt to proceed with circumspection and, when instructed to call Helen Palmer to order, tried to persuade her not to push her differences to breaking point. His brother Eric told in April of 'a breakaway group operating within the party', some of whom he said had been expelled and others merely cautioned. As late as the Eighteenth Congress in 1958, when Lance Sharkey told delegates that the revisionists had now been driven out of the party, he added they would be welcomed back if they saw the errors of their ways.[29]

Since Palmer kept copies of her voluminous correspondence with the secretariat, we have a detailed record of her expulsion. Unsuccessful in pleas for fuller discussion of the implications of 1956, she began submitting articles, probably to the *Communist Review*, as contributions to a reconsideration of the party's position. These included a reappraisal of the legacy of Marx and Engels that challenged the ingrained habit of treating passages with 'scriptural reverence', a practice that she said turned Marxism–Leninism into dogma. A persistent theme was that the party was losing the opportunity to rebuild connections to the Australian people. After thriving during the wartime alliance with the Soviet Union, it had lost credibility in the Cold War because of a slavish imitation of the language and methods of a form of politics that had come to be seen as alien and repugnant. Now, at last, she saw the chance to remove that stigma.[30]

Rebuffed in attempts to circulate her views, Palmer turned by April 1957 to the idea of creating a discussion journal that would publish material the party suppressed and provide a forum to meet the growing interest in a socialist revival. She submitted her plan to the secretariat and persisted despite its warning that any such publication would open the door to revisionism. With unfailing courtesy, she insisted it could only do good and in June submitted a proof copy of the journal *Outlook* as confirmation this was so. The central disputes committee called on Palmer to repudiate any connection with this unauthorised publication or face the consequences. She replied immediately that she could not do so and that in any case compliance with the instruction would create a harmful impression of the party. Helen Palmer was informed of her expulsion on 5 July.[31]

Outlook was modelled on a similar British publication, *The Reasoner*, which two young historians, John Saville and Edward Thompson, established in mid-1956 in response to the CPGB's censure of dissidents. They conceived it as 'a forum for the far-reaching discussion at present going on within and close to the party', particularly discussion of how Stalinism had occurred. Saville and Thompson were summoned before the party executive in the party's King Street headquarters when the second issue appeared in August, and ordered to close the journal down or face suspension. They decided to persist and urged fellow dissidents not to resign but continue the fight for change, though the third issue that appeared at the end of the year brought both the suspension of the two men and their resignations: contrary to their original intentions, the invasion of Hungary convinced them the party was hopelessly discredited. The *Reasoner* was therefore turned into the *New Reasoner* in an attempt to foster a renewed socialist left.[32]

Outlook shared the desire to understand how Stalinism had occurred. Beginning a year later, however, it was aimed from the outset at a wider audience—not simply communists dissatisfied with the party's response to the secret speech but others with no communist past and no interest in a post-mortem. *Outlook*'s readers, Palmer explained in a statement of editorial policy, came from many backgrounds. Some regarded the resolution of theoretical questions as the most urgent task, others wanted information on alternatives to Marxism–Leninism. The first issue reprinted a speech given by Władysław Gomułka on the need to rebuild confidence between government and people, while Palmer herself wrote a searching analysis of the failure of reform in Hungary. Among the discussion material that Palmer obtained and offered to readers was Edward Thompson on socialist humanism and (this a tribute to her persuasive powers) an early appraisal of the changes occurring in Russia by Isaac Deutscher, the former Polish communist who was then working on the second volume of his magisterial biography of Leon Trotsky.[33]

Palmer regarded her expulsion as no more than a temporary setback, for she was convinced she would be reinstated once the changes she sought occurred and regarded *Outlook* as the catalyst that would enable these changes. The journal established support groups in other cities, which conducted their own discussion circles, but it was never intended to function as an alternative to the party.

Melbourne had more dissidents and fewer expulsions. The influence of progressive intellectuals, dissident being synonymous with intellectual, was thought to be one reason for the greater unrest in the southern city. Another was the Olympic Games, which opened in Melbourne on 22 November 1956. Victorian communists had invested considerable political capital in this display of international friendship (when the hammer and sickle flew prominently on city buildings for the first time since the Second World War) and provided both translators and hospitality to Soviet and Eastern European teams, but were discomfited by the number who defected as well as the manifest antagonism of the Hungarian athletes to their Soviet counterparts.[34]

Direct experience of life in the Soviet bloc had a chastening effect on Australian communists. Nonie Sharp, who worked in Prague for the International Union of Students between 1955 and 1956, was struck by the hierarchical and undemocratic character of the people's democracies, as was Geoff Sharp, who took academic leave to join her. Both, however, retained their membership of the Australian party.[35]

The fewer expulsions in Melbourne are all the more striking, since discipline there was in the hands of Ted Hill, the uncompromising state secretary. The explanation seems to lie in the curious irresolution of both Hill and his principal critics. Ian Turner bought a copy of the *New York Times*, read it with a sickening feeling and shared it with Stephen Murray-Smith. Neither doubted the accuracy of the report it contained, and this might well have been the copy of the newspaper that Murray-Smith brandished before Ralph Gibson soon afterwards. Along with their friend Ken Gott, they reacted with horror to the subsequent events in Hungary and soon linked up with Helen Palmer to promote *Outlook*.[36] Beyond that, their expectations, intentions and activities are far from clear. There is little sign they shared Palmer's optimism that the party might be saved. On the contrary, Murray-Smith and Turner were plunged into a state of personal crisis. Unable to contemplate life in the political wilderness, they resolved to stay on and fight for change, but gave no lead to the other dissidents who looked to them for guidance.

Each held positions of importance—Gott as organiser of the Australia–China Association, Murray-Smith in charge of the peace movement, Turner running the Australasian Book Society—and had no intention of giving them up. Murray-Smith left in March 1957 to attend the World Peace Council in Berlin and then spent three months in Prague, Moscow and Beijing, an experience that deepened his disillusionment, so that he openly challenged the report on the cult of personality at the Victorian metropolitan conference later in the year. Beyond such remonstrance, however, he advanced no plan for reforming the party and was already talking about leaving it. So too was Ian Turner, whom sympathetic organisers such as Rex Mortimer and Bernie Taft were urging to stay in and fight for change from the inside.[37]

Ken Gott also decided to hang on, though with even less interest in regeneration—put simply, he would not give Ted Hill the pleasure of going quietly. In August 1957 he established a Socialist Forum with Fred Emery, a psychologist at the University of Melbourne who had recently left the party. They went further than an earlier Socialist Forum in Sydney by opening it to anti-communists such as Frank Knopfelmacher. This member of the University of Melbourne, who had fled Czechoslovakia in 1948, brought a vituperative intensity to political argument. He was also working on behalf of the Association for Cultural Freedom. Gott himself was soon collaborating with Richard Krygier on a number of initiatives.[38]

All three dissidents were told to end their disruption or leave and all three refused to do so. By early 1958, however, Gott was losing patience and told Nita Murray-Smith he saw no future in 'endless compromises'. Never one to mince words, Nita told him she was cross with his influence on 'the boys' (Stephen and Ian). Meanwhile, Amirah was trying to dissuade Ian from leaving. She claimed that 'communism was improving', while an informant who was clearly close to the couple, since he or she was present at the evening meal where this exchange occurred, reported Ian 'was depressed, perhaps even cynical'. He was quoted as saying there had been no improvement and that he could not 'see where anything new can come from', to which Amirah rejoined that he was reading too much of the wrong sort of literature—bourgeois literature.[39]

The failure of the Victorian executive to enforce discipline is striking. It was not until early 1958 that it moved against Gott, and even then it botched his expulsion by failing to secure the endorsement of his branch, which then had to be 'reorganised'. Dorothy Gibson's demand that he repay the £100 she had given him to assist his work as secretary of the Australia–China Association added to the rancour. Ted Hill, convinced that Murray-Smith and Turner intended to take over the Victorian leadership, was seemingly unable to deal with them. He delegated the task to Bernie Taft, knowing that Taft was their sympathiser. It was common at the time to test wavering cadres by instructing them to discipline dissidents, but Taft barely went through the motions. The two miscreants refused to engage in self-criticism and flatly rejected a suggestion they attend a six-week party school in Sydney.[40]

Turner broke the deadlock by sending a protest against the execution in June 1958 of Imre Nagy to *Pravda* and other newspapers in the Soviet Union, China and Poland. This time Ted Hill was determined he must go, and prevailed at the state executive against Taft's warning that Turner enjoyed considerable support. Murray-Smith immediately resigned in protest. There was indeed considerable sympathy for both men, and Hill had to instruct cadres that Turner was a 'despicable type'; soon the two were being smeared with allegations that included a gay relationship. 'We will pour shit on you,' Judah Waten promised.[41]

There was a final twist in this saga. Murray-Smith heard from a contact at the Melbourne *Herald* that it was about to publish a report on Turner's expulsion and went to see Hill about the apparent breach of security. Hill is said to have replied, 'You got yourself into this mess, you can get out of it—if the truth was known, you probably told them yourself.' In fact the *Herald*'s information came from ASIO, which had bugged Hill's office.[42]

Gott was soon replaced in the Australia–China Association, Murray-Smith gave up work for the peace movement and Turner was pushed out of the Australasian Book Society. His decision to take up doctoral research at the Australian National University was motivated, at least in part, by a desire to get out of Melbourne. Friends and admirers had looked up to him from his time at the university, and he had come to find the weight of their expectations intolerable. 'I'd had a gutful,' he explained to Itzhak Gust, his father-in-law. Moreover, he was 'in such a state of revulsion from my previous near-absolute certainty about what ought to be done that I was inhibited from acting'. In a remarkable instance of the latitude that had come to prevail in Victoria, Rex Mortimer organised a farewell for him and Amirah.[43]

The party's announcement of the expulsion of Turner identified him as a revisionist.[44] This term, which had its origins in the nineteenth century as an epithet against those who watered down Marxism, was revived in the 1920s during the battle for supremacy in the CPSU, but now gained a new lease of life. As defined by Lance Sharkey in a 1957 report to the central committee, revisionists committed three basic errors: they denied the need to wage class struggle, they wanted to abandon the Leninist concept of the vanguard party and they rejected democratic centralism. Since the CPA was committed to Khrushchev's policies of peaceful coexistence, a progressive transition to socialism, a greater role for members in decision-making and a broad people's movement, the defence of Marxist–Leninist principles against revisionism called for a verbal dexterity that was in short supply. Laurie Aarons made the best fist of it in his 1959 exposition of the *Organisational Principles and Methods of Work of the Communist Party of Australia*.[45]

Revisionist errors, furthermore, were not simply illusions bred by post-war capitalist prosperity; they were capitulations that served the interests of the capitalist class and caused serious harm in a number of communist parties. Fortunately, Sharkey claimed at the Eighteenth Congress in 1958, the Australian party had been largely spared because of its strong working-class base.[46] Revisionism was attributed to middle-class intellectuals who were deemed inherently susceptible to capitalist ideology. Although neither term, intellectual or middle class, was ever defined, the principal dissidents were not wage-earners and typically had an advanced education. But many such communists refrained from challenging the party's response to the secret speech. Prominent examples include the artist Noel Counihan, who broke with his friend Jack Lindsay over the writer's association with the leading British dissidents, and the barrister Ted Laurie, who publicly defended the invasion of Hungary. We catch the atmosphere in June Factor's memory of Ted Hill chastising the members of Melbourne's university branch. Dressed in a dark suit, his face closed and arms folded, Hill 'made no attempt to hide his contempt for our doubts, our "bourgeois" concern for the niceties of democracy and truth'.[47]

Factor also suggests another characteristic of those who suppressed their doubts: 'I was very young then, and overawed by the powerful rhetoric of the more experienced comrades—the men especially.' Zelda

D'Aprano spoke up at union meetings but her confidence evaporated when the men in charge of the party laid down the line. A resentment of her marginalisation and self-criticism of her failure to challenge it runs through Amirah Turner's account of the arguments at this time. Richenda, the wife of the poet David Martin, echoed Amirah when she remonstrated with him over 'all this anti-Soviet stuff you are getting from the bourgeois press', and Pat Counihan also chastised Martin when he said at their branch meeting that parts of a work by Stalin made no sense. 'No sense? No sense in Stalin? Ah well.' Conversely, it is noticeable that the women who dropped out before their partners did so quietly.[48]

We have seen how some senior members of the party were shaken by the revelations and did their best to minimise the bloodletting. Yet even in Victoria, where sympathy for the dissidents was most pronounced, none was prepared to openly challenge the clampdown. Eddie Robertson and John Sendy, the principal organisers in South Australia, read the *New York Times* report of Khrushchev's secret speech in the public library and were convinced it was authentic, partly because it made sense of actions by Stalin that had troubled them, but they too accepted the embargo on discussing it. As Sendy recalled, 'I believed that if the contents of the secret report became widely known, a wholesale exodus would result.' Eric Aarons was teaching a party school in Queensland when Claude Jones, the state secretary, lent his copy of the *New York Times*. After Eric had stayed up that night to read the paper, the two men agreed its version of the secret speech had to be genuine, but Eric suppressed his doubts when he prepared a publication giving the CPA's line on 1956. This work, *Basic Questions of Communist Theory*, canvassed none of the basic questions raised by that fateful year.[49]

Blake went furthest, during the brief interval in the southern spring of 1956 when it was possible to discuss Stalin's crimes, with an apology at a meeting of Jewish members for his denial of just three years earlier of Soviet persecution of Jews. As he related instances of this anti-Semitism, a member of his audience apparently asked Blake how, if all these dreadful things were true and the Australian party had denied them, it was possible to remain a member. Blake is said to have looked bleakly at his questioner and replied, 'Show me a better party.'

Still bound by its rules, he voiced his condemnation of the invasion of Hungary within the confines of the central committee. That did not save him from censure and removal from his last party post.[50]

Bill Gollan, another member of the central committee, would regret how the party retreated into 'a small, narrow circle within a hostile world'. Having read as a history teacher of Lenin's criticisms of Stalin, he found Khrushchev's revelations all too plausible but went along with the party's suppression of them. As he put it, 'the discipline that was necessary for survival forced us into the wrong position'. Dorothy Hewett, one of many who stayed on because they were unable to imagine life outside the party, put it best: 'some ultimate innocence had been destroyed for ever'.[51]

★

The party lost members, press sales, income and capacity in the aftermath of the secret speech. The magnitude of the loss is difficult to quantify, since the numbers it published from time to time are discontinuous and incomplete. Against the commonly cited claim that a quarter of the membership departed, Ted Hill told a Victorian conference in late 1957 that just sixteen members in that state 'left the Party through the events of 1956', and Lance Sharkey told the Eighteenth Congress in the following year that 'we lost a handful of people' who 'succumbed to revisionist ideology'.[52] The actual figure lies somewhere between these extremes.

The closest we have to an aggregate figure for membership comes from two reports on press sales, in February 1957 and early 1958, that also gave the number of sales per member. They yield a total of 5850 members nationally in 1958, of which New South Wales made up 2920 and Victoria 1530, a reduction of perhaps 1000 from the Seventeenth Congress in 1955. As had been the case earlier in the decade there were repeated drives to rebuild, but recruits failed to keep pace with the departures.[53] And despite amalgamations, branches became smaller and less active. The Eighteenth Congress learned that only a very small percentage of comrades had completed a course of party education.[54]

Press sales were a constant concern. *Tribune*'s circulation fell from 22,428 in 1955 to 16,618 in 1958, when it was losing £200 on every issue. The Queensland *Guardian* was discontinued, leaving just one state-based paper, the Victorian *Guardian*, with a circulation of 6500 and a weekly loss of £50. Both it and *Tribune* began to publish articles at this time reassuring members that street-selling was a more rewarding experience than many evidently felt, but even such a dedicated seller as Paddy Troy, who could be seen every Saturday morning in High Street, Fremantle, found that some customers had little interest in his wares. 'Look, Paddy, here's the money but you keep the paper.'[55]

Donations and fundraising drives could not avert the need for economies. The 40 salaried functionaries working for the central committee and NSW state committee at the beginning of 1956 had to be reduced. Victoria was down to around twenty by the end of the decade, Queensland five, South Australia could support only two and Western Australia one.[56] Some additional cadres were employed off the books, notably organisers of auxiliaries such as the peace movement, who raised their own salaries, but the diminished workforce sapped the party's firepower.

Declining membership had serious implications for the way the party worked. Put simply, the aspiration to function as a vanguard party that gave purpose and direction to the mass of workers was difficult to sustain once numbers fell below a critical point. In its heyday the party had a substantial presence in key industries to support its union officials. As these industrial branches dwindled during the 1950s, the officials became more dependent on the support of other activists whose views had to be accommodated. The problem was exacerbated by special difficulties facing the party's 'stronghold unions' in the mining and maritime industries: mechanisation and competition from alternative forms of fuel and transport cut the workforces of both by a third over the course of the decade, and special tribunals in both industries used their coercive powers to punish transgressions.

Communists in the Miners' Federation had already reached an accommodation whereby Bill Parkinson held the national presidency and a member of the Labor Party served as general secretary; originally an informal arrangement, this division of responsibilities became so widely accepted that the two posts were often uncontested in the union's annual elections. Despite the stability of its leadership, however, the federation was unable to prevent mechanisation, unsuccessful in its bid to avoid job losses by shortening the working week, and powerless to stop pit closures.

Since former Groupers retained a presence in a number of ports, the Waterside Workers' Federation was more turbulent. Although Jim Healy's personal popularity ensured his re-election, he was acutely aware of the forces arrayed against the union. Thus he called off a three-week strike in 1956 to improve wages, the longest national stoppage during this period, in a tactical retreat that allowed the ACTU to secure a settlement. Healy pursued a similar course during a long-running dispute in the Hobart branch that began in 1957, named the 'Hursey case', after a father and son who supported the Democratic Labor Party and refused to pay the union's political levy. The Stevedoring Industry Authority punished the union for refusing to work with the Hurseys, the Packer press painted it as a Soviet-controlled dictatorship that denied any dissident the right to work, and prominent anti-communists sponsored the Hurseys' suit for damages. Healy had to restrain the usually moderate Hobart wharfies from precipitate action, and was finally vindicated in 1959 when the High Court upheld a union appeal and ruled the levy was valid.[57]

Just as new methods of handling cargo reduced the port workforce, so changes in ship design cut crew numbers. Eliot Elliott was less conciliatory than Jim Healy, and his leadership of the Seamen's Union went unchallenged until Bill Bird announced in 1959 that he was resigning his post as Victorian secretary and returning to industry. The party's explanation that Bird was suffering ill health fooled no one: he made no secret of the fact that he was fed up with being told what to do.[58]

One of the strategies Elliott adopted as the workforce fell was to require those shipowners who sold their vessels to overseas operators (so they could be manned by lower-paid foreign crews) to compensate the union for lost earnings. This indemnity money, as it became known, was usually transferred in cash and paid into a union account, but a payment of £1215 received in early 1958 was secreted in the union office for a week. Elliott then took possession of it but failed to get to the bank, and ended up that evening drinking with union members in a waterfront pub, where police officers of the NSW special branch arrested him. They in turn tipped off Alan Reid, a feature writer for the *Daily Telegraph* who was running a campaign against the union, so that a photographer snapped Elliott emerging dishevelled from the police station to accompany an article by Reid that painted him in the worst possible light.[59]

The Senate launched an investigation into indemnity payments. The party's central disputes committee conducted its own inquiry into Elliott's conduct and unearthed alarming additional malpractices. It emerged that union funds had been used to buy a house for the national secretary. Worse, he claimed it was a gift in recognition of the substantial sums he had secured for members in indemnity payments in defiance of a party rule that forbade communist union officials from accepting gifts. Worse still, it was evident that communist members of the union would back him against any disciplinary action, so he continued to go his own way. There could be no clearer illustration of the breakdown of the party's authority.[60]

A further complication was the use of unity tickets. The rules of the ALP forbade any association with communists in union elections. This prohibition was relaxed at the 1955 Hobart federal conference when recognition of the Groups was withdrawn, and subsequently amended to allow the state branches considerable latitude in its interpretation. The ban was strictly enforced in New South Wales, so that in 1957 the state executive expelled three officials of the Sydney branch of the Waterside Workers' Federation for standing on a unity ticket with communists. The Victorian branch of the party, on the other hand, was controlled by industrialists who were determined to prevent any revival of the Groups and thus took little or no action against unity tickets. Other states held positions somewhere between the two extremes. This flexible arrangement came under strain by the end of the decade, partly because of the electoral damage the ALP's association with the CPA caused and partly because the Victorian state executive (strictly, by now, the ALP central executive) became a byword for sectarian intolerance, rebuffing all attempts to popularise the Labor Party.[61]

As part of the realignment in Victoria that accompanied the 1955 Labor Party Split, in 1956 the ALP also readmitted Sam Goldbloom, a leading peace activist who had been expelled at the beginning of the decade for collaborating with the Communist Party. It soon allowed

Labor members to participate in the peace movement, and the central executive itself sponsored a conference that Jim Cairns chaired and Eddie Ward addressed. This was not the case in other states, where the Peace Council was still off limits to members of the ALP.[62]

For that reason, the work of the clergymen who had formed the Peace Quest Forum and held a National Convention on Peace and War in 1953 remained important. They convened another national gathering in Sydney in 1956, the Assembly for Peace, which had no formal link to the party so it was possible for members of the Labor Party to attend. Communists were involved in planning the assembly, however, and Jack Blake, who remained the member of the central committee responsible for peace work, urged that it be given full backing. He received little support from his comrades, principally on the grounds that the party's resources were better used elsewhere. As he put it, peace was not at the top of the leadership's priorities.[63]

Although the party proclaimed the vital importance of peaceful coexistence, it failed to back its words with action, relying instead on an interpretation of world events that echoed that of the Soviet Union. That peace was the responsibility of Jack Blake did not help. He recalled the observation of Max Julius, the Queensland lawyer and peace activist, that being sent to work in any field of activity that Blake is associated with is a little like being sent to 'the salt mines of Siberia'. The peace movement also suffered from association with middle-class intellectuals such as Stephen Murray-Smith, the national organiser. Later in 1956, the central committee transferred responsibility for the peace campaign from Blake to Bill Gollan, who fortunately was one of the few senior members to appreciate its significance.[64]

In an effort to revive flagging momentum, the Victorian Peace Council convened an ambitious Australian and New Zealand Congress for International Co-operation and Disarmament. Alf Dickie would chair the founding congress and Sam Goldbloom serve as the new organisation's secretary. It had the advantage of support from the ACTU as well as the Victorian branch of the ALP, secured a prestigious list of Australian patrons and brought out a clutch of international celebrities, including writers J.B. Priestley and Jacquetta Hawkes from the United

Kingdom, and scientist Linus Pauling and his activist wife Ava from the United States. An event of such magnitude drew condemnation from the Menzies government and a spoiling operation by ASIO, which approached a number of the sponsors with evidence of communist control and persuaded several to withdraw.[65]

Even so, more than 1000 delegates assembled in the South Melbourne Town Hall for the opening of the congress in November 1959, and 5000 joined them the next day at the Olympic Pool to hear the overseas speakers. The trouble came not from ASIO or the protestors who picketed the main sessions, but from participants determined to challenge the communist control of proceedings. There were eight sectional conferences, each of which prepared resolutions for adoption by the full congress. The trade union conference was notable for the studied moderation of the party's delegates, including Jim Healy, who rejected all proposals for industrial action. The citizens' conference saw Jim Jupp, a young Englishman who had recently been recruited to the Department of Political Science at the University of Melbourne, argue in vain that the congress dissociate itself from the World Peace Council. Jupp came from an adamantly anti-communist wing of the British Labour Party and he would soon establish a new journal, *Dissent*, with funds from the Congress for Cultural Freedom to advance that cause.[66]

The greatest difficulty came in the writers' and artists' conference, where the Catholic poet Vincent Buckley introduced Tibor Méray, a journalist who had fled Hungary after the uprising. Buckley did so in conjunction with members of the Association for Cultural Freedom and ex-communists such as Ken Gott, who on his own account was by this time fully anti-communist—Gott tried to enlist Murray-Smith, who told Turner in Canberra that their friend was 'off his rocker'. While Murray-Smith, Turner and for that matter Helen Palmer had their reservations about communist manipulation, they refused to join in the condemnation that preceded the congress. However, when Judah Waten and Frank Hardy refused to countenance any criticism of Hungary in the course of the writers' and artists' conference, Murray-Smith changed his mind and moved an amendment to the resolution extolling 'freedom for every true artist' that read: 'many writers in a number of countries do not have this freedom'. A number of like-minded former communists, including David Martin, Rod Shaw and Bob Gollan, voted with him. He considered the refusal to accept the amendment 'a crowning example of communist sectarianism and moronic strategical conceptions'.[67]

The writers' and artists' conference paid very little attention to literature and art. Its concern was the contribution that cultural practitioners could make to the peace movement and the conditions—the kind of freedom—needed for them to do so. Waten and Hardy held that the role of the creative writer was to rouse workers to an understanding of the part they would play in the overthrow of capitalism. While echoing the dictum 'art is a weapon', they judged a work not so much by its fidelity to socialist realism as its contribution to this purpose.[68]

Back in 1955, Paul Mortier, who was editing *Tribune*'s literary page, wrote a hostile review of *The Thaw*, a novel by the prolific Soviet writer and paragon of socialist realism Ilya Ehrenburg. *The Thaw* depicted the cynicism, self-absorption and abuse of authority by several characters whose privileged positions were under threat as a result of the changes under way following the death of Stalin. That the title alluded to this political thaw and that Khrushchev supported the novel's publication might have escaped Mortier, who castigated Ehrenburg for impugning the glorious achievements of the Soviet Union. Len Fox and Mona Brand were among those Australians who welcomed the novel for acknowledging the abuses that had occurred under Stalin, and Fox asked Bill Brown as editor of *Tribune* if he could reply. Brown, aware that Sharkey and other leaders regarded the book as 'anti-party', said it was inappropriate for *Tribune*'s staff to air their differences. Mona Brand therefore wrote a rejoinder to Mortier, and a debate followed in which David Martin supported Brand and other correspondents joined Mortier in opposing Ehrenburg's negative portrayal of Soviet life.[69]

Paul Mortier, along with Jack Beasley, used *Tribune*'s literary page to promulgate a version of socialist realism that judged literature by its subject matter and standpoint. Since the duty of the artist was to provide a faithful representation of working-class life that would instruct and inspire activists, Mortier warned that 'we need to keep our course clear of the flotsam of bourgeois ideas which keep penetrating it', ideas that included the romantic celebration of national traditions. The cult of mateship, Judah Waten explained, was 'a class collaborationist view'. Denial of the class struggle was the litmus test that distinguished proletarian from bourgeois culture, though the flight from reality also found expression in the literary devices used by reactionary writers. Hence 'the escapist fad of "prose poetry"' found in the novels of Patrick White and Randolph Stow to convey the self-absorption of their morbid heroes. Such writing, with its 'pretentious juggling of words and grammar', was only one of the threats to socialist realism, alongside abstract expressionism, eroticism and the metaphysical or psychological novel.[70] Party members had to guard against such errors. Jack Beasley took to task Dorothy Hewett's path-breaking novel *Bobbin Up*, notable for its unflinching portrayal of life in inner Sydney, for concessions to naturalism. That the Australasian Book Society published the work intensified its merits. 'Sex,' said Ernie Thornton, 'is best left in the bedroom with the door closed.'[71]

Overland came under fire for failure to heed these strictures. It had been established by the Realist Writers' Group with the intention of broadening and popularising working-class literature, a purpose Mortier acknowledged in his promotion of early issues, and it was not until Murray-Smith left the party that his editorship was challenged. An initial step was to cancel the Australasian Book Society's bulk order of 600 copies, a challenge Murray-Smith and Turner met by obtaining a list of the society's subscribers and offering them the journal at a reduced rate. Then came a twin offensive, condemnation in the pages of *Tribune* and an attempt to take control of *Overland*.

Rex Chiplin, who had a weekly column in *Tribune*, opened the criticism with a broadside against the spring 1959 issue for carrying two reviews of Boris Pasternak's *Dr Zhivago*, only one of them positive, printing a poem by Laurence Collinson that was 'thinly disguised pornography', and advertising magazines such as *Outlook* and the *New Reasoner*, all of which indicated that *Overland* had become 'a shackle on the labour movement'. A range of correspondents supported Mortier in letters to *Tribune*, of whom Frank Hardy was the most acerbic. He had argued earlier that creative writers needed some latitude, expressed admiration for *The Thaw*, visited Ehrenburg on a trip to the Soviet Union in 1956 and was regularly consulted by Murray-Smith on the operation of *Overland*. Now Hardy condemned Murray-Smith as a bourgeois renegade who had turned it into an 'anti-communist journal'. There was one defender of the editor, however, who carried even greater weight. Katharine Susannah Prichard, the party's grand old lady of letters and the author of the hostile review of *Dr Zhivago*, wrote that everybody realised how much *Overland*, so important in breaking the ice beyond party circles, owed to Murray-Smith and warned that a sectarian approach would alienate many in the labour movement.[72]

The attempt to remove him as editor fared no better. Les Greenfield, the Sydney organiser who had taken over responsibility for the Book Society from Ian Turner, convened a meeting of the Melbourne Realist Writers late in April 1959 to plan how to 'rescue' *Overland*. If Murray-Smith could not be persuaded to act more cooperatively, the Realist Writers would assert their ownership of the journal. In response to this claim, Murray-Smith countered that since he had established the journal and taken sole responsibility for its production and finances, he was its owner. The Realist Writers pursued their claim by stacking a meeting of the editorial board, but Murray-Smith got wind of the plan and out-stacked them. Throughout this acrimonious dispute, furthermore, he refused to be provoked by Chiplin's censure and continued to publish the work of both communist and non-communist writers. As Judah Waten warned, 'Stephen Murray-Smith is a revisionist—he was a revisionist and he will always be a revisionist.'[73]

The party's campaign for Indigenous rights was perhaps the most successful of its causes in the late 1950s, albeit involving a very small number of members. It was also the least supervised activity, a neglect that might well have contributed to its efficacy. To be sure, *Tribune* and the *Guardian* gave increased attention to cases of injustice, including the conviction and imprisonment of the artist Albert Namatjira in 1958 for supplying liquor to fellow Aboriginal people, the conviction of Max Stuart for murder in 1959, and the death in custody of an Indigenous man in Victoria in the same year.[74] The principal campaign was against the nuclear tests carried out at the inland South Australian site of Maralinga in 1956 and 1957, which were opposed both as a threat to peaceful coexistence and because of their effects on the Indigenous people of the area.

The unlikely catalyst for further action was Bill Grayden, an independent-minded Liberal member of the Western Australian parliament who produced both a parliamentary report and a film on the plight of the Wongi people of the Warburton Ranges to the west of Maralinga. The film deeply affected Doug Nicholls, the leading Indigenous member of the Victorian Council for Aboriginal Rights, and Shirley Andrews organised a meeting for the two men to publicise the cause in Melbourne. The committee she formed for this purpose, named 'Save the Aborigines', was the basis of a new organisation with Doug Nicholls at the helm, the Victorian Aborigines Advancement League, which dealt with the full range of problems encountered by his people in the state. Shirley Andrews encouraged Nicholls to form the new body since it would allow her council to concentrate on national issues and, she hoped, enable the new league to do its work without the taint of communist association.[75]

That the two bodies were complementary became clear with the formation in 1958 of a national body, the Federal Council for Aboriginal Advancement, in which both were active participants. Andrews was closely involved in this initiative with Barry Christophers, a medical doctor recently returned from South Australia, and together with Gordon Bryant, a Labor parliamentarian from the Victorian league, they did much of the legwork for the Melbourne-based national executive. Bryant used his platform in the House of Representatives to mobilise support, Christophers publicised abuses in *Guardian* and correspondence columns of the daily press, leaving Andrews to conduct the research that informed the Federal Council's campaigns. She still thought of equal rights rather than Indigenous rights, but insisted equality had to include economic equality and argued consistently that 'class relationships cannot be altered just by good will'. The two communists worked well with Nicholls and his colleague Stan Davey (a fellow minister of the Church of Christ), though Andrews was less comfortable with some Indigenous leaders in other states.[76]

The party's auxiliaries struggled. Declining sales ended publication of the Eureka Youth League's magazine *Challenge* in 1956. Falling membership narrowed the league to little more than a party youth organisation in which budding communists cut their industrial teeth by organising apprentices (with greatest success in the Victorian metal trades) and acquired familiarity with the dark arts of democratic centralism.[77] It was indicative of its difficulties that the league was beset by personality clashes, including complaints when Charles Bresland was chosen to lead the delegation to the 1957 Youth Festival in Moscow—this would be his third world festival and critics thought someone else should be given a go.[78]

Bresland fell from grace in the following year when he was arrested at a public toilet at Central Railway Station in Sydney, allegedly drunk in a cubicle with his trousers round his ankles. The incident attracted publicity, and the charge of offensive behaviour, used at the time as a euphemism for gay cruising, alarmed a party leadership that was as hostile to homosexuality as the police. The central committee instructed Bresland to claim a political frame-up; instead he pleaded guilty and was dismissed from his post. While it was no secret that a substantial number of communists were gay, their continued membership required them to remain silent on their sexual identity. In a rare challenge to the party's homophobia, a correspondent objected in 1958 to Rex Chiplin's offensive jibe in *Tribune* when it was announced the flamboyant American entertainer Liberace would perform in Australia: 'We just can't keep up with these royal tours.' The offended member complained that this was just the sort of item you would expect to read in a capitalist rag.[79]

Bresland's replacement was Mavis Moten, a recruit from the University of Melbourne Labour Club who worked for the peace movement there before accompanying her partner Alec Robertson to Sydney in 1951 when he became peace organiser in New South Wales. Never one to beat around the bush, she imposed greater order, so that the much smaller number of delegates who went to the Vienna Youth Festival in 1959 did so as 'representative delegates, not as young left wingers fulfilling a personal dream'. Even that achievement indicated the league's original goal as a broad movement of youth could not be revived.[80]

★

This necessarily abbreviated account of communist activity after 1956 reveals a reduced organisation struggling to maintain momentum. The party had suffered a severe shock. While the leadership held fast against calls to acknowledge the full implications of the revelations of 1956, it was not at all sure how to deal with those making those calls—for it could no longer rely on the unreserved loyalty that had given the party its monolithic unity. Although the new course Khrushchev charted for the Soviet Union enjoyed some successes, symbolised by the successful launch of the Sputnik satellite in 1957, the Stalinist past cast a shadow on the credibility of communism here and elsewhere.

Australia severed diplomatic relations with the USSR after the defection of the Petrovs and did not resume them until 1959. Many Australians thought the country should be shunned, an attitude Manning Clark encountered when he was selected to lead a delegation of the Fellowship of Australian Writers on a good-will tour at the end of 1958. The articles he wrote on the workers' homeland were a further provocation: he hailed the Soviets for initiating 'the greatest revolution in human history', claimed the Russian people enjoyed all the freedom they wanted, and was confident that more than 90 per cent of them agreed with Khrushchev's policies. The book that followed early in 1960, *Meeting Soviet Man*, was more ambiguous and managed to offend both communists and anti-communists.[81]

Just how such polemics affected public attitudes is more difficult to gauge. There was no longer the same intense hostility that swept the country at the height of the Cold War. Nor, for that matter, were there the fervent expectations of earlier admirers. Communism as practised in the Soviet Union held little appeal in Australia. Emulating that model was in any case well beyond the Communist Party of Australia. Not only had it long ceased to work for a socialist order, the chance of realising even the limited proposals set out in the program for a people's government was remote.

Yet the dilution of its policies and the collapse of its membership base brought no relaxation of ASIO's conviction that the party posed a serious threat to Australian security. In early 1954, when Colonel Spry briefed the prime minister on the imminent defection of the Petrovs, his secondment from Military Intelligence was due to expire. After speaking on the matter to Menzies, he resigned from the army to continue as director-general in a civilian capacity, though he was promoted to brigadier on the reserve list of officers and expected to be addressed accordingly.

To buttress his position, the government put ASIO on a legislative basis instead of relying on the original prime ministerial directive. The 1956 ASIO Act retained the same charter that restricted the agency to intelligence gathering, though additional legislation in 1960 authorised it to tap telephones, and the Crimes Act was amended in the same year to cover treason, treachery and sabotage in peacetime. There was also a substantial increase in funding, enabling Spry to enlarge the staff and greatly expand the number of agents within the party and its auxiliaries. David Horner's recent commissioned history of ASIO observes that as 'the CPA's capability and intent to undertake subversion was declining' the agency's capacity to combat it was increasing.[82]

Horner describes a variety of operations undertaken by ASIO that relied on an 'extravagant interpretation' of its charter. These included the interception of phone calls (it tapped 181 phones between 1949 and 1960), unauthorised entry to premises, the planting of bugs, and a wide variety of spoiling operations designed to disrupt the activities of the party and the lives of its members.[83] Such operations were given codenames (Boomerang and Hurricane, Cherry Brandy and Ginger Ale), of which the most audacious was Operation Black Snake. In 1958 ASIO learned the party had acquired a property in Minto, near Campbelltown, New South Wales, to use as a national school, though to avoid unwelcome publicity it was called the Bushlovers' Club. The Black Snake himself, ASIO's Ron Richards, attached a sign on a post at a nearby crossroads directing passers-by to the 'Communist Training School'. Although Eric Aarons, who was in charge of the school, insisted to police investigating the incident that he was the manager of the Bushlovers' Club, a hapless member expressed his appreciation that the party had made it easier to find the way to the school.[84]

The 1956 ASIO Act authorised the director-general to communicate intelligence 'to such persons and in such manner' that he considered in the interests of security. Spry complied with ministerial requests for information, such as one in that year from Richard Casey, who was given a list of communists and other persons with 'communist associations' (liberally interpreted) who had written to *The Age* over the past eighteen months, so that he could urge the editor to be more vigilant. The all too frequent requests from W.C. Wentworth were met when Spry judged them expedient, and B.A. Santamaria was also a beneficiary. Such information, along with Spry's briefings of the prime minister, was often damaging to the Labor Party. Other spoiling operations, including leaks to journalists and even the planting of articles, took ASIO beyond its charter and into the realm of propaganda.[85]

ASIO also exceeded its authorised role of vetting applicants for the public service. Hence Spry warned the general manager of the ABC about a number of broadcasters, guest commentators and performers, including one who appeared on the popular children's program *The Argonauts*.[86] The universities attracted particular interest. Appointments of overseas scholars deemed a security risk were blocked by denial of an entry visa, but this was not an option in the case of domestic appointments. Probably the greatest controversy arose in 1956 over the vetoing by the chancellor and vice-chancellor of the NSW University of Technology (later the University of New South Wales) of a selection committee's decision to appoint Russel Ward to a lectureship in history. The two university officers, and Menzies, insisted that ASIO was not involved. Max Hartwell, the chair of the selection committee and an economic historian with no connections to the left, was convinced it was and resigned in protest.[87]

In 1961 ASIO briefed Richard Krygier and James McAuley, the publisher and editor of *Quadrant*, on a dispute at the University of Melbourne concerning the head of the Department of Social Studies and members of her staff. After the university failed to act, Frank Knopfelmacher drew on a dossier of material almost certainly provided by ASIO to make lurid allegations of a communist plot to take over the department. To the surprise of many and the dismay of his colleagues in the history department, Max Crawford, who had recently married the head of social studies, wrote to *The Bulletin* to support the allegation. Donald Horne, the magazine's editor, then published an article that gave further substance to the claim and allowed readers to identify the lecturer in the department said to have organised the takeover.[88] This was Geoffrey Sharp, a dissident who had stayed in the party after 1956; the 'social studies affair', as it became known, caused him lasting damage. Horne claimed later to have paid no attention to approaches from Knopfelmacher and said that his information came from Krygier and McAuley, a very fine distinction since they drew on the same source. He also acknowledged that ASIO provided him with a liaison officer.[89]

The Australian National University (ANU), established after the war to do work of national importance and funded directly by the federal government, was a special case. In 1952 Spry had urged the prime minister that the university should submit all proposed appointments for ASIO's approval, and Menzies prevailed on Douglas Copland, the founding vice-chancellor, to undertake that it would avoid appointing persons who might pose a security risk.[90] The ANU's governing body blocked several such appointments during the following decade—though in contrast to the United States, there was no attempt to police the loyalty of established academic staff. Copland negotiated this policy during the fellowship of English anthropologist Peter Worsley, whom the government denied permission to conduct fieldwork in Papua New Guinea, and the same restriction was imposed on other anthropologists thought likely to undermine the colonial administration there. Such was the sensitivity of this arcane field of research that in 1960 ASIO sought to recruit an informant who could report on the ANU's 'anthologists'.[91]

Canberra, the seat of national government, had long attracted the attention of the security service. The party branch there consisted originally of service workers and public servants, with a sprinkling of scientists working for the CSIR. The receipt of information in 1948 that post-war military planning documents had found their way from the Department of External Affairs to the Moscow headquarters of the NKGB brought heightened surveillance. It centred on members of the national press gallery working for *Tribune*, first Bill Mountjoy, then Doris Beeby and later Rex Chiplin, who were thought to have assisted the transfer of material to Russian intelligence officers.[92]

When Spry took charge of ASIO in 1950, he built up the organisation's

Canberra branch, partly to vet public service appointments and partly to invigilate contacts between public servants and members of the Soviet Embassy. This interest soon extended to left-wing academics working at the ANU. Peter Worsley recalled evenings drinking and singing bush ballads with them and formed a particular friendship with Robert Michell, a scientist working in the patent office whose wife taught English at the embassy. Worsley would not have been surprised that ASIO kept an exhaustive list of those who partied at the home of the Michells, for he sensed the beleaguered atmosphere in this isolated rural town.[93] The owner of every car observed outside the residences of Don Baker, Horrie Brown, Eric Fry, Bob and Daphne Gollan, Ron Heiser and Worsley himself was identified, and fanciful inferences were read into the association of colleagues such as Trevor Swan, Horrie Brown and Noel Butlin, apparently oblivious of the fact that these economists were workmates in the wartime public service and now the university.

In addition, ASIO kept up surveillance of public servants thought to have betrayed secrets, such as Jim Hill and Ric Throssell, and others suspected of covering for or simply associating with them. The children of John Burton and Manning Clark became familiar with the cars parked outside their homes throughout the day, and the men with hats and sunglasses who sat on the front seat with notebooks on their knees to record visitors. John Burton's mettlesome daughter Meredith once approached such a vehicle and the two ASIO operatives hastily lifted newspapers to hide their faces. As Nick Brown observes in his history of the nation's capital, Canberra was not an easy place for 'unobtrusive' surveillance. By the same token, it was not an easy place to be a communist: Daphne Gollan explained at a meeting of the branch in 1959 that the majority of members were public servants and therefore unable to come out into the open.[94]

★

One of the revisionists' heresies was to challenge a fundamental tenet of Marxism–Leninism that explained why capitalism would not survive: the falling rate of profit. Because the accumulation of capital relied on the exploitation of labour for extraction of surplus value, it posited crises of increasing severity as workers were replaced with machines. There was little sign of such difficulties in the 1950s and 1960s, however, as the advanced economies combined substantial investment in new technology with high and sustained rates of growth that maintained full employment, lifted wages and boosted living standards. New techniques of economic management, a greatly expanded public sector and a commitment to welfare provision seemed to resolve the harsh class conflict of the inter-war years, leading social democrats to the conclusion that the idea of abolishing capitalism was obsolete.

Eric Aarons was struck by the increased prosperity when he returned to Australia in 1955 after more than three years in China. There were many more cars, people had more money to spend and they had grown used to spending it freely.[95] The party training classes of which he was national director nevertheless continued to teach that capitalism could not solve the problem of declining profit, and the program adopted at the Eighteenth Congress in April 1958 affirmed that 'an ever growing crisis—economic, political and social' would overtake the major capitalist countries. Lance Sharkey's report to that congress explained how they had enjoyed a temporary boost from the tasks of reconstruction after the Second World War, and then the Korean War and the arms race had staved off a downturn. Australia, in particular, had benefited from high export prices, and its wage-earners were able to make up for the effects of a wage freeze with overtime and consumer credit. Now, with export prices falling, those panaceas were no longer available and an intense class struggle could not be averted.[96]

This in turn was expected to breathe new life into the party's hopes for a broad-based people's movement. As set out in the program adopted at the Eighteenth Congress, conditions had never been more auspicious. With the departure of the Industrial Groups, the labour movement was freed of its most anti-communist influence; 'on the insistence of the rank and file', elements of socialism had been inserted into Labor Party policy and the growing economic difficulties established a wide field for common action. By testing the theories of the Labor leaders against those of the communists, common action would clarify the workers' understanding and 'ultimately lead to the formation of a single mass working class Party' capable of leading the small farmers and the middle class in a people's movement that would establish people's power.[97]

By such tenuous reasoning the party ignored the reverses it had suffered. This history has not been able to deal with communist agrarian policy, and there were no more than a handful of rural producers among the membership. In its response to the secret speech the party had vilified the middle class. It proclaimed a leading role for the working class with scant regard for the changing composition and circumstances of Australian wage-earners.

Laurie Aarons did at least attempt to come to terms with occupational census data. He calculated that the Australian 'big bourgeoisie' numbered 33,000 and the upper middle class 366,000, whereas there were 1.8 million members of the working class, of whom 1.3 million were industrial workers, 160,000 rural workers and 365,000 came from the 'lower strata' of white-collar workers.[98] But this classification failed to consider changes in the compositions of the workforce. Unionisation was highest in the male-dominated mining, manufacturing, building and transport industries, lowest in the burgeoning service industries. The party had not adapted either its rhetoric or its politics beyond traditional male strongholds with their distinctive occupational cultures.

For all the talk of winning people's power, the level of support for communist candidates who stood for public office was derisory. There were occasional successes in local government during the 1950s, including Tom Wright's tenure as an alderman of the Sydney City Council, but these came in multi-member contests where the quota for election was low.[99] State and federal lower house elections, on the other hand, were single-member contests. Paddy Troy stood for the federal and state seats of Fremantle on eleven occasions between 1945 and 1966, almost invariably finishing last and losing his deposit. He came to feel that such candidatures were a futile waste of resources and energy that damaged the party's status and morale.[100]

The same held for other party activities. There was a yawning gap between the claim as a vanguard revolutionary party to provide leadership and direction to the mass of the working class while seeking to exert influence as a responsible section of the union movement, and its rhetoric of overthrowing capitalism and activities as a progressive force in Australian public life. Having rebuffed its revisionists, the CPA was itself about to be accused of succumbing to revisionism.

11

Cannot Stand, 1960–70

Helen Palmer travelled to China in 1952 for a peace conference of Asian and Pacific countries, one of eleven Australians who managed to evade the government's travel ban. They were among 400 peace activists who, after deliberating for a fortnight in the Forbidden City, spent nearly a month on a guided tour of the new People's Republic. Palmer could not but be aware of the special treatment accorded the foreign guests—the shiny motorcade that swept them through the crowded streets in Beijing, the plentiful and varied food they ate in the private dining room of their exclusive hotel. Her observations of land reform, irrigation works and construction projects, improvements in public health and advances in education during the subsequent tour were uniformly positive. She remarked on the enthusiasm of the people she encountered during this carefully arranged itinerary, the helpfulness of the interpreters and the shining eyes of her informants.[1]

Palmer's account accords with those of many Westerners drawn to China after the communist seizure of power in 1949. As with travellers to Russia in the 1930s, these political pilgrims projected their hopes for a more fulfilling way of life onto an exotic country with a wholly new social order and a transformed people. The literature on the phenomenon emphasises the importance that was attached to the eyewitness report, with the assumption that even a short visit enabled the visitor to see, hear and bear witness to the new order. For Australian fellow travellers to the People's Republic, there were additional factors. Inhabiting a European outpost in the Pacific, Australia felt the threat of a resurgent

China with special force. At the same time there was a history of interaction between the two countries and an awareness of the antiquity of Chinese civilisation among sympathisers, who believed its ancient qualities of harmony and common purpose had been remade in the crucible of revolution.[2]

Coming at the end of a protracted civil war, Mao Tse-Tung's proclamation of the People's Republic from the top of the Gate of Heavenly Peace in the Forbidden City on 1 October 1949 altered the balance of forces in the Cold War. While there remained the task of building socialism in a country of 500 million inhabitants racked by poverty and destruction, China was indisputably the principal power in the region. Accordingly, it was there that the World Federation of Trade Unions (WFTU) established its Asian Bureau, headed by Ernie Thornton. It has been suggested that this arrangement was meant to help the Soviet Union keep watch on what the Chinese were up to, for Stalin had already found Mao resistant to direction, but the CPA was oblivious of any such discord.[3]

On the contrary, Australian communists were drawn to the energy and enthusiasm of their Chinese comrades as they set about the task of socialist reconstruction. Working for the International Union of Students in Prague, Ken Gott was familiar with life in the Soviet bloc. In 1951 he attended a meeting of its council in Beijing and, like Helen Palmer, toured China following the 1952 peace conference. He was struck by the contrast: 'Russia was grey, China was red; Russia was inert, China vibrant with life; Chinese were lively, gay, enthusiastic; Russians were dull humourless robots.'[4]

The Australian party established contact with the Communist Party of China (CPC) at the Warsaw peace congress in 1950, when the leader of the Chinese delegation raised the possibility of Australians attending the training school they were establishing in Beijing. In the past, a select number of Australians had attended the International Lenin School in Moscow, but that arrangement lapsed on the eve of the Second World War. Hence thirteen Australian communists set off in June 1951, their passports stamped as not valid for the People's Republic of China, necessitating a circuitous journey to the port of Marseilles (where Gott met them) and then on to Prague (where they joined Ernie Thornton) and Moscow to complete their journey on the Trans-Siberian railway.

The ten men and three women began their studies in the headquarters of the WFTU's Asian Bureau until construction of the new training institute was completed. This was a substantial facility 15 kilometres out of Beijing with accommodation for 250 students from the countries of the region, including Japan, Vietnam, Burma, Malaya, Indonesia, the Philippines, India and Pakistan. All were given Chinese names, undertook Chinese-language classes and wore Chinese uniforms. However, the Chinese staff lived in separate quarters and the Australians struggled with the inflections needed to conduct conversations; the lack of a common language also restricted their interaction with other nationalities.[5]

The Australians studied alone. The lessons their Chinese instructors taught had to be translated into English, while the lectures an elderly Russian delivered on Marxism–Leninism were translated first into Chinese and then into English, mangling but never deviating from the text of Stalin's *Foundations of Leninism* with which the students were completely familiar. Russians also conducted the classes in economics and the history of the CPSU, again closely following standard Soviet texts, whereas Chinese instructors taught the history and methods of their party. Knowing little about the CPC beyond the books of Agnes Smedley and Edgar Snow on the Long March and civil war, the students were intrigued by texts such as Liu Shaoqi's *How to Be a Good Communist.* They learned what the Chinese called the 'mass line', the need for communists to pay close attention to the views of the people—an injunction that clearly appealed to the Australians after their failure to do so in the disastrous miners' strike. They were also impressed by the freshness and zeal of the Chinese instructors, who stressed the importance of not copying their own methods but working out an approach based on local conditions.

The most confronting aspect of the training was self-criticism. All students were required to examine their past and identify examples of where they had gone wrong. The Australians were familiar with the formal statement of self-criticism made by a member who deviated from the party line, but not the intense introspection the Chinese demanded if they were to eliminate every last vestige of bourgeois subjectivity such as individualism, selfishness and egotism and become better communists. Hence John Sendy volunteered incidents when he had served the party at the expense of learning from the masses and ascribed this fault to his lower-middle-class background. Others in the group were expected to provide their views on each self-examination, while the Chinese instructor invariably demanded greater candour: 'You've told us the good reason, now tell us the real reason.'[6]

Such painful ideological remoulding disconcerted some of the Australians, as did the Chinese response to the suicide of an Indonesian student: 'he disgraced the title of Communist by taking a selfish way out'.[7] They were completely isolated, forbidden to tell even parents or partners where they were going or when they might return. They were also relatively young, the oldest still in his mid-thirties, and the only three women came with husbands—the breakdown of one of these marriages added to the sexual tension. They studied ten hours a day for six days a week, and by the third year monotony, boredom and homesickness were slowing progress. The food was unappetising, beer scarce. Even so, Eric Aarons, who led the contingent, was not alone in returning with a conviction that the Australian party would benefit from setting aside its narrow rectitude and listening to the people as the Chinese had done.

A second contingent of a dozen left in August 1955, this time flying to Hong Kong and proceeding by train to Beijing, where they studied until November 1956. They were led by Laurie Aarons, by then a member of the Australian secretariat, and included important cadres such as Ted Bacon, Alec Robertson and Bernie Taft. Partners were excluded, an arrangement made without any consideration of the burden the long absence imposed on them. The only woman present, Joyce Stevens, had to deal with unwelcome attention from the men, but found the course of study rewarding. Previously she had little interest in communist theory, so she felt 'the dunce of the class' when she began, but the Chinese method of using theory to learn from experience made sense to her, and she appreciated the collective form of discussion. Bernie Taft took the opportunity to reflect on the way his loyalty to the party prevented him from questioning its methods. He was less impressed by self-rectification, though it helped him to resolve his dilemma and decide that in future he would stand up and fight for what he believed in. This was the period when the CPC 'let a hundred flowers bloom', and the Australians were impressed by the willingness to consider divergent views.[8]

Thereafter the course was restricted to just six months, with no attempt to teach the Chinese language and the self-criticism concentrated in a final week when all students were required to write up a personal evaluation. Jack Hughes led the third contingent, which had three members of the central committee and lasted from February to August 1957. Rex Mortimer found the 'self-remoulding' a revelation. He had been trained in the Marx School, with its emphasis on mastering communist doctrine, so the Chinese emphasis on ideological purity was both challenging and liberating—it helped him to decide, like Bernie Taft, to challenge the dogmatism in Victoria. He noted also that the senior figures in the group resisted such introspection. They were products of the Depression years, he concluded, tough and rigid men who had survived in a Stalinist school that demanded ruthlessness and deviousness. He added that the respect of younger Australians for these obdurate leaders fell.[9]

Claude Jones and Ralph Gibson led subsequent contingents. The fourth one, which ran over the first half of 1958, found that Mao's works dominated the syllabus. By this time China had embarked on its Great Leap Forward, so the prodigious increase in steel production achieved by small blast furnaces was impressed on the Australians during their tour of the country at the end of the course. Claude Jones was unimpressed by these 'furnaces in everybody's dunny', but appreciated the way you could discuss matters with the Chinese. The Russians would tell you what they had decided you should do, whereas the Chinese would ask you and let you think you had reached the outcome they wanted. Gibson was similarly impressed by the enthusiasm of the people and their willingness to criticise mistakes. The sixth study group, however, was abruptly terminated when the Australian party decided it would not support the CPC in its dispute with the CPSU. The friendliness of the instructors changed overnight to rudeness and contempt.[10]

*

The rift between the two leading communist parties began with their leaders. Mao disapproved of Khrushchev's denunciation of Stalin and used the problems that arose from de-Stalinisation in Poland and Hungary to advance his standing as the senior figure in the communist firmament. While he acknowledged Soviet leadership of the world movement at a conference of 64 parties in Moscow at the end of 1957, and accepted that the Soviet Union had advanced furthest on the socialist road, he had already decided to close the gap by a rapid transformation of his own country. The Great Leap Forward on which China embarked in 1958 required party officials to set impossibly optimistic goals for agricultural as well as industrial output and pursue them through an extreme form of collectivisation. Enforced with great brutality and against the advice of Soviet experts, the Great Leap Forward brought a devastating famine that cost at least 30 million lives.[11]

Unable to challenge the USSR's domestic achievement, Mao turned to criticising its foreign policy. Here Khrushchev enjoyed initial success in a pursuit of peaceful coexistence that he conducted with characteristically exuberant pugnacity, telling his hosts 'we will bury you' during a first visit to the United States in 1959 and banging his shoe on the lectern at the United Nations in the following year. He browbeat the inexperienced President Kennedy at a summit in Vienna in 1961, though failed to secure an agreement on arms control. Thereafter Khrushchev suffered reverses, especially over Germany, where he blustered in an unsuccessful attempt to force Western recognition of the East German regime and then had to allow its rulers to build a wall to stem the large numbers leaving for the West—a wall that made a mockery of his claims for the superiority of the socialist system.[12]

The Soviet Union supported national liberation in Indochina, Algeria and Cuba, but Khrushchev was humiliated in the crisis at the end of 1962 caused by his introduction of nuclear missiles to Fidel Castro's Cuba. Mao capitalised on these setbacks with accusations that Khrushchev had capitulated to the imperialist aggressors, accompanied by reckless provocations of his own that included shelling the islands in the South China Sea controlled by the former Nationalist regime and fighting a border war with India.

Since the two communist parties had signed a declaration of unity at the 1957 conference, they conducted their polemics by proxy, the CPC directing its criticism at the Yugoslav revisionists and the CPSU accusing the Workers' Party of Albania of irresponsible adventurism. The Chinese asserted their fidelity to Marxism–Leninism in a 1960 publication, *Long Live Leninism*; the Russians responded by republishing Lenin's *Left-Wing Communism, an Infantile Disorder*. A second Moscow conference at the end of the year, this one attended by 81 parties, issued a cosmetic restatement of unity that was no more than a temporary truce. Khrushchev used the 22nd Congress of the CPSU in October 1961 to renew his attack on Stalin, whose coffin was removed from Lenin's mausoleum in Red Square, and on those aberrant parties that perpetuated Stalin's errors. All subsequent attempts at reconciliation failed.[13]

The indivisible unity of communism as a world movement had particular importance for a party as small and beleaguered as the Australian one, so it could not but be concerned by the contrary signals given by the two lodestars. At least initially, the leaders of the CPA shared the Chinese misgivings with the direction in which Khrushchev was taking the CPSU, though they did not realise that Mao would go on to shatter the unity of the communist movement.

The three Australians who determined their party's response to this Sino-Soviet split were all in China at the Eighth Congress of the CPC in September 1956. Lance Sharkey and Ted Hill travelled to Beijing for the occasion, and Laurie Aarons joined them from the training school. Since Mao's own cult was already as pronounced as that of the late Russian dictator, it is hardly surprising that he should take the opportunity to defend Stalin's legacy, though his formula that Stalin had been 30 per cent wrong and 70 per cent right was a bizarre quantification of a tyranny that killed millions. While in Beijing, Hill lent Aarons his copy of the *New York Times* version of Khrushchev's secret speech and it occasioned a heated argument between these two members of the secretariat, Aarons convinced it was both authentic and necessary, Hill highly critical because of the damage it did to the communist cause. Lance Sharkey shared Mao's response to criticism of the cult of the individual and for much the same reason.[14]

The three Australians also met with a member of the Soviet delegation, Boris Ponomarev, who was head of the CPSU central committee's international department. He told them the Soviet Union wanted to re-establish diplomatic relations with Australia, which had been severed by the defection of the Petrovs, and to this end might concede that some of the allegations aired in the royal commission were justified. Hill, whose reputation as a barrister was bound up with his attack on the Petrovs' credibility, and Sharkey, who had flatly denied their story of giving him money, were both horrified by such expediency. For his part, Aarons was attracted to the revolutionary élan of the Chinese and the 'mass line' style of party work he had so recently learned.[15]

With many of its leading members having spent time there, the Australian party had close relations with the Chinese one. Moreover, China lay on the route to the Soviet Union, and Australian representatives regularly broke their journeys to confer with Chinese counterparts. *Tribune* picked up the principal statements of the CPC and gave lengthy accounts of the progress of the People's Republic. Leading members praised the Great Leap Forward in glowing terms: it was 'one of the great events in all history', according to Laurie Aarons in October 1958, with growth at 'an astounding, even incredible rate'; an achievement that 'staggers the imagination', his brother Eric added four months later. By then reports of the disastrous famine were beginning to appear in the Western press, reports the party consistently denied. As late as October 1960, when peasants in stricken provinces were reduced to eating the bark from trees, a reporter for the Melbourne *Guardian* wrote that he had travelled thousands of miles in China without meeting a hungry person.[16]

It was the same with stories of conflict between the CPC and CPSU. When Khrushchev first visited China in July 1958 in a futile attempt to settle differences, Mao humiliated his guest by showing off his prowess in the swimming pool while the hapless Russian floundered in a buoyancy vest. Yet according to the *Communist Review* the two sides conducted discussions 'in an atmosphere of exceptional cordiality and warmth' that revealed 'completely identical views'. As the rift between their parties became an open secret, the CPA continued to dismiss reports of discord as malicious inventions of the capitalist press.[17]

It maintained this position even as Sharkey and Dixon set off in September 1960 for the 81 parties conference in Moscow. By this time the political committee had resolved to back the Chinese, or so Ted Hill claimed after it backed away from this decision. He published what he asserted was a stenographic record of a conversation between Mao and the two Australians en route to Moscow in which Sharkey assured the Chinese leader of agreement with his criticisms. 'We fully support the stand and views of the Chinese Party', it read, on 'the nature of imperialism, peaceful transition, general and complete disarmament' and other questions. Although Dixon disputed the accuracy of this transcript, it seems likely that the two Australian leaders did intend to support the Chinese until they discovered at the conference they were so isolated.[18]

There was no mention of any such undertaking in Sharkey's report on the conference for *Tribune*, in which he endorsed the statement of the 81 parties. That the Melbourne *Guardian* ran a report by Mao's deputy, Liu Shaoqi, was an indication that Hill, the Victorian state secretary, was firmly in the Chinese camp. The Australian party's Nineteenth Congress in 1961 gave a hint of these internal differences when it stated that while revisionism remained the chief danger, vigilance was also needed against dogmatism and sectarianism.[19]

The discord became apparent at the 22nd Congress of the CPSU later in that year, when the Australians were put under intense pressure by both sides. The Australian delegates were Lance Sharkey, Ted Bacon and Edgar Ross. Dixon was seriously ill and unavailable, but the absence of Aarons and Hill suggests Sharkey wanted maximum freedom of manoeuvre. When the delegation stopped off at Beijing, he revealed reservations about the Chinese rejection of peaceful coexistence. Did he think the skies would fall in if an open break should occur, they asked him? 'No,' Sharkey is said to have replied, 'but the roof's looking fucking shaky.' Although he refused to discuss his position with the other two delegates, stage whispers during the congress proceedings made his antagonism to Khrushchev evident. In subsequent meetings with both Soviet and Chinese representatives, the Australians insisted they could not commit themselves until they consulted their central committee.[20]

At some point during the time in Moscow the Russians won Sharkey over. He continued to keep his own counsel during the return journey, however, probably because he needed to sound out leading members before declaring himself, but also because of lingering regrets. He told a subsequent meeting of cadres that he disagreed with some of the decisions of the congress; in particular 'the denunciation of Stalin, the removal of his body from alongside our dear Lenin, left me numb with shock'. Yet all but a handful of the communist parties attending the congress had backed the CPSU, and the report of the Australian delegation recommended that, on balance, the CPA should do the same. A special meeting of the political committee in December 1961 went further, declaring its 'profound confidence in, and admiration for, the leading role played in the fight for peace and peaceful coexistence by the CPSU'.[21]

Laurie Aarons was a strong supporter of this resolution. Ted Hill was alone in opposing it, and startled the others with the vehemence of his opposition—this was the occasion when he said that the party should begin preparing for armed struggle. Henceforth Aarons, rather than Sharkey, made the running, for if the preservation of unity finally swayed the general secretary, he could not come to terms with the crashing of his idols—Bacon thought Sharkey returned 'a broken man', Claude Jones found him bewildered and demoralised. As Aarons and Hill conducted the fierce factional conflict that broke out in 1962, they were fighting not just to determine whether the party should be in the Soviet or the Chinese camp but who should lead it.[22]

Hill's style of leadership was evident in the way he ran affairs in Victoria, by personal direction and with minimal consultation. Such was his suspicious vigilance that he ordered the drawers be removed from all desks in the party's head office in Elizabeth Street. Demanding a commitment as absolute and unsparing as his own, he had a circle of loyal officials who referred every important decision to him: Frank Johnson, his unquestioning lieutenant; Flo Russell and Vida Little, who supervised trade union work; and Ken Miller, editor of the *Guardian*.

Opposition to Hill's distrustful dogmatism began among other full-time party workers, and despite his best efforts they were more difficult to control than their counterparts in Sydney, where the secretariat could exercise closer oversight. Bernie Taft refused to submit following his return from China in 1956, as did Rex Mortimer when he returned two years later, and soon there was a group of dissidents. They took care to present their opposition as arising from disagreement with Hill's autocratic methods rather than party policy, and by 1960 were successful in displacing the unpopular Vida Little from her post as secretary of the metropolitan committee. Appeals to Sydney failed to settle the dispute.[23]

'Intra-communist conflict', Mortimer observed, 'is invariably bitter and sordid', and this one employed gossip, deception and mutual espionage in a desperate struggle that took a heavy toll on the adversaries.[24] Hill, whose ailments included sleeplessness, skin rashes, severe abdominal pains and back trouble, was in the Soviet Union for treatment of hypertension during the first half of 1961. Taft suffered insomnia and high blood pressure, while Mortimer was laid low with an ulcer and migraine attacks. Hill seemed to secure Sharkey's support to break the impasse by transferring Taft to Sydney, but the threatened resignation of J.J. Brown of the Australian Railways Union was too high a price to pay, so instead Taft was sent in April 1961 to a study course in Moscow. Some saw this as a Siberian exile. It is more likely that Laurie Aarons and his ally Eddie Robertson, who had recently joined the secretariat, wanted to keep him out of the firing line while they settled matters with Hill. He was then brought back to help reconstruct the party in Victoria.[25]

Hill found no support in the party's inner circle for his criticism of the CPSU, and a meeting of the central committee in early 1962 confirmed his isolation. Realising he had been outmanoeuvred, he delivered a 90-minute statement of defiance. There were two lines in the world communist movement, he began, one Marxist–Leninist and the other utterly erroneous. The errors began with Khrushchev's attack on Stalin at the Twentieth Congress, an ill-considered repudiation of a great Marxist–Leninist and an inspiring leader. The CPC was now 'fighting a stern battle to uphold the truths of Marxism–Leninism', while the CPSU was betraying them in its promotion of peaceful coexistence and peaceful revolution. There was no cult of personality in China, nor were Chinese communists dogmatists, as the Australian party leaders appreciated until they capitulated to the Soviet revisionists at the 22nd Congress.[26]

Such open dissent made it impossible for Hill to remain a member of the secretariat or continue as state secretary. He resigned these posts, but in a ruse that no one at the meeting seems to have rumbled, arranged beforehand for Frank Johnson, the Victorian president, not to vote with him and Flo Russell. Thinking Johnson had deserted Hill, the secretariat installed him as state secretary, a position that enabled him to keep Hill fully briefed on subsequent developments. Meanwhile, Ted Bacon toured the other states to explain the decision to back the Soviets against the Chinese. Although a number of members were surprised to learn of the breach, every state and district committee endorsed the decision.[27]

In Victoria, on the other hand, Hill and his supporters retained control of the state committee and the conflict continued until September 1962, when a 'national commission' consisting of Sharkey, Dixon, Aarons, Claude Jones (the Queensland president) and John Sendy (the South Australian secretary) arrived to restore order. They dismissed several functionaries, and replaced Flo Russell with Bernie Taft as industrial organiser, Frank Johnson with Ralph Gibson as state secretary and Gibson with Sendy as state president.[28] Hill's supporters hotly contested these changes. There was a petition objecting to Taft's appointment, allegations he had a Trotskyist background and that Sendy retained security connections from his war service with the RAAF police, claims the Aarons family had taken over the central committee and complaints that Jews were running the party. On the other side, Ken Miller was removed from the editorship of the *Guardian* after a grilling from the national commission. When his wife rang to ask how he had fared, he said it was like being tied to a tree and used for bayonet practice.[29]

After preliminary skirmishes in branches, sections and districts—and 'the higher up you go', Sendy discovered, 'the worse it gets'—the state conference in April 1963 confirmed the new order.[30] A resolution endorsing the position of the central committee was carried by 146 votes to sixteen and all Hill's supporters were voted off the state committee. Hill, Johnson, Paddy Malone, Miller and Russell were subsequently removed from the central committee. Hill warned during the conference that he had just begun to fight, and his principal supporters resigned from the party, one by one to attract maximum publicity. They included Clarrie O'Shea of the Tramways Union, Malone and Norm Gallagher of the Builders Labourers Federation, Kath Williams of the Liquor and Allied Trades Union, and Ted Bull of the Waterside Workers' Federation.

Summoned to appear before the central committee, Hill replied that he was unable to do so as he was about to leave for China but could see Sharkey and Dixon in his chambers if they made the trip to Melbourne. The two were leaving themselves, however, for talks in the USSR, so Laurie Aarons took over the disciplinary proceedings. Hill was charged with violating party rules that prohibited factional activity and failing to observe decisions of the central committee and state conference. After refusing to attend a meeting of the central disputes committee, he was expelled in August 1963. His trip to confer with the CPC also prevented him from attending the funeral of Ken Miller, who collapsed and died at the end of June. The comrades who had worked with Miller on the *Guardian* over the past thirteen years lamented the loss of this 'warm, complex and sensitive human being', and expressed 'grief that bonds were weakened in the closing months of his life'. Such charity was in short supply as scores were settled in Victoria.[31]

With the encouragement of Beijing, Hill proceeded to form a new party. Greatly to the ire of the existing one, it called itself the Communist Party of Australia, with a defiant subtitle: Marxist–Leninist. While the CPA dismissed the new body as the 'Hill group', Hill declared that the Communist Party of Australia (Marxist-Leninist) was the original Australian party, the revisionists having purified the communist movement by their desertion of the cause. A newspaper, the *Vanguard*, appeared in September, and a journal, the *Australian Communist*, in October. A founding conference in March 1964 elected Ted Hill chairman with Clarrie O'Shea and Paddy Malone vice-chairmen and Frank Johnson secretary. John Nolan, a member of the Queensland state committee, subsequently formed a branch in Townsville (and tried to entice Eddie Mabo across from the CPA branch there). Syd Clare, a waterside worker in Sydney, initiated another branch, as did Charlie McCaffrey, the former secretary of the Ironworkers in Adelaide, but these outposts had little more than nuisance value.[32]

At most the CPA (M-L) had 300 members. Flo Russell had declaimed at the Victorian conference of the CPA in April 1963 that 'the masses would never support the Party while it followed a revisionist policy', but this breakaway one took pride in its smallness, spurning recruitment drives and admitting only those who met the high standards and purity of its ideology. It had few functionaries and kept a low profile in accordance with its leader's insistence on the need for secrecy and the likelihood of repression.[33]

The CPA (M-L) attracted a dozen union officials in Victoria, mostly in the building industry, and set back the CPA's industrial influence there. Paddy Malone, who had built the Builders Labourers Federation into an effective fighting union, was a serious loss. He and the others felt a loyalty to Hill, who handled their unions' legal affairs, and Russell, who coordinated their campaigns. They were less interested in the doctrinal issues involved in the Sino-Soviet dispute than drawn to a militant stance that gave no quarter to the class enemy. Although Cedric Ralph was also attracted to the new party by fervent admiration for Hill, the split crystallised misgivings he had long felt about the character of the old one. Ralph was a member of the Kew branch, which consisted largely of doctors, scientists, journalists, artists and lawyers (like himself) who had joined during and immediately after the Second World War. He considered them humanitarians rather than revolutionaries, people of good will for whom 'revisionism was a virus'. They labelled him an 'Old Bolshevik'.[34]

One of Ralph's complaints before he was expelled from the CPA in September 1963 was that the party refused to publish the correspondence between the CPSU and CPC that set out the issues in dispute. He was not alone in this criticism. Amirah Turner, for example, resigned in protest against the lack of opportunity for branch members to discuss the split, while Dorothy Gibson, who presumably did have discussions with her husband Ralph, still thought the statements of the two parties 'seemed to be saying the same things'.[35] The leaders' failure went further than this. Reluctant to commit the party to either side, they did not even acknowledge there was a dispute until forced to do so, instead relying on the loyalty of members to a monolithic unity that had long ceased to exist. As a result the party came late to an argument over its policies, methods and future direction: in short, what sort of party it should be.

★

The defeat of Ted Hill left Laurie Aarons the leader in waiting. With Dixon out of action for most of 1961 while recovering from a heart attack, Aarons became national vice-president and also picked up the duties of the general secretary during Sharkey's frequent trips abroad. The promotion to secretary of the secretariat of Eddie Robertson—a friend from Aarons' time as South Australian organiser and the man he thought should succeed Lance Sharkey—was meant to lighten the load, but this talented organiser succumbed to heart failure within a year, dead at the age of 37.[36] Eric Aarons took Robertson's place, joined in 1964 by Claude Jones.

The Aarons brothers had spent all their lives in the party. Their father Sam, whose parents were also members, served on the central committee for more than twenty years, and their aunts Millie and Miriam remained active. That did not make Laurie's transition to general secretary any easier. A quietly spoken, self-sufficient man attuned to the feelings of those with whom he dealt, he was now in charge of an organisation in which there was no shortage of strong egos. Whereas he could see the need for change, older functionaries whom he had leapfrogged did not. He would have to tap some on the shoulder as the financial position deteriorated and reinvigorate others who had lost their youthful fire.

There was also the reluctance of Lance Sharkey to hand over. By this time the general secretary was in visible decline, halting, forgetful, given to maudlin recollections of the good old days and in need of constant reassurance. Yet he could still turn nasty in his cups and more than once railed about 'bloody Jews' in Laurie's presence, clearly resentful of his successor. Once revered by the party faithful, Sharkey lost prestige with a disastrous appearance on the ABC's *Four Corners* television program in 1963 and cut a pathetic figure at the CPA's Twentieth Congress in the following year, hunched over the lectern and barely able to read the report Aarons prepared for him. The two men flew to Europe at the beginning of 1965 for meetings with the CPSU and other communist parties, Sharkey staying on and announcing his retirement upon his return at the end of May. The central committee installed Aarons the following week.[37]

With the events leading to the formation of the CPA (M-L) fresh in delegates' minds, the Twentieth Congress was at pains to repudiate any traces of left sectarianism. The principal resolution condemned the isolationist statements and practices of the Hill group and called for 'a mass party of the working class, numbering tens of thousands and with wide contacts among the people everywhere'.[38] During a tour of Europe after the congress, Aarons visited Italy and France to see how the parties there attracted a mass following. They were less demanding and more inclusive, he concluded, not cut off from the rest of society but integrated into the community. In keeping with this orientation, he arranged for future meetings of the central committee to be followed by a press conference with beer and sandwiches laid on for the journalists.[39]

He was not alone in rethinking how the party presented itself. Five years earlier, Rex Mortimer had enlarged in the *Communist Review* on a central committee call to bring its propaganda up to date. He noted that open-air assemblies no longer attracted the audience they had done even ten years earlier, and it required an intensive drive to fill the hall for the now occasional public meeting. The numbers at factory rallies were smaller than they had been at the height of the Cold War, and the party no longer seemed to have speakers with the humour, passion and popular touch to command a hearing.[40]

Mortimer urged members to improve their communication skills and cited the favourable impression Khrushchev made in the United States with his verbal thrusts, an example that might well have caused Hill to write an indignant reply—which, he claimed, Laurie Aarons denied publication.[41] Beyond questions of technique, however, Mortimer's observations pointed to a decline in the older forms of political oratory. With the demise of Friday-night shopping and shift from the high street to the supermarket, there was no longer an audience for a soapbox orator. Television made it harder to draw people out of their homes of an evening to a suburban hall. There were fewer inner-city factories that allowed large groups of workers to gather outside the entrance during their lunch break.

Another problem Mortimer identified was the reputation of communist publicists as 'calamity howlers' who revelled in misery and turned every symptom of economic instability into a full-blown crisis. There were still traces of such catastrophism in the program adopted at the Twentieth Congress, as well as claims that monopoly capitalism was squeezing out small producers and references to the 60 rich Australian families growing richer at the expense of wage-earners.[42] Alongside this familiar dirge, however, was an acknowledgement of 'scientific and technological developments' that were transforming the economy. The proposition that capitalism was on the point of collapse, inherently difficult to reconcile with the doctrine of a peaceful transition to socialism, was abandoned soon after the congress. Attention turned instead to the scientists, technicians, social scientists and other 'intellectually trained people' who were giving capitalism its new lease of life, and who would play a vital role in any transition to socialism. They became the starting point of Laurie Aarons' report to the next congress.[43]

The new state committee in Victoria had already agreed in 1963 to the publication of a theoretical journal aimed at these intellectuals, *Arena*. The idea seems to have originated with Rex Mortimer and Geoff Sharp, who obtained permission for it to be open to members and non-members alike and have financial and organisational independence.[44] This allowed non-communists to serve on the editorial board—ex-communists in the case of Ian Turner and, before too long, Sharp as well. It was he who took interest in the professional intelligentsia furthest with his argument that they differed fundamentally from industrial workers in the degree of autonomy their work required and the non-hierarchical forms of association it used. Such intellectually trained workers were guided by knowledge rather than power, but just as they resisted the uses to which capitalist corporations and state agencies put their knowledge, they were not attracted to centralisation of decision-making, let alone a dictatorship of the proletariat.[45]

Sharp was also prescient in his observation, as early as 1964, that the universities in which this intellectual training was conducted inculcated a critical, independent cast of mind that knowledge workers carried into their careers. Student protest, barely under way in 1964, grew rapidly into a mass movement that rocked campuses all round the world by 1968. It generated a student-based New Left, quite different in appearance, speech and attitudes from the older generation of communists. An ASIO agent who reported the proceedings of a weekend conference in Sydney under the auspices of *Arena* as early as 1964 confessed his bafflement. 'It was very difficult to follow much of what was said', he explained, since many of the participants were 'long-haired academics and university types who used long words which either do not appear in the dictionary or have obscure meanings'.[46] But if the party was to win recruits to replace its ageing membership, let alone become a mass party, it needed to attract this new generation of radicals.

To this end the ponderously authoritative *Communist Review* gave way in 1966 to a bimonthly journal, the *Australian Left Review*, broader in scope, livelier in tone and again open to non-members. When John Sendy wrote in the first issue of the need to democratise party life, he cited the lack of opportunity for proper discussion of congress resolutions.[47] The documents for the 21st Congress were released at the end of the year to allow a full six months for their consideration, and in a break with the ritual whereby district and state conferences rubberstamped the resolutions, a new publication invited all members to share their views. Nearly 200 of them did so in five issues of this *Discussion Journal*.

There was much to discuss. The draft documents were written in a new style, setting out changes that demanded reconsideration of outworn orthodoxies without claiming communists had all the answers. Whereas the party had previously condemned monopoly capitalism for driving down workers' wages, it now talked of the alienation of citizens denied control over their lives and subjected to the 'sordid commercialisation' of social relations. If the industrial working class was still deemed ultimately decisive, dissent among the intellectually trained was seen as a major development. Furthermore, the radicalisation of those undergoing such training was contrasted with the conservatism of trade unions. Communists could no longer assume the prerogatives of a vanguard party or presume that they alone could play the leading role in a united or popular front. Instead they should pursue a 'Coalition of the Left' in which they accepted the legitimacy of other political perspectives and discussed them in a reasoned way. Finally, the congress documents proposed changes to the party's constitution and rules that strengthened provisions for democratic decision-making and gave its principal bodies less threatening names: the central committee would become the national committee, the political committee the national executive, and the secretariat would be known as the national officers.[48]

The *Discussion Journal* was remarkably free of pieties. A minority of contributors gave notice they would defend existing policies. Probably of greater concern were those who felt the new ones fell short of what was needed. Geoff Sharp thought the analysis of knowledge workers deficient. Lloyd Churchward pointed out that a coalition of the left presupposed a mass communist party. Alastair Davidson, whom Laurie Aarons had just assisted in writing his history of the party, judged the prospects of building such a party as poor. Jack Blake argued that the constant talk of doing so ignored the fact that the party had become so self-enclosed there was nothing left to build from. Nor could members be expected to act in new ways until they were told how the old ways were wrong. When Blake talked to party leaders they agreed with his confession he had been a Stalinist, 'but to a man they are not, and never were, influenced by Stalin'.[49]

Paddy Troy went further. For twenty years, he stated, the party had made no headway; indeed, it was not accepted as a party by the Australian people, who regarded it as a kind of appendage of the Soviet Union. The failure of the Communist Party to win acceptance, moreover, was matched by the failure of the Labor Party to win elections. He concluded that communists would do better to abandon their position as a separate political party and concentrate on strengthening the ALP and promoting its socialist objective. That this dedicated veteran wrote so frankly of the wasted years of hostility to 'our ALP friends' surprised many. Claude Jones described Troy as 'a dogmatic leftist' and 'the most reactionary old bloke' he'd ever had to deal with, and suggested that Frank Chamberlain, the state and federal secretary of the ALP, 'would have a fit' if he found his bitter foe in Labor's ranks. Troy received a cool reception at a congress function to honour delegates with more than 30 years of membership.[50]

Held over four days in June 1967, the 21st Congress saw vigorous debate. All the reports and principal resolutions were eventually adopted, though on several occasions a show of hands—unusual in itself as they would once have been endorsed unanimously—had to be followed by a count. The coalition of the left was particularly contentious, some delegates arguing that confining it to the left was too restrictive and others objecting that it watered down the leading role of the party. In its final formulation, the coalition signified joint action and cooperation of all the forces whose aspirations were blocked by 'the owning and controlling class': those opposed to militarism and racism, those pressing for civil liberties and social reform. Such a coalition would bring unions and intellectuals together, for the labour movement needed radical intellectuals while the efforts of intellectuals were ineffective without support from the labour movement.[51]

The congress adopted the rule changes and took some further. The term 'democratic centralism' disappeared from the constitution and it was resolved to establish a charter of democratic rights. At the suggestion of the Western Australian delegates, congress also replaced the central disputes committee by an elected appeals committee, with no member of the national committee able to serve on it. There had been a mutiny in Western Australia against Sam Aarons' unyielding control that forced him to retire from the secretary's post, but the mutineers still insisted on an independent avenue of appeal. They also wanted to replace Sam Aarons on the national committee with Norm Lacey, the new state secretary, but were thwarted when the congress chose Sam's wife Annette. Bill Latter, perhaps the ablest of the party's new generation of union officials in the west, was incensed that he was not allowed to speak before delegates cast their votes for the new committee and resigned.[52]

The elections met Laurie Aarons' goal of rejuvenating the national committee. Lance Sharkey and Len Donald had died; J.B. Miles, Sam Aarons and Alan Finger finally stood down. Among the new members were Max Ogden, a metalworker and secretary of the Eureka Youth League in Victoria; Joe Palmada, the NSW industrial organiser; Malcolm Salmon, who covered international news for *Tribune*; and George Zangalis, a Victorian industrial organiser and Greek community activist.

Laurie Aarons and Richard Dixon were returned unopposed as national secretary and president, with Claude Jones and John Sendy becoming vice-presidents. Eric Aarons remained a member of the national executive, which also underwent renovation: Ralph Gibson, Jack Hughes and J.B. Miles departed; Bernie Taft and Alec Robertson, editor of *Tribune*, were among the replacements. These changes indicated the support for the new policies, though a number who retained their positions harboured reservations. That Judah Waten won election to the national committee was a reminder of the resistance to change.

★

The congress was held in the party's new national headquarters in Day Street, which ran alongside Darling Harbour. It had moved out of the nearby Market Street premises at the beginning of 1964. They were cramped, dilapidated and due for demolition as developers ate into inner Sydney. Day Street, on the other hand, provided a substantial four-storey warehouse that working bees of party carpenters and tradesmen converted into offices, meeting rooms, a coffee lounge and a large hall. A similar arrangement allowed the Queensland branch of the party to occupy a three-storey building in Fortitude Valley in the following year.[53]

The cost of these properties was not cheap and, even with voluntary labour, fitting them out required expenditure the party could ill afford but was unavoidable if it was to rebuild its stocks. The outlay was made possible by the Soviet Union, which provided the CPA with almost US$500,000 in the course of the 1960s. The assistance began with two large payments in 1961 that might well have been part of the inducement for Lance Sharkey to come down on the Russian side in that year. Despite the support, the party remained chronically short of funds. Party-building campaigns were conducted on a regular basis. Encouraging reports from particular districts and states would appear in the party press, but behind closed doors it was a different story.[54]

The decision to build a mass party was taken at the Twentieth Congress after it heard a chastening report on the current position. Membership had remained constant since the previous congress three years earlier. There had been slight gains in New South Wales, South Australia and

Western Australia, offset by losses in Queensland and Victoria. Sales of the party's three weekly newspapers (the Queensland *Guardian* resumed publication in 1960) were static. Expenditure on salaries had been trimmed and the number of functionaries was down to 54. Most were paid no more than £17 a week (just over the basic wage), yet the party was still not paying its way.[55]

Membership statistics at this time when the party was removing the veil of secrecy are even more exiguous than when it was under siege. The aggregate figure of 5274 in mid-1965 was said to be an increase from 4520 in 1963. New South Wales made up almost half, with 2515 members; Victoria had 1375, Queensland 826, South Australia 295, Western Australia 194, Tasmania 51 and the Northern Territory 18.[56] A profile of the party published in 1967 put the membership at about 4500, with the additional information that 70 per cent were men and the average age was 46, and there were 4390 on the books in 1969.[57]

There was a determined effort to revive the party press. Pete Thomas, an able journalist, ran the Brisbane *Guardian* on a shoestring. Rex Mortimer, who became editor of the Melbourne *Guardian* following the defeat of Ted Hill, worked hard to build its circulation. But since the fortunes of communist newspapers depended upon the number of members willing to sell them, both ran at a loss the party could no longer afford and were wound up in 1966. That left *Tribune*, which acquired a new offset press from East Germany in 1967 and adopted a more contemporary graphic layout. Alec Robertson, the editor, breathed new life into the paper's coverage and treatment, yet it too ran at an increasing deficit.

Tribune's new editorial policy was a point of contention. As Robertson pointed out, its previous role as an instrument of party policy restricted the range and depth of analysis, and since only the view of the leadership was entitled to publication, genuine discussion was rare.[58] Now the pages were open to a range of views, and lively debates were conducted in the correspondence columns. The change disconcerted those communists who clung to the notion of a party of one mind, and a number of correspondents warned that the airing of differences was damaging the party's reputation.

One such difference was industrial policy. Full employment made it increasingly difficult for the Arbitration Commission to maintain control of wages—and for unions to control members on the shopfloor who bypassed their officials and took direct action. The use of fines to enforce the no-strike clauses inserted in the awards of militant unions, for so long a crippling deterrent, was challenged in 1969 when a number of unions called a 24-hour stoppage in support of Clarrie O'Shea of the Victorian Tramways Union when he was gaoled for failure to pay such a fine. After threats of a longer, nationwide strike, an anonymous benefactor paid the fine and the government tacitly abandoned its use of such penalties. For years communist-led unions had been campaigning unsuccessfully against the penal powers; now it became apparent that the most simple and effective solution was to defy them.[59]

The 21st Congress had criticised the union movement for lagging behind the new possibilities this increasing labour unrest created. It called for unions to go beyond campaigns for better wages and conditions to challenge monopoly capital's domination of the economy. Before O'Shea made his stand, the national committee was urging communist union officials to fight the penal powers. Some did, notably Laurie Carmichael, the Melbourne district secretary of the Amalgamated Engineering Union (AEU), who was instrumental in planning this action and indeed persuading a somewhat reluctant O'Shea (chosen because the Tramways Union had so few assets for the court to seize) to serve as martyr. Carmichael, who would become assistant national secretary of his union and then assistant national secretary of the ACTU, emerged at this time as the party's most influential and innovative union leader. But others were reluctant to follow his lead. 'Obsolete union structures, authoritarian outlooks and bureaucratic procedures were grimly held onto,' Eric Aarons complained.[60]

Jack Hutson, research officer for the AEU, injected a note of realism. An acute critic of the arbitration system, he offered a comprehensive guide for workers to make the best use of it in his book *From Penal Colony to Penal Powers*. He was all in favour of democratic rights in industry and an increased role for shop stewards, 'who at present have little more legal rights than a stray dog in a factory', but he differed from those who thought the only obstacle to workers' control was a lack of vision. Among the constraints he identified was the small size of the party and its diminished industrial influence.[61]

The loss of Jim Healy, who died from a blood clot on the brain in 1961, was a severe blow. As its candidate in the ballot to elect a new general secretary of the Waterside Workers' Federation, the party chose Tom Nelson, secretary of the Sydney branch, in preference to Ted Roach, the assistant general secretary, or Norm Docker, the federal industrial officer. Either would have been a strong candidate, but their standing would have triggered a spill of the executive positions and, in a sign of its lack of confidence, the party chose not to risk them. That left the door open for Charlie Fitzgibbon, the president of the Newcastle branch and a member of the ALP who had the backing of Arthur Calwell, its new parliamentary leader. Fitzgibbon's victory left rumblings of dissatisfaction among communists on the wharves. A similar problem was averted when Bill Parkinson retired from the presidency of the Miners' Federation in 1967, but only because Jim Comerford withdrew from the contest to give Walter Smart, another communist, a clear run. Comerford became general secretary when the incumbent died in the following year.[62]

The party leaders' call for a bolder industrial strategy aggravated a division in its union ranks. Under the leadership of Jack Mundey, who became secretary in 1968, the NSW branch of the Builders Labourers Federation (BLF) adopted strikingly democratic procedures. It also asserted the right of members 'to have an effective say in all aspects of the industry', including 'what sort of buildings go up and in what sort of environment for the lives of those who use them', and it backed the claim with aggressive industrial tactics that included the use of 'vigilante squads' to shut down sites—and, if necessary, destroy work done on them—that refused the union's demands.[63] These tactics put the BLF on a collision course with the employers and the government. It went further by criticising the Building Workers' Industrial Union (BWIU) for its bureaucracy, protection of craft privileges and lack of fight. Pat Clancy, the federal secretary of the BWIU, and Tom McDonald, the state secretary, were longstanding party members who bridled at the criticism. Other communist union officials shared their resentment.[64]

Another point of contention was the party's courtship of the New Left that emerged from the radicalisation of university students during the 1960s. In the first half of the decade, students campaigned on issues of conscience such as apartheid, the White Australia policy and discrimination against Indigenous Australians, culminating in the Freedom Ride of early 1965, when a busload of Sydney University students challenged segregation in rural New South Wales.[65]

The introduction of military conscription in November 1964 and the commitment of an Australian battalion to the Vietnam War in May 1965 brought a new kind of protest, openly defiant of authority and aggressively confrontational. No longer bound by Cold War shibboleths, activists here and in other Western countries linked Third World liberation struggles to their own rebellion against the oppressive nature of advanced industrial society. A series of events in 1968 seemed to confirm this connection. First came the Tet Offensive, a new-year onslaught by North Vietnamese troops and National Liberation Front guerrillas that showed the United States and its allies were losing the war. Then the assassination of Martin Luther King Jr in April set off riots in American cities. Huge demonstrations, students' occupation of universities and workers' occupation of factories brought France to a standstill in May, and campuses in many other countries were racked by conflict over the remainder of the year.[66]

For traditionalists of the Old Left, as well as stalwarts of the 'first' New Left—those of the *Outlook* circle who for more than a decade had pursued a reasoned alternative to dogmatism—the younger generation's emphasis on spontaneity and antagonism to all forms of authority seemed little more than revolutionary posturing. But the Australian party responded to the student movement with greater enthusiasm than most of its overseas counterparts. Prominent activists provided a running commentary in *Tribune* on the unrest during 1968, and Laurie Aarons issued an invitation to 'all individuals, organisations, journals and groupings considering themselves left, radical, anti-establishment or anti-imperialist' to meet and seek common ground.[67]

Held in Sydney over the Easter of 1969, the Left Action Conference attracted more than 800 participants.[68] Critics alleged this was merely a recruitment exercise to replenish the party's depleted ranks, and Aarons did confer with prominent New Left activists on the heels of the conference, but the claim of one that he offered them half the membership of the national committee and half the posts on *Tribune* is fanciful. None of the four who joined the editorial board of the *Australian Left Review* became a party member. The conference is better understood as an exercise in revitalising the CPA through exposure to the new currents of radical thinking that were not beholden to the communist past.[69]

There was only a modest influx of recruits from the New Left. Those students who joined the various political organisations claiming Marxist inspiration were never more than a fraction of the larger body of protesters. Maoists attracted headlines with their violence, Trotskyists stood out for their obsessive doctrinal wrangles, but followers of the more eclectic and libertarian Students for Democratic Action and Students for a Democratic Society outnumbered both—and although the activists were involved in organising the Vietnam Moratorium of May 1970 and the Springbok tour protest of 1971, these were genuinely mass mobilisations beyond their control. By then the weaknesses of the student movement were becoming apparent: its fragmentation and reliance on a small number of activists, never more than a few hundred on any campus, who exploited the overreaction of authorities to draw the mass of students into action. The movement was heavily dependent on charismatic individuals whose charisma proved ephemeral, as well as on the chain of events that radicalised this generation of students. Those who came just a few years later and did not have that experience were presented with a revolutionary posture that too often confused militancy with radicalism.[70]

The Communist Party attracted some of the more serious New Left activists but not in numbers that arrested the decline in its membership. The newcomers brought an interest in reviving Marxist theory, having discovered the humanist writings of the young Marx and the works of innovative Western Marxists such as György Lukács and Antonio Gramsci, before they returned to the anti-humanist scholasticism of Louis Althusser, so that concepts such as alienation and reification, hegemony and organic intellectuals, and then over-determination and determination in the last instance, challenged the crude determinism of communist orthodoxy. The guardians of that orthodoxy had no intention of accommodating them. As the course of events in France showed, communists were caught by surprise when protest erupted in 1968. It began there with May Day demonstrations that bypassed the Parti Communiste Français (PCF) and Confédération Générale du Travail. Hence the caustic reaction of Georges Marchais, shortly to become leader of the French party, who derided 'these pseudo-revolutionaries who claim to give the working class movement lessons' as spoiled children of the haute bourgeoisie who would go on to 'run daddy's business'. Some members of the Australian party felt the same about their own revolting students. Edgar Ross, who condemned their lax morality as 'permissiveness run mad', considered them a symptom of capitalist decadence.[71]

There was, however, a crucial difference between the two parties. The PCF was hostile to the New Left from the outset. The CPA, despite an initially equivocal response to events in France, embraced them and even sponsored an Australian tour by Roger Garaudy, a leading French communist expelled because of his support for the students. It also welcomed another challenge to the communist order, that of Alexander Dubček, who upon becoming first secretary of the Communist Party of Czechoslovakia at the beginning of 1968 embarked on a far-reaching program of liberal reform, and it was outspoken in its condemnation of the USSR and other Warsaw Pact countries for crushing the Czech experiment in socialist democracy just eight months later. Under new leadership, a party that for so long deferred to the authority of others had become conspicuously independent.

★

The invasion of Czechoslovakia stretched the party's relationship with the CPSU to breaking point. Their differences, which could be traced back to the vacillation in choosing between China and Russia, accumulated over the course of the decade. The CPA expressed concern when Khrushchev was summarily deposed in 1964, and in the same year criticised the treatment of Jews in the Soviet Union.[72] Laurie and Eric Aarons raised both matters on separate visits to Moscow, without success, and Eric caused further offence by refusing to attach the CPA's name to a Soviet attack on the Chinese party.[73] Subsequently, the Australian party regretted the gaoling of two dissident writers, Andrei Sinyavsky and Yuri Daniel, on a charge of 'anti-Soviet propaganda and agitation', though it was not alone in this disapproval—many European communist parties did so too. And when Laurie Aarons was in Moscow in 1967 for the 50th anniversary of the Russian Revolution, he used a seminar on socialism and democracy to urge his hosts to allow greater freedom. There was no further financial assistance to the CPA after 1967.[74]

In all these instances, it was the negligible party that rebuked the dominant one in a reversal of roles reminiscent of the Cold War satire *The Mouse That Roared*. In doing so the leaders proceeded cautiously, since a number of Australian communists regarded any criticism of the Soviet Union as tantamount to lèse-majesté. The loyalists took particular exception to an article by Lloyd Churchward on the shortcomings of Soviet democracy that appeared in a special issue of *Tribune* marking the anniversary of the Russian Revolution. Even though Aarons had just voiced his own criticism, he felt compelled to allow two other delegates in Moscow to express strong disagreement with Churchward's forensic examination of the Soviet system, and the political committee reprimanded Alec Robertson for commissioning it.[75]

Such circumspection ended with the abrupt suppression of the Czechoslovakian reform movement. The CPA's response was heightened by the keen interest it had taken in the Prague Spring. Bernie Taft made the first of several visits to Czechoslovakia in February 1968, and two *Tribune* correspondents, Eric Thornton and Malcolm Salmon, reported events there. Laurie Aarons, along with Taft, was seized with the wider significance of the Czech party's program, which the philosopher Radovan Richta described as building socialism with a human face. Communists had hitherto taken power in underdeveloped countries against fierce resistance that predisposed them to adopt a command economy with centralised decision-making and draconian powers of enforcement. If only to breathe new life into the socialist ideal, revive the stagnant economy and restore popular enthusiasm, the stifling controls had to be removed. Admirers such as Aarons and Taft thus saw the willingness of the Communist Party of Czechoslovakia to devolve decision-making and embrace freedom of thought, expression and assembly as providing a new model of advanced socialist democracy that other ruling parties should follow.[76]

For that very reason, the changes in Czechoslovakia alarmed the communist regimes of Eastern Europe. Dubček had assumed office with the support of Leonid Brezhnev, the general secretary of the CPSU, who could see the stifling effects of the previous regime, but the increasing assertiveness of trade unions, students and churches in exercising their new freedoms called into question the leading role of the party. Fearing the Prague Spring would spread into their countries, the rulers of the USSR, East Germany, Poland, Hungary and Bulgaria met with Czech representatives in the Slovakian capital of Bratislava in early August and obtained an agreement that each would maintain 'the leading role of the working class and its vanguard, the communist party'.[77] But this affirmation did not go far enough, and Brezhnev, whose own position was becoming insecure, pleaded with Dubček to restore censorship and purge his party of dissidents. Eighteen days after the Bratislava declaration, and nineteen days before a special congress of the Czechoslovakian party could meet to approve and consolidate the reforms, 200,000 troops and 5000 tanks of the Warsaw Pact forces invaded the country to arrest Dubček.[78]

Throughout the mounting crisis, the Australian party affirmed its support for the reform movement and warned the CPSU that any interference would be disastrous. Immediately Laurie Aarons heard the news of the invasion at around midday on 21 August, he convened an emergency meeting of the national executive that lasted into the evening. It issued a statement condemning the 'clear violation of the socialist principle of national self-determination' and warning it would 'cause untold harm to the whole cause of socialism'. The statement was published in 80,000 copies of a special issue of *Tribune* and followed by protest meetings in the principal cities.[79]

Yet even before the Soviet Union launched the invasion of Czechoslovakia, some members were defending its right to do so. Anticipating what became known as the Brezhnev doctrine after the

Soviet leader declared later in the year that any threat to any country in the socialist bloc would be treated as a threat to them all, these communists held that, as in Hungary twelve years earlier, it was necessary to prevent a counter-revolution. All members of the national executive supported the CPA's statement of condemnation and only two members of the national committee opposed it, though others argued the criticism of the Soviet Union should be balanced by acknowledgement of the Dubček government's provocations. At state and district conferences in the closing months of 1968, a significant minority of delegates voted against the national executive's position.[80]

In keeping with the party's commitment to open debate, these dissidents were able to continue the argument in the correspondence columns of *Tribune*. After several months of unproductive polemics, Alec Robertson began a forum on 'Socialism and the USSR' with two lengthy articles, one a reasoned defence by Ralph Gibson of its leading role and the other a carefully measured argument by Eric Aarons that by its actions it had forfeited that role and that the only possible basis of future relations between communist parties was independence and equality. If the purpose was to take the heat out of the subject, the contributions that appeared over the following six weeks (and lack of space prevented publication of many more) were sharply polarised. Together with some other sources, this correspondence makes it possible to identify the critics and their grievances.[81]

Most were communist veterans habituated to unwavering support of the USSR. They included Edgar Ross and the South Australian Jim Mitchell (the two members of the national committee who opposed the resolution on Czechoslovakia), Eliot and Della Elliott, Sam Lewis, Edgar Ross, Judah Waten and Alf Watt, the former editor of *Tribune*, and his wife Ray. Others, equally set in their ways but no longer active, suddenly sprang to life. Jack Henry, who had to make up arrears in his party dues so that he could celebrate the invasion of Czechoslovakia as 'good' triumphing over 'evil', 'brotherly love' over a 'foul witches' brew' of revisionism, appeared, along with Les Sullivan, who hadn't been heard of for years, Mick Ryan and Ted Docker. Edgar Ross claimed that J.B. Miles also emerged from retirement to denounce 'the scoundrels down at

Day Street', and had a vinyl record of his conversation with the Old Man to confirm it. The pattern here is of former leading members clinging to nostalgic memories of a monolithic communist movement.[82]

That is not true of Bill and Freda Brown, both full-time party workers and personal friends of Laurie and Carol Aarons. Bill had run foul of party discipline in 1956 by taking the revelations of Stalin's dictatorship too seriously, and the task of admonishing him had fallen to Laurie. Thereafter he was a sedulous supporter of all things Soviet. As the principal organiser in New South Wales and a member of the national executive, Brown had yet to come out in open opposition, but his constant quibbling caused Laurie no end of vexation. Conversely, such former authorities on the theory and practice of communism as Harry Gould and Ernie Campbell broke their silence to pour scorn on Soviet apologetics, as did Ernie Thornton and Rupert Lockwood.[83]

From complaining of the overhasty and one-sided nature of the national executive's statement on Czechoslovakia, the critics were soon alleging the party had fallen into the hands of anti-Soviet renegades. The very slogan 'socialism with a human face', they claimed, insulted other socialist countries by implying that theirs was an inhuman face. The CPA's move into the anti-Soviet camp was variously attributed to intellectuals, Trotskyists, Zionists and student radicals, whose influence was detected in the democratic rights charter developed following the 21st Congress and the adventurist industrial policy the party imposed on its union officials. A common complaint was the lack of respect for members who had given long years of service and now were supposedly denied a hearing. The irony that those making this charge were champions of democratic centralism and were allowed to express their opinion in a party publication escaped them.[84]

Even before the CPA condemned the invasion of Czechoslovakia, the Soviet Embassy was cultivating dissidents. Bill Brown was its best-placed contact and continued to work closely with embassy officials after he lost his organiser's position in October 1968. There was no suggestion at this stage, however, that the critics would leave the party. 'It is our party and we intend to get control of it,' one of Brown's allies said.[85] Nor did the Soviet officials want them to leave. Their strategy was to support the dissidents in their criticism of the directions the party was taking and assist them to dislodge its leaders.

An international conference of communist parties created further discord. The first such meeting since 1960, it was intended to declare support for the Soviet Union against China. The multilingual Bernie Taft made a nuisance of himself as the Australian representative at preliminary meetings of the consultative committee during 1968, though the conference had to be postponed until June 1969 because of the invasion of Czechoslovakia. Taft accompanied Laurie Aarons to Moscow for the occasion, and by meeting beforehand with Italian communists in Rome and Tito in Belgrade the two Australians signalled their intention to rock the boat. Defying the declaration that Czechoslovakia was off limits, Aarons took the opportunity to explicitly criticise the intervention and call for 'full and unequivocal support for the national independence, sovereignty and non-interference in the internal affairs of all nations'. He also criticised the conference documents for failing to give proper consideration to important new developments, including the revolutionary potential of youth. Australia was not alone in refusing to endorse the final resolution—so did a number of European parties, including the Italian—but it was one of the most outspoken.[86]

After the national committee spent a full day discussing Laurie Aarons' report on the Moscow conference, it agreed to adopt it by 27 votes to ten—those ten members having by this time consolidated into a pro-Soviet bloc. The committee also passed a resolution, this time with only two dissentients, warning members against the activities of an 'inner-Party opposition'. The activities included refusal to accept decisions of the national committee, canvassing members to oppose party policies, collecting money to publish material critical of the policies, and holding discussions to gain control of the next party congress.[87]

★

The admonition had no effect. Members of the opposition continued to meet, organise and disrupt efforts to promote the party's policies. Meetings of the national committee remained bogged down in intractable disagreement. Rather than give his opponents time to prepare for the national congress due in mid-1970, Laurie Aarons brought it forward to the end of March.[88] The change, announced only a few weeks before the end of 1969, triggered a scramble to elect delegates to district and state conferences, which in turn elected the congress delegates. The officials were clearly advantaged, since they could call on the assistance of full-time party workers, though every effort was made to allow the opposition to put its case. When Edgar Ross objected in the national committee to the draft of the principal document, Aarons invited him to suggest an alternative and it appeared in the first pre-congress issue of the journal now named simply *Discussion*. In a remarkable departure from past practice, the two sides also conducted a series of formal debates.[89]

The principal document, entitled simply a *Statement of Aims, Methods and Organisation*, recapitulated the ideas put forward in 1967, only in a more radical register. The scientific and technological revolution was now seen as vital because it magnified the contradictions between the forces and relations of production at the expense of humanity and the environment, and thus opened new possibilities for a socialist revolution in Australia. Similarly, the Coalition of the Left was restated in terms far more critical of the earlier united front of the Labor and Communist parties, which was dismissed as a relic of the Cold War based on a very limited program of reform. The coalition was now to embrace 'union militants, students, intellectuals, anarchists and libertarians' on a basis of mutual respect, tolerance and openness that would provide an assurance of democracy in a future socialist society. To this was added a new assessment of the USSR and its satellites as 'socialist-based countries' that had created the economic base for socialism but had not yet established a socialist order and still suffered from over-centralised control, bureaucracy, dogmatism, curtailment of democracy and denial of freedom. They too would experience crises and upheavals if their present policies remained.[90]

Once regarded as an exemplar of orthodoxy, Laurie Aarons had emerged as the most radical of Australian communists. In restoring the word 'revolution' to the party's vocabulary, he called for 'a fearless and critical testing of all our fundamental ideas'. Older ideas, particularly those that had been distorted under Stalinism, no longer served the liberating mission that the *Statement of Aims* encompassed in its call for 'self-management, direct control, socialist democracy, freedom for science and art'. Here again he relied heavily on the scientific and technological revolution, with its need for 'free and inquiring' minds and its potential for serving 'the material and spiritual needs' of humanity.[91]

The alternative, as Aarons saw it, was stagnation and decline if the party failed to adjust its thinking, tactics and methods of organisation to the new circumstances; continued its narrow approach to industrial activity; confined its political program to proposals acceptable to the left of the Labor Party; ignored the revolutionary spirit of the young; and restricted internationalism to uncritical support of every policy and action of the Soviet Union. 'We are speaking,' he told delegates on the opening day of the 22nd Congress, 'of the party's future, of the need to build for that future about which we are optimistic and even confident.'[92]

The 130 delegates were joined at Day Street by 50 observers, some of whom were invited to speak in a further break with tradition. A number of resolutions confirmed the party's international stand: by 112 votes to eighteen, congress endorsed the 1968 statement on the occupation of Czechoslovakia and the 1969 one on the Moscow conference, with a further declaration for good measure that 'no other Party should interfere in any way in efforts to influence Party members or bodies'. The *Statement of Aims, Methods and Organisation* and another document on *Modern Unionism and the Workers' Movement* were adopted by a similar margin. There were further changes to the party's constitution, setting limits on the tenure of the national officers and turning branches into 'centres of united revolutionary action'.[93]

Those seeking to renew the communist project had clearly prevailed. Perhaps the margin of victory was excessive, for it was generally agreed that a substantial minority of members were critical of the party's stand on Czechoslovakia. That did not mean they rejected the policies the congress adopted or embraced the allegations of betrayal made against the leaders, but they did support the opposition group in its affirmation of loyalty to the Soviet Union. Now, as the result of the elections conducted during the congress, the opposition was deprived of a voice. Bill and Freda Brown, Geoffrey Curthoys, Eliot Elliott, Ralph Gibson,

Jim Mitchell, Edgar Ross, Judah Waten and Tom Wright were all voted off the national committee, leaving only Pat Clancy, who along with Bill Brown was dropped from the national executive.

The leaders were in no mood to compromise. The fight against the opposition had absorbed too much time and energy, distracted the party from getting on with urgent tasks and so weakened morale that disheartened members were still dropping out. In 1969, when the executive warned the opposition against violating rules prohibiting factional conduct, it called for 'deeper study' of the issues in dispute as the means of restoring unity. The belief that genuine communists needed only a clear explanation to reach understanding and acceptance was deeply ingrained, as was the expectation that once a decision was reached it was binding. Hence Laurie wrote in the aftermath of the congress that implementation of the resolutions was 'a basic requirement for Party unity'.[94]

The call for unity arises when a political party is unable to resolve its differences. Sometimes unity is sought inclusively by making concessions to accommodate the differences. Communist parties, which with their emphasis on doctrinal purity found it much harder to accept there could be legitimate differences, typically used the organisational rules of democratic centralism to enforce unity through exclusion. The Communist Party of Australia shed most of these monolithic practices in the course of the 1960s. It allowed and indeed encouraged members to debate policy, recognised and tolerated the existence of an opposition, strengthened the democratic provisions in its constitution and reduced the centralist ones. But one vestige of the old order remained following the leaders' crushing victory over the pro-Soviet oppositionists in 1970: the conviction that the party was better off without them. Alone and unaided, the Communist Party of Australia set off on its new path.

Epilogue

The funeral of Jim Healy was reputedly the largest in Sydney since that of Henry Lawson in 1922. Ports around the country came to a halt as news of his death circulated on Thursday 13 July 1961, as they did for his funeral on the following Monday. It was held at the Waterside Workers' Federation's building in Sussex Street, where his body lay in state over the weekend. Loudspeakers played Chopin's Funeral March as mourners filed past to pay their respects, and then broadcast the proceedings to those who stood in the rain, unable to find a place inside. After tributes from trade union leaders, the mourners formed ranks to escort the hearse through the city to Central Railway Station. The ABC put their number at 7000, and many more pedestrians stood in respect as the cortege, a mile long, passed down George Street. Several thousand made the trip out to the Rookwood Cemetery, where Lance Sharkey delivered the final eulogy. He declared that new generations would carry on the work of this most lovable communist, who would be vindicated by the inevitable triumph of the cause to which he devoted his life, the emancipation of labour.[1]

Three years later a plaque honouring Big Jim was unveiled in the main hall of the party's new premises in Day Street, which became the Jim Healy Memorial Hall—fittingly, since it overlooked the waterfront where men laboured as little more than beasts of burden until he helped reclaim their human dignity. Noel Counihan painted a vast mural on one of the walls in the following year depicting the progress of humanity from servitude and suffering to freedom and happiness.[2]

It was here that Lance Sharkey was farewelled in 1967 following his death from a coronary occlusion. The coffin lay in state for the morning of Wednesday 17 May, draped with the Australian and red flags and flanked by four party officials. At 1 p.m. Richard Dixon, who had worked so closely with Sharkey for more than 30 years without ever enjoying his full confidence, delivered the eulogy. He concluded with the passage from the Russian novelist Nikolai Ostrovsky that was used so often in communist obsequies: 'man's dearest possession is life' and since it is given just once he must use it so he can say at the end that he gave his all to 'the finest cause in the world, the liberation of humanity'. There was no talk this time of the inevitable victory of that cause.[3]

Following the eulogy, the coffin was taken past Trades Hall in Goulburn Street, a party stronghold when Sharkey joined it in 1922, and then another landmark, the building in George Street that once had 'Marx House' emblazoned in red. The press estimated 1000 mourners followed it to Railway Square and again many went by car to Rookwood Cemetery for the cremation. Roger Milliss, then working at Day Street for *Tribune*, encountered comrades he had not seen for years, many of whom had left or been pushed out of the party but came to pay their grudging last respects. He was also struck by a mishap that occurred as the coffin was carried from the Jim Healy Memorial Hall. A scratchy record of the Internationale became stuck on the line 'Comrades come rally'.[4]

There were many communist funerals over this decade. Idris Williams and Ted Rowe, two unionists from the glory days, died in 1960. So too did Helen Palmer's uncle Esmonde Higgins, who was one of the party's earliest intellectuals; and four years later his friend Jack Kavanagh, its leader until Miles and Sharkey removed him in the early 1930s. Jean Devanny, with whom Miles had a stormy relationship, died in 1962; and Christian Jollie-Smith, a founder member who did much of the party's legal work, in 1963. Another lawyer died in the same year, Max Julius, from a Brisbane family almost as prolific in communists as the Aaronses. Two dedicated functionaries, Len Donald and Norm Jeffery, were lost in 1965 and 1966. Dave Morris succumbed to cancer in Moscow in 1968, and his widow Bernice returned to Australia with their two sons. J.B. Miles and Katharine Susannah Prichard went in 1969, as did Ernie Thornton and Alex Macdonald, the widely respected secretary of the Queensland Trades and Labor Council. Bruce Milliss died in 1970, Sam Aarons in 1971.

Then there were local heroes. Marj Nunan was a stalwart of the Brunswick branch of the party and an invalid pensioner, suffering from a chronic disorder of the joints. She devoted her energies to campaigning for greater support for pensioners, with protests, petitions and deputations; and, as founder of the Combined Pensioners' Association of Victoria from 1954, she led an annual delegation to the federal treasurer on the eve of the budget. Her funeral, in 1963, conducted by Frank Hartley and Alf Dickie, attracted a crowd of 1500. Another member of the Brunswick branch, Ruth Crow, helped produce *A People's Program for Brunswick* at the end of the war; a quarter century later she and her husband Maurie worked on a larger canvas with their three-volume *Plan for Melbourne*.[5]

After 1971 it was no longer possible to farewell fallen comrades from the party's headquarters. Declining membership and diminished income forced it to give up the large Day Street building for a smaller one around the corner in Dixon Street. Communists had lost keeping places before—such as the honour board for comrades who fought in the Second World War, which had to be removed when Marx House was sold at the end of the 1940s—but the loss of the Jim Healy Memorial Hall in 1971 had a larger significance. As the 22nd Congress proclaimed the CPA's independence with bold new policies, there were hopes it would recover lost ground. Instead it continued to dwindle. The resolutions adopted at that congress were meant to settle differences that had been so contentious and absorbed so much energy. They did not, and even after the traditionalists left, argument continued between those calling for an even sharper break with the past and those who wanted to call a halt.

In keeping with the new openness, Guido Baracchi was one of the speakers at the party's celebration of its 50th anniversary. This founding member, who somehow retained his innocence despite twice being expelled, said the quality he found most heartening in today's communist party was its democracy. Although he and the other founders had talked in 1920 about democracy, 'we didn't know the meaning of the word', whereas the CPA must now be 'the most democratic communist party in the world'.[6] Yet even allowing for its greatly reduced state, the commemoration of the fiftieth anniversary was a pale shadow of that staged 25 years earlier. In 1945 the party presented itself as the guide and inspiration of the Australian people. In 1970 it was clearing away the dogmas that had brought it undone. Back then it was a dutiful member of a world movement; now it was at odds with other communist parties. Former comrades were still honoured for their dedication and sacrifice, but the party itself was no longer memorialised.

*

Once Australian communists began debating the past, it was hard to stop. Late in 1966, just as the executive declared there would be no restrictions on pre-congress discussion, *Tribune* carried a review of the memoirs of an ex-communist, *Once a Jolly Comrade*, in which the former Victorian functionary Keith McEwan related a story of high hopes turning to disillusionment. Bill Wood, the reviewer, who specialised in discrediting works of this kind with orotund mockery, ridiculed McEwan's claim that he had to screw up his courage to write the book because ex-members who publicised their departure were invariably vilified as traitors. 'Actually', Wood stated, 'the few people who drop out of the CPA' did so, like those who left other organisations, for 'a whole variety of reasons'.[7]

This breezy denial of the exodus from the party's ranks prompted Ted Zeffert, an outspoken member of the Western Australian state committee, to point out that a large number of communists had left for a particular reason—because they were denied the right to speak their mind. Besides, there was little point in assuring members that all views were welcome if former members were to be pilloried in this manner. That brought Jack McPhillips into the fray. One of Laurie Aarons' first steps on becoming national secretary had been to replace him as national industrial organiser and, although he left behind a string of election losses in unions that had once been communist, McPhillips remained as domineering and abrasive as ever. He not only rejected Zeffert's assertion that many had left because they were denied the right to dissent but queried the legitimacy of this 'new fangled' and 'much vaunted' entitlement. Too often, he stated, it was mere camouflage for cowardice and desertion.[8]

McPhillips was used to laying down the law and his admonishment would once have settled the argument. On this occasion it continued, as

Roger Milliss reminded readers of the damage such intransigence had caused. He knew of a number of members, many of them still making a valuable contribution to progressive causes, who had been driven out of the party after 1956 for advancing views that were now official policy. McPhillips replied that he knew of no such instance: not one of the small number who left or were expelled at that time was denied the opportunity to state their views, and in any case those who now championed the right to dissent overlooked the requirement of democratic centralism that once an 'authoritative' party body reached a decision, there was an obligation to accept it. This was too much for Mavis Robertson—Mavis Moten during her youth work, Robertson as she took on senior duties and became one of the most forceful critics of the old guard. She gave examples of such victimisation and contrasted the past stifling of debate with the current acceptance of 'the fact that communists, whether leaders or not, have no monopoly of truth or right to deal dogmatically with members'.[9]

Some past wrongs were too difficult to set right. In 1966 Audrey Blake complained of the treatment of her husband in Ralph Gibson's recently published memoirs. Apart from some errors of fact, she objected to the failure to acknowledge Jack's contribution to the party and the attribution to him of sole responsibility for the disastrous prolongation of the miners' strike. This was part of a pattern of denigration, she said, 'about which I feel strongly and bitterly', and needed to be challenged if the party was 'to confront its past and find new ways of advance'.[10]

Her cause for complaint could have been better chosen. There was widespread affection for Gibson, who had served the party with selfless devotion, and a number of members regretted that Audrey should have used the appearance of *My Years in the Communist Party* to rake up these old grievances. Len Fox sprang to her defence. For him the central issue was whether the party could regain the prestige it lost after the war without a thorough examination of its mistakes. That could not happen while Blake and Henry were used as scapegoats for the sectarian excesses of the late 1940s and early 1950s in a power struggle that elevated Ted Hill to the secretariat with such damaging consequences. To this, the former functionary Harry Hatfield rejoined that Hill's ascent began when he worked with Blake in Victoria and that although Blake was not alone in the leftist errors, he was 'particularly responsible for them'.[11]

By the end of 1966 the political committee was considering complaints from both Blakes. Laurie Aarons met them and urged Audrey to reconsider a letter of resignation triggered by Hatfield's article in *Tribune*, but she was adamant she no longer wanted to be in the party. Jack did and gave notice that he wanted the 1953 statement 'For Party Consolidation' that blamed him for left adventurism to be reconsidered. Here the willingness to confront the past faltered. The euphemistically entitled consolidation of the leadership whereby Sharkey and Hill dispatched Blake and Henry was a particularly squalid episode of intra-party intrigue, and the political committee decided that reopening it would bring out little that was new or helpful. As a partial concession, it agreed that Blake's other grievance, his censure for speaking out in the central committee against the invasion of Hungary, could be raised in the pre-congress *Discussion Journal*, and that was where he observed he alone was prepared to acknowledge a Stalinist past.[12]

Consolidation continued to prey on Blake's mind, and in 1980 he spoke on it at a conference in Melbourne on the history of 'Communists and the Labour Movement'. As a result the national committee appointed a commission (Eric Aarons, Bernie Taft and Elliott Johnston, who by then was a Queen's Counsel) to conduct an investigation. Only Jack remained of the members of the secretariat, but the commission interviewed three members of the political committee and listened to recorded interviews with several more. Ted Hill refused to participate, however, and the commission was unable to establish a complete record of events. It found that Blake and Henry shared responsibility for sectarian errors but these were errors of the leadership as a whole; that Blake was submitted to 'extraordinary moral pressure' to make his statement of self-criticism, pressures that were wrong and inimical to the truth; and that a clear injustice had been done.[13]

Some who worked to free the party from its past had given up. Among them was Rex Mortimer, who during the 1960s was both a participant in and commentator on the party's 'painful search for the sources of revitalisation'. In one of his commentaries he tried to give readers of the English theoretical journal *New Left Review* an understanding of the Australian party's puzzling trajectory. His starting point was its influence in trade unions, far greater than that of any other communist party in the English-speaking world, and its theoretical paucity. Except for a few years after 1949, the CPA paid only lip-service to warnings against economism. Lenin's *What Is to Be Done?*, a foundational text in party classes, was completely disregarded in its industrial work. Few Western communist parties, Mortimer explained, had resisted change for so long or so tenaciously as the CPA, crouched behind its besieged trade union bulwarks and denuded of its intellectual battalions. It took the pro-Chinese breakaway in 1962 to administer a shock severe enough to initiate a 'uniquely permissive and forthright discussion' of future directions.[14]

Mortimer, a founder of *Arena*, was an evangelist of the scientific and technological revolution. He claimed it would stimulate unions to give up their preoccupation with better pay and conditions and take on a more active role in determining industry policy. By bringing union militants and left-wing intellectuals together for this purpose, furthermore, the party would dispel the conviction of young radicals that the organised labour movement was 'archaic, sclerotic, intolerant and socially conservative'.[15] But Mortimer became disheartened by his failure to revive the *Guardian* and the collapse of his marriage. As his former wife, a psychologist, told Bernie Taft, 'one has to be an extremely tough person to survive' protracted factional conflict and Rex was not. He continued to serve on the national committee but, after embarking on an academic career, felt increasingly an outsider and resigned from the party in 1969.[16]

There were other departures. Rupert Lockwood wished the new leaders every success in their endeavours but dropped out soon after he returned from Moscow in 1968. He had been there for three years as *Tribune*'s correspondent under an arrangement made in 1961, when the CPA renounced Mao, whereby the host country met all the expenses. The first of these 'special correspondents' was the veteran journalist Rex Chiplin, of whom it was said he never doubted the Soviet Union until he lived in it. The theft of the doormat outside his apartment completed Chiplin's disillusionment and he resigned as soon as he arrived back in Sydney in 1963, reportedly telling an official in Market Street that 'if that is socialism you can stick it up your arse'. Alf Watt, his successor, faithfully reported the richness of Soviet democracy, the wisdom of its leaders (save for Khrushchev, whose sudden fall from grace he attributed to violation of the principles of collective leadership) and the unity and enthusiasm of the people.[17]

Lockwood, who took up the post in early 1965, had the distinction of being under surveillance by both Australian and Soviet security. While most of his reports were based on handouts from the press department of the Foreign Ministry, he made himself unpopular by mixing in the wrong company and taking undue interest in the trials of Soviet dissidents. For a few months after Lockwood returned in March 1968, he accepted invitations to speak at party events and tried to distinguish the Soviet ideal from the grim reality he had witnessed; by the time of the invasion of Czechoslovakia he had retreated into inactivity.[18] While his letter of resignation in October 1969 was brief, the five feature articles he published in the *Australian* three months later gave a characteristically trenchant account of his disenchantment. Lockwood's recourse to the capitalist press drew predictable condemnation, notably from communist members of the Waterside Workers' Federation whose journal he was still editing. A more cogent criticism was that he had left 'just in time to avoid standing up to be counted in the final showdown with the few surviving hard-liners'.[19]

Frank Hardy encountered a similar reaction at the beginning of 1969, when in Frank Packer's *Bulletin* he declared his loss of faith. The Seamen's Union condemned his 'false and vicious anti-Soviet' slander, and several party branches demanded he be expelled.[20] Hardy was at this time championing the Gurindji people who had walked off the Wave Hill pastoral station in pursuit of land rights. He was in London picketing the head office of Vestey's, the pastoral company, when the tanks rolled into Prague, and his indictment of 'Stalin's Heirs' first appeared in the *Sunday Times* following a visit to the Czech capital. The party had encouraged Hardy to use his skills as a publicist to bring the struggle of the Gurindji to national attention, and left-wing unions assisted him in doing so, but here again he angered members by claiming all the credit and complaining of a lack of support.[21]

Some years later Hardy dealt with the disintegrative effects of Czechoslovakia in a novel, *But the Dead Are Many*. It portrays two communists, one a guilt-ridden organiser who is shaken by 1956 and driven to suicide by 1968, the other his closest friend who seeks to understand how they were both so mistaken in clinging to a utopian dream. The two men share an obsession with the show trial and execution in 1938 of an Old Bolshevik whose primer on communism they read as recruits and whose fate prefigures their own disillusionment. As with Hardy's other novels, the people on whom these characters are based are easily recognisable: they are Nikolai Bukharin, the co-author of *The ABC of Communism*, Paul Mortier, who had to give up his party work because of clinical depression in 1964 and committed suicide a year later, and Frank Hardy himself. Mortier's widow Dulcie entrusted Hardy with letters, confidences and (she claimed) money to write the book, and spent hours going over the manuscript with him only to discover that the published version restored passages traducing her husband he had agreed to remove. She was not alone in criticising the book, though Laurie Aarons launched it and Eric gave it a generous review.[22]

Frank Hardy remained an obstreperous party presence into the 1980s, and his funeral service in the Collingwood Town Hall in 1994 drew a large crowd. Gabi Hollows recalled how he persuaded her ophthalmologist husband Fred, an equally unruly communist, to treat the eye disease of Gurindji stockmen, initiating the trachoma program still conducted internationally by the Fred Hollows Foundation. Gough Whitlam, whom Hardy persuaded to take up the Gurindji cause, began a lengthy exposition of the Commonwealth power over Indigenous affairs when he glanced at the coffin, decorated with the Eureka and Indigenous flags, and broke down.[23]

The following year, 1970, marked the end of *Outlook*. It had begun in 1957 as a forum for ex-communists to discuss questions the party would not allow to be discussed, and as some sort of substitute for the feeling of belonging that membership had provided. It eschewed any formal organisation, partly—as Ian Turner put it—as a hangover from communist indoctrination against factionalism; partly because 'we had had a gutful of organisation'; and partly because 'we didn't know what sort of organisation we wanted'. By 1970 there were a number of left organisations, each with its own periodical, and the editorial board realised that *Outlook* had little appeal for the new generation of radicals. As an obituary notice in *Tribune* put it, *Outlook* failed to keep up with the times. From 1957 until the mid-1960s, the writer acknowledged, it was the only means whereby socialists who opposed 'the deformations of socialism in the Soviet Union and China' could express themselves. Though he or she did not say so, *Tribune* itself now offered them that opportunity.[24]

★

From the time of its formation, the Communist Party of Australia drew inspiration and guidance from the makers of the Russian Revolution. As best it could, this fledgling organisation adopted their model of a vanguard party and followed directives disseminated through the Communist International. The degeneration of the Soviet Union under Stalin only increased this dependence: the Australian party attained its greatest following at the peak of popularity for the wartime Soviet ally, just as it declined rapidly with the onset of Cold War hostilities. By then, however, there were other communist countries. Thrown into disarray by Khrushchev's repudiation of Stalinism, some Australians turned to China as an alternative model.

Adherence to another country's communism required adherence to its policies and strategies. Those who favoured the Soviet Union subscribed to the policy of peaceful coexistence between the socialist and capitalist camps, and believed the superiority of the socialist system made it possible to abolish capitalism without a violent upheaval. Those attracted to the People's Republic of China held there could be no lasting accommodation between the imperialist and communist powers, and that capitalists would never submit to a peaceful transition to socialism. Beyond such doctrinal disagreements, moreover, were differences of organisation and method: the top-down vanguard party of the Soviet model with its rigid discipline and the Chinese emphasis on mass mobilisation and requirement for members to constantly monitor their innermost thoughts for any sign of wavering.

The choice between these alternatives, it should be stressed, rested with the CPA. Just as the obligations it imposed on members relied entirely on their willingness to accept them, neither Moscow nor Beijing had any way of enforcing the fealty of Western communist parties. Besides, the circumstances that gave rise to the Russian and Chinese revolutions could scarcely be more different from those in Australia. They occurred in overwhelmingly rural, poverty-stricken societies following long and costly wars that fatally weakened their autocratic regimes. Of necessity, the rules laid down by the Communist International had to be adapted to a prosperous country with an organised working class and a secure system of parliamentary democracy. The endeavour to apply Maoist precepts to Australia verged on fantasy.

Once the Australian party drew back from its flirtation with the Communist Party of China, there could be no return to unquestioning acceptance of guidance by the Soviet party. The falling-out of Moscow and Beijing forced the CPA to consider the arguments of both disputants. Having done so, it would never again give unconditional support for Soviet actions or arguments. By this time, moreover, whatever prestige the Soviet Union possessed as the first and most advanced socialist country had been lost. A series of disagreements in the 1960s over its repression of dissent strained relations between the two parties; the crushing of the Prague Spring damaged them beyond repair.

Initially the CPSU encouraged its Australian supporters to take back control of the CPA. When the decisive defeat of the pro-Soviet faction at the 1970 congress demonstrated that was a forlorn endeavour, it turned to building a party within the party, and after the organisers of this apparatus were expelled the Soviet Union gave a green light to a separate organisation. The Socialist Party of Australia (SPA) was formally established in December 1971.[25] This second split was more damaging than the first. It cost the party some 800 members, including officials of the building and maritime unions, though not all of them joined the SPA—for lifelong adherents such as Tom Wright there could only be one party. Recognition by the CPSU also gave the SPA standing in the international communist movement, but since it was held together by little more than hostility to the CPA and unconditional support for the USSR, it struggled to make headway.

The loss of 800 members was, nevertheless, a serious blow. They were drawn from every state and represented a fifth of the membership. Weekly sales of *Tribune* fell from 12,830 in 1969 to just over 9000 in the aftermath of the congress. The departures also forced a new round of economies, so that the number of functionaries and other employees (including those working for subsidiaries such as the Newsletter Printery in Forest Hill) was cut from 138 to 72. Thirty-seven of these had state responsibilities (twelve in New South Wales, thirteen in Victoria, eight in Queensland) and 35 worked in Sydney on national duties. Contraction made the party even more New South Wales–centric. Twenty-four of the 37 members of the national committee came from the premier state, eight of the twelve members of the national executive.[26]

In 1971, even more than in 1963, there was an expectation the party would benefit from the removal of disruptive elements. A unified body of a single mind and purpose, first expounded in Lenin's *What Is to Be Done?* (1902), was a foundational principle of the Bolsheviks. *Better Fewer, But Better* (1923), his last published work, reiterated the precept that it was better to sacrifice the size of a party organisation than compromise its standards. It was thus possible for Australian communists to regard the departure of Ted Hill and his followers as a painful necessity to rid their party of 'left adventurism'. The decampment of the Muscovites, on the other hand, brought a release of new energy.

It allowed the party to engage more effectively with other activists along the pluralist, democratic lines suggested in its strategy of building a Coalition of the Left. The peace movement provides a good example. As public opinion turned against conscription for the Vietnam War, and the government's entire posture of suppressing communism in Southeast Asia by armed intervention lay in tatters, the anti-war movement planned a nationwide protest. The Vietnam Moratorium Campaign began in November 1969 with a meeting in Canberra of representatives of anti-war groups called by the NSW and Victorian peace organisations through which communists worked.

Their decision to set up organising committees in each state for a nationwide protest came under immediate challenge from student activists who wanted a more confrontational strategy. In the past these militants would have been rebuffed and the communist organisers would have ensured as orderly a demonstration as possible. On this occasion, however, the party determined that all participants should have a voice in planning the Moratorium, and communist participants argued successfully for as broad a campaign as possible, in suburbs, factories, schools and offices as well as an occupation of the city centre, but with no watering down of the demand for immediate withdrawal of Australian forces. This strategy was most successful in Victoria, where the party had good relations with the left of the Labor Party and Jim Cairns led 70,000 protestors into central Melbourne on the afternoon of Friday 8 May 1970.[27]

The new forms of engagement the party's independence fostered are nowhere better illustrated than its embrace of feminism. During the protracted battle with the supporters of the Soviet Union, Freda Brown resisted any interference in her leadership of the Union of Australian Women, which continued to campaign against discrimination by means of resolutions and deputations. Shortly before her resignation in 1971 to join the SPA, she complained that 'The Party is all out in support of Women's Liberation, seems more concerned with abortion, the right to use filthy language etc. than basic questions of prices, etc.'.[28] Mavis Robertson and Joyce Stevens encouraged participation in the Women's Liberation movement as it emerged at this time with its goal of overthrowing the oppression of women.[29]

It was the forerunner of other movements of liberation based on sexuality, ethnicity and other forms of identity, which the party would embrace. Similarly, its new and more inclusive approach in the Vietnam Moratorium was mirrored in a range of other causes, such as environmental activism. Communists had previously applied a class analysis to their work in auxiliaries and fronts, but these 'new social movements' resisted that unifying framework. They were new in the sense that they were not class based and not concerned with materialist grievances arising from the capitalist economy. Each of them involved a coalition of participants from different backgrounds held together by no more than a concern for that issue.

Finally, communist involvement in these new forms of activism revealed the party's altered status. In its heyday the Communist Party was the sole custodian of Marxism as a theory of revolutionary change and the only plausible alternative to the Labor Party as an organiser of working-class politics. By 1970 there were a number of organisations, each offering its own version of Marxism and claiming a presence in the labour movement. A single, monolithic party had become one among many.

The consequences went further. It was noted at the outset of this volume that communism was a unique combination of ideology and practice that offered its adherents a complete and authoritative understanding of all fields of knowledge. Armed with this knowledge and equipped with an iron discipline as codified by Stalin, communists sought to impose leadership over every field of class conflict. But in refusing to entertain any alternative to their doctrine, communists turned it into a lifeless dogma, just as in conducting the class struggle by means of democratic centralism they allowed no alternative to their own position. Even initiatives to build a united front rested on the assumption that other parties would follow the communist lead. It was this assumption of control of the peace movement that Jack Blake rejected in an argument that led many years later to *Revolution from Within*, a book-length critique of Stalinism assisted by Helen Palmer, Geoff Sharp and Bob Gollan. It condemned Stalinism as a perversion of Marxism.[30]

It was also noted in the opening chapter that communism demanded an absolute commitment of time, energy and willingness to endure hostility. The party supported adherents with close ties of comradeship and the prestige of international accomplishments. It also enclosed and isolated them. Hence Jim Healy's admonishment of party members who drank in their own bars rather than mix with workmates with different political convictions. Such exclusiveness ill became a small and dwindling organisation.

For a quarter century after the Second World War, the advanced industrial countries maintained high rates of economic growth, rising living standards and a buoyant labour market. The contrast with the chronic instability before the war confounded communist expectations of deepening crises and sharpening class conflict. Through the gains they won for workers with their industrial militancy, Australian communists might even have dulled the edge of working-class discontent by turning casual, insecure employment into regular, secure jobs with better wages, paid leave and other entitlements. In the party's stronghold industries, they won additional concessions as a trade-off for the introduction of labour-saving productivity improvements.

Years later, when a leading organiser reflected on the collapse of the party in North Queensland, he singled out the advent of containerisation, which closed most of the region's smaller ports; permanency, which ended the practice whereby casual wharfies moved up and down the coast; and cane-cutting machines, which replaced nomadic seasonal workers in the sugar industry. These itinerant workers, he recalled, had nothing to lose by walking off the job, and they were the 'first to put their hands into their pockets for the party'.[31] Those who followed them had financial commitments and family responsibilities that inhibited such audacity. Besides, as permanent residents in rural localities they were exposed to the censure of neighbours. Similar changes eroded the occupational communities based on major ports, coalfields and centres of heavy industry as they shed labour, and car ownership freed the remaining workers from living in such close proximity to their work.

The end of the long boom is usually attributed to a crippling embargo imposed on the West by the oil-producing countries in 1973. In Australia this brought inflation, loss of export income and investment, business failure and a sharp rise in unemployment. The turmoil brought down the Whitlam government at the end of 1975, though trade unions resisted the measures of the Coalition led by Malcolm Fraser until a new Labor government led by Bob Hawke won office in 1983 with an undertaking to put Australia back to work. Many of the fixtures of the post-war class settlement were upended in the course of this decade: the benefits of a mixed economy, the capacity of government to maintain full employment, the need to regulate economic activity, including industrial relations, and a preference for collectivism over untrammelled individualism. The remaining communist union leaders would have a last hurrah with the negotiation of a Prices and Incomes Accord through which the unions participated in economic reconstruction during the 1980s, but by then neoliberalism was ascendant.

When members looked back on the party they served with such devotion, they remembered the causes it took up, the activities it made possible and the comradeship it provided more fondly than they did communist doctrine and organisation. By then the Soviet bloc was in terminal decline, Western communism a spent force, so it was hardly surprising they chose to recall the warm human qualities of an intense political engagement now lost beyond recall. The party itself has an ambiguous status in these memoirs, at once a source of guidance and inspiration and an unforgiving taskmaster that exacted unconditional loyalty.[32]

The temptation in writing communist history is to attribute all that was rewarding and admirable to communists while reserving censure for communism as an ideology and organisation. It is a false dichotomy. Party members were as varied in their personal qualities and as subject to the vagaries of human nature as lesser mortals. It was the party that brought them together, trained them in the practical tasks of political activism, lifted their sights beyond national boundaries, provided them with opportunities for education and cultural engagement, sustained and inspired them. In doing so it also made heavy demands, imposed an ideology that was not open to question, required them to suppress misgivings and blinded them to the reality of communist regimes.

By the 1960s that reality was undeniable. It fostered intense controversy between existing regimes and within nationally based parties: the illusion of a united international commitment fractured. The CPA stood out among the nationally based parties for its insistence on complete independence. The history related in this volume traces a painful passage to autonomy that ended in 1970, with two more decades of activity to follow until it was wound up in 1991. After 1970 it was no longer possible to take inspiration from any of the existing regimes or imagine they offered a model to be followed in Australia. The task was to rescue what remained valid and inspiring from the wreckage of a movement that had betrayed its ideals. That took communists into new policies and practices that require their own history.

The members who stayed the course were but a tiny fraction of those who had held a party card. Now ageing, those who joined in the 1940s could still recall the mass rallies during the war against fascism, the spectacle of national congresses that filled Sydney Town Hall, the hundreds of community plans distributed at the end of the war, the meaning and purpose they found in carrying out their duties. Sooner or later the overwhelming majority left, but not before leaving their mark on this country.

List of Illustrations

Cover: Speaker at a CPA street meeting in Sydney. University of Melbourne Archives, 1991.0152.00052 (front); students protest in Sydney regarding the invasion of Czechoslovakia, August 1968, ON 161, item 359, courtesy SEARCH Foundation (back).

Demonstration for Thomas and Ratliff. State Library of New South Wales, PXE 1034, Box 1. Courtesy SEARCH Foundation.

Second front demonstration. Australian War Memorial, image no. 136742.

Jack Blake addresses meeting on Yarra Bank, photograph by Albert Tucker, National Library of Australia, PICDRAWER PIC/3161.

Australia–Soviet Friendship Society march. Albert Tucker Photographic Collection, Heide Museum of Modern Art & State Library of Victoria, accession no. H2008.98/280.

A New Deal for Youth. State Library of New South Wales, MLMSS 7927, Box 1.

Marx School class. National Archives of Australia, A6122, 2861.

Election candidates. National Archives of Australia, A6122, 2861.

May Day march, 1943. University of Melbourne Archives, 1991-0152-00008.

Demonstration in support of the Red Army. State Library of New South Wales, PXE 1034. Courtesy SEARCH Foundation.

Teheran summit masthead. *Tribune* (Sydney, NSW: 1939–1991), 9 November, 1944, p. 1, viewed 06 Aug 2021, National Library of Australia, http://nla.gov.au/nla.news-article208689827.

The Eureka Oath masthead. *Tribune* (Sydney, NSW: 1939–1991), 13 March, 1945, p. 1, viewed 06 Aug 2021, National Library of Australia, http://nla.gov.au/nla.news-article208691236.

National Congress 1943. State Library of New South Wales, PXA 593 (v. 34). Courtesy SEARCH Foundation.

New Theatre League, photograph by Ivan Ives. Mitchell Library, State Library of New South Wales and courtesy ACP Magazines Ltd, ON 388/Box 017/Item 116.

Ernie Thornton. Mitchell Library, State Library of New South Wales. Courtesy SEARCH Foundation. ON 161/Item 027. IE4515807.

Marx House: National Archives of Australia, A705, 171/94/413.

Police raid on Marx House, photograph by B. Rice. State Library of New South Wales, ON 388/Box 054/Item 033.

Railway Strike. State Library of Queensland, 21219165060002061.

Miners' strike, 1949. University of Melbourne Archives, 1991-0152-00057.

Speaker at a CPA street meeting. University of Melbourne Archives, 1991.0152.00052.

J.B. Miles portrait. State Library of New South Wales, PXA 593/vol. 1. Courtesy SEARCH Foundation.

Lance Sharkey portrait. National Archives of Australia, A6122, 2861.
Jim Healy portrait. Courtesy of Pat Healy.
Lance Sharkey trial. Source unknown.
Faith Bandler. National Library of Australia, nla.obj-153310621. From the collection of Joyce Evans.
Graeme Bell jazz band. University of Melbourne Archives, 1991-0152-00173.
Helen Palmer. Doreen Bridges (ed.), *Helen Palmer's Outlook*, Sydney: Edwards & Shaw, 1982, frontispiece.
Marj Nunan. University of Melbourne Archives, 1991-0152-00177.
Ted Hill and Cedric Ralph. National Archives of Australia, A9626, 225.
Fred Paterson and Dave Morris. National Archives of Australia, A9626, 600.
Eliot Elliot and Bill Bird. National Archives of Australia, A9626, 225.
Labour Club conference. Joyce Evans, *We Had Such High Hopes: Student Activism and the Peace Movement 1949–1952*, Melbourne: Australian Scholarly Press, 2019, p. 19.
Marx Float. University of Melbourne Archives, 1991.0152.00181.
Wharfies' stop-work meeting. University of Melbourne Archives, 1991-0152-00122.
Ralph Gibson. University of Melbourne Archives, 1991-0152-00132.
Paul Robeson. State Library of New South Wales, PXA 593/vol. 1. Courtesy SEARCH Foundation.
Junior Eureka League float. University of Melbourne Archives, 1991.0152.00041.
Jim Healy's funeral procession. State Library of New South Wales, PXA 593 (v. 38). Courtesy SEARCH Foundation.
Roger Wilson. University of Melbourne Archives, 1991-0152-00127.
Wave Hill walk-off. National Archives of Australia, A9626, 212.
Claude Jones and Ted Bacon. Grahame Garner Collection, F3400, Folder 5, item 261, Fryer Library, the University of Queensland Library.
ASIO surveillance photo, Jim Moss et al. National Archives of Australia, A9626, 292.
ASIO surveillance photo, Judah Waten and Rex Mortimer. National Archives of Australia, A9626, 506.
ASIO surveillance photo, Eddie Mabo. National Archives of Australia, A9626, 162.
Pallbearers at Lance Sharkey's funeral. State Library of New South Wales, PXE 1034, Box 1. Courtesy SEARCH Foundation.
Meeting of the National Executive. State Library of New South Wales, PXA 593 (v. 35). Courtesy SEARCH Foundation.
Dick Dixon and Bernie Taft meet Alexander Dubček. State Library of New South Wales, PXA 593 (v. 35). Courtesy SEARCH Foundation.
Rex Mortimer and Rupert Lockwood. State Library of New South Wales, PXA 593 (v. 35). Courtesy SEARCH Foundation.
Laurie Aarons meets Josip Tito. State Library of New South Wales, PXA 593 (v. 35). Courtesy SEARCH Foundation.
Audrey Blake. State Library of New South Wales, PXA 593 (v. 35). Courtesy SEARCH Foundation.

Endnotes

Introduction

1 Stuart Macintyre, *The Reds: The Communist Party of Australia from Origins to Illegality* (Sydney: Allen & Unwin, 1998).

2 See Robert Bozinovski, 'The Communist Party of Australia and Proletarian Internationalism, 1928–1945', PhD thesis, Victoria University, 2008, ch. 1.

3 Audrey Blake, *A Proletarian Life* (Malmsbury: Kibble Books, 1984), pp. 21–35.

4 'Comintern Calls for Peace', *Tribune*, 7 November 1939. The best treatment of these somersaults is Robert Bozinovski, 'The Comintern, the Communist Party of Australia and Illegality', Hons thesis, School of Social Sciences, Victoria University, 2003.

5 Executive Committee of the Communist International (ECCI), 'Proposals for the CPA', 3 November 1939, Russian Centre for the Preservation and Study of Contemporary Historical Documents, Fond 495, Opis 14, Delo 308 (495–14–308); 'Communists State First War Policy Contained Error', *Tribune*, 8 December 1939; L. Sharkey, *The Communist Party Speaks* (Sydney: Central Committee of the CPA, n.d.), p. 5.

6 Kevin Morgan, *Against Fascism and War: Ruptures and Continuities in British Communist Politics, 1935–1941* (Manchester: Manchester University Press, 1989); Monty Johnstone, 'The CPGB, the Comintern and the War, 1939–1941: Filling in the Blank Spots', *Science and Society*, vol. 61, no. 1 (1997), pp. 27–45; A. Rossi, *Les Communistes français pendant la drole de guerre* (Paris: Iles d'Or, 1951).

7 Georgi Dimitrov, *The Diary of Georgi Dimitrov, 1933–1949*, ed. Ivo Banac (New Haven, CT: Yale University Press, 2008), p. 115; G. Dimitrov, *The War and the Working Class* (Sydney: Central Committee, CPA, n.d. [c. January 1940]).

8 *Point of Departure: The Autobiography of Jean Devanny*, ed. Carole Ferrier (Brisbane: UQP, 1986), pp. 222–24; Devanny to Franklin, 22 September 1939, and Devanny to Prichard, 9 January 1940, in Carole Ferrier (ed.), *As Good as a Yarn With You: Letters between Miles Franklin, Katharine Susannah Prichard, Jean Devanny, Marjory Barnard, Flora Eldershaw and Eleanor Dark* (Cambridge: CUP, 1992), p. 47. There is a slight difference in wording of the second letter in a security file on Prichard's son, Richard Prichard Throssell, vol. 1, NAA A6119, 95, ff. 57–58.

9 Central Committee Minutes, July 1939, CPA records, SLNSW, MLMSS 5021, ADD-ON 1936, Box 5; The Communist Party and Illegality, NAA A12389, A30 PART 4, f. 58.

10 Geoffrey Roberts, *Stalin's Wars: From World War to Cold War, 1939–1953* (New Haven, CT: Yale University Press, 2006), ch. 3.

11 'Churchill Invites "Enemy" Attack USSR', *Tribune*, 14 May 1941; 'Soviet-German Relations', *Tribune*, 22 June 1941.

12 'Australian Communist Leader ("In Smoke") Talks', Sydney *Sun*, 16 July 1941.

13 Oriel Gray, *Exit Left: Memoirs of a Scarlet Woman* (Melbourne: Penguin, 1985), pp. 78–79.

14 *Party Builder*, no. 2 (July 1942); Richard Dixon, 'The Party Building Campaign', *Communist Review*, no. 18 (February 1943), pp. 3–4.
15 'Help for Soviet', *Sydney Morning Herald*, 30 June 1941; 'Aid to the Soviet', *Sydney Morning Herald*, 4 July 1941.
16 Jessie Street, *Truth or Repose* (Sydney: Australasian Book Society, 1966); Mavis Robertson and Betty Searle, 'Campaigner for Peace and Friendship', in Heather Radi (ed.), *Jessie Street: Documents and Essays* (Sydney: Women's Redress Press, 1990), pp. 225–37.
17 'Cossacks to Ride', *Sydney Morning Herald*, 14 October 1941; 'Sydney's Heart Is With Russia', Sydney *Sun*, 17 October 1941.
18 '"Racing for Russia" at Newcastle To-Day', *Newcastle Morning Herald*, 1 August 1942; I am grateful to John Arnold for drawing my attention to this horse and to Andrew Lemon for providing the context.
19 *Aid Russia: Report of the Congress for Friendship and Aid to the Soviet Union, Sydney, August 30th and 31st, 1941* (Sydney: NSW Aid Russia Committee, 1941); 'Aid to Soviet', *Sydney Morning Herald*, 1 September 1941; there is a detailed security report in Aid to Russia Committee, NAA A6335, 19, ff. 25–27.
20 Ian Clunies Ross et al., *Soviet Culture: A Selection of Talks at the Cultural Conference, November 1941* (Sydney: NSW Aid Russia Committee, 1941).
21 *National Unity for an Allied Victory: Report of Congress, Sydney Town Hall, February 28th–March 1st 1942* (Sydney: NSW Aid Russia Committee, 1942).
22 'ALP Ban on Soviet Anniversary Celebration', Sydney *Sun*, 6 November 1943; 'Russia's Great Day', *Argus*, 5 November 1943; 'Soviet Day Honoured', *Age*, 8 November 1943.
23 'Prospectus for Australia-Soviet House', n.d., Ralph and Dorothy Gibson papers, NLA MS 7844, box 1, folder 4; 'Ideals of Soviet Russia', *Argus*, 8 November 1944; Australia Soviet House, NAA A6122, 148.
24 *Commonwealth Parliamentary Debates*, 9 September 1942; 'Soviet Russia After 25 Years', *Sydney Morning Herald*, 7 November 1942.
25 'Communist Leader Officially Opens New Building', *Tribune*, 7 September 1944; Rick Oke to Myrtle Aarons, 13 December 1944, Communism—South Australia, NAA A6335, 11, f. 284.
26 'Unique Exhibition Will Glorify Australian Labor's Achievements', *Tribune*, 7 August 1945; *25th Anniversary of the Australian Communist Party* (Sydney: Central Committee, 1945).
27 Raid on Marx House, Sydney, Friday 8th July 1949, NAA A432, 1949, 816, ff. 366–80; 'Sale of Soviet House', *Age*, 4 February 1950.
28 'Town Hall Bans Communist Meeting', *Sydney Morning Herald*, 20 April 1948; 'Meeting on Russia', *Sydney Morning Herald*, 29 June 1949; 'Town Hall Basement Not for "Red" Dean', Sydney *Sun*, 12 April 1950.
29 'Use of Town Hall By Communists', *Argus*, 15 February 1949.
30 'Rodgers Denies Communists Set Up Australia-Soviet House', *Argus*, 11 August 1949; 'Transcript of Proceedings of the Victoria Royal Commission Inquiring into the Origins, Aims, Objects and Funds of the Communist Party, Minutes of Evidence' (Melbourne, 1949–50), p. 2363.
31 Quoted in Odd Arne Westad, *The Cold War: A World History* (London: Allen Lane, 2017), pp. 89–90.
32 'Mrs Street Resigns', *Sydney Morning Herald*, 17 January 1949.
33 Quoted in Stuart Macintyre, *Australia's Boldest Experiment: War and Reconstruction in the 1940s* (Sydney: NewSouth, 2015), p. 145.

34 I draw here on Sean Scalmer, 'Labour's Golden Age and the Changing Forms of Workers Representation in Australia', *Journal of the Royal Australian Historical Society*, vol. 84, no. 2 (1998), pp. 180–98.

35 Quoted in Mark Aarons, *The Family File* (Melbourne: Black Inc., 2010), p. 115.

36 L. Sharkey, *The Trade Unions: Communist Theory and Practice of Trade Unions* (Sydney: CPA, November 1942), p. 9.

37 Roger Milliss, *Serpent's Tooth: An Autobiographical Novel* (Melbourne: Penguin, 1984), p. 124.

38 David Carter, '"History Was on Our Side": Memoirs from the Australian Left', *Meanjin*, vol. 46, no. 1 (March 1987), pp. 108–21.

39 Ralph Gibson to his mother, Christmas Day 1939, in Helen Gwynneth Palmer, vol. 1, NAA A6119, 178, f. 165.

40 David Carter, '"History Was on Our Side"'.

41 Bernard Smith, *Noel Counihan: Artist and Revolutionary* (Melbourne: OUP, 1993), pp. 542–43; see Noel Counihan, 'New Poland Takes Breath Away', *Tribune*, 4 August 1949.

42 Patricia Thompson, *Accidental Chords* (Melbourne: Penguin, 1988), pp. 171, 174, 178; Peter Kirkpatrick, 'John Joseph Thompson', *Australian Dictionary of Biography*, vol. 16, pp. 383–84.

43 Tim Bowden, 'The Making of an Australian Communist: Rupert Lockwood', *Politics*, vol. 9, no. 1 (1974), p. 20.

44 John Passmore, *Memoirs of a Semi-Detached Australian* (Melbourne: MUP, 1997), p. 115.

45 Hal Alexander, 'Red Belt Days', in Hal Alexander and Phil Griffiths (eds), *A Few Rough Reds: Stories of Rank and File Organising* (Canberra: ASSLH Canberra Branch, 2003), pp. 56–62; 'In Memory of Frank Hardy', *The Hummer*, vol. 2, no. 2 (Winter 1994), <www.labourhistory.org.au/hummer/vol-2-no-2/frank-hardy>.

46 John Playford, 'Doctrinal and Strategic Problems of the Communist Party of Australia, 1943–62', PhD thesis, ANU, 1962; Alastair Davidson, *The Communist Party of Australia: A Short History* (Stanford, CA: Hoover Institution Press, 1969).

47 Notably, see Bruce Duncan, *Crusade or Conspiracy? Catholics and the Anti-Communist Struggle in Australia* (Sydney: UNSWP, 2001).

48 Desmond Ball and David Horner, *Breaking the Codes: Australia's KGB Network, 1944–1950* (Sydney: Allen & Unwin, 1998).

49 Mark Aarons, *The Family File* (Melbourne: Black Inc., 2010), p. 167.

50 Raphael Samuel, *The Lost World of British Communism* (London: Verso, 2006), p. 13.

51 Stephen Murray-Smith in Hume Dow (ed.), *Memories of Melbourne University* (Melbourne: Hutchinson, 1983), pp. 122–23.

52 Quoted in Keith McEwan, *Once a Jolly Comrade* (Brisbane: Jacaranda Press, 1966), p. 79; Stephen Murray-Smith, *There's No Iron Curtain: An Australian Journalist in Eastern Europe* (Melbourne: International Bookshop, 1952).

1 Illegality, 1940–41

1 *Constitution of the Communist Party of Australia* (Sydney: Dimitrov Press, 1942), pp. 3, 9.

2 A record of these payments was provided to the army's Intelligence Section of the General Staff, 7 February 1940, NAA A6119, 1799, ff. 106–107.

3 I draw here on the reflections of Rex Mortimer, who was a cadre in the 1950s, 'The Benefits of a Liberal Education', *Meanjin*, vol. 35, no. 2 (June 1976), pp. 115–26,

supplemented by Daphne Gollan, 'The Memoirs of "Cleopatra Sweatfigure"', in Elizabeth Windschuttle (ed.), *Women, Class and History: Feminist Perspectives on Australian History 1788–1988* (Sydney: Fontana, 1980), p. 317; see also Thomas Linehan, *Communism in Britain 1920–1939: From Cradle to the Grave* (Manchester: Manchester University Press, 2007).

4 V.I. Lenin, *What Is to Be Done?* (Sydney: Modern Books, 1932); Joseph Stalin, *On Lenin* (London: Lawrence and Wishart, 1941).

5 Stan Moran, *Reminiscences of a Rebel* (Sydney: Alternative Publishing, 1979), pp. 17–18, 39–48; 'Table Talk', *Daily Telegraph*, 26 September 1946; see also Andrew Metcalfe, *For Freedom and Dignity: Historical Agency and Class Structures in the Coalfields of NSW* (Sydney: Allen & Unwin, 1988), ch. 6.

6 Eric Aarons, *What's Left? Memoirs of an Australian Communist* (Melbourne: Penguin, 1993), p. 59; see also Sean Scalmer, 'The Career of Class: Intellectuals and the Labour Movement in Australia 1942–56', PhD thesis, University of Sydney, 1996, ch. 3.

7 David Plowman, 'Australian Trade Unions: Some Vital Statistics', in G.W. Ford, J.M. Hearn and R.D. Lansbury (eds), *Australian Labour Relations: Readings* (3rd edn, Melbourne: Macmillan, 1980), p. 199.

8 John Playford, 'Doctrinal and Strategic Problems of the Communist Party of Australia, 1943–62', PhD thesis, ANU, 1962, pp. 68–71.

9 There are entries for all these men in the *Australian Dictionary of Biography* (<https://adb.anu.edu.au>), and further sources for them and their unions will be identified later.

10 David McKnight, *Espionage and the Roots of the Cold War: The Conspiratorial Heritage* (London: Frank Cass, 2002), pp. 153–60.

11 Stephen Holt, *A Veritable Dynamo: Lloyd Ross and Australian Labour 1901–1987* (Brisbane: UQP, 1996), chs 4–5.

12 John Sendy, *Ralph Gibson: An Extraordinary Communist* (Melbourne: Ralph Gibson Biography Committee, 1988), chs 5–8; Stuart Macintyre, 'Ralph Siward Gibson', *Australian Dictionary of Biography*, vol. 17, pp. 432–33.

13 Ross Fitzgerald, *The People's Champion: Fred Paterson, Australia's Only Communist Party Member of Parliament* (Brisbane: UQP, 1997), part 2; Stuart Macintyre, *The Reds: The Communist Party of Australia from Origins to Illegality* (Sydney: Allen & Unwin, 1998), p. 460, n. 29.

14 Bill Wood is a central figure in Stephen Moline, *Red* (Melbourne: Australian Scholarly, 2017).

15 Claude Jones, interviewed by Laurie Aarons, June 1980, SLNSW; see Diane Menghetti, *The Red North: The Popular Front in North Queensland* (Townsville: History Department, James Cook University, 1981).

16 Georgi Dimitrov, *The United Front Against Fascism: Speeches at the Seventh World Congress of the Communist International August 1935* (Sydney: Current Book Distributors, 1945), p. 8.

17 Bernie Taft, *Crossing the Party Line: Memoirs of Bernie Taft* (Newham: Scribe Publications, 1994), p. 37; Laurie Aarons, interviewed by Joyce Stevens, 17 September 1980, SLNSW.

18 '295,000 Leaflets', *Tribune*, 10 November 1939; 'More Meetings Each Month', *Tribune*, 28 November 1939.

19 'Business as Usual', *Sydney Morning Herald*, 6 September 1939.

20 'Hisses, Boos in the Domain', *Daily Telegraph*, 4 December 1939; 'AIF Men in Clash With Domain Reds', *Daily Telegraph*, 18 December 1939; 'Soldiers Burn Red

Flag in Domain', *Daily Telegraph*, 25 December 1939; 'Police and Soldiers Clash at Communist Meeting', *Daily Telegraph*, 1 January 1940.

21 Ralph Gibson, *My Years in the Communist Party* (Melbourne: International Bookshop, 1966), pp. 81–83; 'Woman Fined at Footscray', Melbourne *Herald*, 7 December 1939; 'Disturbance at Collingwood', *Age*, 3 February 1942; 'Stones Thrown at Yarra Bank', *Argus*, 19 February 1940; 'Police Guard', *Daily Telegraph*, 8 April 1940.

22 Propaganda Summary, 8 February 1940, Australian Communist Party, NAA A9108, ROLL11/21, f. 93.

23 Jeff Sparrow, *Communism: A Love Story* (Melbourne: MUP, 2007), pp. 241–58.

24 Rawling's account is in his papers, NBA, N57/406; 'Rawling Expelled', *Tribune*, 15 December 1939; L. Sharkey, 'A Girl Who Joined the Party', *Tribune*, 27 February 1940.

25 'Party Secretary in Hospital', *Tribune*, 25 September 1939; 'Knight Again Ill', *Tribune*, 7 November 1939; L.L. Sharkey, *Congress Report on the Work of the Central Committee from the 12th to the 13th Party Congress* (Sydney: Dimitrov Press, 1943), p. [7].

26 'Anti-War Play', *Tribune*, 23 January 1940; Robert Darby, 'New Theatre and the State: The Ban on *Till the Day I Die*, 1936–41', *Labour History*, no. 80 (2001), pp. 1–19; Oriel Gray, *Exit Left: Memoirs of a Scarlet Woman* (Melbourne: Penguin, 1985), p. 50.

27 Dixon's script is in Censorship, Breaches … Broadcasting of Subversive Propaganda by Communist Party, NAA SP109, 3/350/02.

28 'ALP Opposes Fighting in War Against Russia', *Daily Telegraph*, 24 March 1940; McKnight, *Espionage and the Roots of the Cold War*, pp. 162–69.

29 'Clear Lead to Unions', *Tribune*, 19 September 1939; 'War Against Russia Opposed', *Sydney Morning Herald*, 8 March 1940; Jim Hagan, *The History of the ACTU* (Melbourne: Longman Cheshire, 1981), pp. 108–109. Until 1947 the title of this peak body was the Australasian Council of Trade Unions.

30 *Year Book Australia*, 1940, pp. 711–12; 1941, pp. 737–78.

31 The letter, supposedly handed to the Commonwealth Investigation Branch, was published in the Sydney press on 28 April, but it used the wrong title of the union and the wrong address; see William (Bill) Orr, NAA A6119, 403.

32 Robin Gollan, *The Coalminers of New South Wales: A History of the Union 1860–1960* (Melbourne: MUP, 1963), pp. 212–24.

33 Warwick Eather, 'The Trenches at Home: The Industrial Struggle in the Newcastle Iron and Steel Industry 1937–1947', PhD thesis, University of Sydney, 1987, ch. 2.

34 'Watersiders' Claim for Smoko Breaks', *Sydney Morning Herald*, 2 May 1940; 'Wharf Men Load AIF Flour', Melbourne *Herald*, 8 April 1940; Waterside Workers' Federation, vol. 1, NAA A6122, 333, f. 223.

35 'New South Wales Communists', n.d.; H.E. Jones to Inspector D.R.B. Mitchell, 3 April 1940, Mitchell to Jones, 18 April 1940; and Australian Communist Party Policy, all in NAA A9108, ROLL 9/4.

36 'To Lockwood With Love', ABC radio, 13 July 1975, ASIO—History, NAA A12383, A1.

37 Intelligence Section of the General Staff, 'Communist Activities', 27 October 1939, NAA A8911, 46, ff. 434–47.

38 War Cabinet Minutes, 5 January 1940, NAA A5954, 803/1; Conference Called to Decide What Action Necessary Against Communist Party, NAA A8911, 52, ff. 13–19.

39 David Carment, 'Australian Communism and National Security September

1939–June 1941', *Journal of the Royal Australian Historical Society*, vol. 65, no. 4 (1980), pp. 251–52.

40 War Cabinet Minutes, 8, 19 April, 5 June 1940, NAA A5954, 803/2; Cabinet Minutes, 27 May 1940, NAA A2697, ROLL 2, p. 279.

41 George James Caldwell, NAA A6126, 694; 'Official Secrets Charge', *Age*, 5 June 1940.

42 'Sydney Police Act Promptly', Sydney *Sun*, 16 June 1946; 'Raids in Sydney', *Sydney Morning Herald*, 17 June 1940; 'Police Raid in Newcastle', *Newcastle Morning Herald*, 17 June 1940; 'Swift Moves in Melbourne', *Age*, 17 June 1940; 'Police Remove Rifles from Communists', *Courier-Mail*, 17 June 1940; 'Fifty Houses Raided in Toowoomba', *Warwick Daily News*, 19 June 1940; 'Communist Party Declared Illegal', *Cairns Post*, 17 June 1940.

43 Some of these stories were told in a subsequent article, 'Menzies' Police Attacked Our Cultural Liberty', *Tribune*, 29 July 1943; others appear in Simon Bracegirdle, *My Lucky Life* (Brisbane: the author, 1997), Edgar Ross, *Of Storm and Struggle: Pages from Labour History* (Sydney: Alternative Publishing Co-operative, 1982), pp. 80–81, and Moline, *Red*, pp. 128–36.

44 Roy Dalgarno, 'The Winking of an Eye', unpublished memoirs in possession of Lynn Dalgarno.

45 Raphael Samuel, *The Lost World of British Communism* (London: Verso, 2006), pp. 198–202; Julian Goddard, 'John Oldham', in David Bromfield (ed.), *Aspects of Perth Modernism 1929–1942* (Perth: Centre for Fine Arts, UWA, n.d. [1986]), pp. 40–41.

46 National Security (Subversive Associations) Regulations, Administrative Actions Taken, NAA A9108, ROLL 9/7, f. 79; ISGS to Army Command, 17 January 1941, Report on Communist Party Activities, NAA A8911, 46, ff. 222–23.

47 Wally Clayton, interviewed by Ken Mansell, 30 April 1983, SLNSW; Walter Seddon Clayton, A6119, 953, f. 47; 'They Banned the "Tribune"', *Tribune*, 24 May 1941.

48 Ted Bacon, interviewed by Laurie Aarons, June 1980, SLNSW; Ted and Eva Bacon, interviewed by Ken Mansell, 21 April 1983, SLNSW; see Deborah Jordan, Eva Bacon: 1909–1994', in Bob Boughton et al. (eds), *Comrades! Lives of Australian Communists* (Sydney: Search Foundation, 2020), pp. 158–60.

49 Roger Douglas, 'Law, War and Liberty: The World War II Subversion Prosecutions', *Melbourne University Law Review*, vol. 27, no. 1 (2003), pp. 65–115.

50 Douglas, 'Law, War and Liberty', pp. 84–86; Deputy Chief Publicity Censor to Chief Publicity Censor, 14 August 1940, NAA SP109, 316/16.

51 Mrs Phyllis Johnson—Proposed Prosecution, NAA A472, W1456.

52 'Phyllis Johnson Defence', *Tribune*, 7 November 1940; A472, W1456, f. 84; Phyllis Johnson, vol. 1, A6119, 1174; 'Gold Brooch for Mrs Johnson', *Sydney Morning Herald*, 7 January 1941. GPU is the acronym of the Soviet security organisation that operated from 1922 to 1923.

53 National Security (Subversive Associations) Regulations, Administrative Action Taken, NAA A9108, ROLL 9/7, f. 82.

54 Intelligence Section, Eastern Command to Army Headquarters, 14 March 1941, Communist Party of Australia Activities, A8911, 46, f. 193; Detention of Ratliff and Thomas, NAA A367, C70788.

55 Max Thomas, interviewed by Laurie Aarons, 27 March 1980, SLNSW.

56 Thomas interviewed by Laurie Aarons; *The Case of Ratliff and Thomas* (Sydney: Australian Civil Rights Defence League, n.d. [1941]); 'Prime Minister's Statement', *Sydney Morning Herald*, 24 July 1941.

57 'Voluble Anti-Fascist', Sydney *Truth*, 19 June 1941; 'Security Law Breach', *Sydney Morning Herald*, 10 July 1941; Prosecution under National Security (Subversive Associations) Regulations, NAA A467, SF 42/78; Simon Bracegirdle, 'Several Decades as a Communist Activist', in Carole Ferrier and Rebecca Phelan (eds), *The Point of Change: Marxism, Australia, History, Theory* (Brisbane: Australian Studies Centre, University of Queensland, 1998), p. 51.

58 Frederick Woolnough Paterson, NAA A8911, 555; Ross Fitzgerald, *The People's Champion: Fred Paterson, Australia's Only Communist Party Member of Parliament* (Brisbane: UQP, 1997), pp. 125–32.

59 'Homes Raided', *Age*, 5 December 1940; 'The Guardian' Communistic Newspaper, NAA A472, W2179.

60 'Adelaide Police Alleged Anti-Conscription Speeches', *Advertiser*, 22 October 1940; Prosecution of F. Rowan and T. Gouland (sic), NAA A472, W1364.

61 'Communist Literature Seized', *Mercury*, 4 February 1941; George Gordon Wallis, NAA A6119, 1974.

62 A list in NAA A8911, 46, ff. 166–69 gives details of twenty convictions to the end of May 1941, and there were three subsequent cases; for the other states, see Douglas, 'Law, War and Liberty', p. 102

63 'Communist Gaoled', *West Australian*, 15 June 1940; 'Security Act', *West Australian*, 17 February 1941; Dorothy Anne and Oswell Frank Owen, A6119, 1172.

64 Bobbie Oliver and W.S. Latter, 'Spooks, Spies and Subversives! The Wartime Security Service', in Jenny Gregory (ed.), *On the Homefront: Western Australia and World War II* (Nedlands: UWAP, 1996), pp. 176–85; Frank Cain, 'George Ronald Richards', *Australian Dictionary of Biography*, vol. 18, pp. 348–49.

65 Constable Basley to Inspector Doyle, 22 August 1941, Donald Alfred Mountjoy, NAA A6119, 1527, f. 51, and 7 April 1941, A6119, 1177, f. 92. For similar allegations, see 'Subversive Papers', *West Australian*, 19 February 1941; 'Communist Literature', *West Australian*, 19 March 1941; 'Alleged Libel', *West Australian*, 12 June 1941.

66 'Work for Police', *West Australian*, 8 May 1941; Frederick James Thomas, NAA A6119, 1485.

67 'Communist Gaoled', *West Australian*, 30 April 1941; report by Richards, 3 April 1941, John Spencer Simpson, NAA A6126, 415, ff. 52–55; Western Command to Military Board, 22 July 1941, John Bramston Russell Oldham, NAA A6119, 1177, f. 71.

68 'Health Officer's Transfer', *Age*, 25 March 1941; Ian MacDonald, NAA A6119, 2054, ff. 187, 201, 216, 231; see also Kate Hutchinson, *Extreme and Dangerous: The Curious Case of Dr Ian Macdonald* (Melbourne: Australian Scholarly Publishing, 2020).

69 Kevin Morgan, *Against Fascism and War: Ruptures and Continuities in British Communist Politics, 1935–1941* (Manchester: Manchester University Press, 1989), pp. 129, 236; Nancy Taylor, *The Home Front* (Wellington: Government Printer, 1986), vol. 1, pp. 209–23; Ivan Avakumovic, *The Communist Party in Canada: A History* (Toronto: McClelland and Stewart, 1975), pp. 142–47.

70 Communistic Election Leaflets, NAA A467, SF42/114.

2 Underground, 1940–42

1 See Brian Fitzpatrick, *National Security and Individual Insecurity: An Account of the National Security Legislation and Regulations* (Melbourne: Left Book Club of Victoria, December 1939); *The War and Civil Rights: A Survey Prepared by the Australian Council for Civil Liberties* (Melbourne: ACCL, 1940); *The War and Civil Rights. 2nd Series: A Survey of Action Taken in Various Australian States Under the National Security Regulations,*

December 1940 – April 1941 (Melbourne: ACCL, 1941); *The War and Civil Rights. 3rd Series: Campaign for Ratliff and Thomas* (Melbourne: ACCL, 1941).

2 Brian Fitzpatrick, *The Australian Commonwealth: A Picture of the Community 1901–1955* (Melbourne: F.W. Cheshire, 1956), p. 149.

3 'Salute Given in Court', *Age*, 11 June 1940.

4 E.F. Hill, *Communism and Australia: Reflections and Reminiscences* (Melbourne: Communist Party of Australia (Marxist-Leninist), 1989), p. 106.

5 David McKnight, *Espionage and the Roots of the Cold War: The Conspiratorial Heritage* (London: Frank Cass, 2002); Jane Degras (ed.), *The Communist International: Documents*, vol. 1 (London: OUP, 1956), pp. 166–72.

6 Party instructions, 21 March 1940, Report on Communist Activities by Eastern Command, NAA A467, W2569. These instructions were subsequently published in the Brisbane *Truth*, 23 June 1940.

7 Daphne Gollan, 'The Memoirs of "Cleopatra Sweatfigure"', in Elizabeth Windschuttle (ed.), *Women Class and History: Feminist Perspectives on Australian History 1788–1988* (Sydney: Fontana, 1980), p. 318.

8 'To Leading Members of Party Committees', June 1940, ASIO Special Project Branch Documents, NAA A12389, A30 PART 4, ff. 48–49.

9 'To District Committees', NAA A12389, A30 PART 4, ff. 50–51.

10 John Sendy, *Ralph Gibson: An Extraordinary Communist* (Melbourne: Ralph Gibson Biography Committee, 1988), pp. 85–88; Roy Dalgarno, 'The Winking of an Eye', unpublished memoirs in possession of Lynn Dalgarno.

11 Harry Stein, *A Glance Over an Old Left Shoulder* (Sydney: Hale & Iremonger, 1994), p. 62.

12 CIB list of Sharkey's appearances, NAA A6119, 219; Tony McGillick, *Comrade No More: The Autobiography of a Former Communist Leader* (Perth: the author, 1980), p. 166; Mark Aarons, *The Family File* (Melbourne: Black Inc., 2010), pp. 157–58.

13 John Moreland O'Reilly, NAA A6119, 1043; John O'Reilly, interviewed by Stuart Macintyre, 5 March 2006; Stuart Macintyre, 'Communist Party History', in David Clune and Ken Turners (eds), *Writing Party History: Papers from a Seminar Held at Parliament House, Sydney, 20 May 2006* (Sydney: NSW Parliament, 2007), pp. 65–73.

14 Mason and McShane, *Soviet Russia and the War* (Sydney: n.p., n.d.); *What Is This Labor Party* (Sydney: Communist Party of Australia, n.d.); *The Coming War in the Pacific* (Sydney: J. Grace, n.d. [January 1941]).

15 'Sh-h-h! We Are Discovered', *Tribune*, 18 November 1940; Paterson quoted in Ross Fitzgerald, *The People's Champion: Fred Paterson, Australia's Only Communist Party Member of Parliament* (Brisbane: UQP, 1997), p. 124.

16 'Underground Printery', in Jeff Sparrow and Jill Sparrow, *Radical Melbourne 2: The Enemy Within* (Melbourne: Vulgar Press, 2004), pp. 165–69; Les Barnes, 'June 15, 1940', *Recorder*, no. 163 (July 1990), pp. 11–13.

17 P.J. Shears, 'Communist Cave', in author's possession; Ted Bacon, interviewed by Laurie Aarons, June 1980, SLNSW.

18 Communist Publications—Workers' Star, NAA A8911, 90, f. 61.

19 Russel Ward, *A Radical Life: The Autobiography of Russel Ward* (Melbourne: Macmillan, 1988), pp. 139, 188–89; Betty Searle, personal communication, 1 May 1997.

20 Phyllis Johnson, interviewed by Ken Mansell, 6 May 1983, SLNSW; Claude Jones, interviewed by Laurie Aarons, June 1980, SLNSW; Paul Ormonde, *A Foolish Passionate Man: A Biography of Jim Cairns* (Melbourne: Penguin, 1981); Desmond Ball

and David Horner, *Breaking the Codes: Australia's KGB Network, 1944–1950* (Sydney: Allen & Unwin, 1998), pp. 240–41.

21 Edgar Ross, *Of Storm and Struggle: Pages from Labour History* (Sydney: Alternative Publishing Co-operative, 1982), p. 84; Fred Thompson, interviewed by Daniel Connell, 1 October 1989, NLA TRC 2532/4; Michael Patrick Ryan, NAA A6119, 722, f. 215.

22 Richard Dixon to John Simpson, 20 January 1940, NAA A6126, 414, f. 68; Jess Grant in Joyce Stevens, *Taking the Revolution Home: Work Among Women in the Communist Party of Australia 1920–1945* (Melbourne: Sybylla Co-operative Press, 1987), p. 176.

23 Political Committee to Western Australia state committee, Circulars and Statements, CPA records, SLNSW MLMSS 5021, ADD-ON 1936, Box 5 (76).

24 '3000 Rally to No-Conscription Meeting', *Tribune*, 19 April 1940; Central No-Conscription Committee, NAA A472, W1406.

25 Central Committee, 30 October, and n.d. [November 1941], Central Committee Circulars and Statements, SLNSW MLMSS 5021, ADD-ON 1936, Box 5 (76); Central Committee Instructions, 1 January 1941, in Communist Party of Australia Activities, NAA A8911, 46, ff. 222–23.

26 'Ban on Australian Youth Council', *Sydney Morning Herald*, 9 August 1940; 'Police Take Notes', *Argus*, 26 August 1940; 'Raid by Police in Melbourne', *Age*, 25 February 1941; League of Young Democrats, NAA A9108, ROLL 23/1.

27 Bill Wood, 'Progress', Bill Wood papers, NBAC N296/99.

28 Rowan Cahill, 'Rupert Lockwood (1908–1997): Journalist, Communist, Intellectual', PhD thesis, University of Wollongong, 2013; Amirah Inglis, 'John Fisher', *Australian Dictionary of Biography*, vol. 14, p. 172.

29 George Farwell, *Rejoice in Freedom* (Melbourne: Nelson, 1976), p. 208.

30 See Stephen Holt, *A Veritable Dynamo: Lloyd Ross and Australian Labour 1901–1987* (Brisbane: UQP, 1996), pp. 71, 75, which quotes the communist newsletter *Freedom's Voice*, 4 September 1940.

31 Mason and McShane, *What Is This Labor Party*; see Rick Kuhn, 'Lenin on the ALP: The Career of 600 Words', *Australian Journal of Politics and History*, vol. 35, no. 1 (1989), pp. 28–49.

32 'Forgery! Provocation!', *Tribune*, 7 October 1940; see Robert Bozinovski, 'The Communist Party of Australia and Proletarian Internationalism, 1928–1945', PhD thesis, Victoria University, 2008, p. 221.

33 'Curtin Makes a Deal', *Tribune*, 18 December 1940; 'Liberal "History"', *Tribune*, 15 February 1941; Edgar Ross, *Of Storm and Struggle*, p. 87; Wood to Street, 19 April 1941, Jessie Street Part 1, NAA A6119, 360, ff. 136–37.

34 'Communists in the Labor Party', *Age*, 3 May 1940; Peter S. Cook, *Red Barrister: A Biography of Ted Laurie* (Melbourne: La Trobe University Press, 1994); see Paul Strangio, *Neither Power Nor Glory: 100 Years of Political Labor in Victoria, 1856–1956* (Melbourne: MUP, 2012), pp. 229–31.

35 'Election Sensation', *West Australian*, 27 December 1940; see Bobbie Oliver, *Unity Is Strength: A History of the Australian Labor Party and the Trades and Labor Council in Western Australia, 1989–1999* (Perth: Australian Public Intellectual Network, 2003), pp. 154–56.

36 'Mr Curtin Replies to NSW Attack', Perth *Daily News*, 7 January 1941; see John A. McKenzie, *Challenging Faith: An Autobiography* (Fremantle: Fremantle Arts Centre Press, 1993), pp. 118–19; Simpson's contacts with Dinan are recorded in Dinan's security file, NAA A6126, 531, f. 46.

37 'Working for Hitler', *Westralian Worker*, 31 January 1941. This episode was argued at length when Carder sued the *Westralian Worker* for libel in a case reported by the *West Australian* from 28 May to 20 June 1941; see also 'Dinan to Campaign for State Labor', *Progress*, 4 April 1941.
38 Ernie Thornton, *Trade Unions and the War* (Sydney: Federal Council of the FIA, n.d. [1942]), p. 12.
39 *Year Book Australia*, 1941, pp. 741; Military Intelligence, 'Industrial Troubles', NAA A8911, 46, ff. 259–61.
40 Central Committee Minutes, 25 June 1940, Circulars and Statements, SLNSW MLMSS 5021, ADD-ON 1936, Box 5 (76); 'Strike Sequel in Resignation', *Daily Telegraph*, 16 September 1940; William Orr, NAA A6911, 403, ff. 25–39.
41 'Coal Miners' Pledge', *Sydney Morning Herald*, 28 February 1940; 'Unrest in Coalfields', *Tribune*, 7 April 1941. A Royal Commission investigated the secret fund used to make the payment; see Paul Hasluck, *The Government and the People 1939–1941* (Canberra: Australian War Memorial, 1952), Appendix 9.
42 Central Committee, 30 October 1940, 11 March 1941, SLNSW MLMSS 5021, ADD-ON 1936, Box 5 (76); Holt, *A Veritable Dynamo*, pp. 83–89.
43 'A Real Policy for Australia', *Tribune*, 29 July 1940; 'Labor Bellwethers and Scared Capitalists', *Tribune*, 16 February 1941.
44 'The Federal Election', *Tribune*, 27 August 1940; 'Repudiate the Organisers of Disaster', *Tribune*, 4 May 1940; 'War Scare and the ARP Scandal', *Tribune*, 12 March 1941. See also *ARP: Sham or Shelter?* (Melbourne: Left Book Club, December 1940).
45 'Black Pot, Dirty Kettle', *Tribune*, 30 September 1940; 'Profits from Scrap', *Tribune*, 7 October 1940; Mason and McShane, *The Coming War in the Pacific*.
46 'Defend Yourselves, Not Capitalism', *Tribune*, 18 October 1940.
47 Central Committee, n.d. [November 1941], 15 March 1941, Central Committee Circulars and Statements, SLNSW MLMSS 5021, ADD-ON 1936, Box 5 (76).
48 ISGS to Army Command, 17 January 1941; Easter Command to ISGS, 14 March 1941, NAA A8911, 46, ff. 193, 222.
49 ISGS to Army Command, 14 November 1940, NAA, 8911, 46, f. 253; L.L. Sharkey, *Congress Report on the Work of the Central Committee from the 12th to the 13th Party Congress* (Sydney: Dimitrov Press, 1943), p. [7].
50 Sharkey, *Congress Report*, p. [14]; Central Executive Minutes, March 1942, SLNSW MLMSS 5021, ADD-ON 1936, Box 5 (75).
51 D.R.B. Mitchell to H.E. Jones, 5, 13 June, 18, 26 July 1941, Australian Communist Party Policy, NAA A9108, ROLL 9/4, ff. 58, 70, 75, 78–79; 'Communist Party Policy', 27 July 1941.
52 She told Stephen Moline of this incident in 2005 and he relates it in *Red*, pp. 124–28. See also a later meeting in 1940, recorded in Audrey Blake, NAA A6119, 120, f. 3.

3 The Leading War Party, 1942–45

1 'Soviet-German Relations', *Tribune*, 22 June 1941; Bruce Miller quoted in Alan Barcan, *Radical Students: The Old Left at Sydney University* (Melbourne: MUP, 2002), p. 118; Laurie Aarons, interviewed by Joyce Stevens, 17 September 1980, SLNSW.
2 'Pledge Australian Support for Soviet', *Daily Telegraph*, 27 June 1941.
3 Central Executive, 'Some First Thoughts', 23 June 1941, Central Committee Circulars and Statements, CPA records, SLNSW MLMSS 5021, ADD-ON 1936, Box 5 (76); 'Mason' [J.B. Miles], 'Communists and the New Anti-Soviet War', *Tribune*, 30 June 1941.

4 Jack Blake, interviewed by Laurie Aarons, August 1979, SLNSW; Central Committee Circulars and Statements, 5, 9 July 1941, SLNSW MLMSS 5021, ADD-ON 1936, Box 5 (76).
5 Claude Jones, interviewed by Laurie Aarons, June 1980, SLNSW; 'The Wise Farseeing Stalin', *Tribune*, 27 July 1941; Geoffrey Roberts, *Stalin's Wars: From World War to Cold War, 1939–1953* (New Haven, CT: Yale University Press, 2006), ch. 4.
6 'Australian Communist Leader ("In Smoke") Talks', Sydney *Sun*, 16 July 1941; McShane [Sharkey], 'For a People's War for the Defeat of Fascism', *Communist Review*, no. 6 (September 1941), pp. 13–15.
7 'Communist Party Policy', *Tribune*, 27 July 1941; 'Menzies New Order', *Tribune*, 28 August 1941.
8 'Militants' Offer', *Sydney Morning Herald*, 24 September 1941; 'Sabotage of War Effort', *Tribune*, 7 October 1941.
9 Central Committee Circulars and Statements, 25, 28 October 1941, SLNSW MLMSS 5021, ADD-ON 1936, Box 5 (76); 'Leader', *Tribune*, 21 November 1941.
10 Central Committee Circulars and Statements, 28 October 1941.
11 'Let Us Have Action', *Tribune*, 12 December 1941; 'Dangerous National Government Trend', *Tribune*, 19 December 1941; for the British party, see Monty Johnstone, 'The CPGB, the Comintern and the War, 1939–1941: Filling in the Blank Spots', *Science and Society*, vol. 61, no. 1 (1997), pp. 27–45.
12 'Some Notes on the Communist Party in a Just War', *Communist Review*, no. 8 (January 1942), pp. 6–8; 'Urgent Problems of the United Front', *Party Builder*, no. 4 (September 1942), p. 1.
13 Central Committee Circulars and Statements, 5 July 1941; *Party Builder*, no. 1 (June 1942).
14 *Party Builder*, no. 6 (November 1942); Richard Dixon, 'The Party Building Campaign', *Communist Review*, no. 18 (February 1943), pp. 3–4.
15 *Party Builder*, no. 2 (July 1942), no. 3 (August 1942); *Forward*, 29 January 1943.
16 Political Committee Minutes, 29 October 1943, SLNSW MLMSS 5021, ADD-ON 1936, Box 1 (72); Len Donald, 'Victory Campaign Is Answer to Reactionary Offensive', *Communist Review*, no. 32 (April 1944), pp. 480–81; Secretariat to state committees, 18 December 1944, SLNSW MLMSS 5021, ADD-ON 1936, Box 5 (76); *Report of the Work of the Central Committee from the 13th to 14th National Congress* (Sydney: ACP, 1945).
17 Andrew Scott, *Fading Loyalties: The Australian Labor Party and the Working Class* (Sydney: Pluto Press, 1991), p. 29; Ian Hancock, *National and Permanent? The Federal Organisation of the Liberal Party of Australia* (Melbourne: MUP, 2000), pp. 39, 81.
18 'Newsprint for Communists', *Sydney Morning Herald*; Secretariat to state committees, 17 January 1945, SLNSW MLMSS 5021, ADD-ON 1936, Box 5 (76).
19 'Three Million Books Sold', *Tribune*, 15 February 1945.
20 'What's On', *Tribune*, 17 June 1943, 6 January 1944; see also Helen Macallan and John Potts, *Communism on the Air*, Media Papers no. 17 (Sydney: Faculty of Humanities and Social Sciences, New South Wales Institute of Technology, 1982).
21 'Communists' Radio Session', *Tribune*, 24 July 1945.
22 Related by Thornton in Proceedings of the Thirteenth Congress, SLNSW MLMSS 5021, ADD-ON 1936, Box 1 (72).
23 1942 financial statement in proceedings of the Thirteenth Congress.
24 'ACP Financial Statement', *Tribune*, 16 August 1945; a separate statement of Central Committee income for the years 1943 and 1944 appeared in the *Workers' Star*,

26 January 1946. Reserve Bank of Australia Pre-Decimal Inflation Calculator <www.rba.gov.au/calculator/annualPreDecimal.html>.

25 *Handbook for Tutors* (Sydney: CPA, n.d. [1943]); L. Harry Gould, *Glossary of Marxist Terms* (Sydney: Current Book Distributors, January 1943).

26 Jack Beasley, *Red Letter Days: Notes from Inside an Era* (Sydney: Australasian Book Society, 1979), p. 175; Gloria Garton in Joyce Stevens, *Taking the Revolution Home: Work Among Women in the Communist Party of Australia 1920–1945* (Melbourne: Sybylla Co-operative Press, 1987), p. 175.

27 See Robert George Boughton, 'Educating the Educators: The Communist Party of Australia and its Influence on Australian Adult Education', PhD thesis, La Trobe University, 1997, ch. 5.

28 '1000 Wardens Recruited', *Sydney Morning Herald*, 14 December 1940; see Beverley Symons, 'All-Out for the People's War: "Red Diggers" in the Armed Forces and the Communist Party of Australia's Policies in the Second World War', BA Hons thesis, University of Wollongong, 1993, ch. 2.

29 Hughes quoted in Nancy Wills, *Shades of Red: Personal and Political Recollections of a Communist to Mark the Occasion of Our Sixtieth Anniversary 1920–1980* (Brisbane: Communist Arts Group, 1966), p. 36.

30 'Train and Arm the People', *Tribune*, 14 January 1942; 'A People's Army', *Tribune*, 11 February 1942; *They Shall Not Pass: A Preliminary Plan for a People's Defence* (Sydney: Current Book Distributors, 1942).

31 'Let's Have a Real People's Army', *Daily Telegraph*, 1 February 1942; see also 'We Could Fight the Japanese', Sydney *Sun*, 4 January 1942, and Tom Wintringham, 'New Ideas in Home Defence', *Argus*, 2 February 1942.

32 These and two other manuals by Idriess were published as *The Australian Guerrilla* series (Sydney: Angus & Robertson, 1942), along with Lockwood's book in the same year.

33 People's Defence Auxiliary, NAA A472, W6146; Tim Bowden, 'The Making of an Australian Communist: Rupert Lockwood', *Politics*, vol. 9, no. 1 (1974), p. 16; see Michael McKernan, *All In! Australia during the Second World War* (Melbourne: Nelson, 1983), pp. 12–24, and Rowan Cahill, 'Rupert Lockwood (1908–1997): Journalist, Communist, Intellectual', PhD thesis, University of Wollongong, 2013, pp. 198–203.

34 Report of address by Dixon, 5 March 1942, People's Army, NAA A9108, ROLL 4/16, ff. 61–63.

35 Central executive resolutions, 6, 9 December 1941, Central Committee Circulars and Statements; George Gowland, *I Have Joined the AIF* (Sydney: Liberal Rights Committee, 1941); George Edward Duncan Gowland, NAA A6162, 863, f. 22; Bill McDougall, interviewed by Laurie Aarons, n.d. [1980], SLNSW.

36 *Communist Party Program for the Soldiers* (Sydney: CPA, n.d. [1942]); 'RAAF', 'The Armed Struggle and the United Front', *Communist Review*, no. 20 (April 1943), pp. 46–47; *Plan for the Fighting Man*, (Sydney: ACP, August 1944).

37 Symons, 'All-Out for the People's War', ch. 3.

38 'Communists in People's War', *Tribune*, 1 February 1945; *Report of the Work of the Central Committee from the 13th to 14th National Congress*, p. [xii].

39 Betty Reilly, 'A Programme for 800,000 People', *Communist Review*, no. 39 (November 1944), pp. 362–64; W.A. Wood and Len Fox, *Cobbers and Comrades* (Sydney: SLP, November 1942), p. 11.

40 Eric Lambert, *The Twenty Thousand Thieves* (Melbourne: Newmont, 1951; London: Frederick Muller, 1952), p. 363; see Zoe O'Leary, *The Desolate Market: A Biography*

of Eric Lambert (Sydney: Edwards & Shaw, 1974), pp. 27–36; Teri Merlyn, 'Writing Revolution: The British Radical Literary Tradition as Seminal Force in the Development of Adult Education, its Australian Context, and the Life and Work of Eric Lambert', PhD thesis, Griffith University, 2003.

41 Lawrence Louis Sharkey, NAA A6119, 219, f. 108; 'Communists to Confer', *Sunday Telegraph*, 14 March 1943; 'Newsprint for Communists', *Sydney Morning Herald*, 5 June 1943.

42 'Garden's Opportunity', *Tribune*, 1 April 1942; 'Political Roundabout', *Daily Telegraph*, 24 January 1943; Jack Hughes, interviewed by Laurie Aarons, September 1980, SLNSW.

43 'We Must Have Discipline', *Tribune*, 14 January 1942; Ernie Thornton, *Trade Unions and the War* (Sydney: FIA, n.d. [1942]), p. 18; R.D. [Richard Dixon], 'Production for Victory', *Communist Review*, no. 8 (January 1941), pp. 12–13; S.J. Butlin and C.B. Schedvin, *War Economy 1942–1945* (Canberra: Australian War Memorial, 1977), p. 372.

44 'Restraint Must Be Exercised by Government and Unions', *Tribune*, 13 March 1945; Thornton, 'Trade Union Report', Proceedings of the Thirteenth Congress; L. Sharkey, *The Trade Unions: Communist Theory and Practice of Trade Unions* (Sydney: CPA, November 1942), and *Report on the Work of the Central Committee from the 12th to the 13th Party Congress* (Sydney: Dimitrov Press, 1943).

45 Vic Williams, *The Years of Big Jim* (Perth: Lone Hand Press, 1975), ch. 8; Wendy Lowenstein and Tom Hills, *Under the Hook: Melbourne Waterside Workers Remember: 1900–1980* (Melbourne: Melbourne Bookworkers, 1982), pp. 93–98; Craig Thomas Ryan, 'Ships and Sickles: The Communists and Three Australian Maritime Trade Unions, 1928–1945', MA thesis, University of New South Wales, 1989, ch. 3.

46 Brian Fitzpatrick and Rowan J. Cahill, *The Seamen's Union of Australia 1872–1972: A History* (Sydney: Seamen's Union of Australia, 1982), part 2, ch. 2; Richard Morris, 'The Maritime Industry Commission 1942–1952: Towards Order in Shipping Labour Relations', *The Great Circle*, vol. 20, no. 1 (1998), pp. 46–58.

47 John Merritt, 'A History of the Federated Ironworkers' Association of Australia, 1909–1952', PhD thesis, ANU, 1968, ch. 7; Beverley Symons, 'Challenging and Maintaining the Traditional Gender Order: Labour Movement Responses to Women Workers in the Metal Industries, and to Equal Pay in World War II', PhD thesis, University of Wollongong, 1997, chs 6, 8.

48 Daphne Gollan, 'The Duly and Hansford Strike 1943: Find the Strikers', in Margaret Bevege, Margaret James and Carmel Shute (eds), *Worth Her Salt* (Sydney: Hale & Iremonger, 1982), pp. 309–18; Warwick Eather, 'BHP, the Intransigent Rank and File and the 1943 Lockout at the Newcastle Steelworks', *Labour History*, no. 59 (November 1990), pp. 28–44.

49 'Ironworkers New Headquarters', *Tribune*, 10 July 1945.

50 Transport Workers' Union official quoted in Merritt, 'A History of the Federated Ironworkers' Association of Australia', p. 288; 'Thornton's £10,000 Libel Claim', Sydney *Truth*, 25 March 1940; see E. Thornton, *Stronger Trades Unions: Opponents Answered* (Sydney: FIA, November 1943), and J. McPhillips, 'The Wartime Record of the Ironworkers' Union', *Communist Review*, no. 45 (May 1945), pp. 501–503.

51 Donald Pierre Dingsdag, 'The Restructuring of the NSW Coalmining Industry, 1902–1982', PhD thesis, University of Wollongong, 1998, ch. 5; Harold C. Wells, *The Earth Cries Out* (Sydney: Angus & Robertson, 1950).

52 'Textile Girls Idle', *Sydney Morning Herald*, 24 February 1943; 'More Textile Girls Join

Strike', *Daily Telegraph*, 15 February 1943; 'Detrimental', *Daily Telegraph*, 16 March 1943.

53 'Strike at Mills', *Sydney Morning Herald*, 26 August 1941; Joyce Batterham in Stevens, *Taking the Revolution Home*, pp. 206–209; Dorothy Hewett, 'Introduction', *Bobbin Up* (London: Virago, 1985), pp. xi.

54 Tom Sheridan, *Mindful Militants: The Amalgamated Engineering Union in Australia 1920–1972* (Cambridge: CUP, 1975), p. 206; Bradon Ellem, 'Ideology and Union Purpose: The Federated Clerks' Union in New South Wales 1946–58', *Australian Journal of Politics and History*, vol. 43, no. 3 (1997), pp. 344–60; Glenn Mitchell, *On Strong Foundations: The BWIU and Industrial Relations in the Australian Construction Industry 1942–1992* (Sydney: Harcourt, Brace and Co., 1996), esp. pp. 41–45; Audrey Johnson, *Bread & Roses: A Personal History of Three Militant Women and Their Friends 1902–1988* (Sydney: Left Book Club, 1990), esp. pp. 94–98.

55 Jack Lindsay, *Factory Front* (Sydney: Labor Council of NSW, n.d. [1942]); *The Battle for Production* (Sydney: Labor Council of NSW, n.d. [1942]; 'Bungling, Apathy Must End', *Tribune*, 24 March 1943.

56 Bernie Brian, 'The Northern Territory's One Big Union: The Rise and Fall of the North Australian Workers' Union, 1911–1972', PhD thesis, Northern Territory University, 2001, ch. 7; Murray Norris, 'Rebuilding the North Australian Workers' Union', in Hal Alexander and Phil Griffiths (eds), *A Few Rough Reds: Stories of Rank and File Organising* (Canberra: ASSLH Canberra Branch, 2003), pp. 63–109.

57 Bruce Mitchell, *Teachers, Education, and Politics: A History of Organizations of Public School Teachers in New South Wales* (Brisbane: UQP, 1975), pp. 157–60; Clem Lloyd, *Profession Journalist: A History of the Australian Journalists' Association* (Sydney: Hale & Iremonger, 1985), pp. 221–25; James Hagan, 'Craft Power: The Sydney Newspapers Strike and Lockout of 1944', in John Iremonger, John Merritt and Graeme Osborne (eds), *Strikes: Studies in Twentieth Century Australian History* (Sydney: Angus & Robertson, 1973), pp. 159–75; Actors' Equity, vol. 1, NAA A6122, 186.

58 Chris Healy, *The Lifeblood of Footscray: Working Lives at the Angliss Meatworks* (Melbourne: Living Museum of the West, 1986), pp. 89–101; Tom Sheridan, *Division of Labour: Industrial Relations in the Chifley Years 1945–49* (Melbourne: OUP, 1989), pp. 117–24; Mark Hearn, *Working Lives: A History of the Australian Railways Union (NSW Branch)* (Sydney: Hale & Iremonger, 1990), pp. 81–82, 94–95; Eddie Butler-Bowden, *In the Service? A History of the Victorian Railways Workers and their Union* (Melbourne: Hyland House, 1991), pp. 114–20.

59 'United Front Plan Adopted', *Daily Telegraph*, 24 June 1943; 'Powers to Be Reviewed', *Sydney Morning Herald*, 26 June 1943.

60 Thornton, *Trade Unions and the War*, p. 21.

61 Joyce Batterham in Stevens, *Taking the Revolution Home*, p. 209.

62 Symons, 'Challenging and Maintaining the Traditional Gender Order', chs 6–7.

63 *Women for Victory* (Sydney: NSW Legal Rights Committee, October 1942); *Australian Women's Charter* (Sydney: Australian Women's Conference, 1943); Nell Quinlan, 'A Charter for Australian Women', *Communist Review*, no. 34 (June 1944), pp. 268–69.

64 'Don' [Len Donald], 'Communist Party Growth Strengthens Labor and National Unity', *Communist Review*, no. 17 (December 1942), pp. 5–6; Dixon 'The Party Building Campaign'.

65 'Don', 'Communist Party Growth Strengthens Labor and National Unity'; p. 5; K.S. Prichard, 'Party Women Must Study', *Tribune*, 11 November 1943.

66 'Gloria Garton' in Stevens, *Taking the Revolution Home*, pp. 224–31; see also Lyn

Finch, 'Comrades: Women in the Communist Party 1941–1951, an Oral History', MA qualifying thesis, University of Queensland, 1983.

67 Drusilla Modjeska, 'Dorothy Hewett', in Mary Chamberlain (ed.), *Writing Lives: Conversations between Women Writers* (London:Virago, 1988), pp. 86–87.

68 Audrey Blake, 'The Eureka Youth League: A Participant's Report', *Labour History*, no. 42 (May 1982), pp. 94–105; see also Audrey Blake, *A Proletarian Life* (Malmsbury: Kibble Books, 1984).

69 Audrey Elsie Blake, vol. 1, NAA A6119, 120; Harry Stein, *A Glance Over an Old Left Shoulder* (Sydney: Hale & Iremonger, 1994), ch. 7.

70 Organisation Report, the EYL, NAA A6119, 797, ff. 187–94; Barrie Blears, *Together With Us: A Personal Glimpse of the Eureka Youth League and its Origins, 1920 to 1970* (Sydney: the author, 2002), esp. chs 7, 8, 11.

71 Blake, 'The Eureka Youth League', p. 95; Blake and Bacon quoted in Blears, *Together With Us*, pp. 48, 88.

72 Fellowship of Australian Writers, vol. 1, NAA A6122, 189, ff. 204–205; proceedings of the Thirteenth Congress.

73 Bernard Smith, *Noel Counihan: Artist and Revolutionary* (Melbourne: OUP, 1993), pp. 175–77; Oriel Gray, *Exit Left: Memoirs of a Scarlet Woman* (Melbourne: Penguin, 1985), p. 108; Ken Harper, 'The Useful Theatre: The New Theatre Movement in Sydney and Melbourne 1935–1983', *Meanjin*, vol. 43, no. 1 (March 1984), pp. 56–71; *Australian New Writing*, no. 1 (Sydney: Current Book Distributors, 1943), p. 5.

74 Gould in *Culture, Democracy and Australia*, Marx House Publication no. 1 (Sydney: Current Book Distributors, n.d. [1943]), p. 3.

75 Censorship—Newspaper, NAA SP 109/3, 322/22; 'Legal to Stand as Communist', *Daily Telegraph*, 8 April 1942.

76 'Attack on Union Officials', *Sydney Morning Herald*, 23 September 1942; 'Communist Ban Worry to Labor', Sydney *Sun*, 17 October 1942; 'Uncertainty on Ban Lift', *Courier-Mail*, 8 January 1943.

77 Thomas Poole, 'The Establishment of the First Diplomatic Mission in the USSR: Outstanding Landmark or Great Embarrassment?', in John McNair and Thomas Poole (eds), *Russia and the Fifth Continent: Aspects of Russian-Australian Relations* (Brisbane: UQP, 1992), pp. 172–209; Personal Papers of Prime Minister, NAA M1416, 11–18.

78 'Support Curtin's Militia Changes', *Tribune*, 2 December 1942; see Ross McMullin, *The Light on the Hill: The Australian Labor Party 1891–1991* (Melbourne: OUP, 1991), pp. 221–23.

79 'Communist Ban', *Age*, 21 November 1942; 1942 Conference on Communist Party and Revocation of Ban, NAA A8911, ff. 4–6.

80 'Thoughts on Communist Rally', Adelaide *Mail*, 13 March 1943.

81 Proceedings of the Thirteenth Congress.

82 Miles in proceedings of the Thirteenth Congress.

83 Colin A. Hughes and B.D. Graham, *Voting for the Victorian Legislative Assembly 1890–1964* (Canberra: Department of Political Science, ANU, 1975), pp. 277, 282–92.

84 Colin A. Hughes and B.D. Graham, *Voting for the Australian House of Representatives 1901–1964* (Canberra: ANU Press, 1974), pp. 223–42.

85 Political committee, 23 August 1943, SLNSW MLMSS 5021, ADD-ON 1936, Box 5 (76).

86 Documents Obtained from the Police Raid on Australian Communist Party Headquarters, NAA A6122, 2860, ff. 51,103. This file contains a large collection of

the party's 1943 election material.

87 'Labor Council Declares for ALP-Communist Unity', *Tribune*, 19 May 1943; 'The ACTU Aids United Front', *Age*, 24 June 1943.

88 Jane Degras (ed.), *The Communist International 1919–1943* vol. 2 (London: OUP, 1965), pp. 477–79.

89 Stalin's statement to Reuter's Moscow correspondent on 28 May 1943 is reproduced in Fernando Claudin, *The Communist Movement: From Comintern to Cominform* (London: Penguin, 1975), p. 45.

90 Claudin, *The Communist Movement*, ch. 1; see also Paola Spriano, *Stalin and the European Communists* (London:Verso, 1985), ch. 11.

91 'Disbanding of Communism: Stalin Tells of Reasons', *Sydney Morning Herald*, 31 March 1943; L.L. Sharkey, 'Comintern Move Hailed as a Sign of Strength', *Tribune*, 3 June 1943; J.B. Miles, 'Communist Party Has Greater Responsibilities', *Tribune*, 10 June 1943; Bert Birtles, 'The Comintern Is Dead—What Now?', *Daily Telegraph*, 30 May 1943.

92 *Draft Resolution on the Amalgamation of the Communist Party and State Labor Party (NSW)* (Sydney: Consultative Committee, n.d. [October 1944]), and Consultative Committee Minutes, SLNSW MLMSS 5021, ADD-ON 1936, Box 4 (75).

93 McKell, '"State Labor" CP Fusion', *Daily Telegraph*, 16 October 1943; Miles in 'State Labor Delegates Endorse Merger', *Tribune*, 2 December 1943.

94 *Foreign Relations of the United States: Diplomatic Papers, The Conferences at Cairo and Tehran, 1943* (Washington: United States Government Printing Office, 1961), pp. 640–41.

95 'Communist Party CC Hails Victory Pact of Teheran', *Tribune*, 9 December 1943; see also *Teheran, the Key to Victory: Worldwide Democracy and an Enduring Peace* (Melbourne: Australia–Soviet Friendship League, n.d. [1944]).

96 Maurice Isserman, *Which Side Were You On? The American Communist Party during the Second World War* (Urbana: University of Illinois Press, 1993), ch. 9.

97 'Communism in America', *Tribune*, 20 January 1944; L.L. Sharkey, 'What Browder Really Said', *Communist Review*, no. 30 (February 1944), pp. 197–99.

98 'The American Political Situation and the Policy of the C.P.', *Communist Review*, no. 29 (January 1944) reproduced the initial statement issued by Browder; *Choose Between Teheran and Hitler* (Sydney: Central Committee of the ACP, 1944) consists of extracts from his address to the CPUSA National Convention in May.

99 Political Committee Minutes, 24 January 1944, SLNSW MLMSS 5021, ADD-ON 1936, Box 5 (76), record an inconclusive discussion of a message sent by Browder.

100 *Programme of the Australian Communist Party* (Sydney: ACP, 1944), pp. 2–3.

101 J.B. Miles to the secretary of the ALP Federal Executive, 26 January 1944, ALP Affiliation Campaign, SLNSW MLMSS 5021, ADD-ON 1936, Box 5 (76); 'Amalgamation is Step to United Workers' Party', *Tribune*, 20 January 1944.

102 *Communist-Labor Affiliation Means …* (Sydney: ACP, February 1944).

4 Headwinds, 1943–45

1 Fernando Claudin, *The Communist Movement: From Comintern to Cominform* (London: Penguin, 1975), pp. 307–10.

2 *A United Working Class and a National Front for Victory* (Sydney: Central Committee of the CPA, 1943), p. 13.

3 Peter S. Cook, *Red Barrister: A Biography of Ted Laurie* (Melbourne: La Trobe University Press, 1994), pp. 59–61.

4 State committee to Central Committee, 18 April 1942, E.W. Campbell, vol. 1, NAA A6119, 1697, ff. 115–16; see also Bernard Smith, *Noel Counihan: Artist and Revolutionary* (Melbourne: OUP, 1993), pp. 177–79.
5 'Common Cause Inaugurated', Adelaide *Advertiser*, 12 March 1943; Common Cause prospectus, quoted in Stuart Macintyre, 'South Australia: The Pivotal State', in Carolyn Collins and Paul Sendziuk (eds), *Foundational Fictions in South Australian History* (Adelaide: Wakefield Press, 2018), p. 146.
6 Alf Watt, letter to *Advertiser*, 19 May 1943; Joan Finger in Proceedings of the Thirteenth Congress, CPA records, SLNSW MLMSS 5021, ADD-ON 1936, Box 1 (72); see also correspondence between Alf and Rae Watt, Alfred Deaken Watt, vol. 1, NAA A6119, 2129, and Elsie Rae Watt, vol. 1, NAA A6119, 2191.
7 'Communists to Contest 16 Seats in Election', *Tribune*, 8 July 1943; 'WA Communists Must Overcome Submergence', *Workers' Star*, 21 April 1944.
8 'Aus. Reds May Alter Policy', *Sunday Telegraph*, 6 August 1944.
9 Thornton, report to Political Committee, n.d., in Political Committee, 14–15 October 1944, SLNSW MLMSS 5021, ADD-ON 1936, Box 16.
10 Thornton to secretariat, 9 October, and Queensland secretariat to national secretariat, 10 December, in Political Committee, 14–15 October 1944; 'Many Fear Depression', *Daily Telegraph*, 23 November 1944; see John Merritt, 'A History of the Federated Ironworkers' Association of Australia, 1909–1952', PhD thesis, ANU, 1968, pp. 325–29.
11 Report by the political committee to Central Committee Plenum, 10 August 1945, in Political Committee, 14–15 October 1944.
12 Thornton and Miles in proceedings of the Thirteenth Congress; Thornton in Political Committee, 14–15 October 1944; 'Police Must Smash Black Markets, Gangsters!', *Tribune*, 8 February 1945.
13 *A United Working Class and a National Front for Victory*, p. 14.
14 Winston Churchill, *The Second World War. Volume 5: The Closing Ring* (London: Cassell, 1952), p. 321.
15 Roy Dalgarno, 'The Winking of an Eye', unpublished memoirs in possession of Lynn Dalgarno; see also Enzo Traverso, *Fire and Blood: The European Civil War 1914–1945* (London: Verso, 2016), pp. 265–66.
16 'Boss Press Weeps Over Trotsky', *Tribune*, 10 September 1940; 'Trotskyism—The Vilest of Fifth Columns', *Tribune*, 17 February 1943.
17 L.H. Gould and W.A. Wood, *How Russia Smashed its Fifth Column* (Sydney: Current Book Distributors, 1943), pp. 1, 21, 33.
18 Isaac Deutscher, *The Prophet Outcast. Trotsky: 1929–1940* (New York: Vintage Books, 1963), pp. 457–74.
19 Gould and Wood, *How Russia Smashed its Fifth Column*, pp. 1, 32; 'Trotskyism—The Vilest of Fifth Columns'.
20 Erik van Ree, *The Political Thought of Joseph Stalin: A Study in Twentieth-Century Revolutionary Patriotism* (New York: Routledge, 2006), ch. 12; see also Kevin Morgan, *International Communism and the Cult of the Individual: Leaders, Tribunes and Martyrs under Lenin and Stalin* (London: Palgrave Macmillan, 2017).
21 Gerald Peel in *Communist Review*, first series, vol. 6, no. 5 (May 1939).
22 W.J. Thomas, *Stalin and Associates* (Sydney: NSW Bookstall Company, 1941), pp. 22, 31–32; *Australian Women's Weekly*, 12 May 1945.
23 *Commonwealth Parliamentary Debates*, 31 May 1945.
24 Michael Bertram, 'A History of the Institute of Public Affairs', MComm thesis,

University of Melbourne, 1989, ch. 1; Lachlan Clohesy, 'Australian Cold Warrior: The Anti-Communism of W.C. Wentworth', PhD thesis, Victoria University, 2010, pp. 195–200.

25 Michael Lamb, *Red Glows the Dawn* (Melbourne, n.p., n.d. [December 1942]), pp. 25, 37.

26 Patrick Weller and Beverley Lloyd (eds), *Federal Executive Minutes 1915–1955: Minutes of the Meetings of the Federal Executive of the Australian Labor Party* (Melbourne: MUP, 1978), p. 238; see also Paul Strangio, *Neither Power Nor Glory: 100 Years of Political Labor in Victoria, 1856–1956* (Melbourne: MUP, 2012), pp. 249–57.

27 'Minister Not to Attend Soviet Rally', Melbourne *Herald*, 6 November 1943; 'Soviet Minister and ALP President', Melbourne *Herald*, 8 November 1943; 'Political Roundabout', *Daily Telegraph*, 14 November 1943; see *Australia and the USSR: And Some Victorian Leaders* (Melbourne: Australia–Soviet Friendship League, 1944).

28 Ted Hill, *Crisis in the Victorian Labor Party* (Melbourne: State Committee of the ACP, 1944), p. [14].

29 B.A. Santamaria, *Against the Tide* (Oxford: OUP, 1981), pp. 70–76.

30 Bruce Duncan, *Crusade or Conspiracy? Catholics and the Anti-Communist Struggle in Australia* (Sydney: UNSWP, 2001), pp. 25–26, 58–59; Stephen Holt, 'Bert Cremean and the Birth of the Movement', *Quadrant*, vol. 51, no. 6 (June 2007), pp. 30–33.

31 '"Workers' Rights" Radio Front', *Tribune*, 30 September 1943; Lloyd Ring Coleman, NAA A6126, 756, ff. 26–28; H.E. Krygier, 'International Note', *Labor Call*, 17 February 1944–20 December 1945; 'More False Notes in Labor Call', Melbourne *Guardian*, 26 January 1945.

32 Santamaria, *Against the Tide*, p. 75.

33 Hewlett Johnson, *The Socialist Sixth of the World* (London: Victor Gollancz, 1939); see John Butler, *The Red Dean of Canterbury: The Public and Private Faces of Hewlett Johnson* (London: Scala, 2011).

34 'The Church and the Communist', *Age*, 21 August 1944; 'Russia's Great Achievements', *Age*, 28 August 1944; see also C.M. Churchward, *The Rising Tide of Communism: An Appeal to Christian People* (Sydney: the author, November 1943), and Kurt Merz, Ralph Gibson and Farnham E. Maynard, *A Fair Hearing for Socialism* (Melbourne, n.p., n.d. [1944]).

35 Lamb, *Red Glows the Dawn*, p. 15; P.J. Ryan, 'The Christianity of Dean Hewlett Johnson', *Catholic Weekly*, 26 November 1942, and *Dean Hewlett Johnson's Socialist Sixth: A Commentary* (Sydney: Secretariat of the Lay Apostolate, 1943); L.L. Sharkey, *A Reply to Father Ryan* (Sydney: CPA, n.d. [1943]); P.J. Ryan, *Said Comrade Sharkey* (Sydney: the author, n.d. [1944]); W.A. Wood, 'Letter to a Christian', *Communist Review*, no. 42, (February 1945), pp. 435–37.

36 L.L. Sharkey, 'Dr Ryan's Reply Was Weak', *Tribune*, 27 January 1944; *A United Working Class and a National Front for Victory*, p. 11; 'Communism Attacked', *Sydney Morning Herald*, 24 May 1943.

37 'Freedom Disowned by All Churches', Melbourne *Guardian*, 4 August 1944; 'Dr Mannix Repudiates Clerical-Fascist Paper', *Tribune*, 10 August 1944.

38 Santamaria, 'Report on Anti-Communist Campaign', n.d. [1944], Catholic Action, NAA A6122, 129, ff. 60–69; the report is reproduced in Patrick Morgan (ed.), *B.A. Santamaria: Running the Show: Selected Documents 1939–1996* (Melbourne: Miegunyah Press, 2008), pp. 115–29.

39 Duncan, *Crusade or Conspiracy?*, ch. 5; see also Mark Aarons, *The Show: Another Side*

of Santamaria's Movement (Melbourne: Scribe, 2017), ch. 1, and Gerard Henderson, *Santamaria: A Most Unusual Man* (Melbourne: Miegunyah Press, 2015).

40 Aarons, *The Show*, pp. 23–31.

41 *Catholic Action at Work* (Sydney: ACP and Melbourne: International Bookshop, n.d. [December 1945]), pp. 13, 25.

42 *Year Book Australia*, 1944–45, pp. 438–39; 1945–46, pp. 497–98.

43 Robin Gollan, *The Coalminers of New South Wales: A History of the Union 1860–1960* (Melbourne: MUP, 1963), pp. 225–26; Tom Sheridan, *Mindful Militants: The Amalgamated Engineering Union in Australia 1920–1972* (Cambridge: CUP, 1975), pp. 204–26.

44 'Secret Union-Splitting Move', *Tribune*, 5 July 1945 reproduces the circular; 'Progressive Win in Three Unions', *Tribune*, 7 December 1945.

45 See Scott Stephenson, 'Oligarchy Contested and Interconnected: The New South Wales Labor Party and the Trade Unions from 1910 to 1939', PhD thesis, ANU, 2017, for an illuminating comparison of the AWU and the Miners' Federation.

46 Proceedings of the Thirteenth Congress.

47 'Attack on Mr Gourlay', *Advertiser*, 14 November 1944; 'The Advertiser Supports Mr Gourlay', communist handbill in J. Normington Rawling Collection, NBAC N57/547.

48 Bernard Smith, *A Pavane for Another Time* (Melbourne: Macmillan, 2002), p. 94; Daphne Gollan, 'The Memoirs of "Cleopatra Sweatfigure"', in Elizabeth Windschuttle (ed.), *Women Class and History: Feminist Perspectives on Australian History 1788–1988* (Sydney: Fontana, 1980), p. 323.

49 *Catholic Action at Work*, p. 25; Ernie Thornton, *Stronger Trades Unions: Opponents Answered* (Sydney: FIA, November 1943), p. 28.

50 Merritt, 'A History of the Federated Ironworkers' Association of Australia', pp. 325–39; J.T. Lang, *Communism in Australia* (Sydney: Express Newspapers, 1944).

51 Audrey Johnson, *Fly a Rebel Flag: Bill Morrow 1888–1980* (Melbourne: Penguin, 1986), p. 149.

52 John Sebesta, Douglas Fullerton, Stephen Morell and Lyn Smith, 'The French "Turn" in the Antipodes: Early Trotskyists and the Australian Labor Party, 1937–55', *Labour History*, no. 107 (November 2014), pp. 129–48.

53 Hall Greenland, *Red Hot: The Life & Times of Nick Origlass* (Sydney: Wellington Lane Press, 1998), chs 14–15; Susanna Short, *Laurie Short: A Political Life* (Sydney: Allen & Unwin, 1992), chs 5–6.

54 T. Wright, 'Unity and the Trade Unions', *Communist Review*, no. 32 (April 1944), p. 225; Short, *Laurie Short*, p. 80; the fullest account is Daphne Gollan, 'The Balmain Ironworkers' Strike of 1945', *Labour History*, no. 22 (1972), pp. 23–41, and no. 23 (1972), pp. 62–73.

55 Report of Trade Union Convention, 6–7 June 1944, NAA A9816, 1943/924.

56 'Militants Get Control of ACTU Congress', *Sydney Morning Herald*, 14 June 1945; 'Win for Militants at ACTU Congress', *Age*, 15 June 1945.

57 Ray Markey, *In Case of Oppression: The Life and Times of the Labor Council of New South Wales* (Sydney: Pluto Press, 1994), pp. 293–94.

58 'ALP Rejects Link-Up With Communists', *Daily Telegraph*, 11 June 1944; see Jim Hagan and Ken Turner, *A History of the Labor Party in New South Wales* (Melbourne: Longman Cheshire, 1991), pp. 151–53, and D.W. Rawson, 'The ALP Industrial Groups', in J.E. Isaac and G.W. Ford (eds), *Australian Labour Relations: Readings* (2nd edn, Melbourne: Sun Books, 1971), pp. 205–22.

59 Graham Freudenberg, *Cause for Power: The Official History of the New South Wales Branch of the Australian Labor Party* (Sydney: Pluto Press, 1991), pp. 211–13.

60 L. Harry Gould, 'Art Against Fascism', 'Art and the People', 'Decadent Art is Fascist Weapon', *Tribune*, 29 July, 5, 12 August 1943; I draw here on David Carter, 'Re-Viewing Communism: Communist Review (Sydney), 1934–1966: A Checklist of Literary Material', *Australian Literary Studies*, vol. 12, no. 1 (1985), pp. 93–105.

61 Charles Merewether, *Art & Social Commitment: An End to the City of Dreams, 1931–1948* (Sydney: Art Gallery of New South Wales, 1984), pp. 8–48.

62 Janine Burke, *Australian Gothic: A Life of Albert Tucker* (Sydney: Knopf, 2002), p. 227; Bernard Smith, *Noel Counihan: Artist and Revolutionary* (Melbourne: OUP, 1993), pp. 183–87; see also Richard Haese, *Rebels and Precursors: The Revolutionary Years of Australian Art* (Melbourne: Allen Lane, 1981), chs 4–6.

63 Smith, *A Pavane for Another Time*, p. 123; Sheridan Palmer, *Hegel's Owl: The Biography of Bernard Smith* (Sydney: Power Publications, University of Sydney, 2016), pp. 66–67.

64 'Courbet', 'Realists Challenge Surrealists', *Tribune*, 6 July 1944; Noel Counihan, 'The Double-Dealing of John Reed', *Communist Review*, no. 37 (September 1944), pp. 325–27.

65 Noel Counihan, 'Pretentious Penguins Exposed by Hoax', Melbourne *Guardian*, 14 July 1944; Vic O'Connor, 'A Criticism of Adelaide's "Angry Penguins"', *Communist Review*, no. 36 (August 1944), pp. 302–303; see Michael Heyward, *The Ern Malley Affair* (Brisbane: UQP, 1993), and Barrett Reid and Nancy Underhill (eds), *Letters of John Reed: Defining Australian Cultural Life 1920–1981* (Melbourne: Viking, 2001), pp. 230–32, 238–39.

66 *Australian New Writing*, no. 1 (Sydney: Current Book Distributors, 1943), p. 4.

67 Smith, *Noel Counihan*, p. 5; Counihan, 'The Double-Dealing of John Reed', p. 326; see Sean Scalmer, 'The Career of Class: Intellectuals and the Labour Movement in Australia 1942–56', PhD thesis, University of Sydney, 1996, p. 60.

68 Letter to Dave Morris, September 1944, in Bernice Morris, *Between the Lines* (Melbourne: Sybylla Co-operative Press, 1988), p. 66.

69 Nadine Dalgarno, 'What Kind of Music?', *Communist Review*, no. 44 (April 1945), pp. 482–83; Deirdre Moore, 'The Realist Writers', *Overland*, no. 156 (Spring 1999), pp. 24–25; 'Impressive Concert Was Crowded Out', *Tribune*, 1 February 1945.

70 John and Ray Oldham, 'The Modern Ballet We Really Want', *Tribune*, 19 July 1945; Louise Mackay, 'Ballet Controversy', *Tribune*, 23 August 1945; J.S.B., 'Australian Culture and the Ballet', *Communist Review*, no. 51 (November 1945), pp. 68–71.

71 Eric Hobsbaum (sic), 'No Future for the Hero?', *Tribune*, 16 November 1944; 'Film Promises to Capture True Australian Spirit', *Tribune*, 29 March 1945; Gerry Harant, 'We Laid 'Em in the Aisles', *Overland*, no. 156 (Spring 1999), pp. 35–39; John Hughes, *The Archive Project: The Realist Film Unit in Cold War Australia* (Melbourne: Early Works, 2013), pp. 20–29.

72 Jill Roe and Jane E. Hunt, 'Dorothy Jane Adele Helmrich', *Australian Dictionary of Biography*, vol. 17, p. 512.

73 'Ride Out Stranger', *Tribune*, 9 March 1944; Jane Grant, *Kylie Tennant: A Life* (Canberra: NLA, 2006), p. 61.

74 'Attitude of Workers' Rights Association', *Age*, 24 September 1943; '£2000 Claim on Politician Fails', *Courier-Mail*, 9 March 1944; 'Communist Sues the Herald for Libel Damages', Melbourne *Herald*, 20 November 1944; 'Thornton's £10,000 Libel Claim Against J.T. Lang', Sydney *Truth*, 25 March 1945.

75 L. Sharkey, 'Prof. Anderson—A Counter-Revolutionary Humbug', *Communist*

Review, no. 21 (May 1943), p. 55, and 'The WEA and the Inherent Lie', *Communist Review*, no. 22 (June 1943), pp. 5–6; the fullest account of the campaign against B40 is E.M. Higgins, *David Stewart and the WEA* (Sydney: WEA, n.d. [1957]), ch. 11.

76 Gollan in 'Council Outs WEA', *Tribune*, 5 May 1943; Wood in 'WEA and Communists', *Daily Telegraph*, 9 June 1943, and 'Letter to a Liberal', *Communist Review*, no. 38 (October 1944), pp. 344–46; Lance Sharkey, *The WEA Exposed* (Sydney: ACP, June 1944), p. 41; P.H. Partridge, 'The Lecture Has Caused a Controversy', *Daily Telegraph*, 17 June 1943.

77 The fullest accounts are Fay Anderson, *An Historian's Life: Max Crawford and the Politics of Academic Freedom* (Melbourne: MUP, 2005), pp. 124–42; Sheila Fitzpatrick, 'Max Crawford in the Soviet Union: The Historian as Diplomat', in Sheila Fitzpatrick and Carolyn Rasmussen (eds), *Political Tourists: Travellers from Australia to the Soviet Union in the 1920s–1940s* (Melbourne: MUP, 2008), pp. 212–34; and Alan Fewster, *Trusty and Well Beloved: A Life of Keith Officer, Australia's First Diplomat* (Melbourne: Miegunyah Press, 2009), ch. 9; see also John Fisher, NAA A6119, 6655, and Irene Agnes Saxby, vol. 1, NAA A6119, 1553.

78 Desmond Ball and David Horner, *Breaking the Codes: Australia's KGB Network, 1944–1950* (Sydney: Allen & Unwin, 1998), ch. 5.

79 Robert Louis Benson and Michael Warner (eds), *VENONA: Soviet Espionage and the American Response 1939–1957* (Washington, DC: National Security Agency, 1996); Ball and Horner, *Breaking the Codes*, ch. 11; Frank Cain, 'Venona in Australia and its Long-Term Ramifications', *Journal of Contemporary History*, vol. 35, no. 2 (2000), pp. 231–48.

80 Canberra to Moscow, 17 March 1945. This and other Venona documents are taken from the website of the National Security Agency, <www.nsa.gov/News-Features/Declassified-Documents/Venona>.

81 Canberra to Moscow, 25 April 1945; Walter Seddon Clayton, vol. 5, pt 1; NAA A6119, 57, f. 57; Evidence to Royal Commission on Espionage of Frances Bernie, 22 October 1954, pp. 1327–44, NAA A10932, 62.

82 Canberra to Moscow, 5 May 1945; Moscow to Canberra, 3 July, 17, 21 October 1945.

83 Canberra to Moscow, 29, 30 September 1945, 8, 19 March, 24 October 1946.

84 Ball and Horner, *Breaking the Codes*, p. 212.

85 Canberra to Moscow, 6 July 1945; Moscow to Canberra, 13 July 1945; Mark Younger, vol. 1, NAA A6119, 351.

86 W.D. Rubinstein, *The Jews in Australia: A Thematic History*, vol. 2, *1945 to the Present* (Melbourne: William Heinemann Australia, 1991), pp. 6, 11; Philip Mendes, 'Jewish Communism in Australia', in Matthew D. Hoffman and Henry F. Srebnik (eds), *A Vanished Ideology: Essays on the Jewish Communist Movement in the English-Speaking World in the Twentieth Century* (Albany: State University of New York Press, 2016), p. 198. For corrective accounts see David Rechter, 'Beyond the Pale: Jewish Communism in Melbourne', MA thesis, University of Melbourne, 1987, and Max Kaiser, 'Between Nationalism and Assimilation: Jewish Antifascism in Australia in the Late 1940s and early 1950s', PhD thesis, University of Melbourne, 2018.

87 David Rechter, 'The Gezerd Down Under', in Jonathan Frankel (ed.), *Jews and Messianism in the Modern Era: Metaphor and Meaning* (New York: OUP, 1991), pp. 275–83.

88 Communist Party of Australia—Interest and Activity in Jewish Community, NAA A6122, 444; Len Fox, *Australia and the Jews* (Sydney: Current Book Distributors, 1943).

89 *Erlich and Alter: Why the Soviet Union Shot These Two Traitors* (Sydney: CPA, 1943).
90 William Jan Sing Lee, vol. 1, NAA A6119, 2811; Communist Party of Australia, Victorian Chinese Branch, NAA A6122, 619; see also Paul Jones, '"A Consequent Gain in the Tempo of Effort": Chinese Labour and Chinese Industrial Activism in Australia, 1941–1945', in Greg Patmore, John Shields and Nikola Balnave (eds), *The Past Is Before Us: Proceedings of the Ninth National Labour History Conference, the University of Sydney* (Sydney: ASSLH, 2005), pp. 339–47.
91 Brian Fitzpatrick and Rowan J. Cahill, *The Seamen's Union of Australia 1872–1972: A History* (Sydney: Seamen's Union of Australia, 1982), pp. 168–78; Gerald Peel, *Hands Off Indonesia* (Sydney: Current Book Distributors, 1945); E.A.H. Laurie, *Australia in New Guinea* (Sydney: Current Book Distributors, August 1944).
92 'Down With Anti-Foreign Talk', *Tribune*, 25 February 1942; *Smash Japan* (Melbourne: International Bookshop, n.d. [1941), p. 12; Central Committee circular, 28 April 1942, SLNSW MLMSS 5021, ADD-ON 1936, Box 5 (76); 'We Don't Like "Jim Crow"', *Tribune*, 13 May 1942.
93 Rupert Lockwood, *Japan's Heart of Wood* (Sydney: Current Book Distributors, 1943); see also Rowan Cahill, 'Rupert Lockwood (1908–1997): Journalist, Communist, Intellectual', PhD thesis, University of Wollongong, 2013, pp. 170–71.
94 R. Dixon, 'White Australia', *Communist Review*, no. 35 (July 1944), pp. 278–81, and *Immigration and the 'White Australia' Policy* (Sydney: Current Book Distributors, n.d. [1945]), pp. 7, 12.
95 'Attack on "White Australia" Policy', *Sydney Morning Herald*, 5 June 1945; 'A Reply to Mr Thornton', *Sydney Morning Herald*, 7 June 1945.
96 'New Minister Urges Unity', Melbourne *Herald*, 6 November 1943; Canberra to Moscow, 10 August 1945; 'Government of Russia Criticised', *Argus*, 13 March 1946.

5 The Offensive, 1945–49

1 'Curtin's May Day Message', *Daily Telegraph*, 5 May 1945; 'A Great Leader', *Tribune*, 17 April 1945; 'Victory, Progress Are Curtin's Memorials', *Tribune*, 10 July 1945.
2 'Unique Exhibition to Glorify Australian Labor's Achievements', *Tribune*, 7 August 1945; 'Communist Party Buys Painting by Prominent Artists', *Tribune*, 16 October 1945.
3 '5000 at Congress Opening', *Tribune*, 14 August 1945; Laurie Aarons, interviewed by Joyce Stevens, 17 September 1980, SLNSW.
4 A note on terminology. The CPA used the Wade-Giles system for transcribing Chinese names of places and persons (hence Mao Tse-Tung). This has since been replaced by the Pinyin system (Mao Zedung), which I shall use for place names while keeping the older, more familiar form of the names of Chinese communists and places at this time.
5 Miles in proceedings of the Fourteenth Congress, CPA records, SLNSW MLMSS 5021, ADD-ON 1936, Box 2 (73), and *Resolutions of the 14th Congress of the Australian Communist Party* (Sydney: Central Committee of the ACP, October 1945), pp. 11–12, 16. The principal speeches were published separately, and Miles's address appears in J.B. Miles, *Jobs, Freedom, Progress* (Sydney: Central Committee of the ACP, October 1945), p. 10.
6 *Resolutions of the 14th Congress*, pp. 14, 18, 16.
7 J.D. Blake, *Unite for Post-War Progress* (Sydney: Central Committee of the ACP, October 1945), pp. 8–9, 13.

8 R. Dixon, *Our Tasks in the Federal Election* (Sydney: Central Committee of the ACP, October 1945), pp. 13–14.
9 *Jobs, Freedom, Progress: Draft Resolution for the 14th National Congress* (Sydney: ACP, May 1945), p. 1.
10 Bernie Taft, *Crossing the Party Line: Memoirs of Bernie Taft* (Newham: Scribe Publications, 1994), p. 47; Miles, *Jobs, Freedom, Progress*, p. 20.
11 L.L. Sharkey and E.W. Campbell, *The Story of Government Enterprise in Australia* (Sydney: ACP, January 1945), pp. 71–72; Blake, *Unite for Post-War Progress*, p. 9; Miles, *Jobs, Freedom, Progress*, pp. 11–12.
12 The original Russian version appears in Harvey Klehr, John Earl Haynes and Fridrikh Igorevich Firsov, *The Secret World of American Communism* (New Haven, CT: Yale University Press, 1998), pp. 96–98. Duclos's article, 'A propos du dissolution du Parti communiste américain', appeared in the American *Daily Worker* on 24 May 1945 as 'On the Dissolution of the Communist Party of the United States' and was reproduced in the *Communist Review*, no. 47 (July 1945), pp. 541–48; the political committee's response appeared as 'Criticism of Browder Endorsed', *Tribune*, 28 June 1945.
13 'ACP Congress Committee', *Tribune*, 16 August 1945.
14 L.L. Sharkey, 'The American Errors and Our Congress', *Communist Review*, no. 48 (August 1945), p. 570.
15 Miles in proceedings of the Fourteenth Congress; these strictures were omitted from the published version of his speech.
16 Miles, *Jobs, Freedom, Progress*, p. 15.
17 Roger Milliss, *Serpent's Tooth: An Autobiographical Novel* (Melbourne: Penguin, 1984), ch. 5 provides the fullest account, and between 1986 and 1993 John Low published a series of articles on other Katoomba activists in *The Hummer*, which are online (<www.labourhistory.org.au/hummer>); see also Communist Party of Australia—Katoomba Branch, NAA A6122, 760.
18 'Alderman Frank Walford Explains', *Blue Mountains Advertiser*, 17 November 1944; 'Reds Run Chifley's Electorate', *Sunday Telegraph*, 2 December 1945.
19 'Communism and Australia', *Blue Mountains Gazette*, 8 March 1946; 'ALP Delegates Clash in Communist Debate', *Daily Telegraph*, 7 June 1946; 'Labor Man Expelled', *Sydney Morning Herald*, 19 December 1946; 'Bruce Milliss Joins ACP', *Sydney Morning Herald*, 8 June 1947.
20 Canberra to Moscow, 8 March 1946, <www.nsa.gov/public_info/declass/venona>; 'Choice of New Envoy to Moscow', *Sydney Morning Herald*, 8 April 1946; Eric Dark, 'Who Holds the Key to the New Order?', *Sunday Telegraph*, 20 January 1946; E.P. Dark, *Who Are the Reds* (Sydney: the author, 1946).
21 'ALP Reprimands Dr Dark for Article', *Daily Telegraph*, 25 May 1946; 'Katoomba ALP: Branch Charter Withdrawn', *Sydney Morning Herald*, 19 March 1947; Catholic Action NSW State Convention, 18–19 October 1947, p. 14, J. Normington Rawling Collection, NBAC N57/549.
22 J.P. Abbott in *Commonwealth Parliamentary Debates*, 23 April 1947; Barbara Brooks with Judith Clark, *Eleanor Dark: A Writer's Life* (Sydney: Pan Macmillan, 1998), p. 317.
23 Ross Fitzgerald, *The People's Champion: Fred Paterson, Australia's Only Communist Party Member of Parliament* (Brisbane: UQP, 1997), pp. 110–22; Ian Moles, *A Majority of One: Tom Aikens and Independent Politics in Townsville* (Brisbane: UQP, 1979), pp. 59–98.
24 Colin A. Hughes and B.D. Graham, *Voting for the Queensland Legislative Assembly*

1890–1964 (Canberra: Department of Political Science, ANU, 1974), pp. 169, 178, 192, 203.

25 'Growth of Communism in the Herbert Electorate', *Bowen Independent*, 17 September 1943; 'Paterson Farewell Meeting', *Bowen Independent*, 21 July 1944; 'Paterson Play Ground Committee', *Townsville Daily Bulletin*, 28 June 1945; see Paterson's account of his parliamentary work in *Fred Paterson: A Personal History* (Brisbane: Brisbane Labour History Association, 1994), pp. 41–43.

26 Fitzgerald, *The People's Champion*, pp. 155–214; Fred Paterson, *Speeches in Parliament* (Sydney: Central Committee of the ACP, n.d. [1945]).

27 'Communists Fare Poorly', *Courier-Mail*, 8 April 1946; 'Lessons of the Townsville Poll', Brisbane *Guardian*, 12 April 1946.

28 Hughes and Graham, *Voting for the Queensland Legislative Assembly*, p. 228.

29 *Outline for Work With Municipal and Shire Councils*, How to Organise series, no. 8 (Sydney: ACP, 1943); 'Communist Council Has Master Plan for Shire', *Daily Telegraph*, 5 December 1944; see also Martin Mowbray, 'The Red Shire of Kearsley, 1944–1947: Communists in Local Government', *Labour History*, no. 51 (November 1986), 83–94.

30 'Kearsley Shire Elects President', *Tribune*, 21 December 1944; Alan Opie, 'Work of the Communist Councillors', *Communist Review*, no. 62 (October 1946), pp. 297–302; 'Miners Seek Control of Funds for Amenities, Sydney *Sun*, 31 July 1946.

31 H.B. Chandler, 'Communist Victories in Local Government', *Communist Review*, no. 41 (January 1945), p. 406; 'How Citizens' Committees Originated', *Tribune*, 5 April 1946; Ronald McKie, 'What Makes Citizens' Committees Tick', *Daily Telegraph*, 1 April 1946.

32 Joy Wilson, 'Maramanah—In Praise of Communal Living', *Tribune*, 30 July 1946; Elliot Lamb, '1946, Sydney: The Squatting of Maramanah', <www.australianmuseum ofsquatting.org/?p=815>.

33 'Homeless Families Seek ACP Aid', Brisbane *Guardian*, 24 January 1947; 'Camp Pellers Determined to Fight', Melbourne *Guardian*, 24 January 1947; 'Leaflets in Parliament', *Advertiser*, 27 November 1946; see also Iain McIntyre, 'Squats Across the Empire: A Comparison of Squatting Movements in Post-Second World War UK and Australia', in Udo Grasshof (ed.), *Comparative Approaches to Informal Housing around the Globe* (London: UCL Press, 2020), pp. 202–22.

34 Ken Miller, *A Modern Tale of Two Cities: Richmond and Toorak* (Melbourne: A Communist Publication, 1949), pp. 2, 4, 15; Ralph Gibson, *Socialist Melbourne* (2nd edn, Melbourne: International Bookshop, 1951), pp. 28, 31–32.

35 Edgar Ross in proceedings of the Fourteenth Congress; J.B. Miles, 'The Fight on the Industrial Front', *Communist Review*, no. 50 (October 1945), p. 516; Secretariat circular, 15 October 1945, Central Committee Circulars and Statements, SLNSW MLMSS 5021, ADD-ON 1936, Box 5 (76).

36 Stuart Macintyre, *Australia's Boldest Experiment: War and Reconstruction in the 1940s* (Sydney: NewSouth Publishing, 2015), ch. 9.

37 Tom Sheridan, *Division of Labour: Industrial Relations in the Chifley Years 1945–49* (Melbourne: OUP, 1989); ch. 10 discusses the Communist Party. See also Tom Sheridan, *Mindful Militants: The Amalgamated Engineering Union in Australia 1920–1972* (Cambridge: CUP, 1975), chs 7–8.

38 Sheridan, *Division of Labour*, pp. 69, 102.

39 Sheridan, *Division of Labour*, ch. 6; Warwick Eather puts greater emphasis on BHP's

responsibility in 'The Trenches at Home: The Industrial Struggle in the Newcastle Iron and Steel Industry 1937–1947', PhD thesis, University of Sydney, 1987, chs 8–9.

40 'BHP Bows to Unions in Round 1', *Tribune*, 8 January 1946; Sharkey in Central Committee, January 1946, SLNSW MLMSS 5021, ADD-ON 1936, Box 5 (76).

41 Douglas Blackmur, *Strikes: Causes, Conduct and Consequences* (Sydney: Federation Press, 1993), chs 4–7.

42 Central Committee, 31 May–2 June 1946, CPA records, SLNSW MLMSS 2389, Box 1 (72); J.C. Henry, 'The Queensland Meat Strike', *Communist Review*, no. 60 (August 1946), pp. 227–33.

43 'Mass Meeting in Uproar', *Courier-Mail*, 11 July 1946.

44 Central Committee, 31 May–2 June 1946, 1–3 November 1946, SLNSW MLMSS 2389, Box 1 (72).

45 Sheridan, *Division of Labour*, ch. 9.

46 Sheridan, *Division of Labour*, pp. 126–27, 181–202; 'Smashing Strike Win Forces Basic Wage', *Tribune*, 1 November 1946; Stuart Macintyre, 'John Joseph Brown', *Australian Dictionary of Biography*, vol. 17, pp. 149–50.

47 Ted Rowe and Tom Wright, *United Action Wins* (Sydney: Current Book Distributors, n.d. [1947]).

48 Sheridan, *Division of Labour*, ch. 7, and *Mindful Militants*, ch. 7.

49 Sharkey in Central Committee, 1–3 November 1946, pp. 10–13; 16–19 May 1947, pp. 9–12, SLNSW MLMSS 5021, ADD-ON 1936, Box 5 (76), and 14–16 February 1947, SLNSW MLMSS 2389, Box 1 (72).

50 Thornton's address to the FIA national conference is reported in 'Too Many Strikes', *Sydney Morning Herald*, 15 April 1947; Blake in Central Committee, 14–16 February 1947.

51 Michael Hess, 'Black and Red: The Pilbara Pastoral Workers' Strike, 1946', *Aboriginal History*, no. 18 (1994), pp. 65–83; D.M. Wilson, 'Different White People: Communists, Unionists and Aboriginal Rights 1946–1972', PhD thesis, University of Tasmania, 2013, chs 2–3; Donald William McLeod, NAA A6119, 3306 and A6126, 1188.

52 *Workers' Star*, 5 April–30 August 1946; D.W. McLeod, *How the West Was Lost: The Native Question in the Development of Western Australia* (Port Hedland: the author, n.d. [1984]).

53 Tom Wright, *New Deal for Aborigines* (Sydney: Modern Publishers, 1939); Tim Rowse, *Indigenous and Other Australians since 1901* (Sydney: UNSWP, 2017), pp. 174–78.

54 'Moving Natives No Solution', 'Natives Tell of Hardship', 'Discrimination Causes Suffering', *Workers' Star*, 24 March, 6 April, 5 May 1944; Communism—Aborigines, NAA A8911, 209; see also Sharon Delmege, 'From Camp Life to Suburbia: Aboriginal Housing in Perth', *Australian Historical Studies*, vol. 45, no. 3 (2014), pp. 368–87.

55 Joan Beaumont and Allison Cadzow (eds), *Serving Our Country: Indigenous Australians, War, Defence and Citizenship* (Sydney: NewSouth Publishing, 2018), chs 7–9.

56 Dr Alex Jolly, 'Some Clarity on the Question of Tribalized and De-Tribalized Aborigines', *Communist Review*, no. 34 (June 1944), pp. 269–70; 'Jagara' [Fred Rose], *Frederick Engels, Lewis Morgan and the Australian Aborigine* (Sydney: Current Book Distributors, 1946); Tom Wright, *New Deal for Aborigines* (2nd edn, Sydney: Current Book Distributors, 1944).

57 See, for example, 'Aboriginal Comrade', Brisbane *Guardian*, 9 March 1945.

58 Christopher Bayly and Tim Harper, *Forgotten Armies: Britain's Asian Empire and the War With Japan* (London: Allen Lane, 2004).

59 The fullest accounts are Rupert Lockwood, *Black Armada: Australia and the Struggle*

for Indonesian Independence 1942–49 (Sydney: Hale & Iremonger, 1982), and F.C. Bennett, *The Return of the Exiles: Australia's Repatriation of the Indonesians, 1945–1947* (Melbourne: Monash University Press, 2003).

60 Connie Healy, 'Recollections of the "Black Armada" in Queensland', *Queensland Journal of Labour History*, no. 2 (March 2006), pp. 15–27; Ralph Gibson, *The Fight Goes on: A Picture of Australia and the World in the Two Post-War Decades* (Maryborough: Red Rooster Press, 1987), pp. 65–71; Heather Goodall, 'Port Politics: Indian Seamen, Australian Unions and Indonesian Independence, 1945–47', *Labour History*, no. 94 (May 2008), pp. 43–68.

61 'Mercy Ships Defined', *Sydney Morning Herald*, 29 September 1945.

62 'Angry Indonesians Sail for Home', *Sunday Telegraph*, 14 October 1845; 'Indonesians Sail, Thank Australia', *Tribune*, 19 October 1945.

63 John Hughes, 'Indonesia Calling: Joris Ivens in Australia', *Senses of Cinema*, no. 51 (July 2009), online; see also Drew Cottle and Angela Keys, 'From Colonial Film Commissioner to Political Pariah: Joris Ivens and the Making of Indonesia Calling', *Senses of Cinema*, no. 41 (2006), and Hans Schoots, *Living Dangerously: A Biography of Joris Ivens* (Amsterdam: Amsterdam University Press, 2000).

64 'Bottles Thrown in Wharf Riot', *Daily Telegraph*, 8 November 1945; 'Communists Were Hosed', *Courier-Mail*, 8 November 1945; 'Dutch Troops Hurt Girl', *Tribune*, 9 November 1945; 'Moreton Bay's Crew Was Shanghaied', 16 November 1945.

65 'Anti-Dutch Film Banner for Export', 'Export Ban on Film Lifted', *Daily Telegraph*, 1 August, 14 November 1945; Chifley in *Commonwealth Parliamentary Debates*, 6 March 1946; on his conniving, see also David Fettling, 'J.B. Chifley and the Indonesian Revolution 1945–1949', *Australian Journal of Politics and History*, vol. 59, no. 4 (2013), pp. 517–31, and Julie Suares, *J.B. Chifley: An Ardent Internationalist* (Melbourne: MUP, 2019), ch. 5.

66 'Wild Fight in City', *Sydney Morning Herald*, 26 July 1947; Alan Barcan, *Radical Students: The Old Left at Sydney University* (Melbourne: MUP, 2002), pp. 196–203, includes a number of photos.

67 *Student 1941* (Melbourne: Australian Student Labor Federation, 1941), pp. 4–6. These clubs, as well as the Australian Student Labor Federation, also used the spelling Labour; and in addition to six universities in the state capitals, there were smaller university colleges in Canberra and Armidale.

68 Barcan, *Radical Students*, pp. 136–37.

69 Stuart Macintyre, *Australia's Boldest Experiment*, pp. 213–14, 326–33.

70 Ian Turner, 'The Functions of a Labor Club', *Shop*, vol. 1, no. 3, (n.d. [late 1945]), p. 7; 'Red Flag Had to Come Down', *Argus*, 14 August 1947; Ian Turner, 'My Long March', in *Room for Manoeuvre: Writings on History, Politics, Ideas and Play*, edited by Leonie Sandercock and Stephen Murray-Smith (Melbourne: Drummond Publishing, 1982), pp. 122–23.

71 Turner, 'My Long March', p. 122. Other accounts of Melbourne University Labour Club communists include Amirah Inglis, *The Hammer & Sickle and the Washing Up: Memories of an Australian Woman Communist* (Melbourne: Hyland House, 1995); Ken Gott, 'Student Life: The Forties', *Melbourne University Magazine*, Spring 1961, pp. 23–27; Max Marginson and Rivkah Mathews in Hume Dow (ed.), *More Memories of Melbourne University* (Melbourne: Hutchinson, 1985); Stephen Murray-Smith in Hume Dow (ed.), *Memories of Melbourne University* (Melbourne: Hutchinson, 1983); see also John McLaren, *Free Radicals of the Left in Postwar Melbourne* (Melbourne: Australian Scholarly Publishing, 2003), chs 2–4.

72 Paul Strangio, *A Foolish Passionate Man: A Biography of Jim Cairns* (Melbourne: MUP, 2002), p. 52.
73 Stephen Murray-Smith, vol. 1, NAA A6119, 68, ff. 143–45; Robin Gollan, *Revolutionaries and Reformists: Communism and the Australian Labour Movement 1920–1950* (Canberra: ANU Press, 1975), pp. 196–201; report from Melbourne University, October 1947, University Labor Club Melbourne, NAA A6122, 130, f. 14.
74 Walshe quoted in Barcan, *Radical Students*, p. 193.
75 R.D. Walshe, *Student Work for Progress* (Sydney: Arcadia Press, 1947).
76 Barcan, *Radical Students*, p. 185; 'Youth Delegate to England', *Sydney Morning Herald*, 11 July 1945; 'Delegate Left Conference', *Shop*, vol. 2, no. 3 (August 1947), p. 2; 'Delegate Works His Passage', *West Australian*, 20 February 1948; McLaren, *Free Radicals*, ch. 5.
77 Len Donald in Central Committee, 20–22 February 1948, SLNSW MLMSS 5021, Box 85.
78 *Report of the Work of the Central Committee from the 14th to 15th National Congress*, (Sydney: Central Committee of the ACP, April 1948). *Forward*, the party's organisational bulletin from 1943 to 1949, reported the recruitment drives.
79 'Branches Endorse Press Campaign', Brisbane *Guardian*, 19 January 1945; Ted Bacon, interviewed by Laurie Aarons, June 1980, SLNSW; press appeal, Brisbane *Guardian*, 15 November 1946.
80 'Victorian Appeal for Daily Guardian', Victorian *Guardian*, 14 September 1945; Communist Party of Australia, Printing Establishments, Federal Press, NAA A6122, 974.
81 *Left Forum*, October 1947, p. 2; Inglis, *The Hammer & Sickle and the Washing Up*, p. 62; Rowan Cahill, 'Rupert Lockwood (1908–1997): Journalist, Communist, Intellectual', PhD thesis, University of Wollongong, 2013, p. 226.
82 'People's Printing, Publishing Venture Open', *Tribune*, 1 October 1946; 'Printing Soc. Needs Capital', *Tribune*, 14 March 1947; 'No Extra Paper for Communists', *Daily Telegraph*, 17 October 1947.
83 Dixon in Central Committee, January 1946, p. 11; Miles in Central Committee, 31 May–2 June 1946, p. 6.
84 'J.B. Miles Call to ALP', *Tribune*, 14 June 1946, and the reply reproduced in the Melbourne *Guardian*, 23 August 1946; Sydney Metropolitan Organisers' Meeting, 26 August 1946, Herbert Bovyll Chandler, NAA A6119, 71, f. 45.
85 Colin A. Hughes and B.D. Graham, *Voting for the Australian House of Representatives 1901–1964* (Canberra: ANU Press, 1974), pp. 253–64; Sharkey in Central Committee, November 1946, p. 7.
86 Colin A. Hughes and B.D. Graham, *Voting for the South Australian Western Australia and Tasmanian Lower Houses 1890–1964* (Canberra: Department of Political Science, ANU, 1976), pp. 138–42, 373–79; *Voting for the Queensland Legislative Assembly 1890–1964*, pp. 212–19; *Voting for the New South Wales Legislative Assembly 1890–1964* (Canberra: Department of Political Science, ANU, 1975), pp. 338–51; *Voting for the Victorian Legislative Assembly 1890–1964* (Canberra: Department of Political Science, ANU, 1975), pp. 313–23.
87 John Murphy, 'Loyalty and the Communists: An Interview with Bill Gollan', *Labour History*, no. 66 (May 1994), pp. 117.
88 Sharkey in Central Committee, January 1946, pp. 4–5. He drew on the prediction of the Hungarian communist Jenö Varga, first published in the *Communist Review*, no. 53 (January 1946).

89 Central Committee, 14–16 March 1946, SLNSW MLMSS 2389, Box 1. See also the subsequent accounts of Ralph Gibson, *My Years in the Communist Party* (Melbourne: International Bookshop, 1966), pp. 149–50; Jack Blake, 'The 1949 Coal Strike', *Australian Left Review*, no. 70 (August 1979), p. 23; and Taft, *Crossing the Party Line*, p. 56.

90 Dixon in Central Committee, 31 May–2 June 1946; Sharkey in Central Committee, 14–16 February 1947.

6 The Chill, 1947–49

1 John Lamberton Harper, *The Cold War* (Oxford: OUP, 2011), is the best overview; the three volumes of Melvyn P. Leffler and Odd Arne Westad (eds), *The Cambridge History of the Cold War* (Cambridge: CUP, 2010) contain lengthy guides to the enormous literature on the subject.

2 Milovan Djilas, *Conversations With Stalin* (New York: Harcourt Brace, 1962), p. 114.

3 David Reynolds, *From World War to Cold War: Churchill, Roosevelt and the International History of the 1940s* (Oxford: OUP, 2006), part 5.

4 Geoffrey Roberts, *Stalin's Wars: From World War to Cold War, 1939–1953* (New Haven, CT: Yale University Press, 2006), chs 8–9; Vladislav Zubok and Constantine Pleshakov, *Inside the Kremlin's Cold War: From Stalin to Khrushchev* (Cambridge, MA: Harvard University Press, 1996), chs 2–4.

5 Truman quoted in Odd Arne Westad, *The Cold War: A World History* (London: Allen Lane, 2017), p. 92; see also Melvyn P. Leffler, *A Preponderance of Power: National Security, the Truman Administration and the Cold War* (Stanford, CA: Stanford University Press, 1992).

6 Jonathan Haslam, *Russia's Cold War* (New Haven, CT: Yale University Press, 2011), ch. 3.

7 Cominform announcement quoted in Haslam, *Russia's Cold War*, p. 89; see also Guiliano Procacci et al., *The Cominform: Minutes of the Three Conferences 1947/1948/1949* (Milan: Feltrinelli, 1994), and Alessandro Brogi, *Confronting America: The Cold War between the United States and the Communists in France and Italy* (Chapel Hill, NC: University of North Carolina Press, 2011), chs 2–3.

8 Fernando Claudin, *The Communist Movement: From Comintern to Cominform* (London: Penguin, 1975), chs 5–6; Tony Judt, *Postwar: A History of Europe Since 1945* (London: William Heinemann, 2005), p. 144.

9 Eric Hobsbawm, *Interesting Times: A Twentieth-Century Life* (London: Allen Lane, 2002), pp. 133, 180.

10 Belinda Quick, 'Perceptions of the Soviet Union in Australian Political Discourse between 1943 and 1950', MPhil thesis, University of Adelaide, 2014.

11 The articles appeared between 15 and 20 May 1946 and were subsequently expanded into a book, J.J. Maloney, *Inside Red Russia* (Sydney: Angus & Robertson, 1948).

12 Jessie Street, letter to *Sydney Morning Herald*, 8 June 1946; Ernest Thornton, *Soviet Workers and Their Unions* (Sydney: Current Book Distributors, 1946); Irene Saxby 'Another Smashing Rebuff to Maloney', Melbourne *Guardian*, 31 May 1946.

13 *Reply to Maloney: The Real Facts About Russia* (Melbourne: Australia–Soviet House, n.d. [1946]); E.P. Dark, *The Press Against the People* (Sydney: the author, n.d. [1949]), pp. 52–55 documents the cuts made by the *Sydney Morning Herald*.

14 Fay Anderson, *An Historian's Life: Max Crawford and the Politics of Academic Freedom* (Melbourne: MUP, 2005), pp. 168–75; see also Sheila Fitzpatrick, 'Max Crawford in the Soviet Union: The Historian as Diplomat', in Sheila Fitzpatrick and Carolyn

Rasmussen (eds), *Political Tourists: Travellers from Australia to the Soviet Union in the 1920s–1940s* (Melbourne: MUP, 2008), pp. 212–34.

15 *Communism, Australia's Fifth Column* (Sydney: Graziers' Association of NSW, 1945); Michael Carr, *Betrayal: Being a Short History of Australia's Fifth Column* (Sydney: Sane Democracy League, 1946); *The War Has Ceased but Australia Still Has a Fifth Column* (Brisbane: Institute of Public Affairs, 1947).

16 Fay Anderson and Stuart Macintyre, 'Crawford as a Controversialist', in Stuart Macintyre and Peter McPhee (eds), *Max Crawford's School of History* (Melbourne: History Department, University of Melbourne, 2000), pp. 89–112; Drew Cottle and Angela Keys, 'Douglas Evelyn Darby, MP: Anti-Communist Internationalist in the Antipodes', *Labour History*, no. 89 (November 2005), pp. 87–100.

17 Franklin to Katharine Susannah Prichard, 20 November 1947, in Jill Roe (ed.), *My Congenials: Miles Franklin & Friends in Letters* (Sydney: Angus & Robertson, 1993), vol. 2, p. 196 (emphasis in the original); see also Lachlan Clohesy, 'Australian Cold Warrior: The Anti-Communism of W.C. Wentworth', PhD thesis, Victoria University, 2010. OGPU is the acronym of the Soviet security organisation that operated from 1923 to 1934.

18 'Communist Window Smashed', *Sydney Morning Herald*, 6 December 1945; 'Communists Lose Window', *Daily Telegraph*, 12 December 1945; 'Attempt to Fire ACP Bookshop', Melbourne *Guardian*, 3 May 1946; 'Fascist Raid on Communist Bookshop', *Tribune*, 19 May 1948; 'Vicious Stickers on Party Shop', *Tribune*, 4 August 1948.

19 'Redbaiters Bully Girl', *Tribune*, 14 December 1945; 'Disloyal Red Caused Brawl', Brisbane *Telegraph*, 9 January 1948.

20 *Civvy Street: A Booklet of Information for Members of the Services Returning to Civilian Life* (Sydney: ACP, 1945), p. 3.

21 'Soldiers' Legion Bars Communists', *Sydney Morning Herald*, 18 July 1945; 'Reds to Be Expelled', Melbourne *Herald*, 27 July 1948; 'Council Expels Qld Legion', Melbourne *Herald*, 11 July 1949; see also Mark Aarons, *The Family File* (Melbourne: Black Inc., 2010), pp. 105–106.

22 'Attempts to "White-Ant" RSL Feared', *Daily Telegraph*, 11 September 1944; Bergeest's security file, NAA A6126, 619, begins in 1941.

23 Donald Cochrane and Douglas Hocking to RSL president, 30 July 1946, Donald Cochrane, NAA A6119, 1084, f. 17.

24 Lawrence W. Maher, 'King, Country and Kremlin: The RSL Anti-Communist Purge Cases, 1948–1949', *Legal History*, no. 11 (2007), pp. 167–95.

25 L.J. Louis, 'The RSL and the Cold War 1946–50', *Labour History*, no. 74 (1998), pp. 88–104; Arthur Reginald Bergeest, NAA A6126, 619.

26 Arthur Gietzelt wrote under the name Arthur James in *Communist Review*, no. 96 (August 1949), pp. 251–53, and no. 100 (December 1949), pp. 374–76. See also Arthur Gietzelt, *Sticks and Stones* (Shellharbour, NSW: A.T. and D.O. Gietzelt, 2014); '$14,500 to Senator', *Canberra Times*, 5 August 1976; and Arthur [Thomas] Gietzelt, vol. 1, NAA A6119, 381.

27 Chifley, in *Commonwealth Parliamentary Debates*, 25 March 1947, 7 April 1948, and quoted in L.F. Crisp, *Ben Chifley: A Political Biography* (London: Longmans, 1961), p. 192; see also Christopher Waters, *The Empire Fractures: Anglo-Australian Conflict in the 1940s* (Melbourne: Australian Scholarly Publishing, 1995), chs 2–4, and Julie Suares, *J.B. Chifley: An Ardent Internationalist* (Melbourne: MUP, 2019), ch. 8.

28 Wayne Reynolds, *Australia's Bid for the Atomic Bomb* (Melbourne: MUP, 2000), ch. 2.

29 Peter Morton, *Fire Across the Desert: Woomera and the Anglo-Australian Joint Project 1946–1980* (Canberra: AGPS, 1989), ch. 3; Geoffrey Gray, *A Cautious Silence: The Politics of Australian Anthropology* (Canberra: Aboriginal Studies Press, 2007), pp. 207–16.

30 Jim Crawford, 'Land Grab, Background to the Rocket Range Scheme', *Tribune*, 23 May 1947.

31 'Rocket Range Threatened', *Sydney Morning Herald*, 10 May 1947.

32 Central Committee Plenum, 16–19 May 1947, Political Committee Minutes and Resolutions 1942–48, CPA records, SLNSW MLMSS 5021, ADD-ON 1936, Box 16 (76); 'Communist Party Statement', *Sydney Morning Herald*, 14 May 1947; 'Policy on Rockets', *Sydney Morning Herald*, 15 May 1947; Alf Watt, *Rocket Range Threatens Australia* (Adelaide, South Australian State Committee, ACP, n.d. [March 1947]), p. 16.

33 *Commonwealth Parliamentary Debates*, 3, 5 June 1947; H.V. Evatt, *Hands Off the Nation's Defences* (Canberra: Federal Capital Press, n.d. [1947]).

34 Committee of Review—Civil Staffs of Wartime Activities, Report on Commonwealth Investigation Branch and Security Service, NAA A1608, AL29/1/1/14; Jacqueline Templeton, Australian Intelligence/Security Services 1900–1950, chs 9–10, NAA A898, 7B.

35 David Horner, *The Spy Catchers: The Official History of ASIO, 1949–1963, Volume I* (Sydney: Allen & Unwin, 2014), ch. 3; Laurence W. Maher, 'Downunder McCarthyism: The Struggles Against Australian Communism 1945–1960', part 1, *Anglo-American Law Review*, vol. 27, no. 3 (1998), 341–89.

36 Laurence W. Maher, 'Downunder McCarthyism', pp. 359–62; Frank Cain, 'An Aspect of Post-War Relations With the United Kingdom and the United States: Missiles, Spies and Disharmony', *Australian Historical Studies*, vol. 23, no. 92 (April 1989), pp. 186–202; *Commonwealth Parliamentary Debates*, 30 September, 1, 7 October 1948; A.W. Fadden, *They Called Me Artie: The Memoirs of Sir Arthur Fadden* (Brisbane: Jacaranda, 1969), pp. 97–99.

37 David Rivett, 'Science and the Nation', *Meanjin*, vol. 6, no. 3 (Spring 1947), pp. 167–72; Abbott in *Commonwealth Parliamentary Debates*, 30 September 1948.

38 *Commonwealth Parliamentary Debates*, 28 November 1946; see also Donald Alfred Mountjoy, vol. 1, NAA A6119, 1527.

39 'Atom Secrets Opposed', *Sydney Morning Herald*, 15 April 1946; *Commonwealth Parliamentary Debates*, 7 March 1947; Amy Knight, *How the Cold War Began: The Igor Gouzenko Affair and the Hunt for Soviet Spies* (Toronto: McClelland and Stewart, 2005), pp. 79, 141–42.

40 Jean Moran, 'Scientists in the Political and Public Arena: A Social-Intellectual History of the Australian Association of Scientific Workers, 1939–49', MPhil thesis, Griffith University, 1983; Phillip Deery and Lachlan Clohesy, '"Patronised Servants": Australian Scientists in the 1940s', *Journal of the Royal Australian Historical Society*, vol. 99, no. 2 (2013), pp. 114–32.

41 Boris Schedvin, *Shaping Science and Industry: A History of Australia's Council for Scientific and Industrial Research, 1926–1949* (Sydney: Allen & Unwin, 1987), pp. 332–46; see also Marjorie Collard O'Dea, *Ian Clunies Ross: A Biography* (Melbourne: Hyland House, 1997), ch. 14.

42 CPA Activities and Interest in CSIRO, vol. 1, NAA A6122, 223; the relevant security files are NAA A6119, 1064 for Andrews, A6119, 2197 for Pomeroy, A6119, 47 for Rudkin, A6119, 1963 for Nicholls, and A6119, 414 for McArthur.

43 For Burhop see NAA A6119, 50, and the *Australian Dictionary of Biography*, vol. 13, pp. 301–302; A6119, 627 for Berry-Smith, A6619, 846 for Bracewell, A6126, 845 for Freeman, A6126, 586 for Hibbard, A6119, 48 for Kaiser, A6126, 593 for Mills, A6119, 1679 for Payne-Scott and A6119, 2010 for Makinson. Payne-Scott is the subject of a biography: W.M. Goss and Richard X. McGee, *Under the Radar: The First Woman in Radio Astronomy, Ruby Payne Scott* (Heidelberg: Springer, 2010).

44 Richard Ellis Bodenham Makinson, vol. 1, NAA A6119, 1218; see also *Australian Dictionary of Biography*, vol. 15, pp. 290–91, and Phillip Deery, 'Scientific Freedom and Post-War Politics: Australia, 1945–1955', *Historical Records of Australian Science*, vol. 13, no. 1 (June 2000), pp. 1–18.

45 David John Morris, vol. 1, NAA A6119, 61; Bernice Bernice Morris, *Between the Lines* (Melbourne: Sybylla Co-operative Press, 1988); Edwin Harry Medlin, vol. 1, NAA A6119, 2277.

46 J.D. Bernal, *The Social Function of Science* (London: Routledge, 1939); see generally Gary Werskey, *The Visible College* (London: Allen Lane, 1978).

47 John O'Donnell, 'Some Recent Events in Science', *Communist Review*, no. 52 (December 1945), pp. 691–93; ACP Science Committee, 'Methods of Scientific Criticism', *Communist Review*, no. 56 (April 1946), pp. 108–10.

48 'Scientists Show How Environment Kayoes Heredity', *Tribune*, 8 May 1948; 'Lysenko's Materialist Doctrine', *Communist Review*, no. 88 (December 1948), pp. 383–85; Gould to Callaghan, 19 November 1948, John Pierce Callaghan, NAA A6119, 46, ff. 67–69; Makinson to Gould, 23 November 1948, Richard Ellis Bodenham Makinson, NAA A6119, 1218, ff. 49–50.

49 'Biology in the Service of Man', *Communist Review*, no. 94 (June 1949), pp. 182–89; Amirah Inglis, *The Hammer & Sickle and the Washing Up: Memories of an Australian Woman Communist* (Melbourne: Hyland House, 1995), p. 65; I rely here on conversations with Max Marginson.

50 Yoran Gorlizka and Oleg Khlevnik, *Cold Peace: Stalin and the Soviet Ruling Circle 1945–1953* (Oxford: OUP, 2004), pp. 34, 39.

51 Maxim Gorky et al., *Soviet Writers' Congress 1934: The Debate on Socialist Realism and Modernism in the Soviet Union* (London: Lawrence and Wishart, 1977), p. 21.

52 Jessica C.E. Gienow-Hecht, 'Culture and the Cold War in Europe', in Leffler and Westad (eds), *The Cambridge History of the Cold War*, vol. 1, *Origins, 1945–1962*, pp. 398–403; see generally David Caute, *The Dancer Defects: The Struggle for Cultural Supremacy during the Cold War* (Oxford: OUP, 2003).

53 Robin Gollan, *Revolutionaries and Reformists: Communism and the Australian Labour Movement 1920–1950* (Canberra: ANU Press, 1975), p. 248; Jack Beasley, 'Zhdanovism, Socialist Realism and the Communist Party of Australia', in *Red Letter Days: Notes from Inside an Era* (Sydney: Australasian Book Society, 1979), pp. 169–88.

54 A.A. Zhdanov, 'The Soviet Author Is a Man With a Duty to Society', *Tribune*, 8 October 1946; 'On the Errors of Soviet Literary Journals', *Communist Review*, no. 66 (February 1947), pp. 421–30; 'Soviet Fine Arts', *Communist Review*, no. 80 (April 1948), pp. 123–24; 'Authentic Text of the Soviet Music Resolution', *Communist Review*, no. 82 (June 1948), pp. 182–85.

55 John Oldham, 'Picasso and the Arts under Capitalism', *Communist Review*, no. 73 (September 1947), pp. 661–63; Len Fox, 'The Obscurity of Picasso's Art', *Communist Review*, no. 75 (November 1947), pp. 72–30; Paul Mortier, 'Arts and the Class Struggle', *Communist Review*, no. 78 (February 1948), pp. 59–60; R.M. Shaw, 'The Artist in Our Society', *Communist Review*, no. 84 (August 1948), pp. 258–59; for

communist criticism of Picasso see Caute, *The Dancer Defects*, pp. 572–81.

56 J.B. Miles, 'Art for the People', *Communist Review*, no. 84 (August 1948), pp. 260–62; Justine Williams, 'Roaring Nineties', *Workers' Star*, 23 August 1946, and *Anger and Love* (Fremantle: Fremantle Arts Centre Press, 1993), p. 130; Harry Gould, 'USA Party Erred in Culture Too', *Tribune*, 30 August 1945; J.D. Blake, 'Arts and Sciences and the Working Class Struggle', *Communist Review*, no. 60 (August 1946), pp. 247–49.

57 'The Censor Clamps Down in Russia', *Sydney Morning Herald*, 7 September 1946; Lloyd Ross, 'Literature in Uniform', *Sydney Morning Herald*, 8 June 1946; Godfrey Blunden, 'Why Soviet Composers Must Toe the Line', *Sydney Morning Herald*, 19 June 1949.

58 'Manifesto of the Studio', *Tribune*, 15 February 1945; Jean Campbell, *James Cant and Dora Chapman* (Sydney: Beagle Press, 1995), pp. 40–43; Sheridan Palmer, *Hegel's Owl: The Biography of Bernard Smith* (Sydney: Power Publications, University of Sydney, 2016), pp. 94–95.

59 Deirdre Moore, 'The Realist Writers', *Overland*, no. 156 (Spring 1999), pp. 24–29.

60 Waten quoted in David Carter, *A Career in Writing: Judah Waten and the Cultural Politics of a Literary Career* (Toowoomba: Association for the Study of Australian Literature, 1997), p. 54; see also David Carter, '"An Important Social Duty": The Brief Life of Dolphin Publications', *Publishing Studies*, no. 6 (1998), pp. 3–13.

61 Gabriela Zabala, 'The Politics of Drama: The Relationship between the Communist Party of Australia and New Theatre Writers 1932–1980s', PhD thesis, University of New South Wales, 2012, pp. 183, 241; 'Criticism of New Theatre', *Tribune*, 12 November 1949; Ken Coldicutt, 'The Party, Films and I', *Sixty Years of Struggle* (Sydney: Red Pen Publications, vol. 2, 1982), p. 61.

62 Ina Bertrand, '"Goodbye Mr Red": Paranoia and Film Culture After the Second World War', *Journal of Australian Studies*, no. 28 (March 1991), pp. 29–39; Commonwealth Parliamentary Debates, 8 May 1947.

63 'Bell Turns Back on Labor Movement', Melbourne *Guardian*, 13 August 1948; see also Harry Stein, *A Glance Over an Old Left Shoulder* (Sydney: Hale & Iremonger, 1994), pp. 84–91, and Bruce Johnson, 'Naturalising the Exotic: The Australian Jazz Convention', in E.T. Takins (ed.), *Jazz Planet: Transnational Studies of the 'Sound of Surprise'* (Jackson, MO: University Press of Mississippi, 2003), pp. 151–68.

64 'Eureka Youth League Girl for Olympics', *Tribune*, 12 March 1948; 'Miss Strickland Will Rejoin Eureka League', *Argus*, 16 August 1948; 'Tintacks', *Workers' Star*, 12 November 1948; 'Was Never a Communist', Melbourne *Herald*, 7 May 1949; see also Shirley Barbara Delahunty (aka Strickland), NAA A6126, 1367.

65 André Mommen, *Stalin's Economist: The Economic Contribution of Jenö Varga* (London: Routledge, 2011), ch. 12.

66 'Jobs for All Planned', *Tribune*, 7 June 1945; Richard Dixon, 'Full Employment and Capitalism', *Communist Review*, no. 48 (August 1945), pp. 570–71.

67 Len Fox, *Wealthy Men* (Sydney: Current Book Distributors, 1946), n.p. [p. 4]; Brian Fitzpatrick, *The Rich Get Richer* (Melbourne: Rawson's Bookshop, 1944).

68 Fox, *Wealthy Men*, [p. 22].

69 'Southern Bloc Plan to Out Labor', *Tribune*, 12 November 1947.

70 W.A. Wood, 'Pig Iron Bob Talks of Treason', *Tribune*, 22 January 1949; 'Twenty Monopolists in Collins House Can Dictate to Millions of People', *Tribune*, 14 June 1948; Sharkey in 'ACP 15th National Congress, 7–10 May 1948, Speeches and Documents', CPA records, SLNSW MLMSS 2389, Box 2, p. 242. The French Party spoke not of 400 but 200 families.

71 Mommen, *Stalin's Economist*, p. 183; Eugen Varga, 'New Depression Will Break Not Later than 1948', *Tribune*, 10 December 1946; E. Varga, 'The General Crisis of Capitalism', *Communist Review*, no. 70 (June 1947), pp. 551–57.

72 'Australia Enters the Golden Age', *Age*, 28 July 1946; L.L. Sharkey, 'Election Choice—False Promises or a Real Policy', *Tribune*, 20 August 1946; 'Chifley's Pipe Dreams Anger Unionists', *Tribune*, 4 March 1947.

73 L.L. Sharkey, *Labor Betrayed!* (Sydney: Current Book Distributors, July 1946), p. 4; Central Committee Plenum, 1–3 November 1946, SLNSW MLMSS 2389, Box 1.

74 Dixon in Central Committee, 31 May–2 June 1946, SLNSW MLMSS 2389, Box 1.

75 Dixon in Central Committee, 31 May–2 June 1946; Miles in Central Committee, 14–16 February 1947, SLNSW MLMSS 5012, Box 86.

76 Sharkey in political committee, 7 October 1947, 8 December 1947, 10–11 January 1948, SLNSW MLMSS, Box 5 (76).

77 J.D. Blake, *The Communist Way Forward* (Melbourne: State Committee of ACP, December 1947), p. 26.

78 Harry Pollitt, *Looking Ahead* (London: CPGB, August 1947), pp. 103–11; see also Kevin Morgan, *Harry Pollitt* (Manchester: Manchester University Press, 1993), ch. 6.

79 Sharkey in Central Committee Plenum, 14–16 March 1946, SLNSW MLMSS 2389, Box 1; Central Committee Plenum, 14–16 February 1947, SLNSW MLMSS 5021, Box 86; Henry to ACP secretariat, Central Committee Letters to Other Parties 1946–48, MLMSS 2389, Box 1.

80 L.L. Sharkey, 'Critical Comments on Harry Pollitt's Book', *Tribune*, 15 October 1947; Pollitt in *World News and Views*, 20 December 1947.

81 Sharkey in political committee, 1–11 January 1948, SLNSW MLMSS 5021, Box 86; the ACP letter of 31 March 1948 appears in *Communist Review*, no. 85 (September 1948), pp. 270–74.

82 The CPGB reply of 16 July 1948 and the ACP response of 11 August 1948 are in *Communist Review*, no. 85 (September 1948), pp. 274–83.

83 Pollitt to Sharkey, 11 October 1948, Communist Party of Great Britain records, Labour History Archive and Study Centre, Manchester.

84 Edward Upward, *The Rotten Elements* (London: William Heinemann, 1969). There is 1948 correspondence with Edward and Hilda Upward, letters from Ken Gott and Stephen Murray-Smith, 24, 27 October 1948 and an undated letter from 'R' in Central Committee Letters to Other Parties 1946–48.

85 Central Committee Plenum, 14–16 October 1949, SLNSW MLMSS 5021, ADD-ON 1936, Box 16 (76).

86 'India's Heroic Fighters for Freedom', *Tribune*, 31 March 1948; John Callaghan, *Rajani Palme Dutt: A Study in British Stalinism* (London: Lawrence and Wishart, 1993), pp. 224–30.

87 L.L. Sharkey, 'The Present Situation and the Role of Rightwing Socialism', 'The International Situation and Opportunism', *MCP Review*, vol. 2, no. 3 (May–June 1948); Pollitt to Sharkey, 16 July 1948, Sharkey to Pollitt, 2 August 1948, Central Committee Letters to Other Parties 1946–48.

88 'Disruption "Planned for Australia"', *Daily Telegraph*, 27 June 1948; 'Malayan Communists Planned Insurrection', *Canberra Times*, 28 June 1948; 'Egged on by Sharkey, Say Malayan Reds', Melbourne *Herald*, 10 August 1948; 'Problem "Very Difficult"', *Daily Telegraph*, 3 September 1948. Sharkey's role is assessed by Phillip Deery, 'Malaya, 1948: Britain's Asian Cold War', *Journal of Cold War Studies*, vol. 9, no. 1 (2007), pp. 29–50.

89 Peter Edwards with Gregory Pemberton, *Crises and Commitments: The Politics and Diplomacy of Australia's Involvement in Southeast Asian Conflicts 1948–1965* (Sydney: Allen & Unwin, 1992), chs 2–3.
90 'Aust, Agitator in Reds' Asiatic H.Q.', *Daily Telegraph*, 4 September 1948; 'This Is the Strange Story of Asian Airlines Ltd', *Sydney Morning Herald*; see also Drew Cottle and Angela Keys, 'Asian Airlines: An Early Australian Cold War Mystery', in Julie Kimber, Peter Love and Phillip Deery (eds), *Labour Traditions: Proceedings of the Tenth Labour History Conference* (Melbourne: ASSLH, 2007), pp. 62–66, and Clarence Hart Campbell, vol. 2, NAA A6119, 1052.
91 'Sharkey's Congress Call to Fight for Peace, Democracy', *Tribune*, 12 May 1948; Adam Ogston in 'ACP 15th National Congress, 7–10 May 1948, Speeches and Documents', p. 2.
92 'Sharkey's Congress Call to Fight for Peace and Democracy'; see also *The Way Forward: Resolutions of the 15th Congress of the Australian Communist Party* (Sydney: Current Book Distributors, May 1948).
93 Richard Dixon in Central Committee Plenum, 20–22 February 1948, SLNSW MLMSS 5021, Box 85, and ACP 15th National Congress, pp. 63–64; Jack Henry in ACP 15th National Congress, pp. 192–96.
94 Report to the Central Committee, 20 February 1948, Minutes of the Political Committee, 6 July 1948, SLNSW MLMSS 5021, ADD-ON Box 5 (76); R. Dixon, 'Situation in C.P. of Yugoslavia', *Communist Review*, no. 84 (August 1948), pp. 234–37.
95 Tom Sheridan, *Division of Labour: Industrial Relations in the Chifley Years 1945–49* (Melbourne: OUP, 1989), pp. 213–24; Douglas Blackmur, 'The Railway Strike, 1948', in D.J. Murphy (ed.), *The Big Strikes: Queensland 1889–1965* (Brisbane, UQP, 1983), 235–52; Ross Fitzgerald, *The People's Champion: Fred Paterson, Australia's Only Communist Party Member of Parliament* (Brisbane: UQP, 1997), pp. 176–203.
96 'E.J. Rowe Still in Hiding', *Sydney Morning Herald*, 29 March 1948; 'Rowe's Fine Paid Into Court', *Courier-Mail*, 6 April 1948; 'Queensland Reds Freed', *Daily Telegraph*, 20 August 1948.
97 Lance Sharkey, Jim Healy and Ernie Thornton in ACP 15th National Congress, pp. 131, 165–67, 247.
98 Central Committee Plenum, 20–22 February; ACP 15th National Congress, p. 132; Central Committee Plenum, September 1948, SLNSW MLMSS 2389, Box 1; political committee, 8 December 1948, SLNSW MLMSS 5021, ADD-ON 5 (76).
99 ACP 15th National Congress, pp. 227–28; Laurie Aarons, interviewed by Joyce Stevens, 17 September 1980, SLNSW; Ted Bacon, interviewed by Laurie Aarons, June 1980, SLNSW.
100 Ted Bacon, interviewed by Laurie Aarons, SLNSW; Report of the Work of the Central Committee from the 14th to the 15th Congress (Sydney: Central Committee of the ACP, April 1948), p. 29.
101 Claude Jones, interviewed by Laurie Aarons, June 1980, SLNSW.

7 Showdown, 1949–50

1 Fernando Claudin, *The Communist Movement: From Comintern to Cominform* (London: Penguin, 1975), pp. 465–79.
2 Sharkey in Central Committee, 18–20 February 1949, CPA records, SLNSW MLMSS 5021, ADD-ON Box 5 (76); J.C. Henry, 'The Role of Reformism', *Communist Review*, no. 96 (August 1949), p. 230.

3 '20,000 Expected at Community Protest Against High Fares, Prices', *Tribune*, 24 November 1948; Dixon in Central Committee, 18–20 February 1949.

4 David Caute, *The Dancer Defects: The Struggle for Cultural Supremacy during the Cold War* (Oxford: OUP, 2003), pp. 167–69.

5 'Don't Show That Film!', *Herald*, 6 September 1948; 'Film Stirs Pro-Red City Brawl', *Argus*, 25 September 1948; see also Zoe O'Leary, *The Desolate Market: A Biography of Eric Lambert* (Sydney: Edwards & Shaw, 1974), pp. 39–40.

6 'Communists Object', *Sydney Morning Herald*, 2 October 1948; '"Curtain" Went up in Silence', *Brisbane Telegraph*, 1 October 1948.

7 'No Town Hall Use for Peace Lovers', *Tribune*, 30 June 1948.

8 'City Council Cancels Town Hall Booking', *Argus*, 19 February 1949; 'Amplified Talk at Town Hall', *Age*, 24 February 1949; 'Town Hall Ban Part of Drive to War', Melbourne *Guardian*, 25 February 1949; John Rodgers, *Report on the Soviet Union* (Melbourne: Australia–Soviet House, March 1949).

9 See, for example, 'Police State Threat to NSW Workers, Housewives', *Tribune*, 11 December 1949; 'Obstructed Footpath to Sell Communist Paper', *Herald*, 10 August 1949; 'Port Adelaide Police', *Advertiser*, 10 June 1949; 'Police Break Up Red Meeting', *Brisbane Telegraph*, 13 July 1949; 'Esplanade Ban Evaded', *West Australian*, 3 September 1949; Stuart Macintyre, *Militant: The Life and Times of Paddy Troy* (Sydney: Allen & Unwin, 1984), pp. 109–10.

10 'Hall Denial Leads to Reprisals', *Herald*, 18 March 1949; 'Phone Threat to Councillor', *Herald*, 21 March 1949.

11 'Threat to Throw Them in the Yarra', *Argus*, 9 May 1949; 'Police Prevent Clashes between Servicemen and Reds', *Argus*, 23 May 1949.

12 'Reds Rescued from Crowd', *Daily Telegraph*, 10 March 1949; 'Govt. Should Prosecute Bourke Thugs', *Tribune*, 12 March 1949; 'Red Rally Smashed by Crowd', *Courier-Mail*, 29 March 1949; '"Batter Bath" in Wild Rocky Melee', *Brisbane Telegraph*, 29 March 1949; see also Barbara Webster, '"To Fight Against the Horrible Evil of Communism": Catholics, Community and the Movement in Rockhampton, 1943–1957', *Labour History*, no. 81 (November 2001), pp. 155–74.

13 'Communists Not Heard', 'Fight at Communist Meeting', 'Communist Fined at Midland Junction', *West Australian*, 4, 7, 14 April 1949; see also Ralph Gibson, *My Years in the Communist Party* (Melbourne: International Bookshop, 1966), pp. 139–43.

14 Dixon to Acting Attorney-General, 5 April 1949; Acting Attorney-General to Dixon, 4 May 1949, NAA A432, 1949/379, ff. 5, 25.

15 '"Within the Law", Says RSL', *Herald*, 4 April 1949; 'RSL Drive on Reds', *Herald*, 1 August 1949.

16 Andrew Moore, 'Fascism Revived? The Association Stands Guard, 1947–52', *Labour History*, no. 74 (May 1998), pp. 105–21.

17 The fullest account is Vicky Rastrick, 'The Victorian Royal Commission on Communism 1949–50: A Study of Anti-Communism in Australia', MA thesis, ANU, 1973.

18 'Communist on Serious Charge', *Herald*, 7 May 1949; 'Charge Against Red Dismissed', Melbourne *Herald*, 14 May 1949. A fuller report, 'Charge Against Leading Red Dismissed', had appeared in a late edition on the previous day, and the *Herald* noted the girl's admission four days later at the request of Miller, in 'Dismissal of Charge', 17 May 1949. See also Amirah Inglis, 'Witch Hunt: The Trial of Ken Miller and Anti-Communist Hysteria in the 1940s', *Overland*, no. 132 (1993), pp. 13–19.

19 'Court Demonstration Against Sharpley', Melbourne *Guardian*, 2 July 1949; Rastrick, 'The Victorian Royal Commission on Communism', p. 111 cites a subsequent interview with the barrister Murray McInerney.
20 Brian Costar, 'Tom Hollway: The Bohemian', in Paul Strangio and Brian Costar (eds), *The Victorian Premiers 1856–2006* (Sydney: Federation Press, 2006), pp. 233–34.
21 Report of public meeting, 28 April 1948, and address at Marx House, 27 July 1949, Laurence Louis Sharkey, vol. 1, NAA A6119, 219, ff. 73–74; 'Most Australians Would Ban Communist Party', *Herald*, 19 March 1949.
22 'Murdoch Refused to Publish This', Melbourne *Guardian*, 20 April 1949; 'Why the Communist Party Expelled Sharpley', *Tribune*, 20 April 1949; 'Communist Fined for Behaviour', *Herald*, 2 July 1947; 'Transcript of Proceedings: Victoria Royal Commission Inquiring into the Origins, Aims, Objects and Funds of the Communist Party in Victoria and Other Related Matters, Minutes of Evidence' (Melbourne, 1949–50), p. 8; *Royal Commission's Biassed* [sic] *Judge and Perjured Witnesses* (Melbourne: Committee for Free Speech and Democracy, 1949).
23 Peter S. Cook, *Red Barrister: A Biography of Ted Laurie* (Melbourne: La Trobe University Press, 1994), ch. 10.
24 'Judge Finds Contempt in Guardian Articles', Melbourne *Guardian*, 18 November 1949; *Report of Royal Commission Inquiring into the Origins, Aims, Objects and Funds of the Communist Party in Victoria and Other Related Matters* (Melbourne: Government Printer, 1950), p. 4.
25 Bruce Mitchell, *Teachers, Education, and Politics: A History of Organizations of Public School Teachers in New South Wales* (Brisbane: UQP, 1975), ch. 6; *Report of Royal Commission*, p. 94; see also Cheryl Griffin, 'A Biography of Doris McRae, 1893–1988', PhD thesis, University of Melbourne, 2005, and CPA Interest in Schools and Education, NAA A6122, 262.
26 Chifley in *Commonwealth Parliamentary Debates*, 7 April, 18 May 1948.
27 'Speaker Says Communists Here Would Battle for Russians', *Courier-Mail*, 16 September 1948.
28 Laurence W. Maher, 'The Use and Abuse of Sedition', *Sydney Law Review*, vol. 14, no. 3 (1992), esp. pp. 295–301.
29 'Fantastic Upset at Cowra Meeting', *Cowra Guardian*, 19 March 1948, which is contained in Freda Yetta Brown, vol. 1, NAA A6119, 4905, ff. 172–75.
30 'Communists' Peace Policy', *Tribune*, 18 September 1948; circular from secretariat, 1 November 1948, John Bramwell Miles, NAA A6119, 884, f. 46.
31 '"Welcome" for Red Troops', *Daily Telegraph*, 5 March 1949; 'Russia Peaceful Country', *Sydney Morning Herald*, 5 March 1949; 'Sharkey Would Welcome Reds', *Daily Mirror*, 5 March 1949. Lawrence Louis Sharkey, vol. 2, NAA A6119, f. 220 gives details of Sharkey's contacts with the reporters.
32 'Sharkey Convicted', *Sydney Morning Herald*, 21 June 1949; 'Sharkey Sent to Prison', *Sydney Morning Herald*, 18 October 1949; Harold Rich, *The Story of the Sharkey Trial* (Sydney: Release Sharkey Committee, n.d. [1949]).
33 Kevin Martin Healy, vol. 1, NAA A6119, 1105.
34 'Law Called Arbitrary', *Sydney Morning Herald*, 3 November 1949; Maher, 'The Use and Abuse of Sedition', pp. 303–304.
35 Maher, 'The Use and Abuse of Sedition', p. 305.
36 Tom Sheridan, *Division of Labour: Industrial Relations in the Chifley Years 1945–49* (Melbourne: OUP, 1989), pp. 194–212; see also E.F. Hill, 'Lessons of the Victorian Strike Struggles', *Communist Review*, no. 79 (March 1948), pp. 69–72.

37 Catherine Brigden, 'A Vehicle for Solidarity: Power and Purpose in the Victorian Trades Hall Council, 1948–1981', PhD thesis, University of Sydney, 2003, pp. 74–81; see also E.F. Hill, 'Defeat of the Essential Services Act', *Communist Review*, no. 89 (January 1949), pp. 7–10.
38 Jim Hagan, *The History of the ACTU* (Melbourne: Longman Cheshire, 1981), pp. 189–96.
39 'Arrest of Union Leader', *Age*, 4 March 1949.
40 'McPhillips Case', *Age*, 5–6 April 1946; see also Constance Larmour, *Labor Judge: The Life and Times of Judge Alfred William Foster* (Sydney: Hale & Iremonger, 1985), p. 194.
41 Hagan, *The History of the ACTU*, pp. 121–22; 'Court Position in Wright Case', *Daily Telegraph*, 7 May 1949; see also Thomas Wright, vol. 1, NAA A6119, 748, ff. 8–23.
42 Blanche d'Alpuget, *Mediator: A Biography of Sir Richard Kirby* (Melbourne: MUP, 1977), pp. 101–105.
43 Ross in 15th National Congress, 7–10 May 1948, Speeches and Documents, CPA records, SLNSW MLMSS 2389, Box 2, pp. 56–59; see also Edgar Ross, 'Coal Perspectives', *Communist Review*, no. 83 (July 1948), pp. 201–23.
44 The fullest account is Phillip Deery, 'The 1949 Coal Strike', PhD thesis, La Trobe University, 1976; Sheridan, *Division of Labour*, ch. 11 differs over the role of the ACP.
45 'Executive "Appalled" by Sentences', *Age*, 12 July 1949.
46 Foster in 64 *Commonwealth Arbitration Reports* 760, quoted in Larmour, *Labor Judge*, p. 199; advertisements authorised by the prime minister, 30 June, 1 July, 10 July 1949.
47 'Report to Government on Red Papers', *Daily Telegraph*, 9 July 1949; 'Order to Communist Party', *Sydney Morning Herald*, 12 July 1949; 'Communist Party Defeats Plot to Jail All its Leaders', *Tribune*, 23 July 1949.
48 '"Boots and All Fight" Warns Chifley', *Argus*, 4 July 1949; Sheridan, *Division of Labour*, ch. 12 provides a persuasive explanation of the miscalculations of the Miners' Federation.
49 Laurie Aarons quoted in Mark Aarons, *The Family File* (Melbourne: Black Inc., 2010), p. 116.
50 'Communists Slated', *West Australian*, 5 March 1948; 'Angry Protest in Court', *West Australian*, 11 May 1949.
51 'Charge Laid Against Union Leader', *Herald*, 19 July 1948; 'Union Ballot Off: Papers Burnt', *Age*, 18 November 1949; 'Burnt Papers Poll Ruled Invalid', *Herald*, 5 December 1949; see also Lois Farrall, *The File on Fred: A Biography of Fred Farrall* (Melbourne: High Leigh Publishing Company, n.d. [1992]), pp. 161–70.
52 'Court Challenges Bona Fides of Ill Health Claim', *Herald*, 3 March 1949; 'Move to Have Union Ballot Declared Void', *Herald*, 23 March 1950; 'Stalemate in Bid for Clerks' Rooms', *Herald*, 24 March 1950.
53 Don Kenyon, 'A Constitutional Coup: The Case of the Federated Clerks Union', *Politics*, vol. 1, no. 2 (November 1966), pp. 96–106.
54 Phillip Deery, 'Labour, Communism and the Cold War: The Case of "Diver Dobson"', *Australian Historical Studies*, vol. 28, no. 108 (1997), pp. 66–87; see also William Thomas Dobson, NAA A1533, 1954/3374XR parts 1 and 2, and *The Dobson Story: Story of ALP Industrial Groups* (Sydney: J.R. Hughes for Federated Clerks' Union, n.d. [1949]).
55 'Thornton's Vote "Crooked"', *Daily Telegraph*, 30 November 1951; see also John Merritt, 'A History of the Federated Ironworkers' Association of Australia, 1909–1952', PhD thesis, ANU, 1968, ch. 10, and Susanna Short, *Laurie Short: A Political Life* (Sydney: Allen & Unwin, 1992), chs 9–12.

56 Tom Wright, 'The 1949 ACTU Congress', *Communist Review*, no. 99 (November 1949), pp. 334–36; Donald Horne, 'A Reporter at Large at the ACTU Congress', *Daily Telegraph*, 22 September 1949.

57 Sheridan, *Division of Labour*, ch. 10.

58 Ernest Thornton, *Soviet Workers and Their Unions* (Sydney: Current Book Distributors, 1946); E. Thornton, 'British and American Treachery to World Federation of Trade Unions', *Communist Review*, no. 91 (March 1949), pp. 82–84; see also Denis MacShane, *International Labour and the Origins of the Cold War* (Oxford: Clarendon Press, 1992).

59 Ken Tolhurst quoted in Janet McCalman, *Journeyings: The Biography of a Middle-Class Generation 1920–1990* (Melbourne: MUP, 1993), pp. 220–21.

60 Phillip Deery, 'An Australian Communist in Prague', *The Hummer*, vol. 3, no. 8 (Winter 2002); see also John McLaren, *Free Radicals of the Left in Postwar Melbourne* (Melbourne: Australian Scholarly Publishing, 2003), ch. 5.

61 'Youth of 64 Nations Honour Australian Bert Williams', *Tribune*, 10 May 1946; 'Youth Call for Peace', *Daily Telegraph*, 16 August 1949; see also Joyce Evans, *We Had Such High Hopes: Student Activism and the Peace Movement 1949–1952* (Melbourne: Australian Scholarly Publishing, 2019).

62 Peter Worsley, *An Academic Skating on Thin Ice* (New York: Berghahn Books, 2008), pp. 56–57.

63 'Australian Enthusiasm at World Youth Festival', *Tribune*, 3 September 1949; Mona Brand, *Enough Blue Sky: The Autobiography of Mona Brand, an Unknown Well-known Playwright* (Sydney: Tawny Pipit Press, 1995), p. 140; see also Joel Kotek, *Students and the Cold War* (London: Palgrave Macmillan, 1996).

64 'Yugoslavia ACP Branch Raps Tito', *Tribune*, 10 June 1948; 'Aussies Hand Back Yugoslav Badges', *Tribune*, 26 April 1950; Alexander William Sheppard, NAA A6119, 88, vol. 2, ff. 102–19; see also Wendy and Allan Scarfe, *No Taste for Carnage: Alex Sheppard, a Portrait 1913–1997* (Adelaide: Seaview Press, 1998), ch. 12, and Alan Barcan, *The Socialist Left in Australia 1949–1959* (Sydney: Australian Political Studies Association, 1960), p. 10.

65 Arkady Vaksberg, *Stalin Against the Jews* (New York: Alfred A. Knopf, 1994).

66 Judah Waten, 'Anti-Soviet Smear Campaign Exposed', *Tribune*, 20 February 1963.

67 Evelyn Rothfield, *Whither Palestine* (Melbourne: Dolphin Publications, 1947); Ralph Gibson, *War in Palestine* (Melbourne: Victorian State Committee, ACP, 1948); *Australia and Israel* (Melbourne: Jewish Council to Combat Fascism and Anti-Semitism, July 1948); see also Communist Party of Australia—Interests and Activities in Jewish Community, NAA A6122, 444.

68 Philip Mendes, 'Jews, Nazis and Communists Down Under: The Story of the Jewish Council's Controversial Campaign Against German Immigration', *Australian Historical Studies*, vol. 33, no. 119 (2002), pp. 73–92.

69 Jane Persian, *Beautiful Balts: From Displaced Persons to New Australians* (Sydney: NewSouth Publishing, 2017).

70 Constance Lever-Tracy and Michael Quinlan, *A Divided Working Class: Ethnic Segmentation and Industrial Conflict in Australia* (London: Routledge & Kegan Paul, 1988), pp. 171–72; Calwell in *Commonwealth Parliamentary Debates*, 30 September 1948; 'Luxury Hostels for Balts, Tents for Australians', CPA leaflet, Documents Obtained from Police Raid, NAA A6122, 2859, f. 500.

71 'Warning on Balt Migrants', *Tribune* 3 January 1948; Gerald Peel, 'Balts Have Now Become Big Australian Problem', *Tribune*, 2 April 1949; Sharkey quoted by Ted

Bacon, interviewed by Laurie Aarons, June 1980, SLNSW; see also Douglas Jordan, *Conflict in the Unions: The Communist Party of Australia, Politics and the Trade Union Movement, 1945–1960* (Sydney: Resistance Books, 2013), chs 5–6.

72 See, for example, Eric Aarons, *What's Left? Memoirs of an Australian Communist* (Melbourne: Penguin, 1993), pp. 65–67, and Claude Jones, interviewed by Laurie Aarons, June 1989, SLNSW.

73 Edgar Ross, *Of Storm and Struggle*, pp. 102–106. Sheridan, *Division of Labour*, p. 310; Keith Wilson, interviewed by Laurie Aarons, 12–13 May 1979, SLNSW.

74 'Reformists Exposed as Enemies', *Tribune*, 17 July 1949; J.D. Blake, *The Great Coal Strike of 1949* (Sydney: ACP, August 1949), pp. 2, 13, 15.

75 '"Labor" Wars on Women and Children', *Tribune*, 2 July 1949; 'Demonstration Against the Jailings', *Tribune*, 13 July 1949; 'Sharkey Points United Front Path to Win Masses', Melbourne *Guardian*, 26 August 1949; Central Committee Plenum, 14–16 October 1949, SLNSW MLMSS 5021, ADD-ON 1936, Box 16 (76).

76 Central Committee Plenum, 14–16 October 1949.

77 Ted Bacon, interviewed by Laurie Aarons; Jack Hughes, interviewed by Laurie Aarons, September 1980, SLNSW.

78 Jack Hughes, interviewed by Laurie Aarons; see also Jack Blake, 'The 1949 Coal Strike', *Australian Left Review*, no. 70 (August 1979), pp. 12–18.

79 Cedric Ralph, 'One Man's Views of the Twentieth Century', privately printed and held by the family, 1995, vol. 2, ch. 19, p. 11.

80 'Reds Make £20,000 on Marx House', Melbourne *Herald*, 23 September 1949; Herbert Bovyll Chandler, vol. 1, NAA A6119.

81 John Sendy, *The Communist Party: History, Thoughts and Questions* (Melbourne: CPA History Group, 1978), p. 23.

82 'Communists Select 76 Candidates', *Tribune*, 5 February 1949; 'Start Election Drive Now, Ogston Tells Communists', *Tribune*, 21 September 1949.

83 'Crackers, Eggs Thrown at Red Speakers', *Daily Telegraph*, 3 November 1949; 'Police Collusion with Hooligans Is Alleged', *Tribune*, 5 November 1949; 'Bombed Meeting', *Courier-Mail*, 3 November; see also Bill Gollan, interviewed by Laurie Aarons, n.d., SLNSW, and Merv Lilley, *Git Away Back! A Knockabout Life* (Sydney: Currency Press, 1983), pp. 176–77, 240–42.

84 Colin A. Hughes and B.D. Graham, *A Handbook of Australian Government and Politics 1890–1964* (Canberra: ANU Press, 1968), pp. 380–85; Colin A. Hughes and B.D. Graham, *Voting for the Australian House of Representatives 1901–1964* (Canberra: ANU Press, 1974), pp. 268–89.

85 'Unite to Guard Peace, Civil Liberties', *Tribune*, 12 November 1949; 'United Struggle Need After Poll', *Tribune*, 7 December 1949; 'The Federal Elections', *Communist Review*, no. 101 (January 1950), p. 388.

8 Survival, 1950–55

1 Menzies in *Commonwealth Parliamentary Debates*, 27 April 1950.

2 'Communists Must Go', *Argus* 18 January 1949, quoted in A.W. Martin, *Robert Menzies: A Life*, vol. 2, *1944–1978* (Melbourne: MUP, 1999), p. 100; see also A.W. Martin, 'Mr Menzies' Anticommunism', *Quadrant*, vol. 40, no. 5 (May 1996), pp. 47–56.

3 Judith Brett, *Robert Menzies' Forgotten People* (Sydney: Macmillan, 1992), pp. 74–125; see also John Murphy, *Imagining the Fifties: Private Sentiment and Political Culture in Menzies' Australia* (Sydney: UNSWP, 2000), ch. 7.

4 Menzies in *Commonwealth Parliamentary Debates*, 27 April 1950.

5 Menzies in *Commonwealth Parliamentary Debates*, 7 March 1950; the compilation of non-Australian sources on communist doctrine came from the USA and is in Australian Communist Party Dissolution Act—Miscellaneous Papers 1950–52, NAA M1509, 6, ff. 245–624.

6 Ian Hancock, *National and Permanent? The Federal Organisation of the Liberal Party of Australia 1944–1965* (Melbourne: MUP, 2000), pp. 99–100; W.J. Hudson, *Casey* (Melbourne: OUP, 1986); see also *Facts About Communism* (Sydney: Liberal Party of Australia, April 1949).

7 'Menzies Gives Policy', *Sydney Morning Herald*, 11 November 1949.

8 Lawrence W. Maher, 'Dealing with the King's Enemies: The Drafting of the Communist Party Dissolution Bill 1950', *Australian Historical Studies*, vol. 44, no. 1 (2013), pp. 37–53.

9 *Communist Party Dissolution Act 1950*, AustLII, <www5.austlii.edu.au/au/legis/cth/num_act/cpda1950161950387>.

10 Chifley in *Commonwealth Parliamentary Debates*, 9 May 1950; Ross McMullin, *The Light on the Hill: The Australian Labor Party 1891–1991* (Melbourne: OUP, 1991), pp. 256–58.

11 Menzies in *Commonwealth Parliamentary Debates*, 27 April, 9 May 1950; 'Mr J.W.R. Hughes', *Sydney Morning Herald*, 29 April 1950.

12 *Commonwealth Parliamentary Debates*, 4 May 1950; 'Mr Chifley Attacks Prime Minister', Melbourne *Herald*, 5 May 1950.

13 'Red Bill: Onus of Proof Should Be on Government', Melbourne *Herald*, 15 July 1950.

14 Leicester Webb, *Communism and Democracy in Australia: A Survey of the 1951 Referendum* (Melbourne: F.W. Cheshire, 1954) is unsatisfactory but remains the only study.

15 Robert Murray, *The Split: Australian Labor in the Fifties* (Melbourne: Cheshire, 1970, ch. 6; Patrick Weller and Beverley Lloyd (eds), *Federal Executive Minutes 1915–1955: Minutes of the Meetings of the Federal Executive of the Australian Labor Party* (Melbourne: MUP, 1978), p. 478.

16 Rupert Lockwood, 'Seeing Red—and Darker Colours', in Elsa Atkins and Brett Evans (eds), *Seeing Red: The Communist Party Dissolution Act and Referendum 1951, Lessons for Constitutional Reform* (Sydney: Evatt Foundation, 1992), p. 111; Weller and Lloyd (eds), *Federal Executive Minutes*, pp. 412–13, 420, 438.

17 'Protests on Communist Ban', *Age*, 14 February 1950; *A Charter of Freedom: Report of a Conference . . . Held in the Lower Melbourne Town Hall Sat. April 22 1950* (Melbourne: Democratic Rights Council, 1950); 'Human Rights Assembly Challenge to Menzies of Regimentation', Melbourne *Guardian*, 15 September 1950.

18 'Big "No" Campaign Launched', *Tribune*, 22 August 1951; 'Good Start for Referendum Campaign', *Tribune*, 8 August 1951.

19 'Not a Ship Will Sail if Fascist Bill Used', Melbourne *Guardian*, 26 May 1950; '50,000 Stop Work; "Triple Alliance" Union Move Endorsed', *Tribune*, 17 June 1950; 'Rowdy Union Meetings', *Sydney Morning Herald*, 15 June 1950.

20 'Warning of Dangers in Call to the Nation', *Age*, 12 November 1951; see also Laurence W. Maher, 'Tales of the Overt and the Covert: Judges and Politics in Early Cold War Australia', *Federal Law Review*, vol. 21, no. 2 (1993), pp. 151–201, and David Lowe, *Menzies and the 'Great World Struggle': Australia's Cold War 1948–1954* (Sydney: UNSWP, 1999), pp. 115–16.

21 Les Louis, '"Operation Alien" and the Cold War in Australia, 1950–1953', *Labour History*, no. 62 (1992), pp. 1–18.
22 Director-General's memo, 28 July 1950, Detention—Internment Policy, NAA A6122, 1285; Director-General's policy statement, 17 August 1950, Communist Party of Australia—Dissolution Bill, NAA A6122, 1122; see also David McKnight, *Australia's Spies and Their Secrets* (Sydney: Allen & Unwin, 1994), pp. 117–22.
23 Tom Sheridan, *Australia's Own Cold War: The Waterfront Under Menzies* (Melbourne: MUP, 2006), pp. 95, 123–26; Margo Beasley, *Wharfies: A History of the Waterside Workers' Federation of Australia* (Sydney: Halstead Press, 1996), pp. 150–52.
24 'Not a Man, Ship, 'Plane for Korea or Malaya', *Tribune*, 1 July 1950; see also Roger Douglas, 'The Ambiguity of Sedition: The Trials of William Fardon Burns', *Australian Journal of Legal History*, no. 9 (2005), pp. 227–48.
25 Rex Chiplin, 'Secret Treaty Sells Us to US', *Tribune*, November 1951; *Commonwealth Parliamentary Debates*, 27 May 1952; Rex Chiplin, part 1, NAA A6119, 866; Mercia Leonora Zoe Masson, NAA A6119, 915; see also McKnight, *Australia's Spies and Their Secrets*, p. 52; David Horner, *The Spy Catchers: The Official History of ASIO, 1949–1963, Volume I* (Sydney: Allen & Unwin, 2014), pp. 301–304 and the appendix on Masson, pp. 563–80.
26 R.C., 'The "Democratic" Monarchy', *Communist Review*, no. 138 (June 1953), pp. 177–79; see also Laurence W. Maher, 'The Use and Abuse of Sedition', *Sydney Law Review*, vol. 14, no. 3 (1992), pp. 306–11, and McKnight, *Australia's Spies and Their Secrets*, p. 56.
27 McKnight, *Australia's Spies and Their Secrets*, p. 43.
28 Horner, *The Spy Catchers*, ch. 7.
29 Mark Aarons, *The Family File* (Melbourne: Black Inc., 2010), pp. 124–27.
30 Eric Aarons, *What's Left? Memoirs of an Australian Communist* (Melbourne: Penguin, 1993), pp. 72–73; John Sendy, *Comrades Come Rally! Recollections of an Australian Communist* (Melbourne: Thomas Nelson, 1978), pp. 64–65; Harry Hatfield, interviewed by Laurie Aarons, n.d., SLNSW.
31 Keith Wilson, interviewed by Laurie Aarons, 12–13 May 1979, SLNSW.
32 Stuart Macintyre, 'Communist Party History', in David Clune and Ken Turner (eds), *Writing Party History: Papers from a Seminar Held at Parliament House, Sydney, 20 May 2006* (Sydney: NSW Parliament, 2007), pp. 65–73.
33 Wilson, interviewed by Aarons; Aarons, *What's Left?*, p. 75–76; Hatfield, interviewed by Aarons.
34 'Man Dies, Women Faint in Jostle', *Herald*, 23 September 1950; 'Walls and Bridges Defaced—On Red Orders', *Herald*, 21 September 1951; 'Police After "NO" Street Painters', *Courier-Mail*, 22 September 1951.
35 Phillip Deery, '"A Most Important Cadre": Infiltration of the Communist Party of Australia during the Early Cold War', *Labour History*, no. 115 (November 2018), pp. 1–26.
36 'Security's Priority: Get into Party', Melbourne *Guardian*, 19 November 1953.
37 Communist Party of Australia—16th National Congress 1951, NAA A6122, 1075; Spry to Menzies, 31 August 1951, quoted in Horner, *The Spy Catchers*, p. 190; 'Menzies Appeals Vote "Yes"', *Sydney Morning Herald*, 5 September 1951; see also *The Spy Catchers*, chs 8–9.
38 'Editorial: Verification of Members', *Communist Review*, no. 112 (April 1951), p. 739; L.L. Sharkey, 'Report to the 16th National Congress', *Communist Review*, no. 118 (October 1951), p. 936; Communist Party of Australia—16th National Congress 1951, ff. 45–62.

39 Communist Party of Australia—Plans for Operations, NAA A6122, 471, f. 107; Australian Communist Party—Membership, NAA A1209, 1957/4753; 'Building the Communist Party', *Tribune*, 15 October 1952.

40 L. Aarons, 'Problems of Party Growth', *Communist Review*, no. 141 (September 1953), pp. 254–56; L. Aarons, 'Build the Party', *Communist Review*, no. 162 (June 1955), p. 176.

41 Ernest William Campbell, vol. 3, NAA A6119, 1695, f. 53; 'Speed Your Donation to Help Tribune', *Tribune*, 23 November 1950; 'Date for 12-Pager to Be Announced Soon', *Tribune*, 19 April 1951.

42 J.C. Henry, 'Strengths, Weaknesses of Build Party Drive', *Tribune*, 13 August 1952; Central Committee, 22–25 August 1952, Herbert Bovyll Chandler, vol. 5, NAA A6119, 75, ff. 1–16; Aarons, 'Problems of Party Growth'.

43 Claude Jones to William McDougall, 24 February 1950, William McDougall, vol. 1, NAA A6119, 3808, f. 126; Jack Hughes, interviewed by Laurie Aarons, September 1980, SLNSW; 'Queensland Leads in ACP National Fund', *Tribune*, 26 April 1951.

44 'Communist Party's New Rates of Dues', *Tribune*, 28 November 1951; secretariat proposal on finance, 20 January 1953, in Communist Party of Australia—Plans for Operations, ff. 40–41; see also Aarons, *The Family File*, pp. 186–87.

45 Arthur Gietzelt, NAA A6119, 381, f. 92; CP of A Victoria State Committee, NAA A6122, 480, ff. 40–44.

46 'Urgent Need Is Unity', *Tribune*, 25 February 1950; J.D. Blake, 'Unite to Defeat Menzies' Fascist Bill', *Communist Review*, no. 106 (June 1950), p. 547.

47 'Unity and Struggle Can Defeat Reaction', *Tribune*, 10 May 1951; J.D. Blake, 'A Government of National Betrayal', *Communist Review*, no. 103 (March 1950), p. 452; 'Mr Chifley—His Last Speech Was for Unity', *Tribune*, 2 June 1951.

48 *Australia's Path to Socialism: Program of the Communist Party of Australia Sixteenth Congress, August 1951* (Sydney: Current Book Distributors, January 1952), pp. 19, 22.

49 *Australia's Path to Socialism*, pp. 20–21.

50 Kevin Morgan, *Harry Pollitt* (Manchester: Manchester University Press, 1993), pp. 167–70; see also Sharkey's strong endorsement in 'On the Program of the British Communist Party', *Communist Review*, no. 114 (June 1952), pp. 810–11.

51 *Australia's Path to Socialism*, pp. 19–20; L.L. Sharkey, *The Labor Party Crisis* (Sydney: Current Book Distributors, 1952); this first appeared in the *Communist Review*, no. 128 (August 1952), pp. 227–32.

52 J.D. Blake, 'Role of the Working Class in the Struggle for Peace', *Communist Review*, no. 112 (April 1951), pp. 762–65.

53 Transcript of Central Committee, April–May 1951, Communist Party of Australia Central Committee General, vol. 2, NAA A6122, 474, ff. 84–237.

54 J.D. Blake, 'The Party Branch and Political Activity', *Communist Review*, no. 105 (May 1950), p. 528; Blake, interviewed by Laurie Aarons, August 1979, SLNSW.

55 Blake, 'Role of the Working Class in the Struggle for Peace'; J.D. Blake, '1949 to 1966: Stalinism or Independence?', *Australian Left Review*, no. 76 (June 1981), p. 10.

56 Palmiro Togliatti, 'Unity of the Working Class', *Communist Review*, no. 102 (February 1950), pp. 422–28; J.D. Blake, 'Australians Victims of the Cold War', *Tribune*, 24 June 1953; Blake, '1949 to 1966', p. 13.

57 Edward Charles Roach, vols 1–2, NAA A6119, 1212–13; 'Ted Roach Given Rousing Welcome', *Tribune*, 19 December 1951; see also L.J. Louis, 'The Cold/Class War, and the Jailing of Ted Roach', *Labour History*, no. 86 (May 2004), pp. 157–72, and Denis Kevans, *Ted Roach: From Pig Iron Hero to Long Bay Gaol* (ASSLH website, 2020), chs 17–18.

58 Edward Charles Roach, vol. 1, f. 21; Itzhak Gust, *Such Was Life: A Jumping Narrative from Radom to Melbourne* (Melbourne: Makor Community Library, 2004), p. 212.
59 'S.A. Official for High Union Post', *Advertiser*, 15 March 1950; 'Leading S.A. Red Expelled from Party', *Advertiser*, 9 August 1950; 'Carruthers Expelled from A.C.P.', *Tribune*, 16 August 1950.
60 'R.C. Morgan Expelled from Communist Party', *Tribune*, 19 April 1951; Richard Charles Morgan, NAA A6126, 536.
61 'Thompson Leaves B.T.F. Job', *Argus*, 5 April 1952; Donald Thomson, vol. 2, NAA A6119, 1800; see Edward Fowler Hill, vol. 1, NAA A6119, 209, f. 5, and Patrick John Malone, vol. 1, A6119, 2966, ff. 68–75 on the others who were chastised.
62 Aarons, *What's Left?*, p. 71; see also Theo Moody, 'Bill Parkinson', *Australian Left Review*, no. 11 (February–March 1968), pp. 64–69, and Edgar Ross, *A History of the Miners' Federation of Australia* (Sydney: Australasian Coal and Shale Employees' Association, 1970), p. 398.
63 Sendy, *Comrades Come Rally!*, p. 23; Nancy Wills, *Shades of Red: Personal and Political Recollections of a Communist to Mark the Occasion of Our Sixtieth Anniversary 1920–1980* (Brisbane: Communist Arts Group, 1980), p. 78; Tom Brislan in Central Committee, April–May 1951, ff. 127–28.
64 Security report, 7 July 1952, Alfred Deaken Watt, vol. 1, NAA A6119, 2129, f. 62.
65 Ted Rowe in Central Committee, April–May 1951, ff. 160–62.
66 R. Dixon, 'Struggle Against the Right Wing', *Communist Review*, no. 124 (April 1952), pp. 99–101; 'Unite the Working Class to Defeat Menzies', *Communist Review*, no. 127 (July 1952), pp. 195–202; 'Dixon Aims of the Party', *Tribune*, 21 January 1953.
67 L.L. Sharkey, 'Development of the Economic Crisis', *Communist Review*, no. 125 (May 1952), pp. 133–39; 'All Must Fight to Defeat Menzies, Says CC Declaration', *Tribune*, 24 February 1954; see also John Murphy, *Imagining the Fifties: Private Sentiment and Political Culture in Menzies' Australia* (Sydney: UNSWP, 2000), chs 7–8.
68 Laurie Aarons, interviewed by Joyce Stevens, 17 September 1980, SLNSW, and information from Brian Aarons, to whom Sharkey explained the change a decade later.
69 Ted Bacon, interviewed by Laurie Aarons, June 1980, SLNSW.
70 Transcript of Audrey and Jack Blake and Helen Palmer, interviewed by Bob and Ann Gollan, Robin Gollan papers, NLA MS 9372/9/16.
71 Claude Jones, interviewed by Laurie Aarons, June 1980, SLNSW; Hughes interviewed by Aarons.
72 Sharkey in Central Committee, NAA A6122, 474, f. 149; L.L. Sharkey, 'Report to the 16th National Congress', *Communist Review*, no. 118 (October 1951), p. 940; Samuel Aarons, vol. 1, NAA A6119, 108, f. 184; Jones interviewed by Aarons; Cecil Holmes, *One Man's Way* (Melbourne: Penguin, 1986), p. 40.
73 This profile draws on the recollections of Jack Blake, interviewed by Laurie Aarons, August 1979, SLNSW; Bernie Taft, *Crossing the Party Line: Memoirs of Bernie Taft* (Newham: Scribe Publications, 1994), p. 65; Frank Hardy, *The Hard Way: The Story Behind 'Power Without Glory'* (Sydney: Australasian Book Society, 1961), p. 95; Lloyd Edmonds, interviewed by Laurie Aarons, n.d., SLNSW; Wills, *Shades of Red*, p. 78.
74 Blake, '1949 to 1966', pp. 8–17; 'Jack Blake's Final Reminiscences', *The Hummer*, vol. 3, no. 9 (Summer 2002–2003), pp. 25–30.
75 Jones interviewed by Aarons; Hughes interviewed by Aarons.

76 Hughes interviewed by Aarons; Herbert Bovyll Chandler, vol. 8, NAA A6119, 78, ff. 114–19.
77 'Report by J.D. Blake', *Communist Review*, no. 133 (January 1953), pp. 10–14.
78 'Jack Blake's Final Reminiscences'; Blake, '1949 to 1966'.
79 'For Party Consolidation', 'Statement by J.D. Blake', *Tribune*, 10 March 1954; see also Phillip Deery, 'The Sickle and Scythe: Jack Blake and Communist Party "Consolidation", 1949–56', *Labour History*, no. 80 (2001), pp. 215–23.
80 Blake interviewed by Aarons.

9 Revival? 1950–56

1 'What Is Sectarianism?', *Tribune*, 15 June 1955.
2 Keith Wilson, interviewed by Laurie Aarons, 12–13 May 1979, SLNSW.
3 B.J.B., 'Sectarianism: A Critical Quiz for All', *Tribune*, 21 June 1951, SLNSW.
4 A letter by Carmel Shute to *Tribune*, 13 July 1988 is the first recorded usage I have found, but the phrase was in common use well before then.
5 Norman Mitchell, 'Sectarianism—A Way of Life', *Communist Review*, no. 128, (August 1952), pp. 246–47.
6 Waterside Workers' Federation—General, vol. 1, NAA A6122, 333, ff. 161–66; 'Wharf Vote Bans Ships from NZ', Melbourne *Herald*, 23 May 1951; see generally Tom Sheridan, *Australia's Own Cold War: The Waterfront Under Menzies* (Melbourne: MUP, 2006).
7 Central Committee, 22–25 August 1952, James Healy, vol. 4, NAA A6119, 152, ff. 69–76; 'Wharfies Sack Melbourne Branch Executive', Melbourne *Guardian*, 28 January 1954; see also the criticisms of Healy in Denis Kevans, *Ted Roach: From Pig Iron Hero to Long Bay Gaol* (Sydney: ASSLH website, 2020).
8 Andrew Reeves, *A Tapestry of Australia: The Sydney Wharfies Mural* (Sydney: Waterside Workers' Federation, Sydney Port, 1992).
9 Central Committee, 22–25 August 1952, Herbert Bovyll Chandler, vol, 5, NAA A6119, 75, ff. 31–37.
10 '"High Honour" for Big Jim', *Tribune*, 11 May 1955; Thornton's address recalled in John Sendy, *Comrades Come Rally! Recollections of an Australian Communist* (Melbourne: Thomas Nelson, 1978), pp. 177–78. Another version of Healy's address appeared as 'How to Build Unity', *Communist Review*, no. 162 (June 1955), pp. 189–92.
11 Rowan Cahill, *Sea Change: An Essay in Maritime Labour History* (Bowral: the author, 1998); Diane Kirkby and Dmytro Ostapenko, '"Second to None in the International Fight": Australian Seafarers Internationalism and Maritime Unions Against Apartheid', *Journal of Contemporary History*, vol. 54, no. 2 (2019), pp. 442–64.
12 Audrey Johnson, 'Reminiscences of an Old Leftie', *The Hummer*, no. 34 (April–August 1992), <www.labour history.org.au/hummer>.
13 *Ballot Riggers at Work! Defend the Unions* (Melbourne: n.p., n.d. [1953]); see also J.H. Portus, *The Development of Australian Trade Union Law* (Melbourne: MUP, 1958), chs 14–15.
14 Glenn Mitchell, *On Strong Foundations: The BWIU and Industrial Relations in the Australian Construction Industry 1942–1992* (Sydney: Harcourt, Brace and Co., 1996), chs 2–3; see also Tom McDonald and Audrey McDonald, *Intimate Union: Sharing a Revolutionary Life* (Sydney: Pluto Press, 1998).
15 John Playford, 'Doctrinal and Strategic Problems of the Communist Party of Australia, 1943–62', PhD thesis, ANU, 1962, pp. 231–43.
16 Bruce Mitchell, *Teachers, Education, and Politics: A History of Organizations of Public*

School Teachers in New South Wales (Brisbane: UQP, 1975), ch. 6; Jan Friedel, 'Left Wing Melbourne Artists and the Communist Party during the Early Cold War Period', PhD thesis, University of Melbourne, 2013, ch. 6.

17 'Ironworkers' Big Vote for Thornton', 'E. Thornton Victimised Once Again', 'Ernie Thornton Sacked Again', 'Attempts to Sack Thornton', 'Thornton Breaks Long-term Blacklist', *Tribune*, 23 April 1954, 26 January, 9 February, 9 March, 16 March 1955.

18 Tom Sheridan, *Mindful Militants: The Amalgamated Engineering Union in Australia 1920–1972* (Cambridge: CUP, 1975), ch. 8.

19 Lloyd Ross, 'The Labor Scene', Melbourne *Herald*, 6 September 1951.

20 'Rebuff to Reds', Melbourne *Herald*, 4 September 1951; 'Affiliation with ICFU', Melbourne *Herald*, 5 September 1951; Brian Fitzpatrick and Rowan J. Cahill, *The Seamen's Union of Australia 1872–1972: A History* (Sydney: Seamen's Union of Australia, 1982), pp. 190–91; see also Peter Weiler, 'The United States, International Labor, and the Cold War: The Breakup of the World Federation of Trade Unions', *Diplomatic History*, vol. 5, no. 1 (1981), pp. 1–22.

21 L. Aarons, 'Build the Party', *Communist Review*, no. 162 (June 1955), p. 176.

22 Geoffrey Roberts, 'Averting Armageddon: The Communist Peace Movement, 1948–1956', in Stephen A. Smith (ed.), *The Oxford Handbook of the History of Communism* (Oxford: OUP, 2014), pp. 322–37.

23 'Australian Peace Council Launched', *Tribune*, 7 September 1950.

24 The principal studies are O'Byrne, 'The Peace Parsons: The Involvement of the Clergy in Peace Movements during the 1950s', MA thesis, Monash University, 1984; Robert McArthur, 'Christ and the Cold War: An Exploration of the Political Activism of the Reverends Frank Hartley, Alfred Dickie and Victor James, 1942–1972', PhD thesis, University of Melbourne, 2007; and Kim Thoday, 'Christian-Socialist Dialogue during the Early Cold War: A Study of the Protestant Left in Victoria, 1949–1954', MA thesis, Victoria University, 2014. See also Victor James, *Window on the Years* (Melbourne: Unitarian Assembly of Victoria, 1980), and Marian Hartley, *The Truth Shall Prevail: The Reverend Francis John Hartley* (Melbourne: Spectrum Publications, 1982).

25 Conversation with Vernon Rice in 1971.

26 'Resolutions of Australian Peace Congress—Melbourne, April 1950', *Communist Review*, no. 106 (June 1950), p. 554; '25 Australian Delegates for Peking Peace Conference', Melbourne *Guardian*, 7 August 1952; '1952 Vital Year for Peace, Reverend Frank Harley Warns', Melbourne *Guardian*, 29 November 1951.

27 The fullest account of the Melbourne congress is given in the Australian Peace Council's journal, *Peace*, vol. 1, no. 2 (June 1950).

28 'Peace Meeting Calls on US to Stop Operations', *Age*, 29 June 1950; Ian Turner, 'My Long March', in *Room for Manoeuvre: Writings on History, Politics, Ideas and Play*, selected and edited by Leonie Sandercock and Stephen Murray-Smith (Melbourne: Drummond Publishing, 1982), pp. 105–40.

29 'War or Peace . . .? An Appeal to All Men and Women of Goodwill', *Age*, 12 March 1951; Barbara Carter, 'The Peace Movement in the 1950s', in Ann Curthoys and John Merritt (eds), *Australia's First Cold War, 1945–1953*, vol. 2, *Better Red than Dead* (Sydney: Allen & Unwin, 1986), pp. 64–66.

30 Roberts, 'Averting Armageddon', pp. 326–28; 'Oust Menzies—for Peace: 117,000 Sign Against War', *Tribune*, 6 October 1950; 'Signatures for Peace', *Tribune*, 5 March 1952; 'Anti-Atom War Campaign', Melbourne *Guardian*, 17 November 1955.

31 Rowan Cahill, 'Rupert Lockwood (1908–1997): Journalist, Communist, Intellectual', PhD thesis, University of Wollongong, 2013, pp. 258–61; 'Counihan Among Australians for Paris Peace Conference', Melbourne *Guardian*, 14 April 1949, and Noel Jack Counihan, vol. 1, NAA A6119, 179, ff. 153–55; see also Bernard Smith, *Noel Counihan: Artist and Revolutionary* (Melbourne: OUP, 1993), pp. 227–36.
32 Norman Randolph Freehill, vol. 1, NAA A6119, 1424, ff. 84–86; 'Vienna Congress Shows New World Drive for Peace', *Tribune*, 31 March 1953.
33 Craig McLean, 'Fear of Peace? Australian Government Responses to the Peace Movement, 1949–1959', MA thesis, Victoria University, 2001, chs 2–4.
34 J.E. Owen, *The Road to Peace: An Experiment Across Barriers* (Melbourne: The Hawthorn Press, 1954); see also Phillip Deery, 'War on Peace: Menzies, the Cold War and the 1953 Convention on Peace and War', *Australian Historical Studies*, vol. 34, no. 122 (2003), pp. 248–69.
35 Audrey Johnson, *Fly a Rebel Flag: Bill Morrow 1888–1980* (Melbourne: Penguin, 1986), chs 17–18.
36 Bill and Marie Gollan, interviewed by Bob and Ann Gollan, n.d., Robin Gollan papers, NLA MS 9372/9/16; Cecil Holmes, *One Man's Way* (Melbourne: Penguin, 1986), p. 40; see also John Murphy, 'The Australian Intervention in the Vietnam War', PhD thesis, University of Melbourne, 1992, pp. 69–74.
37 'Secret Police Pimping in Railways Exposed by Turner Case', Melbourne *Guardian*, 3 December 1953.
38 Amirah Inglis, *The Hammer & Sickle and the Washing Up: Memories of an Australian Woman Communist* (Melbourne: Hyland House, 1995), pp. 95–96; Turner, 'My Long March', p. 131; Johnson, *Fly a Rebel Flag*, p. 260.
39 Audrey and Jack Blake and Helen Palmer, interviewed by Bob and Ann Gollan, n.d., Gollan papers; J.D. Blake, 'Tasks in the Struggle for Peace', *Communist Review*, no. 140 (August 1953), pp. 227–35, and 'Communists and the Peace Convention', *Tribune*, 16 September 1953.
40 Angela O'Brien, 'Richard Frank (Dick) Diamond', *Australian Dictionary of Biography*, vol. 17, pp. 316–17 suggests 500,000 patrons, while *The 'New' Years, 1932– : The Plays, People and Events of Six Decades of Sydney's Radical New Theatre* (Sydney: New Theatre, 1992), p. 17 claims 450,000.
41 Pauline Armstrong, *Frank Hardy and the Making of* Power Without Glory (Melbourne: MUP, 2000), chs 3–4; Paul Adams, *The Stranger from Melbourne: Frank Hardy—A Literary Biography 1944–1975* (Perth: UWAP, 1999), p. 59.
42 Jenny Hocking, *Frank Hardy: Politics, Literature Life* (Melbourne: Lothian Books, 2005), chs 3–4.
43 Frank Hardy, *The Hard Way: The Story Behind 'Power Without Glory'* (Sydney: Australasian Book Society, 1961); Inglis, *The Hammer & Sickle and the Washing Up*, p. 55; see also Jack Beasley, *Red Letter Days: Notes from Inside an Era* (Sydney: Australasian Book Society, 1979), pp. 53–95.
44 Frank Hardy, 'On the Cultural Front', *Communist Review*, no. 153 (September 1954), p. 274; Jozsef Révai, *Lukacs and Socialist Realism: A Hungarian Literary Controversy* (London: Fore Publications, 1950); John Morrison quoted in 'New Realist Writer Out', *Tribune*, 5 May 1954; David Martin, *My Strange Friend: An Autobiography* (Sydney: Macmillan, 1991), pp. 238–39.
45 Beasley, *Red Letter Days*, pp. 129–68, which also provides a full list of all books published.
46 Frank J. Hardy, *Journey into the Future* (Melbourne: Australasian Book Society, 1952).

47 S.F. Bannister, *Tossed and Blown* (Melbourne: Australasian Book Society, 1953); S.F. Bannister, *God's Own Country* (Melbourne: Australasian Book Society, 1953); Len Fox, 'Has Book Society Gone Off the Right Track?', *Tribune*, 15 July 1953; 'Author Replies to Criticism', *Tribune*, 29 July 1953; J.D. Blake, 'Tribune Discussion Will Keep ABS on Right Track', *Tribune*, 9 September 1953.

48 Leslie James Crawford, NAA A6119, 1041; Stephen Murray-Smith, *Indirections: A Literary Biography* (Townsville: Foundation for Australian Literary Studies, James Cook University, 1981); see also John McLaren, *Free Radicals of the Left in Postwar Melbourne* (Melbourne: Australian Scholarly Publishing, 2003), pp. 123–24.

49 J.D. Blake, 'On the Work of Communist Writers', *Communist Review*, no. 143, (November 1953), pp. 337–41; this was a summary of his address to a conference of communist writers in October 1953.

50 Frank Hardy, 'Make Literature a Mass Question for the Party and the Working Class', *Communist Review*, no. 132 (December 1952), pp. 374–79; 'On the Cultural Front', *Communist Review*, no. 153 (September 1954), pp. 272–75. The term 'culture vultures' was taken from an admonition by Sharkey, 'Report to Cultural Activities', *Communist Review*, no. 152 (August 1954), p. 237.

51 Graeme Davison, 'Rethinking the Australian Legend', *Australian Historical Studies*, vol. 43, no. 3 (2012), pp. 429–51; Keith McHenry, *More Than a Life: John Meredith and the Fight for Australian Tradition* (Dural: Rosenberg Publishing, 2014).

52 Russel Ward, 'The Ethos and Influence of the Australian Pastoral Worker', PhD thesis, ANU, 1957, and *The Australian Legend* (Melbourne: OUP, 1958); see also David Carter, 'The Story of Our Epoch, a Hero of Our Time', in Paul Adams and Christopher Lee (eds), *Frank Hardy and the Literature of Commitment* (Melbourne: Vulgar Press, 2003), pp. 89–111.

53 Jan Friedel, 'Left Wing Melbourne Artists and the Communist Party during the Early Cold War Period', PhD thesis, University of Melbourne, 2013, ch. 7; see also Graeme Smith, 'Making Folk Music', *Meanjin*, vol. 44, no. 4 (December 1985), pp. 477–90.

54 'Secret of Dave Stephens' Wins', *Tribune*, 2 March 1955; 'Percy Cerutty Sees American and Russian Athletes', *Tribune*, 29 August 1952; Janey Stone, 'Coach Who Recreated Himself', *Age*, 19 August 2010.

55 Stephen Murray-Smith (ed.), *The Tracks We Travel* (Melbourne: Australian Book Society, 1953), p. 9; see also Mark Finnane, 'Censorship and the Child: Explaining the Comics Campaign', *Australian Historical Studies*, vol. 23, no. 92 (1989), pp. 22–40.

56 Cyril Pearl, NAA A6119, 1583, ff. 58–62; see also Allan Ashbolt, 'The Great Literary Witch-hunt of 1952', in Ann Curthoys and John Merritt (eds), *Australia's First Cold War, 1945–1953*, vol. 1, *Society, Communism and Culture* (Sydney: Allen & Unwin, 1984), pp. 153–82.

57 Humphrey McQueen, *Gallipoli to Petrov: Arguing with Australian History* (Sydney: Allen & Unwin, 1984), ch. 17; Cassandra Pybus, *The Devil and James McAuley* (Brisbane: University of Queensland Press, 1999), ch. 7.

58 'Meanjin Gives Startling Facts on "Congress for Cultural Freedom"', *Tribune*, 19 January 1955; see also the exchange between Christesen and Latham in *Meanjin*, vol. 13, no. 4 (Summer 1954), and Sean Scalmer, 'The Puzzle of *Meanjin* and the Historical Emergence of an Australian Intelligentsia', *Journal of Australian Studies*, vol. 23, no. 62 (1999), pp. 198–204.

59 Audrey Elsie Blake, NAA A6119, 120, ff. 39–40; Audrey Blake, 'Youth and the People's Movement', *Communist Review*, no. 116 (August 1951), pp. 880–82; Joyce

Stevens, interviewed by Laurie Aarons, 1 July 1980, SLNSW; statement by central committee, 'Eureka League's Importance in the Fight for Peace and People's Government', *Tribune*, 12 March 1952.

60 ASIO report, 27 February 1952, Charles Frederick Wells, vol. 1, NAA A6119, 911; Joyce Evans, *We Had Such High Hopes: Student Activism and the Peace Movement 1949–1952* (Melbourne: Australian Scholarly Publishing, 2010); see also Phillip Deery, 'ASIO and the 1951 Berlin Youth Carnival', *Overland*, no. 168 (Spring 2002), pp. 79–83.

61 Evans, *We Had Such High Hopes*, p. 154.

62 Audrey Blake and Harry Stein, 'Youth Carnival for Peace and Friendship—a People's Victory', *Communist Review*, no. 125 (May 1952), pp. 139–42; statement of income and expenditure, Herbert Bovyll Chandler, vol. 4, NAA A6119, 75, f. 18; 'New Leaders for EYL', *Tribune*, 2 April 1952; see also Harry Stein, *A Glance Over an Old Left Shoulder* (Sydney: Hale & Iremonger, 1994), ch. 10, and Phillip Deery, 'Community Carnival or Cold War Strategy? The 1952 Youth Carnival for Peace and Friendship', in Robert Hood and Ray Markey (eds), *Labour and Community: Historical Essays* (Wollongong: University of Wollongong Press, 2001), pp. 71–77.

63 Barbara Curthoys and Audrey McDonald, *More Than a Hat and Glove Brigade: The Story of the Union of Australian Women* (Sydney: Bookpress, 1996), ch. 1.

64 Audrey Johnson, *Bread & Roses: A Personal History of Three Militant Women and Their Friends 1902–1988* (Sydney: Left Book Club, 1990), p. 134; Jean Blackburn, interviewed by Wendy Lowenstein, 1 July 1994, NLA TRC 2375; see Craig Campbell and Debra Hayes, *Jean Blackburn: Education, Feminism and Social Justice* (Melbourne: Monash University Publishing, 2019), pp. 83–94.

65 Kath Williams, *Equality Will Be Won* (Melbourne: Union of Australian Women, 1956); see also Katherine Keirs, 'Class, Gender and Cold War Politics: The Union of Australian Women and the Campaign for Equal Pay, 1950–66', *Labour History*, no. 117 (November 2019), pp. 159–80.

66 In addition to Curthoys and McDonald, *More that a Hat and Glove Brigade*, see Sue Fabian and Morag Loh, *Left-Wing Ladies: The Union of Australian Women in Victoria 1950–1998* (Melbourne: Hyland House, 2000); Pam Young, *Daring to Take a Stand: The Story of the Union of Australian Women in Queensland* (Brisbane: the author, 1998), and Zora Simic, 'Butter Not Bombs: A Short History of the Union of Australian Women', *History Australia*, vol. 4, no. 1 (2007), pp. 07.1–15.

67 Jess Grant, interviewed by Laurie Aarons, quoted in Joyce Stevens, *Taking the Revolution Home: Work Among Women in the Communist Party of Australia 1920–1945* (Melbourne: Sybylla Co-operative Press, 1987), p. 182.

68 Jean Blackburn, interviewed by Wendy Lowenstein, NLA; Ailsa O'Connor, *Unfinished Work: Articles and Note on Women and the Politics of Art* (Melbourne: Greenhouse, 1982); Dorothy Hewett, *Wild Card: An Autobiography 1923–1958* (Melbourne: McPhee Gribble, 1991).

69 Zelda D'Aprano, *Zelda: The Becoming of a Woman* (Melbourne: Widescope, 1977), pp. 43, 75; see also Patricia Grimshaw, 'Zelda D'Aprano, Leadership and the Politics of Gender in the Australian Labour Movement, 1945–1975', *Labour History*, no. 104 (May 2013), pp. 101–18.

70 Ted Rowe in Central Committee, April 1951, Communist Party of Australia Central Committee General, vol. 2, NAA A6122, 474, ff. 160–61; E.J. Rowe, '"New" and "Old" Australians', *Communist Review*, no. 131 (November 1952), pp. 337–40.

71 Philip Mendes, 'The Cold War, McCarthyism, the Melbourne Jewish Council to

Combat Anti-Semitism and Australian Jewry 1948–55', *Journal of Australian Studies*, no. 64 (2000), pp. 196–206; Max Kaiser, 'Between Nationalism and Assimilation: Jewish Antifascism in Australia in the Late 1940s and early 1950s', PhD thesis, University of Melbourne, 2018.

72 'Rosenbergs, Not Slansky, Victims of Anti-Semitism', *Tribune*, 7 January 1953; see also Phillip Deery, 'Securing Justice? The Australian Campaign to Save the Rosenbergs', *Journal of Australian Studies*, vol. 38, no. 1 (2014), pp. 3–17.

73 Informant's report of meeting, 2 February 1953, Communist Party of Australia—Attitude Towards Anti-Semitism, NAA A6122, 462, ff. 206–208; J.D. Blake, 'Zionism and Anti-Semitism', *Communist Review*, no. 136 (April 1953), pp. 119–24; 'Meeting Hears Blake on Soviet Doctors Case', *Tribune*, 23 August 1956; Jack Blake, interviewed by Laurie Aarons, August 1979, SLNSW.

74 Tom Heenan, *From Traveller to Traitor: The Life of Wilfred Burchett* (Melbourne: MUP, 2006), ch. 5; Laurie Aarons, 'I Saw How Indonesians Defeat Provocateurs', *Tribune*, 13 April 1954; Aarons, interviewed by Stewart Harris, December 1991–January 1992, NLA TRC 2788.

75 Len Fox, *Friendly Vietnam* (Hanoi: Foreign Languages Publishing House, 1958); Mona Brand, *Daughters of Vietnam* (Hanoi: Foreign Languages Publishing House, 1958).

76 'The Dedication and Revolutionary Humanism of Lorraine Salmon', *Tribune*, 25 November 1970; Lorraine Salmon, *Pig Follows Dog* (Hanoi: Foreign Languages Publishing House, 1970).

77 Tom Wright, *New Deal for the Aborigines* (Sydney: Modern Publishers, n.d. [1939]); Murray Norris, 'Rebuilding the North Australian Workers' Union 1942–1951', in Hal Alexander and Phil Griffiths (eds), *A Few Rough Reds: Stories of Rank and File Organising* (Canberra: Australian Society for the Study of Labour History, Canberra Branch, 2003), pp. 63–109.

78 Shirley Andrews, interviewed by Wendy Lowenstein, 1993–94, NLA TRC 3111, quoted in Jennifer Hibben, 'Shirley Andrews: A Prismatic Life', PhD thesis, University of Melbourne, 2012.

79 Sue Taffe, 'Shirley Andrews: An Architect of the National Aboriginal Civil Rights Movement, 1952–1968', *History Australia*, vol. 8, no. 2 (2011), pp. 153–76; Bain Attwood, *Rights for Aborigines* (Sydney: Allen & Unwin, 2003), ch. 6.

80 'A New Stage in the Development of the Aboriginal People', *Communist Review*, no. 153 (September 1954), pp. 282–85; Bacon, interviewed by Laurie Aarons, June 1980, SLNSW; see also Peter Monteath and Valerie Munt, *Red Professor: The Cold War Life of Fred Rose* (Adelaide: Wakefield Press, 2015), and Peter Worsley, *An Academic Skating on Thin Ice* (New York: Berghahn Books, 2008).

81 'Reds Blamed for Strike', *Sydney Morning Herald*, 20 February 1951; information from Jan Richardson, 10 June 2020; Andrews' ministerial correspondence with Paul Hasluck, the responsible federal minister, is in Council for Aboriginal Rights, NAA A452, 1957/479.

82 David McKnight, 'Menzies and the Petrov Commission', *Tribune*, 3 October 1984; see also Nicholas Whitlam and John Stubbs, *Nest of Traitors: The Petrov Affair* (Brisbane: Jacaranda Press, 1974), Richard Hall, *The Secret State: Australia's Spy Industry* (Sydney: Cassell, 1978), David McKnight, *Australia's Spies and Their Secrets* (Sydney: Allen & Unwin, 1994), part I, and Frank Cain, *Terrorism and Intelligence in Australia: A History of ASIO and National Surveillance* (Melbourne: Australian Scholarly Publishing, 2008), chs 5–6.

83 Michael Thwaites, *Truth Will Out: ASIO and the Petrovs* (Melbourne, William Collins, 1980); Robert Manne, *The Petrov Affair: Politics and Espionage* (Sydney: Pergamon, 1987); Desmond Ball and David Horner, *Breaking the Codes: Australia's KGB Network, 1944–1950* (Sydney: Allen & Unwin, 1998); David Horner, *The Spycatchers: The Official History of ASIO 1949–1963, Volume I* (Sydney: Allen & Unwin, 2014), part 3.
84 Spry had to remind Menzies that he first mentioned a possible defection on 3 August 1953 and told the prime minister on 10 February 1954 of his 'high hopes' for Petrov. See Spry to Menzies, 10 August 1954, Correspondence between the Director-General of ASIO and the Prime Minister, NAA A6122, 1427, ff. 32–33.
85 Letters Patent in *Report of the Royal Commission on Espionage* (Sydney: Government Printer, 1955), p. 1.
86 Petrov's dealings with organisers of the Australia–Soviet Friendship Society are recorded in Jean Ada Ferguson, parts 2–3, NAA A6119, 895–6; the interrogation of Hill is documented in James Frederick Hill, vol. 1, NAA A6619, 91.
87 'Petrov Affair Gigantic Frame-up Against People', *Tribune*, 21 April 1954; 'Petrov and U.S. Spies', *Tribune*, 30 June 1954.
88 *Report of the Royal Commission on Espionage*, ch. 1 and Appendix 1.
89 *What Is in Document J* (Canberra: the author, 19 June 1954); *What Is in Document J* (Canberra: Freedom Press, n.d. [July 1954?]); *Royal Commission Exposed* (Sydney: Freedom Press, n.d.); see also Cahill, 'Rupert Lockwood (1908–1997)', ch. 6.
90 Royal Commission on Espionage: Official Transcript of Evidence, NAA A10930, 65–66 (27–28 October 1954) for Dixon; 63 (25 October 1954) for Barnett; 62 (22 October 1954) for Bernie; see also McKnight, *Australia's Spies and Their Secrets*, p. 83.
91 Royal Commission on Espionage: Official Transcript of Evidence, NAA A10930, 82 (6 December 1954).
92 Mark Aarons, *The Family File* (Melbourne: Black Inc., 2010), p. 151; McKnight, *Australia's Spies and Their Secrets*, p. 84; Cedric Ralph, 'One Man's Views of the Twentieth Century', privately printed and held by the family, 1995, vol. 2, ch. 19, p. 29.
93 Royal Commission on Espionage: Official Transcript of Evidence, NAA A10930, 127 (16 March 1954); Horner, *The Spycatchers*, p. 369.
94 'Besieged Petrov Party Outside Commission', *Tribune*, 19 January 1955; L.L. Sharkey and E.F. Hill, *Petrov's 25,000 Dollar Story Exploded* (Sydney: CPA, n.d. [1955]).
95 Royal Commission on Espionage: Official Transcript of Evidence, NAA A10930, 108 (14 February 1955) for Blake; Roger Milliss, *Serpent's Tooth: An Autobiographical Novel* (Melbourne: Penguin, 1984), pp. 160–76; Bernice Merle Morris, vol. 1, NAA A6119, 7062, Bernice Morris, *Between the Lines* (Melbourne: Sybylla Co-operative Press, 1988), part 3, and Betty Searle, 'Invisible Victims of McCarthyism in Australia', *Social Alternatives*, vol. 7, no. 3 (September 1988), pp. 61–63; Ric Throssell, *My Father's Son* (Melbourne: William Heinemann, 1989), part 3; Lynne Strahan, *Just City and the Mirrors:* Meanjin Quarterly *and the Intellectual Front, 1940–1965* (Melbourne: Oxford University Press, 1984), ch. 5; Judith Armstrong, *The Christesen Romance* (Melbourne: Melbourne University Press, 1996).
96 Dorothy Hewett, *Wild Card: An Autobiography 1923–1958* (Melbourne: McPhee Gribble, 1991), pp. 228–30; Royal Commission on Espionage: Official Transcript of Evidence, NAA A10930, 93 (21 January 1955).
97 Robert Murray, *The Split: Australian Labor in the Fifties* (Melbourne: Cheshire, 1970), chs 11–12; Bruce Duncan, *Crusade or Conspiracy? Catholics and the Anti-Communist Struggle in Australia* (Sydney: UNSWP, 2001), chs 14–15.

98 Santamaria to Mannix, 11 December 1952, in Patrick Morgan (ed.), *B.A. Santamaria: Your Most Obedient Servant, Selected Letters 1938–1996* (Melbourne: Miegunyah Press, 2007), p. 75; R. Dixon, 'Labor Fights the Industrial Groups', *Communist Review*, no. 155 (November 1954), pp. 325–28.
99 Evatt's statement, 5 October 1954, quoted in Murray, *The Split*, p. 180; see also *The Split*, part 2, and Duncan, *Crusade or Conspiracy?*, chs 15–18.
100 *Australia's Path to Socialism: Program of the Communist Party of Australia, Seventeenth Congress, May 1955* (Sydney: Current Book Distributors, n.d. [1955]).
101 L. Aarons, 'Build the Party', *Communist Review*, no. 162 (June 1955), pp. 176–80; *Australia's Path to Socialism*, pp. 19–21; '17th Congress Meets', *Tribune*, 11 May 1955; Sharkey, 'Report of the Central Committee', *Communist Review*, no. 162, p. 169.

10 A House Divided, 1956–60

1 N.S. Khrushchev, *Report of the Central Committee of the Soviet Union to the 20th Party Congress, February 1956* (Moscow: Foreign Languages Publishing House, 1956), p. 144. An abridged version appeared in *Communist Review*, no. 172 (April 1956), pp. 99–102.
2 This appeared in 1938, and the English-language edition was entitled *History of the Communist Party of the Soviet Union (Bolsheviks): Short Course* (Moscow: Foreign Languages Publishing House, 1939); Moshe Lewin, *The Soviet Century* (London: Verso, 2005), p. 147.
3 The official text of Khrushchev's secret speech was not published until under Gorbachev in 1989, but unofficial versions were soon circulating. I quote here from the one published in the *New York Times* on 5 June 1956.
4 Vojtech Mastny, 'Soviet Foreign Policy, 1953–1962', in Melvyn P. Leffler and Odd Arne Westad (eds), *The Cambridge History of the Cold War*, vol. 1, *Origins, 1945–1962* (Cambridge: CUP, 2010), p. 318.
5 Paul Lendvai, *One Day That Shook the Communist World: The 1956 Hungarian Uprising and its Legacy* (Princeton, NJ: Princeton University Press, 2008).
6 Kevin Morgan, *Harry Pollitt* (Manchester: Manchester University Press, 1993), ch. 7; Lucio Magri, *The Tailor of Ulm: Communism in the Twentieth Century* (London: Verso, 2011), ch. 6.
7 See the special Stalin memorial issue of *Tribune*, 9 March 1953.
8 John Callaghan, *Cold War, Crisis and Conflict: The CPGB 1951–68* (London: Lawrence and Wishart, 1993), p. 76.
9 Alastair Davidson, *The Communist Party of Australia: A Short History* (Stanford, CA: Hoover Institution Press, 1969), pp. 119–20. For similar contemporary judgements see John Playford, 'Doctrinal and Strategic Problems of the Communist Party of Australia, 1943–62', PhD thesis, ANU, 1962, ch. 8, and I.A.H. Turner, 'The Split in Australian Communism', in J.D.B. Miller and T.H. Rigby (eds), *The Disintegrating Monolith: Pluralist Trends in the Communist World* (Canberra: ANU, 1965), pp. 150–52. The best recent account is Phillip Deery, 'Australian Communism in Crisis—1956', in Jon Piccini, Evan Smith and Matthew Worley (eds), *The Far Left in Australia Since 1945* (London: Routledge, 2018), pp. 21–40.
10 Adam Carr, 'An Age of Certainty: Three Generations of Melbourne Radicals, 1870–1988', PhD thesis, University of Melbourne, 2001, p. 335.
11 Jack Blake, 'Some Facts of History', n.d., Blake papers, SLNSW MLMSS 5971, Box 1/3, Folder 'Consolidation'; Harry Stein, *A Glance Over an Old Left Shoulder* (Sydney: Hale & Iremonger, 1994), p. 120; Bob Gould, 'The Communist Party in

Australian Life', *Labor Review*, no. 34 (2001), p. 29, for the New Zealand source. Hill contributed a disingenuous paean to the Soviet achievement, 'Australian Reports on Soviet Communist Party 20th Congress', to *Tribune* and the *Guardian* in early April.

12 'Moscow Report About Stalin', *Tribune*, 27 March 1956; 'Sharkey on Repudiation of the Cult of the Individual', *Guardian*, 28 March 1956; ASIO report on cadres' meeting, Laurence Louis Sharkey, vol. 10, NAA A6119, ff. 37–40.

13 Jack Blake, 'Some Facts of History', quoted in '"Cracking the Stalinist Crust": The Impact of 1956 on the Communist Party of Australia', MA thesis, Victoria University, 2006, p. 73; 'Sharkey on 20th Congress CPSU', *Tribune*, 30 May 1956; Eric John Aarons, vol. 2, NAA A6119, 437, ff. 132–35.

14 'Sharkey Comments on Togliatti Statement', *Tribune*, 20 June 1956; the CPSU central committee statement appeared as a 9000-word supplement, 'The Stalin Question', in *Tribune*, 18 July 1956; '20th Congress and the Stalin Issue', *Tribune*, 20 June 1956.

15 Bruce Armstrong, interviewed by Rachel Calkin, 25 April 2001, quoted in '"Cracking the Stalinist Crust"', p. 72.

16 W.J. Brown, 'Positive Aspects of the Cult Exposure', *Communist Review*, no. 176 (August 1956), pp. 269–72; 'Congress Lessons on Criticism', *Communist Review*, no. 177 (September 1956), pp. 301–306; 'Independent Thinking and International Solidarity', *Communist Review*, no. 178 (October 1956), pp. 343–48; Paul Mortier, 'Inner-Party Democracy', *Communist Review*, no. 177 (September 1956), pp. 309–11.

17 Bob Walshe, '1956, That "Secret Speech" and Reverberations in Sydney', *The Hummer*, vol. 3, no. 10 (Winter 2003), pp. 1–7; Jim Staples, unpublished letter to the editor of *Tribune*, 22 June 1956, and 'Statement on the Attitude of the Central Committee, Communist Party of Australia, to the Stalin Issue', in Helen Palmer papers, NLA MS 6083, Box 11, File 'Material and Correspondence on Nationalism, Communism and Socialism'.

18 Canterbury section committee to central disputes committee, 21 July 1956, and handwritten note, 3 August 1956; Staples to secretariat, 30 September, 6 November 1956, central disputes committee records (these records form part of the John Rodwell Hughes collection in SLNSW MLMSS 6381, but have yet to be catalogued); Staples, interviewed by Calkin, 28 May 2002, quoted in '"Cracking the Stalinist Crust"', p. 91.

19 Central disputes committee to political committee, 1 March 1957, Hughes collection.

20 Doreen Bridges (ed.), *Helen Palmer's Outlook* (Sydney: Helen Palmer Outlook Committee, 1982); David Martin, *My Strange Friend: An Autobiography* (Sydney: Macmillan, 1991), p. 269.

21 Bill Brown to Helen Palmer, 30 August 1956 (in which he refers to her letter of 19 August), and Palmer to Brown, 25 September 1956; Palmer to Ted Rowe, 27 August 1956; Palmer papers, Box 11, File 'Material and Correspondence on Nationalism, Communism and Socialism'.

22 'Sharkey Comments on Togliatti Statement', *Tribune*, 20 June 1956; '20th Congress and the Stalin Issue', *Tribune*, 20 June 1956.

23 E.F. Hill, 'An Incorrect View of Party Democracy', *Communist Review*, no. 180 (December 1956), pp. 396–402.

24 W.J. Brown, 'W.J. Brown's Position on Cult of the Individual', *Tribune*, 24 October 1956; Report of state conference, 2–4 November 1956, Edward Fowler Hill, vol. 7, NAA A6119, 344, ff. 56–71.

25 L.L. Sharkey, 'Report of the Central Committee', *Communist Review*, no. 180 (December 1956), pp. 387–96.

26 Jean Blackburn, interviewed by Wendy Lowenstein, 1 July 1994, NLA TRC 3111/27; Craig Campbell and Debra Hayes, *Jean Blackburn: Education, Feminism and Social Justice* (Melbourne: Monash University Publishing, 2019), ch. 5.
27 Walshe, '1956, That "Secret Speech" and Reverberations in Sydney'.
28 State executive to all NSW sections and branches, 20 August 1958, Roderick Malcolm Shaw, vol. 1, NAA A6119, 4235, ff. 15–18.
29 Laurie Aarons to Alf Watt, 28 February 1957, Alfred Deaken Watt, vol. 2, NAA A6619, 2130, f. 34, and interviewed by Paul Adams, 20 October 1995, quoted in Paul Adams, *The Stranger from Melbourne: Frank Hardy—A Literary Biography 1944–1975* (Perth: UWAP, 1999), p. 88; Eric John Aarons, NAA A6119, 437, ff. 92–93; 'Sharkey's Speech to Eighteenth Congress', *Tribune*, 9 April 1958.
30 Helen Palmer, 'The Views of Marx and Engels on the State and Revolution', n.d., Palmer papers, Box 12, Folder 'Democratic Centralism'; letter to Sam [Lewis], 13 July 1957, Box 4, 'Correspondence'.
31 Palmer to Sharkey, 7 April 1957; E.W. Campbell (for secretariat) to Palmer, 3 May 1957; central disputes committee to Palmer, 1 July 1957; Palmer to central disputes committee, 2 July 1957; central disputes committee to Palmer, 5 July 1957, Palmer papers, Box 4, Folder 'Correspondence'.
32 Founding statement quoted in Madeleine Davis, 'The *New Reasoner* and the Early New Left', in David Howell, Dianne Kirkby and Kevin Morgan (eds), *John Saville: Commitment and History* (London: Socialist History Society, 2011), p. 32.
33 'Again on Our Editorial Policy', *Outlook*, vol. 1, no. 3 (October 1957), p. 1; Helen G. Palmer, 'Some Afterthoughts on Hungary', *Outlook*, vol. 1, no. 3 (October 1957), pp. 14–17; Isaac Deutscher, *The Prophet Unarmed, Trotsky 1921–1929* (London: OUP, 1959).
34 Amirah Inglis, *The Hammer & Sickle and the Washing Up: Memories of an Australian Woman Communist* (Melbourne: Hyland House, 1995), pp. 144–46; see also Harry Blutstein, *Cold War Games: Spies, Subterfuge and Secret Operations at the 1956 Olympic Games* (Melbourne: Echo, 2017).
35 Geoffrey Bryce Sharp, NAA A6119, 1130; Nonie Sharp, 'A Spoiling Operation: Cold War at the University of Melbourne', *Arena*, vols 47–48 (2017), p. 68.
36 See 'The Long Goodbye' in Ian Turner, *Room for Manoeuvre: Writings on History, Politics, Ideas and Play*, selected and edited by Leonie Sandercock and Stephen Murray-Smith (Melbourne: Drummond Publishing, 1982), pp. 141–49, and Stephen Murray-Smith, *Indirections: A Literary Biography* (Townsville: Foundation for Australian Literary Studies, James Cook University, 1981).
37 Informants' reports, 13 August 1957, 23 January 1958, Stephen Murray-Smith, vol. 3, NAA A6119, 280, ff. 122–23, 134; Inglis, *The Hammer & Sickle and the Washing Up*, p. 150.
38 Informant's report, 7 February, 17 March 1958, Stephen Murray-Smith, vol. 3, ff. 107, 112–13; appraisal, 29 April 1958, Kenneth Davidson Gott—Miscellaneous Papers, NAA A6119, 2678, f. 110; Krygier to Gott, 9 December 1959, Gott papers, NBAC P36/11.
39 Informant's report, 19 March 1958, Stephen Murray-Smith, vol. 3, f. 103; informant's report, 24 June 1958, Ian Alexander Hamilton Turner, vol. 2, NAA A6119, 3743, f. 104.
40 Informants' reports, 14, 21 May 1958, Margaret Beth Gott, NAA A6119, 2665, ff. 14, 27; informants' reports, 2, 7, 15 May, Stephen Murray-Smith, vol. 3, ff. 54, 64, 77.
41 The fullest account is that of Bernie Taft in a letter to Richard Dixon, 25 April 1967,

'Correspondence Regarding Ian Turner's Expulsion', Taft Collection, University of Melbourne Archives, 2010,0053,000387. For the denigration, see informants' report, 24 July 1958, Ian Alexander Hamilton Turner, vol. 2, f. 93; Waten quoted in John McLaren, *Free Radicals of the Left in Postwar Melbourne* (Melbourne: Australian Scholarly Publishing, 2003), pp. 138–39.

42 Informant's report, 12 August 1958, Stephen Murray-Smith, vol. 3, f. 32; David Horner, *The Spy Catchers: The Official History of ASIO, 1949–1963, Volume I* (Sydney: Allen & Unwin, 2014), p. 416; 'Top Red Out of Party; Rift Over Hungary', Melbourne *Herald*, 19 July 1958.

43 Turner to Gust, n.d., quoted in McLaren, *Free Radicals*, pp. 138–39; informant's report, 19 February 1959, Ian Alexander Hamilton Turner, vol. 2, f. 62.

44 'Communist Principles Are Upheld', *Tribune*, 23 July 1958.

45 L. Sharkey, 'For Marxism-Leninism Against Revisionism', *Tribune*, 13 March 1957; L. Aarons, *Party of the Working Class: Organisational Principles and Methods of Work of the Communist Party of Australia* (Sydney: Current Book Distributors, July 1959).

46 'Sharkey's Speech to Eighteenth Congress', *Tribune*, 9 April 1958.

47 Bernard Smith, *Noel Counihan: Artist and Revolutionary* (Melbourne: OUP, 1993), pp. 317–18; Peter S. Cook, *Red Barrister: A Biography of Ted Laurie* (Melbourne: La Trobe University Press, 1994), pp. 121–26; June Factor, in Hume Dow (ed.), *More Memories of Melbourne University* (Melbourne: Hutchinson, 1985), p. 134.

48 Zelda D'Aprano, *Zelda: The Becoming of a Woman* (Melbourne: Widescope, 1977), pp. 74–75; Martin, *My Strange Friend*, pp. 240, 246.

49 John Sendy, *Comrades Come Rally: Recollections of an Australian Communist* (Melbourne: Thomas Nelson, 1978), pp. 100–101; Eric Aarons, *What's Left? Memoirs of an Australian Communist* (Melbourne: Penguin, 1993), pp. 117–19; *Basic Questions of Communist Theory: Documents Relating to the Cult of the Individual and Hungary* (Sydney: Current Book Distributors, 1957).

50 'Meeting Hears Blake on Soviet Doctors' Case', *Tribune*, 22 August 1956 makes no mention of the exchange, which is related in Roger Milliss, *Serpent's Tooth: An Autobiographical Novel* (Melbourne: Penguin, 1984), p. 212; see also Phillip Deery, 'Jack Blake', Search Foundation, <www.search.org.au/jack_blake>.

51 Bill Gollan, interviewed by Laurie Aarons, n.d., SLNSW; John Murphy, 'Loyalty and the Communists: An Interview with Bill Gollan', *Labour History*, no. 66 (May 1994), p. 116; Dorothy Hewett, *Wild Card: An Autobiography 1923–1958* (Melbourne: McPhee Gribble, 1991), p. 251.

52 Edward Fowler Hill, vol. 9A, NAA A6119, 34, ff. 33–36; *Australia's Path to Socialism (Program of the Communist Party of Australia, 18th Congress, 1958)* (Sydney: Current Book Distributors, 1959), p. 40.

53 Adam Ogston, 'The Communist Press', *Communist Review*, no. 190 (October 1957), pp. 320–25; E. Campbell, 'On the Press', *Communist Review*, no. 197 (May 1958), pp. 209–11; Playford, 'Doctrinal and Strategic Problems of the Communist Party of Australia', pp. 318–19 used this information to calculate the 1958 membership.

54 Eric Aarons' report on education in 'The Weapon for Unity', *Communist Review*, no. 198 (June 1958), p. 267.

55 'Plans for Tribune', *Tribune*, 30 January 1957; 'Put Tribune on its Feet', *Tribune*, 6 February 1957; Edward Fowler Hill, vol. 9A, f. 35; address by Ted Zeffert, *Papers in Labour History*, no. 29 (May 2005), p. 27.

56 List of employees, 13 March 1956, William John Brown, vol. 2, NAA A6119, 1112, for NSW; Edward John Hanson, vol. 2, NAA A6119, 6065, f. 127, for Queensland;

and Spoiling Operations, vol. 1, NAA A6122, 1696, for Western Australia; various sources for other states.

57 Tas Bull, *Politics in a Union: The Hursey Case* (Sydney: WWF with Alternative Publishing Cooperative, 1977); see also Margo Beasley, *Wharfies: A History of the Waterside Workers' Federation of Australia* (Sydney: Halstead Press, 1996), ch. 6, and Tom Sheridan, *Australia's Own Cold War: The Waterfront Under Menzies* (Melbourne: MUP, 2006), ch. 11.

58 'Bill Bird Returns to Sea', Melbourne *Guardian*, 26 February 1959.

59 Brian Fitzpatrick and Rowan J. Cahill, *The Seamen's Union of Australia 1872–1972: A History* (Sydney: Seamen's Union of Australia, 1982), pp. 225–34.

60 I draw here on the file of the central disputes committee on Elliott in the Hughes collection.

61 'ALP Decision Damages Unity', *Tribune*, 10 September 1958; David Stephens, 'Unity Tickets and the Victorian Branch of the ALP', *Labour History*, no. 44 (May 1983), pp. 55–74.

62 'Big Hawthorn Rally Calls on Menzies to Press for H-Bomb Ban', Melbourne *Guardian*, 27 June 1957.

63 Jack and Audrey Blake, interviewed by Bob and Ann Gollan, 15 December 1975, Robin Gollan papers, NLA MS 9372/9/16.

64 Report on Assembly, Associations, Conferences Australian Peace Council Assembly for Peace, vol. 6, NAA A6122, ff. 18–21; Jack Blake, '1949 to 1966: Stalinism or Independence', *Australian Left Review*, no. 76 (June 1981), p. 14; see also Bill and Marie Gollan, interviewed by Moira Scollay and Robin Gollan, n.d., Gollan papers.

65 Horner, *The Spy Catchers*, pp. 438–40; see also Ralph Summy and Malcolm Saunders, 'The 1959 Melbourne Peace Congress: Culmination of Anti-Communism in Australia in the 1950s', in Ann Curthoys and John Merritt (eds), *Australia's First Cold War, 1945–1953*, vol. 2, *Better Red than Dead* (Sydney: Allen & Unwin, 1986), pp. 74–95.

66 Informant's report, 15 November 1959, Reverend Francis John Hartley, vol. 3, NAA A6119, 1103, f. 28.

67 Ken Gott, affidavit, 11 June 1968, Kenneth Davidson Gott, vol. 6, NAA A6119, 2667, f. 110; Murray-Smith to Turner, 23 October 1959, quoted in McLaren, *Free Radicals*, p. 148; Murray-Smith to Ralph Summy, 17 October 1966, in Summy and Saunders, 'The 1959 Melbourne Peace Congress', p. 91. The resolution of the writers' and artists' conference is in the papers of Congress for International Co-operation and Disarmament 1959–86, University of Melbourne Archives, 1987.0093, quoted in John Murphy, 'The Australian Intervention in the Vietnam War', PhD thesis, University of Melbourne, 1992, p. 145.

68 See John McLaren, *Writing in Hope and Fear: Literature as Politics in Postwar Australia* (Cambridge: CUP, 1996), ch. 2.

69 Paul Mortier, 'Soviet Literature Has Problems ...'; Mona Brand, 'I Found Much in The Thaw That Was "Interesting, Satisfying"'; Miriam Hampson, Ehrenburg's "Negative Theme"'; anon., 'He Doesn't Know What Ehrenburg Was Trying to Prove'; J. Hutson, 'He Found The Thaw "Aggravating"', *Tribune*, 25 May, 24, 31 August, 21, 28 September 1955; see also Mona Brand, *Enough Blue Sky: The Autobiography of Mona Brand, an Unknown Well-known Playwright* (Sydney: Tawny Pipit Press, 1995), pp. 189–90, and Len Fox, *Broad Left, Narrow Left* (Sydney: the author, 1982), p. 143.

70 Paul Mortier, 'Socialist Realism and the Australian Tradition', *Communist Review*, no. 194 (February 1958), pp. 78–82; Judah Waten, 'What Is the Australian Tradition?',

Tribune, 22 October 1958; Jack Beasley, 'For a Working Class Literature', *Communist Review*, no. 211 (July 1959), p. 278, and 'Miles Franklin and the "Prose Poets"', *Tribune*, 1 July 1959.

71 Jack Beasley, 'Questions of Australian Literature', *Communist Review*, no. 217 (January 1960), p. 35; Thornton quoted in Dorothy Hewett, 'Excerpt from an Autobiography in Progress', *Overland*, no. 160 (Spring 2000), p. 6; see also Nathan Hollier, 'The Critical Reception of Bobbin Up', *Hecate*, vol. 25, no. 1 (1999), pp. 152–64.

72 Rex Chiplin, 'Overland—Where's it Being Taken?', *Tribune*, 13 May 1959; Frank Hardy, 'Some Ideological Problems of Communist Writers', *Communist Review*, no. 174 (June 1956), pp. 182–87, and letter to *Tribune*, 10 June 1959; K.S. Prichard, letter to *Tribune*, 10 June 1959.

73 Informants' reports, Murray-Smith, vol. 3, ff. 10– 41; see also McLaren, *Free Radicals*, pp. 174–77.

74 'Aborigine Left to Die at Pentridge', Melbourne *Guardian*, 11 June 1959.

75 'Pastor Nicholls' Report on Aborigines Shocks 1,000', Melbourne *Guardian*, 28 March 1957; Richard Broome, *Fighting Hard: The Victorian Aborigines Advancement League* (Canberra: Aboriginal Studies Press, 2015), ch. 3.

76 Andrews' criticism of reliance on good will is quoted in Sue Taffe, 'Shirley Andrews: An Architect of the National Aboriginal Civil Rights Movement, 1952–1968', *History Australia*, vol. 8, no. 2 (2011), p. 157; see also Sue Taffe, *Black and White Together: FCAATSI, The Federal Council for the Advancement of Aborigines and Torres Strait Islanders 1958–1973* (Brisbane: UQP, 2005), ch. 3.

77 Keir Reeves, 'Off to the Mystery Picnic: Mobilising Young Engineers in Victoria, 1941–1961', in Andrew Reeves and Andrew Dettmer (eds), *Organise, Educate Control: The AMWU in Australia, 1852–2012* (Melbourne: Monash University Publishing, 2013), pp. 71–83.

78 Barrie Blears, *Together With Us: A Personal Glimpse of the Eureka Youth League and its Origins, 1920 to 1970* (Sydney: the author, 2002), ch. 12.

79 'Clerk on Offensive Behaviour Charge', Sydney *Truth*, 12 January 1958; Charles Desmond Bresland, vol. 4, NAA A61109, 704; 'Rex Chiplin Says', *Tribune*, 1 April 1958; letter to *Tribune*, 14 May 1958.

80 Mavis Moten, 'Vienna Youth Festival', *Communist Review*, no. 217 (January 1960), p. 19.

81 Mark McKenna, *An Eye for Eternity: The Life of Manning Clark* (Melbourne: Miegunyah Press, 2011), pp. 397–410; C.M.H. Clark, *Meeting Soviet Man* (Sydney: Angus & Robertson, 1960).

82 David Horner, *The Spy Catchers: The Official History of ASIO, 1949–1963, Volume I* (Sydney: Allen & Unwin, 2014), p. 427, and see generally chs 15–16.

83 Horner, *The Spy Catchers*, p. 449; David McKnight, *Australia's Spies and Their Secrets* (Sydney: Allen & Unwin, 1994), p. 196, and see generally ch. 16.

84 Horner, *The Spy Catchers*, pp. 437–38; Eric John Aarons, vol. 2, f. 32; 'Minto Mare's Nest', *Tribune*, 25 June 1958.

85 Horner, *The Spy Catchers*, p. 429; Anna Vroland, NAA A6119, 2419, ff. 76–91; W.J. Hudson, *Casey* (Melbourne: OUP, 1986), p. 231.

86 David McKnight, 'Broadcasting the Enemy Within: Political Surveillance and the ABC, 1951–64', *Media International Australia*, no. 87 (May 1998), pp. 35–48.

87 Russel Ward, *A Radical Life: The Autobiography of Russel Ward* (Melbourne: Macmillan, 1988), pp. 237–38; Hannah Forsyth, 'The Russel Ward Case', *History Australia*, vol. 11, no. 3 (2014), pp. 31–52 finds wanting the subsequent claim that Ward was

unacceptable because he had taken advantage of female students when a secondary teacher.

88 'The Crawford Letter', *Bulletin*, 12 April 1961; 'Melbourne University Communist at Work', *Bulletin*, 19 April 1961; see also Fay Anderson, 'Into the Night: Max Crawford, the Labyrinth of the Social Studies Enquiry and ASIO's "Spoiling Operations"', *Australian Historical Studies*, vol. 38, no. 125 (2005), pp. 60–80.

89 Geoffrey Bryce Sharp, NAA A6119, 1130; Donald Horne, *Into the Open* (Sydney: HarperCollins, 2000), p. 110, and correspondence with Anderson. See also Nonie Sharp, 'A Spoiling Operation: Cold War at the University of Melboure', *Arena*, nos 47–48 (2017), pp. 57–75.

90 S.G. Foster and Margaret M.Varghese, *The Making of the Australian National University* (Sydney: Allen & Unwin, 1996), pp. 120–24.

91 Spoiling Operations, NAA A6122, 1889, ff. 72–73.

92 Communist Party of Australia Canberra Branch, vol. 1, NAA A6122, 483, f. 48; Wilfred Athelstone Mountjoy, vol. 2, NAA A6119, 1529; Doris Isobel Beeby, NAA A6126, 243.

93 Peter Worsley, *An Academic Skating on Thin Ice* (New York: Berghahn Books, 2008), p. 82; report on guests of the Michells, 5 August 1954, Communist Party of Australia Canberra Branch, vol. 1, ff. 25–27.

94 Pamela Burton with Meredith Edwards, 'Planet Burton: A Saga of the Lives and Loves of Cecily and John Burton', manuscript under consideration, 2020, p. 231; Nicholas Brown, *A History of Canberra* (Melbourne: CUP, 2014), p. 142; Daphne Gollan reported in Amirah Inglis, vol. 1, NAA A6119, 858, f. 46; see also 'Gregory Pemberton Lifts the Veil on ASIO's Cold War Canberra', *Canberra Times*, 16 September 1990, and Pemberton, 'Snoop City', *Canberra Times*, 16 September 1991.

95 Aarons, *What's Left?*, p. 108.

96 *Eighteenth Congress, April 1958: Report of L.L. Sharkey and Resolution A Land of Plenty Free from War* (Sydney: Current Book Distributors, May 1958), pp. 15–16, 22.

97 *Australia's Path to Socialism: Program of the Communist Party of Australia, 18th Congress, 1958* (Sydney: Current Book Distributors, May 1958), pp. 4, 7.

98 L. Aarons, 'Australian Class Structure', *Communist Review*, nos 192 (December 1957), pp. 406–409, and 193 (January 1958), p. 40–42.

99 Beverley Symons, 'Red Councillors during the Cold War: Communists on the Sydney City Council, 1953–59', in Hal Alexander and Phil Griffiths (eds), *A Few Rough Reds: Stories of Rank and File Organising* (Canberra: ASSLH Canberra Branch, 2003), pp. 110–23.

100 Stuart Macintyre, *Militant: The Life and Times of Paddy Troy* (Sydney: Allen & Unwin, 1984), pp. 135–36.

11 Cannot Stand, 1960–70

1 Helen G. Palmer, *Australian Teacher in China* (Sydney: Teachers' Sponsoring Committee, n.d. [1953?]); the ASIO file Helen Gwynneth Palmer, vol. 1, A6119, 178 includes a copy of the diary she kept in China.

2 Lachlan Strahan, *Australia's China: Changing Perceptions from the 1930s to the 1990s* (Cambridge: CUP, 1996); Agnieszka Sobocinska, 'Australian Fellow-Travellers to China: Devotion and Deceit in the People's Republic', *Journal of Australian Studies*, vol. 32, no. 3 (2008), pp. 323–34.

3 Eric Aarons, *What's Left? Memoirs of an Australian Communist* (Melbourne: Penguin), 1993), p. 81.

4 Gott to 'Bill', 6 July 1964, K.D. Gott papers, State Library of Victoria, MS 3082/4, quoted in John McLaren, *Free Radicals of the Left in Postwar Melbourne* (Melbourne: Australian Scholarly Publishing, 2003), p. 112.

5 This account of the first Australian contingent draws on Aarons, *What's Left?*, pp. 75–101; John Sendy, *Comrades Come Rally! Recollections of an Australian Communist* (Melbourne: Thomas Nelson, 1978), chs 15–16, and Keith McEwan, *Once a Jolly Comrade* (Brisbane: Jacaranda Press, 1966), ch. 2. A slightly expanded version of McEwan's account is in the ASIO file Kenneth Davidson Gott, vol. 6, NAA A6119, 2667.

6 As recalled by Sendy, *Comrades Come Rally!*, p. 84, and Aarons, *What's Left?*, p. 97.

7 McEwan, *Once a Jolly Comrade*, p. 40.

8 Joyce Stevens, interviewed by Laurie Aarons, 1 July 1980, and Keith Wilson, interviewed by Laurie Aarons, 12–13 May 1979, SLNSW; Bernie Taft, *Crossing the Party Line: Memoirs of Bernie Taft* (Newham: Scribe Publications, 1994), ch. 7; Penelope Debelle, *Red Silk: The Life of Elliott Johnston QC* (Adelaide: Wakefield Press, 2011), ch. 1.

9 Jack Hughes, interviewed by Laurie Aarons, September 1980, SLNSW; Rex Mortimer, 'The Benefits of a Liberal Education', *Meanjin*, vol. 35, no. 2 (June 1976), pp. 115–26.

10 Claude Jones, interviewed by Laurie Aarons, June 1980, SLNSW; Ralph Gibson, *My Years in the Communist Party* (Melbourne: International Bookshop, 1966), pp. 235–38; Angus McIntyre, 'The Training of Australian Communist Cadres in China, 1951–1961', *Studies in Comparative Communism*, vol. 11, no. 4 (1978), p. 418.

11 Zhihua Shen and Yafeng Xia, 'The Great Leap Forward, the Peoples Commune and the Sino-Soviet Split', *Journal of Contemporary China*, vol. 20, no. 72 (2011), pp. 861–80; Odd Arne Westad, *The Cold War: A World History* (London: Allen Lane, 2017), ch. 9.

12 David Reynolds, *Summits: Six Meetings that Shaped the Twentieth Century* (London: Allen Lane, 2007), ch. 4.

13 Lorenz M. Luthi, *The Sino-Soviet Split: Cold War in the Communist World* (New Haven, CT: Yale University Press, 2008), chs 2–6.

14 Mark Aarons, *The Family File* (Melbourne: Black Inc., 2010), pp. 180–81, which draws on the testimony of Laurie Aarons.

15 Aarons, *The Family File*, pp. 181–82.

16 Laurie Aarons, 'China's Great Leap—New Victory for Marxism–Leninism', *Communist Review*, no. 202 (October 1958), p. 427; Eric Aarons, 'Some Lessons of Chinese Success', *Communist Review*, no. 206 (February 1959), p. 75; Duncan Clarke, 'Chinese Are Better Fed Than Ever in History', Melbourne *Guardian*, 6 October 1960.

17 'Declaration of the Peking Meeting', *Communist Review*, no. 202 (October 1958), p. 420; 'Unshakable Unity of USSR-China', *Tribune*, 7 October 1959; L.L. Sharkey, 'Press Reaches New Low in Australia', *Tribune*, 8 June 1960.

18 A portion of the transcript was published in E.F. Hill et al., *Defend Marxism–Leninism: Documents of Struggle in the Australian Communist Movement* (Melbourne, n.p., n.d [1963]), pp. 85–89; see also John Herouvim, 'The Communist Party of Australia and the Eighty-One Parties Conference', *Politics*, vol. 21, no. 1 (May 1986), pp. 115–17.

19 L.L. Sharkey, 'The Meeting of the 81 Parties in Moscow', *Tribune*, 1 February 1961; 'China and Soviet Union Always Together—Liu Shao-Chi in Moscow', Melbourne *Guardian*, 15 December 1960; *The People Against Monopoly: 19th Congress of the Communist Party of Australia, 1961* (Sydney: Current Book Distributors, June 1961), p. 37.

20 The principal account is that of Ted Bacon, interviewed by Laurie Aarons, June 1980, SLNSW; Edgar Ross, *Of Storm and Struggle*, ch. 20 claims that Bacon was more critical of the Soviet leadership than Sharkey.

21 'Australian Delegates Say Communism from Strength to Strength', *Tribune*, 8 November 1961; 'Statement by Communist Party', *Tribune*, 20 December 1961.

22 Bacon interviewed by Aarons; Jones interviewed by Aarons.

23 John Herouvim, 'Commitment and Politics: Defending Communism During the Sino-Soviet Split', in Richard Nile and Barry York (eds), *Workers and Intellectuals: Essays on Twentieth-Century Australia from Ten Urban Hunters and Gatherers* (London: Edward Blackwood, 1992), pp. 157–75.

24 Mortimer, 'The Benefits of a Liberal Education', pp. 123–24.

25 Edward Fowler Hill, vol. 13, NAA A6119, 782, ff. 17–22; Taft, *Crossing the Party Line*, chs 8–9; Angus McIntyre, 'The Mentor Relationship and the Dream: The Case of Rex Mortimer', *Biography*, vol. 6, no. 3 (Summer 1983), pp. 238–55.

26 Hill's address is reproduced in *Defend Marxism–Leninism*, pp. 7–30.

27 'Attacks on CP Unity Will Fail', *Tribune*, 18 April 1962; there are informants' reports of the aggregate meetings in Spoiling Operations—Media—vol. 1—Sino-Soviet Split, NAA A6122, 1940, ff. 64–68, 87–88, 95–98, 109–12, 117–21.

28 Sendy, *Comrades Come Rally!*, ch. 27; Taft, *Crossing the Party Line*, ch. 10; Ralph Gibson, notes on report to 1963 state conference, Gibson papers, NLA MS 7844, Folder 9.

29 The allegations appear in reports of meetings in Florence Amy Russell, vol. 4, NAA A6119, 2841, ff. 30–33, and Gibson's notes; for Miller, see telephone intercept report, 26 November 1962, in Patricia Isobel Miller, vol. 1, NAA A6119, 2064, f. 6.

30 Sendy quoted in report on cadres' meeting, 2 December 1962, Florence Amy Russell, vol. 4, f. 30.

31 The exchange between Hill and the secretariat is in Eric John Aarons, vol. 5, NAA A6119, 968, ff. 106–13; 'E.F. Hill and F. Russell Expelled', *Tribune*, 28 August 1963; 'Death of Ken Miller', *Guardian*, 4 July 1963.

32 'On the Question of a Party of a New Type', *Australian Communist*, December 1963, p. 2; Hill quoted in Herouvim, 'Commitment and Politics', p. 172; minutes of meeting of Townsville branch of CPA (M-L), n.d. [1964], CPA Interest in Political Parties—Communist Party of Australia (Marxist/Leninist), vol. 5, NAA A6122, 1730, ff. 19–20.

33 Florence Amy Russell, vol. 4, f. 55; 'Revisionism in the Communist Party of Australia', *Australian Communist*, December 1963, pp. 6–16.

34 Cedric Ralph, 'One Man's Views of the Twentieth Century', privately printed and held by the family, 1995, vol. 2, ch. 19, p. 18; ch. 22, pp. 20–21; ch. 23, pp. 24–25.

35 Amirah Inglis, *The Hammer & Sickle and the Washing Up: Memories of an Australian Woman Communist* (Melbourne: Hyland House, 1995), p. 174; informant's report, 27 February 1960, Amirah Inglis, vol. 1, NAA A6119, 858, ff. 16–17; Dorothy Gibson, 'Autobiographical Papers', Ralph and Dorothy Gibson papers, NLA MS 7844, Folder 21.

36 'Deep Grief at Loss of Leader', *Tribune*, 2 May 1962.

37 Aarons, *What's Left?*, p. 138; Laurie Aarons in *The Family File*, pp. 182, 205; '"New Look" C.P.A', *Current Affairs Bulletin*, vol. 40, no. 2 (28 September 1967), p. 132.

38 'The Way Forward for Australia: Draft Resolution', *Tribune*, 19 February 1964; the final *Resolution, 20th Congress Communist Party of Australia June 1964* (Sydney: D.B. Young, 1964), pp. 39–40 omitted the passage referring to a mass party numbering tens of thousands.

39 'Party Building and the Path to a Mass Party', report to Central Committee, February 1965, CPA records, SLNSW MLMSS 5021, Box 16; minutes of cadres meeting, 11 February 1965, CPA Interest in Political Parties—Communist Party of Australia, vol. 4, NAA A6122, 1729, f. 9.
40 Rex Mortimer, 'Improve Our Style in Propaganda', *Communist Review*, no. 222 (June 1960), pp. 250–52.
41 Herouvim, 'Commitment and Politics', p. 165.
42 Mortimer, 'Improve Our Style', p. 251; *Australia's Way Forward: Program of the Communist Party of Australia* (Sydney: Current Book Distributors, 1964), pp. 5–10; E.W. Campbell's book *The 60 Families Who Own Australia* was published by Current Book Distributors in 1963.
43 L.L. Sharkey, 'Report to 20th Congress', *Communist Review*, no. 270 (July 1964), p. 13; Aarons, 'Party Building and the Path to a Mass Party'; Bernie Taft, 'Can We Build the Communist Party in Present-Day Conditions?', *Communist Review*, no. 279 (April 1965), p. 76; *CPA Twenty-First Congress, Report of the Central Committee Delivered by L. Aarons* (Sydney: n.p., 1967), pp. 5–10.
44 Sendy, *Comrades Come Rally!*, p. 161.
45 Geoff Sharp, 'Politics of the Intelligentsia', *Arena*, no. 5 (1964); Geoff Sharp and Doug White, 'Features of the Intellectually Trained', *Arena*, no. 15 (1968), pp. 30–33; see also Raewyn Connell, 'Theorizing Intellectuals', *Arena*, nos 45–46 (2016), pp. 12–27.
46 Geoffrey Bryce Sharp, NAA A6119, 1130, ff. 15–16.
47 John Sendy, 'Democracy in the Communist Party', *Australian Left Review*, no. 1 (June–July 1966), pp. 34–42.
48 *Communist Party of Australia 21st National Congress, June 1967: Documents* (Sydney: D.B. Young, n.d. [December 1966]), pp. 2–3, 5, 14, 22–23.
49 *Discussion Journal*, no. 1 (March 1967), pp. 1, 29–32, 33–38, 47–51, 92–93.
50 *Discussion Journal*, no. 2 (April 1967), pp. 14–16; information, May 1967, Wilton John Brown, vol. 12, NAA A6119, 5006, f. 114; Stuart Macintyre, *Militant: The Life and Times of Paddy Troy* (Sydney: Allen & Unwin, 1984), pp. 211–12.
51 'Congress Reports', *Tribune*, 21 June 1967; *Australia and the Way Forward: The Political Document Adopted by the 21st Congress of the Communist Party of Australia, June 1967* (Sydney: D.B. Young, 1967).
52 'Two Stand Down in West', *Tribune*, 3 May 1967; 'Amendments from WA', *Tribune*, 17 May 1967; 'Resignation', *Tribune*, 5 July 1967; see also Geoff Davis, 'A Communist Remembers', *Studies in Labour History*, no. 29 (May 2005), pp. 58–59, and Jolly Read, *Marksy: The Life of Jack Marks* (South Fremantle: Read Media, 1998), pp. 212–15.
53 Information, 7 September 1963, Eric John Aarons, vol. 5, NAA A6119, 968, ff. 31–32; information, 24 April 1965, Eva Robinson, vol. 1, NAA A6119, 167, ff. 87–88.
54 Aarons, *The Family File*, p. 192.
55 Sharkey, 'Report to 20th Congress', pp. 221–22; 20th National Congress, CPA Interest in Political Parties—Communist Party of Australia (Marxist/Leninist), vol. 2, NAA A6122, 1727, f. 10.
56 Alastair Davidson, *The Communist Party of Australia: A Short History* (Stanford, CA: Hoover Institution Press, 1969), p. 174, and W.J. Brown, *The Communist Movement and Australia: An Historical Outline—1890s to 1980s* (Sydney: Australian Labor Movement History Publications, 1986), p. 323: both cite *Tribune*, 28 July 1965 as the source of these statistics; I cannot see them there.
57 '"New Look" CPA', p. 131; John Blaxland, *The Protest Years: The Official History of*

ASIO, 1963–1975, Volume II (Sydney: Allen & Unwin, 2015), p. 96; Communist Party of Australia—Organisation July 1970, NAA A12694, 26, f. 19.

58 Alec Robertson, 'Tribune and the Australian Left', *Tribune*, 15 April 1970.

59 Jack Hutson, 'The Penal Powers: To Be or Not to Be', *Tribune*, 21 May 1969; Jack Hutson, *Penal Colony to Penal Powers* (Sydney: Amalgamated Metals Foundry and Shipwrights' Union, 1983), ch. 38.

60 Eric Aarons, 'As I Saw the Sixties', *Australian Left Review*, no. 27 (October–November 1970), p. 68.

61 Jack Hutson, 'Workers' Control', *Australian Left Review*, no. 17 (February–March 1969), p. 11.

62 Margo Beasley, *Wharfies: A History of the Waterside Workers' Federation of Australia* (Sydney: Halstead Press, 1996), pp. 197–99; Tas Bull, *Life on the Waterfront: An Autobiography* (Sydney: HarperCollins, 1998), pp. 96–98; 'Miners' Chief Unopposed', *Tribune*, 4 October 1967.

63 Mundey quoted in Pete Thomas, 'Occupation', *Tribune*, 3 June 1970; Jack Mundey, 'Towards New Union Militancy', *Australian Left Review*, no. 26 (August 1970), pp. 1–8; see also Meredith Burgmann and Verity Burgmann, *Green Bans, Red Union: Environmental Activism and the New South Wales Builders Labourers' Federation* (Sydney: UNSWP, 1998).

64 Tom McDonald and Audrey McDonald, *Intimate Union: Sharing a Revolutionary Life* (Sydney: Pluto Press, 1998), pp. 174–91; see also Glenn Mitchell, *On Strong Foundations: The BWIU and Industrial Relations in the Australian Construction Industry 1942–1992* (Sydney: Harcourt, Brace and Co., 1996), pp. 221–38.

65 Ann Curthoys, *Freedom Ride: A Freedom Rider Remembers* (Sydney: Allen & Unwin, 1993).

66 Richard Gordon and Warren Osmond, 'An Overview of the Australian New Left', in Richard Gordon (ed.), *The Australian New Left: Critical Essays and Strategy* (Melbourne: William Heinemann, 1970), pp. 3–39.

67 '100 Sponsors Behind Easter "Left Action" Conference', *Tribune*, 12 February 1969.

68 'Left Lines up in Easter Movement', *Tribune*, 9 April 1969; Geoff Sorrell, Audrey Blake, Len Fox and Helen Palmer, 'Left Action Conference', *Outlook*, vol. 12, no. 3 (June 1969), pp. 10–11; CPA records, SLNSW MLMSS 5021, Box 28 (159).

69 The participant was Brian Laver, his claim reported in Lani Russell, 'Today the Students, Tomorrow the Workers! Radical Students and the Australian Labour Movement 1960–1972', PhD thesis, University of Technology Sydney, 1999, pp. 273–74; see also C.A. Rootes, 'The Development of Radical Student Movements and Their Sequelae', *Australian Journal of Politics and History*, vol. 34, no. 2 (1988), pp. 173–86.

70 I draw here on Rootes, 'The Development of Radical Student Movements', and John Murphy, 'The Australian Intervention in the Vietnam War', PhD thesis, University of Melbourne, 1992, ch. 12.

71 Marchais quoted in Richard Vinen, *The Long '68: Radical Protest and its Enemies* (London: Allen Lane, 2018), p. 135; Edgar Ross quoted by John Playford in *Tribune*, 25 February 1970, and his *Of Storm and Struggle*, p. 137.

72 Central Committee, 'Changes in the Soviet Union', *Tribune*, 21 October 1964; Philip Mendes, 'A Convergence of Interests: Isi Leibler, the Communist Party of Australia and Soviet Anti-Semitism', *Australian Journal of Politics and History*, vol. 55, no. 2 (2009), pp. 157–69.

73 Aarons, *What's Left?*, p. 151.

74 'Arrests, Jailings Were Unnecessary and Wrong', *Tribune*, 23 February 1966; Aarons, *The Family File*, p. 23; I draw in this paragraph on David McKnight, 'Breaking with Moscow: The Communist Party of Australia's New Road to Socialism', in Jon Piccini, Evan Smith and Matthew Worley (eds), *The Far Left in Australia Since 1945* (London: Routledge, 2018), pp. 59–76.
75 Lloyd Churchward, 'Soviet Democracy', *Tribune*, 1 November 1967; Pat Clancy and Laurie Carmichael, 'Soviet Democracy Today', *Tribune*, 22 November 1967; Sendy, *Comrades Come Rally!*, p. 230.
76 Laurie Aarons, 'Czech Renaissance Lights Way for Us', *Tribune*, 10 April 1968; 'New Stage of Socialism on View, Says Taft', *Tribune*, 17 April 1968; 'Socialism Now Coming of Age, Says Taft', *Tribune*, 24 April 1968.
77 The Warsaw powers' warning to Czechoslovakia and the text of the Bratislava Agreement were published in *Tribune*, 14 July, 7 August 1968.
78 Günter Bischof, Stefan Karner and Peter Ruggenthaler (eds), *The Prague Spring and the Warsaw Pact Invasion of Czechoslovakia* (Lanham, MD: Lexington Books, 2010).
79 'Australian Stand on Czechoslovakian Issue', *Tribune*, 24 July 1968; 'Clear Violation of Socialist Principle', 'Why Communists Condemn Czechoslovakian Occupation', *Tribune*, 28 August 1968.
80 Information, 1 August, 9 October 1968, Wilton John Brown, vol. 14, NAA A6119, 5020, ff. 77, 130.
81 'Socialism and the USSR', *Tribune*, 12 February 1969; Eric Aarons' contribution was markedly less provocative than his earlier 'Czechoslovakia and the USSR: Why?', *Tribune*, 4 September 1968.
82 Apart from letters to *Tribune*, I draw here on Bacon interviewed by Aarons; Ross, *Of Storm and Struggle*, pp. 131–32; intercept report, 28 January 1969, Edward John Docker, vol. 2, A611, 3067, f. 23; and Sam Lipski's well-informed article 'Why the Party is Split Over Moscow', *Australian*, 25 February 1969.
83 Again, this paragraph draws on letters to *Tribune*, as well as Aarons, *The Family File*, pp. 232–33.
84 'Tribune Widens the Debate', *Tribune*, 1 October 1969. The debate was also conducted in *Australian Left Review*.
85 Information on Les Kelton, 2 January 1969, Wilton John Brown, vol. 14, ff. 26–27.
86 *Documents Adopted by the International Conference of Communist and Workers' Parties (Moscow, June 5–17, 1969)* (Moscow: Novosti Press Agency Publishers, 1969), pp. 126–31; 'CPA Stand at Talks', *Tribune*, 11 June 1969; Taft, *Crossing the Party Line*, ch. 18; W.W. Kulski, 'The 1969 Conference of Communist Parties', *Russian Review*, vol. 28, no. 4 (1969), pp. 385–95.
87 'CPA National C'tee Calls for Action on Urgent Problems', *Tribune*, 6 August 1969.
88 'Communist Congress at March', *Tribune*, 26 November 1969.
89 'CPA Congress Lead-up', *Tribune*, 25 February 1970.
90 *Statement of Aims Methods and Organisation: Communist Party of Australia 22nd Congress March 1970* (Sydney: D.B. Young, March 1970). The draft first appeared in *Tribune*, 10 December 1969.
91 Laurie Aarons, 'Big Issues in Congress Clash of Ideas', *Tribune*, 25 February 1970; 'Strategy for Socialism on CPA Congress Agenda', *Tribune*, 1 April 1970.
92 'Strategy for Socialism on CPA Congress Agenda'.
93 'CPA Congress Charts New Paths', *Tribune*, 1 April 1970; 'National Committee Recommendations', *Tribune*, 8 April 1970.

94 'CPA National C'tee Calls for Action on Urgent Problems'; Laurie Aarons, 'After the Congress—What Gives Now?', *Tribune*, 8 April 1970.

Epilogue

1 'Sydney's Greatest Funeral Honors "Big Jim"', 'Sharkey Farewells Healy—"A Model Leader"', *Tribune*, 19 July 1961; John Myrtle, 'Jim Healy's Funeral: A Photographic Perspective', ASSLH, <http://labourhistorycanberra.org/2015/04/jim-healys-funeral-a-photographic-perspective>.

2 'Healy Hall Dedicated to "Big Jim"', *Tribune*, 22 July 1964; H. McClintock, 'A New Chapter in Australian Art', *Tribune*, 21 July 1965.

3 'Tribute to Lance Sharkey', *Tribune*, 24 May 1967.

4 'Funeral of Lance Sharkey', *Tribune*, 24 May 1967; Roger Milliss, *Serpent's Tooth: An Autobiographical Novel* (Melbourne: Penguin, 1984), pp. 407–409.

5 Anthea Bundock, 'Marjorie Estella Nunan', *Australian Dictionary of Biography*, vol. 15, pp. 502–503; Vin Bourke, 'Vale, Marj Nunan', Melbourne *Guardian*, 17 January 1963; Ruth Crow, 'Marge and Mabel of Brunswick', *Tribune*, 2 July 1980; David Nichols, 'Ruth Crow: 1916–1999', in Bob Boughton et al. (eds), *Comrades! Lives of Australian Communists* (Sydney: Search Foundation, 2020), pp. 79–82.

6 'Guido Baracchi: A CPA Founding Father Looks Back on 50 Years', *Tribune*, 10 February 1971.

7 Keith McEwan, *Once a Jolly Comrade* (Brisbane: Jacaranda Press, 1966); W.A. Wood, 'A Sadder (But No Wiser) Communist', *Tribune*, 7 December 1966.

8 Ted Zeffert, '"Jolly Comrade" and Right to Dissent', *Tribune*, 20 December 1966; 'McPhillips Replies', *Tribune*, 1 February 1967; Mark Aarons, *The Family File* (Melbourne: Black Inc., 2010), pp. 245–46.

9 Roger Milliss, 'Desertion and Dissent', *Tribune*, 8 February 1967; Jack McPhillips, 'Not Damaging to Socialism', *Tribune*, 15 February 1967; Mavis Robertson, 'Grain of Salt', *Tribune*, 22 February 1967.

10 Ralph Gibson, *My Years in the Communist Party* (Melbourne: International Bookshop, 1966); Audrey Blake, 'Gibson's Memoirs Sometimes One-Sided', *Tribune*, 10 August 1966.

11 Len Fox, 'Mistakes of 1950s Must Be Confronted', *Tribune*, 24 August 1966; Harry Hatfield, 'Not Sufficient to Delve into the Past', *Tribune*, 7 September 1966.

12 Political Committee Report on Matters Concerning J.B. and A. Blake, 26 January 1967, central disputes committee records, Hughes collection, SLNSW MLMSS 6381.

13 Jack Blake, '1949 to 1956: Stalinism or Independence?', 'CPA NC Resolution', *Australian Left Review*, no. 76 (June 1981), pp. 8–16.

14 Rex Mortimer, 'Communists and the Australian Left', *New Left Review*, no. 46 (November–December 1967), pp. 47–48; see also 'The Communist Challenge', in Henry Mayer (ed.), *Australian Politics: A Reader* (Melbourne: F.W. Cheshire, 1966), pp. 305–19, and 'Dilemmas of Australian Communism', in Henry Mayer (ed.), *Australian Politics: A Second Reader* (Melbourne: F.W. Cheshire, 1969), pp. 382–94.

15 Rex Mortimer, 'A Communist Looks at the Communist Party', *Outlook*, vol. 10, no. 4 (August 1966), pp. 8–11.

16 Intercept of phone conversation between Bernie Taft and Margaret Mortimer, 21 June 1967, Amirah Turner, Part 2, NAA A5119, 859, f. 62.

17 Milliss, *Serpent's Tooth*, p. 298; 'Rex Chiplin's Defection', *Bulletin*, 22 June 1963; Alf Watt, 'USSR's New Leaders', *Tribune*, 25 November 1964.

18 Letters from the Australian embassy to the secretary of the Department of External Affairs, 30 January, 23 February, 20 May 1968, Rupert Ernest Lockwood, vol. 11, NAA A6119, 2334; Rupert Lockwood, 'Wilfred Burchett's Retreat from Moscow', n.d., <http://radicalsydney.blogspot.com/p/wilred-burchetts-tretreat-from-moscow.html>.

19 Rupert Lockwood, 'The Making and Unmaking of a Communist Propagandist', 'The View's Better through a Vodka Glass', 'Blundering in the Communist Fold', 'The Marshal's Loss', 'Bureaucracy Rampant', *Australian*, 24–29 January 1970; Arthur W. Rudkin, 'An Open Letter to Rupert Lockwood', *Tribune*, 4 February; see also Rowan Cahill, 'Rupert Lockwood (1908–1997): Journalist, Communist, Intellectual', PhD thesis, University of Wollongong, 2013, pp. 300–307.

20 'No Penalty on Hardy', *Tribune*, 29 July 1969; Pat Clancy, letter to editor, *Tribune*, 12 February 1969; see also Pauline Armstrong, *Frank Hardy and the Making of* Power Without Glory (Melbourne: MUP, 2000), pp. 167–68.

21 Frank Hardy, *The Unlucky Australians* (Melbourne: Nelson, 1968); 'Action Needed to Help Gurindji, Says Hardy', *Tribune*, 5 June 1968; Bain Attwood, *Rights for Aborigines* (Sydney: Allen & Unwin, 2003), pp. 265–77.

22 Frank Hardy, *But the Dead Are Many* (London: Bodley Head, 1975); Dulcie Mortier, 'Did Anne Hathaway Write Shakespeare?', Women's Labour and History Conference, 1995, quoted in Armstrong, *Frank Hardy and the Making of* Power Without Glory, pp. 175–78; 'Eric Aarons Reviews *But the Dead Are Many*', *Tribune*, 1 October 1975.

23 Jenny Hocking's account of the funeral, *Frank Hardy: Politics, Literature Life* (Melbourne: Lothian Books, 2005), pp. 254–55 suggests a lack of communist recognition; she overlooks the Trades Hall choir, which sang the Internationale as the coffin was carried out.

24 'You Are Reading Our Second Last Issue', *Outlook*, vol. 14, no. 5 (October 1970); Ian Turner, 'The Long Goodbye', *Outlook*, vol. 14, no. 6 (December 1970), p. 4; 'Outlook to Close', *Tribune*, 4 November 1970.

25 W.J. Brown, *The Communist Movement and Australia: An Historical Outline—1890s to 1980s* (Sydney: Australian Labor Movement History Publications, 1986), pp. 277–85.

26 Communist Party of Australia—Organisation July 1970, NAA A12694, 26.

27 'CPA Views of Moratorium Planning', *Tribune*, 4 February 1970; 'Make Moratorium Broad, Militant', *Tribune*, 18 March 1972; see also John Murphy, *Harvest of Fear: Australia's Vietnam War* (Sydney: Allen & Unwin, 1993), ch. 13.

28 Brown quoted in Lisa Milner, *Swimming Against the Tide: A Biography of Freda Brown* (Adelaide: Ginninderra Press, 2017), p. 139; Joyce Stevens, 'Typist or Comrade?', *Tribune*, 3 March 1971; Stevens interviewed by Laurie Aarons, 1 July 1980, SLNSW.

29 Mavis Robertson, 'Freedom of Women', 'The CPA and Women's Liberation', *Tribune*, 2 May 1972, 8 December 1971; Joyce Stevens, 'Typist or Comrade?', *Tribune*, 3 March 1971.

30 J.D. Blake, *Revolution from Within: A contemporary theory of social change* (Sydney: Outlook, 1971).

31 Jones, interviewed by Aarons, June 1980.

32 David Carter, '"History Was on Our Side": Memoirs from the Australian Left', *Meanjin*, vol. 46, no. 1 (March 1987), pp. 108–21; Peter Beilharz, 'Elegies of Australian Communism', *Australian Historical Studies*, vol. 23, no. 92 (1989), pp. 293–306.

Select Bibliography

This bibliography identifies some major primary sources and a very limited selection of secondary sources. A much fuller compilation was provided by Beverley Symons, *Communism in Australia: A Resource Bibliography* (Canberra: National Library, 1994) and Beverley Symons, *Communism in Australia: A Supplementary Resource Bibliography, c. 1994–2001* (Sydney: Sydney Branch of the ASSLH, 2002), so this one is restricted to some of the work that has appeared since 2000. A full bibliography of the material used for the history is available on the website of the Search Foundation.

Archives and Manuscripts

The principal repositories are the National Archives of Australia, which holds security records, the National Library of Australia, which has the papers of many leading members, and the State Library of New South Wales, which houses the national records of the party. The University of Melbourne Archives, the Fryer Library of the University of Queensland, the State Library of South Australia and the State Library of Western Australia hold state collections party records of variable quality. The Noel Butlin Archives at the Australian National University has a wide range of union and personal records.

Oral History

The three main collections are those of Laurie Aarons and Ken Norling, both held by the State Library of New South Wales, and Wendy Lowenstein, held by the National Library of Australia.

Newspapers and Serials

Australian Left Review, 1966–70

Communist Review, 1934–66

Discussion Journal on the Documents for the 21st National Congress of the Communist Party of Australia To Be Held in Sydney June 1967

Guardian (Brisbane), 1943–66

Guardian (Melbourne), 1939–66

Party and *Party Builder*, 1942–43

Progress (Sydney), 1940–46

Tribune (South Australia), 1946–63; South Australian edition, 1951–63

Tribune (Sydney), 1939–70

Workers' Star (Hobart), 1936–51

Workers' Star (Perth), 1936–51

Autobiography and Memoirs

Eric Aarons, *What's Left? Memoirs of an Australian Communist*, Melbourne: Penguin, 1993

Bob Boughton, Danny Blackman, Mike Donaldson, Carmel Shute and Beverley Symons (eds), *Comrades! Lives of Australian Communists*, Sydney: Search Foundation, 2020

Ann Curthoys and Joy Damousi (eds), *What Did You Do in the Cold War, Daddy? Personal Stories from a Troubled Time*, Sydney: New South Publishing, 2014

Roy Dalgarno, 'The Winking of an Eye: Autobiography', n.d., digital memoirs in possession of Lynn Dalgarno

Joyce Evans, *We Had Such High Hopes: Student Activism and the Peace Movement 1949–1952*, Melbourne: Australian Scholarly Publishing, 2019

Itzhak Gust, *Such Was Life: A Jumping Narrative from Radom to Melbourne*, Melbourne: Makor Community Library, 2004

Secondary Works

Mark Aarons, *The Family File*, Melbourne: Black Inc., 2010

Mark Aarons, *The Show: Another Side of Santamaria's Movement*, Melbourne: Scribe, 2017

Hal Alexander and Phil Griffiths (eds), *A Few Rough Reds: Stories of Rank and File Organising*, Canberra: ASSLH Canberra Branch, 2003

Anthony Ashbolt and Rowan Cahill, 'And the Lives Are Many: The Print Culture of Australian Communism', *Twentieth Century Communism*, 12 (2017), pp. 37–61

John Blaxland, *The Protest Years: The Official History of ASIO, 1963–1975, Volume II*, Sydney: Allen & Unwin, 2015

Adam Carr, 'An Age of Certainty: Three Generations of Melbourne Radicals, 1870–1988', PhD thesis, University of Melbourne, 2001

Lachlan Clohesy, 'Australian Cold Warrior: The Anti-Communism of W.C. Wentworth', PhD thesis, Victoria University, 2010

Bruce Duncan, *Crusade or Conspiracy? Catholics and the Anti-Communist Struggle in Australia*, Sydney: UNSWP, 2001

Raymond Evans and Carole Ferrier (eds), *Radical Brisbane: An Unruly History*, Melbourne: Vulgar Press, 2004

Sheila Fitzpatrick and Carolyn Rasmussen (eds), *Political Tourists: Travellers from Australia to the Soviet Union in the 1920s–1940s*, Melbourne: MUP, 2008

Charlie Fox, Bobbie Oliver and Lenore Layman (eds), *Radical Perth, Militant Fremantle*, Perth: Black Swan Press, 2017; new edition, Melbourne: Interventions, 2019

Jan Friedel, 'Left Wing Melbourne Artists and the Communist Party during the Early Cold War Period', PhD thesis, University of Melbourne, 2013

W.M. Goss and Richard X. McGee, *Under the Radar: The First Woman in Radio Astronomy, Ruby Payne Scott*, Heidelberg: Springer, 2010

Cheryl Griffin, 'A Biography of Doris McRae, 1893–1988', PhD thesis, University of Melbourne, 2005

Jennifer Hibben, 'Shirley Andrews: A Prismatic Life', PhD thesis, University of Melbourne, 2012

Jenny Hocking, *Frank Hardy: Politics, Literature Life*, Melbourne: Lothian Books, 2005

David Horner, *The Spy Catchers: The Official History of ASIO, 1949–1963, Volume I*, Sydney: Allen & Unwin, 2014

Dylan Hyde, *Art Was Their Weapon: The History of the Perth Workers' Art Guild*, Fremantle: Fremantle Press, 2019

Terry Irving and Rowan Cahill, *Radical Sydney: Place, Portraits and Unruly Episodes*, Sydney: NewSouth Books, 2010

Marilyn Lake, *Faith: Faith Bandler, Gentle Activist*, Sydney: Allen & Unwin 2002

David McKnight, *Espionage and the Roots of the Cold War: The Conspiratorial Heritage*, London: Frank Cass, 2002

John McLaren, *Free Radicals of the Left in Postwar Melbourne*, Melbourne: Australian Scholarly Publishing, 2003

Lisa Milner, *Swimming Against the Tide: A Biography of Freda Brown*, Adelaide: Ginninderra Press, 2017

Bobbie Oliver, *Unity is Strength: A History of the Australian Labor Party and the Trades and Labor Council in Western Australia, 1989–1999*, Perth: Australian Public Intellectual Network, 2003

Jon Piccini, *Transnational Protest, Australia and the 1960s: Global Radicals*, London: Palgrave Macmillan, 2016

Jon Piccini, Evan Smith and Matthew Worley (eds), *The Far Left in Australia since 1945*, London: Routledge, 2018, pp. 41–58

Andrew Reeves, *Up from the Underworld: Coalminer and Community in Wonthaggi 1909–1968*, Melbourne: Monash University Publishing, 2011

Anne Scrimgeour, *On Red Earth Walking: The Pilbara Aboriginal Strike, Western Australia 1946–1949*, Melbourne: Monash University Publishing, 2020

Tom Sheridan, *Australia's Own Cold War: The Waterfront Under Menzies*, Melbourne: MUP, 2006

Evan Smith, Jon Piccini and Matthew Worley (eds), *The Far Left in Australia since 1945*, London: Routledge, 2018

Jill and Jeff Sparrow, *Radical Melbourne: A Secret History*, Melbourne: Vulgar Press, 2001

Jeff Sparrow and Jill Sparrow, *Radical Melbourne 2: The Enemy Within*, Melbourne: Vulgar Press, 2004

Beverley Symons and Rowan Cahill (eds), *A Turbulent Decade: Social Protest Movements and the Labour Movement, 1965–1975*, Sydney:

Sydney Branch of the Australian Society for the Study of Labour History, 2005

Sue Taffe, *Black and White Together: FCAATSI, The Federal Council for the Advancement of Aborigines and Torres Strait Islanders 1958–1973*, Brisbane: UQP, 2005

Index

INDEX